SPORT

Critical Concepts in Sociology

Other titles in this series

Culture
Edited with a new introduction by Chris Jenks
4 volume set

Crime
Edited with a new introduction by Philip Bean
4 volume set

Globalization
Edited with a new introduction by Roland Robertson and Kathleen White
6 volume set

Islam
Edited with a new introduction by Bryan Turner
4 volume set

Social Networks
Edited with a new introduction by John Scott
4 volume set

Race and Ethnicity
Edited with a new introduction by Harry Goulbourne
4 volume set

Sexualities
Edited with a new introduction by Ken Plummer
4 volume set

Modernity
Edited with a new introduction by Malcolm Waters
4 volume set

Class
Edited by John Scott
4 volume set

Power
Edited by John Scott
3 volume set

Citizenship
Edited by Bryan Turner
2 volume set

The State
Edited by John Hall
3 volume set

SPORT
Critical Concepts in Sociology

Edited by
Eric Dunning and Dominic Malcolm

Volume III

Sport and Power Relations

Routledge
Taylor & Francis Group

LONDON AND NEW YORK

First published 2003
by Routledge
11 New Fetter Lane, London EC4P 4EE

Simultaneously published in the USA and Canada
by Routledge
29 West 35th Street, New York, NY 10001

Routledge is an imprint of the Taylor & Francis Group

Typeset in Times by RefineCatch Limited, Bungay, Suffolk
Printed and bound in Great Britain by
TJ International Ltd, Padstow, Cornwall

British Library Cataloguing in Publication Data
A catalogue record for this book is available from the British Library

Library of Congress Cataloging-in-Publication Data
Sport/edited by Eric Dunning and Dominic Malcolm.
p. cm. – (Critical concepts in sociology)
Includes bibliographical references and index.
Contents: v. 1. Approaches to the study of sport – v. 2. The
development of Sport – v. 3. Sport and power relations – v. 4. Issues
in the sociology of sport.
ISBN 0–415–26292–5 (set) – ISBN 0–415–26293–3 (v. I) –
ISBN 0–415–26294–1 (v. II) – ISBN 0–415–26295–X (v. III) –
ISBN 0–415–26296–8 (v. IV) 1.
Sports – Sociological aspects. 2. Sports – History. I. Dunning, Eric.
II. Malcolm, Dominic, 1969– III. Series.

GV706.5.S7114 2003 306.4'83–dc21 2002037173

ISBN 0–415–26292–5 (Set)
ISBN 0–415–26295–X (Volume III)

Publisher's Note
References within each chapter are as they appear in the original
complete work

CONTENTS

CONTENTS

ACKNOWLEDGEMENTS

Volume 3

The publishers would like to thank the following for permission to reprint their material:

The Black Scholar for permission to reprint H. Edwards, "The sources of the black athlete's superiority", *The Black Scholar*, 3(3) (1971): 32–41.

Sage Publications for permission to reprint D. E. Carlston, "An environmental explanation for race differences in basketball performance". *Journal of Sport and Social Issues*, 7(2) (1983): 30–51.

S. Birrell for permission to reprint S. Birrell, "Racial relations theories and sport: suggestions for a more critical analysis", *Sociology of Sport Journal* 6 (1989): 212–227.

'Introduction: Flying Air Jordan: the Power of Racial Images', from DARWIN'S ATHLETES by John Hoberman. Copyright © 1997 by John Hoberman. Reprinted by permission of Houghton Mifflin Company. All rights reserved.

Reprinted, by permission, from D. Andrews, 1996, 'The Fact(s) of Michael Jordan's Blackness: Excavating a Floating Racial Signifier', in *Sociology of Sport Journal*, 13, (Human Kinetics), pp. 125–58.

D. L. Andrews for permission to reprint D. L. Andrews, "The fact(s) of Michael Jordan's blackness: excavating a floating racial signifier", *Sociology of Sport Journal*, 13 (1996): 125–158. © Human Kinetics Publisher (1996).

Carfax Publishing for permission to reprint A. Bairner and P. Shirlow, "Loyalism, Linfield and the territorial politics of soccer fandom in Northern Ireland", *Space and Polity*, 2(2) (1998): 163–177.

Marxism Today for permission to reprint J. A. Hargreaves, "Taking men on at their own games", *Marxism Today*, 28(8) (1984): 17–21.

Sage Publications for permission to reprint K. Sheard and E. Dunning, "The Rugby Football Club as a type of 'Male Preserve': some sociological notes". *International Review of Sport Sociology*, 8 (1973): 5–24. © International Sociology of Sport Association and Sage Publications, 1973.

S. Birrell and C. Cole for permission to reprint S. Birrell and C. Cole, "Double fault: Renee Richards and the construction and naturalization of difference", *Sociology of Sport Journal* 7 (1990): 1–21.

M. Messner for permission to reprint M. Messner, "Men studying masculinity: some epistemological issues in sport sociology", *Sociology of Sport Journal* 7 (1990): 136–153.

P. Markula for permission to reprint P. Markula, "Firm but shapely, fit but sexy, strong but thin: the postmodern aerobicizing female bodies", *Sociology of Sport Journal*, 12(4) (1995): 424–453.

The American Sociological Association for permission to reprint A. Sack and R. Theil, "College football and social mobility: a case study of Notre Dame football players", *Sociology of Education* 52(1) (1979): 60–66.

Carfax Publishing for permission to reprint R. Holt, "The historical meaning of amateurism: an outline", originally published as "Amateurism and its interpretation: the social origins of British sport", *Innovation*, 5(4) (1992): 19–31.

Sage Publications for permission to reprint P. Bourdieu, "Sport and social class", *Social Science Information*, 17(6) (1978): 819–840. © Sage Publications Ltd and Foundation de la Maison des Sciences de l'Homme, 1978.

D. E. Foley for permission to reprint D. E. Foley, "The great American football ritual: reproducing race, class and gender inequality", *Sociology of Sport Journal*, 7 (1990): 111–135.

Sage Publications for permission to reprint D. S. Eitzen, "Classism in sport: the powerless bear the burden", *Journal of Sport and Social Issues*, 20(1) (1996): 95–105.

J. Loy, D. Andrews and R. Rinehart for permission to reprint J. Loy, D. Andrews and R. Rinehart, "The body in culture and sport". *Sport Science Review*, 2 (1993): 69–91.

A. Klein for permission to reprint A. Klein, "Pumping irony: the crisis and contradiction in bodybuilding", *Sociology of Sport Journal*, 3(2) (1986): 112–133.

S. Guthrie and S. Castelnuovo for permission to reprint S. Guthrie and S. Castelnuovo, "Disability management among women with physical impairments: the contribution of physical activity", *Sociology of Sport Journal*, 18(1) (2001): 5–20.

ACKNOWLEDGEMENTS

Taylor & Francis Limited for permission to reprint B. McPherson, "Retirement from professional sport: the process and problems of occupational and psychological adjustment", *Sociological Symposium*, 30 (1980): 126–143. www.tandf.co.uk.

Disclaimer:

The publishers have made every effort to contact authors/copyright holders of works reprinted in *Sport: Critical Concepts in Sociology*. This has not been possible in every case, however, and we would welcome correspondence from those individuals/companies who we have been unable to trace.

INTRODUCTION
Sport and Power Relations

A key aspect of the development of sport has consisted of the emergence of an ethos which stresses the importance of equality in a twofold sense: on the one hand, equality of opportunities to participate; and on the other, equality in the conditions of competition. In both these senses, the development of modern sport can be said to have occurred as part of the long-term (but by no means simple and unilinear) processes of "democratization" that have characterized the development of the modern West.

In saying this, we are not claiming that modern sports and modern societies are characterized by anything like full equality. Nor are we suggesting that the processes of democratization referred to above are irreversible. Far from it. Like the societies in which it takes place, the participation in sports of competitors, spectators, listeners and viewers remains socially stratified – that is, subject to patterns of inequality, "inclusion" and "exclusion" – in a variety of ways. Participation in the organization, ownership and control of sport – what many regard as key determinants in this as in other areas of social life – remains socially stratified, too. Indeed, there is reason to believe that inequalities regarding sports participation have increased in many countries in recent years.

Four of the primary axes around which patterns of social stratification – the emergence and consolidation of social hierarchies – are conceived by sociologists as having clustered are gender, race, class and the body, the central organizing principles of this volume. All four are forms of power. Hopefully, it will help our student readers if we explore the issues involved a little further.

Popularly, the differences between males and females, racial groups, social classes and people who are "differently abled"[1] are widely believed to have mainly biological roots. As sociologists, however, our concern is more with the ways in which inequalities in these different (but in part overlapping) areas are *socially* produced. We are also concerned with the social production and consequences of beliefs about class, race, gender and "differential embodiment". At first glance, the differences between males and females are obviously biologically rooted. So, too, are the surface ("phenotypical")

1

differences between "blacks" and "whites". However, close observation reveals a more complex picture. For example, just as skin colour differences among and between blacks and whites tend to be questions of overlap and gradation, so the physical differences between males and females tend to be less among children and the old. There are also overlaps between males and females regarding body traits such as size, muscularity, vocal depth and hairiness. Although most of these sorts of differences certainly do have primarily biological roots – the same is true of the skin-colour and hair-form differences of racial groups but not of other supposed "racial" differences – some of them are probably also to some extent social products. For example, in both males and females, muscularity is undoubtedly, in part, a function of involvement in physical activities, and size is probably, in part, a function of diet and personal and societal affluence.

Comparative historical research is revealing regarding the effects of socially constructed beliefs about class, race and gender differentials in potentials for physical performance. It is enough in the present context just to mention two such beliefs. As Patricia Vertinsky has shown (see Volume II), in the nineteenth century it was a widely accepted "medical fact" in Western countries that sports participation would be physically injurious for females. We now know this to be untrue, or at least no more true for females than for males. Despite such knowledge, sports continue to be widely regarded as "male preserves". Indeed, conceptions of which sports are most appropriate for females to participate in, which sports "black" athletes are "naturally" suited or unsuited to, continue to operate as key influences on people's differential access to and experiences of sports. Sport, in fact, is highly significant as a site for the reproduction of ideas about physical differences because, week-in, week-out, sporting performances offer high profile "incontrovertible" supposed "proof" of biologically produced physical differences. The reaffirmation of existing prejudices is then used to legitimate a wider range of ideas about the supposedly "natural" divisions around which contemporary societies are stratified. Examples are the roles of males and females in the division of domestic labour, and the idea that blacks are naturally "physically gifted" but "intellectually challenged". In the contributions to this third volume, these and similar issues are explored in depth by our contributors.

Note

1 Until recently, it was widely believed that inherited "intelligence" varies directly with social class, i.e. that people are genetically more intelligent the higher the position in the class structure that they occupy.

Part 13

SPORT AND 'RACIAL'/ETHNIC POWER

41

THE SOURCES OF THE BLACK
ATHLETE'S SUPERIORITY

Harry Edwards

Source: *Black Scholar* 3(3) (1971): 32–41.

In 1967 and 1968, America was shocked into a new consciousness regarding the totality of black people's commitment to achieving liberation from racism, injustice, and inhumanity. During a sixteen month period ending in October of 1968 at the Olympic Games in Mexico City, a number of dedicated black athletes had taken the struggle of human dignity into the sacred empire of American sports, shattering long-standing myths, exposing countless hypocracies, and laying bare the fact that the sports establishment is nothing more nor less than racist, authoritarian, vulturistic, white America functioning in microcosm. Not since the days of Paul Leroy Robeson (the Rutgers University All-American who turned his back on the recognition derived from playing the role of the "responsible Negro athlete) has white society in general and the sports world in particular, exhibited such anger over the refusal of black men to entertain a decadent social order by performing as uni-dimensional Twentieth Century gladiators.

Since 1968, the countless rebellions, boycotts, and strikes carried out by black athletes and others have made it quite clear that the revolt in sports is a good deal more than a passing fad or political gesture. It has even spread to the ranks of white athletes, a fact attested to in recent books by Dave Meggesy and Jim Bouton who point out and denounce numerous characteristic examples of racism, facism, and inhumane exploitation in both amateur and professional athletics.

Since the onset of the revolt of the black athlete there have been numerous occurences which many interpret as indicative of improvement in the overall racial situation in the sports arena.

- The hiring of unprecedented numbers of black coaches and administrative assistants at predominantly white educational institutions which

5

have traditionally depended heavily upon black athletic talent for sports success;

- The naming of a black manager to a minor league or farm club subsidiary of a major league professional baseball team;
- The naming of three black player-coaches in the National Basketball Association;
- The establishment of athletic boards and committees at many institutions to handle the grievances of black athletes;
- The nomination of pre-1947 baseball stars to a "special" baseball hall of fame roster;
- A highly visible increase in the number of black athletes doing paid television commercials.

There have also been several positive intangibles which have emerged from the black revolt in sports. One of the most important of these has been the development of a heightened consciousness among actual and aspiring black athletes as to their political responsibilities and potentials in the worldwide black liberation struggle. Another intangible result has been a partial desolution of the struggle of the black athlete's image as the purely physical and apolitical automaton, the unquestioningly obedient Uncle Tom. These were images well-established and legitimated by a long line of Negroes who were only too happy to fulfill their assigned roles for money, a few sports trinkets, or a few sentences in the newspaper.

Finally, there is the fact that the black athlete has achieved new prestige and respect among the black masses, not because of his athletic excellence, but because, despite his relatively high status, he has at long last begun to speak out on the social and political issues effecting the lives and destinies of all Afro-American athletes and non-athletes alike. Only time will disclose whether or not these accomplishments of the revolt will have any impact toward positively altering the oppressed and degrading conditions of black people, inside and outside the sports world.

Wide-spread publicity in recent months has been given yet another "accomplishment." Many view it as a concession by the white-controlled sports world – unrecognition of the new spirit of pride, political awareness, and cultural identity among black athletes. This would-be accomplishment is embodied in the fact that diverse and highly influential persons and publications (usually considered part of the "sports establishment" in America) have finally admitted what every objective observer of the sports scene already knew – to wit, that the performance of black athletes, on the average, is significantly superior to that of whites in all sports participated in by both groups in numbers. This admission has not been put forth grudgingly; rather it has been enthusiastically presented and echoed, even by sports commentators and coaches, usually considered conservative or right-wing in their orientation toward the thrust for black dignity in sports.

*

While there can be little argument with the obvious fact that black perform-ances in sports have been and continue to be superior on the whole, to those of whites, there is room for considerable debate over the identity and char-acter of the factors which have determined that superiority and contributed to its perpetuation.

The world of the athlete is one dominated by competition, where the value of one's performance is never absolute but always relative to both the past and the present performances of others. In his newly established role as one of the most visible manifestations of black pride and competence, the black athlete often feels increased pressures to conquer "whitey" in the sports arena. Thus, in their hasty grasp for long-overdue recognition of the general superiority of blacks over whites in athletics, it was perhaps to be expected that many well-meaning black athletes would inadvertently substantiate not only the fact of that superiority itself but also the prevailing arguments put forth regarding the casual factors underlying that situation. Apparently, few paused before making their comments to give serious consideration to the broader implications of these arguments for either black athletes or the black population at large.

The central concern of this essay is to analyze these arguments and their implications. Further, what is considered here to be a more scientifically defensible postulation of the casual factors underlying black athletic superiority will be presented.

The myth of the black male's racially determined, inherent physical and athletic superiority over the white male, rivals the myth of black sexual superiority in antiquity. While both are well fixed in the Negrolore and folk-beliefs of American society, in recent years the former has been sub-ject to increasing emphasis due to the overwhelmingly disproportionate representation of black athletes on all-star rosters, on Olympic teams, in the various "most valuable player" categories, and due to the black athletes overall domination of the highly publicized or so-called "major sports" – basketball, football, baseball, track and field. But seldom in recent times has the myth of racially-linked black athletic prowess been subject to so explicit a formulation and presentation as in the January 18, 1971 issue of *Sports Illustrated* magazine. In an article entitled "An Assessment of 'Black is Best' " by Martin Kane, one of the magazine's senior editors, several arguments are detailed, discussed, and affirmed by a number of widely known medical scientists, athletic researchers, coaches, and black athletes. In essence, the article constitutes an attempt to develop a logical and scientifically defensible foundation for the assertion that black athletic superiority in sports is due to racial characteristics indigenous to the black population in America but not generally found within the white population.

Kane cites the following as evidence of the black athletes superior abilities:

1 – In basketball three of the five players named to the 1969–1970 all NBA team were black, as were all five of the athletes named to the all-rookie team. Blacks have won the league's Most Valuable Player award twelve times in the past thirteen seasons;

2 – In professional football, all four of the 1969 Rookie of the Year awards for the offense and defense were won by blacks;

3 – In baseball, black men have won the National League's Most Valuable Player awards sixteen times in the past twenty-two seasons;

4 – Today there are 150 blacks out of 600 players in major league baseball, 330 blacks out of 1,040 athletes in professional football, and 153 players out of 280 in basketball are black. Of the athletes in professional sports in 1969–70 All-Star teams, 36% in baseball were black, 44% in football were black, and blacks computed 63% of the All-Star talent in basketball.

Clearly there is no argument that black society is contributing more than its 11% share of athletes and star-status performers to professional sports. And where blatant racism and discrimination do not keep blacks from participation almost completely – such as in the Southeastern conference – a similar pattern of black domination prevails in colleges and at other amateur levels where major sports endeavors are pursued.

Attempting to explain this disproportionate representation, Kane mentions, almost in passing, the probable influences of contemporary societal conditions and then launches into a delineation and discussion of the major factors giving rise to black athletic superiority. They are as follows:

Racially linked physical and psychological characteristics
1 – Proportionately longer leg lengths, narrower hips, wider calf bones, and greater arm circumference among black athletes than among whites.

2 – A greater ratio of tendon to muscle among blacks, giving use to a condition typically termed "double jointedness," a relatively dense bone structure.

3 – A basically elongated body structure among black athletes enabling them to function as more efficient heat discipators relative to whites.

Race related psychological factors
1 – The black athlete's greater capacity for relaxation under pressure relative to the capacity of the white athlete.

Racially specific historical occurences
1 – The selectivity of American slavery in weeding out the hereditarily and congenitally weak from among those who came to be the forbearers of today's black population.

Let us now turn to a general consideration of these major factors.

8

Racially-linked physical and physiological characteristics

Kane's attempt to establish the legitimacy of this category of factors as major contributions to the emergence of black athletic superiority suffers from two basic maladies – one methodological, the other arising from a dependence upon scientifically debatable assumptions and presumptions concerning differences between the "races" of men and the impact of these differences upon capacity for physical achievement.

Simply stated, one grossly indefensible methodological tactic is obvious in virtually every case of "scientific" evidence presented in support of a physical or physiological basis for black athletic superiority. *In no case was the evidence presented gathered from a random sample of subjects selected from the black population at large in America.* Thus, supporting data, for the most part, was taken from black athletes of already proven excellence or from blacks who were available due to other circumstances reflective of some degree of uncontrolled social, political, or otherwise continued selectivity. Therefore, the generalization of the research findings on these subjects to the black population as a whole – even assuming the findings to be valid – constitutes a scientific blunder of the highest magnitude and invalidates the would-be scientific foundations of this component of the authors argument.

But there are still other considerations which doubt as to the credibility of Kane's presentation. There is first of all, the problem of justifying the posing of his argument within a context which assumes the biological and genetic validity of delineating human populations into "races." The use of such an approach in an attempt to discover athletically meaningful patterns of differences between the defined groups, does not take complete consideration of the fact that human breeding populations are determined to a great extent by cultural circumstances, and social and political conditions, as well as the factors of opportunity, propinquity, and convenience, not merely by the factor of similarity in morphological characteristics. Thus, to assume a biological and genetic validity to the concept of race implies that, as a population, Afro-Americans have bred endogamously and have maintained their original genotypical and anatomical traits – excepting for an occasional mutation brought about by natural or environmental selectivity.

This of course is nonsense. Virtually every attempt to define or pose problems within a context which either assumes or explicitly postulates the validity of a biological and/or genetic concept of race, has resulted in a troublesome issue of defensibility for the scientist involved, not to speak of the social and political problems that have emerged. This accounts for such widespread disagreement among human biologists and anthropologists concerning the definitions of race and the identification of the races of man. These definitions range all the way from the denial that genetically and biologically discernible races exist at all to those which delineate specific "races"

9

of man numbering from two or three categories to classifications totaling in the hundreds. Invariably, once a biologist or anthropologist has settled upon a definition which suits him, he discovers there is little that he can do with his "races" other than list them. For typically they have defied any effort at deriving consistent patterns of valid relationships between racial heritage and meaningful social, intellectual, or physical capabilities. Hence, Kane treads upon ground of dubious solidity from the moment he couches his argument within the assumption that scientifically valid delineations of racial groupings exist at all.

A more specific analysis of the major points incorporated into this aspect of the author's overall argument only furthers the above assertions. With regard to the alleged physical traits supposedly characteristic of black athletes, the question can justifiably be posed, "what two outstanding black athletes look alike or have identical build?" One of Kane's resource persons answers this question:

"Floyd C. 'Bud' Winter makes it quite obvious that black athletes differ from each other physically quite as much as whites do. He notes that Ray Norton, a sprinter, was tall and slender with scarcely discernible hips, that Bobby Painter, a sprinter, was squat and dumpy with a sway back and a big butt, that Denis Johnson was short and wiry, that Tommy Smith was tall and wiry and so on." Further evidence is plentiful: "What physical characteristics does Lew Alcindor have in common with Elgin Baylor, or Wilt Chamberlain with Al Attles, etc? The point is simply that Wilt Chamberlain and Lew Alcindor have more in common physically with Mel Counts and Henry Finkel, two seven-foot white athletes, than with most of their fellow black athletes."

Even excepting the hyperbolic illustrations just documented, what emerges from any objective analysis of supposed physical differences between so-called races is the undeniable fact that there exist more differences between individual members of any one racial group than between any two groups as a whole. So, a fabricated "average" of the differences between racial group-ings, even if it is scientifically generated, may serve certain heuristic purposes but provides a woefully inadequate basis for explaining specific cases of ath-letic excellence or superior ability. No black athlete conforms to that artificial average. As a matter of scientific fact, black athletes, as is true with the black population as a whole, manifest a wide range of physical builds, body pro-portions, and other highly diverse anatomical, physiological, and biological features, as do other groups including the so-called white race.

Recognition of this essential fact precludes the type of incredible qualifica-tion that Kane is forced to make when faced with exceptions which do not fit the framework which he has developed. A case in point is his assertion that the physical differences between white and black racial groupings pre-disposes blacks to dominate the sports requiring speed and strength while whites, due to racially-linked physical traits, are predestined to prevail in those sporting events requiring endurance. When confronted with the fact that black Kenyans won distance races and defeated highly touted and capable whites in the 1968 Olympic Games, the author makes the ridiculous posthoc assertion that (the Kenyans) Keino and Bikila have black skin but many white features.

Directly pertinent to Kane's presentation of would-be evidence that physiological differences underly black athletic superiority are the facts concerning efficient heat dissipation. In essence, the author attempts to present a case for the notion that due to an elongation of the body, black athletes are more efficient heat dissipators than are whites and thus, excel over whites in sports. First of all, either tall or short individuals may have body builds which enable them to function as relatively efficient heat dispations. The efficiency with which one's body dissipates heat is only incidentally related to the factor of height; it is directly related to the rate of body surface to body mass. Therefore, one way to maximize heat dissipating efficiency is to present a proportionately greater amount of body surface to the air by stretching a given body mass into an elongated shape. Another way of changing the gross mass to surface ratio is to change the overall size of the body. Hence, a decrease in size will decrease the mass (proportional to the cube root of any linear dimension) in relation to the surface area, the end product being the accomplishment of the same thing that body elongation can do.

Substantiation for the accuracy of this formulation is evidenced simply by the Nilotic African or Watusi who is normal in body mass but elongated in shape. Thus, the factor of elongated body proportions become neutralized by the fact that a small white athlete could be as efficient a heat dissipator as an elongated black athlete. In sports where the small athlete can function effectively against other athletes, one would expect at least occasionally to see small and elongated black and white athletes performing at comparable levels of excellence. Evidence of the invalidity of Kane's argument in this regard is the fact that black athletes of a variety of sizes and shapes have dominated sports such as track and field over white athletes who themselves embodied a variety of shapes and sizes and thus body mass to body surface ratio. One last point: given the complexity of variables which determine athletic excellence, even where physical differences exist between individuals, one proceeds on dangerous grounds when he assumes that these observable or decimable differences are the major factors determining differences in demonstrated athletic excellence.

Race-related pyschological factors

Here, the incredibility of Kane's presentation and the supporting statements of those who attempt to substantiate it are almost beyond belief. The

11

academic belief in the existence of a national or a racial "character" was supposedly disposed of by scholars decades ago. Their persistence among the ranks of coaches and other segments of the American population only indicates the difficulty with which racial stereotypes and caricatures are destroyed or altered to comply with prevailing knowledge. Kane and his resource persons, mostly coaches, recreate a portrait of the black athlete as the happy-go-lucky, casual, "what – me worry?" Negro made so familiar to Americans through history books, Stephen Fetchit movies, and other societal outlets. But beside the fact that the overall portrayal itself is inappropriate, not even the specific psychological traits attributed to black athletes are substantiated by contemporary knowledge.

Kane quotes Lloyd C. Winter, former coach of a long line of successful black track and field athletes as stating: "A limber athlete has body control, and body control is part of skill. It is obvious that many black people have some sort of head-start motor in them, but for now I can only theorize that their great advantage is relaxation under stress. As a class, the black athletes who have trained under me are far ahead of whites in that one factor – relaxation under pressure. It's their secret."

In data collected by Bruce C. Ogolvie and Thomas A. Tutko, two athletic psychologists whose work was ironically featured in the same issue of *Sports Illustrated* in which Kane's article appears, a strong case is made for the fact that black athletes are significantly less relaxed than white athletes in the competitive situation. (I am intimately familiar with this data as a result of my Ph.D. dissertation.) Using a test which has been found to have a high degree of reliability in both cross-cultural and simple comparative investigations, the following findings emerged when the psychological orientations of successful black and white athletes were compared:

1 – On the I.P.A.T., successful black athletes showed themselves to be considerably more serious, concerned and "uptight" than their white counterparts as indicated by their relative scores on the item "Soben – happy-go-lucky." Blacks had a mean stern score of 5.1 as compared to a mean score for whites of 5.5 (level of significance of differences is .01; N = 396 whites, 136 blacks).

2 – On the I.P.A.T. item of "Casual-Controlled" successful black athletes, indicating a more controlled orientation. Blacks had a mean stern score of 6.6 as compared with the whites mean score of 6.2 (level of significance of differences is .01; N = 396 whites, 136 blacks).

Sociologically, this pattern of differences given black athletes is expected, as they are aware that they operate at a decided disadvantage competing against whites for highly valued positions and rewards in an admittedly white racist society. Furthermore, sports hold the only promise of escape from the material degradation of oppressed black society. Thus, the assertion that

black athletes are more "relaxed" than whites not only lacks scientific unda-
tion but is ludicrous as even a common sense assumption.

Racially specific historical occurrences

This is perhaps the most odious part of Kane's presentation, perhaps
because he enlists the opinions of undoubtedly well-meaning but
uninformed and unthinking black athletes to support his assertions. Kane
cites the remarks of Yale University graduate Calvin Hill who now plays
football for the Dallas Cowboys professional football team:

> I have a theory about why so many pro stars are black. I think it boils
> down to the survival of the fittest. Think of what the African slaves were
> forced to endure in this country merely to survive. Well, black athletes
> are their descendants. They are the offspring of those who are physically
> and mentally tough enough to survive . . . We were simply bred for phys-
> ical qualities.

Continuing, Kane himself states that "it might be that without special breeding the African has a superior physique." The statements of Kane and his
resource persons evidence confusion as to the scope of characteristics
involved in the selectivity process as it has effected mankind. Natural selection or "the survival of the fittest" has been predicated upon relative strength
and physical attributes to a lesser degree in mankind than in any other form
of animal life. This has been due largely to man's tremendously developed
mental capabilities. The same would have held for the slave. While some may
have survived as a result of greater physical strength and toughness, many
undoubtedly also survived due to their shrewdness and thinking abilities.

Secondly, Kane and his informants speak as if blacks in American society
have somehow remained "pure" as a racial stock. The fact of the matter is
that our best sociological, genetic, and demographical knowledge indicates
that the genetic make up of blacks in America is at least 35% white, not
counting genetic influences from various other so-called racial groupings.
Therefore, to assert that Afro-Americans are superior athletes due to the
genetic make-up or physical prowess of the original slaves would be naive
and ridiculous.

Finally, Kane's argument is that for blacks, demonstration of physical ability alone is all that is required to become a successful athlete. Anyone who is
even vaguely familiar with the internal dynamics of organized sports at
either the amateur or professional levels in America, knows that physical
ability will *maybe* open that door, but before one reaches the level of a Bill
Russell or a Gayle Sayers there is a great number of political psychological
and racial hurdles to conquer. Hence, perhaps the most vaguely related
influence on the determination of black athletic superiority is the genetic or

biological heritage of the black population as a racial group. Undoubtedly of much more importance as a determining factor is the facility with which the black athlete surmounts arbitrary political, psychological, and racial barriers, reflective of the contemporary sickness of American society. For the black athlete, the implications of Kane's article and similar perspectives on black athletic superiority are the following:

1 – These arguments imply that the accomplishments of the black athlete in sports are as natural to him as flight is to an eagle, and thus the facts of a lifetime of dedication, effort, sweat, blood, and tears are ignored. What Kane is essentially telling black athletes is that "you would have been a superior athlete despite yourself." Perhaps it is coincidental but such a stance allows racist whites in American society to affirm the undeniable superiority of the black athlete on the one hand and maintain their definitions of black people as lazy, shiftless, and irresponsible on the other.

2 – The notion that black athletes are by racial heritage physically superior to white athletes provides a basis for maintaining a white monopoly on certain key positions in sports which ostensibly require greater thinking and organizational ability – e.g., quarterback in football, manager in baseball, and head coach in most sports. Thus, no matter how excellent an athlete a black player might be, a white player always gets the nod over him for these "intellectual" positions since the black athlete excels on inborn physical superiority alone. Since the white athlete, under these conditions, would have to work harder toward mastering any given sport, he would probably know the dynamics of the sport better than the black athlete who "naturally" sails through the requirements of the endeavor and, hence, the white athlete would make a better coach or manager.

The major implication of Kane's argument for the black population at large is that it opens the door for at least an informal acceptance of the idea that whites are *intellectually* superior to blacks. Blacks, whether athletes or non-athletes, must not give even passing credence to the possibility of white intellectual superiority. By a tempered or even enthusiastic admission of black physical superiority, the white population of this racist society loses nothing. For it is a simple fact that a multitude of even lower animals are physically superior, not only to whites, but to mankind as a whole: gorillas are physically superior to whites, leopards are physically superior to whites, as are lions, walruses, and elephants. So by asserting that blacks are physically superior, whites at best reinforce some old stereotypes long held about Afro-Americans – to wit, that they are little removed from the apes in their evolutionary development.

On the other hand, intellectual capability is the highest priced commodity on the world market today. If in a fit of black identity or simple stupidity, we accept the myth of innate black physical superiority, we could be inadvertently recognizing and accepting an ideology which has been used as the justification for black slavery, segregation, and general oppression. Further, it was just such an ideology which led to genocide against native Americans in this country and against the Jews in Nazi Germany.

To those black athletes who have spoken out in support of the ideas expressed in Kane's article, I say only that it is a wise warrior who proceeds with caution and discretion when an enemy tosses bouquets in his direction. The argument that blacks are physically superior to whites as athletes or as a people is merely a racist ideology camouflaged to appeal to the ignorant, the unthinking, and the unaware in a period heightened by black identity. If it is accepted by blacks, whites will be released of the pressure to come up with a white hope in sports, year after year, and they can also maintain their gut beliefs in white supremacy – unchallenged. The sacrifice of black human dignity and respect, born of almost 400 years of struggle and despair, is too high a price to pay for white recognition of black athletic prowess. The black athlete has worked hard and diligently to achieve his present status in the athletic world – perhaps harder than his white counterpart, who has fewer number of obstacles facing him.

What then are the major factors underlying black athletic superiority? The factors underlying black athletic superiority emerge from a complex of societal conditions. These conditions instill a heightened motivation among black male youths to achieve success in sports; thus, they channel a proportionately greater number of talented black people than whites into sports participation. Our best sociological evidence indicates that capacity for physical achievement (like other common human traits such as intelligence, artistic ability, etc.) are evenly distributed throughout any population. Thus, it cuts across class, religious, and, more particularly, racial lines. For race, like class and religion, is primarily a culturally determined classification. *The simple fact of the matter is that the scientific concept of race has no proven biological or genetic validity.* As a cultural delineation, however, it does have a social and political reality. This social and political reality of race is the primary basis of stratification in this society and the key means of determining the priority of who shall have access to means – valued goods and services.

Blacks are relegates in this country, having the lowest priority to claiming valued goods and services. This fact, however, does not negate the equal and proportionate distribution of talent across both black and white populations. Hence, a situation arises wherein whites, being the dominant group in the society, have access to *all* means toward achieving desirable valuables defined by the society. Blacks on the other hand are channeled into the one or two endeavors open to them – sports, and to a lesser degree – entertainment.

Bill Russell once stated that he had to work as hard to achieve his status as the greatest basketball player of the last decade, as the president of General Motors had to work to achieve his position. The evidence tends to indicate that Russell is quite correct. In short, it takes just as much talent, perserverance, dedication, and earnest effort to succeed in sports as to become a leading financier, business executive, attorney or doctor. Few occupations (music and art being perhaps the exceptions) demand more time and dedication than sports. A world-class athlete will usually have spent a good deal of his youth practicing the skills and techniques of his chosen sports endeavor.

The competition for the few positions is extremely keen and if he is fortunate he will survive in that competition long enough to become a professional athlete or an outstanding figure in one of the amateur sports. For as he moves up through the various levels of competition, fewer and fewer slots or positions are available and the competition for these becomes increasingly intense because the rewards are greater. (Since the talents of 25 million Afro-Americans have a disproportionately higher concentration in sports, the number of highly gifted whites in sports is proportionately less than the number of blacks.) Under such circumstances, black athletes naturally predominate. Further, the white athletes who do participate in sports operate at a psychological disadvantage (relative to their black counterparts) because they believe blacks to be inherently superior as athletes. Thus, the white man has become the chief victim of his own lie.

Therefore, white racism in American society seems to be responsible for black athletic superiority to whites. That being the case, the real question is perhaps not "why is the number of black athletes so disproportionately high?". The basic factor determining that the number of blacks in sports does not soar still higher is white racism in the sports sphere itself. Sports aggregations at all levels of athletic participation operate under informal quotas as to the number of blacks allowed to make the roster. This is particularly true in the college and professional ranks where the rewards of participation are relatively higher. Also, as was mentioned earlier, certain positions in sports – such as quarterback – are the monopoly of white players.

Each year white America publicizes a "white hope" in sports: in 1968, it was Jim Ryun at the Olympic games; in 1970 it was Jerry Quarry in his fight against Muhammed Ali; in 1971 it was Pete Maravich. If this society is ever to realize its fondest dream in the sports realm – the development of at least relative parity between black and white athletes with regard to sports excellence – it must give Afro-Americans an opportunity for achievement in high status endeavors outside of sports participation.

It is well known that all the great quarterbacks are white because blacks have never, en masse, had an opportunity to play that position. All the great professional football coaches and baseball managers are white because blacks have never had an opportunity to be professional head football coaches or major league baseball managers. So even these "great" white sports figures are contrived phonies, as are the so-called greats in the many other sports closed to blacks. This is due to racism which leads to a de facto denial of opportunity to blacks who have potential for excellence in these activities. The latter is particularly true of sports such as golf, tennis, swimming and auto racing.

The necessity for white America to generate a white hope year after year, and to attempt to justify far-flung and irrational myths (as postulated in Kane's article), will all decrease proportionately to the degree that American society divests itself of the racist restrictions that limit opportunity for blacks across the occupational spectrum. As long as sports provide the only visible, high-status, occupational role model for the masses of black male youths, black superiority over whites shall go unchallenged.

42

AN ENVIRONMENTAL EXPLANATION FOR RACE DIFFERENCES IN BASKETBALL PERFORMANCE

Donal E. Carlston

Source: *Journal of Sport and Social Issues* 7(2) (1983): 30–51.

There is considerable evidence that black and white basketball players differ in their styles of play. Existing physiological, personality, and sociological explanations for these differences appear to be inadequate. An alternative environmental theory is proposed that links player styles and attitudes to environmental factors influencing inner city and on-city playground settings. Specifically, it is hypothesized that factors such as crowding foster the development of functional playing rules and norms, which in turn influence player development. This paper details possible causal relationships between different aspects of the playing environment and player skills, styles, and attitudes.

Both sportswriters (Kirkpatrick, 1968; Kane, 1971; DuPree, 1978a) and social scientists (Worthy and Markle, 1970; Jones and Hochner, 1973; Snyder and Spreitzer, 1978) have observed that systematic differences exist between the performance of white and black athletes. While the nature of the alleged differences varies from writer to writer, it is generally argued that black athletes are faster, jump higher, react more quickly, are more graceful, play with more style, or in other ways out-perform their white counterparts.

Numerous theories have been advanced to explain these performance differences (e.g., Kane, 1971; Worthy and Markle, 1970; Jones and Hochner, 1973; McPherson, 1975), but none of these provides a completely satisfactory explanation for the kinds of differences that have been suggested. The theories of social scientists often gloss over the finer details of athletics, focusing only on the most global or obvious aspects of sports performance. The theories of sports writers attend more closely to the nuances of sports, but fail to provide systematic descriptions of causal mechanisms that might underlie the observed racial differences.

The present paper argues that the oft-observed racial differences in sports performance are not really racial at all, but rather, reflect the differing environments in which black and white players generally develop their skills. While similar arguments have been advanced previously (e.g., Edwards, 1973; Phillips, 1976; Greenfield, 1980) this paper will attempt to present a more comprehensive theory relating differences in athletic performance to specific environmental factors that influence the development of playing skills, styles and attitudes. This theory focuses exclusively on the sport of basketball, a narrowness necessary if the discussion is to progress beyond the vague generalizations that characterize much of the literature in this area. However, while the discussion will be confined to basketball, the mechanisms and effects to be discussed may well have implications for other sports.

Racial differences in basketball performance

One of the most concrete pieces of evidence that racial differences exist in basketball performance is that blacks are represented on basketball teams in much larger proportions than they are in the population at large. While blacks comprise about 11% of the U.S. population, they comprise 27% of NCAA basketball teams (Yetman and Eitzen, 1972) and over 73% of professional basketball teams in this country (Poliquin, 1981). Some writers have suggested that the proportion of black players might be even higher if teams did not have implicit racial quotas (cf. Yetman and Eitzen, 1972).

Blacks are represented in similarly high proportions among those who excel at the professional level. Over a recent 13 year period, 12 of the National Basketball Association's most-valuable players were black (Edwards, 1973). In 1980, 84% of the top 25 players in the N.B.A. were black (Street and Smith's Official Basketball Yearbook, 180); and through the first half of the 1980–81 season, 100% of the top "assist" players, 93% of the top scorers, and 70% of the top rebounders in the N.B.A. were black (Poliquin, 1981). The general manager of The Philadelphia 76'ers states "The black athlete dominates the N.B.A. That's not an opinion, that's a fact." (quoted by Poliquin, 1981).

Analyses of professional basketball statistics further indicate the existence of performance differences between black and white players. Jones and Hochner (1973) found that black players averaged 25% more rebounds than white players, and blacks shot more often than whites relative to the number of assists they made. Finally, these researchers found that black players shot free throws with about 4% *less* accuracy than white players.

Perhaps even more interesting than these performance statistics are the unquantifiable stylistic differences that a number of observers have noted between white and black players (DuPree, 1978; Greenfield, 1980;

19

Kirkpatrick, 1968; Novak, 1976; Wielgus & Wolff, 1980). In their remarkably uniform descriptions, the black playground player is characterized as smooth, flashy and independent, and his game is described as one of spin moves, double pumps, and slam dunks. In contrast, the white player is characterized as hard-working, precise, dull but efficient, and his game is described as one of picks and screens and the high percentage shot. As summarized by Greenfield (1980): " 'White' ball, then, is the basketball of patience and method. 'Black' ball is the basketball of electric self-expression" (p. 318).

These stereotypes are widely held by basketball players, coaches and reporters (cf. Wielgus & Wolff, 1980; Jordan, 1979) although the black style is sometimes labeled "city," "playground" or "ghetto" ball and the white style is termed "noncity," "blue collar," or "midwest." Prototypic exhibitors of the "city" style at the professional level are Julius Erving, Earl Monroe, and George Gervin and prototypic exhibitors of the non-city style are John Havlicek, Dave Cowens and Bill Walton. Of course, there have also been some blacks who exhibited the non-city style (e.g. Wes Unseld) and some whites who played the city game (e.g. Pete Maravich).

The stylistic differences between black and white basketball players are important because they suggest the profound nature of the differences between these groups of athletes. It is not simply that blacks can jump higher or run faster or play better than whites. It is that blacks and whites appear to be playing two different kinds of games, as dissimilar in some respects as they are similar. Existing theories of racial differences in sports performance generally fail to recognize the broad and complex nature of these dissimilarities.

Previous theories

A variety of theories have been proposed to explain performance differences between black and white athletes. Among others, Kane (1971) has proposed that blacks possess physiological characteristics that contribute to superior speed, reflexes and jumping ability. Writers have also proposed that personality differences between blacks and whites may contribute to performance differences. For example, black athletes have been described as more "relaxed" (Kane, 1971) and as more "reactive" (Worthy & Markle, 1970) than white athletes. It has also been suggested that social factors contribute to an exaggerated emphasis on sports participation and excellence among black youngsters (Edwards, 1973; Michener, 1976) and to different patterns of socialization for black athletes (McPherson, 1975).

Although an exhaustive critique of these theories is not possible in this limited space, some common shortcomings will be mentioned. First, most of the theories are based on assumed differences between whites and black athletes that have not been convincingly demonstrated with appropriate samples. For example, as Edwards (1973) notes in his critique, neither physiological nor personality differences have been shown to exist between the black and white populations of the United States as a whole nor between carefully selected samples of black and white athletes. Furthermore, the tremendous heterogeneity in body and personality types within each racial group contrasts markedly with the homogeneity attributed to the athletic styles of each group. In this regard, it should be noted that the "prototypical" exhibitors of city and non-city playing styles listed earlier represent a wide variety of body types and personalities, none of which can be appropriately characterized as "representative" or "typical" for their racial groups.

Second, these theories fail to provide tight linkage between the antecedents they assume and the kinds of performance differences that have been observed. For example, it is unclear how any of the physiological differences that have been described could lead black players to emphasize moves, improvisation, and "electric self-expression," to shoot free throws more poorly, or to pass less often than white players. Even rebounding, which might seem to reflect physiologically-based jumping ability, is probably actually more dependent on skills such as positioning and timing (cf. Davis, 1969). It seems similarly unlikely that personality characteristics can explain more than some peripheral aspects of performance such as demeanor, coachability or aggressiveness. As Edwards (1973) observed: "It will be noted that none of the (personality) factors studied make any direct contribution to the development of actual physical skills or athletic ability (p. 223)".

It is conceivable that the improvisational and exhibitionistic styles of black basketball might reflect global personality traits, but research suggests that black athletes actually score lower on scales measuring impulsivity and exhibitionism than do white athletes (Ogilvie and Tutko, 1968). In any case, there is no evidence that players' off-court personality traits are linked in any meaningful way to their on-court playing personalities.

Similarly, many of the differences in the socialization of white and black athletes that McPherson (1975) observed are only tenuously related to athletic performance. For example, McPherson's finding that black (track) athletes come from larger, sociologically disadvantaged, matriarchically dominated families does not appear to have any direct bearing on athletic skills or styles. Even those sociological factors that might logically lead to variations in athletic style or performance have not been carefully linked to such effects. For example, the overemphasis on sports in black communities (cf. Edwards, 1973; Michener, 1976) might well lead blacks to take up basketball at a younger age, and to devote themselves more thoroughly and exclusively to the sport (see McPherson, 1975, for findings among track athletes). This increased devotion to the sport might explain the greater talent of black players, and consequently, their overrepresentation at the collegiate and professional levels, but it is unclear how it would lead to the various other stylistic and performance differences that have been observed. One might argue that because blacks devote more time to playing basketball, they develop greater facility at difficult skills such as spin moves, pump shots, and dunking the ball. But the assumption that the "expressive" moves and styles of black basketball reflect greater practice has a number of implications that do not appear to be accurate. For example, this implies that white professional players, who have devoted innumerable hours to basketball over their careers, should almost invariably exhibit more of the "black playground style" than black youngsters on the playgrounds, who are relatively new at the game. As this does not appear to be true, the assumption that greater experience with the game necessarily leads to more expressive play seems unjustified. It is similarly unclear why increased playing time would lead to poorer free throw shooting or decreased passing by black players (see Jones and Hochner, 1973). Consequently, the links between various sociological factors and observed differences between white and black basketball players remain rather tenuous.

Finally, as the preceding discussion emphasizes, none of the existing theories for race differences in athletic performance can account for more than a small portion of the differences that appear to exist. Physiological differences between whites and blacks might explain a few differences in physical talents, personality differences might relate to the expressiveness of playing styles, and sociological factors might explain the overrepresentation of blacks in upper levels of play. Consequently, a variety of different theories might be unparsimoniously combined to obtain some explanatory power. Even then, if all of these different theories were substantiated, there would still be glaring gaps in our understanding of race differences in playing styles. Why do black players at the professional level shoot free throws somewhat more poorly than do whites? Why do black players emphasize scoring over other facets of play? Why do white and black youngsters play pick-up games using different rules to govern play? Existing theories are clearly unable to provide satisfactory answers to such questions.

The objective of this paper is to advance such an explanation, based on a variety of different observations and sources. These observations reflect a distillation from personal experiences and observations as a pick-up ball player, interviews with numerous players from a variety of backgrounds, and descriptions in secondary sources, including sports biographies (Auerbach & Fitzgerald, 1977; Cousy & Hirshberg, 1958; Frazier & Berkow, 1974; McPhee, 1965; Russell & Branch, 1979; Wolf, 1972), other basketball books (Holzman & Lewin, 1973; Jordan, 1979; Wielgus & Wolff, 1980) and books on sports sociology (Edwards, 1973; Michener, 1976; Snyder & Spreitzer, 1978). These various sources provide a clear and consistent description of basketball in rural, suburban and inner city communities, and the resultant explanation for basketball styles has a coherence that I believe readers will find compelling. Nonetheless, until empirical evidence is collected to support these observations, this explanation must be considered speculative and preliminary.

A theory of environmental influences on player development

Overview

Most black players learn the game of basketball under conditions differing substantially from those surrounding most developing white players. The inner city basketball courts frequented by blacks are generally crowded with large numbers of players competing for valuable playing time on the limited facilities. On these over-crowded courts, rules and norms have developed to handle the abundance of competitors, and to insure that superior players are able to practice and develop their skills. I contend that these norms subtly shape the skills and styles and attitudes of the inner city player in predictable ways.

In contrast, in the rural and suburban communities where most white players grow up, the number of available courts often exceeds the number of developing players. White players may spend countless hours practicing alone on their own driveway, or playing with a few acquaintances on one of the public courts provided in schools or parks. I will suggest that the skills players develop playing by themselves differ predictably from the skills that are developed in the press of competition. Furthermore, the rules and norms that evolve to govern competitive play in such neighborhoods take maximum advantage of these skills when players do converge for pick-up games. These rules also encourage participation by marginal players, who are needed if enough people are to be attracted to allow a game. It is hypothesized that these various rules, coupled with hours of individual practice, shape players' skills, styles and attitudes, creating the typical white playing style.

In summary, then, it is proposed that the different playing conditions in white and black communities lead to different playing rules and norms, and in turn to the different styles and abilities that observers have noted. In many ways this formulation is similar to Barker's (1960) theory of "overstaffed" and "understaffed" environments. Barker argues that overstaffed environments are characterized by social norms that discourage participation except by the most talented, and by a competitiveness that allows these talented individuals to rise to the top. Understaffed environments are characterized by norms that encourage participation and provide for a more egalitarian reward structure. The present formulation extends these ideas by describing a whole chain of causal factors, beginning with environmental pressures such as crowding, including the development of athletic skills and norms, and ending with the kinds of performance and stylistic differences that writers have observed among basketball players.

Environmental influences

Playing conditions

Inner city games

The inner city provides relatively few basketball courts for a relatively large number of basketball players. The local playgrounds or schoolyards where most courts are located are spread widely through rather densely populated communities, and many of the baskets they provide are no longer really usable. Yet, for a variety of social and economic reasons (cf. Michener, 1971), basketball is one of the more popular activities among inner city males, and consequently, large numbers of players converge on the available courts, hoping to get into games. This crowding leads to competition for spots on teams and provides an audience of would-be players and hangers-on on to watch the games. It is common for 10 to 20 spectators to watch from the sidelines, and when the players in the ongoing game are prominent enough, audiences of 100 or more are possible (see Axthelm, 1970). Crowding, competition for playing time, and audiences are factors that vitally affect the nature of the city game.

Non-city games

The central problem in the rural, small town and suburban communities where most whites learn their basketball, is player scarcity, rather than crowding on the courts. The proportion of middle class and rural youngsters who play basketball is relatively low, particularly in the off-season, when other sports and other diversions draw off sizeable numbers of potential players. Those hard-core devotees who maintain year-round interest in basketball are spread across numerous playground and schoolyard courts and an almost infinite number of driveway courts. Consequently, these players have difficulty rounding up enough other people to play with, and a good deal of the time they resort to solitary practice at the park or in their own driveway (see, for example, Bill Bradley's experience, described by McPhee, 1965). The scarcity of players and the hours spent practicing alone are critical in shaping the typical "white" playing style.

Player development

City players

The city player learns basketball and develops his talents in the endless succession of games that characterize inner city play. Consequently, his skills are shaped in ways that reflect the demands of competition. Almost from the first time a player touches a basketball, someone else is trying to steal it, or block it, and the player needs to learn techniques to defend himself and the basketball from the ever-present defense. A player learns to dribble low, on the side away from the defender, to spin and fake, and to keep his head up, so he can see where the defense is coming from. He learns to deliver his shots and passes in a circuitous manner, keeping the ball close to the protected side of his body, so it won't be tipped away. And he learns to circumvent would-be blockers by faking them off their feet, altering shots in mid-air, and reaching around the basket so the rim and net shield off attacking hands. The moves, fakes, and pump-shots displayed by city players are thus essential components of their styles from the start, because these skills are essential in the games where these individuals learn to play.

City players also learn to accept contact as a routine part of basketball. Jostling, bumping and hacking are almost integral to basketball games, and players who develop their talents in competition naturally learn to handle a high level of such contact. Hence, the city player may be better able to maintain control of the basketball when attacked by a defender, and to learn to shoot while pressured.

Non-city players

The non-city player develops his playing skills largely free from the press of competition. Playing alone on his driveway or at the park, he has little need to protect the basketball on his dribble or his shots. He assumes an upright posture facing the basket, dribbles high in front of his body, delivers the ball carelessly from the front, and learns a simple, straight-forward shooting style that is effective as long as there is no defender. Of course, on occasions he mimics the players he has seen on television, faking and spinning and driving in for a fancy lay-up. But lacking any real defensive pressure, the player fails to make the many subtle physical adjustments that would be necessary to evade an actual defender. Consequently, these moves are unlikely to be effective in real competition, and they contribute little to the player's development.

To entertain himself in the absence of competition, the player is likely to work on his shooting form and effectiveness, consciously altering each aspect of his shot until he achieves the perfect form characteristic of great pure shooters. John McPhee (1965) describes how Bill Bradley consciously analyzed and changed each of his shots to mimic players he admired, and how his practice sessions involved systematically moving from spot to spot on the court, repeating each shot a dozen times. Similarly, former Celtic player Frank Ramsey explains how in practice he would "try to go back to the fundamentally correct way of taking each shot" and to check his technique against the ideal standard (Sharmon, 1968). Such devotion to the form and mechanics of basketball shots is most characteristic of players who spend a lot of time practicing alone.

In essence, then, the non-city player is likely to develop excellent shooting form, and a repertoire of effective shots that he has taken hundreds of times before, while practicing. However, he is unlikely to develop the stance or moves necessary to single-handedly defeat an aggressive defender. And he will be accustomed to taking his shots without hands in his face or body contact throwing him off balance.

In time, the non-city player will face more and more competition, and if he is to excel, he will need to develop better ball handling skills and one-on-one moves. But he is likely to always be most comfortable using his basic, upright, classic shooting form that he developed early in his playing career. Of course, given his inability to adjust and overcome a pressing defender, such a player will be most effective when he can lose the defense and get open for the kind of unencumbered shot that he's been taking his whole life. It is not surprising, then, that a style of play develops in rural and suburban communities that provides these kinds of opportunities, as discussed later in this paper.

Playground rules and norms

When neighborhood "pick-up" basketball games are organized, it is necessary to change the "official" rules to accommodate the unique circumstances of informal competition. There are no pre-existing teams to play one another, no coach to determine who from each team gets to play, no officials to call fouls, and no clock to specify when competition is over. Furthermore, on many playing courts there is only one basket, which must be used by both competing teams, rather than two opposing baskets as found in full court basketball. To handle these circumstances, neighborhood players must adopt a special set of rules to govern play. A number of aspects of play are also governed by implicit social norms, which reflect the expectations of other players, though they are not articulated as explicit rules.

The playing rules and norms are enforced and maintained through the imposition of social sanctions against those who disregard the conventions (cf. Schachter, 1951). Among the most severe kinds of sanctions is physical violence, which sometimes involves outright assault, but more commonly is "disguised" as overly aggressive play. Such physical sanctions are most commonly applied in retaliation for violations of body contact norms. Deviant players may also be excluded from play in different ways, corresponding to the rejection or ostracism discussed by Schachter (1951) and others (e.g., Latane, 1966). Players can also be partially or "psychologically" excluded (cf. Schachter, 1951) by teammates who decline to pass them the basketball. This kind of sanction is commonly used against a player who is taking too many "bad shots." Finally, deviant players may be subjected to various kinds of verbal harassment, including threats, criticism, and ridicule.

On the more positive side, playing behavior is also shaped through positive reinforcements such as compliments and hand slapping. Through combinations of sanctions and positive reinforcements, players can shape each other's behavior, teaching and enforcing the playing rules and norms that exist in different communities.

It is here hypothesized that these rules and norms reflect the different demands of the city and non-city playing environments. In particular, crowding on city basketball courts seems to have led to a system of play that allots playing time according to ability, makes use of skills developed in competition, speeds up games, and allows superior players to dominate play. In contrast, the sparsity of players in non-city environments seems to have led to a set of rules that encourages the participation of marginal players, makes use of skills developed in solo practice, slows down games and prevents superior players from dominating other participants. These differing functions are perhaps most evident in the different systems that have developed for choosing teams in the two types of communities.

Choosing teams

When players gather for informal, pick-up basketball games, there are no established teams to face each other. It is, therefore, necessary for participants to establish a system for determining which players will constitute each team, and which teams will compete in what sequence on the neighborhood court. The systems that have evolved in America's inner cities differ fundamentally from those existing in non-city environments.

In the inner city, the central factor affecting the rules of pick-up games is the overabundance of players who would like to use the basketball court. If all the awaiting players take turns, sharing the facilities equally, the playing time alloted to the best players is likely to be insufficient to allow development and maintenance of their skills. Yet the best players must be able to hone these skills in order to compete successfully for school teams, college scholarships or professional contracts. Consequently, games must be organized so that a) a large number of players can be worked in during the course of the playing day and b) the best players receive the most and the best competition. To accomplish these ends, a system has evolved in most inner city areas where the team to win a pick-up game gets to continue playing against a succession of challengers, until some other team wins (cf. Wielgus and Wolff, 1980). The challenging teams are selected by a series of "captains" who have declared their intention to challenge the winners, by calling out "I've got winners" or "I've got the next game." These claims represent an informal "take-a-number" system providing an orderly succession of captains. When each captain's turn comes up, he is allowed to choose four other players to make up his challenging team. He is given great latitude in doing so, and may include friends or players who participated in the preceeding game or players waiting to play (including those who have only just arrived at the court).

The captain must choose a team strong enough to beat the reigning winners, however, or he will be quickly defeated and find himself sitting on the sidelines, possibly waiting half the day for another opportunity to play. Consequently, the captains are under considerable pressure to put together the best possible group of players for their challenge. A certain amount of politicing takes place on the sidelines as captains try to attract star players to their team, using their priority ("I've got the next game") or their other players ("We've got Wilt; we can't lose") as bargaining chips, and players try to get on the best team they can, using friendship or reputation to close the deal. The challengers then take their turns on the court, trying to dethrone the champions so that they can continue to play, defending against other challenging teams still in line.

These rules encourage the survival of the fittest, with the strongest players coalescing into a team that may hold the court all afternoon, intermediate players being regularly chosen to fill out challenging teams, and weak players sitting out most of the games or enjoying, at best, a few futile minutes of play before being vanquished. The end result of this system is that players generally enjoy playing time proportional to their abilities. The star players, who are most likely to eventually graduate from the playground to organized competition, are most likely to be chosen by the captains. The stars are also able to offer their services to a team that is already strong, and thus to win and hold the court. Yet the system has enough flux so that precocious youngsters can maneuver themselves onto teams and into games, where they may play for some time (if they don't hurt their team too much), accumulating valuable experience against the best players in the neighborhood.

This kind of system will work most effectively in assuring that better players rise to the top if several conditions are met. First, games should move as quickly as possible, particularly when one team consists primarily of inferior players. Quick games are clearly desirable in the inner city simply to allow more players to play. But quick games also allow better players and better teams to rise more rapidly through the ranks, so that the best players come to win and hold the court without prolonged waiting. Second, games should be structured so that they give maximum advantage to the players with the best chances of succeeding in organized basketball. It is desirable for the best players to win, since upset victories by lesser players serve only to deny the better players valuable playing time. Consequently, the inner city game should be played in such a way that better players are favored while lesser players are disadvantaged. A number of rules to be discussed later in this section serve both to speed up games and to give better players a competitive edge.

The central pressure that non-city rules must deal with is not overcrowding but under-manning. As previously noted, it is difficult to get enough players assembled for a basketball game in many communities, particularly at certain times of the year. Consequently, teams are often rounded out by inviting younger brothers or occasional players to join the game, or by soliciting participants from baseball games or other activities going on in the area. Inclusion of such players results in wide variations in the skill levels of those involved in the game. Yet the game must be made appealing to players of marginal ability or they abandon the game for other activities. The rules of the non-city game have consequently evolved in a way that encourages and facilitates participation by marginal players.

For example, teams are generally organized so that they are of roughly equal strength. Initially players may appoint two captains who take turns choosing their teammates, may divide the players by mutual agreement, or may shoot free throws until enough players make the shot to constitute a team. If the adopted system produces teams that clearly differ in talent level, trades will often be made to redress the imbalance. In fact, trades may be made *during* the game if it becomes evident that one team is much stronger than the other. In any case, when the game is over, if one team has won by a wide margin, players will generally re-assign the participants to make two new, more evenly balanced teams.

When games are over, any players who have been waiting on the sideline join the next game automatically. If too many players are waiting (a fairly rare occurrence), then free throw shooting is often used to determine who gets to play and who must sit out. This procedure is fairly time consuming, but the speed of the proceedings is of little concern in non-city environments. Often when new players show up who wish to get in a game, some of the marginal players who were playing drop out on their own accord. In any case, the new arrivals have priority over those players who have just lost a game or those who have played several games previously. Someone who is waiting cannot be made to sit out indefinitely while the same players play over and over again as sometimes happens in city games when a captain chooses those from the losing squad to fill out his team. (This norm does not always apply, however, when an uninvited player stumbles upon a "private" game that players have organized in advance.)

The new players in the game are generally divided up by mutual agreement, or by free-throw shooting, or new teams are made up altogether. The implicit objective is to divide the better players between the two teams, so that they can guard each other, and neither team is put at a strong disadvantage. Players voluntarily match up against opponents of about the same height and ability, so that marginal players are not overwhelmed by superior ones. And to a large extent, the non-city rules serve to minimize the domination of the better players while allowing the lesser players to become more involved.

Special rules for half-court games

Pick-up games are often played at facilities where there is only one usable basket. This is almost always the case on driveway courts, but is also common in playgrounds or schoolyards where there is limited room or where one basket has become unusable. On some occasions, there may be two perfectly good baskets facing each other, but both may be used for separate half-court games. In any of these circumstances, special rules are necessary to allow the single basket to be used by two competing teams.

Change of possession

One area where half-court rules differ between city and non-city communities involves possession of the basketball after a made basket. Inner city players generally play "winners" or "make-and-take" basketball where the team to secure a basket gets to keep possession of the basketball (cf. Wielgus & Wolff, 1980). The offensive team can thus run off a long string of baskets, continuing to score until the defense steals the ball or rebounds a missed shot. This form of basketball tends to go in spurts, with players who are shooting well scoring 3 or 4 consecutive baskets before the defense even gets a chance at a rebound. These spurts speed up the game, making it move faster than games where the teams alternate possession after each basket. Even more important to the inner city game, these rules allow superior teams to dispense with lesser teams more quickly. An inferior team can be defeated 10–0 without ever having possession of the basketball; on the other hand, with alternation of possession, even an inferior team would receive at least 9 ball possessions in a game to 10. The "make and take" rules thus serve to shorten games, and to shorten them most dramatically for teams with lesser ability.

With "make-and-take" rules, there is clearly an advantage to the team that gets the first possession. Whether each team averages a single basket or a string of 3 or 4 on each possession, the team to go first is favored to reach the winning score first. In inner city games, the winning team from the previous game is generally given first possession. This gives the incumbents a slight advantage, so that stronger teams, which have risen to the top, are less likely to be upset by up-start challengers.

The non-city rules parallel those in full-court basketball; after one team scores a basket, the other team takes possession of the basketball. This alternation prolongs games, diminishes the advantage of better teams, and increases offensive opportunities for players on lesser teams. These factors are important for maintaining the interest of marginal players.

Putting the ball in play

After each score in full court basketball, the team which was on defense passes the ball in-bounds from under the opposition basket, and then takes it the length of the court to their own basket. In half-court basketball, the ball is generally brought into play from the mid-court area instead, since only half the court is being used. In the inner city game, the ball may be brought into play by a single player who walks to the mid-court area, turns, and dribbles or shoots the basketball. The inbounding player does *not* need to pass the ball to a teammate to bring the ball into play (although he may be required to "check" the ball with the defense to make sure they are ready for play). Consequently, a "hot shooter" can bring the ball in himself and score several times in a row without anyone else handling the ball.

On the other hand, in non-city pick-up games, the basketball must generally be passed from the mid-court area to another player before anyone can dribble or shoot, just as the ball must be passed in-bounds in full court basketball. This extra pass slows down the game slightly, but it also prevents a single player from "hogging the ball" by continually shooting, rather than passing to teammates. Since two players must handle the ball on each possession, it is always possible to deny possession to a teammate who is taking more than his share of shots, and more players become involved on each possession.

Taking back rebounds

In half-court basketball, players can't rebound an opponent's missed shot and take off towards the basket at the other end of the court. In non-city communities, a convention has developed where a player who rebounds an opponent's shot must pass or dribble the ball to a point in the mid-court area before attempting any further shots. This maneuver, called "taking it back," is required whenever the basketball goes from one team to the other, thus symbolizing the change in direction that would occur with a change of possession in full-court basketball. Only the team which took the original shot can continue to shoot without first taking the basketball back.

In inner city games, players often compete under "no take back" rules. A player from either team may rebound a missed shot and then shoot the ball back at the same basket without doing any dribbling or passing. In fact, under some "no take back" rules, players may tip in an opponent's missed shot, thereby gaining the score for their own team (under other rules, a player must land on the ground with the ball before following in an opponent's shot). The "no take back" rules thus put a heavy emphasis on rebounding, with both teams packed tightly under the backboards attempting to tip or shoot in missed shots. Teams with exceptionally tall or strong players, or with good jumpers, can dominate a game by controlling the rebounds.

The "take-back" game played in non-city neighborhoods is clearly more time-consuming than the "no take back" game, but it also gets more players involved in the play (since rebounds are generally *passed* to mid-court and back), and prevents tall players from dominating the game through their rebounding. Hence, the "take-back" rules are better suited to the leisurely, egalitarian style of games in non-city environments, while "no-take-back" rules are ideal for the faster, survival-of-the-fittest style of city games.

Shooting and passing norms

In the city game, scoring baskets is of paramount importance both to the team and to the individual who scores. The basket brings the team one-point closer to winning the game and keeping possession of the court. Furthermore, in half-court basketball, the scoring team gets the ball back after the basket while the other team must continue playing defense. A score also enhances a player's reputation, and makes him a more attractive choice for future teams.

Since scoring baskets assumes such importance in the city game, most players are inclined to attempt to score first, and to pass only if their moves are stymied or if they can make an eye-opening assist to another player who is in scoring position. A "hot" shooter is generally permitted to take the ball and score on as many consecutive occasions as possible (and in half-court games the occasions really are consecutive, since the offense remains on offense until stopped). Players who shoot at every opportunity are rarely criticized unless they repeatedly take too long in trying to out-maneuver their defender, or take too many "bad shots." Good shots and bad shots are defined in terms of the normative styles of the neighborhood. In the inner city a good shot is any shot in which a player has achieved proficiency. It doesn't matter if the shooter is 35 feet from the basket, if he is tightly guarded, if he is off-balance or even if he misses the basket, as long as the shot is one which he frequently makes. A "bad shot" is one clearly beyond the capabilities of a player. However, this definition is a fairly stringent one, so that shooting does not seem to provoke much criticism in the inner city.

In fact, inner city players may be criticized for *not* shooting under some circumstances. Particularly when the ball is rebounded in close proximity to the basket, players are expected to shoot it back up so that teammates who have moved to rebounding positions have an opportunity to tip in the basket. Passing or dribbling the ball away from the basket is a waste of time which frustrates potential rebounders. In general, routine passing to players who are not in scoring position is discouraged as wasted effort, and players who do not create scoring opportunities by shooting or making assists are unlikely to be passed the ball with any regularity.

In non-city basketball games, shooting and scoring are generally of less importance than in the city. Players rarely need to impress others with their shooting skills in order to play and the game score rarely determines who gets to continue and who must sit out. Passing the ball is made necessary by several rules (including the in-bound rule and the take-back rule in the half-court game) and by the need to keep marginal players involved and happy with the game. Furthermore, a good deal of passing is ordinarily necessary to set up non-city players for the kinds of wide-open shots they have learned during hours of solitary practice. Consequently, non-city players learn to first look for the pass, and only secondarily for the shot. A good deal of routine passing generally occurs as players work the ball around, keeping everyone involved and trying to set-up a wide open shot. Of course, these efforts are interrupted and wasted if the recipient of a pass decides to loft up a "bad" shot. Not surprisingly then, the non-city norms concerning shooting are stricter and more often enforced than those in the inner city.

A "good shot" is generally defined not only as one at which the player is proficient (as in the city), but also as one that is taken on-balance, with good form, and without defensive pressure. In short, the good shot is one that is taken under approximately the same conditions that non-city players encounter in practicing alone. The definition also incorporates the emphasis on good, consistent shooting form which players develop from hours of working alone, trying to shape their shots into classical form. Even when taking "good" shots, non-city players may be criticized for shooting too much, and passing too little. Routine passing is viewed as an important part of the game, and a "gunner" who fails to pass the ball to others is likely to be rebuked.

Picks and screens

An inner city player is generally expected to score without a great deal of help from his teammates. Having developed his skills in the press of competition, the city player has presumably learned how to dribble, drive and shoot while protecting the basketball from outstretched defensive hands. He is expected to have the spins and moves necessary to single-handedly lose his defender and free himself for a shot. And if a defender is able to stay with the would-be shooter, the shooter is expected to fake or jump or double-pump to get the shot off anyway. In this context, picks and screens are unnecessary and possibly counterproductive. Screens intended to free a player to receive the ball are often wasted since the ball handler is more likely to look for driving room than for an open man. Picks set for the ball handler himself may simply bring an extra defender into position to help defend against a shot. Often an inner city ball handler will wave other players away from his side of the court altogether, so that he can take his defender to the basket one-on-one. Hence, inner city norms do not generally require playes to pick or screen for their teammates.

Picks and screens are far more important in the non-city game. Without some assistance from their teammates, non-city players would have difficulty freeing themselves for the kinds of shots they are used to and which are required by the non-city norms. Therefore, players are expected to help each other out on offense more than would be expected in the inner city.

Calling fouls and physical contact

In pick-up games, players must call fouls themselves, since there are no officials to do so. Although circumstances conspire to make the inner city game quite physical, the rules and norms do much to inhibit foul calling. Among the factors contributing to the physical nature of the inner city contest are the necessity for players to win if they wish to continue playing, and the no-take back rule (in half-court), which tends to pack players together in the high contact zone under the basket. However, the norms generally discourage players from calling fouls unless they have the ball and are in the act of shooting. Even then, if a player does call a foul, no foul shots are awarded, and the offended player simply gets the ball back. Consequently, if a player is fouled, but does not lose possession of the basketball, nothing is gained by calling the foul. If a player in the act of shooting calls a foul, and the basket goes in, the basket is disallowed, contrary to "official" basketball rules. Furthermore, a player must call the foul immediately, without seeing whether he made it or not. Hence, most players refrain from calling shooting fouls unless the contact is so severe that the shot has little chance of scoring. It is the offended player's decision whether to jeopardize the basket by calling a foul, and calls by other players (including the offender) are generally discouraged. This combination of forces and rules makes inner city basketball a high contact sport.

The passing and screening game favored in non-city environments spreads players across the court, reducing the number of people crowded into the high contact zone under the basket, and consequently, reducing contact. Additionally, the non-city rules discourage physical contact. Players may call fouls anytime they feel they have been physically offended, whether or not they had the basketball or were in the act of shooting. If a player calls "foul" on a shooting attempt, and the basket goes in, the score is counted and the foul call is nullified. If the basket misses, the player who was fouled generally receives possession of the basketball, although players will occasionally agree to shoot free throws on shooting fouls. Fouls may be called voluntarily by the offending player, or sometimes even by uninvolved players, practices frowned upon in most city games. The circumstances and norms on non-city courts thus tend to reduce the amount of fouling and contact that occurs.

The different rules and norms concerning physical contact are understandable consequences of the different environmental pressures in the different kinds of communities. First, games tend to be slower if a number of fouls are called, and thus the non-city rules slow down the game while the more stringent city criteria for foul calling speed it up. Second, the non-city rules serve to protect players from contact which could disrupt dribbling and shooting skills learned in the absence of defensive pressure, while city players presumably need less protection, having developed their skills in the heat of competition. Third, the non-city rules reduce the advantage held by large, physical and well-skilled players by preventing them from pushing less talented participants around, while the city rules give the better players more latitude. Finally, the non-city rules help to reduce excessive fouling and conflicts which could alienate potential players, a concern not shared on overcrowded city courts.

Effects of the playing environment on player development

The ways in which players are shaped by community playing rules and norms, and other aspects of the playing environment, are summarized and elaborated in the following sections.

Playing skills

Inner city players develop their skills in the press of competition, learning to protect their shots and dribbles from defenders. They are expected by their peers to score without a great deal of assistance from their teammates in the way of passes, picks or screens. They are also expected to shrug off the incidental contact that occurs as they maneuver and launch their shot, and the rules discourage them from calling fouls when they are hindered. They often must challenge better players who hold the court by virtue of previous wins, and must therefore attempt their moves and shots against superior defenders. All of these factors demand and foster the moves and skills generally characterized as "one-on-one" basketball. Players who compete successfully in this environment during their formative years are likely to be superior at the one-on-one game.

On the other hand, non-city players develop their skills in a considerably different milieu. They spend a considerable proportion of their time practicing shots without defensive pressure. When they do find or organize games, the norms prescribe a passing and screening style of play that allows the same kinds of unimpeded shots that have been learned in solitary practice. The rules discourage tight defensive pressure since players can call fouls for the slightest interference. And shooting norms prescribe that shots be taken on-balance, with good form, and only in the absence of defensive pressure. These various pressures impede the development of one-on-one basketball and the various feints and moves necessary to single-handedly defeat the defense. However, they foster the development of pure shooting skills, and the ability to consistently hit the wide-open jump shot.

The different demands made by the inner city and non-city playground environments thus affect the kinds of skills that players in those environments develop. The frequent observation that blacks have better one-on-one moves while whites are better pure shooters (e.g., Axthelm, 1970) can be readily understood in terms of factors in the playing environment, without resort to physiological, personality or societal explanations. The statistical superiority of white professional ball players at free throw shooting (Jones & Hochner, 1973) also makes sense, since the free throw is exactly the kind of unimpeded shot that non-city white players spend their formative years developing.

The superiority of black professionals at rebounding (Jones & Hochner, 1973) is also consistent with the nature of inner city play. In half-court basketball, no-take-back rules place considerable emphasis on rebounding, since players from either team can score off a rebound. The area under the basket becomes congested and players are forced to learn positioning, timing and jumping to compete for the basketball. Even in full court play, rebounding is an important means for a player to gain offensive possession of the basketball, since the likelihood of receiving a pass from a teammate is relatively low. And finally, the physical nature of the city game is ideal preparation for the physical nature of college or professional play under the basket, where a player must venture if he is to rebound effectively. White professionals who have grown up in non-city environments are less likely to have been exposed to no-take-back basketball, highly physical play, or the necessity of rebounding. Consequently, they are less likely to have developed the various skills comprising that ability.

Team style of play

Black basketball has been described as more individualistic and less team oriented than white basketball (e.g., DuPree, 1978). In fact, there are a number of aspects of inner city basketball that tend to emphasize shooting and scoring rather than more team oriented activities like passing and screening. The previous section described the superior development of one-on-one skills among inner city players – skills that reduce the need for passing and screening to free an offensive player. In addition, inner city shooting norms pressure players to look for the shot first, and to take any shot they feel they can make with regularity. Make-and-take rules emphasize shooting by allowing players to run off a series of baskets and possibly to win a game, without the defense ever getting possession. And the need to impress the team captains, who are prone to choosing good scorers for their teams, forces players to take shooting opportunities when they arise.

In contrast, the non-city environment where most white players learn the game places more emphasis on passing and screening. As discussed in the preceeding section, non-city players are more likely to require good passes and screens to free themselves for the shot. Non-city shooting norms pressure players to look for the pass first, and to shoot only under narrowly prescribed conditions. Shooting and other norms require players to make routine passes and to set picks and screens for their teammates. Non-city rules require in-bound passes between baskets and take-back passes between misses. And the sparsity of players makes shooting and scoring less important than in the city, since players do not need to win or impress others in order to continue playing; but it makes passing more important, since marginal players must be kept involved in the game.

One would expect these pressures to dispose non-city players to make relatively more passes between shots than city players do. A good indication of such tendencies would be the ratio of shots to passes attempted by individual players from each environment. Jones and Hochner (1973) have calculated that white professional players do take fewer shots relative to the number of assists they make than do black professionals. While this is consistent with expectation, it must be interpreted cautiously, since assists are a rather special kind of pass (namely one that leads directly to a score) and may not reflect the amount of routine passing players engage in.

Individual styles of play

Inner city players

It is commonly claimed that black basketball players play with more style, flair, finesse, and flamboyance than do white basketball players. To some extent these observations about individual styles of play probably reflect the greater facility that inner city blacks have at one-on-one moves, as discussed earlier. The ability to feint, spin, pump and engage in similar gymnastics are clearly essential to the individualistic city game, and contribute to the apparent "style" of inner city players. But descriptions of black basketball suggest an emphasis on dunks, steals, blocked shots and other spectacular plays that may go beyond the simple components of one-on-one play.

One important aspect of the inner city playing environment may help to explain this emphasis on dramatic play: the presence of an audience. As mentioned earlier, it is not unusual for inner city pick-up games to attract audiences of 10 to 20 people. These audiences can become highly involved in the games, and are particularly appreciative (as are audiences everywhere) of spectacular plays, such as dunks, reverse lay-ups, blocked shots and so on. While the crowd's cheers and comments provide substantial reinforcement for such activities, the contribution which these plays make to one's reputation is even more important in the inner city. In his book, *The City Game*, Peter Axthelm states:

> In its own way, a reputation in the parks is as definable as a scoring average in the N.B.A. Street ballplayers develop their own elaborate

word-of-mouth system. One spectacular performance or one back-wards, twisting stuff shot may be the seed of an athlete's reputation. If he can repeat it a few times in a park where the competition is tough, the word goes out that he may be something special. Then there will be challenges from more established players, and a man who can withstand them may earn a "neighborhood rep." The pro-cess continues in an expanding series of confrontations, until the best athletes have emerged. Perhaps a dozen men at a given time may enjoy "city-wide reps," guaranteeing them attention and respect in any playground they may visit.

(p. 199)

The "rep" which a player develops is more important in determining whether he will be chosen for a street captain's team than any other single factor. A player with a strong reputation can get into the best games on the best courts against the best competition, while lesser players must sit and hope to be chosen.

Under these circumstances, players are likely to attempt dramatic plays in an effort to enhance their reputations. Solid position defense doesn't build a reputation, but blocking a few shots or stealing a few balls will. Making routine passes won't help a reputation, but making dramatic assists might. And taking simple lay-ups won't impress anyone, but flying slam dunks should. Greenfield (1980) states:

The moves that begin as tactics for scoring soon become calling cards. You don't just lay the ball in for an uncontested basket; you take the ball in both hands, leap as high as you can, and slam the ball through the loop. When you jump in the air, fake a shot, bring the ball back to your body, and throw up a shot, all without coming back down, you have proven your worth in incontestable fashion.

(p. 310)

Consequently, the inner city player is more likely to attempt flamboyant moves and shots in pick-up games during his development years, and is more likely to ultimately incorporate these into his repertoire of skills as a player.

Non-city players

Of course, non-city players may occasionally attempt dramatic plays too. But these efforts differ in several critical respects. First, the level of reinforcement is lower for such activities in the non-city environment; there are rarely audi-ences for pick-up games, and one's playing time is not contingent upon one's reputation. Second, the non-city shooting norms dictate against flamboyant shots: since the team has worked collectively to free a player for an open

38

shot, that shot is supposed to be taken while open and on balance. A player who eschews the open jumper to try a spinning reverse lay-up is likely to be criticized if the shot misses. Third, the non-city environment provides numerous opportunities to try spectacular shots *outside* of competition. A player who wishes to show his friends that he can do pump shots or dunk shots can do so during the long intervals between games. However, such moves, made in the absence of competitive pressure, are unlikely to generalize to game situations. Fourth, the non-city norms discourage players from dominating the marginal plays who have been recruited to fill out the teams. Consequently, it would be bad form for a player to repeatedly block a lesser player's shots or to steal the ball from him. All things considered, then, the pressures of the non-city playground environment do more to discourage flamboyant play than to encourage it.

Playing attitudes

It would be surprising if the different character of the inner city and non-city basketball environments didn't produce different attitudes towards the game. Some such attitudinal differences are readily predictable from the observations made in earlier sections. For example, non-city players are likely to develop more team-oriented attitudes towards basketball, while inner city players are likely to be more individualistic. Inner city players are likely to view shooting as the most important aspect of the game, while non-city players are more likely to emphasize passing and other skills. However, there are other attitudinal differences that are less readily discerned from the preceeding sections.

For example, an inner city player is more likely to view basketball as a personal battle against the opponent he is matched up with. The one-on-one style of play makes each player personally responsible if his man scores; there are no zone defenses in inner city basketball, and "switching" men when a player is screened is not very common. So if a player drives past his defender for a score, the defender is embarrassed in front of the watching crowd, and may feel a need to get back somehow. Inner city product Walt Frazier (In Frazier and Berkow, 1974) says "I get close to angry when my man scores on me. So that's my motivation on defense. I take my man's basket personally. I can play passive defense until he starts scoring. Then I start picking him up right away to show him that I'm the man." (p. 49) In this light, steals, for which Frazier was famous, or blocked shots are not only flamboyant plays, but are emphatic public retaliation against one's opponent. Another form of retaliation is discussed by Kirkpatrick (1968):

> Get back in instant playground reprisal. If a man exhibits his best move and scores on a negligent opponent, all hands yell "get back get back" at the defender, whereupon, he must immediately try to get

back at the opponent who just took him. Promptly, with what is often a spectacular retaliatory move of his own, the second man usually does get back.

(p. 7)

In the inner city, then, the one-on-one nature of the game, the crowd pressure, and the importance of winning may all contribute to make the game an intensely personal struggle between opponents. The objective is not simply to play well, not simply to win, but to beat your man: to show that you are better than he is.

In the non-city environment, basketball assumes more recreational proportions: A player need not out-shine his opponent to have a successful performance. This recreational attitude is probably fostered by three factors. First, there is no crowd to cope with, so both pride (for good plays) and shame (for bad ones) are tempered. Second, the team-oriented offenses of the non-city spread the responsibility for any score across several players. Switching is expected on defense (and even zone defenses are used with some frequency), so that no single defensive player is entirely to blame for an opponent's score. Finally, games are generally less intense and less important; since they do not determine future playing time.

The peculiar circumstances of the non-city basketball environment also lead to certain characteristic attitudes regarding shooting form, practice and warm-ups. As noted earlier, a substantial portion of non-city players' basketball time is spent practicing shots alone. During this time, players commonly work on their shooting form, adjusting hand and arm positions, body movements and shooting rhythm until every shot feels just right. One consequence of these efforts is that non-city players often come to believe that shooting is a matter of mechanics, and that for a successful performance, the bodily "machine" needs to be properly tuned, aligned and warmed-up. This "mechanical" attitude underlies the norm requiring that shots be taken on-balance and with proper shooting form. It also underlies the considerable emphasis that non-city players place on shooting practice and game warm-ups, which can be viewed as efforts to tune the "machine" properly. The shooting ritual which Bill Bradley engaged in prior to every game is an exaggerated example of this emphasis.

The shooting slumps that players inevitably experience are therefore explained in terms of some poorly understood mechanical malfunction, and a variety of elaborate superstitions exist about the kinds of factors that might be responsible. Some non-city players believe that tying sneakers improperly, failing to wear knee pads, or having the wrong pre-game meal can upset their delicate mechanical balance. A common set of superstitions deal with mental attitude and its possible effect on performance. Many non-city players engage in a kind of intense, studied concentration prior to games in an effort to "psych up" for the forthcoming contest. Non-city norms discourage levity, irrelevant chatter or anything else that might interfere with the delicate bodily gears. The resultant locker room atmosphere has been described by some as a dreadful combination of fear, purpose and gloom.

The inner city player is more likely to try to keep his composure ("cool") and self-confidence prior to games, viewing the game itself as a contest between players. There is less emphasis on "psyching-up" or "concentrating" intensely (although perhaps, more emphasis on "psyching-out" or rattling the opponent). And, of course, inner city players often view individual shooting practice as irrelevant to game situations, and thus a waste of time. So inner city attitudes towards several aspects of preparation differ somewhat from non-city attitudes.

Conclusions

This analysis suggests that players' skills, styles and attitudes are a coherent reaction to the circumstances under which they learn to play basketball. The formulation thus provides a parsimonious explanation for apparent differences between white and black basketball players, without resorting to indefensible claims regarding physiological or personality differences. The formulation does have some limitations, however, which are spelled out below.

First, although the descriptions of inner city and non-city basketball provided here are based on extensive reading, interviews and observation, there is clearly a need for empirical research to establish their objective validity and generality. I am hopeful that this article will stimulate such studies into the relationships among player backgrounds, styles, abilities and attitudes. I suspect that such research will show my characterizations of inner city and non-city basketball to be prototypes, approximated to different degrees in different communities and in different regions of the country. For example, different kinds of "non-city" locales (rural, small town, suburb) seem likely to vary in playing systems and styles, with crowded suburbs adopting something between the city and non-city styles of play.

Second, the kinds of playing differences that have been described are most likely to be observed at the neighborhood level. College and professional players may have had their styles refined and their attitudes mellowed by years of coaching. Nonetheless, some residual influences are likely to persist, and professional player Darryl Dawkins may be correct when he observes that "Coaching has a little bit to do with your style, but not as much as you might think. It's all in your background." (quoted in DuPree, 1978).

Third, it is unclear how the present formulation, which deals exclusively with basketball, relates to possible performance differences among athletes in other sports. Novak (1976) suggests that the "black athletic style" is most pronounced in sports activities that are closely related to basketball, possibly reflecting carry-over effects among black athletes who played this sport at some point in their lives. It is also possible that careful analyses of other sports (e.g. sandlot baseball) would reveal some of the same kinds of mechanisms discussed here. Finally, it may be that the differences observed in many sports are illusory, reflecting stereotypical generalizations from basketball or naive interpretations of the prevalence of blacks in particular playing positions (as detailed in Edwards' 1973 analysis of racial "stacking"). In any case, the present account argues that racial differences in basketball are a function of factors specific to the basketball environment, suggesting that great care must be taken in generalizing to other sports.

Finally, it may be valuable to highlight several implications of the present analysis. The differing norms and expectations that city and non-city basketball players bring to the court with them can explain a good deal of the conflict and self-segregation that occurs when players meet on common courts, such as a college gym. These differences also relate to the tension that sometimes exists between players from one background and coaches from another. For example, Bill Spivey, an inner city player who ultimately quit his college team, stated: "Cats from the street have their own rhythm when they play. It's not a matter of somebody setting you up and you shooting. You *feel* the shot. When a coach holds you back, you lose the feel and it isn't fun anymore" (quoted in Greenfield, 1980). Our analysis suggests that the roots of such conflicts may be more cultural than racial.

This analysis also has broader implications, beyond simply the explanation of athletic styles. It illustrates the complex interrelationships between man's environment and his behavior. Understanding these interrelationships is important to theorists and researchers in such domains as anthropology, sociology and psychology. Perhaps in a small way, this analysis contributes to those efforts.

References

Auerbach, A. & Fitzgerald, J.A. 1977, *Auerbach: An Autobiography*. (New York: G.P. Putman's Sons).

Axthelm, P. 1970, *The City Game*. (New York: Harper and Row Publishers, Inc.).

Barker, R.G. 1960, "Ecology and Motivation," in M.R. Jones (ed.), *Nebraska Symposium on Motivation*. (Lincoln: University of Nebraska Press).

Cousy, B. (As told to Al Hirshberg) 1958, *Basketball Is My Life*. (New York: Lowell Pratt & Company).

Davis, Ruban M. 1969, *Aggressive Basketball*. (West Nyack, NY: Parke Publishing Company, Inc.).

DuPree, D. 1978a, "It's a Stylish Game They Play," *Los Angeles Times*, Feb. 24. 1978b, "Each Team Does It With Style," *Los Angeles Times*, Feb. 28.

Edwards, H. 1973, *Sociology of Sport*. (Homewood, IL: The Dorsey Press).

Frazier, W. & Berkow, I. 1974, *Rockin' Steady*. (New York: Warner Books, Inc.).

Greenfield, J. 1980, "The Black and White Truth About Basketball: A Skin-Deep

Theory of Style," in Stubbs & Barnet (eds.), *The Little, Brown Reader*, 2nd ed. (Boston: Little, Brown).

Holzman, R. & Lewin, L. 1973, *Holzman's Basketball: Winning Strategy and Tactics*. (New York: Warner Brooks, Inc.).

Jones, J.M. & Hochner, A.R. 1973, "Racial Differences in Sports Activities: A Look at the Self-Paced Versus Reactive Hypothesis," *Journal of Personality and Social Psychology*, vol. 27, pp. 86–95.

Jordan, P. 1979, *Chase the Game*. (New York: Dodd, Mead & Company).

Kane, M. 1971, "An Assessment of Black is Best," *Sports Illustrated*, Jan. 18.

Kirkpatrick, C. 1968, "A Place in the Big City Sun," *Sports Illustrated*, Aug. 5.

Latane, B. (ed.) 1966, "Studies in Social Comparison," *Journal of Experimental Psychology*, Supplement 1.

Loy, J.W. & McElvogue, J.R. 1970, "Racial Segregation in American Sport," *The International Review of Sport Sociology*, vol. 5.

McPhee, J. 1965, *A Sense of Where You Are: A Profile of Princeton's Bill Bradley*. (New York: Bantam Pathfinder Editions).

McPherson, B.D. 1975, "The Segregation by Playing Position Hypothesis in Sport: An Alternative Hypothesis," *Social Science Quarterly*, vol. 55, pp. 960–966.

Michener, J.A. 1976, *Sports in America*. (Greenwich, Ct.: Fawcett Publications, Inc.).

Novak, M. 1976, *The Joy of Sports: End Zones, Bases, Baskets, Balls and the Consecretation of the American Spirit*. (New York: Basic Books, Inc.).

Ogilvie, B. & Tutko, T.A. 1968, "Psychological Consistencies Within the Personalities of High Level Competitors," *Journal of the American Medical Association*, October.

Phillips, J.C. 1976, "Toward an Explanation of Racial Variations in Top-Level Sports Participation," *International Review of Sport Sociology*, vol. 11, pp. 39–53.

Poliquin, B. 1981, "Trouble . . . With a Capital T: Empty Seats Put NBA in a BIND," *The Sporting News*, Feb. 21.

Russell, B. & Branch, T. 1979, *Second Wind: The Memoirs of an Opinionated Man*. (New York: Random House).

Schachter, S. 1951, "Deviation, Rejection and Communication," *Journal of Abnormal and Social Psychology*, vol. 46, p. 190–207.

Sharmon, B. 1968, *Sharmon on Basketball Shooting*. (Englewood Cliffs, NJ: Prentice-Hall, Inc.).

Synder, E.E. & Spreitzer, E. 1978, *Social Aspects of Sport*. (Englewood Cliffs, NJ: Prentice-Hall, Inc. *Street and Smith's Official Basketball Yearbook 1980–81* (New York: Conde Nast Publications Inc.), Oct., 1980.

Tate, L. 1975, "Tatelines: Studies Show Blacks' Jumping Advantages," *The Champaign News Gazette*, March 24.

Wielgus, C., Jr., & Wolff, A. 1980, *The In-Your-Face Basketball Book*. (New York: Everest House Publishers).

Wolf, D. 1972, *Foul! the Connie Hawkins Story*. (New York: Holt, Rinehart & Winston).

Worthy, M. & Markle, A. 1970, "Racial Differences in Reactive Versus Self-Paced Sports Activities," *Journal of Personality and Social Psychology*, vol. 16, pp. 439–443.

Yetman, N. & Eitzen, S. 1972, "Black Americans in Sports: Unequal Opportunity for Equal Ability," *Civil Rights Digest*, vol. 5, pp. 20–34.

43

RACIAL RELATIONS THEORIES AND SPORT

Suggestions for a more critical analysis

Susan Birrell

Source: *Sociology of Sport Journal* 6 (1989): 212–227.

This paper suggests that sport sociology may be ready to move from a generally atheoretical approach to "race and sport" to a critical analysis of racial relations and sport. Four theoretical groups are identified from the writing of racial relations scholars: bias and discrimination theories, assimilation and cultural deprivation theories, materialist and class-based theories, and culturalist or colonial theories. In the past, studies of race and sport have fit within the former two theories. A cultural studies approach that blends the latter theories is advocated in order to move toward the goal of critical theory and develop a comprehensive model for analyzing the complex of relations of dominance and subordination simultaneously structured along racial, gender, and class lines.

In the past few years there has been a promising movement in sociology of sport toward more critical theoretical frameworks and analyses of sport as a cultural form. Marxist and other materialist critiques, critical feminist analyses, and the application of cultural studies approaches to sport have heightened awareness and deepened understanding of sport as a fundamentally class-based and gendered activity and as one of a complex of sites for the articulation of relations of dominance and subordination organized along class and gender lines.

Moreover, there has been a positive move to consolidate the strengths of particular theoretical approaches in order to provide new theories more capable of comprehending the complexity of sport forms and practices. Cultural studies and feminist analyses are premier examples of this theoretical blending. Cultural studies joins Marxist theories and interactionist practice into a "critical qualitative analysis" or "analytical cultural criticism" (Willis, 1982, p. 120) in order to provide a more accurate model of the relationship between human agency and cultural constraint (Gruneau, 1983). Feminist studies is interdisciplinary by design, and at the critical edge of that field a particularly productive blending of materialist analyses and feminist insight works to provide the basis for socialist feminist analyses and "feminist cultural studies" (Cole & Birrell, 1986). Yet notably absent from all these critical positions, in sport studies and in the parent disciplines or fields as well, is any sophisticated, critical analysis of racial relations.

The lack of such an analysis in sport sociology is unfortunate, for sport provides a particularly public display of relations of dominance and subordination. In the first place, sport is specifically structured to produce relations of dominance and subordination on a temporary basis. That is, the point of sport is to display publicly the processes of challenge and struggle between two sides alleged to begin on equal terms but determined to produce and sustain relations of dominance vis-à-vis one another. Moreover, sport as a meritocracy based on skill quietly reaffirms our national common sense: individuals who work hard and possess the right stuff will always prevail. Turned on its head, this lesson becomes even more insidious: those who are at the top must have risen to the top through fair means and thus deserve their position. In contrast, those not at the top do not possess the requisite talent for such privilege. Even the runner-up is a loser.

This commonsense interpretation of sport as a parable of achievement and reward earned through struggle often obscures other relations of dominance and subordination structured along lines not of achievement but of ascription. Placed alongside our commonsense understandings of sport as an important stage of manhood, as an equal opportunity employer for Blacks, and as a reward for and a marker of the good life is the growing criticism of sport as a sexist, racist, and classist institution, as a site for the reproduction of relations of privilege and oppression, and of dominance and subordination structured along gender, race, and class lines.

While many in our field recognize these classic limitations of sport and the exclusivity of sport as a cultural practice, we have diverted little scholarly energy to the analysis of one major aspect of that exclusiveness: we have yet to launch any sort of sophisticated analysis of racial relations in sport. To date our focus on race has been, in reality, a focus on Black male athletes.

This tendency obscures and reduces diversity in sport in four classic ways. First it equates "race" with Black, obscuring other racial identities. Completely absent from our samples, our analyses, and our theories is any consciousness of Chicanos, Asian Americans, Jews, and Native Americans. We say Jackie Robinson broke the color barrier in Major League Baseball, but we really mean that one racial group was finally allowed to play on the same field as the white majority. We applaud the racial opportunities in the NBA, yet we fail to ask where the Asian Americans, Native Americans and Chicanos are. Hispanics are studied only to the extent that they exist in Major League Baseball. In other words, we assess progress toward racial equality ideosyncratically, in terms of each local sport scene.

Second, "Black athlete" usually means "Black male athlete," an equation that obliterates gender. One can count on one hand the number of published analyses that specifically focus on women athletes of color (Green, Oglesby, Alexander, & Franke, 1981; Houzer, 1974). Some unpublished descriptive work on Black women athletes is available (Abney, 1988; Alexander, 1978; Barclay, 1979; Murphy, 1980), and we may find race as a variable in some of our research traditions (e.g., Greendorfer & Ewing, 1981) but no profound analyses have yet been begun. Even less is available concerning Native American women (Oxendine, 1988), Asian American women, Chicanas, and members of other Hispanic groups.

Third, very little mention is made of the interrelationships between race, sport, and sexuality, or between sport and masculinity (Messner, 1987). Finally, class is almost completely obscured through our practice of reading "race" as "race/class" and letting the analysis go at that. Thus we produce an image of race and sport as homogeneous and undifferentiated.

The writing that does explore race and sport is generally superficial. It includes well intentioned but theoretically limited critiques of sport as a racist institution (e.g., Edwards, 1969; Hoch, 1972), personal accounts of the exploitation of Black athletes (e.g., Wolf, 1972), and superficial studies, generally quantitative, that reduce race to a variable. Moreover, we continue to produce studies on centrality and stacking, not because of their theoretical significance but simply because the data are there. Twenty years ago such studies provided major insight into stratification by race, and it is startling to know that such patterns persist today, but there is no theoretical news in this tradition. We need to move to more powerful questions.

In the past, our approach has been to assert that race exists and to ask what effect membership in a particular race or ethnic group has on sport involvement. A more profound approach is to conceive of race as a culturally produced marker of a particular relationship of power, to see racial identity as contested, and to ask how racial relations are produced and reproduced through sport.

The analysis of racial relations in sport remains undeveloped because as a field we remain ignorant of significant developments in the fields of ethnic and racial relations. Since the introduction of ethnic and Black studies programs into the academic curriculum in the United States in the late 1960s, scholars of race and ethnicity have developed sophisticated critiques of the exclusionary practices of dominant academic discourses, and they have offered increasingly profound strategies for reforming and transforming an often resistant curriculum into a more inclusive forum for understanding diversity in the United States. In this paper, the new racial relations scholarship is reviewed and critiqued in terms of its usefulness to the development of a critical analysis of racial relations and sport. Specifically this paper reviews how they conceptualize their field, what models and theoretical perspectives they are exploring and endorsing, what epistemological assumptions ground their perspectives, what paradigmatic challenges they issue, and how they conceptualize race, racism, and racial relations.[1] For the sake of brevity, the comments that follow focus specifically on work in Black/ Afro-American studies and Chicano studies. More inclusive analyses examining the writings of other racially defined groups such as Asian Americans and Native Americans await our attention.

The new racial relations scholarship

The early work of Black and Chicano scholars began with the "archeological" tasks of recovering lost histories and voices, but they soon moved beyond this additive approach which conceived of race as an overlooked variable to be factored into existing theories ("add Blacks and stir"), and they began to conceptualize race as a category of experience marked by exclusionary practices and economic and cultural oppression. Dominant theories of race and racism put forth by white scholars were rejected as racially biased, and the dominant paradigm of social science itself was severely critiqued. As Turner and Perkins argue, "Afro-American experience continues to be locked in the ideological vault of white bourgeois social thought" (1976, p. 9). The attack against bourgeois social science or "mere sociology" (Walters, 1973, p. 202) was directed against the classic stance of objectivity and value-neutrality; the limits of abstracted empiricism, mindless quantification, and scientism; and the control of racial studies by whites.[2]

Black and Chicano scholars called for the transformation of academic discourse through the production of new methodologies and new theories based not on traditional epistemological positions and the experiences of the dominant white, Anglo-European middle-class groups who have controlled academic discourse, but grounded in the diversity of the experiences of people of color themselves. They wanted a Black studies or a Chicano studies that would take the side of the oppressed; that was grounded in the uniqueness of Black or Chicano experience and institutions; that would be critical of Anglo or European institutions while celebrating cultural survival through Afrocentrism or Chicanismo; that would meet the needs of the community by creating a dialectic between research and action; and that would be revolutionary and radical by promoting consciousness raising and working for cultural survival and liberation.[3] In other words, they called for a critical analysis of racial relations.

The epistemological grounding for the new analysis would celebrate the distinctiveness of Black or Chicano culture, replacing the degrading characterizations of Anglo or European research with accurate ones grounded in Black or Chicano experience.[4] Such an approach would recognize racially defined groups not as passive recipients of Anglo-European culture but as active creators of their own social worlds and as groups actively involved in resisting cultural oppression (Mirande, 1985, p. 213). For Chicanos, the analyses would be grounded in "the rationality of the Chicano" (Romano, 1970, p. 12) and "the Chicano world view" (Mirande, 1985, p. 206). For Blacks, it would entail "an examination of the deeper truths of black life" (Jackson, 1970, p. 132). As Walters argued, "Black life has been distinctive and separate enough to constitute its own uniqueness, and it is on the basis of that uniqueness that the ideology and methodology of Black social science rests" (1973, p. 197).

Of particular concern from a methodological standpoint is the epistemological issue known as the insider/outsider debate (Merton, 1972): who can produce a better analysis of Black life—a (Black) insider or a (white) outsider? Those supporting the outsider view frame their arguments around objectivity and fresh insight; insiders argue about authenticity, trust, and access. In Black studies, Walters argues that whites have "technique" but Blacks have the "substance" or "field experience" (1973, p. 202), and Jackson states that "Black studies requires the best interpreters of the black experience—black scholars who have had the experience" (1970, p. 139).

The hallmark of both Black and Chicano studies is a commitment to "ethnographic research that is scholarly and, at the same time socially committed and sensitive to Chicano [or Black] culture" (Mirande, 1985, p. 214). Turner and Perkins urge their colleagues to more radical stances: "Afro-American intelligentsia . . . extend the presuppositions and content of conventional thought, preventing the development of any analytical and critical thinking on the Afro-American question. Until such analysis is made, with the assistance of a critical, reflective, and radical social science, the Afro-American experience will be left to be interpreted by bourgeoisie and liberal intellectuals—black and white—who do not possess the motive of revolutionary self-understanding" (1976, p. 8).

In their call for "revolutionary self-understanding" grounded in the interpretation of life experiences of racially defined groups, racial relations scholars endorse goals and methods similar to critical scholars in cultural studies and feminist studies. Their unproblematic acceptance of insider experience as necessarily authentic, however, represents an epistemological assumption that they, like other critical scholars, will need to examine more closely in the future (Cole, 1988).

Theories of race and racial relations

In addition to delineating proper epistemological grounding and appropriate methodological choices, racial scholars are evaluating the usefulness of the various theoretical perspectives produced to make sense of racial experiences. Although there is disagreement concerning the specifics of particular theories, four general theory groups can be identified: bias theories, assimilation theories, materialist theories, and cultural or colonial theories.

Bias models

The earliest explanations for racism were merely descriptions of the social interaction between members of different racial or ethnic groups, characterized as prejudice and discrimination models. Some writers simply assume prejudice as a universal human trait while others provide fuller descriptions of the attitudes of prejudice that result in the behavior of discrimination. Regardless, this approach provides little theoretical insight. As Alkalimat notes, prejudice and discrimination are static and descriptive concepts that obscure the ideological power of racism and provide only the "lowest level of theory. . . . The fact is that black people have been oppressed by a system unified on the basis of white racism. . . . While the concepts of prejudice and discrimination are helpful on an analytical level of theory because they are so easily operationalized and quantified, racism is the more appropriate theoretical description of the problem precisely because it captures the qualitative character of the oppression" (1972, p. 176).

Sport sociology research focused on race is generally atheoretical in the sense that researchers do not subscribe explicitly to any of the four theories discussed here. However, much work in our field is implicitly framed within a bias and discrimination model. Our substantive focuses on centrality, stacking and positional segregation (Curtis & Loy, 1978; Loy & McElvogue, 1971; Medoff, 1986; and many others), discrimination in salary (Christiano, 1986, 1988) and athletic scholarships (Coakley & Pacey, 1984), and managerial succession (e.g., Fabiano, 1984) all provide more or less passionate endorsements for bias theories. Moreover, one can find the remnants of the bias approach in our textbooks and our most descriptive writing on race and sport. Our understanding of the dynamics of racial relations in sport can move beyond this descriptive level.

Assimilation theories

Assimilation or cultural deprivation theories have been the dominant theories in the study of racial relations. Assimilation theory springs from Park's (1950) classic model that posits a cycle of ethnic relations: contact, conflict, accommodation, assimilation. Cultural conflict is therefore passified through accommodations and assimilation (or cultural annihilation). Mirande (1985) and Omi and Winant (1986) point out that the model reproduces the ideology of the United States melting pot. It assumes an orderly and voluntary desire by the "immigrant" group to conform to dominant cultural values at the same time that it devalues their unique characteristics. The as-yet-unassimilated groups are seen as culturally deprived.

The cultural pluralist model, a variant of this general perspective, appears to value cultural diversity, yet it merely "pays lip service to the preservation of distinct groups within American society" by allowing groups to maintain "cultural, linguistic and religious autonomy while being held 'equal under the law' and integrated into the political and economic system" (Mirande, 1985, p. 187). In other words, the political and economic systems remain unchanged by the cultural diversity of United States citizens.

A more contemporary variant of this model is the cultural deprivation or culture of poverty approach. This approach underlay the Moynihan (1965) report so severely criticized by Black scholars and civil rights activists because it located the cause of poverty in the "maladaptive" Black family, thus blaming the victim. This ideology still operates at the level of common sense in U.S. thought and it is reflected in contemporary racial policies.

In sport, the approach is represented in studies of culture contact among ethnic and racial groups and within studies by anthropologists of play. Research on the contact theory of racial relations (Chu & Griffey, 1982, 1985; Rees & Miracle, 1984), although located within social psychological traditions of race relations, is consistent with assumptions of assimilation theory. These studies in sport have reported disappointing results and led to a call for the reevaluation of the theory (Rees & Miracle, 1984), but not a reexamination of the assumptions that underlie it. Some studies document the gradual erosion of ethnic identity even as groups struggle to retain that identity through connection to sport forms grounded in their own cultural experiences (Day, 1981; LaFlamme, 1977). Other studies, such as Pooley's (1981) classic study of soccer in Milwaukee, actually refute the model, finding evidence that sport maintains ethnic identity and solidarity rather than assimilation into the mainstream. Nevertheless, functionalist theories continue to view the assimilation of "minority" groups into the mainstream of U.S. values as a positive contribution of sport.

The Problem of "Race."

Bias theories and assimilation theories offer only limited, general accounts of race, racism and, to some extent, racial relations. Moreover, assimilation theories contain serious conceptual flaws whose political consequences trouble scholars, such as the lack of conceptual distinction between race and ethnicity. For example, Omi and Winant (1986) critique assimilation theories for applying models designed to explore the relations between ethnic groups to the study of racial relations. This conflation of race and ethnicity obscures the special circumstances of race and the greater inclusiveness of race over ethnicity. As Omi and Winant argue, " 'Blacks' in ethnic terms are as diverse as 'whites' " (1986, p. 23).

The classical distinction made by social scientists has been to regard race as a biological category and ethnicity as a cultural one (McLemore, 1972). The reification of race has been an important topic for critical scholars of racial relations who suggest that race must be problematized and not accepted as a natural or essential identity. Instead they focus on the cultural production of racial relations (Centre for Contemporary Cultural Studies, 1982), racial formation (Omi & Winant, 1986), or racialization (Miles, 1984). Following their direction, race can be understood as a category popularly constructed along assumptions of biological distinctions indexed by color and then naturalized through cultural practices and ideological work.

In a strong critique of using race as a theoretical concept, Miles argues the need to "[formulate] theoretical concepts which are not grounded in everyday commonsense. . . . One of the central political and ideological processes in contemporary capitalist societies is the process of racialisation. . . . The process by which [groups] are racialised and react to that racialisation . . . always occurs in a particular historical context, one in which the social relations of production provide the necessary and initial framework within which racism has its effects" (1984, pp. 232–233).

In the United States, the construction of particular sets of relations along color lines emerged out of the specific conditions of slavery and the need to obscure the differences between members of disparate and distinct African cultures into a homogeneous Black or colored mass, available for exploitation by dominant whites. Indeed the concept of "white" emerges in part from the need to differentiate and then legitimate this work force (Omi & Winant, 1986).

Omi and Winant (1986) provide fascinating evidence of the construction of race through public policy. In the United States such practices include the 1/32 ratio and the principle of hypodescent, both of which function to consolidate white skin privilege through reference to purity. In South Africa, a nation obsessed with issues of racial classification, Chinese are "Asians" while Japanese are "honorary whites," a distinction that is clearly grounded in the historical relations between groups and not in biological fact (Omi & Winant, 1986).

In a very real sense, then, racism creates race; a particular racist ideology is necessary to legitimate the economic and cultural exploitation of subordinated groups. Thus racial identity is a particularly interesting instance of contested terrain. Because people of color, like women, are embodied in the markers of their oppression, the tendency is strong to naturalize oppression through an ontological position referenced through biology. In contemporary life, Black remains a naturalized category because of residual segregation practices, most particularly fears of interracial marriage, and ideologies of racial valorization that remain largely unchallenged.

If race is understood as a social construct, our analysis of racial relations and sport clearly must move beyond the treatment of race as a descriptive variable and address ideological questions about the production of race relations and the specific forms such relations take in particular times. Specifically we must ask, what is the part of sport in the construction of racial relations, and how do dominant forms of sport continue to reproduce particular configurations of racial relations? Focusing on racial relations by connecting the critical theoretical framework these scholars are producing with the insights of cultural studies will advance this important project.

Materialist theories

Although racial scholars have moved beyond the highly descriptive bias theories and the conceptually inadequate assimilation theories, they debate the proper theoretical models to build in their place. Materialist and culturalist (or colonial) theories have received the most serious attention because they provide both a general theory and the flexibility to deal with the more particular historical conditions of specific racial relations. Such careful attention is necessary in order to respect the obvious differences between the chattel slavery of Blacks, the internal colonization of Chicanos in the United States, and the history of empire and colonialism in Great Britain.

A variety of class-based theories have been identified,[5] but the most prevalent approaches are materialist analyses informed by a classical Marxist, class conflict approach. These approaches see racial exploitation as a consequence of capitalist relations of production, and racism as the consequent ideology that justifies oppressive relations of power and control (Acuna, 1981; Almaguer, 1975; Barrera, 1979; Miles, 1984; Staples, 1973). As Staples argues, "White racism arose out of the needs of capitalism, it is a product of capitalism, and it cannot be understood without analyzing the advantages of racism to the capitalist class" (1973, p. 408). Some materialist arguments rest on the assertion that racism did not exist until the late 18th century and the rise of capitalism (Montagu, 1964; Staples, 1973).

Despite increased attention to materialist analyses in sport studies, such studies of racial relations have been confined to descriptive applications of materialist concepts, typified by the work of Hoch (1972) and Edwards (1969). Since the experiences of Afro-Americans in the United States were grounded in the systems of chattel slavery and colonialism, it was quite logical to bring materialist analyses to bear on understanding racial exploitation as a form of oppression occasioned by capitalism. However, others argue that while materialist theories may explain the production of racial relations, such relations are reproduced through other cultural forms (Staples, 1973, 1976). These theorists gravitate toward more culturalist positions.

Cultural theories

The culturalist approach focuses upon cultural suppression and cultural hegemony on the one hand (the colonial models applied to the Black experience; the internal colony model applied to Chicanos) and cultural regeneration, cultural survival, or cultural nationalism on the other. Culturalist theories can be tied to the emergence of Black nationalism in the mid-1960s, when increasing reflection on cultural imperialism in academic circles resulted in a strong critique of the assimilation model. Assimilation with dominant white cultures was seen as a forced and involuntary form of cultural genocide. Dreams of an egalitarian melting pot or a society built on cultural diversity did not match the reality of centuries of subordination and forced deculturation. Racial relations were increasingly understood as the result of cultural imperialism enforced through military and cultural conquest: chattel slavery, colonialism, and neocolonialism disrupted African culture; the conquest of Mexico by white Europeans and the annexation of Mexican lands in southwestern United States resulted in the loss of Aztlan and the colonization of Chicanos within their own land; the white ideology of manifest destiny colonized Native Americans and forced them onto restricted reservations. With conquest came the destruction of traditional economic, political, and family relations and the devaluation of traditional cultural forms such as art, religion, music, and language. Cultural domination and subordination are therefore the key dynamic in the production and maintenance of racial relations of dominance and subordination.

As disruptive as the forces of cultural domination have been, however, the forces for nationalism and cultural survival have endured. Staples (1973), for example, dispels the argument that Blacks were freed by whites following the Civil War. Instead he argues that the incidence of Black sabotage and open revolt were more prevalent than white history has recorded. Mirande (1985) and Romano (1968) offer similar arguments with reference to Chicanos. Omi and Winant (1986) also discuss "cultures of resistance" among Afro-American slaves, and a major focus of their book is on shifting racial relations in the United States brought about by Black nationalism since the 1960s. Afrocentrism and Chicanismo are examples of the cultural pride that is the goal of many academics: racial consciousness raising, accomplished through an analysis of social worlds of Blacks and Chicanos produced by Blacks and Chicanos themselves. Through the blending of research and action, racial groups can attain the goal of nationalism: "Black control of the Black community" (Staples, 1973, p. 413).

The cultural studies solution

Among the community of scholars who debate the proper theoretical approaches to race, a major tension exists between Marxist or materialist positions and culturalist positions. The culturalist model, as presently formulated, has generated several critiques, particularly from Marxists who argue that a focus on cultural oppression is dangerous and counter-revolutionary because it obscures capitalist relations and promotes race war rather than a revolution based on class consciousness (Mirande, 1985, p. 190). Miles (1984) in particular is critical of the work on racial relations produced by the Centre for Contemporary Cultural Studies, which he says practices a "radical sociology of 'racial relations' " which is not compatible with Marxism because it "effectively subordinate[s] production relations to cultural processes" (1984, p. 221). Moreover, Miles accuses the CCCS of taking an extreme culturalist position and reifying race: "They need the idea of 'race' to weld together a population of significantly distinct historical and cultural origins, occupying different class positions, in order to legitimize and encourage the formation of a particular political force" (1984, p. 232). In other words, the CCCS is accused of letting praxis stand in the way of good theory.

Forsythe (1973), on the other hand, argues that Marxist theory is insufficient to produce a detailed understanding of Black life. He documents the racism in Marx' work and demonstrates how Fanon (1963) offers a more comprehensive analysis. Omi and Winant (1986) note the ability of cultural theories to deal with a greater range of racial experiences. Moreover, culturalist positions avoid the heavy-handed determinism of many Marxist arguments and offer more room for an analysis of human agency and cultural resistance.

Although some racial scholars remain staunch Marxists and others are adamant culturalists, the field might benefit from a blending of materialist and cultural analyses of the sort that cultural studies offers, as several scholars have suggested.[6] The analysis would be critical and reflexive; it would take into account the contours of the particular relations of dominance and subordination that exist among groups located at the intersection of class and racial conflicts; it would be grounded in an historical analysis of the origins of such relations; it would carefully attend to the production of ideologies of dominance and subordination; and it would utilize analytical strategies that respect the dialectical relationship between material conditions and cultural reproduction.

Critical analysis of racial relations and sport

Critical analyses of racial relations and sport based on an expanded cultural studies model must be grounded sociohistorically so that the origins of contemporary racial relations are not obscured. Four examples of this sociohistorical work can be suggested.

First, in their discussion of the resistance of racial groups to their total subordination, Omi and Winant (1986) give the example of Blacks under slavery in the United States who "developed cultures of resistance based on music, religion, African traditions, and family ties" (p. 73). Noticeably absent from this account is sport. We should explore why, not just to uncover examples of Black sporting traditions but in order to theorize the place of sport in this particular culture of resistance. Was sport absent, and if so, why? Was the ideology of sport constructed in such a way that sport as constituted could not serve resistant ends? Or were the sport activities of slaves not comprehended as sport within dominant definitions?

Second, we can examine the specific contours of race relations during the period historians call "the rise of sport," 1880–1900–a period perhaps more accurately labeled "sport's formative years" for it represents the years of successful ideological consolidation of dominant sport forms and practices. Materialist scholars have examined this period in terms of the consolidation of class privilege (Gruneau, 1983), and gender relations scholars (Birrell, 1987; Messner, 1988) have explored that period as a hegemonic moment for establishing male privilege and dominance in sport. Surely there is a comparable analysis to be made of racial relations and sport that would enrich our understanding of the cultural meaning and power of sport during this important period. In what ways was sport used to consolidate white skin privilege?

Third, we need to examine more carefully the absences in sport. Women's absence from sport, for example, informs us of the strong territorial imperative of male sport: Men need sport in order to produce an ideology of male dominance, naturalized through men's continually demonstrated "natural" physical superiority (Willis, 1982). Following this logic, we must examine why some racial or ethnic groups are present in sport while others are absent. What are the particular conditions that produce such variation? How does sport pervade the culture of Blacks, and why doesn't it pervade the culture of Chicanos, Asian Americans, or Native Americans in the same way? What is the additional effect of gender on sport involvement in these cultures? How can we pose these questions without falling into an essentialist trap? How can we ground the racial and ethnic differences in sport in the sort of cultural analysis that is sensitive to the interaction of class, gender, and racial antagonisms and grounded in historical experiences?

Fourth, an application of the materialist and cultural traditions of racial relations literature can take us beyond such simple analogies as comparing chattel slavery to the NFL plantation system. And we can ask more profound and particular questions of that experience: How is an ideology of legitimate exploitation produced? What are the effects of changing material conditions in athletics? The extraordinary salaries paid to some professional athletes today offer sweet incentive for a false consciousness of class and gender relations. How is hegemony maintained in the face of material rewards and physical exploitation?

At a more particular level, an analysis of the social conditions surrounding the championship of Jack Johnson or Jackie Robinson's entry into Major League Baseball might focus on the tension between the logic of the capitalist search for profit and prevailing Jim Crow ideologies of racial inferiority. In other words, what happens when the best man for the job is Black? In this case, sport provides an excellent opportunity to examine the tension between these ideologies as they conflict at the local level while being reconciled into a more general theory of Black labor for capitalist gain.

Gender relations and racial relations

As an analytical approach to sport, cultural studies offers a bright promise. It has a general framework for understanding relations of dominance and subordination, an insistence on analyzing the particular conditions of those relations, and an array of conceptual tools to advance the analysis. However, cultural studies continues to privilege class analysis over gender and racial analyses.

An expanded cultural studies must take serious account of racial relations, both as they intersect with gender relations and class relations and as they operate in relatively autonomous spheres. A new theoretical blending would provide a more comprehensive analysis of the relations of dominance and subordination of which class analysis, gender analysis, and racial analysis— or more appropriately, class-gender-racial analysis—are particular forms. Davis' (1981) *Women, Race, and Class* offers an excellent model of the sort of analysis such an approach can produce.

In particular, the absence of gender in the theories reviewed above must be redressed by critical scholars in sport studies. One way to do this is to focus on *physicality* as the connection between gender and race. Following the lead of theorists such as Connell (1987) and Willis (1982), we must explore more thoroughly the way that relations of dominance and subordination, structured along racial and gender lines, are naturalized through a commonsense understanding of difference and value grounded in "inherent" physicality. Feminist scholars are increasingly connecting discourses on physicality to the reproduction of gender through sport. French feminists like Monique Wittig (1979), for example, argue that sex is a socially constructed category and that the notion of two separate and distinct sexes "works" because we systematically eliminate all anomalies. Birke and Vines (1987) argue against "resigning ourselves to ultimate defeat in the face of an inexorable biological destiny" (p. 343). Instead they contend that the interaction between biology and the environment is reciprocal: genes are not the blueprint of developments, gradually unfolding and slightly modified by cultural forces, but our physiology is equally influenced by our own agency. As examples they note the impact of strenuous physical exercise on enhanced growth hormones in children, on amenorrhea, and on muscular development at the molecular level.

These writers provide perceptive commentaries on the production of masculinist hegemony in sport through the manipulation of images of natural physicality. A comparable analysis could be brought to racial relations and sport if we focus on physicality as a key to the construction of dominant images of racially defined groups and thus a major mechanism for the reproduction of racial relations. The recent remarks of Jimmy the Greek, though crude, ably summarize U.S. commonsense on the inherent physical difference of the Black male athlete: "The black is a better athlete to begin with, because he's been bred to be that way. Because of his high thighs and big thighs that go up into his back. And they can jump higher and run faster because of their bigger thighs, you see" ("Sportscaster Greek," 1988).

The definition of race as a biological category has gone unchallenged for centuries, but current theoretical approaches attempt to deconstruct that commonsense by focusing on the processes of racial relations, racial formation, and racialization. Since sport also is thought to derive its essence from its physical nature, it would appear that the connections between dominant discourses on race and sport could offer the grounding for constructing a new understanding of the way that racial relations, and race itself, are produced and reproduced in sport.

Another approach that plays on the intersections rather than connections between gender relations and racial relations would focus on racially located definitions of masculinity and femininity. Dominant readings of masculinity within the Black community and the part that sport may play in their production and reproduction need to be addressed against the historical backdrop of gender relations as they were transformed from their African roots through the conditions of slavery in the U.S. (Davis, 1981; Hooks, 1981). Sojourner Truth's famous question "Ain't I a woman?" reminds us in a powerful way that femininity, like masculinity, is a totalizing concept that requires deconstruction into constituent femininities and masculinities (Brod, 1987) produced within particular communities.

Finally, since so little analysis of women's experiences are included in theories of racial relations, another point of access is through the discourses women of color are producing to make sense of their lives. Because their work cannot be located within traditional paradigms of racial relations scholarship, it is often dismissed or overlooked by sociologists. The move by critical scholars toward interdisciplinary practices will open the way for recognizing these critical autobiographies as the insightful cultural criticisms they are (Birrell, in press).

Cultural studies, racial relations, and sport

The atheoretical approach to racial relations that has characterized the work of sport studies scholars does not have to be reproduced in the future if we engage in the critical discourse on racial relations developing outside our field. Four theoretical groups can be identified in the writing of racial relations scholars, and two of these—materialist and culturalist approaches— offer particularly provocative conceptualizations of racial relations and sport. Most promising is the potential of cultural studies to blend materialist and culturalist perspectives and develop a comprehensive model for analyzing the complex of relations of dominance and subordination simultaneously structured along class, gender, and racial lines. This analytical advance might be gained through a continuing blending of critical theories: cultural studies, socialist feminism, feminist cultural studies, materialist and cultural racial relations theories. A theory of such comprehensive scope must be sensitive to both the autonomy and intersection of racial, gender, and class relations as they are articulated in particular sets of conditions. Until we develop such sophisticated blendings, however, critical scholars need to attend far more carefully to the analysis of racial relations as they are articulated, reproduced, or resisted in sport.

Acknowledgments

I would like to thank Rusty Barcelo for sharing several important sources on Chicano and Chicana scholarship with me, Michael Messner and Don Sabo for offering useful comments on earlier drafts of this manuscript, and Cheryl Cole for critical support at many stages of this project.

This manuscript was prepared during a developmental assignment from The University of Iowa, with the support of colleagues and facilities at University House.

Notes

1 Sources of importance include such journals as *Black Sociologist*, the *Journal of Black Studies, Black Scholar, Sage, Ethnic and Racial Studies, Aztlan, De Colores, Cultural Critique*, and the proceedings of the National Association for Chicano Studies.

2 For more detailed critiques, see Alkalimat (1972), Daniel (1981), Hernandez (1970), Jackson (1970), Mirande (1985), Muñoz (1984), Ralston (1971), Semmes (1981), Staples (1976), Turner and Perkins (1976), and Walters (1973).

3 For suggestions on building a Black studies, see Alkalimat (1972), Daniel (1981), Jackson (1970), McWhorter and Bailey (1984), Ralston (1971), Semmes (1981), Staples (1973), Turner and Perkins (1976), and Walters (1973). For sources on building a Chicano studies, see Mirande (1985), Muñoz (1984), and Romano (1968).

4 In Chicano studies, for example, traditional stereotypes—the Chicano as lazy, passive, and fatalistic; as lacking in achievement drive; as controlled by traditional culture; as the victim of an authoritarian family system and the cult of machismo (Mirande, 1985, p. 2)—are seen as the product of dominant Anglo theory and valorization.

5 These include the market relations approach, stratification theory, class conflict theory, class segmentation, and labor market segmentation (Barrera, 1979; Omi & Winant, 1986).

6 Mirande (1985), Barrera (1979), and Staples (1973) all call for a more complete framework, and Barrera (1979), Blauner (1972), Almaguer (1975), Omi and Winant (1986), and the Centre for Contemporary Cultural Studies (1982) attempt to provide one through their work.

References

Abney, R. (1988). *The effects of role models and mentors on the careers of Black women athletic administrators and coaches in higher education.* Unpublished doctoral dissertation, University of Iowa.

Acuna, R. (1981). *Occupied America: A history of Chicanos* (2nd ed.). New York: Harper & Row.

Alexander, A. (1978). *Status of minority women in the AIAW*. Unpublished master's thesis, Temple University.

Alkalimat, A.I. (1972). The ideology of Black social science. In J. Ladner (Ed.), *The death of white sociology* (pp. 173–189). New York: Random House.

Almaguer, T. (1975, July-September). Class, race, and Chicano oppression. *Socialist Revolution*, pp. 71–99.

Barclay, V.M. (1979). *Status of Black women in sports among selected institutions of higher education*. Unpublished master's thesis, The University of Iowa.

Barrera, M. (1979). *Race and class in the southwest: A theory of racial inequality*. South Bend, IN: Notre Dame University Press.

Birke, L., & Vines, G. (1987). A sporting chance: The anatomy of destiny? *Women's Studies International Forum*, **10**, 337–347.

Birrell, S. (1987, November). *Women and the male myth of sport*. Presented at North American Society for the Sociology of Sport meetings, Edmonton, Alberta.

Birrell, S. (in press). Women of color, critical autobiography, and sport. In M. Messner & D. Sabo (Eds.), *Critical perspectives on sport, men and the gender order*. Champaign, IL: Human Kinetics.

Blauner, R. (1972). *Racial oppression in America*. New York: Harper & Row.

Brod, H. (Ed.) (1987). *The making of masculinities*. Boston: Unwin Hyman.

Centre for Contemporary Cultural Studies. (1982). *The empire strikes back: Race and racism in 70's Britain*. London: Hutchinson.

Christiano, K. (1986). Salary discrimination in major league baseball: The effect of race. *Sociology of Sport Journal*, **3**, 144–153.

Christiano, K. (1988). Salaries and race in professional baseball: Discrimination 10 years later. *Sociology of Sport Journal*, **5**, 136–149.

Chu, D., & Griffey, D. (1982). Sport and racial integration: The relationship of personal contact, attitudes and behavior. In A.O. Donleavy, A. Miracle, & C.R. Rees (Eds.), *Studies in the sociology of sport* (pp. 271–282). Fort Worth: Texas Christian University Press.

Chu, D., & Griffey, D. (1985). Contact theory of racial integration: The case of sport. *Sociology of Sport Journal*, **2**, 323–333.

Coakley, J., & Pacey, P. (1984). Distribution of athletic scholarships among women in intercollegiate sport. In N. Theberge & P. Donnelly (Eds.), *Sport and the sociological imagination* (pp. 228–241). Fort Worth: Texas Christian University Press.

Cole, C. (1988). *The politics of cultural representation*. Paper presented at the North American Society for the Sociology of Sport meetings, Cincinnati.

Cole, C., & Birrell, S. (1986, October). *Resisting the canon: Feminist cultural studies and sport*. Presented at the North American Society for the Sociology of Sport meetings, Las Vegas.

Connell, R. (1987). *Gender and power*. Stanford: Stanford University Press.

Curtis, J., & Loy, J. (1978). Positional segregation and professional baseball. *International Review of Sport Sociology*, **13**, 5–21.

Daniel, T.K. (1981). Theory building in Black studies. *The Black Scholar*, **12**, 29–36.

Davis, A. (1981). *Women, race and class*. New York: Vintage.

Day, R. (1981). Ethnic soccer clubs in London, Canada: A study in assimilation. *International Review of Sport Sociology*, **16**(1), 37–52.

Edwards, H. (1969). *The revolt of the Black athlete*. New York: Free Press.

Fabiano, D. (1984). Minority managers in professional baseball. *Sociology of Sport Journal*, **1**, 163–171.

Fanon, F. (1963). *The wretched of the earth*. New York: Grove Press.

Forsythe, D. (1973). Radical sociology and Blacks. In J. Ladner (Ed.), *The death of white sociology* (pp. 213–233). New York: Random House.

Green, T.S., Oglesby, C.A., Alexander, A., & Franke, N. (1981). *Black women in sport*. Reston, VA: American Association of Health, Physical Education, Recreation and Dance.

Greendorfer, S., & Ewing, M. (1981). Race and gender differences in children's socialization into sport. *Research Quarterly*, **52**, 301–310.

Gruneau, R. (1983). *Class, sports, and social development*, Amherst: University of Massachusetts Press.

Hernandez, D. (1970). *Mexican American challenge to a sacred cow*. Monograph No. 1, Mexican American Cultural Center, University of California, Los Angeles.

Hoch, P. (1972). *Rip off the big game*. New York: Anchor/Doubleday.

Hooks, B. (1981). *Ain't I a woman? Black women and feminism*. Boston: South End Press.

Houzer, S. (1974). Black women in athletics. *Physical Educator*, **31**, 208–209.

Jackson, M. (1970). Toward a sociology of Black studies. *Journal of Black Studies*, **1**(2), 131–140.

LaFlamme, A.G. (1977). The role of sport in the development of ethnicity: A case study. *Sport Sociology Bulletin*, **6**(1), 47–51.

Loy, J., & McElvogue, J. (1971). Racial segregation and American sport. *International Review of Sport Sociology*, **5**, 5–24.

McLemore, L.B. (1972). Toward a theory of Black politics—The Black and ethnic models revisited: A research note. *Journal of Black Studies*, **2**, 323–331.

McWhorter, G.A., & Bailey, R. (1984). Black studies curriculum development in the 1980's: Its patterns and history. *The Black Scholar*, **15**, 18–31.

Medoff, M. (1986). Positional segregation and the economic hypothesis. *Sociology of Sport Journal*, **3**, 297–304.

Merton, R. (1972). Insiders and outsiders: A chapter in the sociology of knowledge. *American Journal of Sociology*, **78**, 9–48.

Messner, M. (1987). *Masculinity, ethnicity, and the athletic career: Motivations and experiences of white men and men of color*. Paper presented at the North American Society for the Sociology of Sport meetings, Edmonton, Alberta.

Messner, M. (1988). Sports and male domination: The female athlete as contested ideological terrain. *Sociology of Sport Journal*, **5**, 197–211.

Miles, R. (1984). Marxism versus the sociology of 'race relations'? *Ethnic and Racial Studies*, **7**(2), 217–231.

Mirande, A. (1985). *The Chicano experience: An alternative perspective*. Notre Dame, IN: University of Notre Dame Press.

Montagu, A. (1964). *Man's most dangerous myth: The fallacy of race*. New York: World.

Moynihan, D.P. (1965). *The Negro family: The case for national action*. Washington: U.S. Department of Labor.

Muñoz, C., Jr. (1984). The development of Chicano studies, 1968–1981. In E.E.

Garcia, F.A. Lomeli, & I.D. Ortiz (Eds.), *Chicano studies: A multidisciplinary approach* (pp. 5–18). New York: Teachers College Press.

Murphy, M.D. (1980). *The involvement of Blacks in women's athletics in member institutions of the AIAW*. Unpublished doctoral dissertation, University of Florida.

Omi, M., & Winant, H. (1986). *Racial formation in the United States*. New York: Routledge & Kegan Paul.

Oxendine, J. (1988). Sports for women and girls. In J. Oxendine, *American Indian sports heritage* (pp. 22–26). Champaign, IL: Human Kinetics.

Park, R. (1950). *Race and culture*. New York: Free Press.

Pooley, J. (1981). Ethnic soccer clubs in Milwaukee: A study of assimilation. In M. Hart & S. Birrell (Eds.), *Sport in the sociocultural process* (3rd ed.) (pp. 430–447). Dubuque, IA: Wm. C. Brown.

Ralston, R. (1971). The role of the Black university in the Black revolution. *Journal of Black Studies*, **3**, 267–286.

Rees, R., & Miracle, A. (1984). Participation in sport and the reduction of racial prejedices: Contact theory, superordinate goals hypothesis, or wishful thinking? In N. Theberge & P. Donnelly (Eds.), *Sport and the sociological imagination* (pp. 140–152). Fort Worth: Texas Christian University Press.

Romano, O. (1968). The anthropology and sociology of the Mexican-Americans: The distortion of Mexican-American history (A review essay). *El Grito*, **2**, 13–26.

Semmes, C. (1981). Foundations of an Afrocentric social science: Implications for curriculum-building, theory, and research in Black studies. *Journal of Black Studies*, **12**, 3–17.

Sportscaster "Greek": Blacks bred to be athletes. (1988, January 16). *Des Moines Register*, p. 1S.

Staples, R. (1973). What is Black sociology? Toward a sociology of Black liberation. In J. Ladner (Ed.), *The death of Black sociology* (pp. 161–172). New York: Random House.

Staples, R. (1976). *Introduction to Black sociology*. New York: McGraw-Hill.

Turner, J., & Perkins, W.E. (1976). Toward a critique of social science. *The Black Scholar*, **7**, 2–11.

Walters, R.W. (1973). Toward a definition of Black social science. In J. Ladner (Ed.), *The death of white sociology* (pp. 190–212). New York: Random House.

Willis, P. (1982). Women in sport in ideology. In J. Hargreaves (Ed.), *Sport, culture and ideology* (pp. 112–135). London: Routledge & Kegan Paul.

Wittig, M. (1979). One is not born a woman. In A. Jaggar & P.S. Rothenberg (Eds.), *Feminist frameworks* (2nd ed.) (pp. 148–152). New York: McGraw-Hill.

Wolf, D. (1972). *Foul: The Connie Hawkins Story*. New York: Warner.

44

FLYING AIR JORDAN

The power of racial images

John Hoberman

Source: J. Hoberman, *Darwin's Athletes: how sport has damaged black America and preserved the myth of race*. New York: Houghton Mifflin (1997), pp. xxiii-xxxv.

The modern world is awash in images of black athletes. The airborne black body, its sinewy arms clutching a basketball as it soars high above the arena floor, has become the paramount symbol of athletic dynamism in the media age.[1] Stereotypes of black athletic superiority are now firmly established as the most recent version of a racial folklore that has spread across the face of the earth over the past two centuries, and a corresponding belief in white athletic inferiority pervades popular thinking about racial difference. Such ideas about the "natural" physical talents of dark-skinned peoples, and the media-generated images that sustain them, probably do more than anything else in our public life to encourage the idea that blacks and whites are biologically different in a meaningful way. Prominent racial theorists of the 1990s such as Charles Murray and Dinesh D'Souza have declared that black athletic superiority is evidence of more profound differences. The world of sport has thus become an image factory that disseminates and even intensifies our racial preoccupations.[2] Centuries of racial classification have made exceptional athletes into ethnic specimens. "Are you a nigger or an Eskimo?" one racist sports fan asked the finest high school basketball player in Alaskan history, displaying a curiosity about human biology that is always latent in multiracial athletic encounters.[3] Interracial sport has thus breathed new life into our racial folklore, reviving nineteenth-century ideas about the racial division of labor that then recur in a trend-setting book like *The Bell Curve*.[4]

Ideas about racial athletic aptitude reign virtually uncontested outside the small number of classrooms in which they are examined. The idea that African Americans are the robust issue of slave-era breeding experiments has

62

served the fantasy needs of blacks and whites alike.[5] ("I propose," Ralph Ellison once wrote, "that we view the whole of American life as a drama acted out upon the body of a Negro giant.")[6] "We were simply bred for physical qualities," the Olympic champion sprinter Lee Evans said in 1971, and better-educated black men have embraced the same eugenic fantasy.[7] Decades of popular scientific speculation about the special endowments of black athletes have shaped the thinking of entire populations. White television sportscasters have long employed a special vocabulary to distinguish "natural" black athletes from "thinking" whites and have referred to black athletes as "monkeys" on more than one occasion.[8] African-American college students who suddenly discover that their assumptions about "natural" black athleticism are illusory can feel as though they are waking from a dream. For their white counterparts too, critical scrutiny of racial stereotypes can take on the power of revelation, because it challenges conventional assumptions about the natural distribution of human abilities. The study of racialistic thinking changes people by exposing unconscious mental habits that permeate everyday life and shape our identities. Conversations with young blacks and whites reveal an unpublicized but thoroughly racialized social universe in which sport functions as a principal medium in which racial folklore flourishes. Here we find the schoolchild who cannot believe that the black college student who is his mentor is not a football player, since television has persuaded him that every black male student is an athlete; here too is the academically precocious child whose athletic skills save him from harassment by his black peers, whose hostility to intellectual development (and even "whitey's" habit of using seatbelts) only intensifies as they enter adolescence. Some black children still face overt hostility in interracial games. In east Texas in the 1990s, black junior high school boys sometimes play football against whites whose parents shout "Niggers!" from the stands as they watch their sons lose.

This racialized universe of everyday encounters receives far less attention than the highly public and officially deracialized theater of professional and collegiate sport, which white administrators present as an oasis of racial harmony. The sports media do not identify or investigate conflicts between blacks and whites, or they portray them as idiosyncratic episodes; young black athletes are immature rather than angry, while older white coaches are curmudgeons whose decency (if not always their authority) remains firmly intact. The realities of race are more evident in the unvarnished world of high school athletics, where far greater numbers of people engage in race relations, absorb ideas about racially specific traits and abilities, and grapple with their own racial dramas in athletic terms. Here, for example, we find a black nerd, the bookish son of a physician, whose conflicts about blackness prompt him to find his athletic identity in ice hockey and other "white" activities. A more common character is the young black athlete who is persuaded, at times by a black coach, that he or she enjoys a physical advantage over whites.

Such black self-confidence has contributed to self-doubts on the other side of the racial divide. A gifted white high school athlete told me that he found himself wondering why the muscles of some black teammates seem to be better defined than his own, and some white professionals are simply fatalistic about their ability to match up against blacks. "You have to be a realist," says Scott Brooks, a guard on the Dallas Mavericks basketball team. "White people can't jump as high." "There aren't many white guys who can jump the way they can," says Pete Chilcutt, white player for the Houston Rockets.[9] White spectators at an interracial high school basketball game may find themselves expecting their team to fail and hearing racial taunts from the other side. White high school players may also perceive a bias in calling fouls that favors black players, as if prevailing stereotypes had persuaded referees that whites are simply incapable of making extraordinary moves while obeying the rules of the game.

Yet it is also possible to face and conquer self-defeating mental habits. A white basketball team in Texas openly confronted the internalized stereotype of black superiority that had ruined one season and proceeded to finish third in the state the following year. This true story of white demoralization and subsequent self-assertion represents a variation on the storyline of the popular film *Hoosiers*, in which a tiny white Indiana high school wins a state championship over a predominantly black city team whose leaping ability is emphasized by the camera. In fact, this storyline has known many variations over the past century of interracial athletic competition, as racial dominance in sport has changed color from white to black.

Racial folklore can also provide modern whites with various compensations for their lost preeminence and the feelings of physical inferiority that are now immortalized in the popular slogan "white men can't jump." A young woman who played high school basketball told me of her coach's habit of giving white players custodial control of presumably less disciplined black teammates. Naive biological racism can also play a compensatory role in the minds of anxious whites. A black teenager who worked as a lifeguard in the Dallas area in 1990 was told by his white counterparts that the peculiar capacity of black skin to absorb water reduced buoyancy and that this explained the scarcity of good black swimmers. When the golfer Jack Nicklaus told an interviewer in 1994 that blacks were anatomically unsuited to play golf ("Blacks have different muscles that react in different ways"), he too was employing an eccentric racial biology to rationalize the absence of black athletes in a segregated country club sport.[10] Such are the culturally acquired mental habits that can preserve the racial balance of power more efficiently than any policies enacted by legislatures and public officials.

While the racial stereotypes that flourish in the sports world can impair white performance, they are capable of damaging African Americans in much more serious ways. The images of black athletes that fill television

screens and the pages of newspapers and magazines only sustain the traditional view of blacks as essentially physical and thus primitive people, and
variations on this theme are absorbed by blacks as well as whites. In this
category we find the young black man who told a Hispanic friend that it was
harder for blacks to master the art of pitching a baseball because blacks are
not as "in control" as whites. Here too is the black football player who grew
up believing that blacks were "genetically superior" athletes while "white
men can't jump, but they are hell in the classroom." Another young black
athlete adopted the habit of calling a white teammate "nigger" in recognition of his superior skills, an awkward variation on the popular idea that
athleticism is literally a black trait. Nor are such ideas about the inherent
limitations of robust black males expressed only by athletes. A young black
woman told me that she had thought of her football-playing cousin as an
insensate "buck" until she learned something about the travails of black
college athletes, at which point she was able to empathize with him as a
person who had feelings of his own. Confinement within the athletic syndrome is maintained by powerful peer-group pressures which ridicule academic achievement while stigmatizing blacks who do not beat "whitey" at
whichever game is at stake. In these and many other ways the sports fixation
permeates the lives of countless people whose ideas about their own developmental possibilities are tightly bound to the world of physical self-
expression.[11]

The interracial sport of earlier decades offered profound emotional gratifications and a measure of hope to most African Americans, and the integration
of college and professional sports played a dramatic (if also overrated) role
in the civil rights movement. Today, however, the sports world is a battle-
ground on which the symbolic integration that reigns on television confronts
a black male stereotype that feeds on media images of black athletes and
other black male action figures. "It is no exaggeration to say," Glenn Loury
has written, "that black, male youngsters in the central cities have been
demonized in the popular mind as have no other group in recent American
history."[12] This aggressive stereotype flourishes in the minds of everyone who
is constantly exposed to images of black athletes who can appear to be
threatening or dangerous. The sports world they inhabit is, after all, an
extraordinary social space in which black men are expected to act out their
aggressions, so the "violent black male" becomes the dangerous twin of the
spectacular black athlete.

While it is assumed that sport has made an important contribution to
racial integration, this has been counterbalanced by the merger of the athlete, the gangster rapper, and the criminal into a single black male persona
that the sports industry, the music industry, and the advertising industry have
made into the predominant image of black masculinity in the United States
and around the world.[13] Convinced that black athleticism alone cannot

sustain market appeal, these commercial interests dramatize and embellish the physical and psychological traits of athletes whose public personalities come to embody the full spectrum of male pathology. From the National Basketball Association comes Charles Barkley, "the frowning clown" whose deodorant advertisements play cleverly on tacit racist ideas about the black man's inherent lack of refinement.[14] Here too is the self-mutilating eccentric Dennis Rodman, whose hair dyes and tattoos have turned his entire body into a kaleidoscopic demonstration of how black self-hatred can be marketed as spectacle to white America, which has always embraced variations of the ridiculous black jester. Here is the young star Alonzo Mourning wearing "a scowling mask of rage" that could be depthless black anger or just the personality quirk of an "intense competitor." Some magazine advertisements confront whites with hard black faces in a safe setting, counterfeit versions of the "bad nigger" of black lore and white nightmares. "You got something to say?" asks a belligerent Shawn Kemp in a Foot Locker ad, presumably thrilling and intimidating insecure white men with his disdain. The broad, sullen face of the football player Greg Lloyd covers two full-color pages of *Sports Illustrated*, every pore visible and glistening to produce the effect of personal confrontation within the safe confines of a photograph, exemplifying the "male restrictions on emotional expression" that reign in the ghetto.[15]

Yet the appeal of such images has less to do with athleticism per se than with a black male style that counts as one of the major cultural myths of our era, for while it is true that black men fill sports teams, hip-hop groups, and prisons in disproportionate numbers, these numbers alone cannot account for the manner in which this notably powerless group of people is presented by various media to the American public.

The black male style has become incarnated in the fusion of black athletes, rappers, and criminals into a single menacing figure who disgusts and offends many blacks as well as whites. The constant, haunting presence of this composite masculine type is maintained by news coverage and advertising strategies that exploit the suggestive mixture of black anger and physical prowess that suffuses each of these roles. Rap music, as the black feminist Trisha Rose once pointed out, "is basically the locker room with a beat" – a perfect fusion of the rhythm and athleticism that are found in so many folkloric images of blackness.[16] In fact, the athlete and the rapper have a relationship that is more reciprocal than popular images might suggest. Shaquille O'Neal serves as a primary symbol of black physical domination in the NBA and is also a highly publicized rap singer. The most aggressive or radical rappers brag about their pugilistic as well as sexual prowess: "I'm like [Mike] Tyson!" crows the rapper L.L. Cool J.[17] The conversation of the rapper Run (Joseph Simmons) of Run-D.M.C. is strewn with sports metaphors, since rappers as well as athletes express "the style and attitude and identity of the street,"[18] while many black youths idolize rap artists, just as they do athletic heroes.[19] "I'm a hip-hop man," says the football star Natrone Means, summing up the effect of his baggy jeans, baseball cap, and diamond earrings.[20] Numerous rappers return the compliment by pursuing physical training regimens to build muscle and endurance for their stage routines. "A lot of us have been in and out of jail," says Tom Guest of Young Gunz. "Once you develop a body in the penitentiary, you want to keep it."[21] The hip-hop dancer who calls himself "Incredible" describes his troupe's production as "the most physically demanding show on or off Broadway" and refers to breakdancing competitions as "musical football without teams," thereby extending the range of black athleticism as an idiom that can encompass black creativity in general.[22]

Criminality, real or imagined, is an essential ingredient of this charismatic black persona. One major producer of "gangsta rap" is a former football star who thrives in the music business by projecting an aura of incipient criminality, thereby combining all three roles into a thuggish identity presented to the world by an awestruck white journalist in the pages of the *New York Times Magazine*.[23] Numerous rappers, including such celebrities as Tupac Shakur and Snoop Doggy Dogg, have been arrested for serious crimes, thereby achieving the "ghetto authenticity" that is glamorized by white-owned corporations and the advertising experts who adapt the black "homeboy" style for consumption by affluent white wannabes. The police blotter also includes many black athletes, some of whom (like O. J. Simpson) have battered wives or girlfriends.

The thoughtful black athlete recognizes the commercial value of violence and understands that he has been cast in two grotesquely incongruous roles, impersonating the traditional sportsman, who honors fair play, while being paid to behave like a predator, a role to which the black athlete brings a special resonance. When the Pittsburgh Steelers linebacker Greg Lloyd blindsided a quarterback who suffered a concussion, he was fined $12,000. "Come to a game early and watch the Jumbotron scoreboard," he objected, pointing out the hypocrisy of the penalty. "You'll see 'NFL's Greatest Hits,' with guys getting their helmets ripped off . . . They're marketing that."[24]

Finally, just as the black athlete may radiate an aura of criminality, so the black criminal can radiate a threatening aura of athleticism. Several states have enacted vindictive anticrime laws that have deprived predominantly black prison populations of weightlifting facilities, on the grounds that more muscular convicts are more dangerous when released – as if muscles were more influential than minds in determining the behavior of black men.[25] But the modern archetype of the black criminal-as-superathlete is now Rodney King, whose beating by a crowd of Los Angeles police officers is best understood as a kind of perverse athletic event that matched a team of unathletic white policemen against a black behemoth descended from the mythical John Henry. "It will be very interesting," an attorney for one of the indicted officers said before the trial, "to see him standing next to these officers, because it will be like a giant standing next to pygmies."[26] Officer Stacy Koon, who was eventually convicted and imprisoned for his role in the attack, stated that Rodney King possessed a "hulk-like super strength" and arms that were like unbendable "steel posts."[27] Related imagery also appeared in the "liberal" media. The same artist who produced the notorious darkened *Time* magazine cover of O. J. Simpson in late June 1994, Matt Mahurin, contributed a strikingly apelike depiction of Rodney King's cranium to the same publication a few weeks earlier. Indeed, it would be interesting to know to what extent folkloric ideas about black primitiveness and physical prowess have shaped police behavior toward black men throughout the twentieth century.

The dissemination of aggressive black male images by corporations and their advertising media threatens to alienate the white public if displays of black assertiveness are not rationed and counterbalanced by others that domesticate and gentrify virile black men. The National Basketball Association, for example, must somehow defuse the "undertone of violence" that surrounds its dynamic but sometimes unstable black players, and it does so with the cooperation of the sporting press.[28] Black as well as white sportswriters have warned black players not to act out degenerate roles that threaten the league's profitability by creating an image of chaos and incipient revolt.[29] The besieged white NBA coach who simply cannot grasp "the bewildering mentality of today's [black] players" has become an emblematic martyr of white failure inside the sports world.[30] The domestication of the black male in our mass media also occurs outside the sports world.[31] Perhaps the most striking images occur in advertisements for fashionable men's clothing, in which a handsome and well-built black man can be racially neutralized as he is absorbed into a white cultural context. Here, for example, we find a statuesque and impeccably groomed black male model posing in a full-page advertisement for the polo sports tie from Ralph Lauren. He is paired with a white counterpart who combines rugged outdoorsiness with evident good breeding. This is one of many men's fashion ads that symbolically induct the stylishly athleticized black male into the squeaky-clean prep school world of inherited money and the symbolic racial vigor of demanding physical exercise. Fitted out in a dark blazer with insignia, this man wears a tie that shows two white polo players in action on their charging horses. Ethnic blackness is dissolved in a sporting world that is exclusively and impeccably white: golfing, fishing, tennis, rowing, sailing, and polo – the sports of dynamic imperial males unwinding from the rigors of colonial administration. Here in its purest form is the dream of the black athlete as a natural gentleman, a cherished white fantasy that culminated in the lionization of a deracialized O. J. Simpson and then met a grotesque end in his fall from grace.

The sports world and the advertising industry that feeds on its celebrities pursue the domesticating strategy on a continual basis. Every black man who smiles for the camera, whether he has scored a touch-down or endorsed a product in a commercial, is participating in the detoxification of his own image in the eyes of a white audience that seldom perceives the redemptive function of these images.[32] This process is one example of what may be called "virtual integration," an effortless commingling of the races (almost always in the service of corporate profits) that offers the illusion of progress to a public that wants both good news about race and the preservation of a racial status quo that seldom forces whites to examine their own racial attitudes. (The aftermath of the O. J. Simpson verdict was one of these rare occasions.) The same passive longing for racial peace once prompted the veteran sportswriter Dan Shaughnessy to beg his readers to believe that the white arm of a Boston Celtics player draped around the shoulder of a black teammate was a sign of hope for race relations in the United States. A standard technique for delivering this message is to place big black athletes in the company of small white children; such juxtapositions appear frequently, for example, on the cover of *Sports Illustrated for Kids*, thereby reassuring the many whites who believe that black men are by nature physically dangerous.[33] The Boston Red Sox slugger Mo Vaughn, who has become a rare black symbol of reconciliation in a racially troubled city, appeared on the cover of *Sports Illustrated* in the company of a small and adoring white boy.[34]

Ralph Ellison pointed out many years ago that such idealized versions of the gentle black man are rooted in white fears of black retribution for the humiliations of slavery.[35] Such symbolic figures also represent an unconscious attempt to resurrect the docile black male of southern racial lore.[36] They are of doubtful social value if only because they cannot resolve the white psyche's anxious oscillation between idealized and demonized images of blacks, who are always denied normal human status. A similar gentling technique appears in a Nike-sponsored, pseudo public-service ad that features the meditative face of Michael Jordan as he contemplates a world without his own celebrity ("Would I still be your hero?"). The cynicism of such corporate advertising is rooted both in its commercial motives and in its entrapment of the black athlete in the vicious cycle of demonization and domestication.

Another domesticating strategy uses the black man's body to accentuate his vulnerability. American publications have a conspicuous tendency to publish naked black male torsos more often than white ones, a practice that expresses the same racial mentality that has long permitted the undressing of racial exotics in *National Geographic* and that plays on the tantalizing themes of miscegenation and human bondage.[37] Yet another pictorial device is the comic-racist celebration of the obese black athlete, who is symbolically neutered the moment he becomes the jolly fat man. The media celebrity once accorded to William (The Refrigerator) Perry of the Chicago Bears is the best-known example of a racist fixation on the black body that becomes acceptable as harmless burlesque. *Sports Illustrated*, the most widely circulated and Middle American sports publication of them all, has published an entire series of such entertainments in recent years, oblivious to the fact that the gratification experienced by its white readers is rooted in an elaborate racist folklore about blacks and their appetites.[38] Here is Nate (The Kitchen) Newton, a Dallas Cowboys guard, surrounded by a dozen bags of fattening snacks and a watermelon, his eager lips pursed for a potato chip. There is Dwayne (Road Grader) White of the St. Louis Cardinals, his dark face averted from the camera as his belly bulges obscenely over an invisible belt. In another photograph Dan (Big Daddy) Wilkinson sits before a heaping plate of food, his large fists grasping an enormous wooden fork and matching spoon, which he holds erect like an African chief posing for *National Geographic*. Nate Newton reveals that he is paid personal appearance fees "so they can see how fat I am" – the bloated black athlete as commercialized human specimen and Garfield-like house creature. "Across the country," *Sports Illustrated* reports, "he is perceived as some kind of enormous, lovable Chia Pet, a big huggybear of a man in the NFL's cast of cartoon characters."[39] Yet even this saccharine nonsense has its social significance, in that these relentlessly upbeat makeovers of black giants for white audiences express a racist wish to find comfort in the domestication of big black men.

The virtual integration of interracial sport is only one aspect of a larger racial coping strategy described by the cultural critic Benjamin DeMott. American mass media, he argues, have been engaged in the relentless promotion of "feel-good images" of black-white sameness that systematically evade all of the deep conflicts between blacks and whites: "Round the clock, ceaselessly, the elements of this orthodoxy of sameness are grouped and regrouped, helping to root an unspoken but felt understanding throughout white America: race problems belong to the passing moment. Race problems do not involve group interests and conflicts developed over centuries. Race problems are being smoothed into nothingness, gradually, inexorably, by good will, affection, points of light." This propaganda of racial bonhomie is also a de facto policy of the American sports industry and is elaborated most effectively and ingeniously in advertisements. The athleticizing of the black male image is thus an integral part of corporate enterprises worth billions of dollars a year. This contributes in turn to the perpetual underdevelopment of people to whom athleticism seems to offer both personal fulfillment and social liberation. At the same time, it is only fair to ask whether these "friendship dogmas" might also serve a useful purpose. As DeMott points out, "friendship ideas do, after all, represent a step forward from yesterday's race-viciousness. Combined with an intelligent address to the problems of non-middle-class blacks, the friendship faith could move us toward a positive interracial future. Some sameness themes radiate real moral energy and carry an inspiring, even lyric charge."[40]

The problem is that "feel-good" initiatives do not seem to transform racial attitudes in socially effective ways. The fifty years of integrated sport that produced a miraculously deracialized O. J. Simpson could not obscure, let alone prevent, the bitter racial antagonisms revealed by his acquittal. Indeed, friendship dogmas may be worse than useless if they are offered as a substitute for social policies that redistribute power toward the powerless, because they help whites avoid "the hard truth that a caste society attempting erratically to dismantle its caste structures can't expect to get the job done without making commitments to developmental assistance on a scale this country has never imagined."[41]

Black athleticism has complicated the identity problems of black Americans by making athletes the most prominent symbols of African-American achievement. This has done much to perpetuate the invisibility of the black middle class, by making black professional achievement a seldom-noted sideshow to more dramatic media coverage of celebrities and deviants. As the critic Walter Goodman once said of local television news in New York City, "If a rule went out excluding entertainers, athletes, and criminals from a night's report, the only black faces you could be sure of seeing would be those of the anchors." The "tabloid style" of such programming virtually prescribes a demoralizing image of blacks as a group: "The opening headlines are about mayhem, not classes for the gifted. The accomplishments come across as flowers in a world of weeds; on local television, social aberration is the norm."[42]

Responses to this process of continuous defamation are strikingly selective, in that members of the black middle class who rightly resent the notoriety of black criminals appear to be unembarrassed by the omnipresence of black athletes, who serve as the reigning symbol of black "genius" for a majority of blacks and whites.[43] "For many years," a black sociologist once noted, "blacks were politically powerless to affect the imagery and metaphor of popular media expression."[44] Yet even after they acquired some influence over their media images, if only the right to censor the worst of them, their lobbying efforts have rarely targeted disproportionate emphasis on athleticism as an obstacle to progress. A black middle class (and its intelligentsia) that remains infatuated with sports cannot campaign effectively against racial stereotyping that preserves the black man's physicality as a sign of his inherent limitations.[45]

This appearance of passivity is, however, misleading, for there are both working-class and middle-class African Americans who do resist the sports propaganda by encouraging their children to pursue more productive cultural and intellectual interests.[46] At this point we do not know how many people offer this sort of guidance to black children. What is more, their voices are unlikely to be heard above the din of a sports industry that profits from the athleticizing of young blacks. Another obstacle is the athleticizing of black life itself, a sense that giving expression to the ordeal of black survival has long required the visceral power of athletic metaphors – or as one black patient told his psychiatrist: "The black man in this country fights the main event in Madison Square Garden every day."[47]

Darwin's Athletes is a racial history of modern sport that explores our racial predicament in its broadest dimensions. The first section of the book describes the origins of the African-American preoccupation with athletic achievement and shows how this cultural syndrome has subverted more productive developmental strategies founded on academic and professional achievement. It argues that Western racism inflicted on African Americans a physicalized (and eventually athleticized) identity from which they have yet to escape. The cult of black athleticism continues a racist tradition that has long emphasized the motor skills and manual training of African Americans. While the idea of black athletic superiority serves the fantasy needs of blacks as well as whites, providing symbolic victories and a renewal of survivalist thinking about black toughness, the sports fixation is also emblematic of an entire complex of black problems, which includes the adolescent violence and academic failure that have come to symbolize the black male for most Americans.

The second section of the book presents the past century of sport as an arena of racial competition. The ascendancy of the black athlete and the growing belief in his biological superiority represent a historic reversal of roles in the encounter between Africans and the West. The Anglo-Saxon racial self-confidence of the nineteenth century prided itself on an athleticism of both physique and temperament, and the conquered racial inferior played a role in confirming the masculinity of the explorer or colonist. Sport in the colonial context was both an instrument of domination and a field of conflict. The European colonialist's emotional stake in his own sense of physical vitality made the issue of racial athletic competition a sensitive one. The decline of the European empires has been accompanied by the decline of the athletic white male as well, and the world of sport is still adjusting to the psychological dislocations brought on by this loss of prestige.

The third section of the book shows how ideas about black athletic superiority belong to a more comprehensive racial folklore that has long imagined black people to be a hardier, physically stronger, and biologically more robust human subspecies than other races. Nineteenth-century racial science took an intimate interest in the black body and intensified a fixation on black physicality from which there appears to be no escape. The rise of the black athlete during this century has thus given the biological racism of the last century a new lease on life. The emergence of African and African-American athletes as the most spectacular stars of the summer Olympic

Games has also led to white fatalism and fears that the twilight of the Caucasian athlete has at last arrived. Images of superior black athleticism have also taken on a special power in the context of a resurgent neo-Darwinian interpretation of the black male and his allegedly criminal propensities. Persistent racial stereotyping has thus made racial athletic aptitude a controversial and even disreputable topic that some would ban from the scientific agenda. The concluding section of this book opposes such censorship and proposes a "postliberal" approach to biomedical racial differences, since a fear of racial biology can only encourage racist interpretations of the genetic research of the future.

Notes

1 "The N.B.A. is visual. It is visceral. What happens to its players seems to deeply affect people. It triggers social debate." See Harvey Araton, "Stern Puts Out Fires and Keeps House in Order," *New York Times*, January 7, 1996.
2 The power of such images to shape the thinking of large numbers of people is impossible to calculate; for this reason alone, it is important to try not to over-estimate or underestimate their influence. In his review of the Whitney Museum of American Art's exhibition titled "Black Male: Representations of Masculinity in Contemporary Art," the critic Adam Gopnik criticized what he regards as a fashionable inflation of the power of stereotypes: "The view that visual clichés shape beliefs is both too pessimistic, in that it supposed that people are helplessly imprisoned by received stereotypes, and too optimistic, in that it supposes that if you could change the images you could change the beliefs. In fact, visual clichés are probably the *weakest* link in the whole chain of racist thought." See Gopnik, "Black Studies," 139. While this is a useful observation, I am convinced that Gopnik's interest in deflating self-absorbed academic analyses of omnipotent "representations" leads him to underestimate the impact of some media images in an unrealistic way. Debunking the power of such images is particularly questionable when they are the aggressive male figures so common in violent television programming, action films, and certain sports, to which black youngsters become even more attached than their white counterparts. See, for example, Nightingale, *On the Edge*, 11, 29, 74, 138, 177.
3 Skip Myslenski, "Alaskan a Cool Court Pioneer," *Chicago Tribune*, December 3, 1994.
4 Gunnar Myrdal pointed out half a century ago that most people favor biological over environmental explanations for apparent differences in ability. "To conceive that apparent differences in capacities and aptitudes could be cultural in origin means a deferment of judgment that is foreign to popular thinking. It requires difficult and complicated thinking about a multitude of mutually dependent variables, thinking which does not easily break into the lazy formalism of unintellectual people." See Myrdal, *An American Dilemma*, 98–99.
5 See, for example, White, "Of Mandingo," 70. A related fantasy of experimentation on black slaves appears in *Farewell Uncle Tom*, a film by Gualtiero Jacopetti and Franco Prosperi, the creators of *Mondo Cane* and *Women of the World*, a pair described by Pauline Kael as "perhaps the most devious and irresponsible filmmakers who have ever lived." *Farewell Uncle Tom* includes "a bizarrely fanciful sequence in which blacks in cages are used for mad scientific experiments." This is one spectacle among others (e.g., mass rape, blacks butchering whites) calculated

to have a visceral appeal for modern audiences. See "Notes on Black Movies," *New Yorker*, December 2, 1972, 163, 164.

6 Ellison, "Twentieth-Century Fiction and the Black Mask of Humanity," in *Shadow and Act*, 28.

7 Quoted in Kane, "An Assessment of 'Black Is Best,' " 79. See also, "Slavery Was 'Great Biological Experiment,' " 58–59.

8 "The popular press and the television medium perpetuate these images with descriptions of African-American athletes as 'Aircraft Carriers' (Al McGuire), 'thoroughbreds' (Brent Musberger), 'superathletes' (Billy Packer) or kids 'who take off flying through the air à la Michael Jordan' (Dick Vitale)." See Harris, "The Image," 25. In 1983 the ABC-TV sports commentator Howard Cosell referred to a black football player as a "little monkey." In March 1996 the CBS-TV sports commentator Billy Packer called a black college basketball player a "tough monkey." See "Breaking the Cosell Rule," *Austin American-Statesman*, March 3, 1996.

9 Schoenfeld, "The Loneliness," 37.

10 "Out of Bounds," *Sports Illustrated*, July 25, 1994, 16. For a thoughtful commentary by a black sportswriter, see Bryan Burwell, "Blame Ignorance for Nicklaus' Comments," *USA Today*, August 11, 1994.

11 Nor is this syndrome confined to African Americans, since it affects the lives of black people in England and Canada as well. On blacks and athletics in England, see Cashmore, *Black Sportsmen*; on the black experience in Canada, see Solomon, *Black Resistance in High School*, 1–15, 63–77.

12 Loury, "The Impossible Dilemma," 22.

13 Writing in his memoir *Time Present, Time Past*, Senator Bill Bradley finds the prominence of black athletic stars to be a positive factor in American life: "It introduces white people who may not know too many African-Americans to a range of individuals. It gets across pretty quickly that David Robinson and Dennis Rodman are very different. That projection forces us to go deeper." Quoted in Robert Lipsyte, "Bill Bradley: A Sense of Where He Is," *New York Times*, February 4, 1996.

14 Charles Barkley, a star player for the Phoenix Suns, is one of a tiny handful of American professional athletes who has an identifiable political identity. He is a doctrinaire conservative Republican who in December 1994 attended a birthday party for the formerly segregationist senator Strom Thurmond in the company of the ultraconservative Supreme Court justice Clarence Thomas. See Tom Kertes, "Charles Barkley Talks about His Republicanism," *Village Voice*, December 27, 1994, 117–18. In 1995 there were some rumors that Barkley planned an eventual run for the governorship of Alabama or a seat in the U.S. House of Representatives. See "Paris Was Fine, Thanks, But It's Nice to Be Home," *New York Times*, June 4, 1995. Also in 1995 a white sportswriter offered a bitterly sarcastic portrait of Barkley, reporting that he had said he hated white people. "Defenders rush to Barkley, pointing out that he is married to a white woman. His best friend on the team, Danny Ainge, is white. Barkley plays golf with Dan Quayle, for crying out loud. How can he hate white people?" See Bernie Lincicome, "Barkley's Bark Shouldn't Pack So Much Bite," *Chicago Tribune*, February 15, 1995. J. C. Watts, another African-American athlete who is a Republican, was elected to the House from an Oklahoma district in November 1994. See "Two Former Football Players try to Master the Gingrich Game Plan," *New York Times*, January 28, 1995.

15 A headline describing Charles Barkley as "a frowning clown" appeared in the *Austin* [Texas] *American-Statesman* (no date); many articles about Dennis Rodman's eccentricities have appeared, only a few of which address his evident emotional problems, e.g., Bryan Burwell, "Rodman Not Talking Trash; He's Crying

for Professional Help," *USA Today*, May 4, 1994; on Alonzo Mourning, see "Angry Hornet Kind and Caring Off Court," *Chicago Tribune*, November 4, 1994; the Shawn Kemp ad appeared in *Sports Illustrated*, October 16, 1995; the Greg Lloyd ad appeared in *Sports Illustrated*, January 8, 1996. On the "behavioral codes" that mandate "managing feelings" among inner-city males, see Nightingale, *On the Edge*, 43, 46, 49.

16 Michele Wallace, "When Black Feminism Faces the Music, and the Music Is Rap," *New York Times*, July 29, 1990.

17 Quoted in Nightingale, *On the Edge*, 182.

18 Amy Linden, "The Grand Old Men of Rap Strike Back," *New York Times*, June 23, 1993.

19 So testified Joe Stuessy, Ph.D., director of the division of music at the University of Texas at San Antonio. See "Expert Links Rap, Murder of Trooper," *Austin American-Statesman*, June 30, 1993.

20 "So Little Known to Be So Good," *New York Times*, October 23, 1994.

21 "Rap, R&B Stars Work to Look as Hot as They Sound," *USA Today*, January 6, 1994.

22 "Fresh Air," National Public Radio, February 8, 1996.

23 Lynn Hirschberg, "Does a Sugar Bear Bite?" *New York Times Magazine*, January 14, 1995.

24 The former coach (and later president) of the Utah Jazz of the NBA, Frank Layden, has ascribed the alleged misbehavior of NBA players to the promotion of the "bad boy" image of the Detroit Pistons during the early 1990s. See Ira Berkow, "New Barbarians Are Really Old Hat," *New York Times*, January 31, 1995.

25 See, for example, "Milwaukee Plan Would Ban Jail Weight Lifting," *Chicago Tribune*, March 24, 1994; "Building a Better Thug?" *Time*, April 11, 1994, 47.

26 "Image-Making Strategy in the Rodney King Case," *New York Times*, December 25, 1992.

27 "L.A. Officer Has Jurors on Edge of Seats," *USA Today*, March 24, 1993, 3A.

28 The phrase "an undertone of violence" was used by Charles Grantham, the black director of the NBA Players Association, who agreed that in the late 1970s the image of the NBA could be summed up in the phrase "blacks on drugs." See Harvey Araton, "Knicks Trade Talk Is Centering on Guns," *New York Times*, March 3, 1994. It has been reported that the commissioner of the NBA, David Stern, has expressed private concern about violence and "trash talking" among players in his overwhelmingly black league. See "Chuck and Coach K," *Sports Illustrated*, June 6, 1994, 15.

29 "It is this bogus, overly macho, preening, smackin' brand of basketball that has turned an original art form [trash talking] into a distorted counterfeit." See Burwell, "Rodman Not Talking Trash."

> A form of insanity is spreading through the NBA like a virus, threatening to infect every team in the league. Alarmingly, its carriers, pouting prima donnas who commit the most outrageous acts of rebellion, include some of the league's younger stars. There is a new outbreak nearly every week, with yet another player skipping practice, refusing his coach's orders to go into a game, demanding a trade or finding some new and creative way to act unprofessionally. Fines are levied, suspensions imposed, but such measures are nothing in the face of the epidemic. The lunacy is contagious. Madness reigns.

See Phil Taylor, "Bad Actors," *Sports Illustrated*, January 30, 1995. A white sportswriter commented, "Root for [coach Don Nelson] not to fall to the monsters of greed, immaturity and selfishness supposedly threatening the tranquility we've known as the Fan-tastic game, the NBA." See Sam Smith, "Classy Nelson Feeling Threat of Brat Plague," *Chicago Tribune*, January 30, 1995.

30 One white sportswriter has commented on the predicament of the white NBA coach as follows:

> It's pretty obvious that coaching anywhere in the NBA these days is something akin to being asked to host the Academy Awards. There just aren't many people on the planet who can handle it. It's the kind of job in which you learn as you go and you get better if you can stick around long enough. In [P.J.] Carlesimo's case, he's been slow to grasp the rhythms of the pro game and even slower to understand the bewildering mentality of today's players.

See Dwight Jaynes, "Firing Carlesimo Is Not the Solution to Blazers' Problems," *Oregonian*, March 1, 1996.

31 The fundamentalist Christian activist Pat Robertson uses the domesticated black athlete – in this case a professional basketball player – as a positive symbolic figure in his apocalyptic novel *The End of the Age*. The author's racial fears are embodied in the black counterpoint to the athlete, a militant black feminist U.S. attorney general. See Christopher Buckley, "Apocalypse Soon," *New York Times Book Review*, February 11, 1996, 8.

32 The negative stereotype of young African-American men has taken on the character of a universal belief that is so pervasive that it can provoke despair in those who would arrest its further development. The black conservative Glenn Loury, to take one of many commentators, has written that black elites "must counter the demonization of young black men in which the majority culture is now feverishly engaged . . . White Americans are, to put it bluntly, frightened by and disgusted with the violent criminal behavior that, with reason, they associate with inner-city black youths. Their fear and disgust have bred contempt; and that contempt in turn produced a truly remarkable publicly expressed disrespect and disdain for blacks." See Loury, "The Impossible Dilemma," 22.

33 "The National Opinion Research Center released a survey on 'Ethnic Images' in 1990, which revealed that over 56 percent of whites thought blacks to be 'violence-prone.' " See Nightingale, *On the Edge*, 24. According to another survey, 24 percent of white American college students, 33 percent at the larger univeristies, are "physically afraid of blacks." See *U.S. News & World Report*, April 19, 1993, 53. The black giant/white child juxtaposition can also be inverted. The cover of the February 1996 issue of *Sports Illustrated for Kids* shows a delighted black boy on a ladder measuring the height of the white giant Gheorghe Muresan, the seven-foot-seven center of the Washington Bullets.

34 For an example of the celebration of Mo Vaughn as a racial reconciler, see Gerry Callahan, "Sox Appeal," *Sports Illustrated*, October 2, 1995, 43–48. Vaughn appears on the cover of this issue.

35 Southern whites, Ellison wrote, "protect themselves from their guilt in the Negro's condition and from their fear that their cooks might poison them, or that their nursemaids might strangle their infant charges, or that their field hands might do them violence, by attributing to them a superhuman capacity for love, kindliness and forgiveness." See Ellison, "Richard Wright's Blues," in *Shadow and Act*, 92.

36 According to Harry Edwards, many whites "felt for years that the professional black athlete was actually genetically predisposed to be *non-violent*." See *The Revolt of the Black Athlete*, 26. This observation is related to the now striking fact that in 1918 the distinguished sociologist Robert E. Park referred to the African-

American population as "the lady among the races." See Frederickson, *The Black Image in the White Mind*, 327.

37 See, for example, the color photograph that appears on the dust jacket of the book Jordan published in 1995. See also the color photograph of Herschel Walker, his bare chest only partly covered by a football, that appears in Allen Barra, "Football's Finest Failure," *New York Times Magazine*, September 24, 1995, 61.

38 See, for example, Michael Farber, "Blue Plate Special," *Sports Illustrated*, April 25, 1994; Steve Rushin, "Big," *Sports Illustrated*, September 4, 1995; "Big Daddy," *Sports Illustrated*, April 25, 1994; Leigh Montville, "The Way He Was," *Sports Illustrated*, June 20, 1994. The same interest in the overeating black athlete can be found in newspaper sports coverage; see, for example, "Newton's Law: Eat and Grow to All-Pro," *New York Times*, January 28, 1993; "Keeping Score, One Pound at a Time," *New York Times*, November 17, 1994; "In Round 2 of Life-as-Champion," *New York Times*, May 24, 1995.

39 Montville, "The Way He Was."

40   The media images I speak of, remote from urban fact, have been teaching mass audiences everywhere that race differences belong to the past, that inequalities of power and status and means have disappeared, that at work and play blacks are as likely as whites to be found at the top as at the bottom, and that the agency responsible for the creation of the near-universal black-white sameness – the only agency capable of producing progress – is that of friendship.

See Benjamin DeMott, "Sure, We're All Just One Big Happy Family," *New York Times*, January 7, 1996.

41 Ibid.

42 Walter Goodman, "Missing Middle-Class Black in TV News," *New York Times*, May 22, 1990.

43 At the same time, it is not always clear who the black middle class will label as "criminals." Some black professionals identified profoundly with their "underclass" brethren who participated in the 1992 Los Angeles riots that followed the acquittal of four police officers who beat Rodney King. See "Middle Class But Not Feeling Equal, Blacks reflect on Los Angeles Strife," *New York Times*, May 4, 1993.

44 Cripps, "The Noble Black Savage," 687.

45 The continuing denial of black complexity may even affect critical assessments of black artists. When the African-American pianist Andre Watts performed Beethoven's Emperor Concerto at Avery Fisher Hall in 1995, one critic, in a review titled "A Beethoven Who's Mostly Muscular," called Watts's version "typically athletic," cautioning the artist that "athleticism merely begins to touch this work's possibilities." See James R. Oestreich, *New York Times*, August 5, 1995. This fusion of athleticism and art in the mind of a white critic shows once again how an omnipresent sense of black athleticism can subvert the African-American struggle for cultural as well as civic responsibility. Nor is reading blackness through the body confined to whites; Ralph Ellison integrated athleticism into black music when he described jazz as "an orgiastic art which demands great physical stamina of its practitioners." See Ellison, "The Charlie Christian Story." In *Shadow and Act*, 233.

46 I am indebted to Yevonne Smith of Michigan State University for bringing this parental resistance to the sports fixation to my attention.

47 Quoted in Grier and Cobbs, *Black Rage*, 71.

References

Books

Cashmore, Ernest. *Black Sportsmen*. London: Routledge & Kegan Paul, 1982.

Edwards, Harry. *The Revolt of the Black Athlete*. New York: Free Press, 1969.

Ellison, Ralph. *Shadow and Act*. New York: Vintage, 1972.

Fredrickson, George M. *The Black Image in the White Mind: The Debate on Afro-American Character and Destiny, 1817–1914*. Middletown, Conn.: Wesleyan University Press, 1971.

Grier, William H., and Price M. Cobbs. *Black Rage*. New York: Basic Books, 1992.

Myrdal, Gunnar. *An American Dilemma: The Negro Problem and Modern Democracy*. New York: Harper & Brothers, 1944.

Nightingale, Carl Husemoller. *On the Edge*. New York: Basic Books, 1993.

Solomon, R. Patrick. *Black Resistance in High School: Forging a Separatist Culture*. Albany: State University of New York Press, 1992.

Articles

Cripps, Thomas. "The Noble Black Savage: A Problem in the Politics of Television Art." *Journal of Popular Culture* 8 (Spring 1975).

Goodman, Walter. "Missing Middle-Class Black in TV News." *New York Times*, May 22, 1990.

Harris, Othello. "The Image of the African American in Psychological Journals, 1825–1923." *Black Scholar* 21 (1990).

Kane, Martin. "An Assessment of 'Black Is Best.'" *Sports Illustrated*, January 18, 1971.

Loury, Glenn. "The Impossible Dilemma." *New Republic*, January 1, 1996.

Schoenfeld, Bruce. "The Loneliness of Being White." *New York Times Magazine*, May 14, 1995.

"Slavery Was 'Great Biological Experiment' Negro M.D. Claims." *Journal of the American Medical Association* 181 (September 1, 1962).

Taylor, Phil. "Bad Actors." *Sports Illustrated*, January 30, 1995.

Wallace, Michele. "When Black Feminism Faces the Music, and the Music Is Rap." *New York Times*, July 29, 1990.

45

THE FACT(S) OF MICHAEL JORDAN'S BLACKNESS

Excavating a floating racial signifier

David L. Andrews

Source: *Sociology of Sport Journal* 13 (1996): 125–158.

This genealogical examination of Michael Jordan's popular signification reveals a complex narrative that incorporates many of the historically grounded racial codes that continue to structure the racial formation of the United States. Borrowing judiciously from cultural studies, poststructuralist, and postmodern theorizing, this paper critically analyzes the imaged persona of Michael Jordan as an important site of mediated popular culture, at which specific racial ideologies are publicized and authorized in support of the reactionary agenda of the post-Reaganite American imaginary. As such, this paper attempts to develop a critical media literacy that encourages readers to interrogate their engagement with the racially oppressive discursive tracts circulated by the popular media.

Cet examen généalogique de la signification populaire de Michael Jordan révèle une narration complexe qui incorpore plusieurs des codes raciaux historiquement fondés qui continuent à structurer la formation raciale des États-Unis. Empruntant judicieusement aux études culturelles et aux théories post-structuralistes et post-modernes, cet article présente une analyse critique du personnage de Michael Jordan comme site important de la culture populaire au sein duquel les idéologies raciales qui sont autorisées et rendues publiques soutiennent l'agenda réactionnaire de l'imaginaire américain post-Reaganien. Comme tel, cet article tente de développer une «alphabétisation médiatique» critique, qui encourage les lecteurs et lectrices à se questionner au niveau de leur engagement avec les tracts discursifs racialement oppressifs circulés par les médias populaires.

The fact of Michael Jordan's blackness, to paraphrase Frantz Fanon (1967), is without doubt one of the most pivotal, yet strangely overlooked questions posed by contemporary American culture. In spite of the pervasiveness of the crass color-blind credo so gleefully expressed by Jerry Reinsdorf, owner of the Chicago Bulls, "Is Michael Jordan black? . . . Michael has no color" (quoted in Kornbluth, 1995, p. 26), close examination of Michael Jordan's popular signification reveals a complex narrative incorporating many of the historically grounded racial codes that continue to structure the racial formation of the United States. Far from his racial identity being nonexistent or extraneous to his social and cultural significance, the imaged persona of Michael Jordan represents an important site of mediated popular culture at which particular racial ideologies are publicized and authorized in support of the multiple inclusions and exclusions that delineate the post-Reaganite American imaginary. Jordan's image exemplifies what Reeves and Campbell (1994, p. 49) identified as "a spectacle of surveillance that is actively engaged in representing authority, visualizing deviance, and publicizing common sense" in a way that has profound implications for the structuring, disciplining, and experiencing of race in contemporary America. For this reason, Michael Eric Dyson was wholly correct in contending that Jordan is "a supremely instructive figure of our times" (1993, p. 71).

While asserting the central importance of Jordan's racial identity, it is also necessary to underscore that his covert racial signification has displayed a distinct lack of uniformity, a condition of instability that clearly corroborates Grossberg's poststructuralist leitmotif that "no element within the cultural field has an identity of its own which is intrinsic to it and thus guaranteed in advance" (1992, p. 39). As Hall noted, anticipating his notion of a conjunctural "Marxism without Guarantees" (Hall, 1983), there are no necessary correspondences, or for that matter noncorrespondences, between meanings and cultural symbols:

> The meaning of a cultural form and its place or position in the cultural field is not fixed once and forever. . . . The meaning of a cultural symbol is given in part by the social field into which it is incorporated, the practices with which it articulates and is made to resonate.
>
> (Hall, 1981, p. 235)

As a cultural construct, Jordan's mediated racial identity is not stable, essential, or consistent; it is dynamic, complex, and contradictory. Thus, it is perhaps more accurate to refer to the facts of Michael Jordan's blackness, and to assert his status as a floating racial signifier who, in Derridean terms, is constantly under erasure (Derrida, 1978).

Borrowing judiciously from cultural studies, poststructural, and postmodern theorizing, this project is prefigured on the understanding of subjectivity as being constantly (re)formed through individuals' shifting and unpredictable engagements (either corroborative, oppositional, ambivalent, or complex permutations of all three) with the telediscursive texts that infuse everyday lives within America's ocular democracy (see Baudrillard, 1988; Clarke, 1991; Dery, 1993). The dominant vectors of the popular media represent points at which power intersects with discourse in an attempt to normalize, and thereby constitute, particular subject positions and the specific forms of authority associated with them (Giroux, 1994; Hall, 1994). With this in mind it is of vital importance to delineate the popular discursive economies that, through dialectic engagement, have a necessarily profound effect upon the formation and experience of human subjectivity. Hence, this paper contributes toward critical media literacy (Giroux, 1992, 1994; Kellner, 1991, 1995; McLaren, 1993, 1994) by encouraging/imploring readers to question, both in a specific and more broader sense, their engagement with the popular media and the effects of such engagements on the creation of the subjective understandings of racial selves and others that have a profound effect upon the structure and experiencing of everyday life (see Cole & Denny, 1995).

The aim of this paper is to provide a contextual interpretation of the dominant racial discourses that have fashioned the mediated icon, Michael Jordan, in accordance with the shifting imperatives of the reactionary post-Reaganite cultural agenda. More specifically, this paper examines how the racial meaning and significance of Michael Jordan is perpetually being deferred, in light of the endless chain of racial signifiers that have been attached to his signified image through the conjunctural and intertextual machinations of the popular print and electronic media. Consequently, I hope to develop a critical understanding of Michael Jordan that highlights "the elasticity and the emptiness of 'racial' signifiers as well as the ideological work which has to be done in order to turn them into signifiers in the first place" (Gilroy, 1991, p. 39); that disrupts the notion of essential systems of racial differentiation; and that confronts race as a conjuncturally informed, and materially manifest, discursive construct (see Smith, 1994). However, before reconstructing the sequential complexities of Michael Jordan's racial articulation, it is first necessary to provide a concise genealogy of the shifting aggregates of popular racial discourse engaged by this process.

An abbreviated genealogy of popular racial signification

As Omi and Winant (1994) persuasively argued, the European conquest of America initiated the on-going process through which American society garnered its peculiar racial formation. As a result, it is necessary to delve into the recesses of European colonialism in order to exhume the derivations of contemporary racial discourse. Although Williams' hypothesis that "Slavery was not born of racism: rather, racism was the consequence of slavery" (1961, p. 6), provided an insightful, if exaggerated, commentary on the emergence of race-based discrimination, it crucially overlooked the presence of earlier European representations of Africans (Miles, 1989). It is perhaps more accurate to contend that these earlier "relatively disorganized" (Omi & Winant, 1994, p. 62) representations of Africanness were subsequently rearticulated within the project of slavery.

During the 18th century, in order to justify the process of systemic slavery (Blackburn, 1988) required of plantation-based colonial capitalism, an overtly racist discourse developed that substantiated the African as a distinctive racial "Other." The significatory violence (Derrida, 1981) of this burgeoning racial biotechnology effectively legitimated the practices of economic exploitation and corporal brutality metered out against enslaved populations within North America and the Caribbean. Justifying the dehumanization of the African Other was particularly necessary in light of the collective celebration of freedom and equality that marked the bourgeois revolutions of the 18th century and that ushered in the adolescence of industrial capitalism:

> Capitalism's reliance on slave labour became an anomaly requiring explanation. It was in this context that the idea blacks were sub-human, and therefore did not demand the equal respect that was increasingly acknowledged as the right of human beings, began to take hold.
>
> (Callinicos, 1993, p. 28)

The required bipolar distinction between the European American Self and the African (American) Other was realized through the mobilization of a system of previously identified, if not fully developed, stereotypical differences that generated an economy of antithetical racial signifiers. As Gilman eloquently noted,

> Stereotypes are a crude set of mental representations of the world. They are palimpsests on which the initial bipolar representations are still vaguely legible. They perpetuate a needed sense of difference between the "self" and the "object" which becomes the "Others." Because there is no real line between self and the Other, an imaginary line must be drawn; and so that the illusion of an absolute difference between self and Other is never troubled, this line is as dynamic in its ability to alter itself as is the self.
>
> (1985, pp. 17–18)

The conflation and subsequent promotion of phenotypical and sociocultural characteristics, as compelling evidence of the inferior status of the African (American) Other, was crucial to the establishment of suggestive racial stereotypes. Distinctions between *them* and *us* were thus enforced through the popular representation of the savage, bestial, and uncivilized black African, in *difference* to the restrained, cerebral, and civilized white European American. In this way a racial hierarchy was implemented that justified systemic slavery to the popular imagination on both sides of the North Atlantic. As the noted Scottish Enlightenment philosopher, David

Hume, stated "I am apt to suspect the negroes, and in general all the other species of men (for there are four or five different kinds) to be naturally inferior to the whites" (quoted in Callinicos, 1993, p. 24). In a similar vein, Thomas Jefferson pronounced, "the blacks, whether originally a different race, or made distinct by time and circumstances, are inferior to the whites" (quoted in Omi & Winant, 1994, p. 64).

Although modern racism developed in tandem with the institution of slavery, the widespread abolition of slavery during the course of the 19th century did not result in the demise of racist discourse. Indeed, the forces of scientific hegemony and accelerated Western imperial expansion, which dominated the post-Enlightenment world, combined to regenerate and scientisize racist ideology in justifying the subjugation of peoples of color within the various imperial orders. Through the spurious appropriation of Darwinian theorizing related to the evolution of species, 19th-century racial science advanced race classifications that announced the "superiority of the white races over the rest in the process of natural selection" (Callinicos, 1993, p. 17). The spread of such popular scientific racial mythologizing (Fryer, 1984) resulted in the phenotypical and sociocultural differences embodied within dominant European representations of the African Other, becoming the focus of scientific investigations intent on identifying inherent, natural, and unalterable biological differences of race (Miles, 1989). The scientisizing of race, keying in on factors such as skin color, hair type, nose shape, and most concertedly cranial dimension and capacity, classified human beings into biologically distinct types that were strategically grafted to equally distinct psychological and sociocultural characteristics around which the hierarchy of races was formulated. As Giroux noted,

> In this racism, the Other's identity warrants its very annihilation because it is seen as impure, evil, and inferior. Moreover, whiteness represents itself as a universal marker for being civilized and in doing so posits the Other within the language of pathology, fear, madness, and degeneration.
>
> (1994, p. 75)

In other words, "savagery became a fixed condition for the 'Negro' or African 'race,' a product of a small brain, and civilization became an attribute of large brained 'white' people" (Stocking, 1968, quoted in Miles, 1989, p. 33).

Dominant theories of race based upon the demeaning conflation of sociocultural and phenotypical differences were granted further legitimacy with the emergence of genetic science in the late 19th and early 20th centuries. As Dumm surmised, "With the emergence of both evolutionary theory and the science of genetics in the nineteenth century, biological theories of race with their specious logic of genetic inferiority came to the fore and dominated 'scientific' discussions of racial difference" (1993, p. 181). Vanguarded at least initially by the eugenics movement founded by Darwin's cousin, Francis Galton, geneticists sought to identify precise definitions of race by searching for consistent patterns of genetic constitution, which would subsequently account for the disparate patterns of *natural* evolution experienced by the different races. The teleological nature of early genetic science meant that as well as being greatly informed by them, this burgeoning scientific discourse unwittingly corroborated the residual stereotypes and representations that structured racial hierarchies throughout the Western influenced world; racial Otherness was now classified in terms of interconnected sociocultural, phenotypical, and genotypical differences.

As well as being a constituent component of imperialist ideologies, racial genetics found an accommodating audience within the climate and institutions of sanctioned segregation that marked the postabolitionist American racial formation. As Omi and Winant noted, "In the wake of civil war and emancipation, and with immigration from southern and Eastern Europe as well as East Asia running high, the U.S. was particularly fertile ground for notions such as social Darwinism and eugenics" (1994, p. 64). The subsequent popularization of hierarchically organized genetic classifications of race provided seemingly rigorous and incontrovertible "scientific" support for the common-sense understandings of racial difference that had invaded popular American consciousness.

Throughout this abbreviated genealogy of racial discourse it should be stressed that, at any given time, the production of (racial) knowledge was not generated by some rational, objective epistemology, rather it was (and indeed is) contingent upon the conjunctural manifestations and subjective interpretations of power, conflict, and struggle. So it was in the immediate post-World War II era, when the notion of racial classifications as fixed, stable, and hierarchically ordered biological entities, became widely discredited within the scientific community. After all, such thinking had provided the philosophical and scientific rationale for the genocidal project of the Third Reich (Mosse, 1978). Within this epoch, the notion of biologically distinct races was exploded by the advances made in the field of genetic science, which identified that the genetic variation within the so-called races was more significant than the genetic variation between these tenuous classifications (Lewontin, Rose, & Kamin, 1984; Omi & Winant, 1994). Put simply, the maturation of genetic science renounced the notion of objectively verifiable racial groupings as having any basis in biological science. The understanding of race as a biologically constituted classification was superseded by a philosophy predicated on the comprehension of race "not [as] a biologically given but rather [as] a socially constructed way of differentiating human beings" (Omi & Winant, 1994, p. 65).

As within previous historic/scientific ruptures, the demise of dominant ideas of race did not result in the disappearance of racially based conceptualizing. Instead, theories of race shifted emphasis and epistemological domains, relocating from the rigid absolutism of the hard natural sciences, to the correlational projections of the soft social sciences. In Dumm's (1993) view this shift was associated with the widespread repudiation of arguments prefigured upon notions of an essential racial hierarchy. In their place, Dumm identified an alternative investigative logic centered upon the articulation of racial phenotypes to "whatever behavior the racist wishes to attribute to the other, whether it be passivity and laziness or violent hyperactivity" (1993, p. 181). Dumm's understanding that race became a "marker tied to a series of associated social phenomena" (1993, p. 181) is partially instructive, however it downplays the politically charged nature of this moment in the evolution of racial discourse.

The social scientists at the forefront of this line of research clearly overlooked the extent to which racial hierarchies had invaded the popular (sub)consciousness—especially their own. This led to a blatant disregard for the influence that the deep-rooted and naturalized notions of an inherent racial order had upon the planning, design, implementation, and analysis of race-based, social-scientific research projects. Race was uncritically engaged and analyzed as "a normalizing category that uses a shorthand of visible markers to communicate its separations" (Dumm, 1993, p. 182). As a consequence, the seductive scientific "objectivity" of this brand of racially focused, social-scientific research resulted, not in the destabilizing of an essential racial order, but in its active, if unintended, reinforcement.

The racially oriented, social-scientific research of the postwar era focused on investigating the perceived diseased, polluted, and corrupted nature of the racial Other (Gilman, 1985). As with any other manifestation of racial pathologizing, this racially corrupt, social-scientific epistemology fortified the stereotypical markers through which the racial self had come to be defined. This substantial and influential body of work thus reinscribed the pathologizing "line drawn between the 'good' and 'bad,'" the normal and the deviant, the cerebral and the physical, the controlled and the violent, the healthy and the diseased, the white and the black (Gilman, 1985, p. 23). As Gilman (1985, p. 25) concluded, "In 'seeing' (constructing a representational system for) the Other, we search for anatomical signs of difference such as physiognomy and skin color . . . [which] are always the antithesis of the idealized self," and which became stereotypical signifiers of the pathologized racial Other.

The work of criminologists, James Q. Wilson and Richard Herrnstein, represents a lucid example of the pathologizing, social-scientific racism that came to the fore in the 1950s, and that still comfortably resides in many fields of inquiry (most recently expounded in Herrnstein & Murray's pernicious tome, *The Bell Curve*, 1994). In 1985, Wilson and Herrnstein published what became a standard work in the field of criminology and a significant contribution to popular discourse related to criminal behavior. These and other conservative architects of the American New Right's punitive law-and-order agenda focused on racial variations in violent crime rates and identified people of color as being significantly more likely to commit violent criminal acts than members of the white majority (Dumm, 1993). Wilson and Herrnstein's (1985) reactionary thesis pivoted on a predictable relationship between biological characteristics and violent behavior. This thesis borrowed from W.H. Sheldon's classification of somatotypes, which identified the athletic, prominently musculatured mesomorph as the body type that displayed a greater propensity for aggressive, violent, criminal behavior. This questionable linkage was racialized by Wilson and Herrnstein's heavily implied correlation between the African American male and the mesomorphic somatotype, which stigmatized the African American male as being pathologically aggressive, violent, and criminal:

> Wilson and Herrnstein follow the lead of (or perhaps, they themselves lead) main-stream modern criminology, dividing populations into the normal and the pathological, reinforcing views of the "abnormality" of minorities, and intensifying a general interpretive framework for criminalizing "otherness."
>
> (Dumm, 1993, p. 182)

As previously noted, Wilson and Herrnstein's racist criminology significantly informed the instantiation of the racist popular politics of the American New Right, which Denzin (1991, p. 7) and Giroux (1994, p. 75) described as the "new cultural racism."

The Reaganite project united the diverse armatures of the New Right through the promotion of cultural rather than overtly political strategies (Grossberg, 1992). By locating itself in the formations of popular sentiment, Reaganism evolved into an affectively oriented, mediated project that downplayed ideological politicking in order to "inaugurate a new national popular through restructuring our investments in the sites of the popular" (Grossberg, 1988, p. 32). Moreover, the New Right's emotive manifesto became inscribed on Reagan's hyperreal body, which became a simulated embodiment of American popular politics. As the most visible corporeal structure in an "era of bodies" (Jeffords, 1994, p. 25), Reagan came to signify the "hard-body" ideology of the hypermasculine, assertive, decisive, and aggressive cultural politics to which he gave his name. This political identity was strategically formulated in contrast to the passive, weak, and indecisive "soft-body" politics embodied by Jimmy Carter and the Carter regime, which was deemed responsible for plunging America into political, economic, military, and moral decline (Jeffords, 1994).

During the 1980s, the domineering and reactionary codes of Reaganite hegemony framed this affective politics through a binary system of embodied identities and differences that symbolically defined the imagery and materialization of the New Right agenda:

In the dialectic of reasoning that constituted the Reagan movement, bodies were deployed in two fundamental categories: the errant body containing sexually transmitted disease, immorality, illegal chemicals, "laziness," and endangered fetuses, which we can call the "soft body"; and the normative body that enveloped strength, labor, determination, loyalty, and courage—the "hard body"—the body that was to come to stand for the emblem of the Reagan philosophies, politics, and economies. In this system of thought marked by race and gender, the soft body invariably belonged to a female and/or person of color, whereas the hard body was, like Reagan's own, male and white.

(Jeffords, 1994, pp. 24–25)

By symbolically nationalizing bodies—equating individual identities and actions with national well-being or decline—Reaganism delineated both the positive and negative signifiers of national popular existence. An emergent cult of hard-bodied supermen, epitomized by single-minded, assertive, and successful figures such as Lee Iacocca, Blake Carrington, Donald Trump, Oliver North, John Rambo, and H. Ross Perot (Merrill, 1988) distinguished the mattering maps of the New Right coalition: maps that represented suggestive disciplinary models for everyday existence in Reagan's America.

On the other side of the New Right's national popular frontier, the new cultural racism conjoined the moral panics surrounding the issues of urban crime, violence, drug abuse, and welfare dependency, under the guise of the irresponsible, indolent, deviant, and promiscuous "soft body" of the essentialized non-White urbanite, whose very existence threatened (and in doing so reinforced) the core values of the Reaganite American nation (Denzin, 1991). In an ironic twist, the New Right also vilified the African American population through

the right-wing appropriation of the celebrated media achievements of a handful of prominent African American "individuals"—Bill Cosby, Whoopi Goldberg, Arsenio Hall, Michael Jackson, Michael Jordan, Eddie Murphy, Keenan Ivory Wayans, and Oprah Winfrey.

(Reeves & Campbell, 1994, p. 100)

The circulation of these high-profile success stories further condemned the struggling African American masses for lacking the personal resolution that, according to Reaganism's doctrine of conservative egalitarianism and colorblind bigotry, was all that was required to achieve in American society (Reeves & Campbell, 1994). As a consequence, the bifocal intersections of this racially charged "enemy from within" ideology (Hall, Critcher, Jefferson, Clarke, & Roberts, 1979; Mercer, 1994) meant that, "Unemployment, poverty, urban decay, school crises, crime, and all their attendant forms of human troubles were spoken of and acted upon as if they were the result of *individual* deviance, immorality, or weakness" (Reinerman & Levine, 1989, p. 127).

As well as shamelessly attacking America's at-risk populations, the New Right also aggressively disparaged the social welfare policies of the 1960s and 1970s, which had actually tried to address the institutionalized racial inequalities that divided American society. Developing upon Moynihan's view of the black family as "a tangled web of pathology" (Department of Labor, 1965, p. 5), influential treatises such as Charles Murray's (1984) *Losing Ground: American Social Policy, 1950–1980* blamed the Great Society reforms for encouraging the purportedly inherent racial pathologies that undermined the work ethic, self-reliance, and moral fortitude of African Americans, and hence inhibited their ability to succeed in American society. According to Murray (1984), misguided social-welfare liberalism created a culture of welfare dependency that ruinously contributed to the depletion of America's moral and economic wealth (Denzin, 1991). Such antiwelfare antagonism spawned a "new [popular] consensus" related to the perceived needs of the African American community, which did not incorporate "government programs but a good dose of sexual restraint, marital commitment, and parental discipline" (Coontz, 1992, p. 235).

This pathologizing disavowal of historically grounded, race-based discrimination and differentiation actively disparaged the relevance of racially oriented welfare policies and justified the slashing of billions of dollars from the welfare budget (see Wacquant, 1994, pp. 258–260), without which, significant swathes of the African American population became ever more entrenched as permanent members of America's expanding underclass. Rather than apportioning blame for the plight of the African American population at the feet of an increasingly negligent and disinterested state, Reaganism mobilized popular, residual racial stereotypes and pathologies that stigmatized and demonized the African American population as a very real threat to themselves (and, by inference, to American society as a whole). In this way "People in trouble were reconceptualized as people who make trouble," and as a result, social control inevitably replaced social welfare as the organizing principle of state policy related to urban America (Reinerman & Levine, 1989, p. 127).

This accusatory racial politics reached maturity during the Reagan-Bush administrations when the hegemony of the New Right fashioned a network of racially focused, affective epidemics that mobilized white fears and insecurities in the face of what became articulated as the increasingly threatening black presence in America. The intrusive reactionary circuits of mediated popular culture circulated this affective orientation for mass consumption through the promotion of stereotypical and divisive, yet common-sense, embodied articulations of race and racial difference. These mass-mediated discourses signified African American culture as being inherently deviant, unproductive, irresponsible, uncivilized, promiscuous, and in contrast to (and thereby threatening toward) the preferred white norm. As Mercer (1994, p. 176) noted, "the rigid and limited grid of representations through which black male subjects become publicly visible continues to reproduce certain *idées fixes*, ideological fictions, and psychic fixations" about the nature of Otherness.

The visible markers of race were displayed and often replayed with accompanying commentary, *ad nauseum*. From the networks' nightly news programs to *Cops*, from *Saturday Night Live* to *Monday Night Football*, popular representations of African American males continued to communicate the separations that the New Right identified as being threats to the American nation. This was ably represented in Giroux's reading of Lawrence Kasdan's (1992) film, *Grand Canyon*. As Giroux (1994) noted, within contemporary popular culture, racial difference confronts the viewer as being strange, unfamiliar, and ominous. This is most frequently depicted in the portrayal of the American inner city as a zone of difference coded with racial fear, fascination, and threat; and the construction of the black youths who populate the urban environment as signifiers of danger and social decay. Perhaps the most infamous image of a soft-bodied African American (Jeffords, 1994) was that of convicted Massachusetts' murderer William Robert "Willie" Horton. His mug shot and a distorted interpretation of his criminal record were used in the notorious television commercials for George Bush's 1988 presidential campaign. In reproaching the crime-fighting record of Bush's opponent, Michael Dukakis (then Massachusetts' governor), these influential texts constructed Horton as "an icon symbolizing the quintessential violent black man," and thus accentuated popular fears and anxieties about black Americans (Feagin & Vera, 1995, p. 119).

The seductive influence of the televisual media, exemplified by the fabrication of Willie Horton, has given racist discourse a residual currency and unwarranted legitimacy that frequently lead to the naturalization of race-based identities and differences within popular consciousness. Mediated racial mobilizations are prominent reference points, reactionary "Social representations—narratives, symbols, images—that privilege race as a sign of social disorder and civic decay [that] can be thought of as part of a socially constructed 'fear of a black planet' " (Clarke, 1991, p. 38). For this reason, the televisual field has been saturated and schematized by the inverted racial projections of white paranoia, which displays an insatiable appetite for images of black men misbehaving (Clarke, 1991). Among other things, this obsessive fear/fascination with the body of the racial Other provided Daryl Gates, onetime Chief of the Los Angeles Police Department, with justification for the spate of African American deaths at the hands of the police through the supposition that "We may be finding that in some Blacks when [the carotid chokehold] is applied the veins or arteries do not open as fast as they do on normal [sic] people" (quoted in Davis, 1992, p. 272), and allowed jurists to view the Rodney King beating as an act of police self-defense against the ever-threatening physical presence of the African American male (Butler, 1993).

The backlash politics that became emblematic of the Reagan administration (Reeves & Campbell, 1994) temporarily assumed a back seat with the election of Bill Clinton and the attendant "post-Bush syndrome" that momentarily afflicted the Republican party (Republican strategist, Azliam Crystal, appearing on NPR's *Morning Edition*, November 10, 1994). In defeat, however, the Republicans were able to regroup and redefine their political identity in opposition to the initially ambitious, but increasingly defensive and conciliatory, Clinton regime. Through the strategic mobilization of the popular media, the new New Right has engaged in a concerted attack against Bill Clinton's presidency. This regressive populism targeted Clinton's policies and the "liberal, democratic machine" (Newt Gingrich, quoted in Balz, 1994, p. AI) as being representative of, and encouraging, an un-American, inevitably flawed, politically correct, and multicultural liberalism that drew its ideological roots from the Great Society reforms (Lauter, 1995). Hence, the new conservative remedy to the threats posed by Clinton's America has been a neo-Reaganite allegiance to a vision of a color-blind society. This hyperreactionary utopia would be realized through the establishment of a color-blind polity (Minzesheimer, 1995) that would aggressively repeal any redistributive legislation designed to redress the racial discrimination and practices upon which America was founded.

As in the Reagan manifesto, the *new* New Right's denial of historically grounded and contemporaneously manifest experiences of racial discrimination and differentiation is designed to legitimate the further slashing of federally funded welfare programs. By dangling the money that would be raised through what is euphemistically called "welfare reform" as the financing for those all-important tax cuts, the new New Right currently seems to be in the process of successfully seducing middle America. This regressive racial politics has its most virulent and troubling expression in the debate surrounding affirmative action policies. Democratic Representative Kweisi Mfume stated, "I am offended at the suggestions that racism is so far past that you don't need remedies anymore. I think people are selling their souls to be the early front-runner in New Hampshire." From the opposite end of the political spectrum, Newt Gingrich conversely pronounced, "Affirmative action (laws), if done by some group distinction, are bad, because it is antithetical to the American dream to measure people by the genetic pattern of their grandmothers" (Minzesheimer, 1995, p. 4A). Evidently, such is the control popular neoconservatism has assumed over the ideological terrain, that the rigorous debating of black poverty and identity that Cornel West (1993a, 1993b, 1994) identified as the prerequisite for future racial equality has been virtually outlawed from public spaces. The regeneration of Reaganite racial discourse has effectively blocked an accurate, historically grounded analysis of the changing political articulation of racial segregation, class inequality, and state abandonment in the American city. It has diverted attention away from the institutional arrangements in education, housing, welfare, transportation, and health and human services that perpetuate the concentration of unemployed and underemployed blacks in the urban core.

(Wacquant, 1994, p. 265)

Reeves and Campbell's (1994, p. 261) discernment of an abatement in the "rugged and ragged individualism" that dominated the Reagan-Bush attitude toward "black urban America" was hopelessly optimistic. If anything, the anti-Black affect (Entman, 1990) of the new New Right appears to be a more strident version of the original model.

As intimated earlier, the popular racial signification of Michael Jordan represents a fluid narrative that, at differing moments, (dis)engages various aspects of the historically accumulated aggregates of popular racial discourse discussed herein. Hence, by explicating the discursive derivations and demonstrating the evolving manifestations of the facts of Michael Jordan's blackness, the following section illuminates a series of conjunctural sketches pertaining to the constitutive inscription of particular racial ideologies onto Jordan's mediated body.

Michael Jordan as a floating racial signifier

In Callinicos' terms, the examination of any racial discourse must be engaged within the contextually specific realms of culture and politics, because "they [racial discourses] emerge as part of a historically specific relationship of oppression in order to justify the existence of that relationship" (1993, p. 18). Certainly, the racial signification of Michael Jordan can be characterized by four distinct yet overlapping moments. Each of the stages in Jordan's semiotic evolution is contingent upon the climate in racial and cultural politics, and each, in differing ways, represents the conjunctural appropriation and fleeting curtailment of the endless play of signifiers that have historically contributed to the violent racial hierarchy (Derrida, 1981) of American popular culture in general, and that of the NBA in particular.

The natural athlete: "born to dunk"

1982 marked the year in which Michael Jordan first came to the attention of the nation's sports media. He capped off his promising rookie collegiate season by hitting the winning basket in North Carolina's defeat of Georgetown in the NCAA championship game. Given the frequency with which this shot has been replayed in the ensuing years, it would be easy to fall into the trap of thinking that Jordan's celebrity status at that time was similar to its current level. On the contrary, at that time, Jordan was a relatively anonymous figure in the minds of the American viewing public. At this fledgling stage of his career in the national media spotlight, Jordan's identity was primarily influenced by his membership of the North Carolina team, as the championship game became the context for the revealing engagement of contrasting racial signifiers to distinguish the competing teams. The media fabricated the event as an intriguing battle between the methodical strategies of Dean Smith (the North Carolina coach) and the hyperactive physical frenzy encouraged by John Thomson (the Georgetown coach): "Carolina was," as Smith put it, "the hunted," and Georgetown—quicker, ravaging, downright frightening in its full-court press—was "the hunter" (Kirkpatrick, 1982, p. 16). Black players on either side, who comprised the dominant racial grouping in the contest, were cast in stereotypical fashion as the contest became an exposition of the mind-body dualism that has historically informed racial discourse.

Closely tied to the stereotypical media representation of the pathologically violent and criminal black body, is the popular fascination with the supposed natural athleticism of the African American Other (see Davis, 1990). Mercer described this as "that most commonplace of stereotypes, the black man as sports hero, mythologically endowed with a 'naturally' muscular physique and an essential capacity for strength, grace and machinelike perfection" (1994, p. 178). In his infamous televised remarks, Al Campanis, the onetime Los Angeles Dodgers vice president for player personnel, voiced these stereotypical views, which many Americans probably would have questioned, were it not for his subsequent firing:

> They are gifted with great musculature and various other things. They're fleet of foot. And this is why there are a lot of black major league ballplayers. Now as far as having the background to become club presidents, or presidents of a bank, I don't know.
> (Al Campanis remarks to Ted Koppel on ABC's *Nightline*, quoted in Omi, 1989, p. 112)

These remarks neatly captured the mind-body dualism that has dominated popular racial discourse related to males of African descent. In a similar though seemingly less offensive way, the popular media's trite celebrations of some inherent African American sporting prowess also draw from the same reservoir of racial signifiers that characterize black urban youth as being habitually violent and therefore threatening. The contemporary constructions of the pathologically criminal and naturally sporting black body are founded upon a common assumption of the innate physicality of the black body, a racist discourse whose genealogy can be traced back to at least the era of systemic slavery:

Classical racism involved a logic of dehumanization, in which African peoples were defined as having bodies but not minds: in this way the superexploitation of the black body as a muscle-machine could be justified. Vestiges of this are active today.

(Mercer, 1994, p. 138)

In this vein, and with specific regard to the 1982 NCAA championship game, the media alluded to the fact that the white coach, Smith, infused his players with a sense of his superior knowledge of the game; whereas his black counterpart, Thomson, merely assembled a group of players and allowed them to do what came naturally, that is, to rely on their natural physical attributes. It was hardly surprising, therefore, that Dean Smith was lauded more widely for his basketball acumen than were James Worthy, Sam Perkins, or Michael Jordan for their input into the victory. When praise was extolled on the North Carolina players, it was usually metered out in recognition of the degree to which they had successfully executed the coach's masterful game plan (Vecsey, 1982a, 1982b).

The racial discourse underscoring the media's narration of the 1982 NCAA championship game clearly displayed aspects of the racial context out of which Michael Jordan, the promotional sign, was initially constructed. Furthermore, throughout the construction of his mediated identity, Michael Jordan's imaged persona has been configured either in congruence with, or in opposition to, the economy of signifiers (as depicted by Lanker, 1982) pertaining to the physical comportment of the African American male. As a collegian, Michael Jordan was portrayed by the media as the latest in a seemingly endless supply of naturally talented and exuberantly physical black bodies. He was, in Cashmore's damning terms, yet another media celebration of "that black magic of nature" (1982, p. 42).

This ubiquitous narrative accompanied Jordan throughout his successful collegiate career, which reached its zenith with him cocaptaining the U.S. team to a gold medal triumph at the 1984 Los Angeles Olympics, where Jordan was referred to in familiar refrain: "The flashiest men's player was Jordan, the 6ft. 6-in. University of North Carolina senior who has won six awards designating him America's best collegian. Born to dunk, he penetrated the zone defenses of opponents to slam at least one goal in each of the eight games" (Henry, 1984, p. 50). Having already been drafted by the Chicago Bulls in the June 1984 NBA draft, Jordan decided to forgo his senior year at the University of North Carolina. The rumored interest shown by the Bull's management in making a trade for Jordan, warranted *Chicago Tribune* sports columnist, Bernie Lincicome, to sarcastically introduce his readership to the Bull's potential "savior" (Logan, 1984):

They [the Bulls] got stuck with Michael Jordan of North Carolina, maybe the greatest natural basketball talent, inch for inch, in this young decade. Nothing they could do. They want you to know that.

They tried to avoid Jordan, tried hard. But nobody wanted to trade with them, swap some big fossil of a center for the third pick in the draft. It was like they were under quarantine or something. So they were forced to do the intelligent thing Tuesday.

They had to take Jordan, even though he is already famous, has had quality coaching, is not a social disgrace and may likely become the next Julius Erving before the old one is in the Hall of Fame.

(Lincicome, 1984, p. 1)

Not only did Lincicome identify Jordan's natural ability, his respectable social standing (in contrast to the way many NBA players were perceived at the time), he also provided him with a pertinent professional basketball ancestry. Although Jordan entered into an NBA that had been revitalized by Johnson and Bird's multifaceted rivalry and the marketing strategies that nurtured it (see Cole & Andrews, 1996), Jordan's already acknowledged tele-visual presence, "his sinewy combat [which] demanded close-ups and super slo-mo," would generate an identity out of difference to the full-court "mark-of-Zorro ricochets" orchestrated by Magic Johnson and Larry Bird (Plagen, 1993, p. 48). Lincicome traced Jordan's basket-ball lineage (and by inference, his racial identity), not to the athletic (and indeed racial) anomaly represented by the genial Magic Johnson, the Laker's 6ft., 9 in, floor general, but to the natural, uninhibited, free-form grace and artistry of Julius Erving (Plagen, 1993). By advancing Jordan as a possible successor to the aging but revered Julius Erving, Lincicome engaged the dubious project of basketball social Darwinism. Others subsequently exalted Jordan as the "highest order of basketball's evolutionary chain," a chain beginning with Elgin Baylor and comprised of Connie Hawkins, Julius Erving, and ending up with the supreme basketball being, Michael Jordan (Ryan, 1993, p. 28).

On entering the league, Jordan took the NBA by storm. He scored 25 points in 10 of his first 15 games, including 37 points in his third game. Less than a month into Jordan's first NBA campaign, Larry Bird described him as the "Best I've ever played against" (quoted in Ryan, 1993, p. 27), and he was compared on national television to Julius Erving, who appeared more than comfortable with the comparison (*ABC Nightly News*, November 4, 1984). However, there was a marked difference in the popular racial articula-tion of Jordan and Erving. Although both were primarily racialized by their supposed natural physical attributes, Jordan's image was not identified in the popular memory for sporting the 1970s black statement, the "bushy Afro," or for being one of the "airborne brothers who defined ABA ball" (George, 1992, p. 181)—overt identifications with black identity that inhibited

Erving's popular acceptance, not as a supreme sportsman but as a national icon. His imaged identity having been fermented within a very different racial climate, that of the color-blind Reagan Revolution, Jordan necessarily emerged as a racially understated version of Julius Erving. As such, even more than Erving, he was always likely to become "the kind of [nonthreatening] figure who goes down easily with most Americans" (Shelby Steele, quoted in Naughton, 1992, p. 137).

Although Jordan's stellar rookie performances during the 1984–1985 NBA season garnered him considerable national publicity, his initial popular identity was crystallized through the innovative promotional initiatives engaged by Nike (see Andrews & Cole, 1996). In the previous fiscal year Nike had experienced an alarming decline in sales and sought to redress this by confronting its anonymous presence in both collegiate and professional basketball. In the spring and summer of 1984, the company surveyed the incoming crop of collegiate players and set their sights on Jordan. According to Sonny Vaccaro, Nike's intermediary with the collegiate game, Jordan "was brilliant. He was charismatic. He was the best player Vaccaro had ever seen. He could fly through the air!" (Strasser & Becklund, 1991, p. 535). Vaccaro, so enthusiastic about Jordan, went so far as to admit, "I'd pay him whatever it takes to get him" (Strasser & Becklund, 1991, p. 536). On Vaccaro's recommendation, Jordan was pinpointed as the figurehead who could reassert Nike's position as the sports shoe industry's market leader. Such confidence in Jordan's playing and marketing potential was confirmed when the company signed him to a $2.5 million contract. Nike was ridiculed for taking such a financial risk on an untried player, at a time when it was experiencing considerable economic troubles. In retrospect, such concerns seem almost laughable, as the Air Jordan phenomenon grossed $130 million in its first year (Strasser & Becklund, 1991, p. 3), a financial boost that reasserted Nike as the preeminent sports shoe manufacturer and elevated the company to the position of an American corporate icon.

Given the exhilarating telegenicism of Jordan's play, Nike's advertising company at the time, the Los Angeles based Chiat/Day agency, chose to develop an innovative campaign for the equally innovative signature Air Jordan shoes. This involved saturating the electronic media with strategically coded images of Michael Jordan wearing Air Jordan shoes. Hence, during early 1985, the first Air Jordan commercial was aired, a slot entitled "Jordan Flight" in which a slow motion Jordan executed a dunk on an urban playground to the sound of jet engines accelerating to take off. With this commercial, and especially his parting salvo, "Who said a man was not meant to fly?" Michael Jordan's identity was constituted in the minds of the American populace as Air Jordan, "the Nike guy who could fly" (Katz, 1994, p. 7). The locus of Nike's Air Jordan initiative keyed on Jordan's physical prowess, and thus corroborated the taken-for-granted assumptions pertaining to the naturalistic element of black corporeality. Jordan's repeatedly valorized sporting body thus became a prominent, if underscored, signifier of racial Otherness, a seemingly material vindication of what popular racist discourse had extolled all along.

Transcendental mediation: Reagan's all-American

The early stages of the Air Jordan promotional phenomenon were evidently dominated by the signification of Jordan's naturally athletic black body. Although racial signifiers pertaining to black physicality have provided a backdrop for the promotional discourse narrating his stellar career, they have been subsumed by a more obtuse relationship to popular racialized codes. In accordance with the prevailing racial politics of the American New Right—founded upon a paranoid defensiveness toward overt expressions of racial difference and a concomitant dismissive attitude toward the existence of race-based discrimination—Nike's subsequent Air Jordan campaigns inspired the multifarious segments of the American mass-culture industry (who subsequently invested in Jordan) into nurturing an intertextually informed identity that explicitly invested in the affective epidemics delineating Reagan's America (see Grossberg, 1992). Thus, Jordan's carefully scripted televisual adventures on the corporate playground were designed to substantiate an All-American (which in Marable's [1993] terms means *white*), hard-bodied identity (Jeffords, 1994) that would appeal to the racially sensitive sensibilities of the American mass market. Jordan's phenotypical features could not be overlooked, but his imaged identity could be distanced from the racial signifiers that dominated popular representations of African American males. Corporate image makers recognized that if he was to become "America's player" (Sakamoto, 1986, p. 10), they could not afford to explicitly associate him with the threatening expressions of black American existence.

To facilitate this evolution from mall America's flavor of the month to enshrined All-American icon, Jordan's marketing directors realized he had to be packaged as a Reaganite racial replicant: a black version of a white cultural model who, by his very simulated existence, would ensure the submergence and subversion of racial Otherness (Willis, 1991). As David Falk, Jordan's agent at ProServ surmised, the intention behind the Jordan project was to promote an "All-American image ... Not Norman Rockwell, but a modern American image. Norman Rockwell values, but a contemporary flair" (quoted in Castle, 1991, p. 30). This process was initiated by Nike's decision to move away from Air Jordan campaigns that solely displayed his physical talents, to slots that furnished Jordan with an identifiable, if superficial, personality. Thus, Nike's move from Chiat/Day to the more innovative Wieden and Kennedy agency, saw the introduction of a series of groundbreaking advertising campaigns in which Jordan interacted with Mars Blackmon, Spike Lee's cinematic alter ego from the film *She's Gotta Have It*.

The apparent willingness of the basketball hero to spend time with his bicycle messenger fan/friend, demonstrated that for all his success, fame, and fortune, Jordan was reassuringly just another "down-to-earth guy" (*New York Times*, February 20, 1989, p. D7). In true Reaganite fashion, Jordan's self-evident wholesome humility, inner drive, and personal responsibility "allows us to believe what we wish to believe: that in this country, have-nots can still become haves; that the American dream is still working" (Naughton, 1992, p. 7). In other words, through his comedic interludes with Mars Blackmon, Jordan was inextricably articulated as a living, breathing, and dunking vindication of the mythological American meritocracy. Through subsequent creative associations (see Andrews, in press) with McDonald's, Coca-Cola (latterly Gatorade), Chevrolet, and Wheaties—all significant All-American corporate icons—Jordan was similarly cast as a "spectacular talent, midsized, well-spoken, attractive, accessible, old-time values, wholesome, clean, natural, not too Goody Two-shoes, with a bit of deviltry in him" (David Falk, quoted in Kirkpatrick, 1987, p. 93).

Unlike the stereotypical representations of deviant, promiscuous, and irresponsible black males that punctuated the ubiquitous populist racist discourse of the New Right, Jordan was identified as embodying personal drive, responsibility, integrity, and success. The flight metaphor dominating the articulation of his imaged persona graphically encapsulated Jordan's decidedly individualistic and American demeanor, "striving for agency, self determination, differentiation from others and freedom from control" (Langman, 1991, p. 205). Here was the prototypical, simulated, Reaganite hard body (Jeffords, 1994), lauded by the popular media for being living proof of the existence of an "open class structure, racial tolerance, economic mobility, the sanctity of individualism, and the availability of the American dream for black Americans" (Gray, 1989, p. 376). This ideology, and indeed the very image of Jordan, cruelly posited that anyone in America could realize the dream regardless of race, color, or creed—the only variable being the individual's desire to take advantage of the opportunities afforded by this great country. For, as Herman Gray identified, the repetitive celebration of this color-blind credo within the popular media does little more than reinforce the notion, propagated within more explicit channels of political communication, that the material and economic failure of the African American constituents of the urban underclass is "their own since they live in an isolated world where contemporary racism is no longer a significant factor in there [sic] lives" (1989, p. 384).

By creating an opposition between Jordan and *them* (the failing and thereby threatening African American throng), the concerted promotion of Jordan as the "embodiment of [Reaganite] American virtue" (Naughton, 1992, p. 154) had the desired effect of downplaying his racial Otherness in a way that mirrored the signification of his equally hard-bodied media contemporary, Heathcliff Huxtable (see Jhally & Lewis, 1992). According to the novelist John Edgar Wideman, Jordan "escapes gravity" and "makes us rise above our obsession with race" because he leaps the great divide between races and classes by being a down-to-earth, middle-class, and apolitical hero (1990, p. 140). This notion of Jordan as a figure who transcends race (and indeed sport) was certainly a common theme, voicing as it did the strategic evacuation of race that characterized the Reagan revolution (Jeffords, 1994). As David Falk avariciously conceded, "He's the first modern crossover in team sports. We think he transcends race, transcends basketball" (quoted in Kirkpatrick, 1987, p. 93). An extended article that astutely deconstructed "The Selling of Michael Jordan" (Patton, 1986), concentrated on the marketing of Jordan as an individual possessing "uncanny moves on the court and 'a charisma that transcends his sport,' " a personal attribute that turned him into "basketball's most lucrative property" (Patton, 1986, p. 48). Likewise Donald Dell, the chief executive of ProServ, commented that Jordan was a rare commercial property because he "has a charisma that transcends his sport. He belongs in a category with Arnold Palmer or Arthur Ashe" (quoted in Patton, 1986, p. 50). Clearly, the use of sport in this context (specifically Jordan's sport, basketball) is as a euphemism for race. Jordan is the figure who has transcended the black identity of professional basketball, and thus garnered a widespread and inclusive simulated appeal that resulted in him becoming America's favorite athlete, a status no black man before him had achieved (Naughton, 1992, p. 137). In doing so, Jordan played a crucial role in making the NBA accessible to the white American populace who had previously been turned off, and turned away, by the game's overtly black demeanor (see Cady, 1979; Cobbs, 1980; Cole & Denny, 1995; and Cole & Andrews, in press).

Michael Jordan's carefully engineered charismatic appeal (Dyer, 1991), which had such an impact on popularizing the NBA to corporate and middle America alike, is not an example of racial transcendence. Rather, it is a case of complicitous racial avoidance, facilitated through the displacement of racial signifiers. Jordan's hyperreal image was charismatic in as much as it set him apart from the popular representations of ordinary black males, by endowing him with "supernatural, superhuman or at least superficially exceptional qualities" (Weber, quoted in Eisenstadt, 1968, p. 329). The most pertinent of Jordan's "exceptional qualities" related to his understated racial identity, as opposed to his superlative basketball displays. After all, the popular imagination would have found nothing exceptional about demonstrations of African American physical excellence. Hence, Jordan's image was coveted and nurtured by the media primarily because of its reassuring affinity with the affective investments of America's white dominated, national popular culture. Although the popular media could not avoid Jordan's African American descent, it could and indeed did, shrewdly sever his identity from any overt vestiges of African American culture.

Some black superstars, the most prominent being Jordan, have been able to pander to the racial insecurities and paranoia of the white majority, primarily because of their ability to shed their black identities in promotional contexts. In doing so, these black mediated icons have achieved a degree of popular approval that superficially would seem to legislate against the presence of race-based discrimination within American society. As Marvin Bressler, the Princeton sociologist, noted, "It has always been possible in the history of race relations in this country to say that some of my best friends are *X*. Such people are very useful in demonstrating our own benevolence. We must be good people—we love Michael Jordan" (quoted in Swift, 1991, p. 58). Nevertheless, the compulsion for African Americans to disavow their blackness, in order to successfully harness rather than alienate popular opinion, is indicative of the ingrained hegemonic racism within American society. American culture simply does not tolerate individuals who are, to put it plainly, "too black."

The notion of acceptable, racially understated representations of black America was vividly illustrated in a scene from Spike Lee's 1989 film *Do The Right Thing*. In the scene in question, Mookie (a pizza delivery man played by Spike Lee, the African American lead in the film) confronts Pino (the Italian American son of the pizzeria's owner) about his bigoted but contradictory attitude toward black people:

Mookie:	Pino, who's you favorite basketball player?
Pino:	Magic Johnson.
Mookie:	Who's your favorite movie star?
Pino:	Eddie Murphy
Mookie:	Who's your favorite rock star? Prince, you're a Prince fan.
Pino:	Bruce!
Mookie:	Prince.
Pino:	Bruce!
Mookie:	Pino, all you ever talk about is "nigger this" and "nigger that," and all your favorite people are so called "niggers."
Pino:	It's different. Magic, Eddie, Prince, are not "niggers." I mean they're not black. I mean. Let me explain myself. They're not really black, I mean, they're black, but they're not really black, they're more than black. It's different.
Mookie:	It's different?
Pino:	Yeah, to me its different.

In this brief interchange, Spike Lee expressed the racial double-standards within American society. Many in the white population are gracious enough to accept, even adulate, African Americans, but only if they do not explicitly assert their blackness: If you're black you are not expected to harp on it, if you do then you are, to use the racist vernacular, a "jumped up nigger."

African Americans are tolerated, even valued, if they abdicate their race and are seen to successfully assimilate into the practices, value system, and identity, of white America. Moreover, African American membership in this exclusive club requires constant affirmative renewal. Any fall from grace (ranging from the judicial severity of a criminal misdemeanor, to the tabloidic scandal of sexual impropriety, to even the supposed democratic right of asserting one's racial identity) cancels membership and recasts the hitherto American person as a criminally deviant, sexually promiscuous, or simply threatening racial Other, exiled to the margins of American society with the bulk of the minority population. The ability of certain black celebrities to downplay their Blackness was the reason for Pino's lauding of Magic Johnson and Eddie Murphy. Spike Lee could have easily substituted Michael Jordan, Bill Cosby, Bo Jackson, or Arsenio Hall, as Pino's favorite stars (Swift, 1991). Conversely, the outspoken championing of black civil rights issues by figures such as Reverend Al Sharpton, Minister Louis Farrakhan, and Reverend Jesse Jackson, greatly disturbed Pino. These radical black activists with "chips on their shoulders"—they were "niggers."

Like the reactionary, color-blind cultural politics that nurtured it, the very notion of racial transcendence, supposedly embodied by Jordan and alluded to by Pino, is a seriously flawed and contradictory concept. Racial discourse is never transcended; it is, in a Derridean sense, always already there (see Smith, 1994). Jordan is not an example of racial transcendence, rather he is an agent of racial displacement. Jordan's valorized, racially neutered image displaces racial codes onto other black bodies, be they Mars Blackmon, Charles Barkley, or the anonymous black urban male who the popular media seem intent on criminalizing. Nike's promotional strategy systematically downplayed Jordan's blackness by contrasting him with Spike Lee's somewhat troubling caricature (Mars Blackmon) of young, urban, African American males. Borrowing from Pino's discriminatory discourse, Jordan was Jordan, he wasn't really black. Mars was a "nigger." The contrast fortified Jordan's wholesome, responsible, All-American, and hence non-threatening persona, and became the basis of his hyperreal identity that was subsequently embellished by the multiplying circuits of promotional capital that enveloped him.

Having been deified (initially in opposition to Mars Blackmon) as the All-American paragon of virtue, Jordan assumed the role of centrifuge of a racial sign system that Nike subsequently built around him. According to Phil Knight, the Nike chairman, the company compartmentalized basketball into distinct playing styles in order to create an expanding network of ties with the buying public:

> we thought about it, we realized that there are different styles of playing basketball. Not every great player has the style of Michael

Jordan, and if we tried to make Air Jordan appeal to everyone, it would lose its meaning. We had to slice up basketball itself,

(quoted in Willigan, 1992, p. 96)

The stylistic differences utilized by Nike, however, engaged contrasting elements of embodied racial discourse. In essence, Nike mobilized stereotypical racial codes in order to fashion identities for the Air Force and Air Flight endorsers/product lines, which would provide ways of demarcating between them and also set them apart from the Air Jordan phenomenon. Within Nike's ever expanding economy of larger-than-life basketball icons (exemplified by the emergence of promotional figures such as Charles Barkley, David Robinson, Scottie Pippen et al.), Jordan's identity was continually reasserted out of racial difference to predominantly African American figures, once again confirming his imperious racial transcendence while displacing dominant racial codes onto the bodies of his Nike underlings (see Andrews, 1993).

Charles Barkley represents one of the most problematic of the racial caricatures Nike has expounded within their basketball campaigns. Unlike David Robinson, whose physical force and aggression were encased in a veneer of humor and moral fortitude within the parodic "Mr. Robinson's Neighborhood" campaigns, Barkley's image promotes sheer, unadulterated aggression. As Knight enthused, "It's not just Charles Barkley saying buy Nike shoes, it's seeing who Charles Barkley is—and knowing that he is going to punch you in the nose" (quoted in Willigan, 1992, p. 100). In his earliest commercial slot, a black and white commercial inspired by the musical *Hell's-a-Poppin'*, Barkley was initially surrounded by a line of chorus girls. He was then confronted by a group of journalists and photographers, one of which he ends up punching. The ensuing newspaper headline predictably reads "Charles-a-Poppin'." Even in the renowned Barkley versus Godzilla commercial, the humorous nature of the narrative cannot detract from the fact that Barkley is being portrayed as little more than an overtly physical and aggressive, almost animal-like individual. Likewise, in the recent "Barkley of Seville" commercial, which in lampooning the excesses of operatic expression, still has Charles killing the referee. Although these narratives are undoubtedly amusing, they do little but reinforce the popular perception of African American males. Despite their humorous overtones, they merely feed the widespread paranoid hostility created by the media's routine use of stereotypically violent and threatening images of young black males.

The pathological signifiers mobilized by Nike to delineate their embodied racial economy, were negatively reinforced by Michael Jordan without impinging upon (indeed they augmented) his racially transcendent image. Thus, in stark contrast to Nike's creation of Barkley as an antihero (an image designed to appeal to sizeable sections of the consuming public),

Michael Jordan was portrayed as a paragon of American virtue. The positive identification of Michael Jordan's image in opposition to those of Barkley, and to a lesser extent, Robinson, Pippen, and others, strategically downplayed his African American identity by engaging binary oppositions between Jordan and the dominant discursive formations of African American Otherness. In this way, Jordan's atypical black body deflects and reinscribes stereotypical signifiers of racial Otherness onto the pathologized black bodies that dominate the media's representation of African American males—ranging from the demonized black male urbanite (ably represented by Mars Blackmon), to the equally problematic caricaturing of Jordan's Nike basketball brethren.

"Look, a negro!": the devil inside[1]

The majority of Michael Jordan's tenure in the media spotlight has been characterized by his portrayal as a figure whose singular virtuosity differentiates him from (and hence underscores) the demonized soft-body signifiers of African American Otherness. Nevertheless, there have been occasions when Jordan's racially neutered identity has been severely questioned by the popular media. Although explicitly referring to British sporting culture, Kobena Mercer provides insights into the Jordan phenomenon, explicitly scrutinizing his identity:

> As a major public arena, sport is a key site of white male ambivalence, fear and fantasy. The spectacle of black bodies triumphant in rituals of masculine competition reinforces the fixed idea that black men are all "brawn and no brains," and yet, because the white man is beaten at his own game—football, boxing, cricket, athletics—the Other is idolized to the point of envy. This schism is played out in the popular tabloid press. On the front page headlines black males become highly visible as a threat to white society, as muggers, rapists, terrorists and guerrillas: their bodies become the image of a savage and unstoppable capacity for destruction and violence. But turn to the back pages, the sports pages, and the black man's body is heroized and lionized; any hint of antagonism is contained by the paternalistic infantilization of Frank Bruno and Daley Thompson to the status of national mascots and adopted pets—they're not Other, they're OK because they're our boys.
>
> (Mercer, 1994, pp. 178–179)

While Jordan conformed to the role of wholesome, nonthreatening, hard-bodied hero, he was deified for being one of "America's boys." However, once his behavior, especially off the court, was deemed to be transgressing the boundaries of what was considered acceptable for the prototypical

All-African American male (George, 1992), the specter of racial Otherness reared its demonized head.

The interrogation of Jordan's Reaganite hard body was virtually inevitable because, although his very symbolic existence indicated that images of African American athleticism are not necessarily representations of black men misbehaving (Clarke, 1991), the new cultural racism was prefigured on the virulent assumption that these innately physical males would be misbehaving were it not for the involvement of their natural physical attributes in the disciplinary mores and stringencies imposed by the dominant (sporting) culture. According to this spurious logic, African American males have found salvation within sporting activity (if only temporary, i.e. Mike Tyson and O.J. Simpson) from themselves. Such reactionary thoughts were echoed by *Chicago Tribune* columnist, Bernie Lincicome, in a startlingly offensive summation of the O.J. Simpson case: "Arguments that sports is responsible for O.J. Simpson's present situation must begin with concessions that without sports, O.J. Simpson is sitting in that chair 30 years ago" (1994b, p. 1). Renouncing such racist diatribes, Giroux (1994) ably illustrated how contemporary American culture is dominated by a fascination with the assumed superior physicality of the black male body and a simultaneous fear of the ever-present threat it poses. Such mass-mediated appeals to middle America's racial paranoia and insecurities dared American popular consciousness to confront the potentiality of Jordan's deviant racial Otherness and, in doing so, posed the unthinkable question, "Perhaps Michael Jordan is black (i.e. pathologically flawed) after all?"

During the 1991–1992 season, Michael Jordan, for the first time, experienced "The underside of stardom" (Isaacson, 1992a, p. 14). As Sullivan noted, "After seven years of nearly perfect marriage with the media and his fans, Jordan endured a season of criticism" (1992, p. 3). At the hands of a salacious mass media, Jordan was rebuked for failing to attend George Bush's honoring of the Chicago Bull's NBA championship win at the White House; castigated for gambling large sums of money on his golf game (Jackson, 1992); criticized for the ruthless and hypercompetitive side of his nature (outlined in Smith's controversial book *The Jordan Rules*, 1992); attacked for his initial reticence to compete for the United States team in the Barcelona Olympics (Cronin, 1991); and chided for his wrangling with the NBA over the commercial rights to his likeness (Banks, 1992; Hiestand, 1992; Mulligan, 1992; Vecsey, 1992), which also led to the ignominious "Reebok flap" at the Olympic medal ceremony (Myslenski, 1992, p. 8). In other words, for the first time, Jordan's "faults and foibles were chronicled, along with his dunks and doggedness" (Sullivan, 1992, p. 3).

Even though Jordan was able to sidestep the controversies that arose during the 1991–1992 season, media interest had been sparked in a new and seemingly profitable spin-off industry from the Jordan phenomenon. Jordan's newfound human frailties represented big business for the tabloid sections of both the electronic and print media. Much to the delight of the salacious media, within a year the undermine-Jordan industry was given fresh impetus. On May 27, 1993, it was reported that Jordan was seen gambling in Atlantic City late into the night on the eve of Game 2 of the Chicago Bulls Eastern Conference Final series against the New York Knicks (Anderson, 1993). In light of this incident, and arguably for the first time, the media began to seriously reevaluate Jordan's imaged identity. The catalyst that initiated this reappraisal was undoubtedly his repeated association with gambling, which had first come to national attention in 1992 when it was revealed that Jordan had gambled and lost a considerable amount of money on a golf game played with one Slim Bouler, who, as it later transpired, turned out to be a drug dealer (Isaacson, 1992b).

The Atlantic City sighting thrust the open secret of Jordan's love of gambling into a racial discourse with which his image had previously been disassociated (Jackson, 1992). In the immediate aftermath of the Atlantic City visit, Jordan's identity as a figure who transcended (displaced) race, was disturbed by the questioning accusations of certain sections of the media. The most inflammable account of the incident predictably came from the New York press, specifically Dave Anderson's intentionally provocative piece, "Jordan's Atlantic City Caper" (1993, p. 11), which first broke the story and pilloried the "best player in basketball history" for letting down his teammates and coaches by gambling until 2:30 a.m. (an hour later refuted by a variety of sources, including Jordan). In a sardonic tone, Anderson identified this display of inappropriate behavior as turning the Knicks "home-court advantage" into their "homecasino" advantage (1993, p. 11), conclusively linking Jordan to the NBA's deviant lifestyle:

> Apologists for the NBA lifestyle argue that players are accustomed to staying up until the early hours, then sleeping late or taking a nap after the shootaround. Some NBA players enjoy frequenting the Atlantic City casinos when their teams visit Philadelphia for a game.
>
> (Anderson, 1993, p. 11)

The NBA had never been completely separated from its popular, racially charged connotation as an aberrant domain. Yet this was the first time Jordan's imperious image had been tainted with the festering detritus of this implicitly racial discourse. However temporarily, Jordan became an imaged sign whose impending fall from grace appeared destined to reinforce the historically inscribed racial discourses that cast African American males as pathologically deficient individuals, whose weaknesses are manifest in addictive and obsessive lifestyles (see Reeves & Campbell, 1994).

Anderson's column not only granted the gambling story a degree of legitimacy because it originated in the august pages of the *New York Times*, it also ignited a furious debate within the popular media—a debate whose underlying current centered on the scrutiny of Jordan's racial identity. In Jefford's (1994) terms, Anderson disrupted the dominant articulation of Jordan's strong and decisive (unraced) hard body à la Reagan, by insinuating that Jordon possessed a pathologically weak and corruptible (raced) soft body à la Bernard King, Eddie Johnson, Terry Furlow, or for that matter Len Bias (see Cole & Andrews, 1996; Donohew, Helm, & Haas, 1989; and Reeves & Campbell, 1994). The *ABC Nightly News* on May 27th, 1993, ended with a segment on the story, introduced with a marked solemnity by Peter Jennings. Within the piece, Dick Shaap identified how, in the first quarter of the game against the Knicks, Jordan played like what he was: "The greatest best basketball player who ever lived." He went on to say that by the last quarter, Jordan "looked human, he looked tired." Shaap then asked the audience to consider whether Jordan was worn down by the Knick's aggressive defense, or was he himself to blame for his own demise, "worn down by a visit to this Atlantic City hotel on the eve of the game." Once again, Jordan's iconic stature was questioned for violating "people's expectations." Without condemnation, Shaap offered some advice: "The most famous and richest active athlete in the world is not supposed to go to a gambling casino and stay out beyond midnight. He is too easy a target." Jordan's status as an exceptional human being and role model (Mariotti, 1993), founded as it was on his imaged identity out of difference to the media's vision of the archetypal black male, was now in doubt. The nation raised its eyebrows as the media suggestively implied that Jordan was perhaps human (a less-than-subtle euphemism for being black) after all (Mariotti, 1993a; Miklasz, 1993).

In early June, the hastened release of Richard Esquinas' book, *Michael & Me: Our Gambling Addiction . . . My Cry for Help!* (Esquinas, 1993), gave further stimulus to the raging debate concerning Jordan's gambling habits. The author maintained the book was circulated sooner than planned because, in the wake of the Atlantic City story, "We wanted to stay in control of information . . . we felt we were losing confidentiality" (Esquinas, quoted in Isaacson, 1993, p. 7). It seemed more likely that the book was distributed in order to take advantage of the popular interest already generated around Jordan's alleged gambling problem. As a result of the popular media's rabid coverage and circulation of the debate over Jordan's alleged predilection for gambling, the story took on "a life of its own," evidencing the "media's apparent inability to put on the brakes when a story is spinning out of control" (Fainaru, 1993, p. 68). In the wake of Jordan's gambling exposé, the media gleefully censured him, and in doing so stimulated popular interest in the story. For this reason, Jordan's attempt to exonerate himself was always likely to elicit a skeptical response from the more avaricious sections of the media:

> I think that was Michael Jordan behind those dark glasses, though it might have been a candidate for the witness protection program. Did

he know the camera was on? Was he wired to a polygraph we couldn't see?

Jordan's first step back as icon and wonder symbol looked more like testimony than conversation . . . the network did him no favors, lighting him like a criminal all the while Jordan was insisting a criminal is exactly what he isn't.

(Lincicome, 1993, p. 1)

Despite the proliferation of stories related to Jordan's penchant for gambling, the currency of mediated narratives within a postmodern culture engorged by information is unavoidably brief. The gambling story that temporarily dominated the media's coverage of Michael Jordan and that threatened to seriously discredit his All-American image, had within a matter of days become a residual and largely neutral aspect of his mediated identity. This process was hastened by the Chicago Bull's victory over the Phoenix Suns in the NBA Final Series. Once more Jordan's on-court exploits took center stage, as the "Bull's three-peat" relegated the gambling issue to the status of a minor problem that was overcome during the course of the teams ultimately triumphant "season of endurance" (Cardon, 1993, p. 5). Jordan's appearance on CBS's *Eye to Eye with Connie Chung* (July 15, 1993) seemed to finally lay the ghost of his gambling problem to rest, as he talked candidly about his life, family, and the gambling controversy. To all intents and purposes Jordan's gambling had become a nonstory; and from being packaged as a role model, a "walking image onto which gambling simply does not project" (Fainaru, 1993, p. 68), Jordan had been reinvented as the All-American hero "who loves motherhood, apple pie and *games of chance*" (emphasis added, Heisler, 1993, p. 1).

Question marks surrounding Jordan's personal integrity did not stay dormant for long. The gambling narrative became violently reactivated around the murder of his father in August 1993. Once James Jordan's body had been positively identified, the media immediately and enthusiastically alluded to a connection between the father's murder and his son's gambling, which implied that the murder was a payback for Michael Jordan's gambling debts (Dobie, 1994). As Margaret Carlson noted, speaking on an edition of CNN's *Reliable Sources* program, which examined the popular media's proclivity for reporting conjecture rather than fact:

I think there was another thing at work in the Jordan murder which was that people were looking for a reason, and they went back to the last story, the last big story, which was this—these gambling charges, and they took the death, and they took the gambling, and they linked the things without any evidence at all, but there's this human desire, I think, here that newspapers pick up on which is to find a reason. They—we don't want to believe that there's absolute, total, random violence, especially when it's someone famous.

(August 28, 1993)

In terms of semiotic analysis, once again the constant erasure and deferral of Michael Jordan's racial signification resulted in the conjunctural rearticulation of his image. From the relative tranquility of postchampionship euphoria, the signification of Jordan "the obsessive gambler" was exhumed and widely attached to the sign of his murdered father. For example, Michael Janofsky, writing in the *New York Times*, appeared to presume a connection between Jordan and his father's murder, and seemed most disappointed with Sheriff Morris Bledsole's failure to corroborate it: "The absence of clues, Bledsole said, made it impossible for him to speculate on the possibility that Jordan's death was connected to any gambling activities of his son" (1993a, p. 25). Writing in the same paper, Ira Berkow added to the speculation: "and now that James P. Jordan is dead, we don't know whether the father is paying for his son's celebrity in some bizarre way. . . . We don't know all the circumstances behind the death of James Jordan . . . but the police are calling it homicide" (1993a, p.25). Perhaps the most irresponsible, and certainly the most hypocritical commentary on the murder came from Jay Mariotti. Writing shortly after James Jordan's body had been identified, Mariotti (1993b, p. 2A) opined, "it would be the height of irresponsibility to start speculating or suggesting factors that may not be factors. Whodunit commentary is impossible until more is unearthed in the Carolinas." And yet, within the same article Mariotti blithely stated, "There are concerns about his gambling habits. . . . Now there is the possibility that his fame may have contributed, in some way, to his father's murder" (1993b, p. 2A).

The reportage of unfounded conjecture and sensationalist supposition was by no means confined to the print media; television coverage of James Jordan's murder also revisited and reinscribed the gambling narrative. The *CBS Evening News* of August 13, 1993, covered the breaking news of the Jordan murder as its lead story. A somber Connie Chung opened the program in dramatic fashion:

> Triumph. Turmoil. And now, tragedy. Michael Jordan has seen it all this year. Today police in North Carolina confirmed the worst fears about the basketball star's missing father. James Jordan shot to death. Killer and motive unknown.

The story then moved into a film segment narrated by Diana Gonzalez, a correspondent situated in North Carolina. She described a "devastated" Michael Jordan's return to North Carolina following his learning of the "mysterious" death of his father. Gonzalez then recounted the events leading up to James Jordan's disappearance/murder, and the closeness of the relationship between father and son. She concluded with a revealing commentary on the case:

> The body of James Jordan was found in an area known for a lot of drug related crime, but as of now police say they have no obvious motive. Authorities have not said whether they will consider the possibility the killing might be connected to the family's gambling activities. Other possibilities include kidnapping for ransom, or simply random crime.

This coverage represented a clear example of what Margaret Carlson (appearing on CNN's *Reliable Sources*, August 28, 1993) referred to as the media's need for immediate gratification, in terms of instantaneously providing a motive for any action within their gaze. The police may have been unwilling to identify an obvious motive, however *CBS News* was more than happy to do so. In one fell swoop Gonzalez' less-than-subtle inferences provided the viewing public with a seemingly compelling rationale for the murder; one which clearly implicated Michael Jordan, without any direct reference to him. Connie Chung, with a picture of James Jordan now providing a backdrop, then contextualized his murder within the narrative of his son's career: "Jordan's murder adds another bitter twist to the darker side of an All-American success story." It was narrative that seemed to be realizing Jordan's dreaded metamorphosis from "Michael Jordan the person to Michael Jordan the black guy" (Michael Jordan, quoted in Breskin, 1989, p. 396).

Back to basics?: Michael Jordan as gingrichite America

Media speculation related to Jordan's potentially deviant (racial) identity abated with the arrest of James Jordan's alleged murderers, one of which was an African American male. In light of this development, the accusatory and racist vectors of the popular media became directed at another black body, that of the indicted African American assailant, Daniel Andre Green. The media's casting of Green as an embodied and highly visible racial sign of "the kind of random violence that all the public was concerned about and afraid of" (Jim Coman, quoted in Janofsky, 1993b, p. 1), neatly absolved Jordan of any responsibility, however indirect, for his father's death. As Janofsky pointed out:

> Today's arrests brought to a swift conclusion a sad and somewhat bizarre case that drew nationwide attention because of the fame of Michael Jordan, the National Basketball Association's premier player, and speculation that the death might be in some way related to Jordan's highly publicized gambling activities.
>
> (1993b, p.1)

With Daniel Andre Green assuming the mantle of a latter day Willie Horton (see Feagin & Vera, 1995), his demonized racial presence provided a semiotic space for, and inverted unity with, the revitalization of Michael Jordan's All-American sign value. In essence, the strategic mobilization of corporeal pathologies associated with the deviant African American Other necessarily resuscitated Jordan's atypical racial persona.

Following the arraignment of his father's alleged murderers and his subsequent retirement from the NBA in October 1993—which was widely reported as being at least partly attributable to the stress and anxiety resulting from his father's murder and the media's reporting thereof (McCallum, 1993)—the articulation of Jordan's simulated existence became infused with a sense of familial sympathy, sorrow, and understanding. As with Wayne Gretzky's "defection" from Canada in 1988 (Jackson, 1993, 1994), Jordan's retirement resonated as a catalyst for the popular expression of national loss and mourning (Jones, 1993; Madigan, 1993; Thomas, 1993). In Bill Clinton's funereal terms, "We may never see his like again. We will miss him—here and all around America, in every smalltown backyard and paved city lot where kids play one-on-one and dream of being like Mike" (quoted in *Inside Sports* special issue, "The End of an Era," October 1993, p. 7). However, unlike the Gretzky scenario—which proved a catalyst for intersecting debates related to Canada's perceived national decline—Jordan's retirement also provided a platform for the national, popular celebration of the American way, as seemingly vindicated by the very nature of his imperious being. Ira Berkow enthused, "His wholesome image, his broad smile and his basketball achievements made him the embodiment of the American dream" (1993b, p. 17). John Leland, in the *Newsweek* special issue "The Greatest Ever," which marked Jordan's retirement, continued this romanticized self-celebratory narrative of contemporary America through Michael Jordan, a discourse which for so long had dominated the populist articulation of his career:

> There is a clip of Michael Jordan that we Americans will be replaying in our heads well into the next century. It is a part of our shared cultural experience, a flash of the American Dream bright enough to join us all momentarily in its promise. It begins with Michael swooping toward the basket. His tongue is out, the ball a willing appendage at the end of his long, muscular right arm. He takes one stride, and then he begins to rise.

> It is a magnificent thing, his rise, as articulate a refutation of the forces that hold human-kind earthbound as the drawings of Leonardo or the joyous music of Louis Armstrong. His legs start to churn in midair, mocking gravity, and he begins, at his apex, to climb even higher: he begins to fly. Jordan made this move scores of times; television multiplied it a hundredfold. And each time he went up he

held out the hope that this time—for the sake of all who believe themselves slaves to gravity—he would never come down.

(1993, p. 9)

Despite the prevalence of such self-satisfied nationalist discourse surrounding the spectacle of Jordan's retirement, some journalists would not let the rumors surrounding Michael Jordan's personal indiscretions dissipate. In the *Newsweek* special issue, Mark Starr resurrected "that gambling thing" (1993, p. 39) in a particularly indicting manner. After chronicling his varied gambling habits, Starr accused Jordan of being a compulsive gambler, a personality flaw that had rendered his basketball legacy, "sadly, a slightly tarnished one" (1993, p. 39). Likewise, Harvey Araton's barbed summation of Jordan's career chided him for a hypocritical lack of personal integrity and responsibility:

> For even as Jordan was saying goodbye, his bitterness over his name being dragged through gambling headlines was obvious. He kept referring to the news media as "you guys," you problem makers, as if the news media had dug up Slim Bouler and Richard Esquinas and every other controversy that dogged Jordan the last two years.
>
> That's the troubling part of the Jordan legacy, his lack of public acknowledgement that the persona he marketed so brilliantly, so lucratively, did not come with responsibility, with accountability.
>
> (1993, p. 1)

Evidently the popular media's representation of Jordan, in the wake of his retirement, was in a state of flux, polarized by the oppositional signifiers of All-American greatness and African American pathological depravity.

Within 4 months of his retirement from the NBA Jordan embarked on his highly publicized baseball odyssey. This somewhat improbable venture resolved the semiotic ambiguity and exorcised the specter of racial contamination implied by the media's prolonged discussion of Jordan's numerous indiscretions. Despite the ever-increasing presence of African American, Hispanic, and Latino players within the game, baseball continues to be a touchstone of white (sporting) culture. Hence, with Jordan's pursuit of what is frequently and often uncritically assumed to be every true-blooded (white) American male's (sporting) dream, the threat posed by his emergent deviant identity to his racially transcendent image almost inevitably subsided. Once again he could be portrayed as the near-mythic All-American hero.

Although there were some notable examples to the contrary (for example, Mariotti, 1994; and most controversially Wulf, 1994), Jordan's sojourn into minor-league baseball was largely characterized as being beneficial to the game as a whole. Perhaps even more important than the direct economic boost Jordan was expected to bring to the game (Banks, 1994; De Lissier & Helyar, 1994; Van Dyck, 1994a), his very presence in a baseball uniform was felt to have improved the game's image by association (Crain, 1994; Lincicome, 1994a; Van Dyck, 1994b; Verdi, 1994a). Jordan was even anointed as the "savior" of the strike-curtailed 1994 major league baseball season: "All the has done since putting on a baseball uniform is bring positive attention to a sport in dire need of it, and dignity to himself by risking his athletic reputation on this baseball fantasy" (Burwell, 1994b, p. 3C). As Burwell intimated, the Jordan-baseball couplet proved to be a mutually beneficial alliance.

When braced with Jordan's revitalizing All-American aura, baseball's residual identity as the national pastime provided the media with a synergetic narrative context, which almost compelled the discursive appropriation of the valorized personal attributes associated with successful engagement with the American dream—most pertinently, naked innocence, hard work, commitment, and desire for success (Verdi, 1994b). Jordan was valorized for being "just a guy who chased his dream" (Myslenski, 1994, p. 1) and someone who was "not afraid to fail" (Michael Jordan, quoted in *Chicago Sun-Times*, 1994, February 8, p. 88) in the pursuit of his dream.

The discursive emendation of the explicitly American, competitive individualism that engulfed Jordan's fledgling baseball career reached its zenith within the crass, popular psychology that comprised the inspirational tome, *I Can't Accept Not Trying: Michael Jordan on the Pursuit of Excellence* (Vancil, 1994). Most of the text for this discussion of Jordan's personal philosophy was garnered from the pictorial coffee-table book, *Rare Air* (Vancil, 1993), which was published the previous year. However, the timing of the later book's release, its very little, and thematic organization, proved an effective intertextual reinforcement of the Alger-esque articulation of Jordan's baseball odyssey.

Perhaps wary of the negative publicity that could potentially accrue if Jordan struggled in baseball (as he plainly did), his coterie of corporate affiliations were initially reticent to develop "Jordan baseball tie-ins" (Jensen, 1994). Soon, however, Jordan's baseball trials and tribulations proved too good a marketing opportunity to miss. Having retired the anthemic "Be like Mike" campaign during Jordan's tenure with the Chicago White Sox' Double-A affiliate, the Birmingham Barons, Gatorade introduced a television commercial that overtly played on his baseball travail. Over grainy, black-and-white, nostalgia-inducing sequences drawn from his imperious basketball career, Jordan—bedecked in baseball garb—solemnly declared, "I always wanted the ball, and I got it where it should go. And, I always drank Gatorade because nothing's better." Switching to color, baseball, and the contemporary, the visual narrative displayed images of Jordan diligently practicing his hitting, base running, and throwing, over which he announced, "Now I'm playing baseball. I still drink Gatorade. I still want the ball. I still know where it should go. And sooner or later, I'm gonna get it there [he smiles] . . . I hope. It's got to be Gatorade!" This commercial keyed on the self-conscious, whimsical admission of Jordan's fallibility with regard to his baseball abilities and ambitions and on an admiration for the strength of character required of Jordan, in pursuit of a dream, to put himself in a position in which failure was a very real and public possibility.

Such a theme also provided the impetus for Nike's somewhat belated contribution to the fabrication of Jordan's baseball-related identity (especially since Jordan's decision to return to the NBA in March 1995 made the television commercial redundant after less than a week). Within this television spot, baseball icons Stan Musial, Willie Mays, and Ken Griffey Jr., were shown surveying Jordan's baseball prowess and admitting to the attendant Spike Lee (resurrecting the Mars Blackmon character), that while Jordan cannot be considered their equals in terms of playing ability, there was no doubting his sincerity, or the fact that "he's trying." Following footage of the ball rolling through Jordan's legs, Bill Buckner, the ex-Boston Red Sox player remembered for committing precisely that error at a crucial point during the 1986 World Series, wryly noted, "He ain't no Bill Buckner . . . But he's trying." Nike pursued this parodic overture within their next Air Jordan commercial, which first aired in May 1995. The spot, which Hiestand (1995, p. 3C) identified as being reminiscent "of your grammar school fiction efforts," reprised images and scenarios drawn from previous Nike commercials, his NBA comeback game against the Indiana Pacers, Bobby Ewing's (Patrick Duffy) resurrection in Dallas, and most importantly from Jordan's baseball detour, which was now cast in a surreal light:

> I had this dream . . . I retired . . . I became a weak-hitting, Double-A outfielder with a below average arm . . . I had a $16 meal per diem . . . I rode from small town to small town on a bus . . . and then I returned to the game I love and shot 7 for 28 . . . Can you imagine it? . . . I can't.

This commercial simultaneously brought Jordan's baseball career to a satirical conclusion and effectively announced his return to the NBA. Through the use of parody and self-deprecating humor, it positioned Jordan's relative failure in baseball as a platform for reasserting his humility, steely determination, and desire to realize even the most challenging goals. Despite a .202 batting average at the Double-A level, Jordan's status as an All-American icon was conclusively reaffirmed. As Grant poignantly summarized, Jordan's "improbable quest" fell short of his goal, "but it wasn't for lack of effort" (1995, p. 110).

Evidently the maturation of Jordan's popular identity in the mid-late 1980s both was influenced by and contributed toward the prevailing climate in popular racial politics. So, his significatory resurrection in the mid-1990s was contingent upon the hyperreactionary, and necessarily racist, reactionary traditionalism of the new populist Republicanism that engulfed public space. According to John Dempsey, writing in *Variety*, the loss of marquee players, impending contract talks, and the rise of overly physical play, had all contributed to the situation in which "the NBA's image dribbles away" (1994, p. 27). This questioning of the NBA's exemplary image, which Jordan had played such a large part in cultivating, intensified following his retirement from the league in October 1993. Thereby, and by disassociation, Jordan's image was further revitalized. The neo-Reaganite climate of racial retrenchment—concretized within the Newt Gingrich orchestrated "Contract with America," which swept the Republicans to a landslide victory in the November 8, 1994 elections for the House of Representatives (see Mollins, 1995a, 1995b, 1995c)—rendered the high profile and overt African American constitution of the Jordan-less NBA, a semiotic space that inevitably became implicated in the rise to ascendancy of the new New Right's accusatory regime of racial signification.

In the wake of the semiotic ambiguity created by Jordan's departure, the NBA became targeted by the reactionary popular media as yet another site for representing African American males as signifiers of danger and social depravity. The process of honing the NBA into a racially acceptable semiotic space, initiated by Bird-Johnson and consolidated by the transcendent persona of Michael Jordan (see Cole & Andrews, in press) was derailed by reactionary diatribes that condemned the new generation of NBA stars for being self-centered, spoilt, brash, arrogant, and irresponsible (Boeck, 1994a, 1994b; Burwell, 1994a; Dempsey, 1994; Diefenbach, 1995; Graham, 1995; Swift, 1994; Taylor, 1995). According to Burwell here was

> an entire generation of slammin', jammin', no jump-shooting, fundamentally unsound kids who have bought into NBA's and Madison Avenue's shallow MTV-generated marketing of the game. People with no soul for the essence of the game turned the poetry into gangster rap.
>
> (Burwell, 1994a, p. 3C)

The much publicized dissension of players such as Dennis Rodman, Chris Webber, Derrick Coleman, and Isaiah Rider, became widely characterized as being indicative of the "league's discipline problems mirror[ing] those of society" (Taylor, 1995, p. 23). Using the NBA as a euphemism for the American nation, the racial paranoia and insecurity pervading popular discourse depicted the unruly and disrespectful behavior of these young African American males as being as threatening to the stability of the NBA as the criminal irresponsibility of the young urban African American male was to American society as a whole. According to Taylor, "A form of insanity is spreading through the NBA like a virus threatening to infect every team in the league"

(1995, p. 19). Or, as Diefenbach described it, "In the NBA, at least for the time being, it is evident: The animals control the zoo" (1995, p. 31). Perhaps Graham most succinctly placed the entire debate within its neoconservative political context, "The players are just the most visible example of what's happening in sports and, in a larger sense, in society: The decline of old-fashioned values" (1995, p. 10). Upholding old-fashioned values, and thereby distinguishing the young deviants, were the residual and ever-revered images of Bird, Johnson, and Jordan (Boeck, 1994a; Diefenbach, 1995).

Thus, despite his commitment to baseball, Michael Jordan's sign-value continued to influence the racial representation of the NBA. The only difference being that his imperious, but absent, image was now used in an almost nostalgic sense to distinguish what the league had become. Even *in absentia*, Jordan's image was a potent agent of racial displacement, deflecting stereotypical racial signifiers away from *his* atypical black body, and onto those of the youthful African American miscreants who now dominated the popular representation of the NBA. This explains the relevance of, and inferences behind, the pointed question asked on the front cover of the December 1994 issue of *Inside Sports*, "Why can't Shaq be like Mike?"

Despite the ubiquitous and intrusive presence of Michael Jordan, his separation from the NBA created the semiotic space for (indeed his physical absence almost necessitated) the creation of a more immediate embodied oppositional referent within the turgid maelstrom the NBA now represented. Grant Hill, the Duke forward, was posited as a future NBA star long before his entry into the league (Wolff, 1993). Having debuted in the Jordan-less NBA in November 1994, Hill produced the type of on-court performances that allowed the popular media, and his expectant commercial sponsors, to legitimately capitalize upon the Jordan-like off-court demeanor that had been manufactured for Hill during the course of his successful collegiate career. Almost overnight Hill was sucked into the vortex of promotional culture. This meant that as well as being a regular performer on NBC's, TBS', and TNT's NBA game coverage, Hill was featured in numerous television (even playing the piano on CBS' *Late Show with David Letterman*), newspaper, and magazine profiles and appeared in commercials for Fila, Sprite, and General Motors, all of which created an economy of mutually reinforcing texts that expedited the signification of Hill as the new Michael Jordan (DuPree, 1994a, 1994b; Feinstein, 1995; Junod, 1995; Lewis, 1995). As a result he became, "Everybody's new NBA favorite [who] is admired not just for the greatness of his game, but for the content of his character" (Feinstein, 1995, p. 58). In a matter of months, Hill was touted as "the savior" of a league that had become "replete with hoodlums" (Junod, 1995, p. 170, 172) because, like Jordan a decade before him, he had been shrewdly promoted as

> a harbinger of the day when the value police will finally break down
> the laws of the locker room and make all those muscled miscreants
> toe the line in the name of God and country . . . [someone who is]
> said to "act white" and "play black," he makes a black man's game
> more palatable to the white folk who have started imputing a connec-
> tion between "in your face" and "in your house."
>
> (Junod, 1995, p. 172)

Or, as Feinstein identified, "To marketers, Hill is a dream come true. He's the
anti-Shaq" (1995, p. 59). The promotional juggernaut that propelled Hill to
the top of the 1995 NBA All-Star balloting and to being corecipient (with
Jason Kidd) of the 1994–1995 NBA Rookie of the Year award, was temporarily interrupted by Jordan's decision to resume his NBA career in March
1995. With the more immediate proximity of Jordan's sign-value actively
redeeming the league's tarnished image, Hill was relegated to the status of an
apprentice Jordan, the "Heir Jordan" (Johnson, 1995, p. 38), ready to assume
the paragonic mantle when his forebear decides to retire once and for all.

Although Charles F. Pierce somewhat prematurely described Grant Hill as
"our first post-Gingrich superstar" (quoted in Junod, 1995, p. 172), Jordan
could be considered America's first Gingrichite superstar who epitomized
the "back to basics" (to borrow a term from John Major) ideology espoused
by the new New Right. Jordan's comeback provided the popular media with
a context for accenting the neo-Reaganitc personal traits and characteristics
that originally framed his mediated identity, implicated him as a lustrous
vindication of Reagan's color-blind ideology, and that set him apart from
popular stereotypes of the African American male:

> In this season of Jordanmania, we are celebrating excellence, which
> is all to the good. With his fierce work ethic, his insistence on prac-
> tices as competitive as games, and his refusal to concede a defeat
> until the buzzer sounds, Jordan is a role model and then some. Even
> the ad slogans most widely associated with Jordan—"Be like Mike"
> and "Just do it"—remind us of how much we can achieve if we
> simply make a real commitment to our dreams.
>
> (Kornbluth, 1995, p. 22)

The reassertion of "SuperMichael" (*Sports Illustrated*, 1995, March 20, front
cover) inevitably positioned Jordan in opposition to the NBA's vilified
"spoilsports and malcontents" (Leland, 1995, p. 54), thus reinforcing both
poles of this racially charged binary opposition. In remarks made during the
postgame press conference following his comeback game, Jordan obligingly
adopted this crusading role:

> I really felt that I wanted to instill some positive things back to the
> game. You know, there's a lot of negative things that have been

happening to the game, and I guess in terms of me coming back, I come back with the notion of, you know, Magic Johnson and the Larry Birds and the Dr. Js—all those players who paved the road for a lot of the young guys. And the young guys are not taking care of their responsibilities in terms of maintaining that love for the game, you know, and not let it waste to where it's so business-oriented that the integrity of the game's going to be at stake.

(*CNN News*, 1995, March 19).

Even Scoop Jackson writing in *Slam*, the youth-oriented and self-styled "In Your Face Basketball Magazine," towed this reactionary line: "Just when the NBA's salvation is in question, Air Jordan returns to save our souls. . . . Michael Jordan's return to the NBA is more like Jesus or Dr. King returning to save our souls, rather than a brotha coming back to shoot hoops" (1995, p. 43).

With Jordan engaged in his stated mission of "reclaiming his throne," and righting the wrongs perpetrated by the NBA's "gimme gimme Generation X'ers" (Araton, 1995, p. 6), it remains to be seen whether a series of subpar performances, which eventually led to the Chicago Bull's second-round play-off defeat at the hands of the Orlando Magic, will lead to a serious reexamination and reconstitution of his popular racial identity. There is a distinct possibility that prolonged evidence of Jordan's physical decline and sporting fallibility may be couched in terms that mobilize residual and deep-rooted racial anxieties around his imaged persona. However, because of the perpetual dynamism and ephemerality of mediated popular culture, the only thing that can be conclusively forecast is that the racial (dis)articulation of Jordan's imaged persona will not achieve any degree of enduring stability or permanence.[2]

In summation, Jordan's conjunctural racial signification will continue to be contingent upon the shifting and overlapping terrains of popular culture and popular cultural politics. As a result, the need to bring this analysis to a degree of closure must be tempered by the realization that the rabid dynamism of mediated culture will inevitably, and rather hurriedly, date such a project. Nevertheless, this discussion of Jordan's on-going simulated metamorphosis can be viewed as signposting "the changing relations of popular culture and daily life, and the changing configurations of our passions and commitments" (Grossberg, 1992, p. 29). More pertinently, this paper has identified the discursive epidemics that delineate Jordan's evolution as a promotional icon and that act as markers of an American cultural racism which oscillates between patronizing and demonizing representations of African American Otherness.

As is the responsibility of any example of critical cultural pedagogy (Giroux, 1992, 1994; Kellner, 1991, 1995; McLaren, 1993, 1994), the goal of this paper has been to formulate the type of knowledge and understanding that would encourage people to interrogate their engagement with racially oppressive mediated discourses. In framing the articulation of cultural texts such as Michael Jordan, these popular discursive tracts inevitably contribute toward the construction of the multiple inclusions and exclusions through which the American racial formation continues to be structured, disciplined, and experienced. Hence, in excavating and reconstructing the evolution of Michael Jordan as a racial sign, paraphrasing Grossberg (1992), it has been my modest aim to develop a better understanding of the popular politics of racial representation within contemporary culture's "empire of signs" (Dery, 1993), which will inform where *we* have been and where *we* are, in order that *we* can get somewhere better.

Acknowledgments

This project has been greatly informed by Cheryl Cole, both as an influential author, enthusiastic collaborator, supportive colleague, and valued friend. Therefore, I would like to take this opportunity to publicly acknowledge my great debt of gratitude to her. I would also like to thank the anonymous *SSJ* reviewer who provided a particularly rigorous and helpful critique.

Notes

1 This section is an elaboration of a position introduced within Cole and Andrews (in press).
2 The October 2, 1995 trade that sent Dennis Rodman to the Chicago Bulls appears certain to represent yet another new chapter in the popular signification of Michael Jordan, with Jordan being positioned in opposition to "Dennis the menace" (Bickley, 1995, p. 92).

References

Anderson, D. (1993, May 27). Jordan's Atlantic City caper, *New York Times*, p. B11.

Andrews, D.L. (1993). *The cult of sporting personality: Nike's affective basketball economy*. Paper presented at the annual meetings of the North American Society for the Sociology of Sport, Ottawa, Ontario, Canada.

Andrews, D.L. (in press). Excavating Michael Jordan: Notes on a critical pedagogy of sporting representation. In G. Rail & J. Harvey (Eds.), *Sport and postmodern times: Culture, gender, sexuality, the body and sport*. Albany, NY: State University of New York Press.

Andrews, D.L., & Cole, C.L. (Eds.). (in press). *Nike nation: Technologies of an American sign*. Minneapolis: University of Minnesota Press.

Araton, H. (1993, October 7). A legacy as Jordan departs; stars as corporate heroes. *New York Times*, p. A1.

Araton, H. (1995, May 15). Be like No. 23, and don't dare say a word. *New York Times*, p. C6.

Balz, D. (1994, October 20). The whip who would be speaker: Gingrich sees role as "transformational." *Washington Post*, p. A1.

Banks, L.J. (1992, February 4). Powerful Jordan packing plenty of promotional pop. *Chicago Sun-Times*, p. 78.

Banks, L.J. (1994, February 6). Baseball can earn, learn from MJ, NBA. *Chicago Sun-Times*, p. B14.

Baudrillard, J. (1988). *America*. London: Verso.

Berkow, I. (1993a, August 14). Jordan's haunting words. *New York Times*, p. 25.

Berkow, I. (1993b, October 7). Suddenly, Michael doesn't play here anymore. *New York Times*, p. B17.

Bickley, D. (1995, October 3). Rough childhood root of problem. *Chicago Sun-Times*, p. 92.

Blackburn, R. (1988). *The overthrow of colonial slavery, 1776–1848*. London: Verso.

Boeck, G. (1994a, December 1). Spoiled—and rotten? "Attitudes" of players worry some. *USA Today*, p. 4C.

Boeck, G. (1994b, December 1). Magic: Game needs stars off court. *USA Today*, p. 4C.

Breskin, D. (1989, March). Michael Jordan: In his own orbit. *Gentlemen's Quarterly*, 318–323, 394–397.

Burwell, B. (1994a, June 3). Pacer's victory could end ugly ball. *USA Today*, p. 3C.

Burwell, B. (1994b, October 7). Get real, purists: Jordan is baseball season's savior. *USA Today*, p. 3C.

Butler, J. (1993). Endangered/endangering: Schematic racism and white paranoia. In R. Gooding-Williams (Ed.), *Reading Rodney King: Reading urban uprising* (pp. 15–22). New York: Routledge.

Cady, S. (1979, August 11). Basketball's image crisis. *New York Times*, p. 15.

Callinicos, A. (1993). *Race & class*. London: Bookmarks.

Cardon, B. (Ed.), (1993). *Chicago Bulls three-peat!* Orlando, FL: Tribune Publishing.

Cashmore, E. (1982). *Black sportsmen*. London: Routledge and Kegan Paul.

Castle, G. (1991, January). Air to the throne. *Sport*, 28–36.

Clarke, S.A. (1991). Fear of black planet. *Socialist Review*, **21**(2), 37–59.

Cobbs, C. (1980, August 19). NBA and cocaine: Nothing to snort at. *Los Angeles Times*, p. C1.

Cole, C.L., & Andrews, D.L. (1996). "Look—Its NBA's *ShowTime*!": Visions of race in the popular imaginary. *Cultural Studies: A Research Volume*, **1**(1), 141–181.

Cole, C.L., & Denny, H. (1995). Visualizing deviance in post-Reagan America: Magic Johnson, AIDS, and the promiscuous world of professional sport. *Critical Sociology*, **20**(3), 123–147.

Coontz, S. (1992). *The way we never were: American families & the nostalgia trap*. New York: Basic Books.

Crain, R. (1994, February 28). Baseball to learn to "Be like Mike." *Advertising Age*, **24**.

Cronin, B. (1991, July 31). Olympics don't fit MJ to a tee. *Chicago Sun-Times*, p. 114.

Davis, L.R. (1990). The articulation of difference: White preoccupation with the question of racially linked genetic differences among athletes (review essay). *Sociology of Sport Journal*, **7**(2), 179–187.

Davis, M. (1992). *City of quartz: Excavating the future in Los Angeles*. New York: Random House.

De Lissier, E., & Helyar, J. (1994, April 8) Is a baseball club with Michael Jordan still minor league. *Wall Street Journal*, pp. A1, A6.

Dempsey, J. (1994, June 27-July 3). NBA's image dribbles away. *Variety*, 27–28.

Denzin, N.K. (1991). *Images of postmodern society: Social theory & contemporary cinema*. London: Sage.

Department of Labor. (1965). *The negro family: The case for national action*. Washington, DC: U.S. Government Printing Office.

Derrida, J. (1978). *Writing & difference*. London: Routledge & Kegan Paul.

Derrida, J. (1981). *Positions*. Chicago: University of Chicago Press.

Dery, M. (1993). The empire of signs. *Adbusters Quarterly: The Journal of the Mental Environment*, **2**(4). 54–61.

Diefenbach, D. (1995, June). Disturbing the peace. *Sport*, 24–31.

Dobie, K. (1994, February). Murder by the roadside in Robeson County. *Vibe*, 72–78.

Donohew, L., Helm, D., & Haas, J. (1989). Drugs and (Len) Bias on the sports page. In L.A. Wenner (Ed.), *Media, sports, & society* (pp. 225–237). Newbury Park: Sage.

Dumm, T.L. (1993). The new enclosures: Racism in the normalized community. In R. Gooding-Williams (Ed.), *Reading Rodney King: Reading urban uprising* (pp. 178–195). New York: Routledge.

DuPree, D. (1994a, October 26). Hill has 'em talking: Pistons rookie stirs Jordan comparisons. *USA Today*, p. 7C.

DuPree, D. (1994b, December 6). Impact draws comparisons to Jordan. *USA Today*, p. 1–2C.

Dyer, R. (1991). Charisma. In C. Gledhill (Ed.), *Stardom: Industry of desire* (pp. 57–59). London: Routledge.

Dyson, M.E. (1993). Be like Mike: Michael Jordan and the pedagogy of desire. *Cultural Studies*, **7**(1), 64–72.

Eisenstadt, S.N. (Ed.). (1968). *Max Weber on charisma & institution building*. Chicago: University of Chicago Press.

Entman, R. (1990). Modern racism and the images of blacks in local television news. *Critical Studies in Mass Communication*, **7**, 332–345.

Esquinas, R. (1993). *Michael & me: Our gambling addiction . . . My cry for help!* San Diego, CA: Athletic Guidance Center Publications.

Fainaru, S. (1993, June 6). Jordan's actions speak louder than words. *Boston Globe*, p. 68.

Fanon, F. (1967). *Black skin, white mask*. New York: Grove Press.

Feagin, J.R., & Vera, H. (1995). *White racism: The basics*. New York: Routledge.

Feinstein, J. (1995, May). Grant the good. *Inside Sports*, 58–59.

Fryer, P. (1984). *Staying power: The history of black people in Britain*. London: Pluto Press.

George, N. (1992). *Elevating the game: Black men & basketball*. New York: HarperCollins.

Gilman, S. (1985). *Differences & pathology: Stereotypes of sexuality, race & madness*. Ithaca, NY: Cornell University Press.

Gilroy, P. (1991). *"There ain't no black in the union jack": The cultural politics of race & nation*. Chicago: University of Chicago Press.

Giroux, H.A. (1992). Resisting difference: Cultural studies and the discourse of critical pedagogy. In L. Grossberg, C. Nelson, & P. Treichler (Eds.), *Cultural studies* (pp. 199–212). London: Routledge.

Giroux, H. (1994). *Disturbing pleasures: Learning popular culture*. New York: Routledge.

Graham, S. (1995, June). The heroes take a fall. *Inside Sports*, 10, 12.

Grant, R.E. (1995). Running down a dream. In *Beckett great sports heroes: Michael Jordan* (pp. 110–114). New York: House of Collectibles.

Gray, H. (1989). Television, black Americans, and the American dream. *Critical Studies in Mass Communication*, **6**, 376–386.

Grossberg, L. (1988). The specificity of American hegemony. In L. Grossberg, T. Fry, A. Curthoys, & P. Patton, *It's a sin: Essays on postmodernism, politics, & culture* (pp. 23–34). Sydney: Power Publications.

Grossberg, L. (1992). *We gotta get out of this place: Popular conservatism & postmodern culture*. London: Routledge.

Hall, S. (1981). Notes on deconstructing "the popular." In R. Samuel (Ed.), *People's history & socialist theory* (pp. 227–240). London: Routledge & Kegan Paul.

Hall, S. (1983). The problem of ideology: Marxism without guarantees. In B. Matthews (Ed.), *Marx 100 years on* (pp. 57–86). London: Lawrence & Wishart.

Hall, S. (1994). Reflections upon the encoding/decoding model: An interview with Stuart Hall. In J. Cruz & J. Lewis (Eds.), *Viewing, reading, listening: Audiences and cultural reception* (pp. 253–274). Boulder: Westview Press.

Hall, S., Critcher, C., Jefferson, T., Clarke, J., & Roberts, B. (1979). *Policing the crisis: Mugging, the state, & law & order*. London: Macmillan.

Heisler, M. (1993, May 28). Jordan's cards under the table. *Los Angeles Times*, p. C1.

Henry, W.A. III. (1984). Faster, higher, stronger. *In Olympic Games 1984: The pictorial record of the XXIII Olympic Games* (pp. 49–51). Upper Montclair, NJ: ProSport.

Herrnstein, R.J., & Murray, C. (1994). *The bell curve: Intelligence & class structure in American life*. New York: Free Press.

Hiestand, M. (1992, January 30). Jordan cuts out of N.B.A. apparel deal. *USA Today*, p. 1C.

Hiestand, M. (1995, April 27). Baseball marketing schemes tardy but on target. *USA Today*, p. 3C.

Isaacson, M. (1992a, June 15). 2nd world championship is "more" to Jordan, *Chicago Tribune*, p. A14.

Isaacson, M. (1992b, October 17). Jordan leaves gambling story up in air. *Chicago Tribune*, pp. B1, B5.

Isaacson, M. (1993, June 4). Jordan mum on book's gambling allegations. *Chicago Tribune*, p. D7.

Jackson, D. (1992, March 29). Jordan's acquaintances in shadowy world. *Chicago Tribune*, pp. A1, A16–A17.

Jackson, S.J. (1993). Sport, crisis and Canadian identity in 1988: The issue of Americanisation. *Borderlines: Studies in American Culture*, **1**(2), 142–156.

Jackson, S.J. (1994). Gretzky, crisis, and Canadian identity in 1988: Rearticulating the Americanization of culture debate. *Sociology of Sport Journal* **11**(4), 428–446.

Jackson, S. (1995, July). The new testament. *Slam*, 42–48.

Janofsky, M. (1993a, August 14). Man shot to death is identified as father of Jordan. *New York Times*, p. A25.

Janofsky, M. (1993b, August 16). Two men are charged with murder of Jordan. *New York Times*, p. C1.

Jeffords, S. (1994). *Hard bodies: Hollywood masculinity in the Reagan era*. New Brunswick, NJ: Rutgers University Press.

Jensen, J. (1994, March 21). Nike, Gatorade resist Jordan baseball tie-ins—For now. *Advertising Age*, **4**, 42.

Jhally, S., & Lewis, J. (1992). *Enlightened racism: The Cosby Show, audiences, & the myth of the American dream*. Boulder, CO: Westview.

Johnson, B. (1995, April 10). Adages, *Advertising Age*, 38.

Jones, C. (1993, October 7). Jordan about to become last year's role model. *New York Times*, p. B20.

Junod, (1995, April). The savior. *Gentleman's Quarterly*, 170–175, 238–240.

Katz, D. (1994). *Just do it: The Nike spirit in the corporate world*. New York: Random House.

Kellner, D. (1991). Reading images critically: Toward a postmodern pedagogy. In H. Giroux (Ed.), *Postmodernism, feminism, & cultural politics* (pp. 60–82). Albany, NY: State University of New York Press.

Kellner, D. (1995). *Media culture: Cultural studies, identity & politics between the modern & the postmodern*. London: Routledge.

Kirkpatrick, C. (1982, April 14). Nothing could be finer. *Sports Illustrated*, 14–16.

Kirkpatrick, C. (1987, November 9). In an orbit all his own. *Sports Illustrated*, 82–98.

Kornbluth, J. (1995, April 22). Here comes Mr. Jordan. *TV Guide*, 22–26.

Langman, L. (1991). From pathos to panic: American national character meets the future. In P. Wexler (Ed.), *Critical theory now* (pp. 165–241). London: Falmer Press.

Lanker, B. (1982, December 27). Pieces of '82. *Sports Illustrated*, 52–69.

Lauter, P. (1995). "Political correctness" and the attack on American colleges. In M. Berube & C. Nelson, (Eds.), *Higher education under fire: Politics, economics, & the crisis of humanities* (pp. 73–90). New York: Routledge.

Leland, J. (1993, October/November). Farewell, Michael . . . and thanks . . . for the memories. *Newsweek: Collector's Issue—The Greatest Ever*, 4–23.

Leland, J. (1995, March 20). Hoop dreams. *Newsweek*, 48–55.

Lewis, D. (1995, January). Who got "next"? *Stam*, 12.

Lewontin, R.C., Rose, S., & Kamin, L.J. (1984), *Not in our genes: Biology, ideology, & human nature*. New York: Pantheon Books.

Lincicome, B. (1984, June 17). Apologetic Bulls "stuck" with Jordan. *Chicago Tribune*, p. D1.

Lincicome, B. (1993, June 10). Jordan's TV appearance criminal. *Arizona Republic*, p. E5.

Lincicome, B. (1994a, March 9). Jordan's majesty is safe, despite baseball's efforts. *Chicago Tribune*, p. D1.

Lincicome, B. (1994b, July 8). Suspicions, guesses and knowledge too good to suppress. *Chicago Tribune*, p. D1.

Logan, B. (1984, June 17). Bulls hope Jordan's a savior. *Chicago Tribune*, pp. D1, D6.

Madigan, C.M. (1993, October 7). Gloom in the cathedral of the sneaker. *Chicago Tribune*, pp. A1, A7.

Marable, M. (1993). Beyond racial identity politics: Towards a liberal theory for multicultural democracy. *Race & Class*, **35**(1), 113–130.

Mariotti, J. (1993a, June 4). Hoopla: What's up Michael? *Newsday*, 181.

Mariotti, J. (1993b, August 15). The ultimate challenge awaits Michael Jordan. *Chicago Sun-Times*, p. 2A.

Mariotti, J. (1994, February 8). Michael at the bat was too painful to watch. *Chicago Sun-Times*, p. 87.

McCallum, J. (1993, October 18). The desire isn't there. *Sports Illustrated*, 28–35.

McLaren, P. (1993). Border disputes: Multicultural narrative, identity formation, and critical pedagogy in postmodern America. In D. McLaughlin & W.G. Tierney (Eds.), *Naming silenced lives: Personal narratives and the process of educational change* (pp. 201–235). London: Routledge.

McLaren, P. (1994). Multiculturalism and the post-modern critique: Toward a pedagogy of resistance and transformation. In H.A. Giroux & P. McLaren (Eds.), *Between borders: Pedagogy and the politics of cultural studies* (pp. 192–222). New York: Routledge.

Mercer, K. (1994). *Welcome to the jungle: New positions in black cultural studies*. London: Routledge.

Merrill, R. (1988). Simulations: Politics, TV, and history in the Reagan era. In R. Merrill (Ed.), *Ethics/aesthetics: Post-modern positions* (pp. 141–168). Washington, DC: Maisonnever Press.

Miklasz, B. (1993, June 4). Jordan gambling with reputation, not poker chips. *St. Louis Post-Dispatch*, p. 1D.

Miles, R. (1989). *Racism*. London: Routledge.

Minzesheimer, B. (1995, February 23). Affirmative action under fire. *USA Today*, p. 4A.

Mollins, C. (1995a, April 17). The politics of disgruntlement. *Maclean's*, 34–35.

Mollins, C. (1995b, April 17). Man of the house. *Maclean's*, 36–37.

Mollins, C. (1995c, April 17). Newt's agenda. *Maclean's*, 38.

Mosse, G.L. (1978). Toward the final solution: A history of European racism. New York: Fertig.

Mulligan, M. (1992, January 30). Nike gets rights to Jordan apparel. *Chicago Sun-Times*, p. 91.

Murray, C. (1984). *Losing ground: American social policy, 1950–1980*. New York: Basic Books.

Myslenski, S. (1992, August 5). Now you see it, now you don't: Reebok flap finally resolved. *Chicago Tribune*, p. D8.

Myslenski, S. (1994, May 1). Jordan: Remember me as just a guy who chased his dream. *Chicago Tribune*, p. C1.

Naughton, J. (1992). *Taking to the air: The rise of Michael Jordan*. New York: Warner Books.

Omi, M. (1989). In living color: Race and American culture. In I, Angus & S. Jhally (Eds.), *Cultural politics in contemporary America* (pp. 111–122). New York: Routledge.

Omi, M., & Winant, H. (1994). *Racial formation in the United States: From the 1960s to the 1990s* (2nd ed.). New York: Routledge.

Patton, P. (1986, November 9). The selling of Michael Jordan. *New York Times Magazine*, 48–58.

Plagen, P. (1993, October/November). Turning hoops upside down. *Newsweek Special Issue: The Greatest Ever*, 48.

Reeves, J.L., & Campbell, R. (1994). Cracked coverage: Television news, the anti-cocaine crusade, and the Reagan legacy. Durham: Duke University Press.

Reinerman, C., & Levine, H.G. (1989). The crack attack: Politics and media in America's latest drug scare. In J. Best (Ed.), *Images of issues: Typifying contemporary social problems*. New York: Aldine de Gruyter.

Ryans, B. (1993, December). Courting greatness. *Sport*, 26–30.

Sakamoto, B. (1986, December 16). Jordan's glamor fills league arenas. *Chicago Tribune*, p. D10.

Smith, A.M. (1994). *New right discourse on race and sexuality*. Cambridge: Cambridge University Press.

Smith, S. (1992). *The Jordan rules: The inside story of a turbulent season with Michael Jordan and the Chicago Bulls*. New York: Simon & Schuster.

Starr, M. (1993, October/November). That gambling thing. *Newsweek Special Issue: The Greatest Ever*, 39.

Strasser, J.B., & Becklund, L. (1991). *Swoosh: The unauthorized story of Nike and the men who played there*. New York: Harcourt Brace Jovanovich.

Sullivan, P. (1992, June 18). MVP Jordan credits Chicago fans. *Chicago Tribune*, p. D3.

Swift, E.M. (1991, August 5). Reach out and touch someone: Some black superstars cash in big on an ability to shed their racial identify. *Sports Illustrated*, 54–58.

Swift, E.M. (1994, June 20). Hot . . . not: White the NBA's image has cooled, the NHL has ignited surprising new interest in hockey. *Sports Illustrated*, 30–40.

Taylor, P. (1995, January 30). Bad actors: The growing number of selfish and spoiled players are hurting their teams and marring the NBA's image. *Sports Illustrated*, 18–23.

Thomas, R.M. (1993, October 7). Across the globe, expressions of regret and gratitude. *New York Times*, p. B21.

Vancil, M. (Ed.). (1993). *Rare air: Michael on Michael*. San Francisco: HarperCollins.

Vancil, M. (Ed.). (1994). *I can't accept not trying: Michael Jordan on the pursuit of excellence*. San Francisco: HarperCollins.

Van Dyck, D. (1994a, February 7). Better believe it: Baseball banking on MJ as "savior." *Chicago Sun-Times*, p. 85.

Van Dyck, D. (1994b, February 25). MJ's charisma lesson for baseball. *Chicago Sun-Times*, p. 108.

Vecsey, G. (1982a, March 30). Dean Smith finally makes the final one. *New York Times*, pp. B9, B11.

Vecsey, G. (1982b, March 31). Kicking the habit. *New York Times*, pp. B7, B9.

Vecsey, P. (1992, November 20). Owning a likeness. *USA Today*, pp. 1C, 4C.

Verdi, B. (1994a, February 10). Question is: Can baseball learn from Jordan style? *Chicago Tribune*, p. D1.

Verdi, B. (1994b, February 15). Jordan's baseball bid a fantasy, but his work ethic isn't. *Chicago Tribune*, p. D1.

Wacquant, L.J.D. (1994). The new urban color line: The state and fate of the ghetto in postFordist America. In C. Calhoun (Ed.), *Social theory and the politics of identity* (pp. 231–276). Oxford: Blackwell.

West, C. (1993a). Learning to talk of race. In R. Gooding-Williams (Ed.), *Reading Rodney King: Reading urban uprising* (pp. 255–260). New York: Routledge.

West, C. (1993b). The new cultural politics of difference. In C. McCarthy & W. Critchlow (Eds.), *Race, identity, and representation in education* (pp. 11–23). New York: Routledge.

West, C. (1994). *Race matters*. Boston: Beacon Press.

Wideman, J.E. (1990, November). Michael Jordan leaps the great divide. *Esquire*, 140–145, 210–216.

Williams, E. (1961). *Capitalism and slavery*. New York: Russell & Russell.

Willigan, G.E. (1992, July/August). High performance marketing: An interview with Nike's Phil Knight. *Harvard Business Review*, 91–101.

Willis, S. (1991). *A primer for daily life*. London: Routledge.

Wilson, J.Q., & Herrnstein, R. (1985). *Crime and human nature*. New York: Simon & Schuster.

Wolff, A. (1993, February 1). The son is shining. *Sports Illustrated*, 58–64.

Wulf, S. (1994, March 14). Err Jordan: Try as he might, Michael Jordan has found baseball beyond his grasp. *Sports Illustrated*, 20–23.

46

LOYALISM, LINFIELD AND THE TERRITORIAL POLITICS OF SOCCER FANDOM IN NORTHERN IRELAND

Alan Bairner and Peter Shirlow

Source: *Space and Polity* 2(2) (1998): 163–177.

It is generally recognised that sport, and particularly soccer, plays an important role in the construction and reproduction of identities in modern society. However, relatively little attention has been paid to the centrality of sporting spaces in the identity formation and reinforcement of soccer fans. Centred around a geography of socio-cultural domination and/or resistance in which power relations are spatialised and imagined in distinct and observable ways, this paper reveals the ways in which sports stadia in Northern Ireland function as key elements in identity politics. In particular, it is argued that those fans who congregate at Windsor Park to support Linfield Football Club and the Northern Ireland national team regard the stadium not only as a built environment which demands collective devotion, but also as a metaphor for an imagined Ulster. As a consequence, the paper argues, Windsor Park has become a site for the reactive cultural resistance of a certain group of men as they endeavour to come to terms with socioeconomic change together with the politico-cultural demands of the Collective Other in the form of Irish nationalism.

Theories of globalisation have created a perception of homogeneity represented in the world of sport by international competitions and organisations, labour migration, commodification through sponsorship, advertising and merchandising and by the world-wide popularity of certain sporting activities. Soccer, in particular, is portrayed as 'the global game'. However, sport sociologists have become increasingly sceptical about the extent to which globalisation has succeeded in eradicating national, regional and ethnic variations in popular responses to sport (Donnelly, 1996; Maguire, 1996).

Given that the soccer fandom is frequently constructed around masculinity and place-centred narratives of devotion and belonging, it is evident that such geographically constructed notions of identity are largely impervious to wider global forces. In Scotland, for example, the rivalry between Rangers and Celtic is still in many instances constructed around the arena of sectarian division and rivalry. Throughout Europe, from Barcelona to Zagreb, there are countless examples of the relationship between soccer clubs and the construction and reconstruction of ethnic and national identities. As such, despite the efforts of administrators and major investors to promote soccer as apolitical, it is evident that such a superficial globalising process is insufficient in tackling the, sometimes conflictual, link between soccer and ethnic identity.

There are, of course, numerous cultural forms and arenas within which the process, by which ethnically constructed communities come to understand themselves and articulate this understanding to the wider world, can take place. In the modern world, however, sport has become one of the most important of these. As MacClancy suggests, sports are

> vehicles of identity, providing people with a sense of difference and a way of classifying themselves and others, whether latitudinally or hierarchically
>
> (MacClancy, 1996, p. 2).

This does not mean that the resultant identities are either self-contained or immutable. Indeed, identities are more likely than not to be dual or even multiple (Kellas, 1991, p. 15). Thus, one's identity as a player of a certain sport or a supporter of a particular team may or may not overlap with other aspects of one's identity. Nevertheless, the fact remains that sport plays an important role in the construction and reproduction of part of the identity of most people (and particularly most men) in the modern world.

Much work, however, needs to be done if we are to understand completelly the processes whereby this comes about. According to Werbner:

> the extent to which 'fun' and the spaces of fun are constitutive of identity and subjectivity—whether ethnic, gendered or generational —remains to be fully theorized, although discussion of youth subcultures, and popular culture have highlighted certain dimensions of this conjuncture
>
> (Werbner, 1996, p. 106).

What is certain is that, of all of the world's major games, soccer is one of the most powerful in terms of identity formation and reinforcement.

A plethora of studies have undertaken examinations of the character of soccer fandom, focusing in particular on the problem of hooliganism (Armstrong and Harris, 1991; Dunning *et al.*, 1988, 1991: Giulianotti *et al.*, 1994; Ingham, 1978; Kerr, 1994; Pearton, 1986; Taylor, 1982; Williams *et al.*,

1989). Few of these have adequately understood the complex relationship which exists between the fans and those places where they congregate to watch their favourite game. More recent analyses have examined the development of a more celebratory and life-enhancing approach to soccer fandom (Giulianotti, 1992; Giulianotti and Williams, 1994; Haynes, 1995; Redhead, 1993). But these too have tended to focus on the relationship between the fans and their teams rather than the places where they gather. Unusually, Canter *et al.* (1989) drew attention to the relationship between football stadia and the environmental psychology of fans. However, their analysis concentrated almost exclusively on the impact of the stadia *qua* stadia, referring to issues of safety, comfort and the potential for violence within these built environments. Little attention was paid to the idea of a football stadium as having a deeper socio-psychological and symbolic meaning which extends beyond its immediate use value.

Bale (1993, 1994) provides a more robust analysis of stadia which extends beyond use values through indicating the multifaceted relationships which they produce in terms of devotion, sanctity and a sense of belonging. This type of analysis is important as it illustrates the value attached to sporting landscapes in the production and reproduction of identity. Unfortunately, his analysis does not adequately explain or comprehend those contexts in which the soccer stadium is an integral part of a much wider socio-political landscape, particularly in societies fragmented by violent political conflict, ethno-sectarian division and territorial disputation. Furthermore, those commentators who have written about sport in divided societies have tended to underestimate the importance of built environments by overindulging in behaviourist accounts and overtly descriptive narratives (Bairner and Sugden, 1998).

This paper aims to indicate how particular sporting arenas within Northern Ireland are themselves more than places of devotion, as witnessed in most Western societies, due to the nature of ethno-sectarian division. We argue that the behaviour of sports fans is influenced not only by their enthusiasm for particular teams, but also by a recognition that a particular stadium is an important symbolic space in terms of a wider cultural resistance or representation. In particular, we focus upon Linfield Football Club, the largest and most successful in Northern Ireland, and its ground Windsor Park, also home of the national team (Bairner, 1997). Both club and ground are synonymous with Protestant identity, tradition and metaphor. As a consequence, we argue that the fans who gather most frequently at this ground take part in activities which extend far beyond devotion to a stadium and to the teams that perform there, activities which implicate many supporters in the wider politics of cultural resistance and of allegiance to a political entity either real or imagined.

Sport and ethnicity

Writing about ethnicity in Australian sport, Jones and Moore observe that "soccer is a public arena in which ethnic identities can be assessed and reinvented in changing circumstances" (Jones and Moore, 1994, p. 18). Whilst players may be able to detach themselves from the political and social context in the course of a game, for spectators, as Duke and Crolley remind us, football matches never take place in isolation.

> The participants (the fans) do not cut themselves off from external matters. In a sense, football does not cut out external factors but it acts more like a sieve than a solid wall, and the sieve is not only selecting but also modifying what it filters
> (Duke and Crolley, 1996, pp. 126–127).

In reality, the relationship between the game and these so-called external matters may be even closer than Duke and Crolley suggest, Sport has been widely recognised as contested terrain. As a consequence, attendance at a soccer match can become an integral part of a broader social process. In this regard, academic attention has tended to focus of examples of soccer's counter-hegemonic role in the promotion of working-class solidarity (Jones, 1988) or progressive nationalism (Hargreaves, 1992). Less interest has been shown where the cultural resistance expressed by soccer fans assumes more reactive forms, except insofar as hooliganism has been linked to right-wing extremism (Giulianotti *et al.*, 1994). This paper seeks to redress the balance by revealing the complex nature of identity politics and the reactive forms of resistance fought out on the abstract terrain of soccer support and in terms of the defence of real sporting spaces.

Undoubtedly, sport does not condition the ethno-sectarian conflict that exists, in Northern Ireland or elsewhere, but it does provide a collateral explanation and an arena within which the different political, cultural and territorial interests of the two communities are articulated and acted out. In this context, ethnic identity and sporting allegiance are used to identify how the perpetuation of sectarianised identities influences the complexity and actuality of sectarianism within Northern Irish society.

Politics and place

Clearly the socioeconomic and cultural history (or historiography) of place is central to any narration or understanding of communal devotion, collective action and socio-cultural modification. Moreover, modes of socio-cultural resistance emanate from ongoing and modified processes of socialisation which, because they are distinctive to place, give specific meaning to life and living in that place (Thrift and Forbes, 1983). In turn, and in reaction to multi-layered forms of social precedent, place and its readings can also engender among individuals and communities an identifiable pool of resistance against the real and imagined processes of socioeconomic and cultural modification which redefine the nature and composition of places and localities.

Comprehending how space has been either socially or culturally fabricated into a distinctive understanding of place, in relation to the manifestation of support for specific soccer teams, provides crucial insights into the production and reproduction of conflict and reactive resistance (Boyle, 1994). However, a valid interpretation of how place and cultural identity are constituted demands an analysis which stretches beyond the nature and form of built environments (such as stadia), through embracing an analysis which includes the examination of other observable processes of socio-cultural modification and alteration (Beck et al., 1994). Material, residual and topophilic relationships are saturated with expressive meaning as they are placed in the subjective and at times introspective context of the iconographies and landscapes of past and present occurrences (Roseberry, 1989; Shirlow and McGovern, 1996).

What ultimately emerges is a geography of socio-cultural domination and/ or resistance in which power relationships are spatialised and imagined in distinct and observable ways. In particular, reactive ideological forms are primarily concerned with the definition and defensive reaction to particular cultural and social forms which are construed as alien, hostile and unacceptable. Undoubtedly, modes of reactive resistance which are played out through the medium of racist and ethno-sectarian discourses are excessively biased and tied to remorselessly negative forms of socio-cultural definition. However, the literature on theories of resistance has tended to ignore the manner, potency and direction of cultural forms of resistance which are located among communities, self-identified as being influenced by fascist or right-wing philosophies (see, for example, Pile and Keith, 1997). Obviously, the omission of communities which promote highly reactive forms of resistance impedes a diagnostic interpretation of the multiplicity of power relationships and their varied locations.

In terms of an understanding of the relationship between resistance and reactive modes of resistance, this paper is taken up with an examination of the extent to which soccer-supporting in Northern Ireland interacts with external factors and plays its part in the construction of the political identity of certain working-class Protestant men.

In assessing the extent to which these phenomena provide examples of cultural resistance, the paper draws on theoretical perspectives concerning space, place and territory which have not previously been used in the debate on the relationship between politics and sport in Northern Ireland (Sugden and Bairner, 1993). This paper conveys a sense of the localised nature of politics of territorial control and resistance, where the imperatives of communal difference, segregation and exclusion have predominated over the politics of shared interests, integration, assimilation and consensus. The paper charts and explains the relevance of space and topophilia in the reproduction of forms of highly politicised identities which are linked to notions of 'besiegement' and cultural dissipation.

Cultures of reactive opposition

In many instances, reactive forms of cultural opposition are tied to notions of cultural dissipation, beseigement and disintegration. Obviously, and as noted by Spradley and McCurdy (1987, pp. 5–6), the reality and perception of fear which is tied to the cultural 'other' means that many individuals:

> . . . cling tenaciously to the values they have acquired and feel threatened when confronted with others who live according to different conceptions of what is desirable. Thus culture is like a 'security blanket' which has great meaning to its owner.

Sectarian and racist discourses are in themselves cultural constructions which are reproduced and reworked through time and space. It is in this sense, too, that the disquisition which constitutes sectarianism, in Northern Ireland is reproduced through what are essentially 'lived experiences'. In particular the defence of boundaries or the perception that communally defined boundaries are, or could be, altered by the in-migration of the sectarian 'other' means that a reactive consciousness is not simply reproduced through ideology itself, but also in physical and spatial terms (Bell, 1990).

In this instance, religious affiliation is established as the primary demarcator of the 'collective other'. However, religion is not recognised as the 'subject' of conflicting interest but as a symbol of conflict, representing a method to distinguish, asseverate, and 'legitimate' rivalry and dogmatic asperity.

Evidently, defining the 'other' leads to the imposition of negative and putative characteristics upon a 'collective other' whose lifestyle, culture and politics must be both resisted and repelled (Jenkins, 1994). Ultimately, the culturally hostile manner of reactive resistance and the desire to challenge pan-cultural contact leads in turn to what are essentially cultures of beseigement which, somewhat depressingly, focus upon imaginings which distinguish the 'we' from the 'they'. Such a conception of peoples undoubtedly fortifies group togetherness, on the one hand, and provides a rationale for group action, on the other (Baker, 1990; Graham, 1994).

The biosphere of cultural opposition is firmly established upon the primary binary opposition of the 'collective self' and the 'collective other', and upon the construction of a necessary relationship between the two. The 'collective self', for the Ulster Protestant/Loyalist community is subjectively defined in terms of 'devotion' to what is imagined as a distinctly Protestant way of life. The 'collective other' is the 'Menace', which can come from a range of social groups or agencies but which is particularly constructed in terms of the Republican-Nationalist communities of Ireland. The mediating practice which defines the necessary relationship between the two is the notion of 'defence'. 'Communal devotion' in this sense is produced and reworked through animosity and identifiable defence strategies.

'Communal devotion' is based upon ethno-political identities tied to what are imagined and perceived as the Ulster/Protestant way of life and living. The 'collective self' is, in other words, built upon the sum of the social relationships experienced by someone growing up within a particular value system. At the same time, through the discourse of 'threat' any challenge to, or change in, the position of the 'collective self' is experienced within the context of traditional lines of division and conflict (Shirlow and McGovern, 1996, 1998). More important is the perception that a loss of socioeconomic or political status is tied not to flaws within the character of the 'collective self', but is due to the encroachment or existence of the 'collective other'. As a result, the potency of such interpretations means that communities must defend themselves. 'Defence' and the protection of territory thus emerges as the primary discourse defining the mediating practice between the 'self' and the 'other', the conceptual ordering of inter-communal relations.

It is in this sense that one must focus upon the relative autonomy of ideology and collective consciousness as a determining factor on social action; the way, in other words, material, political and cultural change is perceived within the context of a pre-existing, if discursive, ideological framework. The role of sectarianism clearly indicates how class relationships in Northern Ireland crosscut politics, economics, ideology and culture.

Contextual background

Highlighting the importance of sport for the construction and consolidation of national identities, Jarvie observes that "it is as if the imagined community or nation becomes more real on the terraces or the athletics track" (Jarvie, 1993, p. 75). Most sports fans cast their sporting heroes and favourite clubs in the role of "proxy warriors", to use Hoberman's phrase (Hoberman, 1986, p. 6). In Northern Ireland, this analogy is complicated by the presence of competing national identities and ethno-sectarian attitudes which are intimately involved in a 'real' conflict with real warriors who are also assigned heroic status by certain sections of the population, most notably working-class young men (Bairner, 1997).

The general relationship between politics and sport in Northern Ireland is already well established (Sugden and Bairner, 1993; Sugden and Harvie, 1995) although there remains considerable scope for more detailed analysis. The broad argument that the organisation of sport in the province not only reflects but can also exacerbate sectarian attitudes and the politics of division cannot be challenged despite the recognition that sport can also be utilised to promote cross-community reconciliation. To support the general thesis, however, it is important to examine particular manifestations of the interplay between sport and politics and to do so from a variety of academic perspectives. One such theme is the relationship between soccer and the construction of collective identities. For example, the importance to unionists (and specifically to unionist men) of the existence of the Northern Ireland national soccer team has been explored in some detail (Bairner and Sugden, 1986; Sugden and Bairner, 1994; Bairner, 1997). It is clear that although Catholics in Northern Ireland are as likely as Protestants to play and watch soccer, a unionist atmosphere surrounds the game at its highest levels, including the administration of senior soccer as well as support for the Northern Ireland team. However, it is one thing to simply record this fact and to pass some critical comments on it. What is more important is to uncover the reasons why Northern Irish Protestants persist in their attempts to exercise a degree of hegemonic control over soccer.

An obvious nationalist response would be that this phenomenon is simply a continuation of traditional unionist discriminatory practice which has been weakened in other areas, such as the allocation of jobs and houses, since the introduction of direct rule from London in order to replace the devolved parliament at Stormont (Clayton, 1996). Adopting a rather different perspective towards the same evidence, it has been argued that, with the loss of self-government and given the fact that most sports are organised on an all-Ireland basis, the national soccer team and its administrative body, the Irish Football Association (IFA) are amongst the few visible indicators of the existence of Northern Ireland as a separate place (Sugden and Bairner, 1993). On its own, however, this explanation cannot explain precisely how significant soccer is in the construction and reproduction of a unionist/loyalist identity although it points in a direction which, if followed, might lead to greater understanding of this process. The key idea raised is that of Northern Ireland as a place, both real and imagined.

Although Northern Ireland is constitutionally part of the UK, it is separated from the rest of Britain not only by a stretch of water but also by distinctive cultural patterns. Physically, it is part of the island of Ireland from which it is separated politically by the will of the majority of its citizens as well as by cultural differences. Within the six counties of Northern Ireland there are additional borders, both visible and invisible, most significantly separating Catholics from Protestants, but also dividing the country from the town and the middle classes from the working classes. As a consequence of these various boundaries, the constitutional impasse in the province can be said to be intimately bound up with territorial politics. As Anderson and Shuttleworth (1998) suggest, the intensifying controversies over Orange marches since 1994 serve to illuminate the importance of the symbolic 'claiming and re-claiming' of territory from which Protestants have retreated, or in which their proportion of the sectarian headcount has diminished. Claiming the right to march through areas against the wishes of a majority of local residents is justified in terms of 'tradition' and basic civil rights. For some, it is a way of demonstrating Protestant supremacy. Above all, it symbolically asserts that all Northern Ireland is British and that Protestants are the privileged upholders of the Union. It is sport's relationship with the politics of space and place in Northern Ireland which needs to be recognised if soccer's role in the construction of the 'collective self' *vis à vis* the 'other' is to be more fully understood.

Sporting venues, in Northern Ireland as elsewhere, consistently emerge as sites for the reproduction of a sense of alienation from the 'other'. The source of the alienation can be social class, with few working-class people feeling comfortable at rugby grounds, for example. Or, it might be gender, since most women are no more likely to feel at ease at the majority of sports stadia in the province than anywhere else. In terms of the politics of division, however, feeling alienated at sporting venues is intrinsically linked to ethno-sectarian identities. Three major examples illustrate the point.

First, there is the alienation of Protestants from nationalist sporting spaces. It is undeniable that Protestants can be made to feel unwelcome at certain soccer grounds in the province. The best example is that of Derry City's Brandywell, particularly since 1985 when the club began to play in the League of Ireland (the league in the Republic of Ireland), having resigned from Northern Ireland's Irish League in 1972. Supported in the past by Protestants in the city, the club's following is now almost exclusively Catholic. The entire west side of the city, where the Brandywell is located, is nowadays regarded as a hostile environment by the overwhelming majority of Derry's Protestant inhabitants and to venture into it for the sake of attending a soccer match is virtually unthinkable. Here is a soccer club which now quite literally plays "across the border" (Duke and Crolley, 1996, pp. 70–76) and which further symbolises the estrangement of nationalists from Northern Ireland as a political entity.

Cliftonville's Solitude ground is also alien territory even when Protestants travel there to support their own team. Established as an amateur club in what was a predominantly middle-class, Protestant area of Belfast, Cliftonville only acquired a nationalist following after population shifts led to a marked decrease in the numbers of Protestants in the area. Into the vacuum stepped Catholics, primarily from the nearby Ardoyne and New Lodge districts, although also from other nationalist parts of the city and beyond. The impression of Solitude as nationalist space is further enhanced by the fact that, on police advice, Linfield fans are not expected to visit there at all. Instead, their team's 'away' games against Cliftonville are played at Windsor Park. As a result, Solitude is transformed into a place where, for Linfield fans, 'real' Protestants do not go.

Furthermore, during the 1996–97 soccer season successful attempts were made on two occasions to prevent Cliftonville fans from attending soccer games at grounds which are regarded as Protestant territory. In response to efforts to have Orange marches rerouted away from nationalist areas, loyalists impeded the progress of Cliftonville supporters as they made their way to games in East Belfast and Portadown on 4 September 1996 and 19 October 1996 respectively. In this way, territorial politics became even more closely involved with sport than ever before and soccer grounds became even more alienating.

However, feelings of alienation from sporting venues in Northern Ireland are by no means confined to soccer grounds. Arguably Gaelic sports grounds are even more alien to Protestants than soccer stadia are to either community. The games themselves are not usually part of the experience of growing up Protestant. Venues and clubs are often named after heroes of Republican historiography. The symbolism is nationalist with the Irish tri-colour aloft and the Gaelic language being used, albeit less extensively than the founders of the Gaelic Athletic Association would have wished.[1] Seldom are overtly sectarian comments to be heard, but one might argue that this omission owes at least as much to the fact that Gaelic games do not involve competition between the two major communities as to inherent political cor-rectness on the part of the followers of Gaelic games. Certainly when nationalists turn their attention to soccer, as in the case of Cliftonville fans, there is far less hesitancy about sectarian chanting. However, as far as senior soccer is concerned it is Catholics rather than Protestants who are more likely to experience a sense of alienation at most major venues.

Indeed, a second obvious example of alienation experienced at sporting venues concerns the overwhelmingly Protestant or loyalist ambience sur-rounding most Irish League games. There are a number of related aspects to this situation. First, of the best-supported clubs in the Irish League, only Cliftonville has a predominantly Catholic following. Of the other major clubs, Ballymena United, Coleraine, Crusaders, Glenavon, Glentoran and Portadown are all mainly supported by Protestants. In the case of Linfield, moreover, it would be reasonable to suppose that the following is almost exclusively Protestant. There are a number of reasons for this preponderance of Protestant support for Irish League soccer which persists despite the fact that all of the clubs, including Linfield, have Catholic players.[2] Amongst these are the British origins of the game which arrived in Ireland at a time when sportive nationalists were constructing a separate Irish sporting culture as a response to what was regarded as British cultural imperialism (Bairner, 1996; Mandle, 1987). This meant that, in the past, many Catholics viewed soccer with suspicion with the result that they were far less involved than Protestants in the game's formal development. This is directly linked to a second reason that most senior clubs tend to be supported by Protestants. Although Catholics today follow soccer with as much enthusiasm as Protest-ants, especially since the Gaelic Athletic Association has become increasingly less antagonistic towards a sport which is now more appropriately described as universal rather than British (Cronin, 1994, 1996; Holmes, 1994), most senior clubs were established in those areas where Protestants were and, for the most part, continue to be in the majority. In this respect, the example of Cliftonville is instructive. The fact that nationalist soccer fans were in search of a team leads directly to a third reason for the disproportionate numbers of Protestants involved in supporting Irish League teams. Over the years, not only Derry City but before them, in 1949, Belfast Celtic, teams which did possess large numbers of Catholic supporters, were obliged to leave the Irish League. With the departure of these clubs, it has become all the more likely than in the past that Irish League soccer will continue to derive the bulk of its support from the Protestant, unionist community in Northern Ireland. The same can also be said about the Northern Ireland national team, albeit for slightly different reasons.[3] Its home fixtures at Windsor Park provide a third and final example of the alienating capacity of sporting venues in the province.

Only those Protestants who are absolutely repelled by vocal expressions of anti-Catholic sentiment would find Windsor Park on the occasion of Northern Ireland games a hostile environment. Catholics respond very differently. They have always represented Northern Ireland at various levels. In addition, it is undeniable that, in the past and even as recently as during the 1982 World Cup Finals in Spain, many of them supported the national team despite the fact that their political outlook would have led them to question the idea of Northern Ireland as a nation or even as a separate place. The fact remained that Catholics as well as Protestants were playing for the team and deserved the support of their co-religionists. This view was taken by large numbers of Catholics although, even at that time, many of the team's Protestant supporters chose to wear the red, white and blue of Linfield or Glasgow Rangers as opposed to the green and white of the national strip and to sing loyalist songs in preference to ones more commonly associated with football supporting. The situation today, however, is markedly different.

Very few Catholics now attend Northern Ireland games and, indeed, few would even admit to supporting the national team (Bairner, 1997). They argue that the loyalist symbolism associated with the side is the main reason for their antipathy. Cynics would add that it cannot be a coincidence that their abandonment of the national team coincided with an upsurge in the fortunes of the Irish Republic's soccer representatives. For the first time, northern nationalists had a worthwhile alternative to supporting Northern Ireland and, given their own political preference for a united Ireland and the fact that the constitution of the Republic continues to lay claim to the six counties of Northern Ireland, for most of them it was a relatively easy choice to make. However, another reason for their growing sense of alienation from the Northern Ireland team brings us back once more to the question of space and its social meaning.

The national team plays its home games at Windsor Park which is situated beside the predominantly Protestant Donegall Road and Village areas of Belfast. The ground is also home to Linfield, the senior club with the most vocal loyalist following. Both because of its location and also its association with a particular club, Windsor Park has always been regarded by nationalists as alien territory. In addition, some fans of Northern Ireland and Linfield have intended it to be so. For many years, the slogan—Taigs[4] Keep Out—which had been painted on a wall close to the stadium represented a sinister warning that Catholics were not welcome at Windsor Park unless, ironically, they had arrived to play for Northern Ireland or, as is increasingly likely today, for Linfield. The message is clear. This is a Protestant place for a Protestant people and Catholics require special dispensation to be there. Indeed, for some Linfield supporters the stadium's symbolic meaning is altered not only by the presence of Catholics but even by the arrival of rural Protestants for international matches. The identification of Protestant Ulster with urban Belfast and its heavy engineering and shipyards appears threatened by the inhabitants of a related but different landscape. The fact that Linfield receives considerable support from outside the city, however, weakens the impact of this sense of a divided Protestant identity.

We are the (loyal) people!

These various observations concerning soccer and territory are particularly relevant to the experience of young Protestant males as they seek to come to terms with the diminished status of the Protestant working class. Unemployed, socially marginalised and with deep-seated fears about the future of Northern Ireland as a separate entity, they look for channels through which to express their loyalist identity and, as a result, to restore their self-esteem. One such vehicle, as Bell observes, are the 'Kick the Pope' bands which accompany Orange marches:

> The bands and their parades seem to provide for the dispossessed Loyalist youth of Ulster a sectarian habitus within which their generational concerns with communal identity and with winning public space become fused with the focal concerns with territoriality and ethnic solidarity
>
> (Bell, 1990, p. 100).

The political strength of Ulster loyalism historically has been its identification with a state which has been able to impose territorial boundaries, directly or indirectly, while being able to afford a relatively relaxed attitude to boundaries within the British Isles (Shirlow and McGovern, 1997). In the past 30 years, this state has been able to enforce a form of effective territorial control in the face of sustained armed resistance. But, Ulster Protestant ideology has an additional myth of siege which implies a contested sense of domicile, which cannot be shared with other British citizens but which also fails to find an exclusive 'homeland' in Northern Ireland.

Supporting a particular 'Protestant' soccer club, such as Linfield and Glentoran, who play at the Oval close to the shipyards in east Belfast, or the Northern Ireland team, provides a similar kind of outlet to that offered by membership of a marching band and soccer stadia offer a context for the celebration of a wider culture (Bairner, 1997). Wearing the colours and singing the songs, young men avail themselves of the opportunity to exhibit their sense of what it means to be Ulster Protestants. Thus, they sing about being up to their knees in Fenian[5] blood or chant the names of loyalist paramilitary organisations in what are amongst the few public spaces where such behaviour is possible (Bairner, 1997).

The identity of most of these soccer fans takes the form of a secular, non-Christian Protestantism, described by Gillespie and his fellow researchers as "a mixture of selective theological dogma, anti-Catholicism and pragmatic loyalism" (Gillespie *et al.*, 1992, p. 135). Despite the lack of religiosity, the commitment of these fans to their native Ulster is undeniable. Less certain, however, is their understanding of Ulster as a landscape.

As Graham (1997) has argued, the territorial definition which has traditionally been proposed by unionists has been essentially negative, with the place being understood not for what it is but rather in terms of what unionists do not wish it to be, namely a part of Ireland. For Graham, therefore,

> Unionism occupies not so much 'a place apart' as 'no place', a failure of legitimation which ensures that it is an ideology which commands little or no external support
>
> (Graham, 1997, p. 40).

But soccer grounds are real places and, in addition, most of the venues for senior soccer in the province are Protestant places, hence their role in identity formation. The imagined community of Ulster as a Protestant place becomes more real for young loyalists as they express their affiliation at Windsor Park or the Oval and, in so doing, struggle

> to resolve at the level of the imaginary, the real contradictions confronting the Protestant working-class in contemporary Northern Ireland
>
> (Bell, 1990, p. 23).

In their own way, by supporting certain soccer teams, these young fans are attempting to defend their home territory and those traditions which make it what it is or what they imagine it to be. This reactive defensiveness is part of a more general 'siege mentality' which afflicts the unionist population and which derives from a sense that everything around them is undergoing fundamental and irrevocable change. Thus, theirs is a form of cultural resistance which remains linked to a parental tradition. The old industries have gone and along with them the sense of community which they helped to create. Political developments are all construed as concessions to the nationalist minority. Through all of this, however, the leading soccer clubs and the Northern Ireland national team have remained constant elements in Protestant working-class culture, although even they are not immune to the forces of change. The presence of Catholic players, including ones recruited from the Irish Republic, in the Linfield team is a relatively novel phenomenon. Combined with the movement of Protestants from inner-city Belfast and the growing number of Saturday afternoon distractions which have affected soccer crowds throughout Ireland and beyond, this has clearly had some impact on attendances. Similarly, the inclusion of Catholic players, or ones only tenuously linked to the province, in the Northern Ireland team does not meet with the approval of every loyalist. Overall, however, clubs like Linfield and Glentoran as well as the national team continue to provide a necessary focus for Protestant working-class identity. In this respect, they perform a function similar to that played in other, less overtly divided societies.

In this case, the blame for poor socioeconomic and/or cultural conditions has been laid at the feet of the 'other'—i.e. Catholics in Northern Ireland. Supporting particular soccer teams allows these fans to express their opposition to rival identities whilst celebrating their own. The places where they engage in these activities thus become quasi-religious sites, important in their own right but also as metaphors for the political territory which is regarded as being in need of defence. These stadia are, therefore, of vital importance in the production of certain identities and in the process of cultural resistance.

Conclusion

It is customary to acknowledge that most individuals possess a number of identities which normally co-exist quite peacefully but occasionally are the cause of internal emotional or spiritual conflict. Furthermore, it is undeniable that the formation of these multiple identities can be traced to a number of different sources. In this respect, for most women in Northern Ireland and even the overwhelming majority of those who belong to the Protestant working class, identification with particular football stadia and teams is largely irrelevant. However, as Kellner (1992) notes, identities are still relatively circumscribed, fixed and limited, despite the fact that the boundaries of possible identities are continually expanding. Indeed, in the context of deindustrialisation and growing unemployment, it can be argued that those men who are discussed in this paper have experienced, if anything, a diminution in terms of potential identities. As a result, it is scarcely surprising that many of them have turned for solace to those activities and places which are familiar to them and in which they feel comfortable and 'at home'. But, as their behaviour reveals, this is more than simply the pursuit of security in a safe environment.

Numerous attempts have been made to understand anti-social behaviour at soccer matches. This paper is unusual in trying to approach the subject in terms of the defence of traditional territory and cultures when these are being threatened and even eroded by larger forces, both specific and global. In such conditions, the soccer ground is more than simply a built environment which is defended by the fans. It represents a metaphor for a wider landscape which is also perceived to be under threat and in need of protection. This indicates that the soccer stadium has been invested with a symbolic value which far exceeds in importance its worth either as a place where sport can be played or as a piece of real estate which could be developed for financial profit. Attendance at soccer games in Northern Ireland as elsewhere is of course embedded in patterns of consumption. In opposition to those theorists, such as Baudrillard (1981), who would have us believe that the triumph of the sign represents the detachment of individuals from their own immediate material reality as opposed to one which has been conjured up in the realm of hyper-reality, the paper shows the extent to which attachment to symbolic space is intimately bound up with shifts in their wider socio-political environment. Indeed, it is for this very reason that the soccer stadium becomes a key site for reactive cultural resistance.

In making these claims about football fans and their relationship with their real and imagined spaces, the paper also endeavours to say something more general concerning the links between sport and the formation of reactive and, in some instances, reactionary identities as elements of cultural resistance. As the symbolic spaces, the soccer stadia are defended in such a way that the 'collective self' is transformed from a group of soccer fans into 'the people' and supporting a soccer team becomes part of a broader movement of cultural resistance against threats to 'the people' and all of its cherished places. The relevance of this conclusion extends far beyond Northern Ireland and into other spatial arenas within which ethno-sectarian conflict is produced and reproduced in the context of the territorial politics of sport.

Notwithstanding the immense political changes which have occurred in the wake of the paramilitary cease-fires and the search for a political settlement, it is evident that new institutional arrangements and non-violent forms of political contestation do not indicate the eradication of ethno-sectarian conflict. Indeed, the most sectarianised members of Linfield's support have vocally expressed their opposition to the 'Good Friday Agreement', the 'Stormont referendum' and the new assembly. Five summers of violence linked to ethnically centred conflicts around the issue of marching testify that the control of territory has remained a central pursuit of republicans and loyalists despite apparent political progress.

In the 1998–99 soccer season, due to alterations in Northern Ireland's political landscape, Linfield will, for the first time in over 20 years, play at Cliftonville's home ground. Whilst this will be interpreted by many as further evidence of political progress, the tensions surrounding this game and the security operation needed to facilitate it underline the reality of persisting sectarian antagonism. The re-establishment of this fixture may indicate a return to 'normality'. However, for many Linfield fans the return to Solitude will be interpreted as a reclaiming of a formerly Protestant area. Thus, somewhat ironically, the place-specific abnormality of Northern Irish society, despite political change, will be given an additional arena within which to operate.

Notes

1 Formed in 1884, the Gaelic Athletic Association is dedicated to the promotion of traditional Irish games and pastimes. At different times in its history, control of the Association has been contested by the various strands of Irish political nationalism. In general, however, it has succeeded in accommodating all forms of Irish national identity. However, its relationship with the game of soccer has been traditionally conflictual despite the fact that the global game also offers an arena in which Irish identity is reproduced.

2 As soccer is played widely by members of both communities, it is scarcely surprising that even those clubs with a predominantly Protestant following employ Catholic players, particularly given the pressures to succeed in the competitive world of semi-professional Irish League soccer. The employment of Catholic players has also been encouraged by certain influential individuals, government agencies, European Commission directives and political pressure from the US.

3 Unlike other major team games which were first played in areas of Ireland which are now part of the Irish Republic, soccer established itself amongst the predominantly Protestant working-class areas of Belfast and its surrounding environment. It was in this region, now part of Northern Ireland, that the Irish Football Association was established in 1880, whereas the organising bodies of most other sports were set up in Dublin. As a consequence following partition in 1921, soccer administrators in the newly established Irish Free State (later Irish Republic) decided that a separate ruling body was required. The resultant division in Irish soccer has remained to the present day.

4 Taig is a derogatory term used to describe Catholics. It is an Irish rendition of the Scottish term Tim.

5 Fenians is a derogatory term used to describe Catholics. It originates from the Irish name for warriors (Fianna) adopted by members of the 19th-century Irish Republican Brotherhood movement.

References

ANDERSON, J. and SHUTTLEWORTH, I. (1998) Sectarian demography, territoriality and policy in Northern Ireland, *Political Geography*, 17, pp. 187–208.

ARMSTRONG, G. & HARRIS, R. (1991) Football hooligans: theory and evidence, *Sociological Review*, 39, pp. 427–458.

BAIRNER, A. (1996) Sportive nationalism and nationalist politics: a comparative analysis of Scotland, the Republic of Ireland and Sweden, *Journal of Sport and Social Issues*, 20, pp. 314–334.

BAIRNER, A. (1997) 'Up to their knees'? Football, sectarianism, masculinity and Protestant working-class identity, in: P. SHIRLOW & M. McGOVERN (Eds) *Who Are 'The People'? Unionism, Protestantism and Loyalism in Northern Ireland*, pp. 95–113. London: Pluto Press.

BAIRNER, A. and SUGDEN, J. (1986) Observe the sons of Ulster: football and politics in Northern Ireland, in: A. TOMLINSON and G. WHANNEL (Eds) *Off the Ball: The Football World Cup*, pp. 146–157. London: Pluto Press.

BAIRNER, A. and SUGDEN, J. (Eds) (1998) *Sport in Divided Societies*. Aachen: Meyer & Meyer.

BAKER, D.G. (1990) *Race, Ethnicity and Power: A Comparative Study*. London: Routledge.

BALE, J. (1993) *Sport, Space and the City*. London: Routledge.

BALE, J. (1994) *Landscapes of Modern Sport*. Leicester: Leicester University Press.

BAUDRILLARD, J. (1981) *For a Critique of the Political Economy of the Sign*. St Louis, MI: Telos Press.

BECK, U., GIDDENS, A. and LASH, S. (1994) *Reflective Modernisation: Politics, Tradition and Aesthetics in the Modern Social Order*. Cambridge: Polity Press.

BELL, D. (1990) *Acts of Union: Youth Culture and Sectarianism in Northern Ireland*. London: Macmillan.

BOYLE, R. (1994) 'We are Celtic supporters . . .' Questions of football and identity in modern Scotland, in: R. GIULIANOTTI and J. WILLIAMS (Eds) *Game without Frontiers; Football, Identity and Modernity*, pp. 73–101. Aldershot: Arena.

CANTER, D., COMBER, M. and UZZELL, D. (1989) *Football in its Place: An Environmental Psychology of Football Grounds*. London: Routledge.

CLAYTON, P. (1996) *Enemies and Passing Friends*. London: Pluto Press.

CRONIN, M. (1994) Sport and a sense of Irishness, *Irish Studies Review*, 9, pp. 13–17.

CRONIN, M. (1996) Defenders of the nation? The Gaelic Athletic Association and Irish national identity, *Irish Political Studies*, 11, pp. 1–19.

DONNELLY, P. (1996) The local and the global: globalization in the sociology of sport, *Journal of Sport and Social Issues*, 20, pp. 239–257.

DUKE, V. & CROLLEY, L. (1996) *Football, Nationality and the State*. Harlow: Longman.

DUNNING, E., MURPHY, P. and WADDINGTON, I. (1991) Anthropological versus sociological approaches to the study of football hooliganism: some critical notes, *Sociological Review*, 39, pp. 459–478.

DUNNING, E., MURPHY, P. and WILLIAMS, J. (1988) *The Roots of Football Hooliganism*. London: Routledge.

GILLESPIE, N., LOVETT, T. and GARNER, W. (1992) *Youth Work and Working Class Youth Culture: Rules and Resistance in West Belfast*. Buckingham: Open University Press.

GIULIANOTTI, R., BONNEY, N. and HEPWORTH, M. (Eds) (1994) *Football, Violence and Social Identity*. London: Routledge.

GIULIANOTTI, R. and WILLIAMS, J. (Eds) (1994) *Game Without Frontiers: Football, Identity and Modernity*. Aldershot: Arena.

GIULIANOTTI, R. (1992) Scotland's tartan army in Italy: the case of the carnivalesque, *Sociological Review*, 39, pp. 503–527.

GRAHAM, B. (1994) No place of the mind: contested Protestant representations of Ulster, *Ecumene*, 1, pp. 257–281.

GRAHAM, B. (1997) Ulster: a representation of place yet to be imagined, in: P. SHIRLOW and M. MCGOVERN (Eds) *Who Are 'The People'? Unionism, Protestantism and Loyalism in Northern Ireland*, pp. 34–54. London: Pluto Press.

HARGREAVES, J. (1992) Olympism and nationalism: some preliminary consideration, *International Review for the Sociology of Sport*, 27, pp. 119–137.

HAYNES, R. (1995) *The Football Imagination: The Rise of Football Fanzine Culture*. Aldershot: Arena.

HOBERMAN, J. (1986) *Sport and Political Ideology*. London: Heinemann.

HOLMES, M. (1994) Symbols of national identity and sport: the case of the Irish football team, *Irish Political Studies*, 9, pp. 81–98.

INGHAM, R. (Ed.) (1978) *Football Hooliganism: The Wider Context*. London: Inter-Action Imprint.

JARVIE, G. (1993) Sport, nationalism and cultural identity, in: L. ALLISON (Ed.) *The Changing Politics of Sport*, pp. 58–83. Manchester: Manchester University Press.

JENKINS, R. (1994) Rethinking ethnicity: identity, categorisation and power, *Ethnic and Racial Studies*, 17, pp. 199–231.

JONES, R. and MOORE, P. (1994) 'He only has eyes for Poms': soccer, ethnicity and locality in Perth, in: J. O'HARA (Ed.) *Ethnicity and Soccer in Australia*, Campbelltown, NSW: Australian Society for Sports History.

JONES, S.G. (1988) *Sport, Politics and the Working Class: Organised Labour and Sport in Inter-War Britain*. Manchester: Manchester University Press.

KELLAS, J.G. (1991) *The Politics of Nationalism and Ethnicity*. Basingstoke: Macmillan.

KELLNER, D. (1992) Popular culture and the construction of postmodern identities, in: S. LASH and J. FRIEDMAN (Eds) *Modernity and Identity*, pp. 141–171. Oxford: Blackwell.

KERR, J.H. (1994) *Understanding Soccer Hooliganism*. Buckingham: Open University Press.

MACCLANCY, J. (1996) Sport, identity and ethnicity, in: J. MACCLANCY (Ed.) *Sport, Identity and Ethnicity*, pp. 1–20. Oxford: Berg.

MAGUIRE, J. (1994) Sport, identity politics, and globalization: diminishing contrasts and increasing varieties, *Sociology of Sport Journal*, 11, pp. 398–427.

MANDLE, W.F. (1987) *The Gaelic Athletic Association and Irish Nationalist Politics 1884–1924*. London: Christopher Helm.

PEARTON, R. (1986) Violence in sport and the special case of soccer hooliganism in the United Kingdom, in: C.R. REES and A. W. MIRACLE (Eds) *Sport and Social Theory*, pp. 67–83. Champaign, IL: Human Kinetics Publishers.

PILE, S. and KEITH, M. (Eds) (1997) *Geographies of Resistance*. London: Routledge.

REDHEAD, S. (1993) *The Passion and the Fashion: Football Fandom and the New Europe*. Aldershot: Avebury.

ROSEBERRY, W. (1989) *Anthropologies and Histories*. New Brunswick, NJ: Rutgers University.

SHIRLOW, P. and MCGOVERN, M. (1996) Sectarianism, socio-economic competition and the political economy of Ulster loyalism, *Antipode*, 21, pp. 399–432.

SHIRLOW, P. and MCGOVERN, M. (Eds) (1997) *Who Are 'The People'? Unionism, Protestantism and Loyalism in Northern Ireland*. London: Pluto Press.

SHIRLOW, P. and MCGOVERN, M. (1998) Language, discourse and dialogue: Sinn Fein and the Irish peace process, *Political Geography*, 17, pp. 171–186.

SPRADLEY, P. and MCCURDY, D.W. (1987) *Conformity and Conflict: Readings in Cultural Anthropology*. Boston: Little, Brown and Company.

SUGDEN, J. and BAIRNER, A. (1993) *Sport, Sectarianism and Society in a Divided Ireland*. Leicester: Leicester University Press.

SUGDEN, J. and BAIRNER, A. (1994) Ireland and the World Cup: 'Two teams in Ireland, there's only two teams in Ireland', In: J. SUGDEN and A. TOMLINSON (Eds) *Hosts and Champions: Soccer Cultures, National Identities and the USA World Cup*, pp. 119–139. Aldershot: Arena.

SUGDEN, J. and HARVIE, S. (1995) *Sport and Community Relations in Northern Ireland*. Colernine: Centre for the Study of Conflict, University of Ulster.

TAYLOR, I. (1982) On the sports-violence question: soccer hooliganism revisited, in: J. HARGREAVES (Ed.) *Sport, Culture and Ideology*, pp. 152–196. London: Routledge.

THRIFT, N. and FORBES, D. (1983) A landscape with figures: political geography with human conflict, *Political Geography Quarterly*, 2, pp. 247–263.

WERBNER, P. (1996) 'Our blood is green': cricket, identity and social empowerment among British Pakistanis, in: J. MACCLANCY (Ed.) *Sport, Identity and Ethnicity*, pp. 87–111. Oxford: Berg.

WILLIAMS, J., DUNNING, E. and MURPHY, P. (1989) *Hooligans Abroad*. London: Routledge.

Part 14

SPORT AND GENDER POWER

47

TAKING MEN ON AT
THEIR GAMES

Jennifer Hargreaves

Source: *Marxism Today* 28(8) (1984): 17–21.

'*I personally am against the participation of women in public competitions . . . At the Olympic Games their primary role should be like in the ancient tournaments – the crowning of the (male) victors with laurels.*'[1]

These are the words of Pierre de Coubertin who founded the modern Olympics in 1896 and was the most powerful member of the central decision making authority of the Olympic Games, the International Olympic Committee (IOC) for over 30 years. De Coubertin was well known for his misogyny and, until his death in 1937, he was intransigent in his opposition to women's sport. It was, he stated, against the 'laws of nature'[2] and 'the most unaesthetic sight human eyes could contemplate'.[3] 'The Olympic Games', he declared, 'must be reserved for men' for the 'solemn and periodic exaltation of male athleticism' with 'female applause as reward'.[4]

De Coubertin's Olympic model was a model of male sport which explicitly excluded women and which was an unambiguous celebration of male supremacy and physical prowess. In the first place, his passion and energy to institute a modern Olympics derived from his desire to reinvigorate the young men of France after his country's defeat in 1870 in the Franco-Prussian war. His plan was rooted in the idealisation of ancient Greek Olympism together with his admiration of the cult of athleticism in English public schools. In both these contexts, the symbolic focus of male power was the male athlete.

De Coubertin was not exceptional for a man of his time with an aristocratic background in believing that male superiority was in 'the natural order of things' – that differences between men and women were biologically determined and hence immutable. 'The eternal role of women in this world', he said, 'is to be a companion of the male and the mother of the family'[5] and, by the same argument, he believed that women were unsuited, because of their innate physical and emotional characteristics, for the Olympic sphere.

Olympic sport was therefore, from the start, a contested zone, between men and women who, like de Coubertin, espoused dominant reactionary ideas about gender divisions, and those men and women who held more liberal views and struggled to advance women's participation in sport.

Elitist traditions

Class, as well as sex, was a fundamental dimension of the development of modern Olympism. De Coubertin had connections with members of the European nobility who were interested in sport and the IOC had strong aristocratic associations from the time of its inauguration. It was composed of a body of upper-class Anglo-Saxon men, and almost every athlete who competed in the first Olympics was rich and leisured. Members of the British team were predominantly public school Oxbridge athletes, and the American team was composed of wealthy young men from Harvard and Princeton. De Coubertin identified Olympism as 'an elite', but he went on to say, 'whose origin is completely egalitarian, since it is determined only by the bodily superiority of the individual and his muscular possibilities'. Such expressions of 'egalitarianism' have provided a basic tenet of Olympism which is very misleading. The term 'elite' is used to signify 'the best', but more realistically elitism in the Olympics carries implications of exclusiveness, exploitation and the exercise of power and privilege. From the start, the modern Olympics were an example of institutionalised sexism and class domination – a conservatising force which made an indelible mark on Olympic development in the twentieth century and undoubtedly hindered the growth of women's participation. However, the original model of Olympic sport was not inviolable – it encapsulated demands for change as well as resistance to them.

The first Olympics, in Greece in 1896, exemplified sport as a bastion of bourgeois male privilege, and the single unofficial female competitor who 'crashed' the marathon – a Greek woman called Melpomene – symbolised the efforts of women to overcome male dominance. In 1908 women were allowed for the first time to take part officially in Olympic competition and 36 women competed in lawn tennis, archery, figure skating and yachting, making up 1.75% of the total number of participants. There were, by comparison, 2,023 men comprising 98.25% of all those taking part. In 1912 archery was withdrawn and two swimming events and one diving event were added to the women's Olympic programme. There has been a gradual expansion of Olympic sport for women since that time, but every advance has been the result of struggle and protest. It was not until 1928, immediately after de Coubertin had resigned as president of the IOC, and 32 years after the first modern Olympic Games, that women's track and field athletics – the major Olympic sports – had their Olympic debut.

The stage has now been reached where there are Olympic events for women in a wide range of sports and the marathon is an official event in the women's programme of the 1984 Los Angeles Olympics, for the first time. It would seem, therefore, that the struggle for Olympic equivalence with men is over, but a closer look would reveal that this is far from true. Females are barred from all events in eight out of the 27 Olympic sports – the biathlon, bobsleigh, boxing, ice hockey, judo, soccer, weight-lifting and wrestling. In addition, there are no athletic events for women in the 5,000 metre and 10,000 metre runs, or in the pole vault, triple jump and hammer events. Women also have fewer events to choose from in rowing, basketball, canoeing, fencing, and handball and are barred from water polo. There are 168 all-male Olympic events, 73 all-female events and 15 mixed events. In all, women comprise only 20% of all competitors in the summer and winter Olympics.

Continuing restrictions

Those people who have been involved in promoting the emancipation of women's sport throughout the world have, by and large, been excluded from positions of power in the Olympic movement where there has been paranoid hostility to an increase in female participation. The sex and class composition of the administrative and decision-making bodies of Olympic sport has not fundamentally changed since de Coubertin's days. The IOC remained an elite and exclusively male body for almost nine decades and even now its membership is composed of 86 men and only three women. The influences of the aristocrat and the 'amateur gentleman' have always been dominant in the National Olympic Committees as well, and in the International Federations of Sport which have the monopoly of power to propose the introduction of new Olympic events. Even the Federation of International Gymnastics, representing the major Olympic sport for women today, is an almost exclusively male body.

The opposition to women's sport from these bodies has never been total – for example, from the time of his inauguration as President of the IOC in 1972, Lord Killanin campaigned, against vigorous opposition, to get a woman elected to the IOC – it took nine years. The IOC and its affiliated associations remain predominantly elitist and undemocratic – a 'world of men' infiltrated by a tiny number of women. The idea that liberal fair-minded men can be persuaded to give women 'what they want' may be the case, but it is a position that reproduces the power relations between the sexes and reinforces the image of man as 'superior and benevolant'; in contrast to the fragile image of the 'child woman'. Women need direct power in the Olympics, sharing equally with men the decision-making procedures. Since 1952 with the entry of the Soviet Union into the Olympics, other vested interests, in particular nationalism, have affected IOC decisions and made the balance of power more complex. Even so, men from Eastern bloc countries where the expansion of women's sport is part of the explicit national sporting ideology are making decisions on behalf of women. It has, ironically, been the men from Eastern bloc countries who have specifically opposed women's entry into long-distance running events, including the marathon.

The most consistent justification for opposition to women's increased participation has been articulated in terms of female biology. The nineteenth-century stereotyped image of women as physically limited by comparison with men has been hard to shift. When it became clear in the 1930s that organised sport for women in Europe and North America had developed a momentum that seemed unstoppable, the focus of opposition changed from the attempt to eliminate Olympic sport for women altogether to an endeavour to limit participation to 'female-appropriate' sports and events. After the Berlin Olympics, Avery Brundage made one of his typically reactionary and explicitly sexist comments when he said, 'I am fed up to the ears with women as track and field competitors . . . her charms sink to less than zero. As swimmers and divers, girls are beautiful and adroit, as they are ineffective and unpleasing on the track'.[6] As President of the IOC in 1949, he again articulated the establishment position, 'I think women's events should be confined to those appropriate to women; swimming, tennis, figure skating and fencing, but certainly not shot-putting'.[7] In 1966 the IOC attempted, unsuccessfully, to eliminate the women's shot-put and discus events because 'often the feminine self-image is badly mutilated when women perform in these two events'.

Sex-role stereotyping of this sort may seem out-of-date in view of the increased numbers of women in more and more sports and the outstanding successes of many women in top-class competitions. It has, nonetheless, remained an integral feature of Olympic sport and has provided the greatest limitation to women's advancement, in particular, in the traditional male sports and events that delebrate masculinity. In 1978, the IOC rejected a proposal to include a 3,000 metre event for women in the Moscow Olympics because they said it was, 'a little strenuous for women' and would adversely affect their metabolism. This was an unequivocally reactionary position in view of the exceptional achievements of women in long distance running events outside the Olympic sphere and a reversal of the decision was gained for this year. The 3,000 metre run is on the programme for the first time, together with the marathon, but the struggle to get the 5,000m and the 10,000m runs on the programme continues.

Women are barred from the triple jump, pole vault and boxing because it remains a popular conception that women's reproductive systems are vulnerable to injury in these sports. It is, however, not generally understood that there are no medical or physiological reasons intrinsic to women which should prevent them, any more than men, from participation. The female reproductive organs are firmly positioned and thoroughly protected inside the body cavity and are probably less susceptible to injury than those of men. And, of course, women, like men, can wear protective apparatus to cover vulnerable parts – they have the same, not a greater, potential than men for injury. The ethics of arguments to ban dangerous sports such as boxing are as appropriate to men as they are to women.

Women's bodies

It is also a popular idea that the uniquely female processes of menstruation, pregnancy and childbirth will adversely affect women's sporting achievements and that, conversely, women's strenuous sports will impair those functions. It is not common knowledge that Olympic medals have been won and Olympic records shattered by female athletes at all phases of the menstrual cycle, and that during early pregnancy, and shortly after childbirth, women have competed successfully in Olympic sport. Fanny Blankers-Koehn, nicknamed 'the flying Dutch housewife', provides one of the best-known examples that supreme athletic ability is not incompatible with normal procreative functioning. In 1948, she won four Olympic medals when she was pregnant and then as a mother went on to set four world records. Some women suffer a reduction in the number of periods during severe training, and research undertaken in Denmark this year shows that 50% of women in training suffered a loss of menstruation.[8] Research has also shown that normal menstruation resumes when intense exercise ceases and with no detrimental effects on fertility. Ingrid Kristiansen, one of the favourites for this year's Olympic marathon, took part in the world cross-country championships last year unaware that she was pregnant at the time. Later, this year, when her son was eight months old, she was the first woman to complete the London marathon in a time close to the world record. Regular exercise has a beneficial effect on female metabolism and the available evidence shows that the experience of premenstrual tension, painful periods and lethargy during menstruation are less common among women who undertake regular exercise. The added bonus is that labour and delivery are generally less complicated for trained athletes.

By their increased rates of participation and improved performances in high level competition, women are themselves changing misleading ideas and dispelling myths about female biology and sporting potential. Although women are on average slower and less powerful than men, it does not follow that biological differences between the sexes should impose restrictions on women's participation, or that events demanding speed and power are only suited to men. Recent research with trained athletes indicates that the superior strength of men is most marked in the arm and shoulder regions but is minimal in the legs. When undergoing similar training programmes women are developing leg strength comparable to their male counterparts and it is estimated that the thigh muscles are stronger in women than men, relative to body size.[9]

There is growing evidence that women may be better suited than men to endurance events because they can avoid fatigue over long periods more efficiently. In long distance running, walking, cycling, sailing, swimming, ice-skating, roller-skating, canoeing and skiing, the trend towards equivalence with, and superiority over, men is most dramatic. There is conjecture that by the year 2000, women will be pre-eminent in many long distance and endurance events.[10] Ironically, the history of women in those sports for which they appear to be best suited has been brief because they have often been the ones where women have encountered the fiercest opposition. Women have been involved in the longer distance road running and track events for little more than a decade and in relatively small numbers in North America and Western Europe. Many of these events are still unofficial competitions and not on the Olympic programme. Above all, the inclusion of the marathon in this year's Olympics is a great symbolic victory for women and the result of a long and bitter battle against mythical past accounts of female inferiority.

Sexual identity

It is paradoxical that at the same time that women who are successful in Olympic sport are challenging traditional sporting identities, they still have to accommodate to the idea that sports may defeminize them and they face insinuations about their sexuality, or are treated as sexual objects for male voyeurism. The Czechoslovak runner, Jarmila Kratochvilova, has been castigated in the western press for her supposed masculinity, whereas descriptions of Mary Decker as the stereotypical 'all female' athlete signify male desire:

> (Mary) Decker is the all-American female retort to the heavy artillery of Eastern Europe which, before she came along, blasted all before it in the women's field. She has become sporting America's favourite daughter; not just a little Mary Decker, hammer of the sickles, but also as pretty, sexy Mary Decker who, in this Amazonian world, wears make-up on the track and shaves her legs . . . In the 3,000 and then the 1500 metres, Decker simply whipped those hard-faced East Europeans with the ambiguous biceps.[11]

The tabloid series *Olympic Golden Girls* depicts the sexual attractiveness of our potential medal winners as they pose erotically, colluding in the 'femininity game'. 'Shirley Strong', we read, 'will jump for joy if she lands an Olympic gold medal',[12] and 'Sonia Legs it for Glory' as she 'shows off those lovely talents that could make her a Golden Girl – the fastest female legs in the land'.[13]

Whereas the sexuality of the nineteenth-century sportswomen tended to be de-emphasised or repressed, it would appear that the sexuality of today's successful Olympic sportswomen in systematically promoted in the public eye. The ideal type Olympians have been transformed into glamour girls – svelte and sexy – whereas the athletes who fail to conform to the desirable body shape are labelled as 'pseudo-men' – unfeminine, gay or butch. What has remained constant is that the sporting prowess of women competitors is treated, by implication, in a less serious fashion than their sexuality – a position exemplified by sex investigations of female athletes.

The inclusion for the first time this year of two new exclusively female Olympic sports – rhythmic gymnastics and synchronised swimming – has been greeted as a victory, but we should consider whether they will do anything to break down the traditional, gender-based assumptions about sport.

Differences between nations

So far, generalisations have been made implying that women's Olympic sport has a homogeneous character. In one sense, this is true – Olympic sport has an international character which transcends national differences and political interests. Athletes from the East and the West are bound up in its nationalist imperatives, its competitive ethos and its history of male dominance as if it had a 'life of its own'. However, factors affecting women's participation have not been uniform for women from different nations or even for women from one nation.

The advancement of female Olympic competition is a manifestation of economic expansion and is most pronounced in societies with centrally planned economies and where women are active members of the labour force. The increased participation of women in advanced industrialised countries in the East and the West has been notable. In the socialist countries as much official encouragement is given to sport for women as is given to sport for men and more attention is focused upon élite female sport than in the West. The Soviet and GDR teams are composed of a higher proportion of female competitors than western teams and East German women win a higher percentage of medals than East German men. However, non-Olympic sports tend to be poorly developed in the socialist countries and special attention is given to those sports and events where medals can be won. Soviet women have been running marathons only since its inclusion in the Los Angeles Olympics was announced whereas western women have been struggling for recognition for long distance events for the past two decades.

In the West, there is still considerable ideological pressure against sportswomen and other factors such as class and race are significant. In Britain, a lower percentage of women participate in sport than in any other country of similar economic status, except Italy, and of those, there is a low percentage of working class participation and some sports are still, unambiguously, class specific. In no way is women's sport democratised as it is in the Eastern bloc and the Olympic team is weighted in favour of middle class women and almost exclusively in, for example, equestrian events.

It is difficult to generalize about the factors inhibiting women's sporting participation on a global scale. They are culturally specific and related to the economic and political systems of different nation-states. Religion tends to be a conservatising influence but the attitudes to sport of, for example, the Protestant, Catholic, Greek Orthodox and Moslem churches vary. The participation of women from developing and Third World countries and repressive regimes is minimal. The commonsense idea that the Olympics are a symbol of women's emancipation in sport throughout the world, and by extension women's wider participation in contemporary societies should, therefore, be resisted.

Drugs and the Olympics

There is another issue, however, which must also be faced – namely, the character of Olympic competition. For those women who are competing in top-level sport, the Olympics have become an increasingly political phenomenon and one which incorporates excesses and corruption.

The 1936 Berlin Games set a precedent in the history of modern Olympism by their blatant use as a forum for Nazi propaganda. Though less extreme, the none the less obvious politicisation of the Olympics since the war has influenced the expansion of Olympic sport for women. Olympic competition intensifies patriotism, and the success of the athletes reflects the apparent success of the social and political arrangements of their nation states. The link between female participation and sporting nationalism has occurred with the appearance of an additional 70% female athletes since the war and has been a pronounced feature of the Olympics since the re-entry of the Soviets into Olympic competition in 1952 which spear-headed the fierce competition between Eastern and Western bloc countries and the promotion of Olympic sportswomen as medal collectors. In 1968 when the GDR entered the Games, the pre-eminence of women from socialist countries strengthened further the political dynamic of female sport. Within ten years, East German women dominated the rest of the world in athletics, swimming, gymnastics and rowing, and held 86% of world records in the 14 standard track and field events.

The emphasis on success, the exaltation of records and the cult of champions are features common to female sport in East and West. Because the peak age of performance for many female sports is during adolescence, the early specialisation, intense training, fierce competition and inevitable high wastage occurs at a very young age. The moral implications of manipulating children in such a way are serious. 'Battered child athletes' is the term employed in the US to describe those children who are psychologically damaged and physically injured by pressure that parents, teachers and coaches are putting on them to become sports superstars. Adults are pushing girls at a younger and younger age into gymnastics, swimming, tennis, ice-skating and even marathon running. 'Over use injuries' in all these sports are increasingly commonplace and there is no proper preventive screening scheme available.[14]

In gymnastics, for example, girls from a very young age are regularly subjected to stress and danger in order to increase the level of technical skill and spectacle: the cost of Olympic sport to a regular percentage of armies of 'child-woman' gymnasts is permanent musculo-skeletal damage, paralysis and even death. Inevitably female Olympic competitors of all ages are impelled to take drugs in order to meet the demands of top-level competition. The 'break' hormone is administered to young female gymnasts in order to delay puberty so that they can remain slight, and underdeveloped on the hips and breasts: it is not known if there are any harmful long term effects from the use of this drug. The *Underground Steroid Handbook for Men and Women* is available in California for prospective Olympic medallists at Los Angeles and describes the side-effects such as growth of the beard and lowering of the voice in women.[15] Pure testosterone is used also in order to artificially boost strength; it develops bulky muscles, stimulates hair growth, suppresses menstruation and it can lead to irreversible sterility. The latest drug in evidence for the 1984 Olympics is the Growth Hormone: when administered it is possible to gain pounds of muscle, but the side effects are irreversible – it may elongate your chin, feet or hands, produce diabetes in teenagers and heart attacks in adults.[16]

These horror drugs expose the hypocrisy and infectious madness inherent in Olympic sport. The Los Angeles Games will not only be 'an expression of American hype and razamatazz' but a 'Mickey Mouse' Olympics[17] boycotted by 12 nations including the Soviet Union and GDR. Strangely, the absence of the East-West confrontation seems in no way to have detracted from the appeal to individuals of Olympic competition. Zola Budd was prepared to leave her homeland to be an Olympic athlete. She has secured a place in the British Olympic team – a political decision reflecting an ideology of competitive individualism. One might ponder upon the connection between the Zola Budd affair and the aspirations of black sportswomen in apartheid South Africa, and the position of British Olympic hopefuls.

Top-level sportswomen are, in the same way as men, sucked into a competitive system in which they are increasingly expected to perform like machines and the Olympic imperative, 'Citius, Altius, Fortius', must, in its present form, reduce their capacity for physical pleasure. However, it would be exaggerated to claim that all female competitors are on a harsh drug regime or have retreated into unthinking expressions of nationalism and non-communication. At the same time as there is growing hypocrisy from those seduced by ideas of Olympic power, glory and profit, there are others including increasing numbers of women from East and West, who are working to eliminate the worst excesses and corruptions of Olympic sport.

Notes

1 Pierre de Coubertin 'Forty years of Olympism: 1894–1934', quoted in *Women At The Olympic Games* Wingate Monograph Series No 7, the Wingate Institute for Physical Education and Sport Netanya (Israel) 1979 p 13.
2 Quoted in *ibid* p 12.
3 *Ibid.*
4 Pierre de Coubertin, quoted in Ellen Gerber et al, *The American Woman in Sport* Addison Wesley NY 1974 pp 137–138.
5 Quoted in 'Women At The Olympic Games' *op cit.*
6 Avery Brundage quoted in *ibid* p 38.
7 *Ibid.*
8 *Guardian*, 4/7/84 p 8.
9 K F Dyer *Catching Up The Men* Junction Books London 1982.
10 *Ibid.*
11 Peter Freedman 'The Fastest Painted Lady in the World' *Sunday Times* 27/5/84.
12 *News of the World* 22/4/84.
13 *News of the World* 29/4/84.
14 Tony Wilkinson 'Marathon Mentality – the risks sportsmen run' *The Listener* 31/5/84 p 2.
15 *Ibid* p 3.
16 *Ibid.*
17 *Observer* 8/7/84.

48

THE RUGBY FOOTBALL CLUB AS A TYPE OF "MALE PRESERVE"

Some sociological notes

Kenneth G. Sheard and Eric G. Dunning

Source: *International Review of Sport Sociology* 8 (1973): 5–21.

Sport is an area of social life which is rich in opportunities for sociological research. So far, however, little work of a genuinely sociological character has been carried out into the problems which it raises.[1] This, it seems to us, is particularly the case as far as the subcultures which arise in connection with sport are concerned. The present paper is an attempt – a preliminary one – to remedy that deficiency. It is the study, not of a sport *per se*, but of the development, functions and subsequent modification of the subculture which has grown up around it.

The sport in question is Rugby Union football. In Britain, players of this sport have gained a reputation for regularly violating a number of taboos, especially those regarding violence, physical contact, nakedness, obscenity, drunkenness, and the treatment of property.[2] Taboo-breaking of this kind tends to take a highly ritualized form. It has come to form an integral part of the subculture that has grown up around the rugby game. One of its functions is that of providing an avenue of satisfaction for the players in addition to the game itself. However, much of the behaviour it involves offends against the "everyday" standards of the upper and middle classes, the social strata to which rugby players mainly belong. It also runs counter to the standards of *mens sana in corpore sano* which have become so firmly embedded in sports ideology though not, in Britain at least, to the same extent in sporting practice. It would be interesting to see whether the type of sports subculture we are about to describe is a uniquely British phenomenon or whether there are counterparts in other countries as well.

Rugby football began to become established in Britain as a game for upper and middle class adults in the years between 1850 and 1870. It seems likely that it grew in popularity in that period largely on account of its comparative roughness and the strenuous physical exertion it involved. It was a game which provided the young man with the opportunity to engage in vigorous physical activity, an opportunity which was increasingly denied him in other fields, particularly that of work. More often than not, his occupation was sedentary, involving mental rather than physical effort. The running entailed in playing rugby enabled him to experience that pleasure which tends to accompany "motility" in any activity which is voluntarily undertaken.[3] At the same time, the competitive rough and tumble of the game enabled him to derive pleasure from the excitement of an organized mock battle and permitted him to measure up better to traditional ideals of masculinity than his everyday occupation. This latter aspect was probably crucial. The fact that the English concept of the "gentleman" is derived, in part, from the ethos of an elite with military roots is probably of some significance with respect to the development of these ideals. Despite the expansion of the empire, the latter half of the nineteenth century witnessed a greater growth of non-military occupations for the middle and upper classes than had occurred in any previous stage in the development of British society. Under the urban-industrial conditions that were coming increasingly to prevail, it became more and more difficult for traditional upper and middle class norms of masculinity to find expression in the normal run of everyday life, and rugby football began to emerge, not without considerable conflict, as one of the principal social enclaves where they could be legitimately expressed.

This analysis may provide the beginnings of an explanation of why, in the second half of the nineteenth century, young adult males from the middle and upper classes should have begun in considerable numbers to take up a rough and energetic contact sport. It does not, however, explain the emergence of those aspects of the rugby subculture which developed off the field of play. The game, came, as we have seen, to embrace a customary disrespect for taboos regarding nakedness. These taboos have to be relaxed to some extent in any activity where a communal dressing room forms the location where the "actors" change from their everyday clothes. What is noticeable about rugby football, however, is the fact that these taboos are contravened and not simply relaxed. The male "strip-tease" became a firmly institutionalized part of the rugby subculture and the singing of a song entitled "the Zulu Warrior" became the traditional signal for a ritualistic strip by a member of the group. This ritual is usually enacted after the match, either in the clubhouse bar or, if the team has been playing away, on the coach which is carrying the players home. Initiation ceremonies also became customary on such occasions. In the course of such ceremonies, the initiate is stripped – often forcibly – and his body, especially his genitals, defiled with shoe polish and vaseline. Drinking to excess also came to be firmly embedded in the rugby club tradition. While drunk, the players sing obscene songs which involve, as a central theme, the mocking, objectification and defilement of

158

women and homosexuals. Articles of property are often either stolen or wantonly destroyed. Perhaps the most striking aspect of this pattern, however, is the fact that it became accepted as normal for members of this group by the rest of society. It did not come to be regarded as either criminal or deviant but, on the contrary, to be condoned as evidence of excusable "high spirits". As long as they confine it largely to the club-house, the players are allowed to behave with impunity in a manner which would bring immediate condemnation and punishment were it to occur among other social strata or even among members of the upper and middle classes in a different social setting. Little effort is made to bring their behaviour into line with the dominant social standards. As far as one can tell, it is even accorded a large measure of tolerance in such public places as the carriages of railway trains and the bars of hotels. It is certainly not condemned as "hooliganism" or regarded as a "social problem" as has recently occurred with respect to the behaviour of those working class youths who smash the light bulbs, tear the seats and defile the lavatories of "football specials".[4]

Rugby Union footballers probably owe this privileged treatment mainly to historical association of their game with the public schools. It originally developed, as its name suggests, at Rugby, which became a leading public school in the early part of the nineteenth century. It began to spread from Rugby during the 1840's and 50's initially to other public schools which had taken that school as their model,[5] later to the universities of Oxford and Cambridge. During most of the second half of the nineteenth century, the game could only be learned in these elite schools and universities. It was seldom adopted by those not introduced to it in such a social setting.[6] Indeed, the earliest adult clubs were founded mainly by "old boys" from the public schools. Players were unambiguously identified as members of the national ruling elite and the game itself came to be regarded as an elite leisure activity. It is unlikely that members of the upper and middle classes would have branded their own sons as delinquents. Members of the lower classes, moreover, were not sufficiently powerful either to label or to punish behaviour of this kind, whatever their feelings about it may have been.

The social status of Rugby Union players and the related class connotations which became attached to the game may help to explain why players were able to flaunt social conventions without fear of punishment but they cannot adequately explain the pressures – whether of a social or a psychological character – which drove young adult males from the middle and upper classes, most of them in their twenties and early thirties, towards such violation of taboos. Nor can they explain why such men should have wanted to break specifically the taboos referred to above. In order to approach such aspects of the problem, it is useful to conceptualize the rugby club as a kind of "male preserve" which came to function as a social setting for the expression, often in an extreme form, of the then current norms of masculinity.

Ned Polsky, in his study of "poolrooms" in the United States, has shown how the poolroom in that country – the "billiard hall" – came to act as an "escape hatch from the world of feminine values".[7] He points out that the open frontier once performed this function but that, with the closure of the frontier and increasing urbanization, the poolroom gradually became the principal refuge for American men who wanted to "curse, spit tobacco, fight freely, dress sloppily, gamble heavily, get drunk, whore around". His main concern was to explain why the poolroom has declined in popularity in recent years. He dismissed several popular explanations in favour of his own which centres on the hypothesis that poolrooms came to form the keystone of a heterosexual but all-male subculture. They became so bound up with this subculture, he suggests, that they could not adapt to changed conditions. When the subculture died, the poolrooms nearly died with it. The traditional poolroom had depended upon men who were heterosexual but, nonetheless, committed to remaining unmarried. They were men whose sexual needs were met partly by masturbation and, partly or mainly, by recourse to prostitutes. Today, Polsky, maintains, American men use prostitutes pre-maritally, extra-maritally and post-maritally but hardly ever any more as a means of maintaining life-long bachelorhood. The social conditions of urban life have led the majority of men to favour marriage. With the decline of the "life-long bachelor" as a social type, came the decline of the traditional poolrooms. Some attempt was made by entrepreneurs to "re-vamp" and glamourize them as a means of attracting a new clientele but it was, argues Polsky, almost bound to fail. This was because it simultaneously alienated such traditional clients as still remained and was too firmly associated, particularly in the minds of women, with the earlier, all-male subculture.

The British rugby club developed as form of male-preserve in a different social setting. Its development, therefore, is not directly equivalent to that of poolrooms in the U.S.A. Britain, for example, had no open frontier during the nineteenth century although it did have an expanding empire which, to some extent, may have served a similar social function. However, the development of rugby football as a male preserve came at the height of imperial expansion and not, as in the case of American pool, with the closure of the frontier. Furthermore, the clientele of British rugby clubs in the late nineteenth century was drawn predominantly from the ranks of the upper and middle classes as compared with the mainly working class clientele of the poolrooms in America. The rugby clubs, however, did embrace a bachelor subculture that was similar in many respects. Most British rugby players, unlike the groups described by Polsky, were not committed to remaining unmarried but the social norms of the class from which they came did dictate the deferral of marriage until the late twenties or early thirties. By that time, it was believed, a man would be earning a salary sufficient for maintaining a wife and children in a manner considered appropriate for a member of his class.[8] Even within marriage, a high degree of conjugal role segregation remained the norm since the balance of power between the sexes[9] had not yet altered sufficiently to lead to the current, increasingly dominant pattern of role-sharing between husband and wife. Consequently, even for the married man, there was less pressure to share his leisure with his wife and children than tends nowadays to be the case. Conditions were ripe, in short, for the emergence of a subculture that was both all-male and composed of heterosexuals. Again, however, although this may provide an explanation of some of the conditions necessary for the emergence of the rugby football club as a type of male preserve, it does not represent an explanation of the sufficient conditions for this process. In particular, it cannot explain why this type of male-preserve came traditionally to involve the contravention of a specific set of social taboos. For a more complete explanation, it is necessary to probe a little deeper.

Lionel Tiger has recently attempted to develop a "socio-biological" theory of the all-male group.[10] He begins by noting that the "male-bond" is a "cultural universal". Its universality, he argues, strongly suggests that the mechanisms which produce it are in large part biological. There is reason to believe, he suggests, that the male-bond became genetically implanted at an early stage in human evolution. The development of co-operative hunting, he maintains, was probably decisive in this respect mainly because groups where men inherited the propensity to form close relations with other men would have been more successful in their hunting and would therefore have had greater potential for survival than groups where men were genetically programmed in some less advantageous way. The genetic inheritance of women, he suggests, followed a different course of evolution. They became programmed to bond with their mates and their children but not with other women. Moreover, as a means of further increasing potential for survival, the propensity to exclude women from their hunting groups became a hereditary part of the males' biological equipment. Women are not physiologically equipped for the efficient performance of the tasks involved in hunting. They cannot run as fast as men. They cannot throw as well. Their temperature control is less adaptable. The menstrual cycle affects their social, psychological, and physical efficiency. They are adapted for child-bearing and child-rearing, and these have always been a full-time occupation. Tiger points out that, despite the apparent success of the suffragettes, women do not seem to have managed yet to gain many top jobs in areas such as government, high finance, major industry, the law and the military. He concludes that this is because men are genetically programmed to rule and women to obey, that men are genetically programmed to co-operate and that women are not, and that the need of men to form "secret societes" and other forms of sex-exclusive association is part of our biological heritage.

In expounding this "socio-biological" hypothesis, Tiger has made a brave and highly imaginative attempt to combat sociological orthodoxy. However, most research to date suggests very strongly that the mechanisms whereby all-male groups are formed are social and not biological in character. We know a good deal, for example, about the ways in which socialization serves to maintain a culture and a social structure in which men are dominant. So far, however, no one has succeeded in identifying the "genetic programme" hypothesized by Tiger.[11] If one compares the short decades which have elapsed since the first strivings in the campaign for women's rights with the centuries during which males have been dominant, it is hardly surprising that relatively little has been achieved so far with respect to ending sexual discrimination in patterns of role recruitment. The failure of women to form effective, solidary groups among themselves is reminiscent of the failure of subordinate groups throughout history to unite in opposition to their oppressors. It is not only women in industrial societes but also the working classes and negroes in societes of this type who have begun, only relatively recently,[12] to organize in order to combat their subordinate status. Would Tiger want to argue that their subordination is "genetically programmed", too? It is a sociological truism that groups with power usually fight hard to retain it and that, as a rule, they only relinquish or share it if they are forced to do so. Moreover, the ideological legitimation of their rule and the techniques of control they utilize to maintain it are often so effective that the legitimacy of their dominance is accepted by members of the subordinate group. In the case of the negro slave, he comes to develop the "Sambo" personality,[13] while the working class "deference voter" who supports the Conservative Party acknowledges the "eternal right" of the upper classes to rule and his own "eternal duty" to obey. In similar fashion, large numbers of women, because of their socialization, a social structure which limits their opportunities, and the sanctions which are brought to bear if they challenge male "superiority", accept the right of men to be dominant in the major spheres of social life. Indeed, in many cases, they learn to need to be dominated and controlled by men.

There can be little doubt that the processes involved in the initial emergence and subsequent transformation of rugby football as a male preserve were social process *sui generis*. It is probably not without significance in this respect that rugby football developed as a game for adults in the second half of the nineteenth century. For it was during that period that the first significant demands began to be made by women for a greater share in political and economic power. Most of the suffragettes came from the ranks of the middle and upper classes, the social strata from which rugby players were predominantly drawn. Their movement reflected a deep ground swell of dissatisfaction with the social opportunities traditionally open to women from the middle and upper classes. We should like to hypothesize that the historical conjuncture represented by the simultaneous rise of rugby football as a game for upper and middle class adult males, and the rise of the suffragette movement within those social strata, may have been of some significance with respect to the emergence of the specific pattern of socially tolerated taboo-breaking – or at least of some central aspects of it – which came to characterize the subculture of Rugby Union football. For women, particularly at these levels in the social hierarchy, were increasingly becoming a threat to men, and men, we should like to suggest, responded, among other ways, by developing rugby football as a male preserve in which they could bolster up their threatened masculinity and, at the same time, mock, objectify and vilify women, the principal source of the threat.

Obscene songs were not widely condemned in England until about the 1850's. From the sixteenth to the middle of the nineteenth century, such songs were common in the theatre and the music hall. As Ivan Bloch has written:

> In the first half of the nineteenth century it was customary among men of the "upper classes" to visit a music hall after an opera performance for "supper and song". A music hall of evil repute was "Little Tom's Tavern" in Whitechapel. But all music halls during the first half of the nineteenth century had a bad reputation owing to the obscene songs performed in them.[14]

Bloch goes on to show how the performance of these songs was only stopped when the doors of the music hall were opened to women. As is frequently the case when women are admitted to a previously all-male institution, manners changed and behaviour began to become more refined – i.e. less "masculine" in terms of previously existing standards.

But women were accorded less opportunity to enter the rugby clubs which were beginning to spring up at that time. Such clubs came to serve as one of the principal social enclaves where the obscene song tradition could be perpetuated and where, at the same time, the threat posed to men by increasingly powerful women could be rendered symbolically harmless. Such songs, moreover, helped to keep the women out and simultaneously to increase the *esprit de corps* of the men. Because obscene songs violated conventional norms and standards, they increased the cohesion of the all-male group by making them, as it were, "partners in crime".

The rugby club in this situation also functioned in part as a perpetuation of the all-male community of the boarding school. Such an all-male community, we can assume from recent research, was accorded positive value by the boys and regarded as something worth defending. Thus, according to a public schoolboy quoted in a recent study:

> Society is warm and close-knit – not ridden by jealousies. Boys aren't catty like girls. Girls couldn't create this sense of community and comradeship – real affection and loyalty to each other. A marvellous sense of togetherness and teamwork.[15]

It was not, however, only the comradeship that was appealing but the fact that the absence of women and girls enhanced the "masculinity" of the group. This was of great importance in the value scheme of rugby players. Another pupil in the same study had this to say of the all-male boarding school:

> It makes us more masculine. If we are to be males, for God's sake let's go the whole hog. Let's learn to understand, command, live with males. We *must* understand our own sex fully and cannot if females are tripping and flirting around.[16]

Remarks such as this are probably indicative of the fact that the balance of power between the sexes is now beginning to veer towards a more egalitarian form of relationship than used formerly to prevail. No one would think it necessary to defend all-male institutions if they were not under attack. We should like to hypothesize that one of the principal initial responses of many men as the attack from women first began to be mounted was to withdraw into the all-male culture and celebrate its values. The rugby clubs became central foci of this culture. In them, the singing of obscene songs which symbolically expressed masculinity in a virulent form, men's fear of women, and their simultaneous dependency on them, became one of the central elements in the club subculture.

The obscene songs and ballads which became traditional in rugby clubs display at least two central characteristics. At first sight, these characteristics may appear to be unrelated. We should like to suggest, however, that they both reflect the increasing power of women and their growing threat to the traditional social position and self-image of men. The first is their embodiment of a hostile, brutal but, at the same time, fearful attitude towards women and the sexual act. The second is the fact that they came to mock homosexuals and homosexuality. The psychiatrist David Stafford-Clark, in a discussion of the "narrative poem", "Eskimo Nell", concluded that:

> What characterises her story on reflection is the absolute joylessness of the whole thing. The deliberate and complete absence of any note of compassion, of humour except for that implicit in the grotesque nature of the sexual descriptions, and the lack of any suggestion of love or delight in life. The poem is the negation of everything except the destructive aspects of sado-masochistic sexuality.[17]

In many of these songs and poems, women tend to be objectified and depicted as a threat to men. In "Eskimo Nell", for example, even the champion womanizer, "Dead Eye Dick", is unable to provide Nell with sexual satisfaction. This is left to his henchman, "Mexican Pete", who performs the task with his "six-shooter". In the "Engineer's Hymn", the central character, an engineer whose wife "was never satisfied", had to build a machine in order to fulfil the erotic component of his marital role. Seldom, if ever, is the "normal" man or women featured in these songs. Super-human or extra-human powers are required before the "hero" can satisfy the "heroine's" voracious sexual appetite. Nothing could be more revealing of the function of these songs in symbolically expressing but also, to some extent, in symbolically reducing the fear of women who were experienced as powerful and demanding. Such fears are likely to have grown as the power of women began, factually, to increase. They were probably particularly strong in the case of public schoolboys, for they had been brought up largely in an all-male environment. In such an environment, the opportunities available for learning to relate to women of equal social status from outside their own families were relatively restricted. Such relationships, moreover, were surrounded by a complex etiquette which placed women "on a pedestal" but, at the same time, expressed their subordination to men.[18]

The rugby club can reveal itself to the outsider as a very close, affectionate gathering of males who bathe together, strip in all-male company, and generally indulge in what may appear to be homo-erotic behaviour, perhaps of an unconsciously motivated kind. Even the game-situation of the scrummage where the players grasp each other in a hot, sticky mass, their heads between each others thighs, has become the butt for frequent jokes. Thus, as the other side of the coin, the feminine or homosexual male has come to be mocked in rugby songs. For, especially given the growing power of women, homosexuality, or the fear of it, represents another source of threat to the male's sense of masculine identity. One of the songs, traditional in rugby circles, has as its chorus:

> *For we're all queers together,*
> *Excuse us while we go upstairs,*
> *For we're all queers together,*
> *That's why we go round in pairs.*[19]

The function of this song appears to be to counter the charge before it is made, to stress and reinforce masculinity by mocking, not only women but also homosexuals. In an age when women were beginning to become more powerful and able to challenge their factual subordination, if not their symbolic objectification, with a growing measure of success, men who clung to the old style and continued to enjoy participation in all-male groups would have had doubts cast on their masculinity. Many of them probably began to doubt it themselves. Doubts of this kind must have been doubly threatening in a situation such as that of the rugby club where the principal function was the expression of masculinity and the perpetuation of traditional norms in this regard. In the case of public schoolboys, the threat is likely to have been even greater for, in the public schools, as an author has recently written:

... the incidence of homosexuality is likely to be high: in some schools, either over-homosexuality or partially repressed homosexuality is the general practice. Nearly everywhere homosexual friendships are frequent and it is not infrequent ... for such friendships to reach the point of physical action.[20]

In all probability, much of the homosexuality that occurs in public schools is merely a temporary substitute for heterosexual behaviour. It has not been proved that boys' boarding schools produce more adult homosexuals than non-boarding schools. But the fact remains that, at these schools, boys do frequently experience desire for other boys. This must have the effect on many of making them apprehensive concerning their masculinity. When, as is the case with rugby footballers, they participate in a subculture which epitomizes rugged manliness and still "unnatural" desires of this kind, the resultant conflicts are likely to accentuate the need to prove their masculinity.

From the very beginning, the ethos of rugby football has consistently stressed masculinity. In 1863, at one of the series of meetings held in London in order to set up a uniform code of rules for football on a national level, F. W. Campbell of the Blackheath Rugby club spoke as follows in defence of "hacking", the practice which the majority of members of the embryo Football Association wished to abolish:

> As to not liking hacking as at present carried on, I say that ... it savours far more of the feeling of those who like their pipes and grog or schnappes more than the manly game of football.[21]

H. H. Almond, headmaster of Loretto Academy, the Scottish public school, wrote in 1892 that, "... the great end of the game (is) to produce a race of robust men, with active habits, brisk circulations, manly sympathies and exuberant spirits".[22]

It is probably significant in the light of this concern with masculinity that rugby-playing and beer-drinking have long been regarded as synonymous. As early as 1893, *The Cambrian* reported a speech by a Mr Michael Craven in which he stated that rugby football was "the fascination of the devil and twin sister of the drinking system and that without the latter it would have a job to succeed".[23] More recently, Morgan and Nicholson have pointed out that:

> The schoolboys who are boldest at going into pubs for a beer are so often to be the best footballers that the amateur sociologist could be forgiven for hazarding a bit of cause and effect. In College the beer drinking competitions were always staged under the aegis of the Rugby Club.[24]

Many commentators seem to regard drunkenness as the greatest single factor behind the "vandalism" which occurs in rugby-playing fraternities. However, it would be dangerous to assume that the mere fact of men in groups, drinking heavily together, will produce the type of behaviour which is characteristic of rugby players after the match. Here is an example from one of our case records:

> An after-rugger match striptease ended in uproar as an under-graduate footballer was carried naked past girl students in a university bar. Yesterday, the rumpus was condemned as "disgusting behaviour" by a female student leader at Keele University . . . She wrote: "Soon after the bar opened at 6 o'clock, the players were singing characteristic songs. So far all was normal. But the high spirits zoomed into orbit. A player in the bar removed all his clothing except for his underpants. Then two players undressed to vocal accompaniment. They made obscene movements. They began throwing beer at each other, smashing glasses and throwing sugar. Then the students (both sexes) sitting at the tables were treated to the sight of a naked man being carried around the snack bar. He was drunk but consenting."[25]

It seems fairly clear that, in cases such as this, the drinking serves, partly as a means of testing, expressing and accentuating masculinity, and partly as a means of loosening internalized restraints. The loosening of restraints with alcohol appears to be a necessary precondition for the ritual enactments which follow. The rituals in the case described above centrally involved the mocking of the female stripper and, symbolically through her, of the "fallen" woman who is easy prey to men. It is significant that they took place in the actual presence of women and that many of the women present appeared to regard them simply as a matter of course. As far as one can tell, such women did not have, or gain, a reputation as "easy" sexual objects among the players they were accompanying. It is perhaps even more significant that some of the women present reacted vocally and with disgust. This would seem to reveal that, increasingly, women are willing and able to fight against their symbolic reification and ritual vilification by men.

Asked to justify his participation in such activities, a student rugby player interviewed by one of the authors replied:

> I don't try to personally. If one analyzes it outside the context of being there, then you're dissatisfied with what you've done, but when you've had ten or eleven pints and you're in this situation then the way to justify it is to say you were pissed out of your mind at the time. One isn't necessarily proud of what one has done but you do tend to look back on it and say "we had a good night there".

This appears to indicate that the activities of the rugby club offend against the "everyday" values of its own members as well as against those of the dominant groups in society at large. The very fact, however, that this type of activity runs counter to dominant values and that this is recognized by the participants themselves, probably serves even further to reinforce the close-knit character of the group. Such fellowship and closeness are enhanced by the consumption of alcohol so that "respectability" and "propriety" can make way for a value that is more highly regarded than both – masculinity and, since traditional standards of masculinity are increasingly threatened in modern society, as its corollary, the mocking, objectification and ritual vilification of women.

However, great changes have begun to take place in British rugby clubs in recent years. They are no longer clear-cut male preserves. Much of the behaviour which, formerly, was typical of them is now either dead or in the process of dying out. Rugby players tend to remain a special "type" but the type has begun to alter. Their off-the-field behaviour has begun to change, largely in the direction of greater restraint and greater control.

The breakdown and loosening of the structures and ideologies that once held rugby players together into close-knit, all-male groups is a complex social process. We should like to suggest that one of the more important aspects of it has been the continuing emancipation of women in British society.[26] A stage has now been reached where women are frequent and, what is more important, *welcome* visitors to rugby clubs. In part, it was financial necessity that began to bring about this change. But this economic fact reflects wide changes in social structure, particularly in the position of women within that structure.

Ten or so years ago, if a young person wanted to go dancing, he or she typically went to a youth club, a church hall or a commercial dance. Today, young people can usually find ample opportunities for dancing at any of the rugby clubs in their district. The senior clubs especially, faced with the prospect of falling gates and rising costs, opted for dances as a means of raising money. Fear of the dangers supposedly inherent in professionalism[27] and the corresponding emphasis placed on Rugby Union as a "players game", ruled out, at least until recently, attracting more spectators to the game through the introduction of a more competitive framework designed to enhance excitement.[28] The junior and the "old boy" clubs, with little or no chance of spectator appeal but with valuable contributions to make as social centres, had only one acceptable course open to them and that was to hold dances. Other ways of raising funds such as bingo and football pools had lower class connotations and did not, therefore, represent a feasible alternative.

Dances, of course, brought women into the male preserve with official approval. This does not mean that their presence had been entirely disallowed before. On the contrary, they have always been welcome to make tea, prepare and serve meals, and to cheer on their men-folk. But traditionally, their presence was only tolerated if they were content to remain in a subordinate position. They had to leave the club-house when ordered to do so by the men. In fact, a particular exclusion ritual grew up in order to let them know that they had overstayed their welcome and that beer-drinking and the singing of obscene songs were about to commence. The signal was a song entitled "Good Night, Ladies". Any women who insisted on remaining after the enactment of this ritual suffered loss of status. In any event, their presence was only tolerated as long as they passively accepted the objectification of themselves by men.

The more emancipated women who have now begun to enter the club-houses, whether in order to attend the dances or simply in order to drink with their men, are increasingly not prepared to accept this subordinate position. They tend to be more independent, better off financially, more desirous of equality, more aware of the power which their desirability as mates gives them in relation to men. They are unwilling to accept behaviour which they regard as aggressively intentioned or, alternatively, they use obscenities themselves as a sign of their emancipation. However, the principal consequence of the admission of increasing numbers of women into rugby clubs has been to prevent the rugby club Saturday night from assuming its traditional shape. Writing for a Sunday paper in 1969, Lionel Tiger observed that:

> One of the most obvious distinguishing characteristics of men is their great ability, even urge, to get together with their own sex. The cheerful, noisy Rugby players at the wash-up and sing-in . . . have featured on the covers of best-selling Rugby song-books. The half-million copies that have been bought are a tribute to the appeal of the all-male get together.[29]

However, he appears to have missed the point. The majority of such books are sold outside rugby circles. In this respect, they form part of that overall cultural change which began in the early 1960's and led to the advent of the so called "permissive society". Previous generations of rugby players found books of this kind unnecessary. "True" rugby men even today – the guardians of a dying tradition – hold them in amused contempt. Traditionally, the obscene songs were passed from generation to generation by word of mouth. Each club had its own version of the favourite songs and these were picked up *in situ* by the younger members who perpetuated the tradition. But, in large part because women are now beginning to become an integral part of rugby club life, newcomers are not exposed to the songs with the same intensity as previously. The tradition is difficult to maintain in its earlier, oral form. Insofar as such books are sold to rugby players, this is indicative, not of the strength but of the growing weakness of the rugby club as a male-preserve.

Excessive drinking and the antics which accompanied it have also begun to decline in rugby clubs in recent years. This is clearly due, in part, to the advent of a more competitive framework in the game and to the greater emphasis on coaching and training which this has begun to entail. Physical fitness is increasingly at a premium and this limits the degree to which players can engage in heavy drinking. But, we would venture to suggest, the decline of heavy drinking is also connected with the changing pattern of relations between the sexes. Women today, especially in the middle classes, demand increasingly to be regarded as central in the lives of their men. The young man, whose status among other young men is now increased by having a regular girl friend, is forced to go in search of a mate on Saturday nights instead of drinking at the rugby club. Even the young married man is much more willing than previously to share his leisure with his family and more inclined to accord with the wishes of his wife. This appears to be indicative, not only of the increasing power of women in our society, but also of the increasing willingness of men to succumb to that power. Gradually, men are ceasing to regard women as objects and are coming, more and more, to regard them as persons. Increasingly, they *want* to be with their wives and girl friends rather than with other men. According to a student rugby player interviewed in the course of our researches:

> I tend to go out with my girl friend on Saturday nights. I always put my girl friend before rugby crowd, because I don't think that the boozing and socialising in rugby after the game is so important that you've got to give something up in order to be there. I think it's alright if you've nothing better to do.

Today, middle class men have to be more attentive towards their wives and girl friends and more responsive to their needs and wishes. During the 1960's, this developed to a stage where growing numbers even of the more "traditional" men began to become afraid to admit that they would rather spend their time in an all-male group than with a member of the opposite sex. Women, for their part are beginning to become aware that, by gaining entry to the rugby clubs, they have begun to breach a bastion of male dominance. At times, they are openly exultant. In a letter to the student newspaper attacking the University rugby club, a female student at Leicester University recently wrote:

> Let's face it, the cult of the hairy-legged hard man is dying a natural death and the minority who are still desperately prodding the corpse can do little to save the species from extinction.

It appears likely that, with the increasing emancipation of women and the altering focus of marriage and family life, the old-style rugby player will become just an historical curiosity. All the signs seem to indicate that he is gradually being replaced by a much more restrained model, one who is more "conformist" with respect to the dominant social standards and much more serious and dedicated in his approach to the game. It is true that obscene songs and rowdy behaviour still occur in rugby circles but, increasingly, they are being limited to special occasions. The "hot pot suppers" and the Easter tours are, in most cases, the only situations where the rugby club still tends frequently to get out of hand but even these last sanctuaries are beginning to be invaded. At Leicester University, it was recently proposed, admittedly tentatively, that women be allowed to attend the annual dinner of the rugby club and, at Easter 1969, the "old boy" side with which one of the authors is associated allowed women to accompany the team to an Easter rugby tournament on the Isle of Man. Wives and girl friends went along and enjoyed the "family occasion". This remained a type of male dominance, of course, in that the women accompanied the men rather than vice versa. Nonetheless, it provides a clear enough indication of the degree to which male dominance in British society has begun to be eroded. Of course, it shows at the same time how far women still have to go in order to achieve something approaching a measure of full equality with men. For one of the reasons' why, in this case, they had to follow the men, is the fact that few comparable leisure activities are available to women. This, in its turn, we should like to suggest, is largely the result of centuries of male dominance and an overall social structure which, by and large, continues to reflect and reinforce that dominance. It also reflects the development of patterns of socialization which fit women for the performance of subordinate roles and which limit their aspirations, not only in the occupational field but in the sphere of leisure activities as well.

Notes

1 Günter Lüschen, in his *The Sociology of Sport: A Trend Report and Bibliography*, (Current Sociology Series, the Hague and Paris, 1968), lists 892 books and articles on the sociology of sport. However, as Lüschen himself points out, most of the contributions listed were written, not by sociologists, but by specialists in physical education. At a fairly generous estimate, only something like twenty to thirty of the articles referred to were written by sociologists and published in sociology journals. Some of the books listed are by recognized sociologists but none of them deals with the sociology of sport as such. They were included by the author because he considered them relevant to the field.

2 Behaviour of this kind is not found in such a highly developed form in Rugby League, the semi-professional offshoot of Rugby Union football played mainly, in the North of England. There is insufficient space here for a detailed examination of the reasons why such behaviour did not become so firmly established in Rugby League. It must be enough simply to say that the semi-professional nature of the latter game with its correspondingly greater emphasis on fitness and training, and the fact that most of its players traditionally come from the working classes, are among the major factors.

3 For a discussion of this concept, see Elias N. and Dunning E., "Leisure in the Sparetime Spectrum", in: Albonico R. and Pfister-Binz K. (eds.), *Sociology of Sport: Theoretical and Methodological Foundations*, Magglingen, 1972.

4 For a highly imaginative discussion of "soccer hooliganism" as a social problem, see Taylor I., "*Football Mad*": *A Speculative Sociology of Football Hooliganism*, in: Dunning E., (ed.), *The Sociology of Sport: A Selection of Readings*, London, 1971. Taylor has developed his ideas further in another article, *Soccer Consciousness and Soccer Hooliganism*, which appears in Cohen S. (ed.), *Images of Deviance*, Harmondsworth, 1971.

5 Principal among them were schools such as Marlborough, Cheltenham, Haileybury and Sherborne which were not founded or did not become public schools until the middle of the nineteenth century.

6 From about 1880 onwards, members of the working classes, particularly in Lancashire and Yorkshire, did begin to play rugby in increasing numbers. As their participation increased, however, so did the tendency towards the professionalization of the game. It was this which led to the break between Rugby Union and Rugby League.

7 Polsky N., *Poolrooms: End of the Male Sanctuary*, "Transactions", March 1967, p. 38. "Pool" is an American version of the game which, in Britain, we call "billiards".

8 Banks J. A., *Prosperity and Parenthood*, London, 1958.

9 This term is taken from an as yet unpublished paper by Norbert Elias entitled *The Balance of Power Between the Sexes*. As far as we know, he is the first sociologist to attempt to conceptualize the relations between the sexes in terms of an explicit "power model".

10 See his *Men in Groups*, London, 1969.

11 We do not wish to give the impression that Tiger is unaware of the speculative nature of much of his work. As he writes himself: "My method . . . owes more to the enthusiastic shotgun than the sabre". (*op. cit.*, p. 141). Or again, ". . . we do not know the actual cortical-amygdaloid processes involved in bonding among men, or even the neurological differences among males and females in this respect". (*ibid.*, p. 51).

12 The term "recently" as used here with respect to the working classes refers, of course, to the last one hundred and fifty years.

13 See Elkins S. M., *Slavery: A Problem in American Institutional and Intellectual Life*, Chicago, 1969.

14 Bloch I., *Sexual Life in England, Past and Present*, London, 1958, p. 607.

15 Lambert R., *The Hothouse Society*, London, 1968, p. 105.

16 *Ibid.*, p. 309.

17 Stafford-Clark D., *The Twentieth Century*, Summer edn., 1965, pp. 17–22, no title. While we agree with Stafford-Clark's analysis of "Eskimo Nell", we would not wish to argue that all rugby songs similarly lack humour and compassion. Nor would we accept that all the songs negate "everything except the destructive elements of sado-masochistic sexuality. This is a recurrent element, it is true, but rugby songs are part of a complex oral tradition which frequently displays considerable able humour and both verbal and rhyming skill. We do not wish to claim that our own analysis offers more than a possible explanation of one or two strands in this complex tradition. Thus, many of the songs and rhymes mock, not only women and homosexuals, but also men and male sexuality, even human sexuality as such. Others reveal a mixture of fear and disgust at the possibilities of contracting venereal disease. Yet another possible strand is revealed in one of the favourite songs, "The Sexual Life of the Camel". This song not only displays considerable humour and literary skill but is sung to the tune of the "Eton Boating Song". It

172

does not seem too far-fetched to suggest that the use of this tune may have been introduced by pupils at Rugby or by Old Rugbeians as a means of mocking their traditional rivals, the Etonians.

18 Of course, access to female servants and to prostitutes was probably never restricted to the same extent nor surrounded by such a complex etiquette. This was probably the case only as far as women who were status equals were concerned.

19 It may be of some significance that the tune to which this song, too, is traditionally sung is that of the "Eton Boating Song".

20 Wilson J., *Public Schools and Private Practice*, London, 1962, p. 70.

21 Green G., *A History of the Football Association*, London, 1953, p. 29.

22 Mackenzie R. J., *Almond of Loretto*, London, 1906, p. 73.

23 Quoted in Morgan W. J. and Nicholson G., *Report on Rugby*, London, 1958, p. 18.

24 *Ibid.*, p. 26.

25 As we shall try to show, the presence of women on this occasion did not result simply from the fact that the venue was a university bar rather than the bar of a rugby club. None of the rituals which have grown up as a means of excluding women from such events was brought into play. Their presence was actually tolerated, even welcomed, if not without ambivalence. This is indicative, we should like to suggest, of the fundamental changes which have begun to take place in the relations between the sexes.

26 It may seem as if we are committing the logical error here of principally explaining both the rise and decline of the male preserve in rugby football in terms of the same "factor", the increasing power of women. What we are, in fact, suggesting is that the relationship between them is "curvi-linear", that the same social process had different consequences at different stages. This is perfectly logical, especially if one thinks in terms of social processes rather than in terms of discrete, ahistorical "factors" or "variables".

27 i.e. principally of the fact that, as Gregory Stone would put it, profession alism might lead to a change in the balance between "play" and "display" in favour of the latter, with the consequent destruction of rugby as a "sport" and its transformation into a mass, commercial spectacle. For a discussion of these concepts, see Stone G. P., *American Sports: Play and Dis-Play*, in Dunning, *op. cit.*, pp. 47–65.

28 The introduction of formal competitions such as "leagues" and "cups" was resisted by the Rugby Union authorities until the 1971–72 season. Now they have begun, reluctantly, to give way in the face of mounting pressure from players and the press.

29 *Observer Colour Magazine*, 29th June, 1969.

49

DOUBLE FAULT

Renee Richards and the construction and naturalization of difference

Susan Birrell and Cheryl L. Cole

Source: *Sociology of Sport Journal* 7 (1990): 1–21.

This study examines the implications of the entrance of Renee Richards, a con-structed-female transsexual, into the women's professional tennis circuit. The pur-pose of our analysis is to show how our culture constructs woman and produces particular notions of gender, sex, and difference by examining a case in which these ideological processes are literally enacted: the construction of a "woman," Renee Richards, from a man. We do this by exploring the cultural meaning of transsexualism in the U.S.; by examining critically how issues of transsexualism, sex, and gender are framed by the media in the Renee Richards case; and by exploring the particular problematic posed by Richards' entrance into the highly gendered world of professional sport. Although Renee Richards appears to chal-lenge fundamental cultural assumptions about sex and gender, closer analysis reveals that the various media frames invoked to explain the meaning of Renee Richards reproduce rather than challenge dominant gender arrangements and ideologies.

In July of 1976, a reporter covering a local tennis tournament in La Jolla, California, became suspicious when the defending champion in the women's division was soundly thrashed by a 6-ft 2-in. newcomer by the name of Renee Clarke. Searching further, the reporter discovered that Renee Clarke was actually Renee Richards, a constructed-female transsexual[1] who less than a year before had been Richard Raskind, a man ranked highly by the United States Tennis Association in the 35-and-over men's division. The media clamor that ensued might have died down had Richards not accepted an invitation to play in a national tournament in South Orange, New Jersey, that his/her[2] old friend Eugene Scott was organizing as a warm-up to the U.S. Open. The United States Tennis Association (USTA) and the Women's Tennis Association (WTA) promptly withdrew their sanctions from the

South Orange tournament. In protest of Richards' participation, 25 of the 32 women originally scheduled to play in South Orange withdrew to enter an alternative tournament hastily arranged and sanctioned by the USTA and the WTA. Undaunted, the 41-year-old Richards advanced through three rounds before losing in the semifinals to 17-year-old Lea Antonopolis. Thus begins one of the more sensational and most illuminating incidents in contemporary sport.

A few days later, Richards announced his/her intention to play women's singles in the 1976 U.S. Open at Forest Hills, and the antagonism between Renee Richards and the women's tennis world was formalized. The USTA, the WTA, and the U.S. Open Committee responded by requiring that all women competitors take a sex chromatin test known as the Barr body test. Richards refused, and the U.S. Open went on without him/her. One year later s/he took the case to the New York Supreme Court, which ruled that "this person is now female" and that requiring Richards to pass the Barr body test was "grossly unfair, discriminatory and inequitable, and violative of her rights" (*Richards v. USTA*, 1977, p. 272). The court's decision cleared the way for Richards to play in the women's singles at the 1977 U.S. Open where s/he lost in the first round to Virginia Wade, 6–1, 6–4. Richards' modest professional career continued until 1981 when s/he retired from competition at age 47. After a successful year as Martina Navratilova's coach, s/he left professional tennis and returned to his/her ophthalmology practice.

The entrance of Renee Richards into women's professional tennis created confusion and controversy for the players, the fans, organized tennis, and the public. Adding drama to the general controversy over the sexual status of transsexuals was Richards' decision to participate as a woman in a cultural activity still accepted as legitimately divided into two sex categories. The confusion that followed Richards' action illuminates sport as an important element in a political field that produces and reproduces two apparently natural, mutually exclusive, "opposite" sexes.

The controversy over Richards' contested entrance into women's sport was addressed at length in the press and later reexamined in Richards' auto-biography, *Second Serve* (1983), and the television movie, *Second Serve*. These sources framed the Renee Richards story within traditional liberal rhetoric as a story about fairness and human rights focused around the prob-lematic status of the transsexual. By focusing on the question of individual sex legitimacy, that is, whether Renee Richards is a man or a woman, the media obscured the broader political and social issues.

The purpose of our analysis is to show how our culture constructs woman and produces particular notions of gender, sex, the body, and difference by examining a case where these ideological processes are literally enacted: the construction of a "woman," Renee Richards, from a "man." In Richards' rather spectacular case, the construction can be examined on two dimen-sions: the relatively private technical construction of Richards accomplished by an array of medical and legal experts, and the more public construction of Richards accomplished through the discursive practices of the print media and the autobiographical construction offered by Richards in the book and television movie, *Second Serve*.

In this paper we examine the media's construction of the controversy surrounding Renee Richards; we offer a critical reading of discursive practices that construct and control transsexualism, sexuality, sex, and gender; and we explore the particular problematic posed by Richards' entrance into the highly gendered world of professional sport. Moreover, by asking how it is possible to "change" sexes, what it means to want to change, and what it means to be able to change, we argue that transsexualism simultaneously illuminates and mystifies the cultural constructions of woman and man by positioning a seemingly anomalous case within hegemonic discourses of sex difference, sex and gender identity, and the gendering of bodies.

Although initially Renee Richards appears to be newsworthy because s/he is a sexual anomaly who challenges taken-for-granted assumptions about sex and gender, our critical reading suggests how the media frames invoked to explain the meaning of Renee Richards reproduce rather than challenge dominant gender arrangements and ideologies, specifically the assumption that there are two and only two, obviously universal, natural, bipolar, mutually exclusive sexes that necessarily correspond to stable gender identity and gendered behavior. And while the media coverage of the controversy surrounding Richards' desire to play women's professional tennis is seemingly confined to the immediate event, we will suggest that the media enter into and depend upon a broader discourse produced by a constellation of institutions empowered to enforce boundaries between woman and man based on essential conceptualizations of gender, sex, and difference.

Transsexualism and the technological construction of woman

Within the dominant discourse of sex research, the category of transsexual is assigned to a person who believes he or she was born into the wrong body, a belief Jan Morris describes as "a passionate, lifelong, ineradicable conviction" (1974, p. 8). The anatomical structure of the body that indexes sex, particularly the genitals, is in direct conflict with the preoperative transsexual's sense of self as a gendered individual. In contrast to transvestites, who habitually cross-dress, "true transsexuals feel that they *belong* to the other sex, they want to *be* and *function* as members of the opposite sex, not only to appear as such" (Benjamin, 1966, p. 13). Such an identity depends on the belief that there are two neatly distinct and absolute categories of sex/gender. As Jan Morris understands it, "I was born into the wrong body, being feminine by gender but male by sex, and I could achieve completeness only when the one was adjusted to the other" (1974, p. 26).

176

Anxieties constructed through sex, gender, and sexuality in our culture reside ultimately in the body and our attitudes toward our own body as well as the bodies of others. Foucault (1979) suggests, "The body is directly involved in a political field; power relations have an intimate hold upon it: they invest it, train it, and torture it, force it to carry out its tasks, to perform ceremonies and emit signs" (pp. 25–26).

The gender dysphoria that transsexuals suffer often drives them to seek "sex reassignment," a lengthy process that requires the services of a number of experts in normalizing disciplines: surgeons, gynecologists, endocrinologists, plastic surgeons, psychiatrists, speech therapists, and lawyers. These experts enact a discourse that legitimates sex reassignment by working together to alter what is presented as the unalterable. In this sense, gender dysphoria and transsexualism are not neutral categories but elements in a social system that controls and regulates the body, sex, and gender relations.

For the constructed-female transsexual—estimated as comprising about 80 to 90% of the 10,000 transsexuals in the United States (Grimm, 1987)—the sex reassignment process begins with extensive psychotherapy to ensure that surgery is advisable. This is followed by a lengthy period during which the preoperative transsexual must live as a member of the opposite sex as proof of his or her ability to accomplish appropriately gendered behavior. Finally a series of operations is performed during which the sex signifiers are exchanged: male sex organs are removed and an artificial vagina is constructed and implanted. Massive doses of female sex hormones, breast implants, cosmetic plastic surgery on the face and Adam's apple, and speech therapy further sustain the apparent change.

The knowledge that organizes our understanding of transsexualism has been divided into two major approaches (Bolin, 1987): clinical approaches that characterize the psychiatric and psychological research and are based on a medical model in which transsexualism is constituted as an individual problem, "a syndrome subject to treatment" (p. 41); and sociocultural approaches taken by ethnomethodologists and anthropologists, which focus on "the relationship of . . . transsexualism to the culture at large" (p. 47).

Clinical approaches (e.g., Benjamin, 1966; Money & Ehrhardt, 1972; Money & Tucker, 1975; Stoller, 1975), are concerned with transsexual etiology or the biological and/or psychological variables that have caused transsexualism.[3] They subscribe to some form of sexual essentialism while locating the problem within the individual and the dysfunctional family, "with the family as the largest unit of external etiological influence" (Bolin, 1987, p. 59). However, by focusing on the individual as the pathological victim of a disconcerting sexual syndrome, the body and transsexualism are removed from the technologies of gender[4] and the broader network of social relations in which we experience and understand our lives. In this view, the transsexual is blamed for failing to adjust to a rigid system of gender stereotypes. Therapeutic management programs designed to create gender reversal and surgical treatment, though an object of some dispute, are viewed as legitimate treatments to cure transsexuals. Gender dysphoria is represented as a state that can be most effectively corrected through the combination of biomedical and legal authorization of the exchange of the material signifiers that reconstitute sex status.

Sociocultural approaches view transsexualism not as an individual malady but as an epiphenomenon that can be understood only within the context of a particular culture. Sociocultural researchers (e.g., Bolin, 1988; Garfinkel & Stoller, 1967; Kando, 1973; Kessler & McKenna, 1978; Williams, 1986) are interested in "what transsexualism reveals about the cultural construction of gender and the sex/gender system" (Bolin, 1987, p. 47). For example, while the disproportionate number of transsexuals are male to female, historically the reverse was true (Bullough, 1975), testimony to the cultural and historical specificity of transsexual emergence.[5] And the ethnocentricity of our two-sex/two-gender paradigm is revealed through ethnographic descriptions of different sex/gender arrangements in other cultures such as the Berdasch and the Amazonia (Williams, 1986).[6]

The existence of transsexualism is discomforting because it simultaneously disrupts and confirms our commonsense about the nature of sex, gender, and the relationships between them. Transsexualism unravels and rebinds our cultural notion that there are two and only two, mutually exclusive, naturally occurring, immutable, *opposite* sexes. The acute gender dysphoria that impels a transsexual to consider surgical remedy suggests that radically reconfiguring the body through the removal and construction of sex signifiers is easier than living in a culture in which rigid gender ideologies do not permit men to act in stereotypically feminine ways.

The transsexual's solution to gender dysphoria is to change sexes: an individual solution to a systemic problem. Gender dysphoria is the personal manifestation of a larger cultural problem, in this case the institutionalization of a system that reduces sex to two mutually exclusive, natural categories. By seeking surgical remedy, the transsexual acquiesces to a system that locates individuals as either male or female subjects. Ironically the transsexual's personal relief reinforces the very system that produces transsexualism.

Contesting sex: the legal construction of woman

In her critique, *The Transsexual Empire*, Jan Raymond (1979) raises important critical issues: Who is empowered to legitimate transsexual surgery as a valid medical procedure and treatment? Who is authorized to decide who qualifies for sex reassignment and what will the proof of qualification be? Who will determine the legal status of the postoperative transsexual? Raymond bases her argument on the cultural construction of gender identity and transsexualism.[7] The successful male candidate for sex reassignment surgery, for example, must demonstrate stereotypical female behavior patterns and attitudes to those "authorities" who hold the power to reconstruct his body.

By conceptualizing transsexualism within a scientific/clinical discourse as an exceptional pathological condition traceable to early childhood abnormalities, and by dealing with it on a case by case basis, those who have power through and within the technologies of gender, especially the transsexual empire, give themselves license to offer a technological solution to the cultural problem of inflexible gender role prescriptions. For a culture organized around rigid gender roles and for the individuals most discomfitted by those demands, the transsexual empire prescribes the small but expensive Band-Aid of reconstructive surgery.

The Renee Richards case offered a particularly public opportunity to examine Raymond's thesis, but the power of the transsexual empire is one of the major issues obscured by the news media in that case. The coverage of Richards' entrance into women's tennis fails to acknowledge the existence of the male-dominated transsexual empire of surgeons, lawyers, and psychologists whose technological and discursive practices make it legally and, Raymond would argue, morally possible to change one's body/sex. While medical technology makes sex reassignment possible, the legal system insists upon and is the final arbiter of sex identity.[8] Renee Richards was positioned as a woman through legal discourses and was granted the legal right to play tennis as a woman because the New York Supreme Court accepted as its criterion of womanhood a female-appearing phenotype brought about by cosmetic surgery and sustained by massive amounts of female hormones.

In formulating their decision, the court was persuaded by the argument of the expert witnesses Richards called upon in his/her behalf: the surgeon who performed the sex reassignment operation, his/her gynecologist, and John Money, a psychologist from Johns Hopkins—considered the most prominent sex reassignment expert in the U.S. and a major architect of the transsexual empire. In effect, the court accepted as voices of legitimation those very people responsible for producing Richards as a postoperative transsexual in the first place.

Opposing Richards in court were the defendants—the USTA, the WTA, and the U.S. Open Committee, who argued that "there is a competitive advantage for a male who has undergone 'sex-change' surgery as a result of physical training and development as a male" (*Richards v. USTA*, 1977, p. 269). To support their case, they submitted affidavits from an expert witness defending the validity of the Barr body test; from three women professional tennis players: Francoise Durr, Janet Newberry, and Kristien Shaw; and from the Director of Women's Tennis for the USTA, Vicki Berner. Those who would articulate oppositional discourses, however, lacked access to both the institutions and the means of challenging them directly. Thus the Renee Richards case offers literal and dramatic evidence that when an individual's sex is contested, and when the discourses of womanhood are contested, male dominated institutions have disproportionate power to decide what is and is not a woman. Acting in concert, the medical and legal institutions have the power to authorize, regulate, and control the body and sex.

Media conventions and frames, and the construction of woman

The construction of Renee Richards began with the transformation of Richard Raskind to Renee Richards through extensive psychological and medical procedures. Thus Renee Richards exists as Renee Richards at least in part because it is technologically possible. The construction continues more publicly in the news media's coverage of the controversy and in Richards' autobiography, *Second Serve* (1983), and the television movie adaptation of the autobiography in 1985. By drawing upon examples from both the news media and the autobiographies, we argue that dominant liberal conventions shape the narrative and thus public understandings of Renee Richards and transsexualism.[9]

The media produce news, not truth. While the media appear simply to report what happened, they actively construct news through frames, values, and conventions. Having made the initial decision that an incident is worthy of treatment as news, reporters and editors make choices that foreground some elements of the potential narrative and obscure others, and they define and delineate issues through a series of choices including headlines, descriptive word choices, photographs, who to authorize with an interview, and what to report (Hartley, 1982). Gitlin (1980) suggests that the hegemonic frames, codes, and conventions in U.S. news include an emphasis on elements of drama and personality; conventions of balance, brevity, and stereotyping in which the complexity of an event is collapsed into two opposing positions and authorities representing each side are offered the opportunity to comment; temporality; and suspicion of difference and disorder as threat. In the production of news, the frame constructed and choices made offer a preferred reading of the events. As Hall (1977) summarizes the effect,

> It is masked, frequently by the intervention of the professional ideologies—those practical-technical routinizations of practices (news values, news sense, lively presentation, "exciting pictures," good stories, hot news, etc.) which, at the phenomenal level, structure the everyday practices of encoding and set the encoder within the bracket of a professional-technical neutrality which, in any case distances him [sic] effectively from the ideological content of the material he is handling and the ideological inflections of codes he is employing. Hence, though events will not be systematically encoded in a single way, they will tend, systematically, to draw on a very

limited repertoire: and that repertoire . . . will have the overall tendency of making things "mean" within the sphere of the dominant
ideology.

(p. 344)

Following convention, the newspapers recognized the tennis controversy
as news because its immediacy and finiteness mark it as newsworthy within
the media's ideological code. The coverage of the Renee Richards story
began in the national news media on July 24, 1976, the first news mention of
Richards during the South Orange tournament, and it ended on August 18,
1977, the date the papers reported the court decision that granted Richards
the right to participate as a woman in the 1977 U.S. Open. By using the
official proclamation of the law to provide closure for the story, the newspapers implied that the end of the tennis controversy marked the logical
resolution to the issue of transsexualism itself.

To the newspapers, the threshold of newsworthiness had passed. Indeed
only Richards' intentions to enter women's sport had qualified the story as
news in the first place: The mere existence of a transsexual in society has not
been news since Christine Jorgensen (1967). Thus the newspapers focus on
what seems to be a concrete event: the controversy surrounding Renee
Richards' decision to enter women's tennis. But by isolating the event in the
present, the historical and cultural context and significance are excluded
from the frame. In other words, the ideological codes that journalists follow
in their apparent impartiality actively mystify the ideological determinants
of the story.

The media identified two issues that guided their coverage: Is it fair to
allow Renee Richards to play women's professional tennis? And is Renee
Richards a man or a woman? Both issues are clearly embedded in ideological frames of liberalism and sexual essentialism. The central narrative
was constructed around liberal notions of human rights, and fairness clearly
was defined in terms of Richards, not in terms of the women players who
had to accommodate him/her as one of them. Richards was represented as
the central character within a drama of heroic confrontation between an
individual and the tennis bureaucracy. Richards was thus positioned within
a familiar cultural discourse of heroic narrative, a story worthy of Frank
Capra, about an individual's struggle to prevail against the tyranny of the
system.

Generally obscured in the newspapers' construction of this drama of
human rights were any serious consideration of the women players' case,
particularly the social and historical context within which sport in North
America has developed as an activity that privileges males; the meaning of
the sex test ordered by the USTA; the meaning of the antifeminist sentiment
that was packaged as pro-Richards rhetoric; and the wider implications of
the Richards controversy, including the cultural meaning of transsexualism,

sex, and gender, and the power of the male-dominated medical and legal professions to construct and legitimate the female.

The news coverage and the autobiographies differ in the relationship between the issues of whether Richards should be allowed to play women's tennis and whether Richards is a man or a woman. The news media focused on the former and implicated the latter, while the autobiography and film used the former as an occasion to focus on the latter. The news media clearly defined the issues in terms of tennis, and the Renee Richards story unfolded as news almost entirely on the sport pages of newspapers and the sport sections of magazines. In contrast, the autobiographies rely on the familiar autobiographical convention of exposing personal truths to address broader issues of transsexualism. In the entire book of 373 pages, tennis comprises only 46 pages, a proportion that is matched in the film as well. Tennis, it is clear, is merely the occasion for the unfolding of a deeper personal narrative.

Yet even taken together, the news media's exposition of the tennis controversy and the autobiographies' analyses of transsexualism as personal history do not offer a critical understanding of transsexualism. Both accounts work within the constraints of a dominant discourse that constructs two essential, universal, and opposite sexes. By maintaining a tight frame around Richards and by presenting Richards as an isolated case, they endorse an individualistic, clinical model and neglect the larger cultural context of gender arrangements. Beneath the surface of their narratives, the ideology of gender relations lies undisturbed and important questions go unasked: What is a woman? On what basis should we make our decision? Who shall be empowered to decide? How have women been constructed? What is the connection between sex and gender, since transsexual gender identity makes it clear that one cannot necessarily be mapped from the other? These issues are not centralized in the narrative; they are too controversial and complex to be treated within the media conventions of balance, immediacy, objectivity, and appeals to authority.

The gendering of Renee Richards

The news media focused primarily on whether Richards should be allowed to play women's tennis, but the issue of whether Richards is a man or a woman formed an implicit frame for their narratives. Indeed, the most significant framing device the papers used in their construction of the story was the gendering of Richards as a female. The framing of Richards as female was accomplished through their choice of personal pronouns and through the descriptions of Richards they drew for their readers.

While there was some doubt in their minds about which sex category Richards belonged in and whether Richards was a transvestite or a transsexual (*The New York Times*, July 24, 1976), in fact they resolved the problem for themselves and their readers by referring to Richards as "she" from the very first day of coverage. This choice of personal pronoun was made a full year before a legal decision was made,[10] and it is one of the primary ways that the public came to know Richards. By framing Richards as "she," the press resolved the very issue it was purporting to cover: the contest over his/ her sex. In a similar manner, the casting of Vanessa Redgrave to portray Richards in the television movie tells viewers from the very first minute that Renee Richards is truly and naturally a female.

An individual contesting his or her sex creates a linguistic dilemma in cultures in which pronouns and adjectives denote gender. The dilemma is reflected in the quotes from women protesting Richards. Glynnis Coles was quite consistent: "I don't think he should be playing ... As far as I'm concerned he's just a man who's had an operation" (*The Washington Post*, January 1, 1978). But Diane Fromholtz' complaint captured the ambiguity most protesters could not work through: "People are laughing at us, at the way she walks on and acts like a female" (*The Washington Post*, January 1, 1978). With the very act of refuting Richards' claims to be female, Fromholtz genders Richards female. The most telling statement was Roz Reid's protest on behalf of his wife, Kerry Melville Reid: "We don't believe Renee is a woman. Kerry will never play her again" (*The Washington Post*, January 1, 1978).

Officials also had difficulty with the ambiguity. Early in the controversy W.E. Hester, vice-president of the USTA, stated, "I don't know on what grounds we could admit her and on what grounds we can refuse to admit him" (*Los Angeles Times*, August 12, 1976). The USTA first described Richards as "a man [who had] won a woman's tournament" (*The New York Times*, July 24, 1976) and "a biological male" (*The New York Times*, August 14, 1976), then, as more sophisticated discourses developed, as a "person not genetically female" (*The New York Times*, August 15, 1976). Phillippe Chatrier of the International Tennis Federation, determined to bar Richards from international competition, said "Mr.—Miss Richards should not be allowed to play" (*Winston-Salem Journal*, October 22, 1977).

Richards was also gendered by the press in terms of the descriptions they offered of him/her, many of which captured the ambiguity that the press and the public were trying to resolve. *The New York Times* noted, "Dr. Richards displays traits associated with both sexes. The soft husky voice is mostly male but the high cheekbones, shapely legs, graceful gold pierced earrings and peach nail polish ... are distinctly female" (August 19, 1976). And Neil Amdur reported Richards' declaration that "I'm as much a woman as anyone on the U.S. tour" and added,

> At 6 feet 2 inches, Dr. Richards who weighs 147 pounds is considerably taller than most women, even women athletes. She has tight muscles in her calves, the kind you might expect to see on a male sprinter or a halfback in football. Yet her facial features, the high

cheekbones, the brown eyes and the sharply defined eyebrows—are distinctly feminine. She carries herself considerably smoother than many female athletes . . . Her voice is soft, somewhat raspy but firm in the manner of a confident professional.

(*The New York Times*, August 21, 1976)

Elsewhere the press followed their convention of mentioning details of physical appearance of women athletes they generally ignore in male athletes. By reporting on physical appearance, the press legitimates physicality as a valid means for assessing one's sex status, thus confusing the issue of the sex/gender relationship and obscuring the cultural production of such relationships.

Richards' autobiography makes even more explicit the cultural confusion about sex, gender, and sexuality. Throughout the book Richards dwells on his/her appearance and the confirmation of his/her true female self, his/her "success as a girl" that is reflected in male attention to his/her female-appearing body: "Renee fed on [the attention] because [it] represented a casual and ready acceptance of her femaleness. 'Men held doors open for me, young boys and sometimes older men looked me over appreciatively'" (p. 31). On a trip to Casablanca, Richards was mistaken for a woman and picked up for the first time. His/her suitor had "eyes that appraised me with obvious interest. This was the first time I had ever been openly, unreservedly ogled by a man. I quite liked it . . . The more he appreciated me the more I felt like a girl" (p. 220).

Elsewhere in the autobiography Richards enacts male-defined conceptions of feminine behavior. These include the almost total objectification of his/her new body, an exhibitionism evident throughout the book and symbolized by sitting naked for an hour in the locker room while being interviewed by reporters after the South Orange tournament (*The Washington Post*, August 22, 1976), and his/her desire to relate to men in submissive ways. Of one male friend who had known him/her only as Renee, s/he says, "He'd always treated me with overtones of male superiority, and I loved it, considering this treatment a compliment of my validity as a woman" (p. 321).

His/her submission to men is most marked in the accounts of intimacy in which s/he clearly equates sexuality, specifically sexual passivity and submission, with being a woman. In his/her adolescent years, for example, s/he enacted mock rapes with a male high school friend under the guise of wrestling naked on his bed.

Eventually I would have to surrender to his compelling strength. There was something about this situation that pleased me . . . I struggled like hell because that was crucial to my feeling. I had to know that his dominance was real . . . It was very sensual to surrender like that. (p. 45)

His/her trip to Europe was full of sexual encounters with strange men: a truck driver who helped by scraping ice off the windshield of his/her Maserati, then made sexual advances ("After all, he had done me a favor and deserved something for his trouble . . . It's not every day that a truck driver gets to make out with a classy dame in a Maserati" p. 237); a dangerous episode with a stranger in Marrakech; and a *ménage à trois* in Majorca. Finally, after the reconstructive surgery, Richards "waited three months, resigning myself to a lengthy virginity" (p. 287) before being "deflowered" by a former homosexual lover:

> I got a real sense of satisfaction out of being the object of his desire . . . Tremendously exciting also were his encompassing size, the smell of him, his hairiness, and his weight pressing down on me . . . [H]e finished quickly, and I loved that as well. I was warmed by his sense of urgency and the forceful thrusts that accompanied his climax. I didn't have an orgasm myself . . . Nonetheless, I loved it. I was at last fully capable of the woman's role.
>
> (pp. 294–296)

By offering his/her body as a source of sexual pleasure for men, Richards apparently believes s/he has been re-sexed as a woman. S/he has clearly incorporated the dominant cultural discourse on femininity, gendered bodies, and femaleness into his/her consciousness.

Constructing the oppositions

Since conventions limit journalists' abilities to deal with the complexity of the issues posed by controversy, and since reporters are required to cover and present only two sides of a story, the controversy over Renee Richards' entrance into women's professional tennis was reduced and assembled into two mutually exclusive and opposing positions. Support for Richards came from his/her old male tennis friends such as Gene Scott and Bobby Riggs, and from two prominent women, Gladys Heldman, who provided several opportunities for Richards to play on a women's tour she was promoting, and Billie Jean King, who invited Richards to play women's doubles with her on that tour.

Opposition came from the rank and file of the women's tour, some of whom refused to play Richards. Their position was represented by Beth Norton in a letter to the WTA quoted in the *Winston-Salem Journal* in which she protested

> the unfairness of forcing young girls to compete with a middle-aged transsexual who previously has been a nationally ranked men's player . . . [and who had] 30 years experience playing men's and boy's

tennis . . . It is only fair that her rights should not impose upon the rights of girls earning a professional living in the women's tour. The rights of all of us as individuals should be taken into consideration.

(February 14, 1978)

However, the voices of the individual women tennis players who opposed Richards were generally silenced by the media,[11] who represented opposition to Richards as "the tennis establishment," "organized tennis," or most often by the impersonal device of initials: the WTA, the USTA, the USOC. The use of initials and the fact that most spokespersons for these groups were men not only depersonalized the opposition but obscured sex and gender in a situation that is in fact *about* sex and gender. Richards' sex status was constantly foregrounded while the sex of his/her opposition was obscured.

The autobiographies obscure the opposition even more, never acknowledging adverse reaction from anyone other than the USTA and the WTA. Richards claims "most of the women . . . were on my side" (1984, p. 346). S/he reports receiving 40,000 letters after the La Jolla tournament, of which "nine-tenths was positive" (p. 324), and s/he notes a pattern of support from the fans: "I was treated respectfully and if there were hecklers I never heard them" (p. 350). The newspapers confirmed this impression (*The New York Times*, August 28, 1976).

Thus opposition to Richards was framed as organizational impulses to protect the carefully nurtured image of women's tennis by protecting the women players from unfair competition.[12] What might have been reported as a series of individual dramas that paralleled the structure of the sport itself—Richards vs. Antonopolis, Richards vs. Smith, Richards vs. Evert—was instead packaged as Richards vs. The Establishment. The controversy was framed within the classic American liberal tradition of the heroic struggle of one individual against the bureaucracy. Given such a plot, the American tradition is to root for the beleaguered underdog.

Richards solidified his/her role as an underdog by being positioned and by positioning him/herself as a spokesperson for a minority group. S/he first discovered this possibility at the La Jolla tournament when a woman of color said,

Renee . . . I don't want you to withdraw. I am a member of a minority myself . . . I've found that when people don't know what pigeonhole to put you in, your only alternative is to show them what you are and act as if you have the right to be that. You won't be doing yourself a favor if you run away from this tournament. You'll be giving in to stupidity. Hold your head up and play.

(Richards, 1983, p. 317)

Richards noted, "This was the first time anybody had ever put the issues in broader perspective," and s/he began to consider him/herself "a kind of standard bearer" (p. 317). S/he was deluged with letters of support from "people who were members of minorities. Among others, I heard from blacks, convicts, Chicanos, hippies, homosexuals, people with physical handicaps and, of course, transsexuals" (p. 325). Notably absent from his/her list of oppressed groups is women. The support surprised Richards, who admitted,

> I've never even been political [but] . . . I was susceptible to this flood of sentiment. Until you have pawed through thirty thousand letters pleading with you to stand up for your rights and, in so doing, stand up for the rights of the world's downtrodden, you don't know what pressure is. Left to my own devices, I probably would have resolved my personal pique at being summarily barred from competition— but, my god, the whole world seemed to be looking for me to be their Joan of Arc.
>
> (p. 325)

The broadened support an identity as Joan of Arc could provide him/her was not lost on Richards, who returned to that theme throughout the book and regularly spoke to it during interviews with the press. In a story head-lined, "Renee Richards Pursuing Tennis Career for a Cause" (August 19, 1976), *The New York Times* positioned Richards as a champion for all trans-sexuals, and later they broadened Richards' underdog status by quoting him/her: "[The USTA] have done the same thing with me that they've done with every other minority" (September 1, 1976).

However, Richards' inability to recognize *women* as an historically oppressed group whose interests should be protected, or whose interests might, indeed *do*, interfere with his/her own, contradicts his/her stance as a spokesperson for human rights. Richards acknowledged in the auto-biography that much as s/he desired to live life as a woman, s/he had little sensitivity to the political implications of that life: "My idea of how a lady is treated was formed prior to women's liberation" (p. 291). Like many trans-sexuals, s/he displays an exaggerated, stereotypical notion of feminine behavior drawn from masculine hegemonic notions of gender. This attitude was exacerbated by the requirement that s/he prove to psychiatric and med-ical authorities that s/he was ready for the drastic surgical step of sex reassignment by demonstrating almost hyperfeminine behavior.

Moreover, Richards is clearly unaware of the advantages of Raskind's life of white male privilege, including attendance at a boys' prep school, gradu-ation from Yale, completion of medical school, a successful surgical practice, the thrill of being approached by a scout from the New York Yankees, and access to highly competitive tennis which s/he took as his/her natural right as a male. His/her own sister, who so longed for such opportunities, was sum-marily denied them. Yet Richards never acknowledges the implications for women of his/her entrance into their world. As one colleague has suggested to us, "Renee Richards should have had his consciousness raised before he had his sex changed."

Support for Richards as suspicion of women

Richards' apparent inability to recognize the political position of women problematizes the media's construction of him/her as a symbol for human rights. But while Richards was positioned by the press as a symbol of human rights, support for him/her can be read for meanings overlooked by the media: Indeed it is difficult to read the support for Richards as anything other than opposition to women. Richards' entrance into women's profes-sional sport occasioned an outburst of antifeminist sentiment that was unexamined by the press.

The vehemence of this opposition to the women players can be read within a Foucauldian (1979) context of anxiety, suspicion, and surveillance. Terry (1989) has argued that "we witness daily technological developments designed to keep a watchful eye on those entities considered suspicious . . . in an effort to contain 'danger' and restore 'security' " (p. 14). Given the chal-lenges transsexuals pose to the dominant gender system, medical and legal surveillance systems work together to contain what they consider to be dan-gerous. In a similar manner, growing anxiety about changes in women's social positions and participation in traditional masculine practices such as sport have intensified suspicion of women.

The historical struggles of women and sport are particularly important in locating the sources of the tension around the women players, since Richards entered women's sport in the wake of the women's liberation movement and dramatic gains for women, and for women in sport, throughout the 1960s and 1970s. Billie Jean King's defeat of Bobby Riggs in 1974 in "the battle of the sexes" and the success of Gladys Heldman and King in organizing resist-ance to male control of the women's tennis circuit in the early 1970s marked the end of men's complete dominance in tennis. Ironically, Richards' desire to play on the women's tour depended upon the recent struggles of women players and organizers whose successes gave the tour increased economic viability. Thus Richards stood to benefit directly from the hard-won opportunities for women in sport at the very moment s/he was challenging them.

While the media's narratives make general references to the history of sex discrimination in tennis and to past confrontations, in effect they provided space for male voices to frame women's successes within an atmosphere of suspicion, and readers were not given a context in which to understand these challenges to the women's integrity. By directing attention to the event's immediacy and presenting the controversy apart from its historical context, the origins of opposition are obscured. Jameson (1983) notes,

> the disappearance of a sense of history, the way in which our entire contemporary social system has little by little begun to lose its capacity to retain its own past, has begun to live in a perpetual present and in a perpetual change which obliterates traditions of the kind which all earlier social formations have had in one way or another to preserve . . . One is tempted to say that the very function of the news media would thus be to help us forget, to serve as the very agents and mechanisms for our historical amnesia.
>
> (p. 125)

The support for Richards can be read within a context of anxiety and suspicion of women's recent gains in sport. Gene Scott's support of Richards was particularly revealing of this suspicion: "The women players are always talking about sex discrimination but when it comes to a real issue they run and hide. If we followed them we'd still be reading by candlelight" (quoted in Kennedy, 1976, p. 19).

Although Scott's comments allude to a history of struggle around women and sport, to him the "real" issue is not the hard-won rights of the women players but the rights of constructed-female transsexuals. Equally telling was Scott's comment to *The Washington Post*:

> I think the women players today are basically sheep followers. They have worked hard and gotten a terrific recognition factor and lots of spectators. The prize money has escalated out of all proportion. But they did all this by cultivating a reputation of being in a mood of change and imagination. [Their reaction to Renee Richards] shows this is all bunk. They're actually afraid of new ideas.
>
> (August 21, 1976)

This quote betrays Scott's feelings about women's equality when he complains that "the prize money has escalated out of all proportion." He dismisses the women players' opposition to Richards as childish whimpering: "I've heard the women whine for years about Chris Evert's dominating on clay" (*The Washington Post*, August 21, 1976).

Ilie Nastase's comment also reveals more disdain for the women players than support for Richards: "If she wears a dress, why not? Now you see how strong the women players are. She could be their mother, yet they complain. They're afraid" (quoted in Kennedy, 1976, p. 18).

Richards was proud to report that Nastase "was one of my earliest supporters; he once made a remark that I was more feminine than some of the women already on the tour" (p. 332). Such comments represent the women players as imperfect women by casting suspicion on their femininity and sexuality and belittling women's historical struggles. Through similar homo-phobic comments about the women players, Richards attempted to establish his/her own claim to female status. Explaining why s/he refused to take the sex chromosome test, for example, Richards argued "in my case such tests were irrelevant. Of all the potential competitors my sex was the least in doubt. It was a matter of public record based on legal documentation" (p. 343). Admitting that at 6-ft 1-in. "I looked so damn fearsome," Richards continued, "Still Betty Stove was six feet tall and hefty besides. So were some lesser known pros, yet their *sexuality* had never been questioned" (our emphasis, p. 344). Throughout the autobiography, Richards used the con-cepts sex status and sexuality interchangeably. That confusion suggests the homophobia that also forms the basis for the men's anxieties. Elsewhere the confusion can be understood as a central feature in Richards' construction of him/herself as a gendered being.

In all the coverage of the Renee Richards controversy, not one mention was made of a male player who did *not* support Richards, a rather extra-ordinary detail that may indicate either the press' reluctance to report opposition among male players or the depths of antiwoman sentiment on the tour. As one woman player who opposed Richards complained, "They want to see anybody beat us, even a transsexual" (quoted in Steinem, 1977, p. 85). Thus "support" for Richards came in a form that simultaneously cast suspicion on or discredited the women players. Steinem pointed out the tactic as well:

> When the women players themselves questioned the fairness of their facing someone trained physically and culturally for 40 years as a man, they were ridiculed as poor sports, anti-civil libertarians, or cowards who feared they couldn't win.
>
> (p. 85)

The press sometimes joined in the trivialization of the women's oppos-ition. *The Washington Post* acknowledged "Few on Tour Support Richards" and "Opposition to Richards Apparently Growing" (January 1, 1978). They estimated that 80% of the women opposed Richards: "some of it friendly, some impersonal, some viciously hostile." Yet in one of the few stories deal-ing with the reactions of individual women players, *The Post* chose to report instances of "downright cruel" behavior, including two British players who appeared at a tournament wearing T-shirts with the message, "I am a real woman."

A final example of producing sympathy for Richards by casting suspicion on or blaming women can be found in Richards' autobiography. The book is an extended narrative of personal etiology in which Richards recounts in detail the anguish of gender dysphoria, his/her analysis of the causes, and his/her 41-year search for remedies, including the mutilation of his/her penis in a denial of the signifier of manhood, vivid accounts of sexual adventures into hyperheterosexuality, transvestism, homosexuality, and quasi-lesbianism, and the cruel series of promises and rejections from the medical establishment, the psychiatric community, and family and friends as s/he finally sought sex reassignment.

In the book and movie, a major focus of blame and suspicion was Richards' mother. The book begins, for example, with the words, "My mother was a head-strong woman" (p. 1), and within two pages the reader has been acquainted with the sex role reversals traditionally believed to be the root of transsexualism and male homosexuality: the domineering mother, the submissive father. Richards paints a picture of a childhood full of gender confusion—an older sister named Michael who wanted to be a boy, and his mother and sister's habit of dressing him in girl's clothes, including a traumatic incident at age 4 when he was humiliated by being made to appear in public dressed as a girl. Richards argues that "my early life is strewn with unsubtle touches that beg to be seen as reasons for my sexual confusion. If they aren't the true cause they ought to be" (p. 5).

Most of these incidents are depicted in the film as well, and a rather fore-shortened analysis is offered by his/her psychiatrist mother (Louise Fletcher in a tight performance reminiscent of her portrayal of Nurse Ratched in *One Flew Over the Cuckoo's Nest*). When confronted by her son's admission of deep sexual confusion, she prescribes psychiatric therapy and states simply, "Maybe it's my fault . . . You probably identified with me instead of your father. Quite *natural* really. I was so strong" (our emphasis). To underscore her strength, she is portrayed in her first scene as a feminist, and her first line, delivered to someone on the phone while her son awaits her attention, is "But women have *always* had to fight." In both the book and the film, strong women come in for more than their share of blame for Richards' condition while cultural constructions of rigid gender and sex ideologies go unaddressed.

Competitive equality and the "natural inferiority" of women

Opposition to Richards was framed in terms of the issues of competitive equality and the domino effect. As the USTA saw it, "The entry into women's events . . . of persons not genetically female would introduce an element of inequality and unfairness into the championships" (*The New York Times*, August 15, 1976). USTA counsel Peter Leisure argued in court, "It would be unfair to have women who have worked hard and prepared for this tournament beaten by a person who is *more than woman* (our emphasis, *The New York Times*, August 11, 1977). Added to the fear that Richards' formerly male body provided an insurmountable natural advantage over the women players was the fear that Richards would "open the way to problems in the future from young male players with transsexual tendencies" (*The New York Times*, December 31, 1976). As Richards viewed the issue,

If I was allowed to play, then the floodgates would be opened and through them would come tumbling an endless stream of made-over Neanderthals who would brutalize Chris Evert and Evonne Goolagong. . . . Some player who was not quite good enough in men's tennis might decide to change only in order to overpower the women players.

(p. 345)

These debates over fairness were translated into issues related to the body and power. The body, one of the most seemingly natural elements of social life, was foregrounded by the press. Descriptions emphasizing Richards'/ women's physical appearance and women's physical inferiority were presented uncritically and circulated by the media. The logic they employed seemed to say that if Richards is weaker than s/he was or if s/he adorns his/ her body in stereotypical feminine ways, then Richards is weak enough and feminine enough to be allowed to play.

Because the media focused on men's "natural" ability rather than the years of privileged access to sport that Richard Raskind had enjoyed, they foregrounded physical definitions of sex and gender and obscured cultural ones. Richards also constructed the argument in physiological and biomechanical terms. S/he noted with characteristic humor, "they think of me as a bionic woman" (*The New York Times*, August 18, 1976), but s/he refuted this view. Noting the changes in his/her body as the result of hormonal treatments, s/he said "The tone of the muscles . . . seemed to be softer now" (p. 172). Of his/ her tennis game s/he remarked "I didn't notice much decrease in my general abilities though I was definitely less strong. After six months of hormone therapy I estimate that I had about four-fifths of my previous strength" (p. 178). In fact Richards argued that his/her heavier male bone structure and hormonally reduced muscle mass actually meant "I was playing with a handicap" (p. 344). S/he argued that his/her losses proved a point: "they served to inform the public that I was not an unbeatable behemoth out to prey on helpless little girls" (p. 350).

The discourse on bodies within the Richards controversy demonstrates the cultural significance of constructing women's bodies as different from and representing them as physically inferior to men's bodies. The challenge of Richards' presence in women's sport works to naturalize women as physically inferior, and that assumption of the natural inferiority of women is evident in Richards' thinking throughout the autobiography. Playing social tennis in Europe while undergoing hormonal treatment prior to his/her operation, Richards was pleased at his/her partners' reaction to his/her superior skill but "when I missed a ball, they were quick to blame it on my being a woman. I didn't mind these jibes because they affirmed my womanliness" (p. 238).

Richards' mediocre performances on court were also used by the press to suggest his/her acceptability as a woman. After Richards lost to Antonopolis in South Orange (August 28, 1976), *The New York Times* asked, "So what was all the fuss about?" Billie Jean King argued in Richards' defense, "she does not enjoy physical superiority or strength so as to have an advantage over women competitors in the sport of tennis" (*Richards v. USTA*, 1977, p. 272). And the USTA eventually decided against an appeal because Richards "did not represent the physical threat that officials and players once feared" (*The New York Times*, August 18, 1977). Richards him/herself noted that "none of the fears that drove them to ban me ever proved waranted. I certainly haven't dominated the world of women's tennis" (p. 365).[13]

Richards' inability to dominate women's tennis is offered as proof of his/her status as a woman. Radically reconfiguring his/her body through the exchange of material sex-signifiers has apparently cost Richards his/her natural superiority as a (former) male. Through reference to his/her weakened condition, the news media and Richards construct Richards as less-than-male and thus an acceptable challenge for women players.

Representation and constraint

In this paper we have tried to show how meanings of sex, gender, difference, and power are literally inscribed onto the body and then how that body is represented through the discourse of news and the autobiographical constructions of individual subjectivity. The ambiguity of Richards' constructed-female transsexual body triggered a crisis in representation in terms of sport and the gendered body. However, the media not only ignored the contradictions posed by Richards but positioned him/her as a hero and a signifier of resistance while women as a group became targets for the exercise of power through criticism. Homophobic and sexist discourses were constructed to contain women as suspicious. Dyer (1982) reminds us that,

> A major legacy of the social and political movements of the Sixties and Seventies has been the realization of the importance of representation. The political chances of different groups in society—powerful or weak, central or marginal—are crucially affected by how they are represented, whether in legal and parliamentary discourse, in educational practices, or in the arts. The mass media in particular have a crucial role to play, because they are a centralised source of definitions of what people are like in any given society. How a particular group is represented determines in a very real sense what it can do in society.
>
> (p. 43)

The Renee Richards case provides a dramatic moment for examining these issues.

Our examination of the media's representation of the controversy around Renee Richards is an attempt to illuminate the everyday practices of the media and the processes through which representations define femininity. In this case, the media accepted as unproblematic the assumptions of liberalism, dominant images of femininity, and ideologies of sport. While the contradictions embedded in and through the processes of transsexualism potentially trigger a crisis in representations of sex and gender, the conventions of the media make it difficult to articulate and interpret the controversy outside of dominant discourses.

This is not to suggest that all readings are symmetrical with encodings or preferred readings. The varied and complex lived experience of social actors no doubt produce readings that depart from the frame constructed by the commercial media. But the tight frame and the narrative constructed around the controversy, combined with a neglect of the historical position of women and sport, the meaning of the possibility of transsexualism, and the technologies of gender, work to constrain the possibility of alternative readings. These conventions produce what Hall (1977) has suggested is the endemic tendency of the media: support of the status quo.

Renee Richards, sport, and the production of difference

Renee Richards' determination to enter women's sport, the support and opposition to that move, and the representation of the controversy that the media constructed provide fascinating insight into our cultural understandings of sex difference, gender behavior, and the role that sport plays in their production and reproduction.

The entrance of a transsexual into women's sport posed an interesting dilemma that was symbolized by the fact that Richards had to sue to gain the legal right to enter sport as a woman. After all, Jan Morris did not have to sue to be allowed to be a writer, Christine Jorgensen did not have to sue to become an entertainer, and Richards continued his/her career as an ophthalmologist. The particular difficulty of this dilemma reveals sport not only as a gender producing, gender affirming system but as a difference and power producing system. For sport works to differentiate winners from losers, the men from the boys, the men from the women. As a significant gendering activity, sport not only reproduces gender and sex differences but it produces a logic of differentiation.

Because sport celebrates physically within a competitive frame, working to determine winners based on physical superiority, it is a major site for the naturalization of sex and gender differences. Moreover, sport's logic continually reproduces men as naturally superior to women (Connell, 1983; Willis, 1982). The sex test instituted for the 1968 Olympic Games is a clear example of the manner in which sex categories are vigilantly maintained in sport. The sex test arose from the suspicion that superior female athletic performances, such as those of Ewa Klobukowska, were actually accomplished by women who were not truly women or by craftily disguised men. The implication is that superior athletic prowess is the natural domain of males.

The prestige of athletic victory, the "natural" inferiority of women constructed through sport's power as metaphor, and thus the easier competition assumed in the women's division all lead to the logical conclusion that enterprising men might try to pass as women. Renee Richards represented one form that challenge might take. Although Richards asked, "How hungry for tennis success must you be to have your penis chopped off in pursuit of it? How many men would do it for a million dollars?" (p. 345). In fact the U.S. obsession with sport makes it not at all unlikely that some man would willingly sacrifice his penis for victory; drug abuse, steroid use, blood doping, urine transplants, overtraining, and risking life-threatening or severe injuries are all a part of the modern sport scene.

A critical reading of the Renee Richards incident illuminates the part sport plays in the reproduction of an ideology of sex difference/power, gender and sex identity, and the regulation of the body. As Willis (1982) and others argue, sport is a central site for the naturalization of sex and gender difference, that is, sport produces a narrative structured around physical superiority in which sex differences are understood as, and thus reproduced as, real and meaningful. Transsexualism appears to challenge the neatness and logic—indeed the "reality"—of a sex/gender system marked by biological difference. This reveals not only the social construction of gender but the social construction of the sex-gender connection. Moreover, transsexualism demonstrates that it is not only the categories of difference that are culturally produced but the notion of difference itself.

It would seem as though the re-sexing of an individual such as Richards deconstructs notions of natural sex identity, but in fact by remaining gendered, Richards reaffirms the concept of sexual difference. By apparently changing sex, Renee Richards appears to upset our dominant ideology of gender relations, but in fact s/he stabilizes that ideology by merely shifting categories, by demonstrating dramatically the cultural necessity of a gendered home and that the "mistakes of nature" can be technologically regulated by humankind.

As Joan Scott and other poststructuralists point out, "meaning is made through implicit and explicit contrast" (1988, p. 36), through antithesis and difference. Primary among these binary oppositions that structure our discourses and thus our consciousness, indeed the archetype of that ideological practice, is sexual difference. When sex difference is contested, the entire ideological enterprise of meaning through difference is shaken. While Renee Richards demonstrates the disproportionate power that male-dominated institutions have in the construction and legitimation of woman, even more profound is the illumination that the Renee Richards incident casts on our cultural mandate to maintain sexual difference. There are no alternative categories for Richards or other nonconforming subjects to inhabit in the law, medical science, language, or sport. Their order depends upon the maintenance of the familiar binary opposition of male/female. The Renee Richards case is not only about tennis and transsexualism, not only about the construction of woman, but about the construction of difference itself.

Acknowledgments

An earlier version of this paper was presented at the 1987 meetings of the North American Society for the Sociology of Sport. The paper was substantially revised during a developmental leave provided by The University of Iowa and generously supported by the staff and colleagues at University House. The senior author gratefully acknowledges this collegial support. We would also like to thank Nancy Theberge, Linda Yanney, Nancy Romalov, and the reviewers for *SSJ* for bringing important sources to our attention and for useful critical feedback.

Notes

1 A major purpose of this paper is to problematize one fiction of science, the discourse of transsexualism, including the assumptions about the ontological status of sex and femininity, and to ask how sex reassignment or sex change is possible. We problematize some terms through the use of quotation marks at first mention. We use the phrase "constructed-female transsexual" because it reflects the constructedness of sex and gender.

2 The pronoun used to describe Richards is a significant political move. We have opted to refer to Renee Richards as s/he to denote Richards' bisexed lived experience and his/her difference from those who have lived only one sexual identity. Had we countered the mainstream positioning of Richards as female by repositioning him as male, the choice of a singular pronoun would deny either Richards' past or present positioning.

3 This is true as well of the autobiographies of transsexuals (e.g., Jorgensen, 1967; Martino, 1977; Morris, 1974; Richards, 1983) which struggle to comprehend their own personal etiology, which dwell on the personal anguish of gender dysphoria, and which end on a note of personal triumph.

4 According to de Lauretis (1987), the concept of technologies of gender "takes . . . its conceptual premise from Foucault's theory of sexuality as a 'technology of sex' and proposes that gender, too, both as a representation and self-representation, is the product of various social technologies, such as cinema, as well as by institutional discourses, epistemologies, and critical practices; [meaning] not only academic criticism, but more broadly social and cultural practices" (p. ix).

5 According to Bullough (1975), strict religious sanctions and "a kind of mystic view of the inferiority of the female" made it almost impossible for men to assume the female role without harsh reprisals. Thus the majority of preoperative transsexuals, or transvestites, prior to the 19th century were women.

196

6 We persist in our two-sexes/two-gender paradigm despite the counterexamples in our own culture: tomboys, sissies, transvestites, female impersonators, drag queens, gay men, lesbians, gender blending women (Devor, 1987). These anomalies are repositioned within dominant discourse through a variety of cultural practices: labeling homosexuals as queers, refusing to take transvestites and drag queens seriously, waiting for tomboys to grow out of their inappropriate behavior, and completely misunderstanding the meaning of the Berdasch by imposing an ethnocentric model on them (Williams, 1987).

7 Raymond's book clearly illuminates the relationship between sex stereotypes and the medical empire's understanding and treatment of transsexuals. But although her argument is based on an understanding of the cultural constructedness of gender, she contradicts her explanation of the cultural construction of gender identity and transsexualism when she argues that female-transsexuals can never be real women because women's biology makes females unique.

8 While a number of criteria traditionally have been available to distinguish between the sexes—including chromosomes, anatomy or morphological structure, genital or gonadal evidence, endocrine or hormonal balances, and psychological factors (Money & Ehrhardt, 1972)—the law accepts genital anatomy as its means of "official sex designation" (Dunlap, 1979, p. 1132).

9 Our analysis is of three metropolitan newspapers of national reputation: *The New York Times, The Washington Post*, and the *Los Angeles Times*. We analyzed all news stories, editorials, photographs, and cartoons featuring Renee Richards that appeared between July 24, 1976, the first news mention of Richards during the South Orange tournament, and August 12, 1982, when Richards returned to his/her medical practice. We also included articles in popular magazines such as *Sports Illustrated, Ms., Time*, and *Newsweek*.

10 The legal system also accomplished gendering through language. In the very case which was to determine Richards' legal sex status, the court referred to Richards as "she" in the very first sentence: "A professional tennis player who had undergone sex reassignment surgery which allegedly changed her sex from male to female" (*Richards v. USTA*, 1977, p. 267).

11 Reactions of feminists outside of tennis were not covered by the news media. Writing in *Ms.* magazine, Gloria Steinem (1977) noted the deeper cultural meaning of transsexualism underlying the Richards story and she decried the diversionary effect that attention to Richards had on women's issues. Marcia Seligson (1977), by focusing upon the promotional efforts launched in Richards' behalf and the opportunism s/he displayed, expressed serious doubts about his/her sincerity and commitment.

12 The USTA's opposition to Richards represented male protectionism not of women's rights but of commercial profit. The economic rationality of the tour depends upon a clear division of competitors by sex because one tenet of profit maximization is to provide a product that clearly differentiates itself from the competition. Richards had to be challenged because s/he problematized the division of sport into two separate markets.

13 Richards' *dominance* of the tour is not the point. None of the top players ever lost to Richards but many of the less experienced players did. Allowing Richards to play in the U.S. Open in 1977 did not displace King or Evert but some lower ranked professional woman player whose interests were equally worthy of protection. The USTA's action makes it clear that it was not the rank and file players they sought to protect but the top stars, and thus the economic vitality of the tour.

References

Benjamin, H. (1966). *The transsexual phenomenon*. New York: Julian.

Bolin, A. (1987). Transsexualism and the limits of traditional analysis. *American Behavioral Scientist*, **31**, 41–65.

Bolin, A. (1988). *In search of Eve: Transsexual rites of passage*. South Hadley, MA: Bergen & Garvey.

Brod, H. (1987). Cross-culture, cross-gender: Cultural marginality and gender transcendence. *American Behavioral Scientist*, **31**, 5–11.

Bullough, V.L. (1975). Transsexualism in history. *Archives of Sexual Behavior*, **4**, 561–571.

Connell, R. (1983). *Which way is up?* Sydney: Allen & Unwin.

de Lauretis, T. (1987). *Technologies of gender: Essays on theory, film, and fiction*. Bloomington: Indiana University Press.

Devor, H. (1987). Gender blending females: Women and sometimes men. *American Behavioral Scientist*, **31**, 12–39.

Dunlap, M.C. (1979). The constitutional rights of sexual minorities: A crisis of the male/female dichotomy. *Hastings Law Journal*, **30**, 1131–1149.

Dyer, R. (1982). The celluloid closet. *Birmingham Arts Lab Bulletin*, **1**, 43.

Foucault, M. (1979). *Discipline and punish: The birth of the prison*. New York: Vintage.

Garfinkel, H., & Stoller, R.J. (1967). Passing and the managed achievement of sex status in an "intersexed" person. In H. Garfinkel (Ed.), *Studies in ethnomethodology* (pp. 116–135). Englewood Cliffs, NJ: Prentice-Hall.

Gitlin, T. (1980). *The whole world is watching*. Berkeley: University of California Press.

Grimm, D.E. (1987). Toward a theory of gender. *American Behavioral Scientist*, **31**, 66–85.

Hall, S. (1977). Culture, the media and 'ideological effect.' In J. Curran, M. Gurevich, & J. Woollocott (Eds.), *Mass communication and society* (pp. 315–348). London: Edward Arnold.

Hartley, J. (1982). *Understanding news*. New York: Methuen.

Jameson, F. (1983). Postmodernism and consumer society. In H. Foster (Ed.), *The antiaesthetic: Essays on postmodern cultures* (pp. 111–125). Post Townsend, WA: Bay Press.

Jorgensen, C. (1967). *Christine Jorgensen: A personal autobiography*. New York: Bantam.

Kando, T. (1973). *Sex change: The achievement of gender identity among feminized transsexuals*. Springfield, IL: C.C. Thomas.

Kennedy, R. (1976, Sept. 6). She'd rather switch—And fight. *Sports Illustrated*, pp. 16–19.

Kessler, S.J., & McKenna, W. (1978). *Gender: An ethnomethodological approach*. New York: Wiley.

Los Angeles Times. (Selected articles.) August 12, 1976–January 1, 1978.

Martino, M. (1977). *Emergence: A transexual autobiography*. New York: Signet.

Money, J., & Ehrhardt, A. (1972). *Man and woman, boy and girl*. Baltimore: Johns Hopkins University Press.

Money, J., & Tucker, P. (1975). *Sexual signatures: On being a man or a woman*. Boston: Little, Brown.

Morris, J. (1974). *Conundrum*. New York: Henry Holt.

New York Times, The. (Selected articles.) July 24, 1976–August 18, 1977.

Raymond, J. (1979). *The transsexual empire.* Boston: Beacon Press.

Richards, R., with Ames, J. (1983). *Second serve.* New York: Stein & Day.

Richards v. United States Tennis Association, 400 N. Y. S. 2nd 267 (1977).

Scott, J.W. (1988). Deconstructing equality-versus-difference: Or, the uses of post-structuralist theory for feminism. *Feminist Studies,* **14**, 33–50.

Seligson, M. (1977, Feb.). The packaging of Renee Richards. *Ms.*, pp. 74–76, 85.

Steinem, G. (1977, Feb.). If the shoe doesn't fit, change the foot. *Ms.*, pp. 76, 85, 86.

Stoller, R. (1975). *Sex and gender, Vol. 2: The transsexual experiment.* New York: Jason Aronson.

Terry, J. (1989). The body invaded: Medical surveillance of women as reproducers. *Socialist Review,* **19**, 13–45.

Washington Post, The. (Selected articles.) August 12, 1976-January 1, 1978.

Williams, W.L. (1986). *The spirit and the flesh: Sexual diversity of American Indian culture.* Boston: Beacon.

Williams, W.L. (1987). Women, men, and others. *American Behavioral Scientist,* **31**, 135–141.

Willis, P. (1982). Women in sport in ideology. In J. Hargreaves (Ed.), *Sport, culture and ideology* (pp. 117–135). London: Routledge & Kegan Paul.

Winston-Salem Journal. (Selected articles.) August 5, 1977-February 14, 1978.

50

MEN STUDYING MASCULINITY

Some epistemological issues in sport sociology

Michael A. Messner

Source: *Sociology of Sport Journal* 7 (1990): 136–153.

This paper evaluates a growing genre of studies of masculinity and sport. It is argued that sport sociology, like sociology in general, has become more gender conscious but not necessarily more feminist. Feminist critiques of objectivism and value-free sociology and feminist calls for a values-based feminist standpoint are discussed. Two responses to feminism by male scholars—antifeminist masculinism and profeminism—are discussed and critically analyzed. Finally, it is argued that studies of masculinity and sport are more likely to tell a true story if they are grounded in an inclusive feminism, which utilizes multiple standpoints that take into account the intersections of class, race, gender, and other systems of domination and subordination.

Feminist scholarship has posed fundamental challenges within various academic disciplines (Spender, 1981; Stacey & Thorne, 1985). At its most radical, feminist thought has laid bare the implicit androcentric bias of dominant modes of inquiry. Gender, we have learned, is a basic organizing principle of social life, and therefore the social construction of gender must become a basic theoretical category through which we understand the world. In its less radical manifestations, feminist thought has at least sensitized scholars that gender is a variable that must be taken into account in our research. This increased awareness of the importance of gender has led to a new focus on men and masculinity, and much of the new scholarship on men and masculinity is being done by men. Increasingly, college courses are being taught by men about men; professional networks of "men's studies" scholars are forming; texts, anthologies, monographs, and journal articles have begun to demarcate a new subfield (Brod, 1987b; Carrigan, Connell, & Lee, 1987; Franklin, 1984; Hearn, 1987; Kaufman, 1987; Kimmel, 1987a; Kimmel & Messner, 1989; Pleck, 1982; Pleck & Pleck, 1980; Tolson, 1977).

This new phenomenon raises critical questions. As men increasingly jump on the bandwagon of gender analysis and begin to examine their own lives in terms of the social construction of masculinity, do women's voices—and their critical, antipatriarchal perspectives—get lost in the shuffle? Does the "new" men's studies simply degenerate into a more sensitive version of the "old" men's studies? (Banner, 1989; Klein, 1983) This paper analyzes these general questions by examining the emergent literature on masculinity in sport sociology. It will be argued that at the heart of the debate is an epistemological issue: From whose standpoint can we develop a more true understanding of men and masculinity? This is a crucial and timely question within sport sociology today for two reasons: First, despite the obviously gendered basis of sport as a social institution, it is only very recently that studies of masculinity and sport have begun to appear in the literature. And second, as these studies begin to appear, it is clear that access to much of the subject matter of masculinity and sport is open primarily (in some cases, perhaps exclusively) to male researchers. It becomes crucial, then, to critically evaluate this emergent genre of men studying masculinity within sport sociology.

I will begin to evaluate these studies of masculinity and sport with the observation that the new men's studies is not all of one piece. There are different, and oppositional, strands of thought now emerging and claiming the terrain of men's studies. I will first identify three existent strands of thought: gender-conscious sociology, antifeminist masculinism, and profeminism.[1] I will then outline a fourth, emergent perspective, inclusive feminism. Utilizing examples from sport studies, it will be argued that these four perspectives, while overlapping in some ways, have distinct epistemological bases and as a result are often at odds with each other.

Beyond objectivism to a feminist standpoint

For the most part, feminism has not faced outright resistance within sociology; rather, it has been largely co-opted and ghettoized. This has occurred mainly because the dominant disciplinary paradigms—role theory and structural functionalism—have been able to absorb gender as a variable while leaving the dominant epistemological basis of mainstream sociology—positivism—unchallenged and unquestioned (Stacey & Thorne, 1985). Social scientists have become increasingly gender-conscious, that is, we have become sensitized to add gender to our already long list of variables to be measured; yet this incorporation of gender into our analysis has taken place largely within the dominant assumptions of the discipline. As a result, as Carrigan et al. (1987) point out in their critical examination of the recent spate of books about men, studies of the male sex role have often proceeded from an objectivist standpoint that ignores, and thus inadvertently affirms, men's institutionalized power and privilege over women. This sort of criticism is based on the relatively recent feminist critique of value-free social science and the concomitant call for a feminist standpoint epistemology.[2]

Advocates of a feminist standpoint reject the objectivist assumption that there exists an object-world that is equally knowable to all who follow a proper, presumably scientific, method.[3] Yet they do not revert to solipsism. Rather, following a theory of knowledge adapted from critical Marxism, feminists argue that there *is* in fact a knowable object-world, but it is not static and it is not equally knowable from all standpoints by all people (Rose, 1986). As Freire (1970) has argued, the object-world tends to appear static in the "false" knowledge produced by those who hold power and privilege. "True" knowledge is produced when oppressed people are engaged in the process of trying to change the world. In other words, the social world itself is constantly being constituted through human practice; true knowledge about the social world is thus produced through the dialectical interaction between subject and object.

Since the production of knowledge is a social process, it is thus always based in relations of power. Hartsock (1983) has argued that the gendered division of labor has led men and women to develop different kinds of knowledge, or different standpoints. Men's overall social power, and in particular their control over cultural and intellectual apparatus, has allowed them to universalize their knowledge as "truth." Traditional men's studies amounts to the passing off of men's knowledge as "human knowledge" (Spender, 1981, p. 1). As a result, this knowledge is false knowledge because it is insisted that men's partial view of reality be accepted as the whole (Daly, 1973, p. 8). Spender, drawing from Smith (1978), describes the social process of the production of this falsely universalized masculine knowledge:

> Men . . . attend to and treat only as significant what men say with the result that women have been "largely excluded from the work of producing the forms of thought, and the images and symbols in which thought is expressed and ordered." There is a circle effect as men check with each other, validating each other's explanation of the world.
>
> (Spender, 1981, p. 3)

Mainstream researchers might object to the call for a feminist standpoint as an injection of bias into social science. Feminists would respond that they simply make their values explicit, while mainstream social science keeps its biases hidden behind a facade of "scientific" methods. Put another way, paraphrasing Rich (1979), objectivity is the name men give to their subjectivity.

The feminist observation that men's knowledge-making is a social process based in the material conditions of a privileged masculine culture has been accompanied by a counterobservation: women too make knowledge, but their knowledge has not been universalized as human knowledge. Adherents of a feminist standpoint have argued that women's oppressed, marginalized status, their Otherness, gives them a privileged standpoint from which to "stand back and criticize the norms, values, and practices that the dominant culture (patriarchy) seeks to impose on everyone" (Tong, 1989, p. 219).

Sport studies and the call for a feminist standpoint

A look at the past several years of sport sociology journals, books, and conference proceedings suggests that this new and growing subfield is certainly becoming more gender conscious (Melnick & Sabo, 1987). Within the context of the gendering of sport studies, what has the call for a feminist standpoint meant? Following Hartsock, Smith, and Harding, Hall (1985, p. 32) has argued that due to women's social experience of oppression and marginalization, "the standpoint of women provides for a more accurate and comprehensive representation of reality than the standpoint of men." Examining sport from the standpoint of women's marginalization and oppression reveals "not only how women are constructed as subordinate, but also how male sport structures operate to keep them that way" (Hall, 1985, p. 33). Traditional objectivist research in sport studies is thus partial and distorted knowledge that ultimately serves to obscure these oppressive realities.

Is the call for a feminist standpoint ultimately a methodological question? On the one hand it has been argued that the quantitative methods most commonly employed by mainstream social scientists are clearly congruent with the positivist, objectivist epistemological standpoint that feminists criticize as "prejudiced . . . patriarchal abstraction" (O'Brien, 1989, p. 35). And qualitative methods and interpretive theories are more in tune with the normative social science advocated by feminists (Stacey & Thorne, 1985). Sport sociologists, perhaps partly because of their stigmatized status within the larger discipline, have tended to mimic the "hyperempirical methodology" of the mainstream (Gallmeier, 1989; Klein, 1986). As a result, the objectivist epistemologies common within (especially U.S.) sport sociology have tended to smuggle in the standpoint, and thus support the material interests, of the dominant masculine culture. DiIorio (1989) encourages sport sociologists to employ ethnographic and other qualitative methods that explore the gendered *meanings* of sport. Qualitative methods, she argues, are more consistent with asking "woman centered" questions about sport and thus building critical and liberatory sport studies.

Though choices of method are clearly important, it would be a mistake to indict all quantitative sociology as inherently patriarchal and oppressive. There are numerous examples of excellent surveys in sport studies that critically illuminate the existence of oppression and inequality in sport (e.g., Sabo & Women's Sports Foundation, 1989). Similarly, qualitative methodologies, even those that are aimed at exploring issues of gender, are not inherently critical or feminist. For example, I will examine one recent work that explicitly tackles the masculinity issue, Fine's *With the Boys: Little League*

Baseball and Preadolescent Subculture (1987), a rich, participant-observation based study that has won praises and book awards. Fine makes an important contribution in moving us beyond a static, top-down socialization theory, wherein adults are assumed to instill social values into young boys, toward a more dynamic conception of boys as active agents in the construction of their own masculine culture and identities. Despite this valuable contribution to the study of the social construction of masculinity, Fine's book has been roundly criticized in several reviews in academic journals (Klein, 1988; Messner, 1989; Thorne, 1987).

A common thread in the criticisms of Fine is the contention that when he takes on the issue of assessing the effects of Little League baseball on boys, he concludes, "I know of no systematic research study that has shown any harmful psychological side effects of Little League" (Fine, 1987, p. 200). My response when I read this statement was, "what about your own research?" His chapter 5, Sexual Aggressive Themes of Preadolescent Boys, chronicles in great detail how Little League baseball provides a structured context within which male dominance (including the ideology of male superiority, devaluation of the feminine, aggressive objectification of females, and so on) as well as intermale dominance hierarchies (including verbal sparring, cruel insults aimed at more vulnerable boys, destructive homophobia, and racism) are constructed. Given the fact that these realities are clearly documented in Fine's descriptive data, it is interesting to speculate why he concludes that Little League baseball has no harmful side effects. Klein, in his review of the book, is similarly bothered by Fine's

> refusal to make statements or critically comment on subjects that need to be addressed. Pages of description of young boys making homophobic and sexist pronouncements just ask to be analyzed. Fine gets around this by claiming that these boys have their own subculture and what they mean by "fag" or "whore" is not the same as what we mean. He forgets that eventually what they mean by those terms will in all likelihood be what we in the adult world mean by them. This is the breeding ground of those unfortunate adult attitudes. . . . Fine does little in the way of critiquing his subject matter, and so winds up affirming something he might not really want to. This is the inevitable pitfall of value-free social science.
>
> (Klein, 1988, p. 293)

Fine's critics suggest further that his value-free approach, the apparent basis of his refusal to criticize sexism and homophobia, raises questions concerning the extent to which he *identifies with* the masculine culture he is studying. As Thorne points out in her review, *With the Boys* is more than the title of the book; it also "refers to the author's approach to gathering information" (Thorne, 1987, p. 67). The issue of identification is crucially important as more and more studies on masculinity and sport are done in the late '80s and into the '90s, for the worlds of boys' and men's sports are largely a world apart from women. Men researchers, simply put, have much easier and direct entrée to these worlds.

Clearly, Fine does not employ the dominant (quantitative) methods or the dominant (functionalist) theory of U.S. sociology. Rather, he employs primarily qualitative (participant observation) methods and symbolic interactionist theory in his analysis and interpretation of boys' relationships with Little League baseball. Fine's research demonstrates the point that advancing our understanding of gender and sport is decidedly *not* simply a matter of deciding on a proper methodology. Rather it involves, first and foremost, moving beyond a false value-neutrality.

How have men in sport studies responded to feminist critiques of sport and the call for viewing sport through feminism? Just as in the larger discipline of sociology, the dominant response has probably been to become "gender conscious," yet to remain (like Fine) working within established epistemological, methodological, and theoretical frameworks. In addition to an increase in "gender-conscious sociology," there have been two other highly significant responses to the feminist challenge. In what follows, I will describe two categories of values-based sport scholarship that men are producing, largely in response to feminism. The first category explicitly advocates a view of the world from a masculine standpoint, and I thus call it antifeminist masculinism. The second category, profeminism, attempts to view men's experience through a feminist standpoint.

Antifeminist masculinism

Though the dominant response to the call for a feminist standpoint has been a defense of scientific objectivity, there has also resulted a small but vocal assertion of men's right to name their own experience. For instance, when Banner (1987) delivered an address in which she criticized the new men's studies for appearing to be "too much a movement of men speaking to men," this raised the hackles of Robinson (1987), a self-proclaimed masculinist who objected to Banner's insistence that men's studies maintain a woman-centered analysis. Robinson wrote,

> *the* "woman-centered" analysis seems to have the effect of universalizing feminist analysis as the gender-analytical norm and woman-centered analysis as the normative criterion. But where does that leave us men? Must our analysis of men, women, and gender be woman-centered too? Do we have no right to our masculine experience?

This masculinist (re)assertion of men's "right to our own masculine experience" has taken several forms. One manifestation has emerged within conservative academic biology and sociobiology, which argues against the possibility of the feminist vision of equality between the sexes by reasserting a traditional biological essentialism. Goldberg's (1974) *The Inevitability of Patriarchy*, for instance, argues that feminism is doomed to fail because it runs against the basic biological differences between the sexes, differences that predispose men to aggressively dominate naturally weaker and subordinate women. This perspective ignores a wealth of historical, anthropological, and indeed even biological data which suggests that male dominance is a cultural and historical construction (Fausto-Sterling, 1985; Lee & Daly, 1987).

In contrast to sociobiologists, who see male-dominant cultural arrangements as consistent with (indeed as springing from) biological differences between the sexes, conservative writer Gilder (1973, 1986) views culture as muting the naturally destructive aggression of men. Gilder views men, especially single men, as barbarians who need to be tamed by civilization. In particular this means that women, in their roles as mothers and wives in nuclear families, must constrain and domesticate men's sexually aggressive nature. Gilder thus sees feminism as a danger to the entire fabric of civilization, as it directly threatens women's important role as guardians of morality, thus undermining the gendered public-domestic split that Gilder sees as necessary (Clatterbaugh, 1989).

The perceived moral and/or biological imperative to defend Victorian gender arrangements against the feminist challenge has led masculinists to a defensive glorification of men's homosocial retreats from women's emotional control, and from the general feminization of social life.[4] Feminist historians and sociologists have argued that organized sport as we now know it was constructed in the 19th and 20th centuries as an institution that supports and ideologically legitimates an otherwise challenged and faltering masculine domination of women (Bryson, 1987; Messner, 1988). The feminist critique of masculine domination within sport, and of the ideological use of sport to naturalize and support male domination, has been accompanied by a massive upsurge of female sport participation in the past two decades (Birrell, 1987–88).

As a result of women's movement into sport as well as feminist critiques of sport, some masculinists have been moved to defend sport as a male preserve. Gilder asserts that "Sports are possibly the single most important male rite in modern society," which women endanger. "The woman reduces the game from a religious male rite to a mere physical exercise, with some treacherous danger of psychic effect" (Gilder, 1973, p. 218). Athletic performance, for males, embodies "an ideal of beauty and truth," while women's participation represents a "disgusting . . . perversion" of this truth (p. 216). Despite his insistence that sports are an important institution for male socialization, the key to Gilder's assertion of the importance of maintaining sport as a male rite is his essentialist view of males as naturally aggressive, in need of civilizing. Drawing from Tiger, he claims that,

The tendency to bond with other males in intensely purposeful and dangerous activity is said to come from the collective demands of pursuing large animals. The female body, on the other hand, more closely resembles the body of nonhunting primates. A woman throws, for example, very like a male chimpanzee.

(Gilder, 1973, p. 221)

Sport, then, to Gilder, emerges as a means for men to bond together and mute or channel their natural aggressions. Though probably reflecting popular ideology about gender and sport, Gilder's perspective is rarely expressed within sport scholarship. However, there have been some masculinist defenses of sport in academic journals. Carroll (1986), for instance, lauds the "virtue and grace" of sport and defends it against its critics, especially feminists. He concludes that in order to preserve sport's "naturally conserving and creating" tendencies, especially in the realms of "the moral and the religious,"

women should once again be prohibited from sport: they are the true defenders of the humanist values that emanate from the household, the values of tenderness, nurture and compassion, and this most important role must not be confused by the military and political values inherent in sport. Likewise, sport should not be muzzled by humanist values: it is the living arena for the great virtue of manliness.

(Carroll, 1986, p. 98)

Though there are obviously some very important differences between biological, moral, and men's-rights masculinisms (Clatterbaugh, 1989), I categorize them all under the rubric of antifeminist masculinism because they all share a common epistemological basis. In short they all begin from masculine standpoints, where men's power and privilege over women is defended as naturally rooted in biology (Goldberg), or defined as a necessary cultural myth created to keep a naturally barbaric male essence in check (Gilder), or explained away as a feminist lie perpetrated so women can seize and hold power over men (Baumli, 1985).

Though weak by scholarly standards, masculinism has been politically salient as a unifying ideology for insecure and angry men (and some women) intent on saving the family against feminism. The theme of organizing men's anger toward women has led to significant financial support and media attention for men's rights (especially child custody) organizations. Similarly, Gilder's neo-Victorian perspective was laughed at when he first introduced it in the early 1970s, but with the rise of the Reagan counterrevolution it became a major basis for state family policy in the 1980s. In terms of sport, masculinist ideology often is taken as common sense to many; within academic sport studies, though, it is easily discredited as weak scholarship (Jennifer Hargreaves, 1986) and is thus for the most part marginalized.

Profeminism

Ironically, the emergence of masculinism reveals the powerful influence that feminism has had on academic thought. Feminists, in criticizing the andro-centric biases implicit in objectivist social science and in calling for an up-front values-based social science, have created a context for a values-based (masculinist) backlash. In essence, once an argument has been made that true knowledge is grounded in human experience, the space has been created for a kind of epistemological relativism: Since we all have experiences, then arguably all of our knowledge is equally valid. As the masculinist Robinson (1987) put it, "where does that leave us men? . . . Do we have no right to our masculine experience?" Feminists might answer this question "yes and no." Yes, like all human beings, as men we have a right to have our own experi-ences. But no, this does not mean that our experiences, as men, are equally accurate or reliable bases upon which to construct theoretical generalizations about social life. As Harding has argued, feminists are not arguing for a sort of relativism, whereby women's views are simply added to men's already existing views:

> women's and men's experiences are not equally reliable guides to the production of complete and undistorted social research. . . . Femi-nist researchers are arguing that women's and men's characteristic social experiences provide different, but not equal grounds for reli-able knowledge claims. . . . We all—men as well as women—should prefer women's experiences to men's as reliable bases for knowledge claims.
>
> (Harding, 1987, p. 10)

A conclusion that one might draw from this point is that men are not capable of doing social science, that men's work is inherently doomed to replicate patriarchal bias, either overtly as masculinism or covertly as objectivism. However, Harding argues that this would be a faulty conclusion, that "neither the ability nor the willingness to contribute to feminist understanding are sex linked traits" (p. 11). In fact, she sees promise in the possibility that men can contribute to the construction of a "phallic critique," especially in "areas of masculine behavior and thought to which male researchers have easier and perhaps better access than do women researchers . . . such as board rooms, military settings, or locker rooms" (pp. 11–12).

Indeed, the emergent new men's studies has largely aimed at contributing to feminist thought rather than countering it (Brod, 1987b; Kaufman, 1987;

Kimmel, 1987a). Brod, in his essay "The Case for Men's Studies," defines the profeminist men's studies standpoint:

> Like women's studies, men's studies aims at the emasculation of patriarchal ideology's masquerade as knowledge. . . . If men are to be removed from center stage and a feminist vision fulfilled, that feminist vision must be explicitly focused on men to move them off center. Men's studies views men precisely in this manner. While women have been obscured from our vision by being too much in the background, men have been obscured by being too much in the foreground. . . . The "woman question" must be supplemented by the "man question" for either to be addressed fully.
>
> (Brod, 1987a, pp. 40–41)

As Harding, Brod, and many others agree, men studying men can potentially make an important contribution to the overall feminist project. Yet the fact remains that gender studies is a political minefield for male scholars. As we have already seen in the feminist critiques of Fine's work, it is not enough for a male scholar to use his access to masculine worlds to describe and reflect on gender issues. For men to do feminist research, they must consciously adopt a feminist standpoint. How does sport sociology look when men do this? There is an emergent genre of this kind of work in sport sociology (Crosset, in press; Kidd, 1987; Messner, 1987; Messner & Sabo, in press-a; Sabo, 1985, 1986; Whitson, in press). I will focus here on one example of this profeminist sociology of masculinity in sport.

Sabo's (1986) article "Pigskin, Patriarchy and Pain" is perhaps the paradigmatic example of a profeminist male's reinterpretation, in light of feminism, of his own experience as an athlete. In the article, Sabo begins his analysis within his own body, describing the years of severe back pain that he had endured as a result of having played football. And he then poses a simple question: "How did I, a well-intending and reasonably gentle boy from western Pennsylvania, ever get into so much pain?" (p. 24). He then proceeds to answer this question by first detailing his own boyhood socialization. He felt insecure and "uncomfortable inside my body," and he soon found that working out, building his body up, and playing football was a way to overcome these insecurities. But he had to constantly prove himself to coaches and peers:

> calisthenics until my arms ached; hitting hard and fast and knocking the other guy down; getting hit in the groin and not crying. I learned that pain and injury are "part of the game." The coaches taught me to "punish the other man," but little did I suspect that I was devastating my own body at the same time.
>
> (p. 24)

But Sabo does not simply conclude, as a masculinist might, that his personal pain is yet another example of male victimization. Instead he analyzes his personal experience of pain within a larger institutional framework: "My pain, each individual's pain, is really an expression of a linkage to an outer world of people, events and forces" (p. 24). And the structure of that outside world is patriarchy, which beckons boys and men to dominate women and to dominate other males:

> Patriarchy is a form of social hierarchy. Hierarchy breeds inequity and inequity breeds pain. To remain stable, the hierarchy must either justify the pain or explain it away. . . . Male athletes adopt the visions and values that coaches are offering: To take orders, to take pain, to "take out" opponents, to take the game seriously, to take women, and to take their place on the team. And if they can't "take it," then the rewards of athletic comraderie, prestige, scholarships, pro contracts, and community recognition are not forthcoming. Becoming a football player fosters conformity to male-chauvinistic values and self-abusing lifestyles. It contributes to the legitimacy of a social structure based on patriarchal power.
>
> (Sabo, 1986, p. 25)

Sabo, Kidd, Crosset, and many other men doing profeminist sport studies are former athletes and thus have experiential access to aspects of the world of sport that few if any women have. And to a certain extent they are viewing sport through their own experience. Yet it is in stepping outside their experiences and viewing sport from the margins, through feminism, that a new truth is revealed about men's experience in sport. Painful and broken bodies (Messner, in press: Sabo, 1986), the denial or disparagement of men's feelings (Kidd, 1987), and the impoverishment of relationships in the single-minded pursuit of "success" (Messner, 1987) are all heavy costs that men pay for adherence to their role as athletes. Yet men are not simply being victimized by sports: These costs are linked to the promise of masculine power and privilege. And it is this link that a profeminist men's studies makes. To return to Sabo's analysis of what he calls the pain principle, in essence he is describing *the social process of the masculinization of the male body through sport*. This process results in the construction and naturalization of men's power over women, and in pain (both physical and emotional) for men.

Revealing the links between the costs and the privileges of masculinity is one of the major contributions being made by profeminist men's studies and also the point of greatest political tension (recall Banner's point that men's studies is too little about male power and privilege and too much about "explicating patriarchy's victimization of men or plumbing for male sensitivity" [Banner, 1989, pp. 704–705]). Yet it is these sorts of concrete examinations of men's lives that reveal the social mechanisms through which men's power over women is constructed. And a sensitive analysis, one that is atten-tive to the prices men pay for their power, can begin to reveal the ways that a feminist transformation of the world might be viewed as in men's interests. On the other hand, an overemphasis on men's victimization by narrow def-initions of masculinity, as in some forms of men's liberation, tends to obscure the fact that given the social structure of power, "the liberation of women must mean a loss of power for most men" (Carrigan et al., 1987, p. 167). Profeminist men's studies, then, faces a tricky balancing act. And given the fact that the men who are doing these studies share in the institutional power and privilege of all men, for the foreseeable future women scholars "are wise to look especially critically at analyses produced by members of the oppressor group" (Harding, 1987, p. 11).

Inclusive feminism

Just as some men have begun to employ a feminist standpoint in their studies of men and masculinity, there has been a major movement within feminism against the notion that there *is* a feminist standpoint. By the early 1980s a critique was emerging from women of color, who argued that feminism, in the industrialized societies, has essentially been a movement of and by white, middle-class women who have tended to falsely universalize their own issues and interests (i.e., their own standpoint) as "women's" issues and interests. This has contributed to the marginalization and alienation of working-class women and women of color from feminism (Davis, 1981; Dill, 1979; Hooks, 1981).

The initial response of feminist scholars to the criticism of their class and race biases was to conduct more studies of working-class women and women of color. Yet many of these studies still employed a theoretical framework that a priori privileged gender oppression over other forms of oppression. As a result, as Baca Zinn and her coauthors pointed out in an influential (1986) *Signs* article, women of color still felt that their experiences and needs were being falsely subsumed under the rubric of a middle-class feminist agenda. The experiences and life-chances of poor and minority women are, the critics argued, *at least* as much shaped and limited by class and race domination as they are by gender. Many white feminist activists and scholars felt confused by minority women's insistence that their interests might best be served through alliances with men, waged against race and class oppression. For their part, many poor and minority women felt uneasy about being lumped together with white, privileged women as mutual victims of patriarchy.

More recently, feminist scholars have responded to this dilemma by mov-ing beyond an additive approach (whereby studies of women of color are simply added to studies of white, middle-class women) toward a conceptual-ization of women's lives that takes into account what Stacey and Thorne (1985, p. 311) call a more "inclusive knowledge [which] would as equally attend to race, class, and sexuality as to gender." Moving toward this more complex, inclusive feminism means overcoming the latent reductionism that feminist thought may have inherited from Marxist theory in particular and Enlightenment thought in general (i.e., the assumption that there must be *one* dynamic of oppression and resistance—gender, class, race—that is the "motor of history"). In contrast, Harding (1986, pp. 163–164) argues that the fractured nature of social reality, and indeed the fractured nature of contemporary identity even among feminists (black women, Asian women, working-class women, lesbian women, black lesbian women, etc.) should serve as a warning sign against the development of theories that privilege one form of social domination (and identity) over others. Instead, Harding argues,

> we should explicitly recognize the ambivalences and contradictions within both feminist and androcentric thinking, and learn how to cherish beneficial tendencies while struggling against the social conditions that make possible regressive tendencies in both. I am not suggesting that we should *try* to produce incoherent theories, but that we should try to fashion conceptual schemes that are more alert to the complex and often beneficial ways in which the modernist world is falling apart.
>
> (1986, pp. 163–164)

An excellent example of recent feminist scholarship that does deal with some of these ambivalences and contradictions is Rothman's (1989) article in which she illuminates the ways that women from privileged racial and class groups can and often do exploit the bodies and the labor of poor women in order to themselves "have some of the privileges of patriarchy." In the class-privileged, dual-career family with children, she argues,

> both the mother and the father are sources of power—but it may be that neither is the daily care giver. The child is asked to switch identification from the nurturant care giver to the powerful parent, mother or father. And so, in this situation, the source of power is not sex, but class. . . . Racism and classism enter into this equation, too. Poor women, women of color, are often valued for their nurturant qualities.
>
> (Rothman, 1989, pp. 100–101)

In Rothman's analysis, the experience of white, privileged women is viewed through the standpoint of poor women and women of color who work for them. Viewing this reality from the standpoint of poor women of color reveals not an undifferentiated group of women who are equally oppressed by patriarchy, but rather cross-cutting and contradictory systems of inequality, power, and privilege. The fact that some women can "buy off" some of their gender oppression with their class and racial privilege, can themselves oppress and exploit lower class and minority women (and even men), does not of course mean that all women are not oppressed. It simply reveals the complexity of interlocking, yet semiautonomous, systems of power and inequality and warns us of the dangers inherent in simplistic and reductionistic theories of oppression and liberation.

As a result of recognizing these complexities, recent feminist thought has become "deeply skeptical of universalizing claims" (Harding, 1987, p. 188). Yet feminist theorists are quick to point out that the development of a non-hierarchical theory does not mean the acceptance of a sort of watered-down relativism or theoretical anarchy. Rather, it means developing concrete studies that illuminate the "complex web of hierarchical social arrangements that generate different experiences for women" (Baca Zinn et al., 1986, p. 297). It involves a commitment by white, middle-class feminists to learn from the work of women of color and lesbian scholars, whose "outsider within" status has already challenged and enriched social scientific discourse (Collins, 1986). And it involves the development of theories that allow us to conceptualize varied and shifting forms of domination and resistance in such a way that we do not privilege one at the expense of distorting or ignoring the others (Messner & Sabo, in press-b).

One of the most obvious dangers in this new direction in feminism is that men will see in it an opportunity to begin illuminating the various social contexts in which women, by virtue of their class and racial privileges, oppress or exploit men. Carrigan et al. point out that

> The global subordination of women is consistent with many particular situations in which women hold power over men or are at least equal. . . . [But] to cite such examples and claim that women are therefore not subordinated would be crass. The point is, rather, that contradictions between local situations and the global relationships are endemic. They are likely to be a fruitful source of turmoil and change in the structure as a whole.
>
> (1987, pp. 177–178)

Recent men's-studies theorists have suggested that rather than approaching the study of men and masculinity from this "crass" perspective (documenting instances of men's local subordinations to women), the proper approach is to examine the relationships among and between various masculinities and femininities (Brod, 1987b; Connell, 1987). Carrigan et al. (1987, p. 178) suggest, in fact, that "the fissuring of the categories 'men' and 'women' is one of the central facts about patriarchal power and the way it works. In the case of men, the crucial division is between hegemonic masculinity and various subordinated masculinities."

I would argue that the study of the concrete ways that various masculinities are constructed in relation to each other through sport holds the potential to make a key contribution to the construction of a more inclusive feminism. What follows are some brief examples of recent work that moves us in the direction of integrating analyses of masculinity with class, race, and sexual inequalities.

Class oppression and masculinity in sport

Marxist sport sociology, like Marxism in general, has usually ignored gender oppression or subordinated it within a class dynamic (e.g., Gruneau, 1983; Hoch, 1972). Recently though, neo-Marxist analyses of sport have taken greater account of gender issues. An example of the promise—and the limits —of this work is John Hargreaves' (1986) analysis of the historical development of sport in Britain. Hargreaves makes an important contribution to our understanding of how working-class masculinity, as constructed through organized sport, played a key role in the recomposition of a working class that resisted but ultimately contributed to the construction of a new bourgeois hegemony.

Racial oppression and masculinity in sport

Past studies of racial domination in sport have also tended to ignore or downplay gender issues (Edwards, 1971). Recently though, the work of Majors (1986, in press) has begun to examine masculinity issues more carefully. Majors argues that black men use sport as a context in which to develop and embody what he calls "cool pose," an expressive masculine style that acts as a form of resistance to racial oppression.

Sexual oppression and masculinity in sport

Very little work has been done on gay men and sport, partly because the world of sport is so homophobic; gay athletes have been an extremely invisible group. Recently though, some research has begun to emerge on this topic. Pronger (in press) utilizes a phenomenological analysis of "gay jocks" to argue that since sport is essentially an institution in which heterosexual masculinity is constructed and naturalized, gay male athletes within this institution develop "ironic" sensibilities about themselves, their bodies, and sporting activity itself. Gay men are sexually oppressed through sport, Pronger argues, but the ironic ways that they often redefine the athletic context can be interpreted as a form of resistance against heterosexism.

The three recent works I have outlined above demonstrate both the promise and the dangers of the new focus on masculinity in sport studies. On the one hand, each of these authors is utilizing a social constructionist view of masculinity, inspired by feminist thought, to inform his analysis. But these are not for the most part feminist analyses. Rather, they are studies in which the concept of masculinity is used to shed light on dominance and resistance *among men*. Working-class men construct and draw on an aggressive masculinity in order to resist class oppression and exploitation (Hargreaves). Black men construct and draw on an expressive and "cool" masculinity in order to resist racial oppression (Majors). Gay men construct and draw on an "ironic" masculinity in order to resist sexual oppression (Pronger).

These studies suggest that marginalized and subordinated (working-class, black, gay) men have often found sport to be an arena in which they can construct a masculinity that is, in some ways, resistant to the oppressions they face within hierarchies of intermale dominance. Yet in foregrounding the class, race, and sexual oppression of men by men, these studies portray masculinity primarily as a liberatory form of resistance against oppression. What is obscured is the feminist observation that masculinity itself is a form of domination over women. Once again, we risk framing masculinity as the hero while rendering women's oppression invisible. Looked at through feminist standpoints, these studies might reveal that in adopting as their expressive vehicle many of the aspects of hegemonic masculinity as it is defined in sport, working-class, black, and gay men often continue to contribute to the subordination of women as well as further limiting their own relationships and personal development.

Conclusion

I will now return to the question I asked at the outset: From whose standpoint can we begin to develop a more true picture of masculinity and sport? From the point of view of those who advocate a feminist standpoint, men who study masculinity should be attempting to help break the circle of the conventional social production of patriarchal knowledge. This does not mean, however, that our own experiences as men or theories constructed by men are meaningless. To the contrary, it is precisely our experiences as men and our access to masculine worlds that give us the potential to construct a powerful critique of masculinity. Rather, it simply means that we should not trust men's experience and ideas as the major basis of Truth. Clearly, to return to Spender's point, men should, in producing knowledge, "check with women."

On the other hand, if men scholars are to check with women, advocates of an inclusive feminism might rightfully ask, "*Which* women? Black women? Lesbians? Working-class women? Feminist academicians?" Clearly, an inclusive feminism rejects the notion of a single, privileged historical Subject. In fact, as Harding (1986) has argued, feminist thought has entered an era of transitional epistemologies, where multiple standpoints are used to examine, understand, and transform reality. Yet the adoption of the multiple standpoints implicit in an inclusive feminism leaves the researcher with a puzzling dilemma: To avoid a sort of watered-down relativism, a choice must often be made to foreground gender, class, sexuality, race, or some other form of oppression. And foregrounding one form of oppression risks setting up a linear hierarchy of oppression, thus replicating the problem of reductionism that feminists are attempting to overcome. Birrell (in press) suggests that for the time being, feminist women should foreground racial oppression since this is the level of oppression that feminist thought has largely rendered invisible in the recent past. This means, Birrell argues, building theory through listening to "critical autobiography" of women of color.

Similarly I would argue that male scholars must, for the foreseeable future, always forefront gender oppression. There are two reasons for this. First, until very recently gender has been the biggest blind spot in men's studies of men. Now that our studies of men and sport are becoming more gender conscious, it is crucial that men who enter the terrain of gender studies recognize the social basis of our privileged access to information, our privileged roles as "experts," as well as the *limits and potential distortions* in our analysis, if we continue to approach our subject matter simply from masculine standpoints. To avoid the distortions and pitfalls of masculinism, or gender-conscious objectivism, I suggest that in all our work we explicitly begin from the position that feminist visions of an egalitarian society are desirable. Consciously adopting this standpoint requires both an ethical commitment to the building of a just and egalitarian world and a thorough grounding in—and constant dialogue with—the feminist literature on the subject (Deem, 1988; Diamond & Quinby, 1988; Whitson, 1989).

The second reason I see it as desirable to foreground gender in our studies of men and sport is that it is today within feminist theory that the greatest strides are being made toward understanding the linkages among various systems of inequality. In foregrounding gender oppression, current inclusive feminist theories warn us against the false universalization of men's experiences and invite us to critically examine intermale dominance hierarchies. Studies of gay men, for example, can put non-gay masculinities in an entirely new focus (Kinsman, 1987). And in my research on former athletes I spend considerable time examining how athletic careers help to construct class and race inequalities among men, but I do so within the broader context of examining how these inequalities among men help to construct the overall gender order (Messner, 1989a). Through an inclusive feminism that recognizes the importance of working from multiple standpoints, we can begin to build an understanding of how class, racial, and sexual struggles within hierarchies of intermale dominance serve to construct men's global subordination of women. These sorts of studies might begin to reveal some of the contradictions within and among these various systems of domination and subordination, eventually contributing to the development of what Weeks (1985) calls a politics of radical pluralism.

Acknowledgments

Parts of this paper were presented at the National Women's Studies Association meetings, August 1989, Towson, MD, and at the North American Society for the Sociology of Sport meetings, November 1989, Washington, DC, Some of the ideas in this paper have emerged from two separate projects I have been working on with Don Sabo and Maxine Baca Zinn. I am very grateful for this cross-pollination of ideas. And I thank Lois Banner, Bob Connell, Ann Hall, Pierrette Hondagneu-Sotelo, Don Sabo, and Barrie Thorne for constructive criticisms and suggestions on earlier drafts of this paper. Finally, editorial suggestions by three anonymous *SSJ* reviewers have improved this paper considerably.

Notes

1 There are similarities and differences in the categories I employ here and the three that Kimmel (1987b) employs (antifeminism, masculinism, and profeminism). The similarity is that we are both examining men's responses to feminism. But Kimmel examines men's more general historical and cultural responses to feminism while I evaluate men's responses to feminism within academia. Clatterbaugh's (1989) typology of men's studies is also helpful.

2 The point that a value-free social science implicitly smuggles in the values of those who presently hold social power is not a new one (Mills, 1959). Alvin Gouldner (1970) has argued that value-free sociology tends to mask a set of unexamined domain assumptions that are heavily value-laden and thus tend to affirm the status quo.

3 Though a feminist standpoint is a dominant epistemological perspective within feminism, it is not the only one. As Harding (1986) has noted, there are also feminist empiricists who operate largely within a positivist framework and who assume that a proper "scientific" methodology best illuminates the ways women are oppressed. As Harding notes, though, feminist empiricists *do* begin with value-laden profeminist orientation, so in this sense they tend to undermine conventional positivist assumptions.

4 In fact, several historical accounts of "crises of masculinity" have pointed out that around the turn of the century men's fears of "social feminization" led to their creation (or increased salience) of homosocial institutions such as the Boy Scouts of America (Hantover, 1978), the military (Filene, 1975), and organized sport (Messner, 1988). For a more general discussion, see Kimmel (1987b).

References

Baca Zinn, M., Weber Cannon, L., Higgenbotham, E., & Thornton Dill, B. (1986). The costs of exclusionary practices in women's studies. *Signs: Journal of Women in Culture and Society*, **11**, 290–303.

Banner, L. (1987, November). *Margaret Mead, men's studies, and feminist scholarship*. Address delivered to the American Studies Association, New York.

Banner, L. (1989). Review of eight books about men. *Signs: Journal of Women in Culture and Society*, **14**, 703–708.

Baumli, F. (Ed.) (1985). *Men freeing men: Exploding the myth of the traditional male.* Jersey City: New Atlantis Press.

Birrell, S. (1987–1988). The woman athlete's college experience: Knowns and unknowns. *Journal of Sport and Social Issues,* **11**, 82–96.

Birrell, S. (in press). Women of color, critical autobiography, and sport. In M.A. Messner & D.F Sabo (Eds.), *Sport, men and the gender order: Critical feminist perspectives.* Champaign, IL: Human Kinetics.

Brod, H. (1987a). The case for men's studies. In H. Brod (Ed.), *The making of masculinities: The new men's studies* (pp. 39–62). Boston: Allen & Unwin.

Brod, H. (Ed.) (1987b). *The making of masculinities: The new men's studies.* Boston: Allen & Unwin.

Bryson, L. (1987). Sport and the maintenance of masculine hegemony. *Women's Studies International Forum,* **10**, 349–360.

Carrigan, T., Connell, B., & Lee, J. (1987). Hard and heavy: Toward a new sociology of masculinity. In M. Kaufman (Ed.), *Beyond patriarchy: Essays by men on pleasure, power, and change* (pp. 139–192). Toronto and New York: Oxford University.

Carroll, J. (1986). Sport: Virtue and grace. *Theory, Culture & Society,* **3**, 91–98.

Clatterbaugh, K. (1989). Masculinist perspectives. *Changing Men: Issues in Gender, Sex, and Politics,* **20**, 4–6.

Collins, P.H. (1986). Learning from the outsider within: The sociological significance of black feminist thought. *Social Problems,* **33**, 14–32.

Connell, R.W. (1987). *Gender and power.* Stanford, CA: Stanford University Press.

Crosset, T.W. (in press). Masculinity, sexuality and the development of early modern sport. In M.A. Messner & D.F. Sabo (Eds.), *Sport, men and the gender order: Critical feminist perspectives.* Champaign, IL: Human Kinetics.

Daly, M. (1973). *Beyond God the father.* Boston: Beacon Press.

Davis, A. (1981). *Women, race and class.* New York: Random House.

Deem, R. (1988). "Together we stand, divided we fall"; Social criticism and the sociology of sport and leisure." *Sociology of Sport Journal,* **5**, 341–354.

Diamond, I.D., & Quinby, L. (1988). Introduction. In I.D. Diamond & L. Quinby (Eds.), *Feminism and Foucault: Reflections on resistance* (pp. ix–xx). Boston: Northeastern University Press.

DiIorio, J.A. (1989). Feminism, gender, and the ethnographic study of sport. *Arena Review,* **13**, 49–60.

Dill, B.T. (1979). The dialectics of black womanhood. *Signs: Journal of Women in Culture and Society,* **4**, 543–555.

Edwards, H. (1971, November). The myth of the racially superior athlete. *The Black Scholar,* **3**, 58–60.

Fausto-Sterling, A. (1985). *Myths of gender: Biological theories about men and women.* New York: Basic Books.

Filene, P. (1975). *Him/her/self: Sex roles in modern America.* New York: Harcourt Brace Jovanovich.

Fine, G.A. (1987). *With the boys: Little League baseball and preadolescent subculture.* Chicago: University of Chicago Press.

Franklin, C.W. II. (1984). *The changing definition of masculinity.* New York: Plenum.

Freire, P. (1970). *Pedagogy of the oppressed.* New York: Herder & Herden.

Gallmeier, C.P. (1989). Toward an emergent ethnography of sport. *Arena Review,* **13**, 1–8.

Gilder, G. (1973). *Sexual suicide*. New York: Bantam.

Gilder, G. (1986). *Men and marriage*. London: Pelican.

Goldberg, S. (1974). *The inevitability of patriarchy*. New York: Wm. Morrow & Co.

Gouldner, A. (1970). *The coming crisis of western sociology*. New York: Basic Books.

Gruneau, R. (1983), *Class, sports and social development*. Amherst: University of Massachusetts Press.

Hall, M.A. (1985). Knowledge and gender: Epistemological questions in the social analysis of sport. *Sociology of Sport Journal*, **2**, 25–42.

Hantover, J. (1978). The Boy Scouts and the validation of masculinity. *Journal of Social Issues*, **34**, 184–195.

Harding, S. (1986). *The science question in feminism*. Ithaca: Cornell University Press.

Harding, S. (Ed.) (1987). *Feminism and methodology*. Bloomington: Indiana University Press.

Hargreaves, J[ennifer], (1986). Where's the virtue? Where's the grace? A discussion of the social production of gender through sport. *Theory, Culture & Society*, **3**, 109–122.

Hargreaves, J[ohn]. (1986). *Sport, power and culture: A social and historical analysis of popular sports in Britain*. New York: St. Martin's Press.

Hartsock, N.C.M. (1983). The feminist standpoint: Developing the ground for a specifically feminist historical materialism. In S. Harding & M.B. Hintikka (Eds.), *Discovering reality: Feminist perspectives on epistemology, metaphysics, methodology, and philosophy of science* (pp. 283–310). Boston: D. Reidel Pub. Co.

Hearn, J. (1987). *The gender of oppression: Men, masculinity, and the critique of Marxism*, Brighton, Sussex: Wheatsheaf Books.

Hoch, P. (1972). *Rip off the big game*. Garden City, NY: Doubleday & Co.

Hooks, B. (1981). *Ain't I a woman. Black women and feminism*. Boston: South End Press.

Kaufman, M. (Ed.) (1987). *Beyond patriarchy: Essays by men on pleasure, power, and change*. Toronto and New York: Oxford University.

Kidd, B. (1987). Sports and masculinity. In M. Kaufman (Ed.), *Beyond patriarchy: Essays by men on pleasure, power, and change* (pp. 250–265). Toronto and New York: Oxford University.

Kimmel, M.S. (Ed.) (1987a). *Changing men: New directions in research on men and masculinity*. Newbury Park, CA: Sage.

Kimmel, M.S. (1987b). Men's responses to feminism at the turn of the century. *Gender & Society*, **1**, 517–530.

Kimmel, M.S., & Messner, M.A. (Eds.) (1989). *Men's lives*. New York: Macmillan.

Kinsman, G. (1987). Men loving men: The challenge of gay liberation. In M. Kaufman (Ed.), *Beyond patriarchy: Essays by men on pleasure, power, and change* (pp. 103–119). Toronto and New York: Oxford University.

Klein, A.M. (1986). Pumping irony: Crisis and contradiction in bodybuilding subculture. *Sociology of Sport Journal*, **3**, 112–133.

Klein, A.M. (1988). Review of *With the boys: Little League baseball and preadolescent subculture*, by G.A. Fine. *Sociology of Sport Journal*, **5**, 290–293.

Klein, R.D. (1983). The 'men problem' in women's studies: The expert, the ignoramus, and the poor dear. *Women's Studies International Forum*, **6**, 413–421.

Lee, R., & Daly, R. (1987). Man's domination and woman's oppression: The question of origins. In M. Kaufman (Ed.), *Beyond patriarchy: Essays by men on pleasure, power, and change* (pp. 30–44). Toronto and New York: Oxford University.

Majors, R. (1986). Cool pose: The proud signature of black survival. *Changing men: Issues in gender, sex and politics*, **17**, 5–6.

Majors, R. (in press). Cool pose: Black masculinity in sports. In M.A. Messner & D.F. Sabo (Eds.), *Sport, men and the gender order: Critical feminist perspectives*. Champaign, IL: Human Kinetics.

Melnick, M.J. & Sabo, D.F. (1987). Analysis of free communications presented at the first seven NASSS annual meetings: Some patterns and trends. *Sociology of Sport Journal*, **4**, 289–297.

Messner, M. (1987). The meaning of success: The athletic experience and the development of male identity. In H. Brod (Ed.), *The making of masculinities: The new men's studies* (pp. 193–210). Boston: Allen & Unwin.

Messner, M. (1988). Sports and male domination: The female athlete as contested ideological terrain. *Sociology of Sport Journal*, **5**, 197–211.

Messner, M. (1989a). Masculinities and athletic careers. *Gender & Society*, **3**, 71–88.

Messner, M. (1989b). Review of *With the boys: Little League baseball and pre-adolescent subculture*, by G.A. Fine. *Gender & Society*, **3**, 138–140.

Messner, M. (in press). When bodies are weapons: Masculinity and violence in sport. *International Review for the Sociology of Sport*.

Messner, M.A., & Sabo, D.F. (Eds.) (in press-a). *Sport, men and the gender order: Critical feminist perspectives*. Champaign, IL: Human Kinetics.

Messner, M.A., & Sabo, D.F. (in press-b). Toward a critical feminist reappraisal of sport, men and the gender order. In M.A. Messner & D.F. Sabo (Eds.), *Sport, men and the gender order: Critical feminist perspectives*. Champaign, IL: Human Kinetics.

Mills, C.W. (1959). *The sociological imagination*. London: Oxford University.

O'Brien, M. (1989). Abstract thought and feminist theory. In M. O'Brien (Ed.), *Reproducing the world: Essays in feminist theory* (pp. 33–44). Boulder, CO: Westview Press.

Pleck, J.H. (1982). *The myth of masculinity*. Cambridge, MA: MIT Press.

Pleck, E.H., & Pleck, J.H. (Eds) (1980). *The American man*. Englewood Cliffs, NJ: Prentice-Hall.

Pronger, B. (in press). Gay jocks: A phenomenology of gay men in athletics. In M.A. Messner & D.F. Sabo (Eds.), *Sport, men and the gender order: Critical feminist perspectives*. Champaign, IL: Human Kinetics.

Rich, A. (1979). On lies, secrets, and silence: Selected prose, 1966–1978. New York: Norton & Co.

Robinson, D. (1987). Letter published in the *Bulletin of the American Studies Association*.

Rose, H. (1986). Women's work: Women's knowledge. In J. Mitchell & A. Oakley (Eds.), *What is feminism: A re-examination* (pp. 161–183). New York: Pantheon.

Rothman, B.K. (1989). Women as fathers: Motherhood and child care under a modified patriarchy. *Gender & Society*, **3**, 89–104.

Sabo, D. (1985). Sport, patriarchy, and male identity: New questions about men and sport. *Arena Review*, **9**(2), 1–30.

Sabo, D. (1986). Pigskin, patriarchy and pain. *Changing Men: Issues in Gender, Sex and Politics*, **16**, 24–25.

Sabo, D., & Women's Sports Foundation. (1989). The Women's Sports Foundation report: Minorities in sports. New York: Women's Sports Foundation.

Smith, D. (1978). A peculiar eclipsing: Women's exclusion from man's culture. *Women's Studies International Quarterly*, **1**, 281–296.

Spender, D. (1981). *Men's studies modified: The impact of feminism on the academic disciplines*. Oxford: Pergamon Press.

Stacey, J., & Thorne, B. (1985). The missing feminist revolution in sociology. *Social Problems*, **32**, 301–316.

Thorne, B. (1987, Summer). Review of *With the boys: Little League baseball and preadolescent subculture*, by G.A. Fine. *Baseball History*, pp. 67–69.

Tolson, A. (1977). *The limits of masculinity: Male identity and women's liberation*. New York: Harper & Row.

Tong, R. (1989). *Feminist thought: A comprehensive introduction*. Boulder, CO: Westview Press.

Weeks, J. (1985). *Sexuality and its discontents: Meanings, myths, and modern sexualities*. London: Routledge & Kegan Paul.

Whitson, D. (1989). Discourses of critique in sport sociology: A response to Deem and Sparks. *Sociology of Sport Journal*, **6**, 60–65.

Whitson, D. (in press). Sport in the social construction of masculinity. In M.A. Messner & D.F. Sabo (Eds.), *Sport, men and the gender order: Critical feminist perspectives*. Champaign, IL: Human Kinetics.

51

FIRM BUT SHAPELY, FIT BUT SEXY, STRONG BUT THIN

The postmodern aerobicizing female bodies

Pirkko Markula

Source: *Sociology of Sport Journal* 12(4) (1995): 424–453.

This paper aims to reconstruct the cultural dialogue surrounding the female body image in aerobics. To do this I have used several methods: ethnographic fieldwork, interviews, and media analysis. I found that the media ideal is a contradiction: firm but shapely, fit but sexy, strong but thin. Likewise, women's relationships with the media image are contradictory: They struggle to obtain the ideal body, but they also find their battles ridiculous. I interpret my findings from a Foucaultian perspective to show how the discourse surrounding the female body image is part of a complex use of power over women in postmodern consumer society. In addition, I assume a feminist perspective that assigns an active role to the individual aerobicizers to question the power arrangement.

Cette étude tente de reconstruire le dialogue culturel qui entoure l'image du corps de la femme en danse aérobique. J'utilise plusieurs méthodes: le travail ethnographique de terrain, les entrevues et l'analyse médiatique. Mes résultats indiquent que l'idéal des médias est une contradiction: ferme mais "bien faite," en forme mais sexy, forte mais mince. De même, la relation entre les femmes et l'image projetée par les médias est contradictoire: elles luttent pour avoir un corps idéal mais elles trouvent cette lutte ridicule. J'interprète mes résultats à partir d'une perspective foucaldienne afin de démontrer comment le discours entourant l'image du corps de la femme fait partie de l'utilisation complexe du pouvoir sur les femmes au sein d'une société de consommation post-moderne. De plus, j'adopte une perspective féministe qui donne aux adeptes de la danse aérobique un rôle actif qui leur permet de remettre en question la disposition du pouvoir.

Introduction: the feminine beauty ideal

She is fit . . . she's got an incredible body, she is completely tight, she has no fat on her body.

(Anna)

Popular women's magazines are saturated with images of beautiful, thin, and tight models. These polished images are often accompanied with advice on how we readers can achieve a body that resembles these images. When the magazines motivate us to work toward the model look, they provide us with an opportunity for a positive change: to obtain our best body ever.

Many feminist scholars, however, consider this glossy festival of feminine beauty a disservice to women. They point out that women's bodies come in a variety of shapes and weights. Paradoxically, the media portray only thin and tight models. Therefore, these scholars conclude, this fashion ideal is oppressive precisely because of its singularity: If only slim and toned women are attractive, most women with normal figures are classified as unattractive (e.g., Bartky, 1988; Bordo, 1990; Coward, 1985; Martin, 1987; Spitzack, 1990; Wolf, 1990). Consequently, to look attractive in this society, the majority of us have to engage in activities—like dressing, applying makeup, dieting, exercising, or, most drastically, reconstructive surgery—to mask or alter our body shapes. Because the sole purpose of these practices is to change our bodies to resemble the narrowly defined beauty ideal, many feminists deem them as vehicles of oppression (e.g., Bartky, 1988; Bordo, 1989; Cole, 1993; Martin, 1989; Wolf, 1990).

Regardless of the feminist opposition to such practices, many women still engage in these potentially degrading activities. For example, they continue to read women's magazines for beauty tips or exercise to lose weight. Can one simply assume that most women are unaware of how they contribute to their own suppression through their everyday behavior? Or is a woman's everyday life a more complex phenomenon? Perhaps one's behavior is not purely a function of ignorance or lack of education. Although several researchers have examined the discourses surrounding feminine practices, few studies examine how individual women experience their bodies in everyday life. In this paper, therefore, I plan to investigate how women encounter and sense the body ideal in one potentially oppressive female activity, aerobics. I map women's body experiences within aerobics through an ethnographic study. Similar to other feminist scholars, I examine the body ideal, but I limit myself to the exercise context. Furthermore, I am interested in how women react to this body ideal. Are women single-mindedly occupied with improving their bodies in aerobics classes? Or do they celebrate their own figures ignoring the ideal imposed on them by the mass media? Or do they struggle to disregard the image but, at the same time, exercise to reshape their bodies?

First, however, I survey the literature examining women's need to become thinner by dieting and to become tighter by exercising. This journey will lead to my analysis of what kind of body ideal aerobics promotes and an interpretation of what some aerobicizing women think of this ideal.

"No fat on her body"

Several writers have examined women's dieting in today's society (Arveda, 1991; Bordo, 1989, 1990; Chernin, 1981; Imm, 1989; Spitzack, 1990). Their findings suggest that women in general are more obsessed with dieting, body weight, and slimness than men are and that women's ideal slenderness also seems to be more narrowly defined than men's (Arveda, 1991; Bordo, 1990; Cole, 1993). Women diet to obtain the desired extremely slender body rather than accept the natural dimensions of their own bodies. Pamela Imm (1989) suggests that many women participate in aerobics because they are unhappy with their body shape and feel fat. She points out that particularly women who exercise excessively (6 or more hours per week) view their bodies negatively although they are not heavier than the other participants. Why are women required to be so thin? Why do we submit to rigid, constant dieting regimes?

Carol Spitzack (1990) examines women's dieting practices from a Foucaultian perspective. She locates women's body reduction within the net of disciplining discursive power. Her main argument is that women accept the disciplining body control (diet) because it is masked under promises of liberation. In other words, women are persuaded to believe that after they lose weight their lives suddenly change and they can pursue new challenges, unobtainable earlier due to their excess weight. However, Spitzack (1990) proceeds, this voice of liberation only masks a continuous control over women by the dominant patriarchal and capitalist powers. This control process starts with individual confession that one has excess weight. After realizing her problem, a woman is capable of improvement; now she is ready to lose weight. This change requires, thus, individual initiative and willingness to take control of one's life. This confession mentality, Spitzack (1990) argues, also necessitates an ongoing surveillance and monitoring of one's own body. For example, women keep constantly looking for the excess fat that needs to be eliminated. The female body has become a site of constant self-scrutiny. Therefore, instead of liberating their lives, dieting practices increase the body discipline required from women. In this way, the dominant practice, without openly suppressing women, invisibly controls them.

Margaret Duncan (1994) applies Spitzack's formula to analyze women's body image in two issues of *Shape* magazine. She focuses her analysis on the text of "Success Stories," a recurring feature that introduces *Shape* readers to women who have successfully lost weight through diet and exercise. Duncan (1994) traces a similar pattern to Spitzack's (1990) study: *Shape*'s text urges individual readers to confess that they have a problem, advises them to take the initiative to change from fat and unhealthy to thin and healthy, and advocates how good they will feel after such a body change. Through the "Success Stories," Duncan (1994) concludes, *Shape* practices oppressive disciplinary control over women.

"She is completely tight"

Dieting, thus, is an important part of the disciplinary practices designed to oppress women in this society. The desire to lose weight is maintained through the unobtainable female body ideal: Women are expected to be thin to be considered attractive and accepted in this society. Susan Bordo (1990) adds another component to this ideal: Now it is not enough to eliminate the excess, soft fat from our bodies; we are also required to achieve an athletic, tight look as well. Therefore, women must become more disciplined: In addition to dieting to lose weight, we now exercise to build muscle.

This new requirement—the tight, athletic look—creates a paradoxical body ideal that oscillates "back and forth between a spare 'minimalist' look and a solid, muscular athletic look" (Bordo, 1990, p. 90). Slenderness, Bordo (1990) suggests, can be associated with reduced power and femininity, whereas muscularity symbolizes strength, control, willfulness and masculinity. Therefore, these two ideals, Bordo (1990) continues, can promote different ideas about femininity in the same body: The muscularity could indicate women's liberation from the narrow definition of the female body as frail, whereas the thinness of this ideal restores the connotation to traditional femininity. This observation of such coexisting, disparate images characterizes many so-called postmodern studies examining the women's body ideal. If the women's body ideal simultaneously expands and limits the notions of femininity, it is no longer enough to label women's body practices only as disciplining or as empowering. Rather, in Helen Lenskyj's (1994) words, "a particular social practice cannot be understood purely as conformity or rebellion: rather, the ambiguities and contradictions need to be considered" (p. 258). Women's bodybuilding lends itself well to an analysis in which the disciplined exercise routine is interpreted both as oppressive and liberating (Lenskyj, 1994).

The bodybuilding body

Women's bodybuilding has captured many researchers' attention, because the bulging muscles of these competitors so clearly oppose the traditional frail feminine body ideal. These women lift weights to become visibly big. Hence, bodybuilding has clear potential to challenge the traditional notion of femininity. However, some research demonstrates that this emergent resistance has turned to serve the dominant power by sexualizing and objectifying the transgressive female bodybuilder body (Balsamo, 1994; MacNeill, 1988). Particularly, filmed or televised bodybuilding competitions that closely resemble beauty contests contribute to such an oppressive practice.

Other scholars have disengaged from debating whether bodybuilding is liberating or oppressing women. Rather, they argue that women's bodybuilding is a contradiction in itself: It simultaneously complies with and resists the dominant powers in the society (Bolin, 1992a, 1992b, 1992c; Daniels, 1992; Guthrie & Castelnuovo, 1992; Miller & Penz, 1991). Sharon Guthrie and Shirley Castelnuovo (1992) observe that women bodybuilders are compliant with the dominant discourse of feminine beauty in that they worry about their body shapes and invest tremendous energy to body care. In addition, their pink posing costumes, their blond, fluffy hair styles, and their feminine posing routines and music choices are in line with the traditional femininity. However, women bodybuilders resist the same femininity by actively creating a new female body shape. As a result, they do not feel compelled to model themselves after the more traditional feminine body form.

Anne Bolin (1992a, 1992b, 1992c) expands this analysis by locating the more compliant practices on the public—front stage—arena and the more resistant practices on the private—backstage—arena. When on the front stage during a competition, the women bodybuilders use the feminine accessories to comply with the judges' requirements of proper femininity. This, Bolin (1992a) demonstrates, is necessary if one wants to win the competition, and bodybuilders are there to win. Therefore, enforced notions of femininity for them are simply a necessary means to a higher goal: a victory. On the backstage, outside of the competition, women bodybuilders do not worry about looking feminine. They train seriously to build more muscle mass in the hard-core gyms devoted only to bodybuilding. They wear training gear far from skimpy posing outfits: sweat pants, sweat shirts, baggy tee shirts, and shorts. Bolin (1992b) concludes,

> Theirs is a transformative experience. . . . The presentation of an appearance that the judges will regard as feminine is just a matter of strategizing one's training, diet, and accessorizing with insignias of femininity. This exposes femininity as a cultural construction with boundaries, while femininity as a lived attribute knows no such limits.
>
> (p. 395)

What about the aerobicizing body? Some bodybuilders consider that aerobics supports the dominant oppressive beauty ideal. For example, they regard "the aerobics instructor body" as a derogatory term when they discuss women bodybuilders like Cory Everson, who deliberately keeps her muscles smaller and softer to comply with the traditional femininity required by the media (Bolin, 1992a). Nevertheless, some scholars argue that aerobics, similar to bodybuilding, creates a double image that embodies traditional conceptions of both feminine and masculine characteristics.

The aerobicizing body

Margaret MacNeill (1988) observes that although aerobics helps to uphold a feminine look, it also promotes healthy life and vitality that assumes a tight, thin, and muscular body. Regina Kenen (1987) characterizes such an aerobics image as a "hybrid" of a patriarchal image (the feminine look) and a feminist image (strong, muscular look). Interestingly, Kenen (1987) argues that women need to obtain the feminine look to successfully manipulate the power source—the men. This form of resistance has provoked lively discussion among feminist scholars. They observe that instead of initiating open resistance women effectively obtain power through similar manipulation of the traditional channels (e.g., Abu-Lughod, 1990; Bolin, 1992a; Dubisch, 1986; Gottlieb, 1989; Strathern, 1981). Therefore, what looks like oppression to the researcher's eye might serve as a means for power for the women involved. Kenen (1987) also points out that the media equate the feminist image with sex appeal and turn it to serve the patriarchal powers. Here the aerobics image is truly ambiguous: The traditional feminine image is resistant, but the strong "feminist" image sexualizes women.

In their approach to the double image, Elizabeth Kagan and Margaret Morse (1988) place the aerobicizing body in the postmodern context. They concentrate on the images in Jane Fonda's exercise videotapes. Like Kenen (1987), they contend that Fonda's body incorporates the slender femininity with a new powerful self-determining subject in motion. However, these writers assume that women participate in aerobics basically to fight against their aging and sagging bodies. This preoccupation results in a compromising aerobics body image: The subjectivity and its will are delegated to shape the body to a commercially supported ideal of femininity. Like those who studied women's bodybuilding (Balsamo, 1994; MacNeill, 1988), Kagan and Morse (1988) conclude that the emergent potential for liberation is revisited to serve the purposes of patriarchy by linking women's physical activity to attractiveness.

Kagan and Morse (1988) like MacNeill (1988) focus on the body discourse transmitted through media. What about the everyday practice in aerobics classes? Do the aerobicizers there struggle to confront a contradictory body image? To find answers to these questions I set myself to listen to the voices of the aerobicizing women.

Method

Like Kagan and Morse (1988), I locate my research of aerobics within the postmodern cultural condition. Central to my study is the view that this culture is communication between different voices. Michael Bakhtin's (1981) examination of the dynamics of cultural dialogue serves as a foundation for my analysis.

In every dialogue, Bakhtin (1981) argues, several voices, some more dominant than others, struggle over each other to give meanings to cultural phenomena. Cultural dialogue, therefore, implies a certain authority and assumes certain power relations in its exchange. Bakhtin (1981) locates dominant voices in the public, official sphere, from where they claim the rights for the correct interpretation of the phenomenon at hand. For example, the magazines and aerobics videotapes are claiming the rights for public representation of the perfect female body image. The private voices, like the aerobicizers', must use other channels available to them to replace the official interpretation with their own meaning. I believe, therefore, that the meaning of aerobics in this culture is created by many voices that contradict with each other and work to replace each other. All these meanings, the public as well as the private, are produced within cultural discourses.

For example, our understanding of the body is formed within such discourses as health, medicine, and femininity. However, I believe it is insufficient to examine the discursive construction of the body ideal at the public arena. Like Spitzack (1990), I aim to examine how the discursive dialogue of the public arena materializes in the women's everyday experiences. To find out, I have to listen to the voices of the individual women. I assume, along with many other feminists, that women actively make sense out of their social world and construct different meanings in different social contexts. In this paper, individual women engage in a dialogue with the discursive representations: They strive to make sense of the "fit body ideal." Here I focus on the ambiguities and contradictions in women's body experience (Lenskyj, 1994), as I do not believe that any experience can be classified as purely empowering or purely oppressive. However, I believe, following Spitzack (1990), that aerobicizers' critical voices have the potential to alter the course of dominant practices.

I also assign an active role for myself when I aim to uncover women's meanings about the aerobicizing body. The reported meanings are my subjective interpretations based on my fieldwork within aerobics. In this study, therefore, the aerobicizers and I have negotiated a shared understanding of the aerobicizing body in American culture. I also acknowledge that I am a human observer whose personal, social, and historical background structures research considerably (e.g., Bruner, 1993; Clifford & Marcus, 1986; Denzin, 1992; Rosaldo, 1989).

Fieldwork

I used several methods to reconstruct the dialogue surrounding the body image in aerobics: fieldwork, interviews, and media analysis. My research derives predominantly from my ethnographic fieldwork among aerobicizers from 1990 to 1992. Although ethnography is most often associated with anthropology, today its methods have been increasingly used to study the

228

state of Western society as the minutiae of everyday life (de Certeau, 1984) have attracted researchers across the social sciences. Many taken-for-granted, commonplace phenomena like aerobics are now considered especially fruitful topics, because they, in their popularity, unveil central aspects of our culture to a critical inquiry (Dunn, 1991; Featherstone, 1988; Foley, 1992; Johnston, 1986; McRobbie, 1994).

Aerobics handed itself quite easily to ethnographic fieldwork because aerobicizers gather regularly together in a public, yet well-defined place—the gymnasium. My field was mainly the university community in a small Midwestern town: Most aerobics classes were organized by the university and the participants were in some way associated with the university. This is only one context for aerobics classes. Kenen (1987) has found that the setting influences the aerobics praxis. For example, commercial health clubs exacerbate the negative, oppressive practices more than do public-sector classes like the YMCA. I do not intend to generalize my findings over the private aerobics sector (the health clubs) or different geographical regions of the U.S., although I attended private health clubs in the community and in other parts of the country to complete my ethnography. In this study I focus on women's experiences within a university community. On average, I participated in seven 1-hour classes weekly.

In addition to my field observations, I conducted both informal and formal interviews to closely trace the individual experiences. I interviewed the aerobicizers informally whenever possible: before and after classes, in the locker rooms, in the street, in coffee shops, in the classes, or any other time I met one of the participants. The formal interviewing technique used in this study can be characterized after Michael Quinn Patton (1980) as open-ended topical interviews. I had prepared a list of topics instead of setting up detailed questions. I selected the topics—the structure and nature of an aerobics class, the body image, health, and nutrition—based on findings in the literature (Kagan & Morse, 1988; Kenen, 1987; MacNeill, 1988; Martin, 1987), an earlier pilot study, and my ongoing participant observation. Therefore, the discussion regarding the body was only one part of my larger research project on aerobics (Markula, 1993b). I wanted to adopt a conversational model (e.g., Spitzack, 1990) in which both the researcher and respondent assume equal responsibility for the discussion. Basically, we discussed the above-mentioned topics during each interview, but the conversation could also follow a particular concern of the interviewee. Body matters were such a concern for many of the aerobicizers, and we usually discussed body image extensively. The length of each interview varied from 30 minutes to 2 hours. I interviewed most participants once, but certain "informative" or verbal participants were interviewed twice. All the interviewees assumed anonymity, and I refer to them here by their pseudonyms. I interviewed 35 exercisers (33 women and 2 men). This imbalanced gender ratio was common in the aerobics classes I participated in; the vast majority of the participants were women. Consequently, in this paper I focus on women's views. The exercisers in my study were mostly students but also were secretaries, staff members, and researchers. This research, therefore, is based on the experiences of a select group. The typical aerobicizer in my study was a white, well-educated, 18- to 45-year-old female, a description which—according to nationwide surveys—also characterizes an average aerobics exerciser around the U.S. (Rothlein, 1988).

In addition to recording the aerobicizers' private voices, I wanted to record the public voices constructing the aerobics body. Therefore, to support my investigation, I analyzed how aerobics was presented in the media. My research drew from images in aerobics videotapes but mainly I examined exercise images in such magazines as *Health, Women's Sport and Fitness, Shape*, and *Self*. I selected *Health* and *Women's Sport and Fitness* because they were likely to contain frequent articles on women's exercise. In addition, because they were available since 1979 I had a chance to examine the change in media representation of the female body through these magazines. I selected the other two monthly magazines, *Shape* and *Self*, because of their self-proclaimed specialization in women's fitness matters. For example, *Shape*, published by bodybuilding tycoon Joe Weider, promised to provide "mind and body fitness for women" (*Shape*, March 1994, p. 2). Moreover, individual aerobicizers I spoke with recommended these two magazines for me. I investigated issues of both magazines starting from 1986. In these magazines I focused specifically on articles about aerobics or women's exercise. Their topics varied from aerobics shoe and video guides to articles advising strength and toning exercises. I read the text of each article and examined the accompanying pictures, which I also compared to the text.

Several of the women I interviewed also exercised using videotapes. I have, therefore, included the women's views about the video bodies in my study. Among the numerous exercise tapes available the women talked most about Jane Fonda's "Workout" series and Kathy Smith's exercise videos.

To analyze how the contradictory body image evolves in aerobics, I first look at the meanings the magazines construct around the female body image. I then proceed to identify how these meanings materialize in aerobicizers' everyday experiences: How do the media discourses structure women's ideas about their bodies? In addition, I am interested in women's responses to the dominant media discourses: Do women question the media representation of the body? To conclude, I will explain why the media portray a certain female image and why women react to this ideal the way they do. I will start by sketching the ideal body of the exercising female in the media.

Shapely, slender, and softly curvy

Since the early days of aerobics, women's bodies seem to occupy a central space in the fitness discourse. For example, in the 1960s the father of the aerobics running program, Kenneth Cooper, felt that women's exercise should primarily improve bodily appearance: "The way it works out, women earn a double payoff from aerobics; they go to the program to improve their looks and they get fitness and health as fringe benefits" (Cooper, 1970, p. 134).

In the 1970s and early 1980s women were increasingly urged to exercise to take care of their bodies. In addition to light aerobic activities such as jogging, swimming, or tennis, calisthenics, light strengthening exercises, and stretching were often recommended. The ideal feminine body was described as shapely, slender, and softly curvy (Fairclough, 1980; Hoover, 1980; Lenskyj, 1986). Muscles did not fit with this image: Muscle bulk was seen as masculine and unsuitable for the "proper" feminine look. Fear of visible muscle growth and the fear of lost femininity due to physical activity were commonly addressed in the exercise articles. One way of countering the muscle bulk was to exercise correctly: Magazines advised slow, controlled repetitions. Women were also blessed with another way of avoiding bulging muscles. Magazines comforted their readers that female hormones prevented any extensive muscle development despite engagement in physical activity. It was, therefore, a physiological fact that women had soft, small muscles and curvy bodies. Conversely, it was naturally unfeminine to display well-defined muscles. The following quote summarizes the sentiment that surrounded women's conditioning:

> Today, the leg to strive for embodies the virtues of predecessors—it should be shapely, smooth and supple—but it also must be strong. . . . No, we are not talking about big, muscular legs like Richard Gere's. A woman's legs can have power without having bulk. . . . The way to strength without mass is to exercise against low resistance, but with a higher number of repetitions. . . . Muscles will increase a bit in size, but combining the resistance/repetition formula with your body's female hormones will prevent your legs from becoming locker room curiosities.
>
> (Farah, 1984, p. 38)

The whole concept of a muscular woman was redefined when Jane Fonda published *Jane Fonda's Workout Book* in 1981. Jane Fonda aimed for a fit, trim, and muscular body, and a new ideal stepped into the aerobics movement. If the idea of women having muscles was "just abhorrent" (Tucker, 1990, p. 97) earlier, muscles now became acceptable, even a desired part of the ideal female body. Starting from the 1980s "fashion magazines were abuzz with the news that muscles were chic" (Tucker, 1990, p. 97). Muscles are still a central feature of the ideal female body. Exercise reserves, therefore, a prominent place in women's lives: The only way to obtain the desired, trim muscles is to exercise. The magazines sensed a need for exercise advice.

Special workout articles, which encouraged women to develop their muscle tone, started to appear in the magazines. For example, in 1990 *Shape* began its "Spot Training" columns, which focused on training for muscle tone with free weights or machines. Muscle tone is also a prominent part of aerobicizers' everyday exercise experience. In what follows, I discuss the discourses surrounding women's toning exercises.

Toned and trim

When toned muscles became an important part of the ideal feminine body, special shaping exercises became an integral part of the aerobics class. Some aerobicizers call these exercises "toning"; others refer to them as "floorwork" (most of the training is done while lying on the floor). This muscle work resembles the spot training exercises depicted in *Shape* and *Self*. The most important principle underlining these exercises is to focus on one muscle group —or body "spot"—at a time. This focus ensures that the participant effectively tones the intended, isolated body part. This is how one gets the best results: The particular muscle is toned without wasting time and energy to condition the unintended muscles. Aerobicizers' comments reflect this philosophy:

> I don't see how you can really work the abs and do a good job if you are doing something else.
>
> (Sheila)

> When you are toning, you concentrate on one muscular area; I think it's the best way to do it, because . . . it's kind of hard to the mind to do two things at once.
>
> (Trisha)

> You can concentrate more in one area, if you are only working one area, that makes sense.
>
> (Anna)

Aerobicizers have faith in toning exercises: These workouts do, indeed, effectively tone the body. At the same time, many of them view toning as hard, repetitious, and boring:

> Toning is boring to me, period. I hate toning, the worst part of the class.
>
> (Trisha)

> Boring, body toning is intensely boring . . . with these little boring ah, ah, ah, sit-up aerobics . . . they are doing body toning grimacing and looking unhappy.
>
> (Antoinette)

Although it is torturous, hard, and horrible, most exercisers would incorporate toning into their class. They find it a necessary yet uncomfortable and difficult way to achieve muscle tone. Some of the exercises are particularly difficult as they are aimed for muscles infrequently used in everyday life. These muscles have to be trained in strange positions, which adds to the discomfort. Sheila talks about the so-called "doggy lifts," also referred to as "elbows and knees":

> I really don't like the elbows and knees, I don't know why it is . . . we always do it, maybe it's just a strange way to do it . . . I think people don't like it because it's just an abnormal way to do things, we don't sit like that or do anything like that. I feel like I'm walking around like a dog; it's just not very comfortable feeling.

Sheila points out a contradiction: "elbows and knees" (which is designed to train the gluteus maximus) is frequently done in her class although it's an abnormal move. The whole exercise makes her feel uneasy and she wonders why it is included in her class. Kagan and Morse (1988) explain this contradiction. They argue that exercises like "elbows and knees" do not improve functionality: We do not need these movement patterns to perform everyday chores. Rather, these exercises are designed to improve our appearance. Thus, toning in aerobics class dissociates body parts from their functional roles. Sheila was right when she pointed out that doggy lifts are abnormal because she never does such a movement in "real" life. The meaning of such exercises, Kagan and Morse (1988) believe, is to change the body to look like the ideal, toned body. In this way women are assigned to manipulate their body parts for the sake of appearance. Apparently, not all the exercisers are prepared to work only for their "looks": Sheila questioned the rationale for performing "elbows and knees" because that exercise did not have a functional meaning for her. In addition, many aerobicizers lined at the water fountain to avoid this uncomfortable exercise. Paradoxically, in the line we complained about our problematic body parts that needed more tone.

"Hot moves to shape your trouble spots"

Magazines deepen the fragmented image when they assign special parts of our bodies as problem spots. Problem areas—abdomen, thighs, underarms, and the "butt"—are particularly resistant to manipulative toning, albeit they need it the most. Already in 1980, one article pointed out that "the main areas of concern for most women are the upper arms (batwings), abdomen (stretch marks and flab) and outer thighs (saddlebags)" (Stallings, 1980, p. 49). Fifteen years later these particular parts still trouble women. Jane Fonda, for example, advertised her 1992 video "Lower Body Solution" as "designed especially for the #1 problem areas for women; abs, buns, and thighs" (e.g., *Self*, March 1992, p. 178). In every issue magazines introduce workouts to "hit" one or more of these parts. A myriad of special exercises such as abdominal tighteners, waist cinchers, lower belly flatteners, back-of-the-thigh hardeners, seat shapers, bottom lifters, fanny firmers, hip slimmers, and front-of-the-thigh definers are designed to firm women's problematic body parts. These movements are promoted as simple, effective, and easy to perform. Therefore, even the busiest women can manage to fit exercise into her daily schedule.

Magazines advocate these workouts based on one assumption: Women need to look good. They assume further that their readers presently find their bodies imperfect. This imbalance results in great anxiety, which only their workout program can cure. In this sense, the magazines see themselves contributing to women's well-being.

> If you balk at pool-party invitations; if you lie awake at night wondering how to cover your thighs while keeping cool and looking great; if you seriously consider moving to Antarctica as soon as the hot weather sets in—this workout is for you.
>
> (Sternlicht, 1990c, p. 34)

> Weak triceps can make wearing a sleeveless shirt or evening dress an embarrassment. By adding triceps exercises to your workout, you can make the back of your arms shapely and strong.
>
> (Sternlicht, 1990a, p. 46)

> Both women and men alike are self-conscious of their derrieres, whether their buttocks are large or flat, high or low, round or saggy. But relax. It's fairly easy either to develop this area and give it more roundness or to firm it up and give it more sleekness.
>
> (Sternlicht, 1990b, p. 38)

One participant in my study also confirms that women exercise because their bodies are flawed:

> I think everyone there has a certain area that they want to work on; it's obvious to them or it's obvious to you, they wouldn't be there if they hadn't a complex about [some area]. They don't like something . . . like a stereotype, we don't like our arms, that's why we signed up . . . we are trying to get rid of our arms.
>
> (Sarah)

In the magazine texts, the problem spots cause the biggest anxieties; the thighs, the triceps (underarms), and the butts are what women are most embarrassed about. Are their predictions well placed? When I asked the aerobicizers to identify any problematic parts of their bodies, their answers resonate with the magazine discourse. The problem spots trouble the aerobicizers the most. For example, Jane, Cecilia, and Laura quickly identified their problem parts:

Pirkko: Do you feel that you have certain problem areas in your bodies?
Jane: My lower half, I sit all day.
Cecilia: My stomach, that's the hardest part.
Laura: After having a baby, stomach muscles are the worst.

Many aerobics classes I participated in included exercises for these particular parts. The instructors, like the magazines, presumed that women want to tackle those particular areas. I asked Becky, an aerobics instructor, to describe a typical toning session. She found that "a lot of them [the participants] want to work on their sides, the outer thighs or . . . the seats more. . . . I think stomachs are probably one [problem area], hips, outer thighs, those are the main ones." When questioned why these areas are so problematic, she explained, "That's where we have most of our fat cells, that's where we store most of the fat." Obviously, storing fat is a highly undesirable, yet natural, process. The storage places are the problem spots whose fat levels women carefully monitor. These areas require special toning as they appear especially prone to excess fat and flab.

As other scholars, I contend that these spots "where we store most of the fat" are the very parts of our bodies that identify us as females: the rounded bellies, the larger hips, the thighs, the softer underarms. These "female parts" are also the ones we hate the most and fight the hardest to diminish. Logically then, we hate looking like women. Bordo (1990) argues that women grow up despising their feminine form, because the ideal feminine shape in this society resembles that of a young boy: wide shoulders, tight muscles, narrow hips (also Bartky, 1988; Chernin, 1981; Coward, 1985). The majority of women, regardless how hard they try, can never achieve this type of body. Most women simply are not born with male bodies. Kim Chernin (1981) adds that the unattainable boyish ideal is one of the major causes for women's anxieties with their bodies. The dissatisfaction with one's feminine shape can lead to an extreme fear of fat and, consequently, a distorted body image. Ronda Gates (1991) reports that devoted aerobicizers and fitness professionals, more than anyone, have a distorted understanding of their bodies. They are afraid of fat: "If 22 percent of fat is optimum, 18 percent is better" (Gates, 1991, p. 28), these exercisers conclude (see also Imm, 1989). According to Chernin (1981), this attitude generates desperate attempts to control one's body weight that precede serious eating disorders like anorexia nervosa and bulimia nervosa.

Magazines advocate muscle tone as a vital feature of an ideal female body, and the aerobicizers seem to accept this model. Paradoxically, although they work hard to "sculpt" their trouble spots into the desired tone, they also question the meaning of the uncomfortable toning exercises. I examine next what is meant by toned muscles: What kind of muscle definition is desirable?

Sleek and sexy

Although a "good female body" is a muscular body, the magazines discourage extreme muscularity. Exercise articles primarily promote a toned and shapely look. Magazine workouts, thus, aim to "tone" one's muscles, not to build muscles. One article puts a clear limit on female muscle size: "Strong muscles mean more shape in arms and shoulders, definition in the legs and a flat, but not concave middle" (Kaufman, 1989, p. 124). The ideal body is layered with long, sleek, unbulky muscles. Such muscles are also defined as "sexy." For example, workouts are advertised with such slogans as "The Ultimate Guide to Sexy Muscles" (*Self*, March 1991, cover), "Three Easy Ways to a Strong and Sexy Stomach" (*Self*, February 1991, cover), "Sculpted and Sexy" (Rover, 1992, p. 48), "Shoulders are Sexy" (Laurence, 1992, p. 103).

"Is it all right for women to have muscular arms?"

Evidently, muscles—particularly the problem spots—need to be toned, tight, and firm. Most problem spots are located in the lower body. Toning the upper body in general and arms in particular is a more complex enterprise. Magazines encourage upper body workouts: "Firm Triceps and Shapely Biceps are in Vogue" (Sternlicht, 1991, p. 48) and "It's all right for women to have muscular arms" (Sternlicht, 1991, p. 48). For women in aerobics classes, however, muscular arms are not "all right." Many women fear large arm muscles if they do upper body workouts in their classes. Arm toning is complicated, because one of the problem areas is the triceps region, under the upper arm. Aerobicizers want firm triceps without bulking up. Sarah, for example, trains her arm muscles, but says, "I am afraid that I bulk up when I do arms. . . . I used to swim and I was huge, like bulky and I hated it." Sarah continues to explain why women hate "big arms":

> Girls don't really work out their arms, because if you work your arms, you get big arms, you look like a guy. It seems to be okay if you have strong legs, but if you are athletic and you have big arms, it's like she looks like a guy. It's more socially acceptable to have big legs than the arms.

Women do not want to look masculine, Sarah explains, and that is what muscular arms do to you: You end up looking like a guy. Considering that the ideal female body nowadays "looks like a young guy" more than a

236

woman, this distaste of big arms seems unjustified. Apparently, although women should possess broad shoulders, they should not be muscular.

Not only muscle size but also the location of the muscles defines the exerciser's femininity. Sarah in her earlier quote points out that muscular legs—firm thighs—are socially acceptable, unlike muscular arms. Kathy adds that tight legs are not only acceptable but desirable:

> I personally would like to work on my arms more, but it seems that a lot of girls would rather work on their thighs, their outer, inner thighs and their butt, but they don't feel that they need their arms built up. . . . The thing that guys look at or a lot of women are concerned, tends to be your butt or their thighs. They don't say, "I have fat arms" . . . and you don't have guys going by and saying, "Look at those sexy arms."

Well-toned legs are sought after because men notice them. Women do not urgently shape their arms because men do not care about seeing them. Obviously, arms are not as vital a part of an attractive woman as legs are. In addition, Kathy implies that women are exposed to a gaze that sets the standards of the desirable female form. We shape our bodies to please that gaze. Kathy clearly identifies the gaze as male; other aerobicizers do not really recognize a source for the controlling gaze. They are objects of a gaze that is just ubiquitously "societal": "It's a product of society" (Colleen); "It's socially acceptable" (Sarah). The preferences of this gaze often contradict the exercisers' own will, but they feel pressured to please the gaze. Most exercisers comply with, as Kelly puts it, what "most people presumably think women are . . . softer lines," and she continues, "which is too bad." Kelly indicates, hence, that she does not agree with such definitions of femininity. She weight trains herself, as do Andrea, Becky, Colleen, and Trisha. Trisha has even tried bodybuilding, and Kelly would like to start:

> I would like to do bodybuilding myself and we've [she and her body-builder husband] actually been in bodybuilding competitions . . . and I would like to do that. But I think I am a minority; a lot of women feel that's not the way a woman should look, but I wouldn't mind looking like that.

> (Kelly)

Interestingly she adds, "within reason, of course. I don't want to look like Arnold Schwarzenegger. I would like to build my muscles a little more than they are [now]." None of the women in my study desires to have big muscles, not even the exercisers who work out with weights. All the weight trainers also indicate that women cannot become too muscular even with the help of weights and definitely not without serious commitment and work. Becky and

Colleen rely on a biological explanation: "I don't think women should worry about getting too muscular, because they just don't have the hormone" (Colleen), which Becky specifies as testosterone. Trisha reflects her own experience:

> It takes so much, I didn't realize . . . it's just really, very disciplined sport. . . . I think a lot of women have a misconception that if I go to the gym and lift weights I'll look like Rachel McLish, Cher or somebody, [but] it takes a lot. This one lady spent 40 hours a week in the gym—that's a career—but that is ridiculous and I think there are lot of people who think if you lift like six weeks you can see the difference. . . . I think women see men going do sit-ups, 100 sit-ups every day and their stomachs look like Rambo's; the women can do 100 sit-ups the rest of their lives and their stomachs still wouldn't look like that.

Although women do not want big muscles, everybody admires toned muscles. Most aerobicizers also admit needing more tone, also in their upper bodies. Kathy and Kelly indicate that they want to include more arm work in their classes but find themselves different from the majority of the women in this matter. Others, like Helen and Sarah, acknowledge that they benefit from arm exercises, although they prefer toning their legs to upper body work. Maria's comment summarizes the feelings of many exercisers in my study: "I just want my legs to be more toned and the upper arms, when you get older, you know, the little wonderful thing that flabs down here (points at her triceps area)." Maria is 21 years old, but already worries about how her aging body is changing. I discuss this concern more in depth later in this paper.

Some women, like Antoinette, Becky, Colleen, or Christy, do not want to appear muscular but still want to be strong. Antoinette reasons that it is good to be strong,

> because if I'm physically strong, I can do things that I want to do: I can unscrew jam jars—I don't have to ask some guys to do it for me— I can put the trash out; I can lift things. I don't like feeling weak and helpless and end up asking other people to do things for me.

Maria and Molly want to be strong to excel in the sports they love. For these women, it's not the appearance, the muscle size, that matters but the actual functionality of the muscles. Christy, a former competitive swimmer, likes to be strong and to have strong arms but believes that "you don't have to have muscle definition to have good strong muscles." Therefore, the aerobicizers might conform with the toned look of the ideal body, but for functionality, not only for looks.

"I was bulky and I hated it!"

The aerobicizers admire other participants or instructors with tight and firm muscles, but built, big muscles are disliked. The muscle size, therefore, is an intricate matter. The women I interviewed define toned muscles quite differently from built muscles. For example, Kelly points out that "when you are toning you are just keeping the muscle firm and when you are bodybuilding you are actually enlarging the muscle and building what they call definition, when you can see one muscle from the other." To the aerobicizers, toned muscles can be visible but not big and massive. Toned muscles are lean, in use, and tight. But when exactly does the tone turn into bulk? This, apparently, is a hard question to answer. Trisha considers that "there is a real fine line between looking good and being too muscular." Many women are perplexed: They begin to work out their muscles but end up feeling ashamed of their bodies. Andrea tells a story of a confused friend who started weight training but is not sure about the results:

> *Andrea*: We were going to go out and she was wearing a dress and she was like "I can't take off my jacket" . . . they [the arms] were definitely tight, but I don't think they were that unattractive, but she said she is always used to having great, thin arms, not the actual muscle, so I guess for some girls, maybe for the majority, it just is not very attractive.
> *Pirkko*: Why did she start lifting weights?
> *Andrea*: I'm not sure. I think she did it because she was working on her upper body more, she just tried to get rid of her arm fat. I think eventually she started to work more on the arms, so she wouldn't overwork her legs.

Andrea's friend felt that she was unattractive; the never-resting eyes of society glanced at her arms disapprovingly. Some of the exercisers sense a contradiction here: They recognize that they want to be strong—it is good to be strong—but concurrently they feel bad about it. For example, Melissa is struggling with her feelings about being strong:

> It is really contradictory, because the very things that I do in aerobics, like my class always has this long session of push-ups, I'm strong and I feel uncomfortable with that, but at the same time I'm proud of that, not proud, that makes me feel good about myself to be strong, but I don't know. . . . I'm not satisfied and I don't know what I want to look better; it doesn't make sense.

Feeling simultaneous pride and shame does not make sense to Melissa. Many of these women can, thus, see the unfair expectation placed on them.

It is, however, almost impossible to resist the societal pressure to conform. Aerobics does not seem to help women to expand the boundaries of the ideal feminine body to the same extent as, for example, women's bodybuilding does. However, Helen and Sarah compare aerobics to ice skating and ballet, physical activities they have been involved in earlier. They prefer aerobics because, unlike ice skaters or ballet dancers, aerobicizers can be proud of their muscles:

> I've been in ballet forever, and I prefer aerobics to it, because in ballet you are supposed to be skinny and have no muscles. I mean, muscles are not valued, just flexibility. In aerobics muscles are valued, because it shows that you've been doing aerobics for a while and if you have big claves . . . [they think], "Oh, she is dedicated."
>
> (Sarah)

For these women, aerobics has been a liberating experience, because they no longer feel ashamed of their well-defined leg muscles. Both, however, express an added desire "to look thinner" (Helen). Therefore, along with the refined regulations regarding ideal tone, the perfect female body is also required to be thin.

"I like to be sort of petite"

The connection between women's exercise and slimness dates back to the advent of aerobics. When aerobics began, its initial purpose was to facilitate weight loss (Cooper, 1968, 1970; Sorensen, 1979). Presently, weight loss is always listed as an advantage of a regular exercise program. Occasionally strength training is also sold to the audience by linking it with weight loss. Theoretically, increased muscle mass burns calories even at rest. Therefore, a muscular person will consume more calories in everyday life than her or his weaker counterpart (e.g., Barrett, 1991). This logic implies that women should build muscles to assist weight loss, not to increase strength.

Weight loss is important for the exercisers in my study, more so than the firm muscles. For example, one should first worry about being thin; once sufficiently thin, one can work on muscle tone. Cari's comment illustrates this sentiment:

> I'm trying to burn out some fat and just stay in shape, maybe if I got down to when I was satisfied [with my weight], maybe then I worked on shaping, but I'm a long way from there; right now, I'm just trying . . . to burn out some of those fat cells.

Cari supposes that shaped muscles are something slim exercisers work on; for her the ideal body is thin, and tone is a fringe benefit. The present body ideal is definitely slim. However, slimness does not mean soft, meatless flesh but requires firm, tight, and sleek muscle tone. Bordo (1990) confirms that "unless one goes the route of muscle building, it is virtually impossible to achieve a flab-less, excess-less body unless one trims very near to the bone" (p. 90). Consequently, Cari could not achieve a fashionably small body by only losing weight. Jiggling flesh, even on a thin body, feels loose—like fat. Hence, without toning one will always feel big. Magazine texts appeal to similar reasoning: They construct their strengthening exercises to reduce women's bodies like their diet regimens are designed to downsize their female readers. For example, Laurence (1992) reasons,

> Broad shoulders, squared and relaxed, create a regal, imposing carriage that signifies power and presence. They can also make your waist seem smaller, more delicate, and the sight of silk sliding over a creamy shoulder carries its own potency.
>
> (p. 103)

Although broad shoulders signify "power and presence," above all, they make one's waist appear smaller. Some aerobicizers complete their toning exercises based on this rationale: Toned muscles actually will make one smaller. Even the much-feared arm exercises become acceptable when they, instead of strengthening, diminish women's arms. Eileen defends the arm exercises done in her aerobics class: "It's not that their arms are going to get bigger [by doing toning], they are just going to be tighter, they actually will look smaller, because they'll be tighter and not flabby."

Apparently, women do not want to be associated with big anything: Big muscles, big bones, and big bodies are generally feared. Somehow, we ought to fight the big body. This struggle to reduce the body is problematic. Sheila discusses a dilemma she has faced:

> *Sheila*: I tend to build muscle pretty fast, especially when I do biking. . . . I like to slim down my legs, most slim down the muscle. I do have a lot of muscle I could slim down.
> *Pirkko*: By doing what?
> *Sheila*: I don't know, it's hard. When I was a freshman, I managed to do it. I have a slow metabolism; I have to not eat, and I have to do more exercising. When I did I was only eating dinner as a meal, and I was trying to make it light and have a few snacks during the day.
> *Pirkko*: It didn't bother you to get more muscles by doing all those exercises?
> *Sheila*: You have to eat enough less, so that you are using more calories. It's hard to do for me. You have 50 pounds of equipment [when you play ice hockey] and you go skating around, it's going to

build up my muscles unless I don't eat anything, so, I try to keep a balance so that I don't gain weight but it's hard, it's a battle. ... I mean, I have a petite frame, I just don't have petite muscles.

Sheila tries to control her rebellious body—prevent it from becoming any bigger—by dieting and exercising, which creates a predicament: Her muscles tend to develop due to her workout. She is trapped in a vicious cycle where only a strict diet, as she believes, can free her. An ascetic diet regime is the only way to reveal her petite frame. Her hobby, however, is ice hockey, which is not a sport for small and frail females. A hockey player, like Sheila, needs strong muscles. She, therefore, has to be strong and delicate, big and small all at the same time.

It is evident that aerobicizers' lived experiences reflect the double body image detailed by the scholars studying the aerobics image in the media (Kagan & Morse, 1988; MacNeill, 1988). Earlier studies also debated whether this image resists or complies with those in power. I believe that, like the bodybuilding body, it is an ambiguous image: It embraces potential for both empowerment and oppression. Similar to the women bodybuilders (Bolin, 1992a, 1992b), the aerobicizers aim to challenge the traditional beauty ideal by toning their muscles, but they also engage in oppressive feminine practices like dieting. Unlike bodybuilders, however, the aerobicizers dislike big muscles, especially in the upper body. Moreover, the aerobicizers aim to become smaller: They tone their muscles to look smaller when bodybuilders even diet to appear more muscular (Bolin, 1992b). Many aerobicizers think bodybuilders are disgusting:

I've seen women's bodies that I find repulsive, because they are so muscular,

(Cari)

They have this huge bulging muscle that I think is really unattractive.

(Molly)

Women bodybuilders, that looks bad.

(Eileen)

I don't like ... the women bodybuilders, to lift weights to become big, I personally don't like that.

(Daedra)

The magazines support the aerobicizers' views regarding bodybuilding. For example, although the fitness articles promote upper body work, they clarify that their weight training will not result in bulging arm muscles (Barrett, 1991; Brick, 1990). Why this fear of big muscles?

Feminist research explains that such rejection of big muscles serves women's oppression in society. Namely, patriarchal domination over women is based on the assumption that men are naturally—biologically—stronger and bigger than women. Physically stronger males are also alleged to be naturally determined, intellectual, active leaders who should dominate the weak, passive, and small women. To retain this power arrangement in patriarchal society, it is necessary, thus, to define the female body differently from the male body: ideally, the weak female's muscles are sleek and firm, whereas the powerful male's muscles are visible and big. The aerobics body fits in this scheme nicely, whereas the bodybuilding body challenges this gender dichotomy, because it resembles the big, muscular male body and minimizes the biological gap separating the sexes (Holmlund, 1989). A simple conclusion would be that aerobics supports the patriarchal ideology but bodybuilding resists it. However, Bolin (1992b) adds an interesting dimension to this discussion.

She points out that not only bodybuilding but other sporting lifestyles can challenge and minimize the biological differences between the sexes. She uses triathlon, long-distance running, and rock climbing as examples in which there is a considerable overlap in the contours of male and female physiques. It is noticeable that these athletic male bodies are small. Therefore, the resistant female body does not have to be bulky to challenge the patriarchal, dualistic definitions of gender. In this light, a well-toned aerobicizer's body could be seen to resemble a male athlete's body and defy the dominant patriarchy over the female body.

In addition to having toned muscles, the aerobicized body is thin. The aerobicizers accordingly are afraid of fat, more than they are afraid of big muscles. For example, Becky explains that she appreciates muscles, because they make "the person look very fit." However, when asked why she exercises, she answered, "I was once fat. I don't ever want to be fat again." Being overweight was a bigger concern for more of the aerobicizers than extensive muscles. As we know, bodybuilders also need to be unnaturally thin to show their muscle development. Therefore, even women bodybuilders, although challenging femininity through developing big muscles, do not aim to overcome the requirement of feminine thinness. Being fat is still probably the furthest from the ideal feminine body of the 90s. A strong, overweight woman, theoretically, would offer the most direct resistance to the patriarchal notions of femininity in this society, as her body would directly oppose the toned and thin ideal. If we define resistance only through clear binary oppositions like this, aerobics—or any other physical activity—would never offer an avenue for true resistance. I believe that instead of classifying women's practices exclusively into resistance or oppression, it is more fruitful to concentrate on the richness of everyday experiences.

Women in aerobics classes keep struggling to make sense of the contradictory requirements of the female body. There is an additional element in the ideal female body that needs to be analyzed. This ideal implies that besides being thin and toned, our bodies must stay young. This adds another component to our bodywork load.

"I am not sure if it's too late"

The ideal female body is also a youthful body. Women over 30 seldom appear in fitness magazines. The flabless, firm muscles do not cover an old, wrinkly, bent, gray-haired body. Nevertheless, everyone will grow older, and the natural signs of aging are opposite to the requirements of the beautiful body. Some women in my study have turned to aerobics to specifically fight the effects of age: "I have this cellulite and these fat cells. I'm not sure if it's too late; at least I'm attempting to do something" (Cari). Cari feels somewhat optimistic about the power of exercise to overcome her aging body, although her late start worries her. Others feel that age exacerbates the problems they have with their body shapes. Some exercisers become desperate when their bodies show signs of old age. When the aging progresses, women have to work incredibly hard to obtain the ideal figure. Particularly, the problem areas—underarms, thighs, hips, and abdomen—seem to get flabbier and more resistant to shaping. This experience is tangible for some aerobicizers. Colleen, Ann, and Rosi describe their bodies:

> When you get older . . . your muscles aren't that dividing any more. . . . It seems relatively easy when you are a young person to have toned muscles.
>
> (Colleen)

> My body is getting older, it's harder to keep my weight in control, and I get really fat if I don't exercise.
>
> (Ann)

> You gain so much weight, you don't know how to get rid of it.
>
> (Rosi)

Why do we have to fight the naturally aging body so hard? To explain our urge to remain youthful, Mike Featherstone (1991) locates the body in the context of so-called consumer culture. He argues that in present consumerism the perfect body—youthful, physically beautiful, and healthy—makes its owner more marketable. For example, "good looks" increase a person's exchange value in the job market: A physically attractive person gets hired before someone else. Like the aerobicizers, Featherstone (1991) observes that the desired body shape can be achieved only with effort and body work. Cosmetic, beauty, fitness, and leisure industries have emerged to guide people in their quest for perfection. Sagging flesh, for example, should be treated in

244

exercise programs provided by the fitness industry. But even with the help of specific programs, the consumer has to work hard for the results. Video queen and marketing master Jane Fonda (1981) emphasizes individual hard work as a means to a better body:

> Notice I've said "vigorous" and "exercise hard." I don't use these words idly. Namby-pamby little routines that don't speed up your heart beat and make you sweat aren't really worth your while.
>
> (p. 49)

> If you are serious about wanting to lose weight once and for all, about changing the shape of your body, about improving your self-image and your morale, you must get over being soggy. There are not short cuts. No sweatless quickies. You must be committed to working hard, sweating hard and getting sore . . . You have to work for it.
>
> (pp. 55–56)

Fonda's own body demonstrates how effective vigorous work is. She, although over 50, displays the ideal young boyish body discussed earlier: broad shoulders, narrow hips, long legs. Her body is "reminiscent of adolescence" (Coward, 1985, p. 41) in late middle age; it is a "version of an immature body" (Coward, 1985, p. 41) possessed by a mature woman. Spitzack (1990) reads two meanings in Fonda's fantastic teenager body. First, many women view Fonda in hopeful terms: Her body suggests that women over 50 can be viewed as attractive and can have a "good body." Consequently, older women are still attractive and maintain their marketability in consumer society. But second, women fear that this means an ongoing attention to appearance. Some had looked forward to middle age because of less focus on "looks," but now women need to continue monitoring their bodies to maintain an adolescent body, like Fonda's body, to a mature age.

In consumer society, we need to invest in body care to secure our positions in the market. Featherstone (1991) adds that this creates an expanding market for commodities that aid body work. Looking after one's body, he illustrates, is like looking after a car. As a car needs a whole array of things to function, the body needs products from soaps to diet teas to keep its shape. Such products as cosmetic surgery, diet pills, or cosmetic devices (Coward, 1985; Spitzack, 1990) are marketed particularly at women. I would place aerobics in this line of products: It is advertised to help women battle their aging, bulging, and sagging bodies in a manner similar to other body industry products. Evidently, if women start worrying about their bodies growing old at 20, and aerobics is one of the solutions to discipline such a body, aerobics classes will be securely filled with customers, because we all will age and our bodies will need more and more work to resemble the ideal body.

Featherstone (1991) also points out that good looks are promoted by the media. Fitness magazines, TV programs, and exercise videos portray a stylized image of the body in consumer culture. Feminist research (Kagan & Morse, 1988; MacNeill, 1988) has found that these media images sexualize and object-ify women as they emphasize appearance rather than fitness. The aerobicizers have obviously come face to face with the perfect media bodies in these sources. How do they find the media representation of the exercising women?

"You don't see them sweating"

Women's ideas about exercise often resonate with the fitness discourse in the media: They work on their problem spots; they long for a toned body, but not for visible muscle definition; they struggle to fight fat and age, exactly as urged by the media texts. However, the same aerobicizers criticize the por-trayal of exercisers in the media. Many women are consciously suspicious of this representation. To illustrate, Eileen, Anna, and Andrea consider the media exercisers unreal, even irritating:

> TV doesn't seem realistic; it's like they go out and get models to do it, because they are all tall and very skinny, in shape and kind of disgusting in a way; they have their hair perfectly done and their make-up is perfect; you don't see them sweating. It's the same image they project, very thin, lean . . . they are just generally thin, they are just models.

This portrayal makes the exercisers doubt the expertise of the demonstra-tors. They suspect that these "models" are there because of their looks, not because they know something about exercise. Christy verbalizes her skepti-cism: "They [the demonstrators] don't have to be necessarily fit, they could just be someone who looks good in a leotard and who are told, 'Put your body in this position.' " Christy refers to the way many exercises are pre-sented in the magazine pictures: The demonstrator is in a still pose waiting for the camera to capture the moment. Often a series of these pictures is arranged on the page to illustrate a continuous exercise routine. The real-life aerobicizers feel, therefore, that even unfit, thin models can pose a couple of seconds for a beautiful picture, but they would not be able to follow a con-tinuous aerobics class.

If my interviewees are skeptical of the magazine representations, they view exercise videotapes with an even stronger suspicion. Unlike the static pictures, a video shows a continuous aerobics class lasting 30 to 60 minutes. The video exercisers should, thus, demonstrate a good fitness level. The aer-obicizers I interviewed are distrustful: The videotapes are a media trick because the video exercisers appear too perfect to be real. Sarah, for example, is annoyed with the exercise videos:

246

> It kind of makes me mad because I keep hearing that they stop, put on more make-up and jump another five minutes and then come back, wipe off the sweat, and you never see them really ugly; there is something wrong.

While being disturbed, women have also accepted that the media display only perfect bodies. For example, Daedra explains,

> I expect that anyone demonstrating any exercise in any magazine is going to have to be close to that ideal body. I don't think I expect anything but that.

Flawless models do not irritate all the aerobicizers. For some women, the perfect media exercisers are a positive incentive that keeps them exercising.

Regardless, many women in this study like to see "normal people" demonstrating the exercises. Or they prefer to follow a fitness expert who knows what she or he is doing. The body size is not as important as fitness level and professional instruction. These exercisers welcome a larger-size leader or participant in exercise class. Actually, a little "chunkiness" makes the person more human and easier to relate to. Therefore, the media class should resemble more closely the "real-life" classes they participate in. Sarah summarizes her requirements for an instructor:

> You can be an aerobics teacher and not have a body. My only requirements for an aerobics teacher are that they can do the routines with us and that they've got energy doing that. . . . I don't care if they are like 200 pounds, but if they can jump as high and are energetic. . . . There is this picture in our minds like Jane Fonda, perfect body, [but] like [our teachers], they've got nice bodies, but are not beautiful, but as long as they can keep up with us, lead us, that's fine.

Sarah notices the discrepancy between the media images of an aerobicizer ("there is this picture in our minds like Jane Fonda, perfect body") and her instructors. She still prefers her instructors. Some exercisers have discovered that the recent exercise videos include different types of people in their model classes. For example, Fonda instructs some "overweight" exercisers in one of her latest tapes; in Kathy Smith's video class exercisers in different fitness levels aerobicize together. However, my interviewees regard these tapes as exceptional.

The interviewees do not like the thin and toned media ideal: It is too perfect, it is no longer real. This conscious rejection seems odd as the women keep working toward the same ideal in their aerobics classes. Therefore, women's relationship with the contradictory body ideal is ambiguous:

Against their own judgment, many aerobicizers still desire to look like the flawless models. It seems a lot easier to judge the body image at the intellectual level than engage in the resistant action in real life. Recall how aerobicizers like Melissa or Sheila struggle to keep weight training. They choose to be strong, but when their bodies grow more muscular and less feminine, they find it hard to face the judgment of the policing gaze without shame. Likewise I, a feminist researcher, am petrified that I will become fat regardless of my knowledge that the ideal thinness is an unrealistic goal designed to keep women dieting. One has to be extremely secure to be able to confront the everyday challenges put forward by the dominant discourses and even more confident to engage in an openly resistant action. We struggle to resist the body ideal but are not able to ignore it or achieve it. Our bodies remain imperfect.

Many of my interviewees feel that they are continuously required to improve some part of their bodies. Occasionally—like Antoinette here—they reflect their unhappiness with a touch of irony: "We talk about it [the body] a lot. My roommates and I sit around all the time, which is hilarious, because we are all in pretty good shape . . . but we think we are overweight or out of shape or we have too much fat," Antoinette and her friends realize that they actually look acceptable, but they still want to work on their bodies. Considering that the same women criticize the present body ideal for being unrealistically thin, their desire for change appears quite contradictory. Daedra is aware of her problematic relationship with the ideal body:

> I think it's [the body ideal] really unhealthy, but . . . the ideal body is
> the perfect woman . . . with no fat, a beautifully shaped body. . . .
> You have to work your butt off for that type of body . . . and a lot of
> people can just never look that way because of the way they are. I
> think a lot of girls have fallen into a trap that they have to look
> certain way. . . . I'm falling into that trap.

She recognizes how "unhealthy" and unrealistic the body ideal is but admits, at the same time, that she longs to have such a body herself. She is trapped into a false fight with her body. Why do we fall into the illusionary body ideal? Why do we need to change our bodies that really do not need a change? Why do women drive themselves for the image they find fallacious? In her discussion of dieting practices Spitzack (1990) connects the present beauty ideal to health. This connection provides a starting point for my discussion of women's antagonistic relationships with their bodies.

The panoptic power: be positive and you can change!

Spitzack (1990) first locates the body image in patriarchal consumer society. Her discussion confirms my notions that the present image of the perfect female body jointly serves visions of traditional femininity—women's muscles are toned and firm but not "hulkish," visible, or big—and the economic interest of consumer society. However, Spitzack (1990) argues further that the influence of these powerful agencies on the female body becomes more obvious when discussed in connection with the discourse of health.

Spitzack's key to understanding women's situation in society is the "aesthetics of health." Women's present beauty standard is defined through health: The "healthy look" and "natural beauty" are now fashionable, albeit culturally constructed, descriptions of a good-looking woman. Basically, a beautiful body in this society is a healthy body, not only a slender body as 10 years ago. This shift away from thinness should provide more diverse models for women, but most descriptions of the healthy look still center on the requirements of physical attractiveness. In reality, the healthy body "mandates even greater restrictions on female bodies" (Spitzack, 1990, p. 37). For example, toned muscles now cast the required healthy glow on the slender women. Bradley Block's (1988) article in *Health* magazine can serve as a case in point. He proclaims that the great body today is a healthy body and, therefore, there is no single great body "look." The article introduces six women who demonstrate the growing diversity. However, when we take a closer look at these women, we find that they are all thin, young, and toned. The only variable is their height. Therefore, the healthy body is only a new, fashionable rubric for the physically attractive body.

Spitzack (1990) adds high self-esteem, self-confidence, and increased assertiveness to the measures of "the healthy look." This connection is evident in aerobics. Many women in aerobics classes assert that exercise makes them feel better not only about their physique but also about "themselves," much like the *Shape* "Success Story" heroines in Duncan's (1994) study. For example, Eileen tells how aerobics boosts her self-confidence:

> When I do aerobics, I feel toned; if I'm not even any more toned, at least I feel my muscles are tighter and I feel better about myself.

In this sense, aerobics indirectly makes the participants' self-confidence grow, which at first glance seems to empower the exercisers. Eileen, however, connects positive feelings about herself to her looks: When one looks better, one feels better. Here a conversation by Sarah and Helen further reveals how good looks and positive self-image are inevitably linked with each other:

> *Helen*: It feels better, when the jeans fit looser.
> *Sarah*: You can loosen your belt buckle . . . and you feel more confident . . . you can look better, you feel better . . . you look skinnier, you feel more confident about your body.

Helen: The reason [to go to aerobics] is to look better, not just for a better body, but for self-image . . . you definitely see a difference in your body, maybe other people don't but you feel a lot better.
Sarah: You just feel like you are doing your best for the body; this is straining, but it's also good for us, so you feel better.

Helen obviously believes that good looks consist not only of a "skinny" body but also of a good self-image, which again is a result of the improved body. Therefore, better self-confidence derives from an attractive body.

Similar to the aerobicizers, magazine texts connect self-confidence with good looks. Many articles claim that a better body ignites positive self-esteem. Magazines describe confidence and self-esteem to characterize the beauty ideal of the 90s. Now women who have confidence and a positive attitude look good. Furthermore, the new beauty reflects our growth and self-acceptance; women now "want to look and feel good" (Lazarus, 1991, p. 62). In one article Rita Freedman (1991), a psychologist, points out the unquestionable link between a woman's self-esteem and her body image: "Improving your body image is quite likely to improve your self-esteem—so, working on self-esteem will usually improve your body image also. Body-loathing leads to self-loathing, while body-love leads to self-love" (p. 98). Consequently, women should not try to turn themselves into something they are not. Instead, magazines encourage readers to find their normal, healthy body weights and accept their current measurements. For example, magazines advise women to focus on the positive points of their mirror reflections, not the flawed parts (Freedman, 1991; Wise, 1990). In addition, exercise clothing—although quite revealing—can be designed to accentuate the positives about one's body: "Magicians do it with smoke and mirrors, but body-wear designers use lines, stitching, nips and cuts to improve upon reality. These exercise pieces perform their own magic to accentuate your positives" (p. 92) writes Kathleen Riquelme (1994) in *Shape* to introduce "the latest and greatest in figure-flattering bodywear" (p. 92). The article is named ironically "Grand Illusions" as if to acknowledge that women have to trick themselves to feel positive with bodywear magic. Women need magic to mask the real body like magicians need to create an illusion by hiding the traces of their tricks.

Partly, such a discourse sounds quite strange after readers are advised to accept themselves as they are. Why do we need illusions if we are to accept our "real" bodies? Is it something to do with the models wearing these clothes that create "larger-than-life" illusions? Their perfectly thin bodies are not imaginary; they are real. We readers know we don't look like them, but with the right clothing we can at least make the best of our "bottom-heavy-figures" (Riquelme, 1994, p. 92).

Partly, this discourse is very encouraging: Every woman should accept her body, feel confident about it, and derive increased self-esteem from her appearance even if it is achieved through clothing magic. These positive feelings and increased powerfulness can free women from the regulative mechanism of the masculine ideology and consumerism. Spitzack (1990) argues, however, that this seemingly liberating discourse is in itself an illusion.

Illusions surrounding the women's fitness movement have been tackled previously by other feminist researchers (Kagan & Morse, 1988; Lenskyj, 1986; MacNeill, 1988; Theberge, 1987). According to these scholars, as pointed out earlier, the potentially liberating impulses in aerobics have been turned to serve the masculine ideology by cementing the effects of exercise with an improved appearance. Spitzack (1990) agrees that such claims of liberation only "mask increasing control with a rhetoric of freedom" (p. 42). For example, to maintain a healthy body, women are required to detect their bodily flaws more carefully. While constantly scrutinizing, one has to appear assertive and confident about one's body. Rather than being free, women are prisoners of more detailed regulations of beauty. Why do women accept this controlling discipline?

Spitzack (1990) believes that this control is implemented over women through a confession that women have secret problems. As I demonstrated earlier, the magazine texts were indeed convinced that their readers all possessed hidden body anxieties. Similar to Duncan's (1994) and Spitzack's (1990) dieters, exercisers were urged to admit that their bodies are imperfect and then take action to change for the better. One article advises the reader to follow these exact steps: "The most important thing I have learned is that you have to accept the way you look now in order to make a change . . . you have to think positively about yourself, your appearance and your ability to accomplish your goals" (Glenn, 1992, p. 13). Another article assures us that we women are not helping ourselves by self-disgust, which only "creates a feeling of punishment" (Weaver & Ruther, 1991, p. 81) and defeats our attempts to change through exercise or weight loss programs. To successfully change our female bodies, we have to enjoy the process.

In sum, self-acceptance in exercise discourse promotes only bodily change; feeling positive about oneself is a necessary precondition for a model body. One is to accept one's body shape only to reform it. Focus on women's psychological well-being disguises increased attention to women's appearance and makes a deeper obsession with the body possible. This practice, Spitzack (1990) observes, is analogical to the treatment of another obsession, alcoholism. For instance, similar to Alcoholics Anonymous (AA), Overeaters Anonymous (OA) is patterned to help overeaters overcome their addiction. Exercise discourse advocates similar logic. Curiously, unlike other addictions, the confession of body problems does not free one from the obsessive behavior. On the contrary, it precedes a more thorough internalization of the addiction. To further implement the logic of confession, magazines, as I interpret them, urge women to take responsibility for their change.

The Foucauldian concept of panoptic power explains some meanings embedded in this discourse.

In his analysis of contemporary society, Foucault (1979) argues that the body is a target of subtle disciplinary practices that seek to regulate its existence. Different disciplinary practices—which Foucault ties to modern forms of the army, the school, the hospital, the prison, and the manufactory—produce "docile bodies" ready to obey the regimes of power in society. Each person has internalized the control mechanisms through the body discipline. Individual citizens are, therefore, governed not by visible and openly repressive power sources, but by themselves. Foucault (1979) illustrates this power arrangement with an analogy to the Panopticon, a model prison whose circular design leaves all inmates in their individual cells permanently visible for the invisible supervisor in the center tower. Each prisoner is disciplined through his or her awareness of the supervisor rather than the supervisor's actual presence. The inmates are controlled by their own awareness of power. Spitzack (1990) finds dieting practices effectively disciplining women's bodies. She adds that the power over them is the most effective and captivating when the dieting discourse persuades the individual women to control their bodies on account of society. This logic is evident in aerobics.

Individual aerobicizers have taken the responsibility to control their bodies. They, sometimes questioningly, aim to change to resemble the ideal body. In addition, women feel good when their body shapes begin to approximate the ideal. However, societal standards, not women's own standards, define this ideal. Therefore, even the heightened self-esteem derived from a better body ultimately serves the purposes of the powerful to continue the oppression of women in society. Aerobics, like dieting, is part of a complex use of power over women in postmodern consumer society. The panoptic power arrangement, whereby the individuals control themselves on behalf of the powerful while the power source itself remains invisible, ensures that women are so occupied with obtaining the healthy look that they do not have time to wonder why they are doing it. Such a conclusion sounds quite depressing. Is the power over us so extensive and does it penetrate so deeply into our lives that whatever we think we are doing for our own benefit is actually harnessed to serve the purposes of an invisible power?

Conclusion

The invisible discursive power seems to effectively shape our thoughts and our behavior regarding our bodies. But if this grip were complete, women would passively follow the confessional logic without ever questioning it. Aerobicizers in this study have an active voice. They do not quietly dedicate their lives to body reconstruction, but they question the body ideal and are particularly skeptical about the media presentation of exercising women. This questioning leaves many women puzzled: They want to conform with the ideal, but they also find the whole process ridiculous. As a result, women's relationship with the body ideal is contradictory. This awareness, nevertheless, demonstrates that women have not internalized the panoptic power arrangement entirely. Aerobicizers do not, however, visibly resist the patriarchal body ideal by actively aiming to build transgressive bodies like the women bodybuilders. Aerobics does not offer an avenue for a large-scale revolution, at least not in the public arena. Nevertheless, in aerobics, much like women's bodybuilding (Bolin, 1992a), the private setting is quite different from the official discourse and does not necessarily follow the practices set by the dominant powers.

Although many aerobics classes revolve around body shaping (e.g., the toning moves are designed to improve appearance rather than functionality; the muscles are built to increase the caloric expenditure, not to gain strength), many aerobicizers participate for reasons other than improving their bodies. For example, aerobics is a source of enjoyment and not only because of the improved body (Markula, 1993a, 1993b, in press); it provides a safe environment for being physically active (Markula, in press); it supplies women with increased energy to carry on with their work (Markula, 1993b); it allows women to spend time on themselves (Markula, 1993b); and it is an opportunity to meet and make friends (Markula, 1993b). All these reasons, whose resistant potential I have discussed in detail in other contexts, demonstrate that aerobics does not entirely serve as a vehicle for the oppressive dominant body discourses. Furthermore, the real-life aerobics class does not appear similar to the video classes. For instance, the instructors are not all picture-perfect (recall Sarah's earlier comment about her instructor); the aerobicizers themselves do not wear skimpy clothes like the video or magazine exercisers (Markula, 1992); and not all classes include nonfunctional moves geared around body shaping (Markula, 1993b).

Central to my examination of the body in aerobics has been the view that culture consists of communication between different voices. In this paper, individual aerobicizers' voices engage in a dialogue with the media voices of aerobics. Following Bakhtin (1981) I assume that cultural dialogue implies certain power relations: Some voices are public and more dominant than other, private, voices. For example, the voices of the magazines and aerobics videotapes can dominate the public representations of the perfect aerobics body. It seems obviously that this public discourse around the aerobics body is a voice of oppression. However, individual aerobicizers struggle to give different meanings to the ideal aerobicizing body. Like Spitzack's (1990) dieters, aerobicizers privately question the logic of this discourse whose contradictory beauty requirements leave many of these women confused. This leads me to ask, if the public voice authoritatively shapes the meaning of women's exercising bodies, are women's private voices heard? Bakhtin (1981) believes that individual voices can use alternative channels to replace the official meanings with their own meanings. I believe this study is one attempt to bring women's private voices to a public stage and give them the lines in the body dialogue they deserve. I hope these voices are loud enough to ignite a change.

Acknowledgments

I would like to thank Jim Denison and the two anonymous reviewers for their helpful comments and suggestions. I am also grateful for the support of M.K. Howard and K.S.W. Davidson during the preparation of this paper.

References

Abu-Lughod, L. (1990). The romance of resistance: Tracing transformations of power through Bedouin women. *American Ethnologist*, **17**(1), 41–55.

Arveda, K.E. (1991). One size does not fit all, or how I learned to stop dieting and love the body. *Quest*, **43**, 135–147.

Bakhtin, M.M. (1981). Discourse in novel. In M. Holquist (Ed.), *The dialogical imagination* (pp. 259–442). Austin: University of Texas Press.

Balsamo, A. (1994). Feminist bodybuilding. In S. Birrell & C.L. Cole (Eds.), *Women sport, and culture* (pp. 341–352). Champaign, IL: Human Kinetics.

Barrett, E. (1991, March). The ultimate guide to sexy muscles. *Self*, pp. 137–143.

Bartky, S.L. (1988). Foucault, femininity, and the modernization of patriarchal power. In I. Diamond & L. Quinby (Eds.), *Feminism and Foucault: Reflections on resistance* (pp. 61–86). Boston: Northeastern University Press.

Block, B.W. (1988, July). Great American body. *Health*, pp. 27–35.

Bolin, A. (1992a). Beauty or beast: The subversive soma. In C. Ballerino Cohen (Ed.), *Body contours: Deciphering scripts of gender and power* (pp. 54–77). New Brunswick, NJ: Rutgers University Press.

Bolin, A. (1992b). Flex appeal, food, and fat: Competitive bodybuilding, gender and diet. *Play & Culture*, **5**, 378–400.

Bolin, A. (1992c). Vandalized vanity: Feminine physiques betrayed and portrayed. In F. Mascia-Lees (Ed.), *Tatoo, torture, adornment and disfigurement: The denaturalization of the body in culture and text* (pp. 79–99). Albany: State University of New York Press.

Bordo, S. (1989). The body and the reproduction of femininity: A feminist appropriation of Foucault. In A.M. Jaggar & S.R. Bordo (Eds.), *Gender/body/knowledge: Feminist reconstructions of being and knowing* (pp. 13–33). New Brunswick, NJ: Rutgers University Press.

Bordo, S. (1990). Reading the slender body. In M. Jacobus, E. Fox Keller, & S. Shuttleworth (Eds.), *Body/politics: Women and the discourse of science* (pp. 83–112). New York: Routledge.

Brick, L. (1990, May). The get set for summer workout. *Shape*, pp. 81–87.

Bruner, E. (1993). Introduction: The ethnographic self and the personal self. In P. Benson (Ed.), *Anthropology and literature* (pp. 1–26). Urbana: University of Illinois Press.

Chernin, K. (1981). *The obsession: Reflections on the tyranny of slenderness*. New York: Harper & Row.

Clifford, J., & Marcus, G.E. (1986). *Writing culture: Poetics and politics of ethnography*. Berkeley: University of California Press.

Cole, C. (1993). Resisting the canon: feminist cultural studies, sport, and technologies of the body. *Journal of Sport & Social Issues*, **17**, 77–97.

Cooper, K.H. (1968). *Aerobics*, New York: Simon & Schuster.

Cooper, K.H. (1970). *New aerobics*. Philadelphia: Lippincott.

Coward, R. (1985). *Female desires: How they are sought, bought and packaged*. New York: Grove Weidenfeld.

Daniels, D.B. (1992). Gender (body) verification (building). *Play & Culture*, **5**, 370–377.

de Certeau, M. (1984). *The practice of everyday life*. Berkeley: University of California Press.

Denzin, N. (1992). *Symbolic interactionism and cultural studies: The politics of interpretation*. Cambridge, MA: Blackwell.

Dubisch, J. (1986). Introduction. In J. Dubisch (Ed.), *Gender and power in rural Greece* (pp. 3–41). Princeton, NJ: Princeton University Press.

Duncan, M.C. (1994). The politics of women's body images and practices: Foucault, the panopticon, and *Shape* magazine. *Journal of Sport & Social Issues*, **18**, 48–65.

Dunn, R. (1991). Postmodernism: Populism, mass culture, and avant-garde. *Theory, Culture & Society*, **8**, 111–135.

Fairclough, E. (1980, May). Legs. *Women's Sports*, pp. 34–53.

Farah, A.D. (1984, January). Legs. *Health*, pp. 38–42.

Featherstone, M. (1988). In pursuit of the postmodern: An introduction. *Theory, Culture & Society*, **6**, 195–213.

Featherstone, M. (1991). The body in consumer culture. In M. Featherstone, M. Hepworth, & B.S. Turner (Eds.), *The body: Social process and cultural theory* (pp. 170–196). London: Sage.

Foley, D.E. (1992). Making the familiar strange: Writing critical sports narratives. *Sociology of Sport Journal*, **9**, 36–47.

Fonda, J. (1981). *Jane Fonda's workout book*. New York: Simon & Schuster.

Foucault, M. (1979). *Discipline and punish: The birth of the prison*. New York: Vintage Books.

Freedman, R. (1991, July). Mind over mirror. *Shape*, pp. 66–68.

Gates, R. (1991, March). Body image: The problem with trying to be perfect. *IDEA Magazine*, pp. 28–29.

Glenn, J. (1992, March 2). Healthy mind, healthy diet. *The Daily Illini*, p. 13.

Gottlieb, A. (1989). Rethinking female pollution: The Beng of the Cote D'Ivoire. *Dialectical Anthropology*, **14**, 65–79.

Guthrie, S.R., & Castelnuovo, S. (1992). Elite women bodybuilders: Models of resistance or compliance. *Play & Culture*, **5**, 401–408.

Holmlund, C.A. (1989). Visible difference and flex appeal. *Cinema Journal*, **28**(4), 38–51.

Hoover, S. (1980, January). Exercise and all that jazz. *Women's Sports*, pp. 10–18.

Imm, P. (1989). *Exercise habits and perceptions of body image in female exercisers*. Paper presented at fourth Annual IDEA Conference, Los Angeles, CA.

Jacobs, C. (1991, March). Winning at the losing game. *Shape*, pp. 74–77.

Johnston, R. (1986). The story so far: And further transformations? In D. Punter (Ed.), *Introduction to contemporary cultural studies* (pp. 277–313). London: Longmans.

Kagan, E., & Morse, M. (1988). The body electronic: Aerobic exercise video. *The Drama Review, 32*, 164–180.

Kaufman, E. (1989, December). Put some muscle into it. *Self,* pp. 123–128.

Kenen, R.L. (1987). Double messages, double images: Physical fitness, self-concepts, and women's exercise classes. *Journal of Physical Education, Recreation, and Dance, 58*(6), 76–79.

Laurence, L. (1992, January). Shoulders are sexy. *Self,* pp. 102–105.

Lazarus, J. (1991, September), Beauty and the best. *Shape,* pp. 62–64.

Lenskyj, H. (1986). *Out of bounds: Women, sport and sexuality.* Toronto, ON: Women's Press.

Lenskyj, H. (1994). Sexuality and femininity in sport contexts: Issues and alternatives. *Journal of Sport and Social Issues, 18*, 356–376.

MacNeill, M. (1988). Active women, media representations, ideology. In J. Harvey & G. Cantelon (Eds.), *Not just a game* (pp. 195–212). Altona, MB: University of Ottawa Press.

Markula, P. (1992, November). *Bodywear that lets the body speak: Pleasures of fitness fashion in aerobics.* Paper presented at the Thirteenth Annual Conference of the North American Society for Sociology of Sport, Toledo, OH.

Markula, P. (1993a). Looking good, feeling good: Strengthening mind and body in aerobics. In L. Laine (Ed.), *On the fringes of sport* (pp. 93–99). Sankt Augustin, Germany: Akademia Verlag.

Markula, P. (1993b). *Total-body-tone-up: Paradox and women's realities in aerobics.* Unpublished doctoral dissertation, University of Illinois, Urbana–Champaign.

Markula, P. (in press). Postmodern aerobics: Contradictions and resistance. In A. Bolin & J. Granskog (Eds.), *Athletic intruders.* Newbury Park, CA: Sage.

Martin, E. (1987). *The woman in the body: Cultural analysis of reproduction.* Boston: Beacon Press.

Martin, E. (1989). The cultural construction of gendered bodies: Biology and metaphors of production and destruction. *Ethos, 3–4*, 143–159.

McRobbie, A. (1994). *Postmodernism and popular culture.* London: Routledge.

Miller, L., & Penz, O. (1991). Talking bodies: Female bodybuilders colonize a male preserve, *Quest, 43*, 148–163.

Patton, M.Q. (1980). *Qualitative evaluation methods.* Beverly Hills, CA: Sage.

Riquelme, K. (1994, March). Grand illusions, *Shape,* pp. 92–97.

Rosaldo, R. (1989). *Culture and truth: The remaking of social analysis.* Boston: Beacon Press.

Rothlein, L. (1988, May). Portrait of an aerobic dancer. *Women's Sports and Fitness,* p. 18.

Rover, E. (1992, January). Biceps strengthener. *Self,* p. 48.

Sorensen, J. (1979). *Aerobic dancing.* New York: Rawson, Wade.

Spitzack, C. (1990). *Confessing excess: Women and the politics of body reduction.* Albany: State University of New York Press.

Stallings, J. (1980). Fantasy, fact. *Women's Sports,* p. 49.

Sternlicht, E. (1990a, January). Testing your triceps. *Shape,* pp. 46–48.

Sternlicht, E. (1990b, February). Behind every great shape . . . is a great behind. *Shape,* pp. 38–40.

Sternlicht, E. (1990c, July). Try this for thighs. *Shape,* p. 34.

Sternlicht, E. (1991, May). Up in arms. *Shape,* pp. 48–50.

Strathern, M. (1981). Culture in a netbag: The manufacture of a subdiscipline in anthropology. *Man*, **16**(4), 276–292.

Theberge, N. (1987). Sport and women's empowerment. *Women's Studies International Forum*, **10**, 387–393.

Tucker, S. (1990, July). What is the ideal body. *Shape*, pp. 94–112.

Wolf, N. (1990). *The beauty myth*. London: Vintage.

Weaver, G., & Ruther, K. (1991, March). Learning to love exercise. *Shape*, pp. 81–86.

Wise, E. (1990, July). Feeling fat. *Shape*, pp. 20–21.

Part 15

SPORT AND CLASS POWER

52

COLLEGE FOOTBALL AND SOCIAL MOBILITY

A case study of Notre Dame football players[*]

Allen L. Sack and Robert Theil

Source: *Sociology of Education* 52(1) (1979): 60–66.

This study examined the social origins and career mobility of college football players who graduated from Notre Dame between 1946 and 1965. It was found that Notre Dame football players came from much lower socioeconomic backgrounds than regular Notre Dame students. In terms of social mobility, both ballplayers and regular students from lower socioeconomic backgrounds have moved well beyond their social origins. Only in educational attainment do the two groups differ significantly. Among ballplayers, first teamers experienced greater income mobility than second teamers and reserves. First team ballplayers were also found to be over-represented as top ranking executives in their companies.

It is a widely held belief that college football has been an effective avenue for upward social mobility. Thousands of boys, so the argument goes, would never have risen above their humble origins if they had not received athletic scholarships. One has only to point to such parvenu celebrities as Joe Namath, O. J. Simpson, or Franco Harris for evidence in support of this view. The main purpose of this study is to determine whether conventional wisdom concerning big time college football and social mobility holds up under empirical investigation.

There are a number of empirical studies which show that athletic participation in high school is positively related to academic achievement (Schafer and Armer, 1968; Phillips and Schafer, 1971) and to educational expectations (Bend, 1968; Rehberg and Schafer, 1968; Schafer and Rehberg, 1970; Spreitzer and Pugh, 1973; Snyder and Spreitzer, 1977). All of this research suggests that sport involvement in high school in some way enhances an athlete's chances of attending college and of becoming upwardly mobile later in life. Few studies, however, have examined the consequences of sport participation at the college level for an athlete's career mobility.

It is hard to deny that commercialized college football, as played at schools like Notre Dame, Texas, or the University of Nebraska, makes far greater demands on an athlete than is typically the case in high school. Thus, it is reasonable to expect that athletes will face many obstacles in obtaining their college educations they did not encounter at the high school level. In other words, even if athletes benefit in a number of ways from high school sport, their experiences might be quite different at the big time college level.

Sage (1967) and Webb (1968) provide evidence that college athletes are less successful academically than non-athletes. Sage compared two groups of former high school athletic stars; one group chose to play college sport while the other did not. Sage found that non-athletes received better grades, were more occupationally oriented, and were less concerned about fraternities and campus social life than athletes. Webb, in a study of Michigan State athletes, found that only 49 percent of the team athletes as opposed to 70 percent of the regular Michigan State students had actually graduated when five years had lapsed since the graduation of their original college classes.

The argument that college sport often interferes with an athlete's intellectual development is supported by a number of former college athletes (e.g., Meggysey, 1970; Scott, 1971; Shaw, 1972; Edwards, 1973; Sack, 1977). All of these writers found the demands of "big time" college sport to be incompatible with the pursuit of a first rate education. While the views of former athletes and the work of Sage and Webb do not provide enough solid empirical evidence to make firm conclusions, they do at least suggest that participation in college sport might in some ways hinder career mobility.

Many of the studies of college athletes, as Loy (1969) points out, have either focused on their social origins (McIntyre, 1959; Webb, 1968) or on their careers after graduating from college (Coughlan, 1956; Litchfield and Cope, 1962; Crawford, 1962). There have been few attempts, however, to compare an athlete's status of origin with his status later in life.

Loy (1969), in his study of athletes from UCLA, attempted to correct this shortcoming. By using mailed questionnaires, Loy was able to gather data on the social origins as well as the present social statuses of 845 life pass holders at UCLA. To obtain a life pass, an athlete must have competed at the college level for 4 years and have earned at least 3 varsity letters. Loy utilized the Duncan Socioeconomic Index (SEI) to rate an athlete's first job after graduation (status of entry), present job (status of destination) and his father's job when the athlete entered college (status of origin). By comparing the mean SEI scores for fathers and sons, Loy was able to derive a measure of social mobility.

Loy's use of data on origins and destinations was a marked improvement over earlier studies, but he failed to deal adequately with a number of other important methodological problems. Most importantly, he failed to use a control group of college students who were not varsity athletes. Thus, there is no way of knowing whether the mobility experienced by ballplayers in his study was a consequence of athletic participation or whether ballplayers and non-ballplayers alike experienced mobility during this period due to factors unrelated to athletic involvement.

Loy's study was also deficient in that it only included subjects who had at least 3 varsity letters. Thus, average and reserve ballplayers were excluded. The tendency to focus on star athletes when discussing sport and social mobility is a major problem with many studies in this area. An adequate study of how participation in college football affects social mobility must include all ballplayers who experienced the rigors of commercialized college sport. It is important to emphasize that most big time college ballplayers never reach the star category and many never earn a letter. There is also a sizeable number of athletes who receive scholarships, attend practice for 4 years, but never dress for a game. To exclude such ballplayers would be a gross oversight.

Methods

In the present study, the social origins and career mobility of 2 groups of college graduates were examined—former Notre Dame football players and Notre Dame students who were not varsity athletes. Social rank was measured in a number of ways. The Hollingshead Two Factor Index of Social Position (ISP) and the Duncan SEI were used as measures of social status. In addition, income and educational attainment helped to locate respondents in the stratification system. Social mobility was measured by examining the status, educational and income attainment of respondents who came from similar social origins. By social origin was meant the father's social rank when the respondent entered Notre Dame.

The sample consisted of 344 Notre Dame football players who graduated between 1946 and 1965. It also included 444 randomly selected regular students who graduated from Notre Dame during that same period.[1] The years 1946–1965 were chosen because graduates during that era should now be well established in their careers. A 20 year span was chosen to insure that a large number of football players could be included. The oldest subjects in the study were around 55, the youngest 35. Care was taken to include first team, second team and reserve ballplayers in the sample. It should be noted that Notre Dame was an all-male university during this period.

Data were gathered by use of a mailed questionnaire. Current mailing addresses of ballplayers and regular students were obtained from the Alumni Records Office at Notre Dame. Lists of football players were derived from rosters in football *Dopebooks* that were published yearly during the period under investigation. Only seniors were taken from each roster. A systematic sample of regular students was drawn from names in alumni files. Of the 788 questionnaires mailed out, 759 actually reached the respondents. The returned questionnaires numbered 482, with 218 coming from ballplayers and 264 from regular students. The overall response rate of 64 percent was about equal for both ballplayers and regular students.[2]

Findings

It is clear from Table 1 that Notre Dame players came from lower socio-economic backgrounds than average Notre Dame students. In education, income and in social status (Hollingshead ISP), the fathers of ballplayers rank much lower than the fathers of regular students.

Table 2 indicates that both ballplayers and regular students have experienced considerable status mobility. The mean Hollingshead ISP scores of

Table 1 Percentage distribution of indicators of social origin by type of student.

Father's Education	Players (N = 215)	Students (N = 261)	Total
16 years or more	15.8	36.7	130
12–15 years	29.3	33.3	150
Less than 12	54.9	30.0	196
Father's Income[a]	Players (N = 202)	Students (N = 238)	Total
$40,000 +	15.9	39.5	188
$20–39,000	28.2	29.0	126
Less $20,000	55.9	31.5	126
Father's Class (ISP)	Players (N = 205)	Students (N = 248)	Total
Upper	23.4	53.2	180
Middle	25.4	25.4	115
Lower	51.2	21.4	158

[a] Father's income is based on 1977 dollars.

Note: In this and in all subsequent tables, the total number of ballplayers and students should be 218 and 264 respectively. Where this is not the case, it is because of missing data.
χ^2 is significant at .001 for all three indicators.

Table 2 Mean Hollingshead ISP scores of ballplayers and regular students controlling father's ISP.[a]

	Father's ISP score					
Student Type	I (11–17)	II (18–31)	III (32–47)	IV (48–63)	V (64–77)	Total
Players	15.3(12)	19.5(35)	19.9(51)	20.3(74)	19.5(31)	19.6(203)
Students	16.6(57)	18.5(74)	18.0(63)	17.4(46)	18.2(6)	17.7(246)
Total	16.4(69)	18.8(109)	18.9(114)	19.2(120)	19.0(37)	18.6(449)

[a] In Hollingshead's ranking system, ISP scores range from a high of 11 to a low of 77.

respondents whose fathers were from classes IV and V reveal that both ball-players and regular students have moved well beyond their social origins.[3] A two way analysis of variance indicates that the main effect of student type on respondents ISP is not statistically significant, nor are there any significant interactions. Thus, ballplayers were no more or less mobile than regular students. The main effect of father's status on son's status, however, is statistically significant at the .03 level.[4]

It is obvious that the rather high social status enjoyed by the respondents can be largely attributed to their being college graduates. The fact that the Hollingshead ISP as well as other indices of social status rely heavily on education as a factor impairs somewhat their usefulness in assessing differences in social rank within a sample of college graduates. It should be noted, however, that the use of educational attainment, independent of the occupational factor in Hollingshead's index, reveals some important differences among Notre Dame graduates.

Table 3 indicates that Notre Dame football players were less likely than regular students to have earned graduate or professional degrees, regardless of father's educational attainment. Of the regular students whose fathers did not graduate from high school, 44 percent earned advanced degrees. This was true of only 29 percent of the ballplayers from similar origins. This would suggest that the former experienced greater educational mobility. It would also appear that for players and regular students alike, there was a positive relationship between father's and son's educational attainment.

A two way analysis of variance examining the effects of father's income and student type on son's income found no statistically significant main effects or interactions. It is clear, however, that both ballplayers and regular students experienced considerable income mobility. Even respondents whose fathers made less than $15,000 a year (adjusted to 1977 dollars) now have a mean annual income of over $30,000 (see Table 4). A three way analysis of variance using father's income, father's education, and rank on football team, i.e., first team, second team or reserve, as independent variables and son's income as the dependent variable, uncovered only one statistically significant main effect. That was the effect of rank on team. The absence of any

Table 3 Percentage of respondents who earned advanced degrees by type of student and father's education.

	Father's education							
Student Type	16 or more years	(N)	12–15 Years	(N)	Less than 12 Years	(N)	Total	(N)
Players	38.2	(34)	34.9	(63)	28.8	(118)	32.1	(215)
Students	55.2	(96)	50.6	(87)	43.6	(78)	50.2	(261)
Total	50.8	(130)	44.0	(150)	34.7	(196)	42.0	(476)

statistically significant interactions means that the relationship between rank on team and son's income holds up regardless of father's education and income.

Table 5 clearly illustrates this relationship between a ballplayer's rank on the football team in his senior year and his present income. Whereas 41 percent of the first team ballplayers are now making $50,000 or more, this is true of only 30 percent of the second teamers and 13 percent of the reserves. Table 5 also indicates that there is very little difference in income attainment when regular students are compared with ballplayers as a whole.

A player's rank on the team, while influencing income, had little effect on a player's social status or educational attainment. A two way analysis of variance examining the effect of father's ISP and rank on team on son's ISP revealed that only father's ISP had a statistically significant main effect. Furthermore, while 42 percent of the second teamers, 33 percent of the reserves and only 29 percent of the first team ballplayers earned advanced degrees, this difference was not statistically significant at the .05 level.

Table 4 Mean income of ballplayers and regular students controlling father's income (in thousands of dollars)[a]

			Father's income			
Student Type	−$15,000	$15–$19,999	$20–$29,999	$30–$39,999	$40,000+	Total
Players	35 (70)	33 (42)	37 (46)	41 (11)	44 (31)	37 (200)
Students	36 (35)	35 (40)	36 (43)	36 (24)	38 (94)	36 (236)
Total	35 (105)	34 (82)	36 (89)	38 (35)	36 (125)	37 (436)

[a] The means in this table were calculated on the basis of midpoints of intervals. Income categories ranged from 1 to 8 with 1 being 0–$4,999 and 8 being $50,000+. All entries are rounded to nearest thousand.

Table 5 Percentage distribution of respondent's present income by type of student and rank on football team.

	Student type		Rank on team		
Income	Players	Students	1st	2nd	Res.
$50,000+	29.6	24.3	41.0	29.8	13.1
$30–49,999	29.2	35.2	25.3	26.3	36.1
Less $30,000	41.2	40.5	33.7	43.9	50.8
Total	(216)	(259)	(95)	(57)	(61)

χ^2 for student type and income is not significant at .05.
χ^2 for rank on team and income is significant at .05.

Discussion

From the above findings it can be concluded that both Notre Dame football players and regular students have experienced considerable upward social mobility. Only in educational attainment beyond a college degree do the two groups differ significantly. The fact that the respondents were all at least college graduates has undoubtedly contributed to their general success. Among ballplayers, rank on the team appears to have had a marked impact on income mobility.

The finding that ballplayers earned fewer advanced degrees than other students may indicate that athletes set a lower priority on academic accomplishment. Then again, the demands of commercialized college football may force even academically oriented ballplayers to do only enough studying to get by. What many people fail to realize, or refuse to acknowledge, is that big time college football demands as much time and energy as professional football. When presented with the statement, "playing football at Notre Dame is as physically and psychologically demanding as playing in the National Football League," 64 percent of the respondents who had actually played pro ball agreed or strongly agreed. Only 32 percent were in disagreement and 4 percent were undecided.

Given the fact that big time college athletes work as hard as professionals, it is not surprising that many of them take academic shortcuts. When asked if they cheated in school work while at Notre Dame, 69 percent of the ballplayers and only 43 percent of the regular students admitted having done so. Ballplayers were also found to be under-represented in fields that require considerable scholarly commitment (such as science and engineering) and had lower grade point averages than regular students. As a result of the lower priority athletes are often forced to give to education, it is to be expected that they would earn fewer advanced degrees than other students.

The finding than first team ballplayers experienced greater income mobility than second teamers and reserves, while not surprising, is nonetheless open to a variety of interpretations. One could argue that the fame the first team athletes receive gives them entree to high paying positions which demand people with celebrity status. This fame is even enhanced if an athlete has a successful career in professional football. Paul Hornung, Daryl Lamonica, Myron Pottios, and Nick Pietrosante are just a few of the many Notre Dame graduates in the sample who were able to capitalize on their stellar careers in professional football.[5]

It might also be argued, however, that the interpersonal skills and character traits which make successful athletes are precisely those which make successful entrepreneurs. Athletes who rise to the top in the often brutal competition of big time college football may be best suited for careers in business. This study uncovered no significant status differences among first team, second team and reserve ballplayers. Likewise, the careers pursued by all three categories of ballplayers were fairly similar. There is one occupational difference though that is worth noting. Of the first team ballplayers, 34 percent are presently top executives in their companies, i.e., presidents, vice presidents, assistant vice presidents, or treasurers. This was true of only 13 percent of the second teamers and 14 percent of the reserves.

Whether the income and business success of first team athletes is the result of their celebrity status or their ability to thrive in highly competitive situations is a question worthy of further research. Further research should also explore in greater detail other differences among star, journeyman, and marginal college athletes. This is especially important in studies of sport and social mobility. An issue that was not raised here is how do ballplayers fare who do not graduate from college? It would also be useful to compare the career mobility and academic accomplishments of athletes who attend a wide variety of academic institutions. A comparison of big time college athletes with athletes in the Ivy League might be particularly revealing in this regard. These are just a few of the many possibilities for further research in this area.

Notes

* This is a revised version of a paper delivered at the annual meeting of the American Sociological Association at San Francisco, September, 1978. The authors are indebted to the University of New Haven for providing financial support for this study and to Gina R. Sack. Thomas Mordecai and Cynthia Kranyik for assistance in gathering, coding, and processing the data.

1 Of the 482 respondents who returned the questionnaires, 12 reported that they never received their degrees. Only one of those was a former football player.
2 It should be noted that the age distributions for football players and regular students who returned the questionnaires were almost identical. (Chisquare = .52, P < .98).
3 The use of Duncan's SEI yielded very similar results. The mean SEI scores of ballplayers and regular students who came from lower status origins were 74 and 78 respectively. Given the fact that the mean SEI scores for the fathers of both group were in the 30's, it is clear that the respondents have experienced considerable status mobility.
4 In this and all subsequent ANOVA, effects have been estimated using the least squares approach to unequal cell N's. Post-hoc between—group comparisons were made using the Scheffe approach, a conservative test appropriate to the non-orthogonal design.
5 It should be noted that 59 percent of first team athletes, 28 percent of second teamers and only 8 percent of the reserves went on to play pro ball. Nonetheless, a two way analysis of variance examining the effects of team rank and playing pro ball on present income revealed that only team rank had a statistically significant main effect.

References

Bend, E. 1968 The Impact of Athletic Participation on Academic and Career Aspiration and Achievement. New Brunswick, N.J.: The National Football Foundation Hall of Fame.

Coughlan, R. 1956 "What happens to football players?" Sports Illustrated (September 24) (October 1).

Crawford, A. B. 1962 Football Y Men: 1872–1919. Men of Yale Series. New Haven: Yale University Press.

Duncan, O. D. 1961 "A socioeconomic index of all occupations." Pp. 109–138 in Albert J. Reiss, et al., Occupations and Social Status. New York: Free Press.

Edwards, H. 1973 Sociology of Sport. Homewood, Ill.: Dorsey.

Litchfield, E. E., and M. Cope 1962 "Saturday's hero is doing fine." Sports Illustrated (July 8):66–80.

Loy, J. W. 1969 "The study of sport and social mobility." Pp. 249–268 in George H. Sage (ed.), Sport and American Society. Reading, Ma.: Addison/Wesley.

McIntyre, T. D. 1959 Socioeconomic Background of White Male Athletes from Selected Sports at The Pennsylvania State University. Unpublished M.Ed. thesis. The Pennsylvania State University.

Meggysey, D. 1970 Out of Their League. Berkeley: Ramparts.

Phillips, J., and W. E. Schafer 1971 "Consequences of participation in interscholastic sports: A review and prospectus." Pacific Sociological Review 14 (July):328–338.

Rehberg, R., and W. E. Schafer 1968 "Participation in interscholastic athletics and college expectations." American Journal of Sociology 73 (May):732–740.

Sack, A. L. 1977 "Big time college football: Whose free ride?" Quest 27 (Winter):87–96.

Sage, J. N. 1967 "Adolescent values and the non-participating college athlete." Paper presented at the convention of the Southern Section of the Canadian Association of Health, Physical Education, and Recreation. San Fernando, Ca.

Schafer, W. E. and J. J. Armer 1968 "Athletes are not inferior students." Transaction 5 (November):21–26, 61–62.

Schafer, W. E., and R. Rehberg 1970 "Athletic participation, college aspirations, and college encouragement," Pacific Sociological Review 13 (Summer):182–186.

Scott, J. 1971 The Athletic Revolution. New York: Free Press.

Shaw, G. 1972 Meat on the Hoof. New York: St. Martin's.

Snyder, E., and E. Spreitzer 1977 "Participation in sport as related to educational expectations among high school girls." Sociology of Education 50 (January):47–55.

Spreitzer, E., and M. Pugh 1973 "Interscholastic athletics and educational expectations." Sociology of Education 46 (Spring):171–182.

Webb, H. 1968 "Social backgrounds of college athletes". Paper presented at the National Convention of the American Association of Health, Physical Education, and Recreation. St. Louis, Mo.

53

THE HISTORICAL MEANING OF AMATEURISM

An outline

Richard Holt

Source: *Innovation* 5(4) (1992): 19–31. Originally published as "Amateurism and its interpretation: the social origins of British sport. Updated for this publication.

For around a hundred years – the period spanning the third quarter of the nineteenth century to the third quarter of the twentieth – most sports were run by organizations and individuals proclaiming amateur status. Even sports in which professionals played a prominent part were frequently run by amateurs; the Football Association, for example, was an amateur body formed in 1863 which determined the rules of the sport, disciplined players, set their terms of employment and chose national teams, leaving only the organization of fixtures to the professional Football League. The 1870s and 1880s were crucial in amateur control of most other sporting bodies. Athletics was reformed under the aegis of the amateur Athletic Association in 1880; the Amateur Boxing Association was set up in the same year; in 1882 the Amateur Rowing Association was formed and the Amateur Swimming Association took on its final amateur form in 1886. This by no means exhausts the list of newly "amateur" sports. Henceforth amateurs ruled both morally and in a practical organizational sense. What was "amateurism" and why did it take such a hold on British sport at this moment in history?

Definitions

It is perhaps surprising that there is no major monograph devoted to the broad emergence of amateurism despite specialized histories of the achievements of the major amateur sporting bodies, which by now have all had their centenaries, and of "athleticism" in the "Public Schools".[1] How can we account for the emergence of distinctive forms of organization combined with a new system of values in sport in mid-Victorian Britain? What is the relationship between the new institutions of amateur sport and the ideals of "fair play" and "sportsmanship" with which they were associated? It should be made clear at the outset that new research is needed. The purpose of this article is simply to indicate what kinds of explanations have been offered and how some existing approaches might be combined to produce a better account of what became a kind of distinguishing feature of late Victorian and Edwardian culture.

Amateurism, as we shall see, has been widely but not directly discussed; it is usually seen in terms of something else, a dimension of "hegemony", or "Darwinism", "imperialism", "the Civilizing Process" or even a part of a revival of "chivalry". As yet we have no very clear idea of who the major figures in the amateur sports movement were beyond knowing that an aristocrat could often be found to act as a public figurehead. But whether the leading amateurs, members of national and local committees, were largely from landed families or from merchant, legal or administrative ones is unclear. For, in terms of the social meaning of amateurism, this seems to be the historical issue: was amateurism a development and adaptation of existing aristocratic sporting forms and values to suit the new conditions of the mid-nineteenth century? Or was it rather a new phenomenon arising from the firm belief in the virtue of competition, from the success of "*laissez faire*" economics and leading to the opening of higher education and public service to the principle of meritocracy? Was it a question of the old landed elite evolving under the influence of the dynamic Victorian middle class, or was this middle class itself divided and partially assimilated into an upper class value system of which amateurism was an important element? Or is this model too crude? Could it be that intermarriage and occupational fluidity, notably between land, the liberal professions and the City, was forming a genuinely mixed elite for whom amateurism based on shared public school experiences helped to provide a unifying set of values?

According to the *Oxford English Dictionary* the term "amateur" came into use in the nineteenth century to signify "one who cultivates anything as a pastime as distinguished from one who prosecutes it professionally"; the word "amateurism" as "the characteristic practice of amateurs" seems to have come into use in the 1860s and was common thereafter. The stress is on enjoyment rather than the "call to seriousness", which characterized much of mid-Victorianism. "Amateur" was a word often used to describe those who put on plays for pleasure as opposed to professional actors; it was also used derogatively for someone who did something badly (in an "amateurish" fashion). But it was in sport that the word became part of public discourse as a formal definition of status. An amateur sportsman was one who did not take money for the playing of sport; however, as the rules of the new bodies made clear, amateurism was far more than a question of payment or non-payment as the following definition by division into structure, principles and ethos tries to indicate:

Structure

This has been the least discussed aspect of amateurism; the creation of public voluntary bodies to regulate sport on a national basis instead of private clubs such as the Marylebone Cricket Club, the Jockey Club and the Royal and Ancient Golf Club of St. Andrews which were all eighteenth century upper class, closed and self-perpetuating institutions. All of these, significantly, survived and ensured a continued, if modified, upper class influence; but the new sporting bodies were not "clubs" but rather "unions" or "associations" of a number of clubs, which could affiliate without reference to the social class of their own members; this was the period when a large number of other national administrative institutions such as trade unions and modern political parties also came into existence; the growth of a national rail network was a pre-condition for mobility and better communications; amateur sporting bodies were among the first examples of bureaucratic rationality in sport as Allen Guttmann (1978) has observed.[2]

Principles

These were:

(1) the creation of "fair" competition by establishing common rules;
(2) the avoidance of excessive violence and injury by disciplinary codes which, for example, outlawed "hacking" (the deliberate kicking of opponents);
(3) to encourage participation; most amateur bodies placed much more stress on playing than on spectating; in some amateur sports, notably rugby union, spectators were scarcely tolerated.
(4) to exclude from competition those who profit financially from sport; originally this was designed to exclude those who were at an unfair advantage because of their occupation; for example, a waterman or a swimming teacher; it was only when the commercial possibilities of sport became obvious around 1880 that the systematic payment of players became an issue;
(5) abolition of gambling; opposition to the use of sport for betting was an important aspect of amateurism that contrasts starkly with earlier aristocratic attitudes; the Amateur Athletic Association prosecuted competitors in the 1880s for betting and the Football Association continued to oppose all forms of gambling, including the "football pools" up to 1930s, by which time betting on football matches had become almost a national institution.

Ethos

The spirit of amateur sport is often confused with its principles; a belief in sportsmanship and "fair play" was closely associated with amateurism from the beginning but was in fact logically separate from it; the ideals of honourable, dignified and respectable behaviour, not boasting in victory or complaining in defeat, not fanatical nor too partisan; maintaining self-control and dignity; performing stylishly and with courage; the manner of victory as more important than the margin; all this was more a matter of being a gentleman than of strict compliance with the principles of amateurism. Many working class amateurs, who accepted rules and did not take money or gamble, ignored or rejected this wider set of values, which were articles of faith amongst those who ran amateur sport.

Interpretations

The most obvious way of "explaining" the rise of amateurism is to link it to the growth of the Victorian public school; in this way amateurism can be seen as little more than the extension of the "athleticism" of the public school which has been widely discussed, notably in the work of J.A. Mangan.[3] It is tempting to see the setting up of bodies like the Football Association (FA) or the Amateur Athletic Association (AAA) solely in terms of former public school pupils or Oxford and Cambridge graduates continuing the games they had enjoyed at school and university. The FA certainly had a large number of Etonians and Harrovians amongst its early members and the very name of the Rugby Union speaks for itself. Those who set up the amateur associations were almost entirely drawn from the public schools; as were the members of the MCC, who revised cricket in the 1860s and 1870s to clarify the distinction between the position of the amateurs ("the Gentlemen") and the professionals ("the Players").

It is not so much that such an approach is wrong; it is rather that it does not take us very far in the wider understanding of amateurism. While playing down the personal role of Thomas Arnold at Rugby as a pioneer of sport, Mangan gives much weight to the intervention of other headmasters, notably Cotton of Harrow in the early 1850s and stresses the value of sport in creating order in schools, which earlier in the century had witnessed revolts by pupils. A new generation of middle class parents had new requirements of education, and athletic sports arose to help fulfil these expectations. Mangan succeeds admirably in showing how the new sports became part of a reformed educational system reinforced by clothes, songs and rituals that became increasingly linked to a Darwinist and imperialist ethic in the later part of the century. The question is whether we are witnessing a controlled broadening of an upper class system of education with its love of physical vigour and contempt for money, or a new cult of bourgeois competition?

Recent research by Chandler has thrown new light on the question. He has stressed the gradual and pupil-led growth of sport, starting in the early nineteenth century amongst the sons of the gentry; it was the "great schools", notably Eton, Harrow, Winchester, Shrewsbury and Westminster with the addition of the newer Rugby, whose pupils themselves developed modern sports, especially cricket and rowing, before reforming headmasters like Cotton of Marlborough and Vaughan at Harrow made sport officially respectable and strengthened it. Hence the initial impetus came from the most aristocratic private schools; this pioneering period lasted until around 1860 and was followed by a second phase in the 1860s and 1870s when Oxford and Cambridge took over; the role of sport was greatly increased in the two ancient universities, which had a crucial role in producing a "gentrified" elite. Chandler shows that a very small number of schools had a huge impact on Oxbridge sport with Eton supplying never less than one in six and as many as one in three of all cricket and rowing first teams ("blues") between 1829 and 1880. The pupil controlled system worked perfectly at Oxbridge and was supremely important in the spread of amateurism.[4]

"Athleticism" cannot be seen as an imposition on a declining gentry by educational reformers. Traditional values of courage and honour were repackaged to fit new circumstances but how seriously were they changed or challenged? Matthew Arnold's upper classes were athletic "Barbarians" and the same kind of rule was given to them in Veblen's *The Theory of the Leisure Class*[5]. More recently Martin Wiener's *English Culture and the Decline of the Industrial Spirit* stressed middle class subservience to gentry values expressed through the public school's anti-urban dislike of commerce and their cult of manliness through sport. "In no country do the professions so naturally and generally share the cast of ideas of the aristocracy as in England" notes Wiener citing Matthew Arnold, and an observer of comparative higher education writing in the 1860s agreed "a middle class cut in two in a way unexampled anywhere else; a professional class brought up on the first plane, with fine and governing qualities, but without the idea of science; while that immense business class ... is in England brought up on the second plane, cut off from the aristocracy and the professions, and without governing qualities."[6]

This observation leads to what is probably the most detailed and important contribution to the discussion of British amateurism. The work of Norbert Elias on the "Civilizing Process" and its specific application to sport by Eric Dunning and other members of the "Leicester School" of "figurational" or "process" sociology, who argue that amateur sport was a crucial step in the process by which physical contests were "civilized" (i.e. turned into pleasurable, exciting but relatively safe and self-controlled activities); this in turn represents an important stage in a much longer and wider process of "civilization".[7] Elias is concerned to explain long-term shifts in sensibility by linking changes in the structure of the state with the development of the personality. I do not propose here to enter into methodological and theoretical debates which are examined elsewhere by Dunning and others.[8] For an historian a sociological approach which looks at the slow transformation of manners from the handbooks of sixteenth century courtiers to the peaceful, "civilized" competitiveness in politics and leisure displayed by the eighteenth century British elite is of major interest. Did the theory and practice of amateur sport in the nineteenth century arise out of the culture of a demilitarized, educated and economically sophisticated English elite?

Elias himself did not develop these ideas very extensively beyond a discussion of early forms of football and a rather unsatisfactory attempt to link the rise of fox hunting as a "civilized" alternative to the brutality of older hunts where the huntsman killed the prey himself. Peaceful physical contests were a wider manifestation of a more controlled culture which also favoured a system of party political government and substituted verbal for physical aggression.[9] Dunning and Sheard took up this idea, systematized it and applied it ingeniously to the history of the game of rugby. If any sport could be said to provide a "civilized" substitute for the violent encounters of previous centuries both in sport and battle, then rugby was it. Dunning and Sheard argue that amateur sport grew out of the withdrawal of the gentry from folk-football and other sports during the course of the eighteenth and early nineteenth centuries. They suggest that the upper classes withdrew into "status exclusivity" because they were challenged by "bourgeois power and that new sports grew out of this disaffection with the old"; however, as D. A. Reid has pointed out, there is little evidence for the "bourgeois challenge" hypothesis.[10] Linda Colley has argued that the later eighteenth century saw the creation of a new kind of British national identity. This was based upon a ruling oligarchy that recovered its confidence after the fear of a Catholic–French-supported return of the Stuart monarchy (Jacobitism) subsided and survived the loss of the American colonies. They "reinvented their culture", including elements like fox hunting and public school education and revived their thinning blood lines by marriage.[11] From one of the leading historians of the period since Plumb (upon whom Elias was much too dependent), this is clearly an important advance. Whether it can be brought into the ample ambit of the "civilizing process" – which, as Dunning honestly admits, its critics attack as so inclusive as to claim a "vacuous interconnectedness" for everything – remains to be seen. For the Leicester School, it seems to me that nothing is so imperative as to ground their views in the mass of excellent empirical work going on in the field of history. As it stands, Dunning and Sheard's pioneering *Barbarians, Gentlemen and Players* is just too schematic: consider the terminology, which speaks of the "Establishment of the sufficient conditions for incipient modernisation"; this leads from "Industrialisation" through "Embourgeoisement" to the "Struggle for the reform of public schools". This culminates, it is true, empirically enough in Thomas Arnold at Rugby and the "ban on aristocratic sports" and "mild encouragement of team sports".[12] Maybe we should ask why his reforms were so well received among the upper classes instead of assuming a process of "embourgeoisement" was taking place.

None of this necessarily invalidates the wider "civilizing process" approach. On the contrary, the idea of an accelerating shift in manners whether from commercial rationality, the influence of the Enlightenment or the Evangelical revival – or whatever other historical force that can be pressed into explanatory service – fits well with rising standards of self-control amongst well-born or well-educated persons. The facts of parliamentary life meant that even if urban middle class protestants – a formidably active minority – attacked certain traditional sports as "cruel", so-called "brutal" sports could not in fact be banned until the nobility and the gentry chose to do so via the House of Commons and the House of Lords; the "natural rulers" were under no greater pressure to interfere in popular culture than they were to abandon agricultural protection. If change came, it was because a significant element within the landed elite believed it to be inevitable and right. There was, therefore, a split in the gentry between the "backwoodsmen" – the old country-squires who abhorred education and reform of all kinds – and the rest whose manners are the subject of Jane Austen's work, among others. Such persons were presumably influenced in part by the kind of increased sensitivity to the suffering of animals that Keith Thomas has discussed in *Man and the Natural World*.[13]

As is often the case, history and sociology have been going along parallel lines: for the shift from animal to human exertion as the basis for sport was a very profound transformation; the amateurs' emphasis on active participation and sportsmanship was clearly relevant and important. More stress is now being given to cultural attitudes as opposed to economic change, especially evangelism, than was the case in the last generation when a "rise of the bourgeoisie" thesis and class consciousness dominated historical thinking through the works of Hobsbawm and E.P. Thompson. Hence the mores of the elite are once more at the centre of the stage.[14] Historians have to listen to Elias and the advocates of his "approach" – historians have much more difficulty with the words "method" or "theory"; but any school of thought which depends so much on observing long-term historical change should obviously be in closer touch with current historical scholarship. To take a final example, the work of the distinguished architectural and social historian Mark Girouard on the widespread revival of chivalry amongst the upper classes seems highly relevant here.[15] In *Return to Camelot* Girouard shows how powerful the concept of honour remained and how amateurism in the sense of sportsmanship and fair play fitted into this revitalized aristocratic code of good behaviour, even suggesting the kinds of emblems and colours worn by the new sportsmen had their origins in chivalric emblems.

Leaving aside this thorny question of the origins of amateurism, the main contribution of Dunning and Sheard concerns the different interpretations of it according to social status.[16] The Football Association, composed of old boys from the highest status schools like Eton, was an amateur body which was in the end willing to accept professionals under strict controls (as was done in cricket). Rugby, however, where the older aristocratic influence was possibly less important and individuals less secure in their status – more research is still needed here – adopted a stricter approach, which outlawed all forms of professionals. This brings Dunning and Sheard to the second part of their argument, which stresses the split in the middle classes between the southern public school amateur group with strong links to the liberal professions and old money, and the northern industrial grouping who accepted the creation of commercially run clubs and payment of players. Far from uniting the middle classes, sport helped to split them socially and geographically into two camps. It was the challenge from the northern clubs with substantial working class support to the rule of the southern gentlemen that brought about the split within rugby in 1894. In England amateurism, therefore, remained firmly in the camp of an aristocratic elite which had expanded to incorporate the law, medicine, the civil service and merchant banking as well as the more established institutions of the armed services and the Church. Clergymen were not to be found foxhunting (decreasingly) but on the cricket field (increasingly).

The role of amateurism in what might be called the selective "assimilation" or "diffusionist" view of British history needs to be set alongside the rather different "social control" approach, which was a major theme of Victorian social history in the 1970s and 1980s.[17] From this perspective modern sports, coinciding with the mid-Victorian hey-day of free trade, can be seen as an expression of a robust bourgeois culture of fitness, competition and discipline. For the new bourgeoisie, whose values were epitomized by Samuel Smiles' *Self Help*, the problem was that the poor were not persuaded of the virtues of competition and had to be re-educated. This was the meaning of the term "rational recreation" used to describe the kinds of leisure activity which middle class activists wanted the poor to take up. Ideally, they would spend their few hours of free time attending lectures at a Mechanics Institute or a Workingmen's Club where alcohol and gambling were not permitted. But healthy exercise was also promoted, especially as football teams or boxing clubs were so obviously more acceptable to working class youths than more intellectual kinds of activity. Peter Bailey gave an excellent account of this process using the town of Bolton as a case study and a series of other collections around the same theme explored the extent to which the working classes could be changed from above.[18] In broad terms most of the empirical research on social control and popular culture has stressed the limitations of such initiatives. While an active minority of reformers – often Evangelicals of a "muscular Christian" type drawn not so much from the industrial middle classes as from the public school elite – tried to change popular culture partly through sport, workers themselves soon learned to "play the game in their own way". They took over clubs that had been created for them and ran them in their own fashion. Hence amateur sporting bodies may have provided a useful structure for competition but the ethos of sportsmanship and fair play was not necessarily disseminated or respected. It was possible to accept "amateurism" without the ideology that was supposed to go with it.

Growing out of this interest in efforts at "social control" – the concept was not originally a Marxist one but came to be associated with a leftist, class-based approach to nineteenth century history – has come the more theoretically refined notion of "hegemony". This has been most fully elaborated in relation to sport in the work of Richard Gruneau and in John Hargreaves' study of British sport where amateurism is seen as an important part of "the hegemonic subject".[19] There is no space here to discuss the conceptual debate within Marxism itself concerning Gramsci's concept of the way in which bourgeois intellectuals within a liberal democratic state must seek to assert moral leadership over the proletariat, and the process of negotiation by which elements of the dominant ideology are assimilated or resisted. Accepting for a moment this contentious assumption, can we say that amateur sport was "hegemonic"? Hargreaves credits amateur sport with simultaneously unifying the middle and upper classes whilst dividing manual workers into the respectable, who accepted the new values of sportsmanship and the rough, unskilled elements who did not. Here he comes close to the wider debate within social history over the creation of a Victorian "labour aristocracy" cut off from the rest of the working class by higher wages and a respectable culture that assimilated bourgeois values. Skilled workers tended, in fact, to be more radical than unskilled; high wages did not easily equate with respectability, which in any case was more widely diffused than has been supposed. The whole debate seems underpinned by the Marxist-Leninist need to explain the lack of popular revolution by the lack of a "revolutionary vanguard" in Britain.[20]

In a dense but brief discussion – *Sport, Power and Culture* tries to cover both the nineteenth century and the current political economy of sport – Hargreaves seems at certain points to be saying amateurism is the ideology of a rising bourgeoisie and at others to be accepting the continued importance of a reformed upper class. Quoting Hughes on Tom Brown, he says that the hero's father wants his son inculcated with the "virtues of Victorian bourgeois morality". But Tom Brown was the son of a country squire, who presumably wanted his boy imbued with the ideals of honour and service; he was hardly likely to be looking for a Cobden or a Bright, a free-trading, Liberal meritocrat, critical of Land, the Empire, of inherited privilege and even the Church of England. This is no mere quibbling with words. The crucial point here, to which I will return, is that there was no simple consensus over dominant values in Victorian England; there were "the model lives" of engineers anatomized by Smiles and there were other model lives of service and soldiery read about in children's literature. There was a range of projects which might conceivably be described as "hegemonic" ranging from the efforts of Oxbridge undergraduates to start boys' clubs in the East End of London to municipal socialism and the provision of public facilities like parks and swimming baths for cleanliness and wholesome recreation.[21]

There really is not very much evidence for extensive promotion of sport by either the southern public school set or the northern business group. Activists are often self-publicists and write books that historians can read. But for the most part it seems that middle class amateurs were generally more concerned with playing together than with workers. Workers played because they wanted to and in their own ways; this had little to do with the ideals of amateurism. It is certainly true that amateur sport set up national structures with open access – a point that will be developed later – but there was no "Sport For All" programme in Victorian times. Legally amateur officials would not exclude anyone for class reasons but neither did they encourage working class participation; they possibly saw themselves as "facilitators" but were not really propagandists. Hence there seems to have been little crossing of class barriers through sport. Furthermore, the moral urgency of the rational recreation movement waned as middle-class, middle-aged leisure came to centre around the suburb with its golf and tennis clubs. Sport was shorn of some of its idealism and settled into a pattern of comfortable consumption. The athletic amateurs of the late nineteenth century certainly imbued public school sport with an imperialist ethos of conquest and service and no doubt some of this filtered down the social pyramid. But we should be under no illusion that most middle class sportsmen seem to have wanted to keep as far away from the working classes as possible.

This does not mean that the hegemonic approach is without its uses; the problem lies in the scope of the claims that different schools make for their theories – a perpetual complaint between the more and the less systematic elements within what the French call the "human sciences". Why should "theories" be true or false, all right or all wrong? Why can't we pick and choose from the concepts we need to make sense of the rich diversity of our material? Providing, of course, we take the trouble to try to understand their intellectual provenance and be as careful and explicit in our usage as sociologists are supposed to be. How many times does it have to be said that there are really no theories and solutions that command more than the most partial assent, there are only problems, more or less well defined and shifting back and forth in the interplay of argument and research, which produce responses that are more or less convincing in terms of their "cumulative plausibility" (a phrase which describes the kind of "explanation" which most historians try to achieve). To be fair, this is very much the direction in which social science is now going. As Pierre Bourdieu has remarked, it is easier to deal with the celebratory tradition of sports writing than with the analytic schools who insist that transformations in sport must mean something in terms of *tous les grands mots* like "class struggle", "feminism", "capitalism" without the initial research having been done on the structures of the subject itself.[22] The priority must be to establish what the particular structure of sport was at a particular time and see what follows from that. Following this line of reasoning, consider this review by a distinguished historian and sociologist of an important new work – *Plausible Worlds: Possibility and Understanding in History and the Social Sciences* by Geoffrey Hawthorn (1991):

> Hawthorn's treatment is an exemplary specimen of recent social science "cool". It is chastened in its claims, distrustful of theory, tentative about interpretation, disarmingly modest in its post-Wittgensteinian sensitivity to communities of language. The "old" social scientist believed his own knowledge was power – progressive and benevolent power. The new one has long since learned to distrust the benevolence. He or she . . . aspires to knowledge as play, or even, in Hawthorn's case, renounces knowledge. "Success in history and the social science, as perhaps in life itself, consists in understanding more and knowing less".[23]

More simply, it is the exclusivity of truth claims that makes life hard for those of us who cannot bring ourselves to acknowledge the *a priori* rightness of any particular Big Idea. Sport was a vast and complex phenomenon and, as Allen Guttmann has recently observed in relation to the Dunning and Elias school of thought, "no key turns all locks".[24]

With such important reservations in mind, it could be argued that cricket, for example, the only genuinely national sport in England, enshrined values and practices that were "hegemonic" though not in the straightforward sense of reproducing "bourgeois" values. Cricket, however, certainly embodied a set of national and imperial values in which the public school elite were presented as rightly superior to the rest of the English, whose job it was to support the team. It is a shortcoming of Hargreaves' analysis of amateurism that he is not able to discuss individual sports in any depth. By making sports as a whole "hegemonic", it is difficult to make crucial distinctions between them. While it is hard to see how football in any meaningful sense strength-ened the moral authority of the status quo, it is perfectly evident that the strict subordination of professionals in cricket and the glorification of the "gentlemen amateur" of the "The Golden Age" before 1914 gave a moral lesson and language to the English – and to the Empire – which it would be perverse to argue was without any effect. As Ross McKibbin, the most sophisticated analyst of working class culture and politics, has argued, "the use of a vocabulary of 'fairness' derived from amateur sport was important in all aspects of public life and was actively encouraged by the politically predominant classes".[25] It was not the main reason for the failure, for example, of Marxism in Britain but it was a factor along with others. Moral authority rested with the "natural" rulers as represented by the MCC with peers and baronets at the helm supported by lawyers, doctors, civil servants and the massed ranks of those who were "something in the City", who could preside in a "neutral" way over the fortunes of the game as they would over the State.

The most recent addition to the literature on the meaning of amateurism has come from the ingenious idea of comparing the role of sport in the formation of the middle classes in Britain and Germany in the nineteenth century by Christiane Eisenberg.[26] Eisenberg points out that in Germany the term "middle class" was much easier to define than in Britain. In Germany the "middle" was composed of those with some property and education who were neither workers nor peasants on the one hand and were clearly separated from the powerful nobility on the other; the German bourgeoisie developed a high culture; the British, who were more active commercially and industrially, allegedly took over the older popular and elite traditions of sport in the early nineteenth century, refining and reforming them, before handing them back to the wider public in the later nineteenth century. Just as the German middle classes were musical the British were sporting; in particular, they cherished the ideal of competition; competition is a "good thing" and ought to be encouraged systematically through the practice of sport.

This has the simple merit of restoring the economic realities of the mid-Victorian boom to the centre of the stage. Instead of stressing the hegemonic implications of sport for class relations, perhaps a simpler emphasis on the role of sport in promoting the competitive principle is more important. Eisenberg's approach, however, is "neo-liberal" rather than Marxist in the sense that economic competition is seen in a positive light, promoting not unbridled egoism but a softening of social relations and new kinds of solidarity, expressed in part through the clubs and associations that made up the world of sport. The landed elite believed in agrarian capitalism and to a certain extent in competition. They had carried through an agricultural revolution and were willing to invest their profits in commerce. The athletic interests of the upper classes took on new forms in the public schools where their numbers were swelled by the sons of the liberal professions, who became increasingly important as time went by and were less distracted by horse racing and hunting than the gentry. On the contrary, in Germany the aristocracy kept itself pure – duelling kept its key role in defining noble status – and the middle classes were excluded from noble leisure pursuits. If Eisenberg underestimates upper class involvement, she is surely right to stress the distinctiveness of sports associations "based on principles of universal admittance and managed by a democratically elected general committee".[27]

All too often the broad political context of social change is left out of the analysis of sport. It is not that party politics directly affected sport but rather that the political history of the period reveals a similar interplay between established elites and new forces which is evident in amateurism. The Old

Tory dominance, which had lasted from the 1760s to the 1820s, came to an end with Catholic Emancipation and the Great Reform Act. It is hardly a coincidence that the political resistance to "civilized" reforms collapsed shortly afterwards with the banning of bullbaiting and cock-fighting in 1835. This was the same point at which Thomas Arnold became the symbol of a new elite of "Christian gentlemen". But this was no simple "triumph of the bourgeoisie". It was rather the victory of the Whigs with all that term implied for the creation of a progressive coalition between the great land-owners and the professional and commercial middle classes. After the Tory Party split in 1846 over the Corn Laws, the more reforming business-orientated element under Peel, himself the son of a Lancashire landed family that had made a fortune from textiles, was drawn in to a broad coalition that eventually formed the Liberal Party. This complex realignment of forces blending the more progressive elements in the older elite with the good num-ber of the newly educated middle classes dominated British politics from 1846 to the election of a Tory government under Disraeli in 1874.

This seems to have been the same kind of blend that made up the early amateur sporting bodies. Cautious meritocracy, a certain almost puritanical belief in exertion and the promotion of excellence through vigorous competi-tion was a refrain common to advocates of amateurism and the supporters of Gladstone. Wider access was given to Oxbridge, the armed services and the civil service. Hence the importance, as Eisenberg stresses, of open access to sport. Without the Liberal impetus it would have been easier to segregate sportsmen formally by occupation. This, of course, is not to equate Liberal-ism and amateurism. The gradual process of democratization was accepted by the Tory party under Disraeli, who exploited the patriotism and class anxieties of a significant portion of the middle classes to create what came to be known as "Villa Toryism"; this was particularly powerful in the southern suburbs, especially London, binding together the old Tory families from the countryside with those who joined the tennis and golf clubs that spread around the fringes of the great cities.[28]

Both political parties were composed of alliances of middle and upper class elements and it may be that the great sporting associations were rather similar. Here we await new research with the proviso that finding out whether the majority of leading amateurs were from gentry or from middle class families may be difficult because of the frequent lack of formal distinctions (the "de" or "von" in France and Germany); categorization is hard precisely because the gentry and liberal professions seem to have intermarried quite extensively, although the few hundred families represented in the House of Lords were closed to all but the most fabulously wealthy heiresses. It was precisely this social interpretation just beneath the very top level, which was reflected in a new sporting code that was neither just a revival of the idea of prowess or chivalry nor new kind of bourgeois imposition – a Foucault type "instrument of normalisation" where a new elite laid down through rules what was "normal" in play as they did in matters of sanity, sexuality and crime. Amateurism was never as prescriptive as this; its rules laid down only what was forbidden, not how a game had to be played; socially, the amateur approach was to combine the democratic principle at the level of national organization with informal club segregation. Hence order and access, hierarchy and liberty were combined within what has been described as a "mature class society". This acceptance of class difference within a democratic framework gave a factory worker the same freedom (but not the same chance) to win an Amateur Athletic Association medal as an Oxbridge undergraduate.

Conclusion: The wider historical context

Amateurism, in conclusion, was many things; it was part of a "civilizing process" of self-restraint; but it was also a way of promoting the spirit of competition for its own sake; hostility to betting seems to place amateur sport clearly in the camp of the protestant work ethic and the industrial bourgeoisie rather than the aristocracy, who continued to gamble on horses; yet disapproval of payment for honest work as a professional player was something the northern businessmen, who became directors of football or rugby league clubs could not understand or accept. Contempt for payment and for commerce have clear echoes of a pre-industrial code of honour; the liberal professions followed the gentlemanly code learned in public school, but shorn of its excesses of drinking and gambling. Payment spoiled the fun and defeated the moral purpose of games which was to improve the body and the character; for, as Haley has shown, eminent Victorians, men like Leslie Stephen, the Cambridge don and literary critic, mountaineer and rowing coach, believed strongly in the interconnection of mind and body;[29] mens sana in corpore sano meant something more specific then than it does now. We cannot ignore the fact that educated Victorian men, often first generation office-bound inhabitants of the Great Indoors, partly played sport for their health and approved of the amateur doctrine of active participation for this reason. This kind of motive could presumably be set alongside the view of amateur sport as a vehicle for "scientific and bureaucratic rationality" identified by Weber and applied to sport with grace and clarity in the work of Allen Guttmann; only limitations of space prevented a fuller discussion of this dimension, which obviously boosts the claims of the professional bureaucrats – civil servants and solicitors – to having a special place in amateur sport. None of this denies that a game like cricket certainly enshrined a philosophy of moral superiority, which was widely shared by elite amateurs, that could be called "hegemonic" on the one hand and also "civilized" (in its avoidance of excess violence and stress on self-control) on the other.

Analysing "amateurism" in this way shows just how complex it was; there were differing discourses depending on who was talking; the gentry patron, the local politician or the imperial civil servant and so on. In terms of the values of amateur sport, the older aristocratic ones of courage – rugby was especially valued for this – and honour (now called "sportsmanship") co-existed with a newer ideal of beneficent healthy competition, where individual effort and ability were rewarded, preferably within the context of the team. Aristocratic and bourgeois culture were thoroughly mixed up in amateur sport. The spirit or ethos was mainly aristocratic but the principles and structures were not. No wonder the liberal aristocrat, the Baron de Coubertin, exasperated at French social and political divisions, decided that British amateurism was the way to reunite and invigorate first his own country, and then the wider world.[30]

References

1 With the exception of G. Williams and D. Smith, *Fields of Praise: the Official History of the Welsh Rugby Union 1881–1981*, (Cardiff, 1991) – the only centenary history by social historians; for research in public school sport see Mangan below; on amateurism itself there is P. McIntosh, *Fair Play: Ethics in Sport and Education* (London, 1979), which takes a broadly philosophical rather than historical approach.

2 Allen Guttmann's *From Ritual to Record: the Nature of Modern Sports* (New York. 1978) stresses bureaucratic innovation.

3 J. A. Mangan, *Athleticism in the Victorian and Edwardian Public School* (Cambridge, 1981) is the classic exposition; see also his *The Games Ethic and Imperialism* (London, 1986).

4 T.J.L. Chandler, "Emergent Athleticism: Games in Two English Public Schools, 1800–1860", *International Journal of the History of Sport*, Dec. 1988; also his "Games at Oxbridge and the Public Schools, 1830–1880", *International Journal of the History of Sport*, Sept. 1991.

5 A. Briggs, *Victorian People* (London, 1965 edn) remains useful; T. Veblen, *The Theory of the Leisure Class*, introd. C. Wright-Mills (London, 1970) deserves re-assessment.

6 M.J. Wiener, *English Culture and the Decline of the Industrial Spirit* (London, 1981), p.16.

7 N. Elias, *The Civilizing Process: The History of Manners* (Oxford, 1978 edn) for a general statement of his views; on sport see Eric Dunning's pioneering volume *The Sociology of Sport: a selection of readings* (London, 1971); this has been supplemented in his later book with Norbert Elias, *Quest for Excitement; Sport and Leisure in the Civilizing Process* (Oxford, 1986).

8 For example, E. Dunning and C. Rojek have also edited an important new collection, *Sport and Leisure in the Civilizing Process: Critique and Counter Critique* (London, 1992) which is particularly revealing.

9 N. Elias in *The Quest for Excitement*, pp.129–131; see critique by Stokvis in Dunning and Rojek, *op.cit.*

10 E. Dunning and K. Sheard, *Barbarians, Gentlemen and Players: a Sociological Study of the Development of Rugby* (Oxford, 1979); also D.A. Reid, "Folk Football; the Aristocracy and Cultural Change: A Critique of Dunning and Sheard", *International Journal of the History of Sport*, Sept. 1988, p.225.

11 L. Colley, *Britons* (Yale, 1992).

12 Dunning and Sheard, *op.cit.* p.68.

13 Keith Thomas, *Man and the Natural World: Changing Attitudes in England 1500–1800* (London, 1983).
14 The attack on the class conflict interpretation of the period has been led by J.C.D. Clark, *English Society, 1688–1832: Ideology, Social Structure and Political Practice* (Cambridge, 1985).
15 M. Girouard, *Return to Camelot: Chivalry and the English Gentleman* (Yale, 1981), esp. pp.129–144 and 231–249.
16 Dunning and Sheard, *op.cit.*, esp. chap.7.
17 F. M. L. Thompson, *The Rise of Respectable Society: a social history of Victorian Bntain 1830–1900* (London, 1988) provides a good survey.
18 P. Bailey, *Leisure and Class in Victorian England* (London, 1978); see also his useful survey of the literature in Leisure, Culture and the Historian, *Leisure Studies* 8, 1989.
19 P. Gruneau, *Class, Sports and Social Development* (Mass. UP, 1983); John Hargreaves, *Sport, Power and Culture: a social and historical analysis of popular sports in Britain* (Cambridge, 1986).
20 The debate is summarized in H.F. Moorhouse, "The Marxist theory of the Labour aristocracy", *Social History* 3, 1978; for a synthesis see J. Benson, *The Working Class in Britain 1850–1939* (London, 1989).
21 R. Holt (ed.) *Sport and the Working Class in Modern Britain* (Manchester, 1990), esp. D. Bowker, "Parks and Baths".
22 P. Bourdieu "Sports, classes sociales et sub-cultures", conference introduction in *Sports et societes contemporaines: VIlle Symposium de ICSS.* (Paris, 1983), p. 325.
23 Charles Maier reviewing G. Hawthorn, *Plausible Worlds: Possibility and Understanding in the Social Sciences* (Cambridge, 1991), in *The London Review of Books*, 13 February 1992, pp. 11–12.
24 A. Guttmann, "Chariot races, Tournaments and the Civilising Process", in Dunning and Rojek, *op.cit.* p. 158; I have developed my own ideas more fully in my appendix to *Sport and the British* (Oxford, 1989).
25 R. McKibbin, *The Ideologies of Class: Social Relations in Britain 1880–1950* (Oxford, 1992), p.22.
26 C. Eisenberg, "The Middle Class and Competition: some considerations on the beginnings of modern sport in England and Germany", *International Journal of the History of Sport*, Sept. 1990.
27 *ibid*, p.272.
28 M. Pugh, *The Making of Modern British Politics 1867–1939* (London, 1982) offers the best general survey.
29 B. Haley, *The Healthy Body in Victorian Culture* (Cambridge, Mass, 1978), esp. chap. 3 for Stephen and chap. 6 for sport.
30 For a full account of Coubertin and England, see J.J. MacAloon, *This Great Symbol* (Chicago, 1981); more briefly, R. Holt, *Sport and Society in Modern France* (London, 1981), chap. 4.

54

SPORT AND SOCIAL CLASS

Pierre Bourdieu

Source: *Social Science Information* 17(6) (1978): 819–840.

I speak neither as an historian nor as an historian of sport, and so I appear as an amateur among professionals and can only ask you, as the phrase goes, to be 'good sports' . . . But I think that the innocence which comes from not being a specialist can sometimes lead one to ask questions which specialists tend to forget, because they think they have answered them, because they have taken for granted a certain number of presuppositions which are perhaps fundamental to their discipline. The questions I shall raise come from outside; they are the questions of a sociologist who, among the objects he studies, encounters sporting activities and entertainments (*les pratiques et les consommations sportives*) in the form, for example, of the statistical distribution of sports activities by educational level, age, sex, and occupation, and who is led to ask himself questions not only about the relationship between the practices and the variables, but also about the meaning which the practices take on in those relationships.

I think that, without doing too much violence to reality, it is possible to consider the whole range of sporting activities and entertainments offered to social agents – rugby, football, swimming, athletics, tennis, golf, etc. – as a *supply* intended to meet a *social demand*. If such a model is adopted, two sets of questions arise. First, is there an area of production, endowed with its own logic and its own history, in which 'sports products' are generated, i.e. the universe of the sporting activities and entertainments socially realized and acceptable at a given moment in time? Secondly, what are the social conditions of possibility of the appropriation of the various 'sports products' that are thus produced – playing golf or reading *L'Équipe*, cross-country skiing or watching the World Cup on TV? In other words, how is the demand for 'sports products' produced, how do people acquire the 'taste' for sport, and for one sport rather than another, whether as an activity or as a spectacle? The question certainly has to be confronted, unless one chooses to suppose that there exists a natural need, equally widespread at all times, in all

286

places and in all social milieux, not only for the expenditure of muscular energy, but more precisely, for this or that form of exertion. (To take the example most favourable to the 'natural need' thesis, we know that swimming, which most educators would probably point to as the most necessary sporting activity, both on account of its 'life-saving' functions and its physical effects, has at times been ignored or refused – e.g. in medieval Europe – and still has to be imposed by means of national 'campaigns'.) More precisely, according to what principles do agents choose between the different sports activities or entertainments which, at a given moment in time, are offered to them as being possible?

I. The production of supply

It seems to me that it is first necessary to consider the historical and social conditions of possibility of a social phenomenon which we too easily take for granted: 'modern sport'. In other words, what social conditions made possible the constitution of the system of institutions and agents directly or indirectly linked to the existence of sporting activities and entertainments? The system includes public or private 'sports associations', whose function is to represent and defend the interests of the practitioners of a given sport and to draw up and impose the standards governing that activity,[1] the producers and vendors of goods (equipment, instruments, special clothing, etc.) and services required in order to pursue the sport (teachers, instructors, trainers, sports doctors, sports journalists, etc.) and the producers and vendors of sporting entertainments and associated goods (tee shirts, photos of stars, the *tiercé*,[2] etc.). How was this body of specialists, living directly or indirectly off sport, progressively constituted (a body to which sports sociologists and historians also belong – which probably does not help the question to emerge)? And, more exactly, when did this system of agents and institutions begin to function as a *field of competition*, the site of confrontations between agents with specific interests linked to their positions within the field? If it is the case, as my questions tend to suggest, that the system of the institutions and agents whose interests are bound up with sport tends to function as a field, it follows that one cannot directly understand what sporting phenomena are at a given moment in a given social environment by relating them directly to the economic and social conditions of the corresponding societies: the history of sport is a relatively autonomous history which, even when marked by the major events of economic and social history, has its own tempo, its own evolutionary laws, its own crises, in short, its specific chronology.

Thus one of the most important tasks for the social history of sport could well be to establish its foundations by constructing the historical genealogy of the emergence of its object as a *specific reality* irreducible to any other. It alone can answer the question – which has nothing to do with an academic question of *definition* – as to the moment (it is not a matter of a precise date) from which it is possible to talk of sport, i.e. the moment from which there began to be constituted a field of competition within which sport was defined as a specific practice, irreducible to a mere ritual game or festive amusement. This amounts to asking if the appearance of sport in the modern sense of the word is not correlative with a *break* (which may have taken place in several stages) with activities which may appear to be the 'ancestors' of modern sports, a break which is itself linked to the constitution of a field of specific practices, endowed with its own specific rewards and its own rules, where a whole specific competence or culture is generated and invested (whether it be the inseparably cultural and physical competence of the top-level athlete or the cultural competence of the sports manager or journalist) – a culture which is in a sense esoteric, since it separates the professional from the layman. This leads us to cast doubt on the validity of all those studies which, by an essential anachronism, pursue analogies between the *games* of European or extra-European precapitalist societies, erroneously treated as pre-sporting practices, and *sports* in the strict sense, whose historical appearance is contemporary with the constitution of a field of production of 'sports products'. Such a comparison is only justified when, taking a path diametrically opposed to the search for 'origins', it aims, as in Norbert Elias' work, to grasp the specificity of sporting practice or, more precisely, to determine how certain pre-existing physical exercises, or others which may have received a radically new meaning and function – as radically new as in the case of simple invention, e.g. volleyball or basketball – become sports, defined with respect to their rewards, their rules, and also the social identity of their participants – players or spectators – by the specific logic of the 'sporting field'.

So one of the tasks of the social history of sport might be to lay the real foundations of the legitimacy of a social science of sport as a *distinct scientific object* (which is not at all self-evident), by establishing from what moment, or rather, from what set of social conditions, it is really possible to speak of sport (as opposed to the simple playing of games – a meaning that is still present in the English word 'sport' but not in the use made of the word in countries outside the Anglo-Saxon world where it was introduced *at the same time* as the radically new social practices which it designated). How was this terrain constituted, with its specific logic, as the site of quite specific social practices, which have defined themselves in the course of a specific history and can only be understood in terms of that history (e.g. the history of sports laws or the history of *records*, an interesting word that recalls the contribution which historians, with their task of *recording* and celebrating noteworthy exploits, make to the constitution of a field and its esoteric culture)?

The genesis of a relatively autonomous field of production and circulation of sports products

Not possessing the historical culture needed to answer these questions, I have tried to mobilize what I knew of the history, particularly of football and rugby, so as at least to try to formulate them better. (There is of course no reason to suppose that the process of constitution of a field took the same form in all cases, and it is even likely that, as with Gerschenkron's model of economic development, the sports which came into existence later than others consequently underwent a different history, largely based on borrowings from older and therefore more 'advanced' sports.) It seems to be indisputable that the shift from games to sports in the strict sense (which, as Defrance points out, must be distinguished from gymnastics[3]) took place in the educational establishments reserved for the 'élites' of bourgeois society, the English public schools, where the sons of aristocratic or upper-bourgeois families took over a number of *popular* – i.e. *vulgar* – *games*, simultaneously changing their meaning and function in exactly the same way as the field of learned music transformed the folk dances – bourrées, sarabands, gavottes, etc. – which it introduced into high-art forms such as the suite.

To characterize this transformation briefly, i.e. as regards its *principle*,[4] we can say that the bodily exercises of the 'élite' are disconnected from the ordinary social occasions with which folk games remained associated (agrarian feasts, for example) and divested of the social (and, *a fortiori*, religious) functions still attached to a number of traditional games (such as the ritual games played in a number of precapitalist societies at certain turning-points in the farming year). The school, the site of *skhole*, leisure, is the place where practices endowed with social functions and integrated into the collective calendar are converted into *bodily exercises*, activities which are an end in themselves, a sort of physical art for art's sake, governed by specific rules, increasingly irreducible to any functional necessity, and inserted into a specific calendar. The school is the site, *par excellence*, of what are called gratuitous exercises, where one acquires a distant, neutralizing disposition towards language and the social world, the very same one which is implied in the bourgeois relation to art, language and the body: gymnastics makes a use of the body which, like the scholastic use of language, is an end in itself. (This no doubt explains why sporting activity, whose frequency rises very markedly with educational level, declines more slowly with age, as do cultural practices, when educational level is higher. It is known that among the working classes, the abandonment of sport, an activity whose play-like character seems to make it particularly appropriate to adolescence, often coincides with marriage and entry into the serious responsibilities of adulthood.) What is acquired in and through experience of school, a sort of retreat from the world and from real practice, of which the great boarding schools of the 'élite' represent the fully developed form, is the propensity towards activity for no purpose, a fundamental aspect of the ethos of bourgeois 'élites', who always pride themselves on disinterestedness and define themselves by an elective distance – manifested in art and sport – from material interests. 'Fair play' is the way of playing the game characteristic of those who do not get so carried away by the game as to forget that it *is* a game, those who maintain the 'rôle distance', as Goffman puts it, that is implied in all the rôles designated for the future leaders.

The autonomization of the field of sport is also accompanied by a process of *rationalization* intended, as Weber expresses it, to ensure predictability and calculability, beyond local differences and particularisms: the constitution of a corpus of specific rules and of specialized governing bodies recruited, initially at least, from the 'old boys' of the public schools, come hand in hand. The need for a body of fixed, universally applicable rules makes itself felt as soon as sporting 'exchanges' are established between different educational institutions, then between regions, etc. The relative autonomy of the field of sport is most clearly affirmed in the powers of self-administration and rule-making, based on a historical tradition or guaranteed by the State, which sports associations are acknowledged to exercise: these bodies are invested with the right to lay down the standards governing participation in the events which they organize, and they are entitled to exercise a disciplinary power (banning, fines, etc.) in order to ensure observance of the specific rules which they decree. In addition, they award specific titles, such as championship titles and also, as in England, the status of trainer.

The constitution of a field of sports practices is linked to the development of a philosophy of sport which is necessarily a *political* philosophy of sport. The theory of amateurism is in fact one dimension of an aristocratic philosophy of sport as a disinterested practice, a finality without an end, analogous to artistic practice, but even more suitable than art (there is always something residually feminine about art: consider the piano and watercolours of genteel young ladies in the same period) for affirming the manly virtues of future leaders: sport is conceived as a training in courage and manliness, 'forming the character' and inculcating the 'will to win' which is the mark of the true leader, but a will to win within the rules. This is 'fair play', conceived as an aristocratic disposition utterly opposed to the plebeian pursuit of victory at all costs. (And then one would have to explore the link between the sporting virtues and the military virtues: remember the glorification of the deeds of old Etonians or Oxonians on the field of battle or in aerial combat.) This aristocratic ethic, devised by aristocrats (the first Olympic committee included innumerable dukes, counts and lords, and all of ancient stock) and guaranteed by aristocrats, all those who constitute the self-perpetuating oligarchy of international and national organizations, is clearly adapted to the requirements of the times, and, as one sees in the works of Baron Pierre de Coubertin, incorporates the most essential assumptions of the bourgeois ethic of private enterprise, baptized 'self-help'

(English often serves as a euphemism). This glorification of sport as an essential component in a new type of apprenticeship requiring an entirely new educational institution, which is expressed in Coubertin's writings, particularly *l'Education en Angleterre* and *l'Education anglaise en France*,[5] reappears in the work of Demolins, another of Frédéric Le Play's disciples. Demolins founded the École des Roches and is author of *A quoi tient la supériorité des Anglo-Saxons* and *l'Education nouvelle*, in which he criticises the Napoleonic barracks-style lycée (a theme which has subsequently become one of the commonplaces of the 'sociology of France' produced at the Paris Institut des Sciences Politiques and Harvard). What is at stake, it seems to me, in this debate (which goes far beyond sport), is a definition of bourgeois education which contrasts with the petty-bourgeois and academic definition: it is 'energy', 'courage', 'willpower', the virtues of leaders (military or industrial), and perhaps above all personal initiative, (private) 'enterprise', as opposed to knowledge, erudition, 'scholastic' submissiveness, symbolized in the great lycée-barracks and its disciplines, etc. In short, it would be a mistake to forget that the modern definition of sport that is often associated with the name of Coubertin is an integral part of a 'moral ideal', i.e. an ethos which is that of the dominant fractions of the dominant class and is brought to fruition in the major private schools intended primarily for the sons of the heads of private industry, such as the École des Roches, the paradigmatic realization of this ideal. To value *education* over *instruction, character* or *willpower* over *intelligence, sport* over *culture*, is to affirm, within the educational universe itself, the existence of a hierarchy irreducible to the strictly scholastic hierarchy which favours the second term in those oppositions. It means, as it were, disqualifying or discrediting the values recognized by other fractions of the dominant class or by other classes (especially the intellectual fractions of the petty-bourgeoisie and the 'sons of schoolteachers', who are serious challengers to the sons of the bourgeoisie on the terrain of purely scholastic competence); it means putting forward other criteria of 'achievement' and other principles for legitimating achievement as alternatives to 'academic achievement'. (In a recent survey of French industrialists,[6] I was able to demonstrate that the opposition between the two conceptions of education corresponds to two routes into managerial positions in large firms, one from the École des Roches or the major Jesuit schools via the Law Faculty or, more recently, the Institut des Sciences Politiques, the Inspection des Finances or the École des Hautes Études Commerciales, the other from a provincial lycée via the Ecole Polytechnique.) Glorification of sport as the training-ground of character, etc., always implies a certain anti-intellectualism. When one remembers that the dominant fractions of the dominant class always tend to conceive their relation to the dominated fraction – 'intellectuals', 'artists', 'professors' – in terms of the opposition between the male and the female, the virile and the effeminate, which is given different contents depending on the period (e.g., nowadays short hair/long hair; 'economico-political' culture/'artistico-literary' culture, etc.), one understands one of the most important implications of the exaltation of sport and especially of 'manly' sports like rugby, and it can be seen that sport, like any other practice, is an object of struggles between the fractions of the dominant class and also between the social classes.

At this point I shall take the opportunity to emphasize, in passing, that the *social definition of sport* is an object of struggles, that the field of sporting practices is the site of struggles in which what is at stake, *inter alia*, is the monopolistic capacity to impose the legitimate definition of sporting practice and of the legitimate function of sporting activity – amateurism vs. professionalism, participant sport vs. spectator sport, distinctive (élite) sport vs. popular (mass) sport; that this field is itself part of the larger field of struggles over the definition of the *legitimate body* and the *legitimate use of the body*, struggles which, in addition to the agents engaged in the struggle over the definition of sporting uses of the body, also involve moralists and especially the clergy, doctors (especially health specialists), educators in the broadest sense (marriage guidance counsellors, etc.), pacemakers in matters of fashion and taste (couturiers, etc.). One would have to explore whether the struggles for the monopolistic power to impose the legitimate definition of a particular *class* of body uses, sporting uses, present any *invariant* features. I am thinking, for example, of the opposition, from the point of view of the definition of legitimate exercise, between the professionals in physical education (gymnasiarchs, gymnastics teachers, etc.) and doctors, i.e. between two forms of specific *authority* ('pedagogic' vs. 'scientific'), linked to two sorts of *specific capital*; or the recurrent opposition between two antagonistic philosophies of the use of the body, a more ascetic one (*askesis* = training) which, in the paradoxical expression *culture physique* ('physical culture') emphasizes culture, *antiphysis*, the counter-natural, straightening, rectitude, effort, and another, more hedonistic one which privileges nature, *physis*, reducing culture to the body, physical culture to a sort of 'laisser-faire', or return to 'laisser-faire' – as *expression corporelle* ('physical expression' – 'anti-gymnastics') does nowadays, teaching its devotees to unlearn the superfluous disciplines and restraints imposed, among other things, by ordinary gymnastics.

Since the relative autonomy of the field of bodily practices entails, by definition, a relative dependence, the development within the field of practices oriented towards one or the other pole, asceticism or hedonism, depends to a large extent on the state of the power relations within the field of struggles for monopolistic definition of the legitimate body and, more broadly, in the field of struggles between fractions of the dominant class and between the social classes over morality. Thus the progress made by everything that is referred to as 'physical expression' can only be understood in relation to the progress, seen for example in parent-child relations and more generally in all that pertains to pedagogy, of a new variant of bourgeois morality, preached by certain rising fractions of the bourgeoisie (and petty bourgeoisie) and favouring liberalism in child-rearing and also in hierarchical relations and sexuality, in place of ascetic severity (denounced as 'repressive').

The popularization phase

It was necessary to sketch in this first phase, which seems to me a determinant one, because in states of the field that are nonetheless quite different, sport still bears the marks of its origins. Not only does the aristocratic ideology of sport as disinterested, gratuitous activity, which lives on in the ritual themes of celebratory discourse, help to mask the true nature of an increasing proportion of sporting practices, but the practice of sports such as tennis, riding, sailing or golf doubtless owes part of its 'interest', just as much nowadays as at the beginning, to its distinguishing function and, more precisely, to the *gains in distinction* which it brings (it is no accident that the majority of the most select, i.e. selective, clubs are organized around sporting activities which serve as a focus or pretext for elective gatherings). We may even consider that the distinctive gains are increased when the distinction between noble – distinguished and distinctive – practices, such as the 'smart' sports, and the 'vulgar' practices which popularization has made of a number of sports originally reserved for the 'élite', such as foot-ball (and to a lesser extent rugby, which will perhaps retain for some time to come a dual status and a dual social recruitment), is combined with the yet sharper opposition between participation in sport and the mere consumption of sporting entertainments. We know that the probability of practising a sport beyond adolescence (and *a fortiori* beyond early manhood or in old age) declines markedly as one moves down the social hierarchy (as does the probability of belonging to a sports club), whereas the probability of watching one of the reputedly most popular sporting spectacles, such as football or rugby, on television (stadium attendance as a spectator obeys more complex laws) declines markedly as one rises in the social hierarchy.

Thus, without forgetting the importance of taking part in sport – particularly team sports like football – for working-class and lower middle-class adolescents, it cannot be ignored that the so-called popular sports, cycling, football or rugby, *also* function as spectacles (which may owe part of their interest to imaginary participation based on past experience of real practice). They are 'popular' but in the sense this adjective takes on whenever it is applied to the material or cultural products of mass production, cars, furniture or songs. In brief, sport, born of truly popular games, i.e. games produced by the people, returns to the people, like 'folk music', in the form of spectacles produced for the people. We may consider that sport as a spectacle would appear more clearly as a mass commodity, and the organization of sporting entertainments as one branch among others of show business (there is a difference of degree rather than kind between the spectacle of professional boxing, or Holiday on Ice shows, and a number of sporting events that are perceived as legitimate, such as the various European football championships or ski competitions), if the value collectively bestowed on practising sports (especially now that sports contests have become a measure of relative national strength and hence a political objective) did not help to mask the divorce between practice and consumption and consequently the functions of simple passive consumption.

It might be wondered, in passing, whether some recent developments in sporting practices – such as doping, or the increased violence both on the pitch and on the terraces – are not in part an effect of the evolution which I have too rapidly sketched. One only has to think, for example, of all that is implied in the fact that a sport like rugby (in France – but the same is true of American football in the USA) has become, through television, a mass spectacle, transmitted far beyond the circle of present or past 'practitioners', i.e. to a public very imperfectly equipped with the specific competence needed to decipher it adequately. The 'connoisseur' has schemes of perception and appreciation which enable him to see what the layman cannot see, to perceive a necessity where the outsider sees only violence and confusion, and so to find in the promptness of a movement, in the unforeseeable inevitability of a successful combination or the near-miraculous orchestration of a team strategy, a pleasure no less intense and learned than the pleasure a music-lover derives from a particularly successful rendering of a favourite work. The more superficial the perception, the less it finds its pleasure in the spectacle contemplated in itself and for itself, and the more it is drawn to the search for the 'sensational', the cult of obvious feats and visible virtuosity and, above all, the more exclusively it is concerned with that other dimension of the sporting spectacle, suspense and anxiety as to the result, thereby encouraging players and especially organizers to aim for victory at all costs. In other words, everything seems to suggest that, in sport as in music, extension of the public beyond the circle of amateurs helps to reinforce the reign of the pure professionals. When Roland Barthes, in an article entitled "Le grain de la voix",[7] contrasts Panzera, a French singer of the inter-war period, with Fischer-Dieskau, whom he sees as the archetypal product of middle-brow culture, just as others contrast Cartot, perfect even in his imperfections, with the too-perfect pianists of the age of long-playing records, he is exactly reminiscent of those who contrast the inspired rugby of a Dauger or a Boniface with the 'well-oiled machinery' of the Béziers team or France captained by Fouroux. This is the viewpoint of the 'practitioner', past or present, who, as opposed to the mere consumer, the 'hi-fi freak' or armchair sportsman, recognizes a form of excellence which, as even its imperfections testify (Cortot's famous 'mistakes'), is but the extreme limit of the competence of the ordinary amateur. In short, there is every reason to suppose that, in music as in sport, the purely passive competence, acquired without any personal performance, of publics newly won by records or television, is at least a negative, i.e. permissive, factor in the evolution of production (one sees, incidentally, the ambiguity of a certain style of 'ultra-left' critique: denunciation of the vices of mass production – in sport as in music – is often combined with aristocratic nostalgia for the days of amateurism).

More than by the encouragement it gives to chauvinism and sexism, it is undoubtedly through the division it makes between professionals, the virtuosi of an esoteric technique, and laymen, reduced to the role of mere consumers, a division that tends to become a deep structure of the collective consciousness, that sport produces its most decisive political effects. Sport is not the only area in which ordinary people are reduced to fans, the extreme caricatural form of the militant, condemned to an imaginary participation which is only an illusory compensation for the dispossession they suffer to the advantage of the experts.

In fact, before taking further the analysis of the effects, we must try to analyse more closely the determinants of the shift whereby sport as an élite practice reserved for amateurs became sport as a spectacle produced by professionals for consumption by the masses. It is not sufficient to invoke the relatively autonomous logic of the field of production of sporting goods and services or, more precisely, the development, within this field, of a sporting entertainments industry which, subject to the laws of profitability, aims to maximize its efficiency while minimizing its risks. (This leads, in particular, to the need for specialized executive personnel and scientific management techniques that can rationally organize the training and upkeep of the physical capital of the professional players: one thinks, for example, of American football, in which the squad of trainers, doctors and public-relations men is more numerous than the team of players, and which almost always serves as a publicity medium for the sports equipment and accessories industry.)

In reality, the development of sporting activity itself, even among working-class youngsters, doubtless results partly from the fact that sport was predisposed to fulfil, on a much larger scale, the very same functions which underlay its *invention* in the late nineteenth century English public schools. Even before they saw sport as a means of 'improving character' in accordance with the Victorian belief, the public schools, 'total institutions' in Goffman's sense, which have to carry out their supervisory task twenty-four hours a day, seven days a week, saw sport as 'a means of filling in time', an economical way of occupying the adolescents who were their full-time responsibility. When the pupils are on the sports field, they are easy to supervise, they are engaged in healthy activity and they are venting their violence on each other rather than destroying the buildings or shouting down their teachers; that is why, Ian Weiberg concludes, "organized sport will last as long as the public schools".[8] So it would not be possible to understand the popularization of sport and the growth of sports associations, which, originally organized on a *voluntary* basis, progressively received recognition and aid from the public authorities,[9] if we did not realize that this *extremely economical* means of mobilizing, occupying and controlling adolescents was predisposed to become an instrument and an objective in struggles between all the institutions totally or partly organized with a view to the mobilization and symbolic conquest of the masses and therefore competing for the symbolic conquest of youth. These include political parties, unions, and churches, of course, but also paternalistic bosses, who, with the aim of ensuring *complete and continuous containment* of the working population, provided their employees not only with hospitals and schools but also with stadiums and other sports facilities (a number of sports clubs were founded with the help and under the control of private employers, as is still attested today by the number of stadiums named after employers). We are familiar with the competition which has never ceased to be fought out in the various political arenas over questions of sport from the level of the village (with the rivalry between secular or religious clubs, or more recently, the debates over the priority to be given to sports facilities, which is one of the issues at stake in political struggles on a municipal scale) to the level of the nation as a whole (with, for example, the opposition between the Fédération du Sport de France, controlled by the Catholic Church, and the Fédération Sportive et Gymnique du Travail controlled by the left-wing parties.) And indeed, in an increasingly disguised way as State recognition and subsidies increase, and with them the apparent neutrality of sports organizations and their officials, sport is an object of political struggle. This competition is one of the most important factors in the development of a social, i.e. socially constituted, need for sporting practices and for all the accompanying equipment, instruments, personnel and services. Thus the imposition of sporting needs is most evident in rural areas where the appearance of facilities and teams, as with youth clubs and senior citizens' clubs nowadays, is almost always the result of the work of the village petty-bourgeoisie or bourgeoisie, which finds here an opportunity to impose its political services of organization and leadership[10] and to accumulate or maintain a political capital of renown and honourability which is always potentially reconvertible into political power.

It goes without saying that the popularization of sport, down from the élite schools (where its place is now contested by the 'intellectual' pursuits imposed by the demands of intensified social competition) to the mass sporting associations, is necessarily accompanied by a change in the functions which the sportsmen and their organizers assign to this practice, and also by a transformation of the very logic of sporting practices which corresponds to the transformation of the expectations and demands of the public in correlation with the increasing autonomy of the spectacle vis-à-vis past or present practice. The exaltation of 'manliness' and the cult of 'team spirit'[11] that are associated with playing rugby – not to mention the aristocratic ideal of 'fair play' – have a very different meaning and function for bourgeois or

aristocratic adolescents in English public schools and for the sons of peasants or shopkeepers in south-west France. This is simply because, for
example, a sporting career, which is practically excluded from the field of
acceptable trajectories for a child of the bourgeoisie – setting aside tennis or
golf – represents one of the few paths of upward mobility open to the children of the dominated classes; the sports market is to the boys' physical
capital what the system of beauty prizes and the occupations to which they
lead – hostess, etc. – is to the girls' physical capital; and the working-class
cult of sportsmen of working-class origin is doubtless explained in part by
the fact that these 'success stories' symbolize the only recognized route to
wealth and fame. Everything suggests that the 'interests' and values which
practitioners from the working and lower-middle classes bring into the
conduct of sports are in harmony with the corresponding requirements of
professionalization (which can, of course, coexist with the appearances of
amateurism) and of the rationalization of preparation for and performance
of the sporting exercise that are imposed by the pursuit of maximum specific
efficiency (measured in 'wins', 'titles', or 'records') combined with the mini-
mization of risks (which we have seen is itself linked to the development of a
private or State sports entertainments industry).

II. The logic of demand: sporting practices and entertainments in the unity of life-styles

We have here a case of a supply, i.e. the particular definition of sporting
practice and entertainment that is put forward at a given moment in time,
meeting a demand, i.e. the expectations, interests and values that agents
bring into the field, with the actual practices and entertainments evolving as
a result of the permanent confrontation and adjustment between the two. Of
course, at every moment each new entrant must take account of a determin-
ate state of the division of sporting activities and entertainments and their
distribution among the social classes, a state which he cannot alter and which
is the result of the whole previous history of the struggles and competition
among the agents and institutions engaged in the 'sporting field'. For
example, the appearance of a new sport or a new way of practicing an
already established sport (e.g. the 'invention' of the crawl by Trudgen in
1893) causes a restructuring of the space of sporting practices and a more or
less complete redefinition of the meaning attached to the various practices.
But while it is true that, here as elsewhere, the field of production helps to
produce the need for its own products, nonetheless the logic whereby agents
incline towards this or that sporting practice cannot be understood unless
their dispositions towards sport, which are themselves one dimension of a
particular relation to the body, are reinserted into the unity of the system of
dispositions, the habitus, which is the basis from which life-styles are generated. One would be likely to make serious mistakes if one attempted to study

sporting practices (more so, perhaps, than with any other practices, since their basis and object is the body, the synthesizing agent *par excellence*, which integrates everything that it incorporates), without re-placing them in the universe of practices that are bound up with them because their common origin is the system of tastes and preferences that is a class habitus (for example, it would be easy to demonstrate the homologies between the relation to the body and the relation to language that are characteristic of a class or class fraction).[12] Insofar as the 'body-for-others' is the visible manifestation of the person, of the 'idea it wants to give of itself', its 'character', i.e. its values and capacities, the sports practices which have the aim of shaping the body are realizations, among others, of an aesthetic and an ethic in the practical state. A postural norm such as uprightness ('stand up straight') has, like a direct gaze or a close haircut, the function of symbolizing a whole set of moral 'virtues' – rectitude, straightforwardness, dignity (face to face confrontation as a demand for respect) – and also physical ones – vigour, strength, health.

An explanatory model capable of accounting for the distribution of sporting practices among the classes and class fractions must clearly take account of the positive or negative determining factors, the most important of which are *spare time* (a transformed form of economic capital), *economic capital* (more or less indispensable depending on the sport), and *cultural capital* (again, more or less necessary depending on the sport). But such a model would fail to grasp what is most essential if it did not take account of the variations in the meaning and function given to the various practices by the various classes and class fractions. In other words, faced with the distribution of the various sporting practices by social class, one must give as much thought to the variations in the meaning and function of the different sports among the social classes as to the variations in the intensity of the statistical relationship between the different practices and the different social classes. To answer this question, one might be tempted to turn to the *specialists*, who, like nutritionists for food and drink, claim to possess a purely technical definition of what bodily exercise ought to be by reference to a purely technical definition of what the body ought to be. In reality, the sociology and social history of sport, which establish the variations, according to the period, society or social class, of the functions assigned to bodily exercise, also enable us to characterize the illusion that there exists *a* technical definition, i.e. one that is socially neutral and objectively based (on nature), of sporting exercise, as the occupational ideology of the professionals who produce and sell sporting goods and services. As is clearly seen in the case of a diet, which will vary depending on whether the objective – which the dietitian's technique cannot of itself determine – is to get fatter or thinner, to approach a weight defined in terms of an ideal which varies with time, place and milieu, the 'choice' of the 'aims' of sporting exercise is determined by a system of principles which orient the whole set of practices, i.e.

sexual practices and eating habits, aesthetic preferences and style of dress, and so on.

It would not be difficult to show that the different social classes do not agree as to the effects expected from bodily exercise, whether on the outside of the body (bodily hexis), such as the visible strength of prominent muscles which some prefer or the elegance, ease and beauty favoured by others, or inside the body, health, mental equilibrium, etc. In other words, the class variations in these practices derive not only from the variations in the factors which make it possible or impossible to meet their *economic or cultural costs* but also from the *variations in the perception and appreciation of the immediate or deferred profits* accruing from the different sporting practices. (It can be seen, incidentally, that specialists are able to make use of the specific authority conferred by their status to put forward a perception and appreciation defined as the only legitimate ones, in opposition to the perceptions and appreciations structured by the dispositions of a class habitus. I am thinking of the national campaigns to impose a sport like swimming, which seems to be unanimously approved by the specialists in the name of its strictly 'technical' functions, on those who "can't see the use of it".) As regards the profits actually perceived, Jacques Defrance convincingly shows that gymnastics may be asked to produce either a strong body, bearing the outward signs of strength – this is the working-class demand, which is satisfied by body-building – or a healthy body – this is the bourgeois demand, which is satisfied by a gymnastics or other sports whose function is essentially hygienic.[13]

But this is not all: class habitus defines the meaning conferred on sporting activity, the profits expected from it; and not the least of these profits is the social value accruing from the pursuit of certain sports by virtue of the distinctive rarity they derive from their class distribution. In short, to the 'intrinsic' profits (real or imaginary, it makes little difference – real in the sense of being really anticipated, in the mode of belief) which are expected from sport for the body itself, one must add the social profits, those accruing from any distinctive practice, which are very unequally perceived and appreciated by the different classes (for whom they are, of course, very unequally accessible). It can be seen, for example, that in addition to its strictly health-giving functions, golf, like caviar, *foie gras* or whisky, has a *distributional significance* (the meaning which practices derive from their distribution among agents distributed in social classes), which, unanimously recognized and acknowledged on the basis of a practical mastery of the probability of the various classes practising the various sports,[14] is entirely opposed to that of *pétanque*,[15] whose purely health-giving function is perhaps not very different but which has a distributional significance very close to that of Pernod and all *strong* drinks, and all types of food that are not only economical but *strong* (also in the sense of *spicy*) and supposed to give strength because they are heavy, fatty and spicy. It is no accident that the

'strong-man' was for a long time one of the most typically popular entertainments – remember the famous Dédé la Boulange who performed in the
Square d'Anvers, alternating feats of strength with a mountebank's patter –
or that weight-lifting, which is supposed to develop the muscles, was for
many years, especially in France, the favourite working-class sport; nor is it
an accident that the Olympic authorities took so long to grant official recognition to weight-lifting, which, in the eyes of the aristocratic founders of
modern sport, symbolized mere strength, brutality and intellectual poverty,
in short the working classes.

We can now try to account for the distribution of these practices among the
classes and class fractions. The probability, of practising the different sports
depends, to a different degree for each sport, primarily on economic capital
and secondarily on cultural capital and spare time; it also depends on the
affinity between the ethical and aesthetic dispositions characteristic of each
class or class fraction and the objective potentialities of ethical or aesthetic
accomplishment which are or seem to be contained in each sport. The relationship between the different sports and age is more complex, since it is only
defined – through the intensity of the physical effort required and the disposition towards that effort which is an aspect of class ethos – within the
relationship between a sport and a class. The most important property of the
'popular sports' is the fact that they are tacitly associated with youth, which
is spontaneously and implicitly credited with a sort of *provisional licence*
expressed, among other ways, in the squandering of an excess of physical
(and sexual) energy, and are abandoned very early (usually at the moment of
entry into adult life, marked by marriage). By contrast, the 'bourgeois'
sports, mainly practised for their functions of physical maintenance and for
the social profit they bring, have in common the fact that their age-limit lies
far beyond youth and perhaps comes correspondingly later the more prestigious and exclusive they are (e.g. golf). This means that the probability of
practising those sports which, because they demand only 'physical' qualities
and bodily competences for which the conditions of early apprenticeship
seem to be fairly equally distributed, are doubtless equally accessible within
the limits of the spare time and, secondarily, the physical energy available,
would undoubtedly increase as one goes up the social hierarchy, if the concern for distinction and the absence of ethico-aesthetic affinity of 'taste' for
them did not turn away members of the dominant class, in accordance with a
logic also observed in other fields (photography, for example).[16] Thus, most
of the team sports – basketball, handball, rugby, football – which are most
common among office workers, technicians and shopkeepers, and also no
doubt the most typically working-class individual sports, such as boxing or
wrestling, combine all the reasons to repel the upper classes. These include
the social composition of their public which reinforces the vulgarity implied

by their popularization, the values and virtues demanded (strength, endurance, the propensity, to violence, the spirit of 'sacrifice', docility and submission to collective discipline, the absolute antithesis of the 'rôle distance' implied in bourgeois rôles, etc.), the exaltation of competition and the contest, etc. But in the case of a sport like *pétanque* it seems that only the logic of distinction can explain the class distribution. This sport, the least distinguished and least distinctive of all, since it requires practically no economic or cultural capital and demands little more than spare time, regularly culminates among the lower middle classes, especially among primary-school teachers and clerical workers in the medical services. Thereafter it declines, particularly sharply in categories where there is the strongest desire to stand apart from the vulgar, as among artists and members of the professions. To understand how the most distinctive sports, such as golf, riding, skiing or tennis, or even some less recherché ones, like gymnastics or mountaineering, are distributed among the social classes and especially among the fractions of the dominant class, it is even more difficult to appeal solely to variations in economic and cultural capital or in spare time. This is firstly because it would be to forget that, no less than the economic obstacles, it is the hidden entry requirements, such as family tradition and early training, and also the obligatory clothing, bearing and techniques of sociability which keep these sports closed to the working classes and to individuals rising from the lower-middle and even upper-middle classes; and secondly because economic constraints define the field of possibilities and impossibilities without determining within it an agent's positive orientation towards this or that particular form of practice. In reality, even apart from any search for distinction, it is the relation to one's own body, a fundamental aspects of the habitus, which distinguishes the working classes from the privileged classes, just as, within the latter, it distinguishes fractions that are separated by the whole universe of a life-style. On one side, there is the *instrumental* relation to the body which the working classes express in all the practices centred on the body, whether in dieting or beauty care, relation to illness or medication, and which is also manifested in the choice of sports requiring a considerable investment of effort, sometimes of pain and suffering (e.g. boxing) and sometimes a *gambling with the body itself* (as in motor-cycling, parachute-jumping, all forms of acrobatics, and, to some extent, all sports involving fighting, among which we may include rugby). On the other side, there is the tendency of the privileged classes to treat the body as an *end in itself*, with variants according to whether the emphasis is placed on the intrinsic functioning of the body as an organism, which leads to the macrobiotic cult of health, or on the appearance of the body as a perceptible configuration, the 'physique', i.e. the body-for-others. Everything seems to suggest that the concern to cultivate the body appears, in its most elementary form, i.e. as the cult of health, often implying an ascetic exaltation of sobriety and dietetic rigour, among the lower middle classes, i.e. among junior executives, clerical workers in the medical services and especially primary-school teachers, who indulge particularly intensively in gymnastics, the ascetic sport *par excellence* since it amounts to a sort of training (*askesis*) for training's sake.

Gymnastics or strictly health-oriented sports like walking or jogging, which, unlike ball games, do not offer any competitive satisfaction, are highly rational and rationalized activities. This is firstly because they presuppose a resolute faith in reason and in the deferred and often intangible benefits which reason promises (such as protection against ageing, an abstract and negative advantage which only exists by reference to a thoroughly theoretical referent); secondly, because they generally only have meaning by reference to a thoroughly theoretical, abstract knowledge of the effects of an exercise which it itself often reduced, as in gymnastics, to a series of abstract movements, decomposed and reorganized by reference to a specific and technically-defined end (e.g. 'the abdominals') and is opposed to the total movements of everyday situations, oriented towards practical goals, just as marching, broken down into elementary movements in the sergeant-major's handbook, is opposed to ordinary walking. Thus it is understandable that these activities can only be rooted in the ascetic dispositions of upwardly mobile individuals who are prepared to find their satisfaction in effort itself and to accept – such is the whole meaning of their existence – the deferred satisfactions which will reward their present sacrifice.

In sports like mountaineering (or, to a lesser extent, walking), which are most common among secondary or university teachers, the purely health-oriented function of maintaining the body is combined with all the symbolic gratifications associated with practising a highly distinctive activity. This gives to the highest degree the sense of mastery of one's own body as well as the free and exclusive appropriation of scenery inaccessible to the vulgar. In fact, the health-giving functions are always more or less strongly associated with what might be called aesthetic functions (especially, other things being equal, in women, who are more imperatively required to submit to the norms defining what the body ought to be, not only in its perceptible configuration but also in its motion, its gait, etc.). It is doubtless among the professions and the well-established business bourgeoisie that the health-giving and aesthetic functions are combined with social functions; there, sports take their place, along with parlour games and social exchanges (receptions, dinners, etc.), among the 'gratuitous' and 'disinterested' activities which enable the accumulation of social capital. This is seen in the fact that, in the extreme form it assumes in golf, shooting, and polo in smart clubs, sporting activity is a mere pretext for select encounters or, to put it another way, a technique of sociability, like bridge or dancing. Indeed, quite apart from its socializing functions, dancing is, of all the social uses of the body, the one which, treating the body as a sign, a sign of one's own ease, i.e. one's own mastery, represents the most accomplished realization of the bourgeois uses of the body: if this way of comporting the body is most successfully affirmed in dancing, this is perhaps because it is recognizable above all by its *tempo*, i.e. by the measured, self-assured slowness which also characterizes the bourgeois use of language, in contrast to working-class abruptness and petty-bourgeois eagerness.

Notes

This article is a translation of a paper given at the International Congress of the History of Sports and Physical Education Association, held in March 1978 at the Institut National des Sports et de l'Education Physique, Paris. The original title was "Pratiques sportives et pratiques sociales".

The translation is by Richard Nice.

1 Cf. J. Meynaud, *Sport et politique*, Paris, Payot, 1966.
2 One of the options available in the French state-run system of betting on horses. (Translator's note.)
3 J. Defrance, "Esquisse d'une histoire sociale de la gymnastique (1760–1870)", *Actes de la Recherche en Sciences Sociales* 6, 1976, pp. 22–46.
4 For a more detailed analysis, see C. Pociello, "Pratiques sportives et pratiques sociales", *Informations Sociales* 5, 1977, pp. 33–45.
5 Cf. J. Thibault, *Sports et éducation physique, 1870–1970*, Paris, Vrin, 1973.
6 P. Bourdieu, M. de Saint Martin, "Le patronat", *Actes de la Recherche en Sciences Sociales* 20/21, 1978, pp. 3–82.
7 *Musique en jeu* 9, nov. 1972, pp. 57–63.
8 I. Weinberg, *The English public Schools*, New York, Atherton Press, 1967, pp. 69–70.
9 Cf. Meynaud, op. cit., pp. 58 sq.
10 Cf. P. Bourdieu, "Célibat et condition paysanne", *Etudes Rurales* 5–6, 1962, pp. 32–136.
11 Cf. Weinberg, op. cit., pp. 111–112.
12 Cf. P. Bourdieu, "The economics of linguistic exchanges", *Social Science Information* 16 (6), 1977, 645–668.
13 Defrance, op. cit.
14 Cf. P. Bourdieu, "Le jeu chinois", *Actes de la Recherche en Sciences Sociales* 4, 1976, pp. 91–101.
15 *Pétanque*: a form of bowls played particularly in Southern France. (Translator's note.)
16 Cf. P. Bourdieu et al., *Un art moyen, essai sur les usages sociaux de la photographie*, Paris, Editions de Minuit, 1965.

55

THE GREAT AMERICAN
FOOTBALL RITUAL

Reproducing race, class and gender inequality

Douglas E. Foley

Source: *Sociology of Sport Journal* 7 (1990): 111–135.

An ethnographic study of one football season in a small South Texas town is pre-sented to explore the extent that community sport is, as various critical theorists have suggested, a potential site for counterhegemonic cultural practices. Football is conceptualized as a major community ritual that socializes future generations of youth. This broad, holistic description of socialization also notes various moments of ethnic resistance engendered by the Chicano civil rights movement. Other moments of class and gender resistance to the football ritual are also noted. Finally, the way players generally resisted attempts to thoroughly rationalize their sport is also described. In spite of these moments of resistance, this study ultimately shows how deeply implicated community sport – in this case high school football – is in the reproduction of class, gender, and racial inequality. The white ruling class and the town's patriarchal system of gender relations are preserved in spite of concessions to the new ethnic challenges. When seen from a historical community perspective, sport may be less a site for progressive, counterhegemonic practices than critical sport theorists hope.

This analysis of a football season is part of a larger study of the popular culture practices of youth in one South Texas town (Foley, 1990). Theoretic-ally, it has a great affinity with a Gramscian perspective (Critcher, 1986; Deem, 1988; Gruneau, 1983; Hargreaves, 1986; McKay, 1986; Whitson, 1984) of sport as a site of contested popular cultural practices. Although there are significant differences between these authors, the Gramscian per-spective advocated by the Birmingham Centre for Contemporary Cultural Studies (CCCS) generally informs many new critical studies of sports. The cultural studies perspective has been employed to study a wide array of popular or leisure practices (Bennett, Mercer, & Wollacott, 1986; Chambers, 1986; Fiske, 1989a, 1989b). Increasingly, sport sociologists are arguing that sports must also be studied as an autonomous cultural activity with the potential to challenge the commercialization and rationalization of sports activities.

This study seeks to ground recent critical perspectives of sports in the everyday cultural practices of one small, historical community. It explores the way high school sport reproduces social inequalities with the kind of detailed ethnographic data used in other microstudies of sport subcultures (Donnelly & Young, 1988; Fine, 1987). Like those microethnographic studies, this one is concerned with describing sports as a socialization process. Unlike other socialization studies, however, a historical[1] community with a social structure, not a group of people practicing a particular sport, is the focus. In addition, the reproduction and resistance perspective of popular culture theory is used rather than a functionalist or symbolic interactionist perspective (Donnelly & Young, 1988; Loy & Ingham, 1973).

The anthropological concept of a dramatic community ritual (Turner, 1974) is also used to give a holistic portrait of how major popular or leisure cultural practices (in this case, football) socialize people into community structures of inequality. The following description of the ritual complex surrounding high school football games concentrates on the rites, ceremonies, and events that socialize youth in the community and that symbolically stage class, gender, and racial inequality. Two basic premises not generally used in anthropological studies of ritual, but commonly shared by critical theorists of sport, guided this study. First, capitalist societies and their sport scenes are marked by multiple systems of dominance (Birrell, 1984, 1989; Deem, 1988; Hall, 1984, 1985; Messner, 1988). Consequently, a multiple-system-of-dominance perspective was used to explore the intersections of class, gender, and racial practices and relations and the way in which they are dialectically related in local community sport rituals. Second, any ideological hegemony constructed by a capitalist class is never secure and is often contested through various popular culture practices. Consequently, this study also explores the extent to which community sport scenes are sites of resistance and counterhegemonic popular or leisure cultural practices.

The setting of this field study was "North Town," a small (8,000 population) South Texas farming/ranching community with limited industry, considerable local poverty, and a population that was 80% Mexican-American. North Town was one of three towns in this winter-vegetable-producing area where a Chicano third party emerged to challenge the segregated racial order. The third party, the Partido Raza Unida, has since disbanded, but their impact was felt in all walks of life and sport was no exception. "North Town High" had an enrollment of 600 students and its sports teams played at the Triple-A level in a five-level state ranking system.

During the football season described here, I attended a number of practices, rode on the players' bus, and hung out with the coaches at the fieldhouse and with players during extensive classroom and lunchtime observations. I also participated in basketball and tennis practices and interviewed students extensively about student status groups, friendship, dating, and race relations. The participant-observation and interviewing in the sports scene involved hundreds of hours of fieldwork over a 12-month period. The larger community study[2] also included three full-time research assistants, and the fieldwork took place over a 2-year period. The traditional anthropological field methods used in this study are reported in great detail in Foley, Mota, Post, and Lozano (1988) and Foley (1990).

The ritual complex

The weekly pep rally

Shortly after arriving in North Town I attended my first pep rally. Students, whether they liked football or not, looked forward to Friday afternoons. Regular 7th-period classes were let out early to hold a mass pep rally to support the team. Most students attended these events but a few used it to slip away from school early. During the day of this pep rally I overheard a number of students planning their trip to the game. Those in the school marching band (80) and in the pep club (50) were the most enthusiastic. Students were plotting secret rendezvous with boyfriends and girlfriends or were fantasizing about fateful meetings with their secret loves. Fewer students and townspeople than usual would follow the team on this first long road trip.

Nevertheless, as on most Fridays, teachers and students were talking about The Game. Some teachers engaged the players in lively banter during classes about "whipping" Larson City. In senior English class a long analysis of last year's bad calls, missed kicks, and fumbles ensued. The history of this event had already been reconstructed, and those students interested in it shared that moment with the players. Players and nonplayers collectively plotted and reveled in mythical feats of revenge. There was much brave talk about "kicking their asses this year."

Some high school students considered the idea of young males in padded armor crashing into each other as dumb and boring. Some adults also thought that the sport was silly or too rough or a waste of time. Generally, however, most North Town students, like the adults, looked forward to football season and the Friday night games. The games enlivened the community's social life. Adults, especially the local chamber of commerce types, articulated this view even more than the students. Community sports was the patriotic, neighborly thing to do. Many students felt deep loyalties to support their team, but others used these community events to express their disgust for the game and the players, hence for "respectable" mainstream society.

This Friday afternoon the pep rally started like most school pep rallies. As the last bell rang, the halls were crammed with students rushing to put books

306

away and to find their friends. Various students claimed their rightful territory on the bleachers facing the microphones. Months later, when I knew them better, I could see the pattern to this mad scramble for seats: It was age-graded. The older, most prominent students took the center seats, thus signaling their status and loyalty. Younger first- and second-year students sat next to the leaders of the school activities if they were protégés of those leaders.

In sharp contrast, knots and clusters of the more socially marginal students, the "draggers," and the "punks and greasers," usually claimed the seats nearest the exits, thus signaling their indifference to all the rah-rah speeches they had to endure. The "nobodies" or "nerds," those dutiful, conforming students who were followers, tended to sit in the back of the center regions. Irrespective of the general territory, students usually sat with friends from their age group. Teachers strategically placed themselves at the margins and down in front to assist in crowd control.

The pep rally itself was dominated by the coaches and players, who were introduced to the audience to reflect upon the coming contest. In this particular pep rally the team captains led the team onto the stage. All the Anglo players entered first, followed by all the Mexicano players. Coach Trujillo started out with the classic pep talk that introduced the team captains, who in turn stepped forward and spoke in an awkward and self-effacing manner, thus enacting the ideal of sportsman – a man of deeds, not words. They all stuttered through several "uhs" and "ers," then quickly said, "I hope y'all come support us. Thanks." Generally students expected their jocks to be inarticulate and, as the cliché goes, strong but silent types. Coach Trujillo then elaborated upon how hard work, loyalty, and dedication would bring the school victory. He also brought up last year's defeat at the hands of Larson City to jibe the present seniors that this would be their "last chance to beat the Raiders."

Between the brief comments made by players and coaches, the cheerleaders and pep squad tried to involve the student body through cheers. A small contingent of the 80-piece marching band tooted and banged out the proper drum rolls for the speakers and cheerleaders. Other band members dispersed among the crowd and helped the pep squad lead cheers. Being a part of the band was also an important way of establishing one's loyalty to school and community. Later, during the game, the marching band would entertain the crowd at halftime while the players rested. Halftime performance also showcased the youth of North Town.

The marching band and band fags

The quality of the marching band was as carefully scrutinized as the football team by some community members. The band director, Dante Aguila, was keenly aware of maintaining an excellent winning band. Like sport teams, marching bands competed in local, district, and statewide contests and won rankings. The ultimate goal was winning a top rating at the state level. In addition, each band sent its best players of various instruments to district contests to compete for individual rankings. Individual band members could also achieve top rankings at the state level.

A certain segment of the student body began training for the high school marching band during their grade-school years. Band members had a much more positive view of their participation in band than the players did. The band was filled with students who tended to have better grades and came from the more affluent families. The more marginal, deviant students perceived band members as "goodie goodies," "richies," and "brains." This characterization was not entirely true because the band boosters club did make an effort to raise money to help low-income students join the band. Not all band students were top students, but many were in the advanced or academic tracks. Band members were generally the students with school spirit who were proud to promote loyalty to the school and community. The marching band was also a major symbolic expression of the community's unity and its future generation of good citizens and leaders.

The view that band members were the cream of the crop was not widely shared by the football players. Many female band members were socially prominent and "cool," but some were also studious homebodies. On the other hand, "real men" supposedly did not sign up for the North Town band. According to the football players, the physically weaker, more effeminate males tended to be in the band. Males in the band were called "band fags." The only exceptions were "cool guys" who did drugs, or had their own rock and roll band, or came from musical families and planned to become professional musicians. The males considered to be fags were sometimes derided and picked on as "sissies." Occasional gender jokes were made about their not having the "balls" to date the cute female band members.

The main masculinity test for band fags was to punch their biceps as hard as possible. If the victim returned this aggression with a defiant smile or smirk, he was a real man; if he winced and whined, he was a wimp or a fag. The other variations on punching the biceps were pinching the forearm and rapping the knuckles. North Town boys generally punched and pinched each other, but this kind of male play toward those considered fags was a daily ritual degradation. These were moments when physically dominant males picked on allegedly more effeminate males and reaffirmed their place in the male pecking order. Ironically, however, the players themselves rarely picked on those they called band fags. Males who emulated jocks and hoped to hang out with them were usually the hit men. The jocks signaled their real power and prestige by showing restraint toward obviously weaker males.

Cheerleaders and pep squads

As in most pep rallies, on the Friday I am describing, the cheerleaders were in front of the crowd on the gym floor doing dance and jumping routines in unison and shouting patriotic cheers to whip up enthusiasm for the team. The cheerleaders were acknowledged as some of the prettiest young women in the school and they aroused the envy of nobodies and nerds. Male students incessantly gossiped and fantasized about these young women and their reputations.

One frequently told story was about a pep rally when students started throwing pennies at Trini, a cheerleader. Initially this curious story made no sense to me. Trini struck me as the perfect all-American girl next door. She was widely acknowledged as cute and perky, got above average grades, and was on her way to college, a good career, and marriage. She also dated an Anglo from another town. That fact, and the relentless gossip about her being a "slut" and "gringo-loving whore," had hurt her; but being strong willed, she would not quietly accept these put-downs. She lashed back by criticizing people for being small-townish and small-minded.

The rest of the girls, four Mexicanas and two Anglos, were more or less alike both physical and socially. One Anglo girl was particularly athletic, which often prompted Anglos to make negative remarks about a Mexicana who was popular but considered a bit plump. Students invariably had their favorites to adore and/or ridicule. Yet they told contradictory stories about the cheerleaders. When privately reflecting on their physical attributes and social status, males saw going with a cheerleader as guaranteeing their coolness and masculinity. Particularly the less attractive males plotted the seduction of these young women and reveled in the idea of having them as girlfriends. When expressing their views of these young women to other males, however, they often accused the cheer-leaders of being stuck-up or sluts.

This sharp contradiction in males' discourse about cheerleaders makes perfect sense, however, when seen as males talking about females as objects to possess and dominate and through which to gain status. Conversations among males about cheerleaders were rhetorical performances that bonded males together and established their rank in this patriarchal order. In public conversations, males often expressed bravado about conquest of these "easy lays." In private conversations with intimate friends, they expressed their unabashed longing for, hence vulnerable emotional need for, these fantasized sexual objects. Hence, cheerleaders as highly prized females were dangerous, status-confirming creatures who were easier to relate to in rhetorical performances than in real life. Only those males with very high social status could actually risk relating to and being rejected by a cheerleader. The rest of the stories the young men told were simply male talk and fantasy.

Many young women were not athletic or attractive enough to be cheerleaders, nevertheless they wanted to be cheerleaders. Such young women often joined the pep squad as an alternative, and a strong esprit de corps developed among the pep squad members. They were a group of 50 young women in costume who came to the games and helped the cheerleaders arouse crowd enthusiasm. The pep squad also helped publicize and decorate the school and town with catchy team-spirit slogans such as "Smash the Seahawks" and "Spear the Javelinos." In addition, they helped organize after-the-game school dances. Their uniforms expressed loyalty to the team, and pep squad members were given a number of small status privileges in the school. They were sometimes released early for pep rallies and away games.

Teachers were often solicitous to pep squad members and labeled them good students. Pep squad members were usually students who conformed to the school rules and goals, thus were good citizens, but being in the pep squad also afforded them an opportunity to break home rules. Students and some teachers joked with pep squad members about "getting out of the house" to go to the games for romantic reasons. On road trips these young women momentarily escaped parental supervision and had opportunities to publicly attract and flirt with young men from other towns. This helped establish their gender status among other students as more "hip," even though being in the pep squad was a "straight" activity.

Homecoming: A rite of community solidarity and status

Ideally, North Town graduates would return to the homecoming bonfire and dance to reaffirm their support and commitment to the school and team. They would come back to be honored and to honor the new generation presently upholding the name and tradition of the community. In reality, however, few ex-graduates actually attended the pregame bonfire rally or postgame school dance. Typically, the game itself drew a larger crowd and the local paper played up the homecoming game more. College-bound youth were noticeably present at the informal beer party after the game. Some townspeople were also at the pregame bonfire rally, something that rarely happened during an ordinary school pep rally.

That afternoon, bands of Anglo males riding in pickup trucks began foraging for firewood. Other students not involved in hauling the wood gathered in the school parking lot. They wanted to watch what was brought for burning and meanwhile shared stories about stolen outdoor wooden outhouses, sheds, posts, and packing crates. It was important to the onlookers just which community members donated burnable objects, how cleverly objects were procured, and what outrageous objects were to be burnt this year. This was obviously a traditional event that entertained and bestowed status on both the procurers and donors of burnable objects.

Three groups of boys with pickup trucks eventually created a huge pile of scrap wood and burnable objects that had been donated. The cheerleaders, band, and pep squad members then conducted the bonfire ceremonies.

310

Several hundred persons, approximately an equal number of Anglo and Mexicano students, showed up at the rally along with a fair sprinkling of older people and others who were not in high school. Nearly all of the leaders were Anglos and they were complaining that not enough students supported the school or them. The cheerleaders led cheers and sang the school fight song after brief inspirational speeches from the coaches and players. Unlike the school pep rally, the police arrived to survey the fire. Rumors circulated that the police were there to harass people because some crates might have been stolen from a local packing shed. It was also rumored that some of the football players were planning to get drunk after the bonfire died down.

The huge blazing fire in the school parking lot made this pep rally special. The fire added to the festive mood, which seemed partly adolescent high jinks and partly serious communion with the town's traditions. The collective energy of the youth had broken a property law or two to stage this event. Adults laughed about the "borrowed" packing crates and were pleased that others "donated" things from their stores and houses to feed the fire. The adults expressed no elaborate rationale for having a homecoming bonfire, which they considered nice, hot, and a good way to fire up the team.[3] Gathering around the bonfire reunited all North Towners, past and present, for the special homecoming reunion and gridiron battle. Whatever the deeper symbolic meaning, those attending seemed to enjoy the pep rally. Several of the organizers and friends remained behind to watch the fire burn down. They gossiped about friends and acquaintances and told sport stories.

After the homecoming game, a school dance was held featuring a homecoming court complete with king and queen. The queen and her court and the king and his attendants, typically the most popular and attractive students, were elected by the student body. Ideally they represented the most attractive, popular, and successful youth. They were considered the best of a future generation of North Towners. Following tradition, the queen was crowned during halftime at midfield as the band played and the crowd cheered. According to tradition, the lovely queen and her court, dressed in formal gowns, were ceremoniously transported to the crowning in convertibles. The king and his attendants, who were often football players and dirty and sweaty at that, then came running from their halftime break to escort the young women from the convertibles and to their crowning. The king and his court lingered rather uneasily until the ceremony was over and then quickly returned to their team to rest and prepare for the second half.

This particular homecoming halftime ceremony took place as it always did, but with one major difference. The customary convertibles for the queen and her court were missing; consequently, the queen and her court, on this occasion all Mexicanas, had to walk to their crowning. This evoked numerous criticisms among Mexicano students and parents in attendance. Many felt it was a "gringo plot" to rob them of their chance to be leaders in

311

the community. The *Chicano Times*, a radical San Antonio newspaper, screamed out headlines that accused the school officials of blatant discrimination. The administrators and teachers in charge of organizing the event denied these charges but were left embarrassed and without any acceptable defense.

In this particular instance, this rite of solidarity became instead a source of divisiveness in North Town. A number of Better Government League (BGL) Anglos perceived the Mexicanos as politicizing the event and causing trouble. Another way of interpreting their criticism, however, was as an attempt to preserve the pomp and splendor of the ceremony that marked the social status of the town's future leaders. Those Mexicanos seeking to become integrated into and leaders of the community were not willing to be treated differently. They demanded that football and its homecoming ceremony serve its traditional purpose of creating continuity and unity. Mexicanos were trying to preserve a cultural tradition that would finally serve their children the way it had those of Anglos.

The powder-puff football game: another rite of gender reproduction

A powder-puff football game was traditionally held in North Town on a Friday afternoon before the seniors' final game. A number of the senior football players dressed up as girls and acted as cheerleaders for the game. A number of the senior girls dressed up as football players and formed a touch football team that played the junior girls. The male football players served as coaches and referees and comprised much of the audience as well. Perhaps a quarter of the student body, mainly the active, popular, successful students, drifted in and out to have a laugh over this event. More boys than girls, both Anglo and Mexicano, attended the game.

The striking thing about this ritual was the gender difference in expressive manner. Males took the opportunity to act in silly and outrageous ways. They pranced around in high heels, smeared their faces with lipstick, and flaunted their padded breasts and posteriors in a sexually provocative manner. Everything, including the cheers they led, was done in a very playful, exaggerated, and burlesque manner.

In sharp contrast, the females donned the football jerseys and helmets of the players, sometimes those of their boyfriends, and proceeded to huff and puff soberly up and down the field under the watchful eyes of the boys. They played their part in the game as seriously as possible, blocking and shoving with considerable gusto. This farce went on for several scores, until one team was the clear winner and until the females were physically exhausted and the males were satiated with acting in a ridiculous manner.

When asked why they had powder-puff football games, most male students could not articulate a very deep meaning for the event. Most said things like, "It's good for a laugh," "It's fun," "It's a good break from

312

school; school's boring." Others hinted at something more than recreation and teenage fun:

> I don't know, I guess it gives guys a chance to have a little fun with the girls. . . . It makes the girls see how rough it is to play football. . . . The guys get to let off a little steam, tease their girlfriends a little, maybe show them who's the boss.

Some girls earnestly suggested the following meanings for the event:

> It gives us a chance to show the guys that we can compete too. We aren't sissies. We can take getting hit too. . . . We can show them that football isn't just for guys. . . . Girls are athletic, too. We can run and throw the ball pretty good, too. . . . God, I don't know, just to have a break from sixth period. . . . The guys get to have all the fun, why shouldn't we?

Teachers tended to look on the game as a silly, harmless event that helped build school spirit. One boldly suggested that maybe these big jocks were putting on bras because they secretly wanted to be girls. That tongue-in-cheek interpretation of football players has already been seriously proposed by one prominent folklorist (Dundes, 1978). Alan Dundes understands the butt-slapping and talk about "hitting holes" and "penetrating the other team's endzone" as a form of male combat that masks latent homosexuality. Such an interpretation would undoubtedly shock North Towners, who generally regarded this sort of thing as simply fun and silliness.

This interpretation also completely misses the cultural significance of such an event. Anthropologists have come to call such curious practices "rituals of inversion" (Babcock, 1978), specially marked moments when people radically reverse everyday cultural roles and practices. During these events people break, or humorously play with, their own cultural rules. Such reversals are possible without suffering any sanctions or loss of face. These moments are clearly marked so that no one familiar with the culture will misread such reversals as anything more than a momentary break in daily life.

Males of North Town High used this moment of symbolic inversion to parody females in a burlesque and ridiculous manner. They took great liberties with the female role through this humorous form of expression. The power of these young males to appropriate and play with female symbols of sexuality was a statement about males' social and physical dominance. Conversely, the females took few liberties with their expression of the male role. They tried to play a serious game of football. The females tried earnestly to prove they were equal. Their lack of playfulness was a poignant testimony to their subordinate status in this small town.

This moment of gender role reversal was a reflection of sexual politics, not of sexual preference. A psychological interpretation overlooks the historical pattern of patriarchy in the entire football ritual. The powder-puff football game, although seemingly a minor event, was an important part of the total football ritual. This ritual generally socialized both sexes to assume their proper, traditional gender roles. On the other hand, one could argue that the assertive, serious way they played the game may also be teaching these young women some new lessons in competing with males. Perhaps the girls were also trying to invert this inversion ritual, thus turning boys into real rather than symbolic buffoons. Generally, however, the women seemed to participate unwittingly in staging this expression of male dominance and privilege.

The coach: A Mexicano coach on the firing line

The North Town adult primarily responsible for making high school football an important, well-attended ritual was the head coach. Unfortunately, a good deal of local politics made it difficult for Coach Roberto Trujillo, North Town's first Mexicano head coach, to do his job. Coach Trujillo's father ran a dance hall that alternately hosted Anglo country and western as well as Mexicano "conjunto" (country, polka, and Caribbean) music. More important, his father had been a charter member in the new BGL political organization, which opposed North Town's new Chicano civil rights organization, Partido Raza Unida (PRU). The Trujillos' alliance with the Anglo BGL made both father and son "vendidos" (sellouts) in the eyes of most Raza Unida members. Coach Trujillo, in reality not a politically involved person, had a reputation as "a nice man but a little weak." He was the perfect compromise candidate for the BGL liberals who controlled the school board. He was a native son, college educated, polite, respectful, and generally mild mannered. His coaching record, though not exceptional, was considered acceptable. Most important, he was from a successful middle-class Mexicano family who renounced the extreme views of the PRU. Coach Trujillo was the BGL liberals' model of an accommodating, reasonable Mexican.

A number of other BGL Anglos were outraged, however, at his appointment over an Anglo coach, Jim Ryan, also a native son and one who had the distinction of leading North Town to their only regional finals. He was a likeable "good ole' boy" who was very approachable and had deep South Texas roots. Liberal BGLers viewed him as a poorly educated redneck who lacked the new ethnic tolerance they sought to project as school board leaders. Coach Ryan was a staunch conservative who constantly railed against what he termed communists, welfare loafers, and PRU radicals. Many Mexicano players actually considered him a good disciplinarian and coach, but a number of them also felt that he was indeed partial toward Anglo players.

Coach Trujillo, on the other hand, was considered too friendly and soft on the players. Stories circulated about his easy practices and indecisive play calling. What many of the critics wanted was a military-style coach, a stern disciplinarian. They constantly criticized the star North Town players as being lazy and too soft. Trujillo was in the proverbial coach's hot seat for all the classic reasons, and for uniquely racial ones as well. He had the double jeopardy of being neither manly enough nor white or brown enough to lead North Town youth into battle. He was constantly challenged to prove himself both to the Mexicano activists and to the more redneck Anglos.

Coaches as storytellers: reproducing and resisting inequality

The first out-of-town trip proved to be revealing on the subject of race relations. The players took their seats as if some crusading liberal had written the script. All the Mexicano players quietly seated themselves at the back of the bus. Then all the Anglo players brashly seated themselves in the front of the bus with the coaching staff. At first I was taken aback by this event, which seemed an unmistakable sign of Anglo racial dominance. Yet I wondered how such a seating arrangement could possibly signify subservience in a town full of politically assertive Mexicano adults. Before we reached Larson City, at least 10 racial jokes were hurled between the front and the back of the bus. One giant Anglo tackle, the high school principal's son, cracked perhaps the best joke. He bellowed out, "Shewt, if we lose this game, *we* are going to ride home in the back of the bus." This brought a nervous reply from Coach Trujillo that he might have to join them (the Anglos) there too. Having just heard the story of his compromised political position with Mexicanos, I thought the comment was his way of downplaying the controversy over him. Or perhaps he was as subservient to Anglos as the Raza Unida leaders claimed.

As we neared Larson City, to my great surprise Trujillo cracked the following joke with the Anglo players: "We are going to have to take some of you boys to Boystown to show you how the *other* half lives." Anyone familiar with Texas border culture knows that the whorehouse sections of Mexican border towns are called Boystown. The classic rite of passage for South and West Texas males[4] is to lose their virginity in one of these Boystowns. This embattled Mexicano coach was joking about Anglo males using Mexicana prostitutes. He was suggesting to the Anglo players that they were about to become men and friends with his race, if they would let him make men out of them. The coach was evoking a common male bonding ritual and using humor to displace the racial tensions. He was also saying that they were all heading for "the border" of race relations in search of a new understanding.

During the fieldwork, I spent a great deal of time watching for examples of coaches serving as mediators of racial conflict, and at least one other coach

315

and Coach Trujillo did indeed take it upon themselves to mediate racial attitudes and images. They directly intervened as peacemakers in at least two incidents of conflict between players and students. More important, they often tried to redefine the reality of North Town race relations by telling a story or homily to their players. An excellent example of their role in redefining racial/ethnic relations was a story I overheard Coach Trujillo tell several Anglo players after practice one day. He had just finished putting the boys through a brutal 2–1/2 hour fullpads scrimmage. This occurred during the dog days of late September and the temperature on the playing field was at least 100°F. The boys were exhausted and began joking and complaining about what a dictator the coach was. One quipped, "Man, I thought Hitler was a German."

Coach Trujillo read this ethnic reference as an invitation to launch into a racial treatise on the sense of equality and character of the Mexicano people, and himself in particular. Trujillo had been the first Mexicano player with a scholarship to play for a "lily-white" West Texas college. He then recounted his own version of the brutal two-a-day summer practice story that all football players tell. Usually this tale is told to illustrate one's pain threshold and ability to survive hot, sweaty practices. Often such practices do seem like the nightmarish inventions of a sadistic coach. Only "real men" survive these hot summer practices, and the worse the practices, the better the telling of the tale. Young players usually recount these practices to older relatives and former players who hang out in local gas stations and restaurants.

Coach Trujillo created an interesting variant of this tale that also had a racial lesson. After the exhausted players returned to the locker room, one of the Anglo players had the gall to toss the coach's equipment away from the coach's locker, thus invading his hard-earned resting space. The coach confronted the offending lockermate and reminded him that they were all in it together. They were all survivors of the football wars; consequently he was deserving of equal respect and space. With a twinkle in his eye, the coach explained, "I was telling this guy in a nice way, 'Hey, redneck, that's my space.'" According to Coach Trujillo, this bold, honest confrontation with the Anglo, and by extension American society, brought instant respect from the other players sitting nearby. They could see that he was ready to fight for his rights, which he had earned the hard way. Seeing this hulking white monster of a lineman being cowed by this little brown bulldog was a new experience for the Anglo players. They purportedly responded with warmth and admiration, and this was the beginning of the coach's acceptance among the Anglo players.

In a way, Coach Trujillo's story was much like the miraculous conversion tales born-again Christians often tell. In a trying and difficult moment, he acted with courage and humility to be accepted as an equal. He risked everything and stood up for the ideal that the races should live together in harmony rather than discord. According to his tale, from that day forward a new era of race relations began for his college and their football team. He relived his past to model what he wanted for his own players. He was no Hitler, nor were his people any different from Anglos. Moreover, he and his people were ready to fight for their rights. The coach told several homilies like this one. It is not clear how effective such moral lessons were, but this was how he dealt with the race problem.

But in the end, Coach Trujillo said he "threw in the towel." Despite a good season, second in the conference, and a 7–4 record, he resigned and left his hometown feeling, in his own words, "sick of the strife and the pressure on my family." The coach claimed that he had "lost a lotta friends" and had gotten an ulcer. He compared the South Texas racial situation unfavorably to other places he had been, such as Colorado and Michigan, and feared that North Town might never change. Being a political centrist, he had very little good to say about either political group:

> My daddy wants out of the BGL. He can see that the Anglos just won't change. They just want to use him, and one or two Anglo board members still think I am just a Meskin'. They'll never change. They always overreact to a Mexicano getting ahead. Look at the school elections. They handled the whole thing very poorly. Some kids were left off the ballot by mistake, and they should get rid of the rule that disqualified some of our best kids. They are just trying to protect their kids and hold us back. And the Anglos should not have quit the band trying to pressure the new Mexican-American band director. I'm sick of the Raza Unida too. They use these pressure tactics and call people "vendidos" and shoot off their mouths. The indictments of voters is real bad, and the Anglos are pressuring to control the school board votes, but Raza Unida has gone too far. I believe they did try to steal the city election, and they did shoot a gun at the mayor's house.

When Coach Trujillo reflected on his past, he came across as a man trapped in a painful process of cultural change. Unlike the new generation of students, he was not part of the civil rights movement and remained unsure how much to assert himself. The movement left him filled with a longing for change but a certain fear about breaking the cultural rules he hated. In the end, Coach Trujillo decided the situation was impossible to change or live with, so he moved on, but not without a great deal of sadness. He was unable to develop the type of relationship with North Town community leaders that would solidify his place in the local power structure.

Prominent citizens and their booster club: reproducing
class privileges

North Town was the type of community in which male teachers who had athletic or coaching backgrounds were more respected than other teachers. For their part, the other teachers often told "dumb coach" jokes and expressed resentment toward the school board's view of coaches. North Town school board members, many of them farmers and ranchers – rugged men of action – generally preferred that their school leaders be ex-coaches. Consequently a disproportionate number of ex-coaches became school principals and superintendents. The superintendent, himself an ex-coach, sported a 1950s-style flattop and loved to hunt. The junior high principal, also a former coach, owned and operated a steak house. The high school principal was an ex-coach but he lacked the capital to start a business. Three of the present coaching staff had farms or small businesses. School board members invariably emphasized an ex-coach's ability to deal with the public and to discipline the youth.

Once gridiron warriors, coaches in small towns are ultimately forced to become organization men, budget administrators, and public relations experts. These administrative Minotaurs are half-man, half-bureaucrat who are paid a small sum of money for hundreds of hours of extra work. Ultimately they must appease local factions, school boards, administrators, booster clubs, angry parents, and rebellious teenagers. The successful North Town coaches invariably become excellent public relations men who live a "down home" rural lifestyle; they like to hunt and fish and join local coffee klatches or Saturday morning quarterback groups. They must be real men who like fraternizing with the entrepreneurs, politicians, and good ole' boys who actually run the town. This role as a local male leader creates a web of alliances and obligations that put most coaches in the debt of the prominent citizens and their booster club.

North Town's booster club, composed mainly of local merchants, farmers, and ranchers, had the all-important function of raising supplementary funds for improving the sports program and for holding a postseason awards banquet. The club was the most direct and formal link that coaches had with the principal North Town civic leaders. Some prominent merchants and ranchers were absent from these activities, however, because they disliked sports or because they left it to those with more time and enthusiasm. North Town had a long history of booster club and school board interference in coaching the team. One coach characterized North Town as follows: "One of the toughest towns around to keep a job. Folks here take their football seriously. They are used to winning, not everything, not the state, but conference and maybe district, and someday even regional. They put a lot of pressure on you to win here."

The booster club that coach Trujillo had to deal with was run by a small clique of Anglos whom the BGL liberals considered "good ole" boys and redneck types." They became outspoken early in the season against their "weak Mexican coach." They fanned the fires of criticism in the coffee-drinking sessions over which of the two freshman quarterbacks should start, the "strong-armed Mexican boy" or the "all-around, smart Anglo boy." The Anglo boy was the son of a prominent car dealer and BGL and booster club activist. The Mexican boy was the son of a migrant worker and small grocery store manager. The freshman coach, Jim Ryan, chose the Anglo boy, and the PRU accused him of racial prejudice. In a similar vein, conflict also surfaced over the selection of the varsity quarterback. Coach Trujillo chose the son of an Anglo businessman, an under-classman, over a senior, the son of a less prominent Anglo. The less educated Anglo faction lambasted the coach for this decision, claiming he showed his preference for the children of the more socially and politically prominent BGL types.

One of Coach Trujillo's former players, who was a coach and community political leader, eloquently recounted to me "what physical education courses never teach you" about coaching:

> I will never forget Coach Bowman. He was a hard-core sargeant-type who didn't give a damn about pleasing the booster club. During a real rough practice the Smith kid got beat up pretty bad by a Hispanic kid and Coach stopped starting him. His mother came into the office one day to chew out Coach Bowman, and she caught him sitting there in his shorts with his legs up on the desk puffing away on this stogie. He told her that her son was a "goddamn sissy and didn't deserve to start." From then on his days were numbered, and the booster club got him fired. . . . And it works both ways. Hispanics do the same thing. When we had the big school board change and Coach Fuentes was brought in, he gave me a list of three kids, a quarterback, line-backer, and running back, who he wanted me to play on the freshman team. They were all the kids of school board members or buddies of the politicos. It was bad, man. I threatened to walk off the field and let him coach, so he finally gave in.

The former player went on to explain how local pressures and influences on coaches get played out. He advised me to watch who got invited to the parties after the games and who got invited to hunt on certain ranches:

> I'll tell you where you really see all this stuff, Doc. You never got invited to the parties, so you didn't see this. Every Friday night after the games, the prominent people in this town throw a barbecue and invite us coaches. The whole staff has gotta go and behave right if you wanna keep your job. That is where a coach can make or break himself. . . . No there wasn't but one or two Mexicanos at these parties. It was all Anglos, until the Mexicano school board came in.

319

Then everything changed. Nobody invited Coach Fuentes and his staff to these parties. They started going to parties on the other side held by the Mexicano politicos. Most Anglos also dropped out of the booster club at that time too. . . . Really, there is no way that this town can have a good football program without a good mix of kids and the Anglo parents ramrodding the booster club. It is sad to say, but the Mexicanos will probably always be too divided to run the thing right. The booster club was in bad shape when they ran it. . . . The other important thing is getting invited by the people who have got money to hunt bird or deer on their land. It is kind of an honor for you to do this, and for them to have you. And if you've got good connections with star players and name coaches from the university or the pro ranks, then you bring them in to speak to the booster club. Local people like going hunting with a real sports celebrity even better. It's all part of the way it is down here, Doc. To survive, you gotta get along with certain people.

The pattern of community pressures observed in North Town was not particularly exceptional. A good deal of the public criticism and grumbling about choices of players had racial overtones. The debate over which Anglo varsity quarterback to play also reflected community class differences among Anglos. North Town students and adults often expressed their fears and suspicion that racial and class prejudices were operating. It would be an exaggeration, however, to portray the North Town football team as rife with racial conflict and disunity. Nor was it filled with class prejudice. On a day-to-day basis there was considerable harmony and unity. Mexicanos and Anglos played side by side with few incidents. A number of working-class Mexicano youths and a few low-income Anglos were also members of the football program. At least in a general way, a surface harmony and equality seemed to prevail.

The only rupture of such public accommodations came when Coach Trujillo and Coach Ryan exchanged sharp words and nearly got into a fistfight during practice. This led to Trujillo making what many Mexicano political activists considered a humiliating public apology to Ryan. The two coaches were also severely reprimanded by the principal and superintendent. Ultimately everyone, especially the two feuding coaches, tried to downplay the conflict for the good of the team. Powerful social pressures controlled any public expression of racial disunity and class conflict on the team.

Local sports enthusiasts are fond of arguing that coaches select players objectively, without class or racial prejudices, because their personal interest, and that of the team, is served by winning. Unfortunately, this free-market view glosses over how sport actually functions in local communities. Small-town coaches are generally subjected to enormous pressures to play everyone's child, regardless of social class and race. Success in sport is an important symbolic representation of familial social position. Men can reaffirm their claim to leadership and prominence through the success of their offspring. A son's athletic exploits relieve and display the past physical and present social dominance of the father. In displaying past and present familial prominence, the son lays claim to his future potentional. Every North Town coach lived and died by his ability to win games *and* his social competence to handle the competing status claims of the parents and their children.

Socially prominent families, who want to maintain their social position, promote their interests through booster clubs. The fathers of future community leaders spend much time talking about and criticizing coaches in local coffee shops. These fathers are more likely to talk to the coaches privately. Coaches who have ambitions to be socially prominent are more likely to "network" with these sportsminded community leaders. A symbiotic relationship develops between coaches, especially native ones, and the traditional community leaders. Preferential treatment of the sons of prominent community leaders flows from this web of friendships, hunting privileges, Saturday morning joking, and other such exchanges.

Moreover, considerable pressure to favor the sons of prominent citizens comes from within the school as well. The school and its classrooms are also a primary social stage upon which students enact their social privilege. These youths establish themselves as leaders in academic, political, and social affairs, and teachers grant them a variety of privileges. This reinforces the influence of their parents in the PTA, the sports and band booster clubs, and the school board. Both generations, in their own way, advance the interests of the family on many fronts.

The spectators: male socialization through ex-players

Another major aspect of the football ritual is how the spectators, the men in the community, socialize each new generation of players. In North Town, groups of middle-aged males with families and businesses were influential in socializing the new generation of males. These men congregated in various restaurants for their morning coffee and conversation about business, politics, the weather, and sports. Those leading citizens particularly interested in sports could be heard praising and criticizing "the boys" in almost a fatherly way. Some hired the players for part-time or summer jobs and were inclined to give them special privileges. Athletes were more likely to get well-paying jobs as road-gang workers, machine operators, and crew leaders. Most players denied that they got any favors, but they clearly had more prestige than other high school students who worked. Nonplayers complained that jocks got the good jobs. On the job site the men regaled players with stories of male conquests in sports, romance, and business.

Many players reported these conversations, and I observed several during Saturday morning quarterback sessions in a local restaurant and gas station.

One Saturday morning after the all-important Harris game, two starters and their good buddies came into the Cactus Bowl Café. One local rancher-businessman shouted, "Hey, Chuck, Jimmie, get over here! I want to talk to you boys about that Harris game!" He then launched into a litany of mistakes each boy and the team had made. Others in the group chimed in and hurled jokes at the boys about "wearing skirts" and being "wimps." Meanwhile the players stood slope-shouldered and "uh-huhed" their tormentors. One thing they had learned was never to argue back too vociferously. The players ridiculed such confrontations with "old-timers" privately, but the proper response from a good kid was tongue-biting deference.

This sort of pressure on players began early in the week with various good-natured jests and comments. The most critical groups were the cliques of explayers who had recently graduated. Those who went off to college usually came back only a few weekends to watch games. If they continued to play, they returned as celebrities and tended to say very little. Being college players, they tended to be above any carping criticism of high school players. Usually, the more relentlessly critical groups were those ex-players who had never left town.

Some ex-players led the romanticized life of tough, brawling, womanizing young bachelors. These young men seemed suspended in a state of adolescence while avoiding becoming responsible family men. They could openly do things that the players had to control or hide because of training rules. Many of these ex-players were also able to physically dominate the younger high school players. But ex-players no longer had a stage upon which to perform heroics for the town. Consequently they often reminded current players of their past exploits and the superiority of players and teams in their era. Current players had to "learn" from these tormentors and take their place in local sports history.

Players talking about their sport: the meaning of football

The preceding portrayal of the community sports scene has already suggested several major reasons why young males play football. Many of them are willing to endure considerable physical pain and sacrifice to achieve social prominence in their community. Only a very small percentage are skilled enough to play college football, and only one North Towner has ever made a living playing professional football. The social rewards from playing football are therefore mainly local and cultural.

However, there are other more immediate psychological rewards for playing football. When asked why they play football and why they like it, young North Town males gave a variety of answers. A few openly admitted that football was a way for them to achieve some social status and prominence, to "become somebody in this town." Many said football was fun, or "makes a man out of you," or "helps you get a cute chick." Others parroted a chamber of commerce view that it built character and trained them to have discipline, thus helping them be successful in life. Finally, many evoked patriotic motives – to beat rival towns and to "show others that South Texas plays as good a football as East Texas."

These explicit statements do not reveal the deeper psychological lessons learned in sports combat, however. In casual conversations, players used phrases that were particularly revealing. What they talked most about was "hitting" or "sticking" or "popping" someone. These were all things that coaches exhorted the players to do in practice. After a hard game, the supreme compliment was having a particular "lick" or "hit" singled out. Folkloric immortality, endless stories about that one great hit in the big game, was what players secretly strove for. For most coaches and players, really "laying a lick on" or "knocking somebody's can off" or "taking a real lick" was that quintessential football moment. Somebody who could "take it" was someone who could bounce up off the ground as if he had hardly been hit. The supreme compliment, however, was to be called a hitter or head-hunter. A hitter made bone-crushing tackles that knocked out or hurt his opponent.

Players who consistently inflicted outstanding hits were called animals, studs, bulls, horses, or gorillas. A stud was a superior physical specimen who fearlessly dished out and took hits, who liked the physical contact, who could dominate other players physically. Other players idolized a "real stud," because he seemed fearless and indomitable on the field. Off the field a stud was also cool, or at least imagined to be cool, with girls. Most players expected and wanted strong coaches and some studs to lead them into battle. They talked endlessly about who was a real stud and whether the coach "really kicks butt."

The point of being a hitter and stud is proving that you have enough courage to inflict and take physical pain. Pain is a badge of honor. Playing with pain proves you are a man. In conventional society, pain is a warning to protect your body, but the opposite ethic rules in football. In North Town bandages and stitches and casts became medals worn proudly into battle. Players constantly told stories about overcoming injuries and "playing hurt." A truly brave man was one who could fight on; his pain and wounds were simply greater obstacles to overcome. Scars were permanent traces of past battles won, or at the very least fought well. They became stories told to girlfriends and relatives.

The other, gentler, more social side of football was the emphasis on cama-raderie, loyalty, friendship between players, and pulling together. Players also often mentioned how much fun it was to hang out with the guys. Some of them admitted to being locker room and "gym rats," guys who were always hanging around the fieldhouse and gym. They told stories of their miracu-lous goal line stands, of last-minute comebacks against all odds, and of tear-ful, gut-wrenching losses on cold muddy fields. Most of the players talked about the value of teamwork and how satisfying it was to achieve something together with other guys. Difficult, negative experiences were also shared. Long grueling practices without water and shade, and painful injuries – these were part of being teammates. Only other football buddies who had been in the football wars could appreciate the sacrifice and physical courage demanded in practices and games.

There were also shining tales of good sportsmanship. Players told stories about being helped up and helped off the field by opponents. They also prided themselves in learning how to lose gracefully and be good sports. At the high school level, winning was still the most important thing, and most coaches drilled that into their players. But if you could not win, the very least you could do was try as hard as possible, give all of yourself to the cause. The one cliché that North Town players constantly parroted back to me was "winners never quit, and quitters never win." Most North Town players prided themselves on giving their best effort. If they did not, the townspeople would lose respect for them and grumble, as they did during two conference losses. As the chamber of commerce claimed, North Town youth acquire their aggressive, competitive spirit on the town's athletic fields.

Another positive, pleasurable part of the game that most players mentioned was the emotional thrill of performing before large crowds. Many stories were told about "butterflies" and "getting the adrenalin pumping." Players coming back to the bench during the game were quite aware of the crowd. They threw down their helmets in exaggerated anger and disgust. They shouted at each other, slapped high-fives, and smashed each others' shoulder pads. Meanwhile they cast furtive glances at girls in the pep squad or at older brothers prowling the side-lines. They had to constantly express their spirit and commitment to the game, even during sideline breaks. Others limped and ice-packed their injuries and grimaced broadly for all to see.

Many players, particularly the skilled ones, described what might be called their aesthetic moments as the most rewarding thing about football. Players sitting around reviewing a game always talked about themselves or others as "making a good cut" and "running a good route," or "trapping" and "blindsiding" someone. All these specific acts involved executing a particular type of body control and skill with perfection and excellence. Running backs made quick turns or cuts that left would-be tacklers grasping for thin air. Ends "ran routes" or a clever change of direction that freed them to leap into the air and catch a pass. Guards lay in wait for big opposing linemen or aggressive linebackers to enter their territory recklessly, only to be trapped or blindsided by them. Each position had a variety of assignments or moments when players used their strength and intelligence to defeat their opponents. The way this was done was beautiful to a player who had spent years perfecting the body control and timing to execute the play. Players talked about "feeling" the game and the ball and the pressure from an opponent.

Team sports, and especially American football, generally socialize-males to be warriors. The young men of North Town were being socialized to measure themselves by their animal instincts and aggressiveness. Physicality, searching for pain, enduring pain, inflicting pain, and knowing one's pain threshold emphasizes the biological, animal side of human beings. These are the instincts needed to work together and survive in military combat and, in capitalist ideology, in corporate, academic, and industrial combat. The language used – head-hunter, stick 'em, and various aggressive animal symbols – conjures up visions of Wall Street stockbrokers and real estate sharks chewing up their competition.

Other males: brains, farm kids, and nobodies

What of those males who do not play high school football? Does this pervasive community ritual require the participation of all young males? Do all nonathletes end up in the category of effeminate "band fags"? To the contrary, several types of male students did not lose gender status for being unathletic. There were a small number of "brains" who were obviously not physically capable of being gridiron warriors. Some of them played other sports with less physical contact such as basketball, tennis, track, or baseball. In this way they still upheld the ideal of being involved in some form of sport. Others, who were slight of physique, wore thick glasses, lacked hand-eye coordination, or ran and threw poorly, sometimes ended up hanging around jocks or helping them with their schoolwork. Others were loners who were labeled nerds and weirdos.

In addition, there were many farm kids or poor kids who did not participate in sports. They were generally homebodies who did not participate in many extracurricular activities. Some of them had to work to help support their families. Others had no transportation to attend practices. In the student peer groups they were often part of the great silent majority called "the nobodies."

Resistance to the football ritual: the working-class chicano rebels

There were also a number of Mexicano males who formed anti-school oriented peer groups. They were into a "hip" drug oriented lifestyle. These males, often called "vatos" (cool dudes), made it a point to be anti-sports, an activity they considered straight. Although some were quite physically capable of playing, they rarely tried out for any type of team sports. They made excuses for not playing such as needing a job to support their car or van or pickup. They considered sports "kids' stuff," and their hip lifestyle as more adult, cool, and fun.

Even for the vatos, however, sports events were important moments when they could publicly display their lifestyle and establish their reputation. A number of vatos always came to the games and even followed the team to other towns. They went to games to be tough guys and "enforcers" and to establish "reps" as fighters. The vatos also went to games to "hit on chicks from other towns." During one road game, after smoking several joints, they swaggered in with cocky smiles plastered on their faces. The idea was to attract attention from young women and hopefully provoke a fight while stealing another town's women. Unlike stealing watermelons or apples from a neighbor, stealing women was done openly and was a test of courage. A man faced this danger in front of his buddies and under the eyes of the enemy.

Ultimately, only one minor scuffle actually occurred at the Larson City game. Some days after the game the vatos told many tales about their foray into enemy territory. With great bravado they recounted every unanswered slight and insult they hurled at those "geeks." They also gloried in their mythical conquests of local young women. For the vatos, fighting, smoking pot, and chasing females were far better sport than huffing and puffing around for "some fucking coach." As the players battled on the field, the vatos battled on the sidelines. They were another kind of warrior that established North Town's community identity and territoriality through the sport of fighting over and chasing young women.

The contradiction of being "in training"

In other ways, even the straight young men who played football also resisted certain aspects of the game. Young athletes were thrust into a real dilemma when their coaches sought to rationalize training techniques and forbade various pleasures of the flesh. Being in training meant no drugs, alcohol, or tobacco. It also meant eating well-balanced meals, getting at least 8 hours of sleep, and not wasting one's emotional and physical energy chasing women. These dictates were extremely difficult to follow in a culture where drugs are used regularly and where sexual conquest and/or romantic love are popular cultural ideals. Add a combination of male adolescence and the overwhelming use of sex and women's bodies to sell commodities, and you have an environment not particularly conducive to making sacrifices for the coach and the team. North Town athletes envied the young bachelors who drank, smoked pot, and chased women late into the night. If they wanted to be males, American culture dictated that they break the rigid, unnatural training rules set for them.

Contrary to the vatos' caricature of jocks as straight and conformist, many North Town football players actually broke their training rules. They often drank and smoked pot at private teen parties. Unlike the rebellious vatos, who publicly flaunted their drinking and drugs, jocks avoided drinking in public. By acting like all-American boys, jocks won praise from adults for their conformity. Many of them publicly pretended to be sacrificing and denying themselves pleasure. They told the old-timers stories about their "rough practices" and "commitment to conditioning." Consequently, if jocks got caught breaking training, the men tended to overlook these infractions as slips or temptations. In short, cool jocks knew how to manage their public image as conformists and hide their private nonconformity.

One incident, when two of the players were caught drinking at a school livestock show, illustrates how many of the adults preferred to handle this cultural contradiction. The sons of two ranchers, Roddy, a senior tackle, and Bob, a senior linebacker, were suspended from school for this incident. Since football season was over, this only jeopardized their graduation, not the winning of a conference championship. The main line of argument made on their behalf was that "boys will be boys," and "these are good kids."[5]

Fathers who had experienced this training contradiction themselves made the boys-will-be-boys argument on behalf of their sons. They gave their sons and other players stern lectures about keeping in shape, *but* they were the first to chuckle at the heroic stories of playing with a hangover. They told these same stories about teammates or about themselves over a cup of coffee or a beer. As a result, unless their youth were outrageously indiscreet – for example passing out drunk on the main street or in class, getting a "trashy girl" pregnant – a "little drinking and screwing around" was overlooked. They simply wanted the school board to stop being hypocritical and acknowledge that drinking was all part of growing up to be a prominent male.

In the small sports world of North Town, a real jock actually enhances his public image of being in shape by occasionally being a "boozer" or "doper." Indeed, one of the most common genres of stories that jocks told was the "I played while drunk/stoned," or the "I got drunk/stoned the night before the game" tale. Olmo, a big bruising guard who is now a hard-living, hard-drinking bachelor, told me a classic version of this tale before the homecoming game:

> Last night we really went out and hung one on. Me and Jaime and Arturo drank a six-pack apiece in a couple of hours. We were cruising around Daly City checking out the action. It was real dead. We didn't see nobody we knew except Arturo's cousin. We stopped at his place and drank some more and listened to some music. We stayed there till his old lady [mom] told us to go home. We got home pretty late, but before the sun come up, 'cause we're in training, ha ha.

Olmo told this story with a twinkle in his eye, especially the part about being in training. I asked him how it was possible to play well if he had "hung one on" the night before. This launched him into the story that he wanted to tell about drinking before and even during games. This story had become part of local sports lore because other players also told it to me. Stories of players' sexual exploits were recounted in the same vein that drinking stories were. A real man could be "in shape" because his extraordinary will could overcome these allegedly debilitating vices. A real man could have it all and become complete through drugs, sex, violence, and glory.

Most players secretly admired such rule-breaking behaviors. Olmo was a model of ideal male behavior and, to a degree, other players who were cool emulated him. Homebodies, the farm kids, and goodie-goodies rarely broke training, but the pressures on them to do so were enormous. Drinking parties, like North Town's post-homecoming bash, made celebrities out of the players. Kids clustered around the bonfire and around various pickups and shared beer and pot with their warriors who had beaten the enemy.

Conclusions: some theoretical considerations

A number of critical sports theorists have begun to ask whether the legitimation of the ruling elites of both capitalist and communist states through mass sports rituals actually does create an ideological hegemony. Moreover, they ask, if sport is some dehumanizing form of ideological dominance, why do so many people enjoy and increasingly participate in organized popular sports? This raises the issue of whether sport scenes also become the site for resistance to ideological hegemony.

The answer that sports theorists (Critcher, 1986; Gruneau, 1983; Hargreaves 1986) give, following a Gramscian perspective of popular culture studies, is that ruling-class cultural hegemony is never secure. These theorists generally argue that popular and leisure cultural practices such as sports always have the potential for autonomy and resistance to ruling-class hegemony. This is so, not because sport is inherently ludic but because the politicization and commercialization of local sports practices provoke some form of class consciousness and class resistance. In other words, the elite are never quite successful at appropriating popular cultural practices such as sport and recreation and turning them into mind-numbing, nationalistic forms of political conformity.

Other social theorists sympathetic to this perspective of class dominance (Birrell, 1984, 1989; Hall, 1984, 1985; McKay, 1986; Messner, 1988) suggest even more emphatically than the previously cited critical theorists that the ground of resistance to mass sport must be situated in multiple forms of dominance. In this view, the cultural practices of gender and racial dominance must *also* be included with a class theory perspective of sports. A multiple-dominance view of sports suggests that the commercializing and rationalizing tendencies in sports can at least be mediated and somewhat democratized through the more active participation of previously marginalized groups. Some feminists also argue that since women are more nurturing and humanistic, a massive new presence of women in organized sports will at least have a humanizing effect.

Finally, other popular culture theorists (Fiske 1989a, 1989b) suggest an additional ground for resistance and autonomy that is more general than class, gender, or racial consciousness. Fiske argues that all popular cultural forms have the potential to be pleasurable because they are profane, expressive cultural acts. Sport, like dance, music, or visual art, is a form of personal expression within a set of conventions or rules for self-expression. Within certain limits, these cultural performances manipulate the conventional symbols and expressive practices in new, self-gratifying ways. Students of popular cultural practices outside sport have shown a variety of creative resistance in the expressions of street graffiti, low-rider cars, pop art, informal clothes such a jeans, pop music, youth culture styles, and other unconventional popular expressive forms. This perspective generally suggests that the ultimate ground for resistance to the rationalization and commercialization of various expressive popular culture practices is the human preference to control and produce self-expression. Mass-produced overly standardized forms of self-expression such as commercialized art or sport will invariably run into some resistance because human beings are symbol-producing animals who invariably prefer to innovate with and invent expressive forms to represent themselves and create a social identity. Gruneau proposes some caution here that we "seem to have discovered resistance virtually everywhere in capitalist consumer cultures" (1988, p. 25).

This general question of how autonomous a cultural domain-organized sport is must be addressed, as Gruneau (1983) forcefully suggests, through historical studies of sport practices. Bourdieu (1988) also outlines a complementary programmatic statement for the sociology of sport that calls for intensive studies of the "habitus" of sport practices. I would add to these programmatic statements the addendum that a critical sociology of sport needs to conceptualize local studies of sports as historical community studies. Whatever resistance exists against sport rituals of socialization, it must be understood within the context of the local traditions of structural dominance.

In this particular study there were definitely signs of working-class resistance to the way the football ritual socializes youths to enact various forms of social inequality. The most dramatic example was the way the rebellious vatos used the games to parody football as a ritual of class and racial privilege. According to them, football was not the only way to prove one was a real man and warrior. Moreover, even the most straight, conformist youths who played football, especially those who knew they would never play beyond the community level, did not simply go along with the increasing rationalization of their sport. They were far less likely to follow modern scientific training practices than coaches and the booster club hoped. As Fiske (1989a, 1989b) suggests, leisure culture practices such football have pleasurable expressive and aesthetic moments. The real joy of playing hometown football is still some kind of ludic or expressive moment that may survive more on the local level than in big-time college and professional sports.

In addition, in a town experiencing the Chicano civil rights movement, there were many signs of an ethnic resistance to the reproductive character of local sports. Many Mexicanos protested strongly when the Anglos enacted the homecoming ceremony in a way that marginalized them. The same could be said for the Mexicano players who defiantly sat in the back of the bus and who made it difficult for Anglo coaches to unquestioningly put Anglo players in the high status positions. Moreover, Coach Trujillo clearly played a mediating role in resisting racial dominance until he was forced out. Finally, even the Mexicana cheer-leader, Trini, was making her own statement about the reproductive character of the football ritual.

Yet, all of the previously mentioned signs of resistance notwithstanding, the football ritual remains a powerful metaphor of American capitalist culture. In North Town, football is still a popular cultural practice deeply implicated in the reproduction of the local ruling class of white males, hence class, patriarchal, and racial forms of dominance. The larger ethnographic study (Foley, 1990) details how the football ritual was also tied to student status groups, dating, friendship, and social mobility patterns. Local sports, especially football, are still central to the socialization of each new generation of youth and to the maintenance of the adolescent society's status system. In addition, this ritual is also central to the preservation of the community's adult status hierarchy. The local politics of the booster club, adult male peer groups, and Saturday morning coffee klatches ensnare coaches and turn a son's participation in the football ritual into an important symbolic reenactment of the father's social class and gender prominence.

Despite continuous claims about the autonomous and liberating effects of organized sports, this study appears to indicate that organized sports, as presently practiced at the community level, is still a rather archaic, conservative force in our society. This is not to claim that sport is an inherently conservative popular culture practice in the sense that Critcher (1986) seems to suggest. Following Gruneau (1983) and Bourdieu (1988), I would argue that sport, like all cultural practices, is never intrinsically reactionary or progressive. Each cultural context or habitus of practices has a history and set of traditions that can either endure or change, depending upon what the people living out that tradition choose to do. These data suggest the emergence of some forms of human agency and autonomy. There were Mexicano, female, and working-class challenges to the maintaining of traditional forms of dominance through local sports practices.

Nevertheless, it is clear that such challenges have done little to transform the everyday culture that this major community ritual enacts. The football ritual continues to stage North Town's contemporary system of class dominance and its archaic system of patriarchal dominance. The transformation of sports at the community level will require a deeper cultural change in this community socialization process that re-creates each new generation. Without political movements that are stronger than the Chicano civil rights movement, local sport scenes like North Town's will not easily become sites of progressive, counterhegemonic forces.

Notes

1 The distinction here is between a community and a subculture or lifestyle group. A historical community is a geopolitical territory that has its own political, economic, and cultural systems – a collective of people who share a set of memories and traditions about past political, economic, and cultural practices. A subculture of sports enthusiasts such as surfers or skiers do not live in and share a community mode of production and its traditional social structure of class, gender, and racial dominance.
2 The community study includes a historical analysis of how the county's political economy evolved into a fully capitalist mode of agricultural production and a major recomposition of social classes. This economic transformation engenders ethnic politics and the gradual dismantling of this capitalist racial order. The community study also analyzes how these broader transformations affect the local youth scene and race relations in the high school.
3 The firing-up-the-team pun was actually a fairly good explanation of the bonfire. It was a kind of tribal fire around which the community war dance was held. The event was preparing these young warriors for battle, and the cheerleaders and band replaced painted dancers and tom tom drums. In addition, the fire was a kind of community hearth. At least some people were literally returning to the "home fires" of their village and tribe.
4 This South Texas rite of passage was beautifully portrayed in Peter Bogdanovich's *The Last Picture Show*, which is based on a novel by Larry McMurtry.
5 This is of course the classic defense often used to condone the drinking and vandalism of privileged college fraternity kids.

References

Babcock, B. (Ed.) (1978). *The reversible world: Symbolic inversion in art and society*. Ithaca, NY: Cornell University Press.

Bennett, T.C., Mercer, C., & Wollacott, J. (1986). *Popular culture and social relations*. Milton Keynes: Open University Press.

Birrell, S. (1984). Studying gender in sport: Issues, insights, and struggle. In N. Theberge & P. Donnelly (Eds.), *Sport and the sociological imagination* (pp. 125–135). Fort Worth: Texas Christian University Press.

Birrell, S. (1989). Race relations theories and sport: Suggestions for a more critical analysis. *Sociology of Sport Journal*, **6**, 212–227.

Bourdieu, P. (1988). Program for a sociology of sport. *Sociology of Sport Journal*, **5**, 153–161.

Chambers, I. (1986). Popular culture: The metropolitan experience. London: Methuen.

Critcher, C. (1986). Radical theorists of sport: The state of play. *Sociology of Sport Journal*, **3**, 333–343.

Deem, R. (1988). "Together we stand, divided we fall"; Social criticism and the sociology of sport and leisure. *Sociology of Sport Journal*, **5**, 341–354.

Donnelly, P., & Young, K. (1988). The construction and confirmation of identity in sport subcultures. *Sociology of Sport Journal*, **5**, 223–240.

Dundes, A. (1978). Into the endzone for a touchdown: A psychoanalytic consideration of American football. *Western Folklore*, **37**, 75–88.

Fine, G.A. (1987). *With the boys: Little League baseball and preadolescent culture*. Chicago: University of Chicago Press.

Fiske, J. (1989a). *Understanding popular culture*. Boston: Unwin Hyman.

Fiske, J. (1989b). *Reading the popular*. Boston: Unwin Hyman.

Foley, D. (1990). *Learning capitalist culture: Deep in the heart of Tejas*. Philadelphia: University of Pennsylvania Press.

Foley, D., with Mota, C., Post, D., & Lozano, I. (1988). *From peones to politicos: Class and ethnicity in a south Texas town, 1900–1987*. Austin: University of Texas Press.

Gruneau, R. (1983). *Class, sports, and social development*. Amherst: The University of Massachusetts Press.

Gruneau, R. (1988). Introduction: Notes on popular culture and political practice. In R. Gruneau (Ed.), *Popular cultures and political practices* (pp. 11–32). Toronto: Garamond Press.

Hall, M.A. (1984). Toward a feminist analysis of gender inequality it sport. In N. Theberge & P. Donnelly (Eds.), *Sport and the sociological imagination* (pp. 82–103). Fort Worth: Texas Christian University Press.

Hall, M.A. (1985). Knowledge and gender: Epistemological questions in the social analysis of sport. *Sociology of Sport Journal*, **2**, 25–42.

Hargreaves, J. (1986). *Sport, power and culture: A social and historical analysis of popular sports in Britain*. London: St. Martins Press.

Loy, J.W., & Ingham, A.G. (1973). Play, games, and sport in the psychosocial development of children and youth. In G.L. Rarick (Ed.), *Physical activity – Human growth and development* (pp. 257–302). New York: Academic Press.

McKay, J. (1986). Marxism as a way of seeing: Beyond the limits of current critical approaches to sport. *Sociology of Sport Journal*, **3**, 261–272.

Messner, M. (1988). Sports and male domination: the female athlete as contested ideologicla terrain. *Sociology of Sport Journal*, **3**, 261–272.

Turner, V. (1974). *Dramas, fields, and metaphors: Symbolic action in human societies*. Ithaca, NY: Cornell University Press.

Whitson, D. (1984). Sport and hegemony: On the construction of the dominant culture. *Sociology of Sport Journal*, **1**, 64–78.

56

CLASSISM IN SPORT

The powerless bear the burden

D. Stanley Eitzen

Source: *Journal of Sport and Social Issues* 20(1) (1996): 95–105.

Robert Hutchins, in his 1976 critique of U.S. governmental policy, characterized the basic principle guiding internal affairs as: The powerless disproportionately bear the burden (p. 4). Examples of this principle (see Eitzen
& Baca Zinn, 1994, p. 48) outside of sport are (a) the draft, which is really a
tax on the poor because they are more likely to be drafted and more likely
than the more advantaged to be killed or injured during military duty; (b) the
poor who absorb, disproportionately, the costs of societal changes such as
being dislocated by urban renewal, the building of expressways, and parks;
(c) the common solution for runaway inflation is to increase the amount of
unemployment; and (d) society's tolerance of a "moderate" unemployment
rate, not just during economic downturns, because this benefits the capitalist
class by creating a reserve army of the unemployed, which depresses wages
and weakens unions.

A common argument is that sports provide the poor with a mechanism for
upward mobility. This is true, of course, but in a very limited way for the
truly gifted. In reality though, sports, just as the other institutions of society,
provide a setting where the "poor pay more." Two assumptions guide this
inquiry. The underlying assumption is that the stratification system of society has consequences for sport, with advantage begetting advantage and disadvantage begetting disadvantage. Second, I am committed to moving sport
and society in a more humane direction. Therefore, I seek policies that move
us toward equity.

What follows are examples of how the relatively powerless in society bear
more than their share of the burden. Although there are many instances of
this in sport, this article is limited to four examples: (a) subsidized public
arenas, (b) the unequal costs of spectatorship, (c) the exploitation of big-
time college gladiators, and (d) the unequal financing of public schools and

333

their sport programs. The issues raised in this article are broader than sport. Examining them in the sport context is intended to sharpen our focus about inequities in society.

Subsidized public arenas

When cities build stadiums for sports teams, several decisions have negative consequences for the economically disadvantaged. The first decision is whether to build or refurbish a sports arena. This expensive subsidy for team owners may have economic benefits for the business climate in the community, but there is also a downside. That is, when communities subsidize teams with arenas, skyboxes, practice facilities, access roads to expressways, low rents, and the like, they may deplete their budgets leaving less money for schools, parks, street maintenance, and police protection. Thus, whereas the cities budget monies to aid sports teams and businesses that benefit from them, city services that help everyone, especially the poor, may be reduced (for the situation in Cleveland, see Bartimole, 1994).

The building of public arenas involves another inequity. These arenas, although subsidized by public moneys from all residents, have sexist connotations. That is, these arenas "constitute a massive subsidization and celebration of the interests of men" (Kidd, 1990, p. 32). In the words of Mariah Burton Nelson (1994):

> We live in a country in which the manly sports culture is so pervasive we may fail to recognize the symbolic messages we all receive about men, women, love, sex, and power. We need to take sports seriously— not the scores or the statistics, but the process. Not to focus on who wins, but on who's losing. Who loses when a community spends millions of dollars in tax revenue to construct a new stadium and only men get to play in it, and only men get to work there?
>
> (p. 8)

To answer Nelson's question: The losers are women—an already disadvantaged social category.

The second decision concerning the new arena is how it will be financed. Often a seat tax is imposed on all events within the city (orchestra, ballet, theater, and sports). This tax is regressive because the same amount is charged, regardless of the cost of the seat. Thus the poor pay more if they attend events. Another strategy is a sales tax to finance the building of arenas. The problem with a sales tax, of course, is that is it is a regressive tax, with the poor paying more in relative terms.

The third decision by city leaders involves the location of the new arena. Urban arenas are usually located on relatively inexpensive land. When this occurs poor people are often displaced. Two examples of this dismantling of poor neighborhoods for new arenas are occurring in Atlanta as that city prepares for the 1996 Olympics (Appelbome, 1994) and the building of Coors Field in lower downtown Denver. In the latter case, the placement of the new stadium has not only displaced the poor by the razing of their cheap apartment buildings for the field itself but it has also driven up property values dramatically in the surrounding area, thus raising rents and intensifying gentrification. This, of course, further displaces the poor as affluent renters and businesses take over the surrounding area. The result is that, although the new arena and its surroundings increase community pride, it also reduces the stock of low-cost housing, displaces poor individuals and families, destroying their social networks and viable neighborhoods in the process (Timmer, Eitzen, & Talley, 1994).

Policy recommendations

Municipalities have three options regarding the subsidization of professional teams. I will take these in ascending order (by my values), with the policy implications for each alternative. If city governments choose to build public arenas at public expense to lure or retain professional teams, then I recommend the following policies to negate the tendency of present policies to burden the powerless disproportionately: (a) progressive taxation to fund the subsidies, with a floor that exempts from taxes those below a certain threshold (e.g., $20,000 in annual family income); (b) a special tax on those businesses that benefit especially from having a professional team in the community (e.g., restaurants, hotels, transportation); and (c) when neighborhoods and low-cost housing are demolished for the building of new arenas, the cities must relocate those affected adversely in a suitable area with amenities such as parks better than what they left, provide low-cost housing, and compensate those affected for their sacrifice.

A second option for cities is city, county, or regional ownership rather than the current arrangement where individuals own a team. Under the present system, owners sometimes threaten to leave if they do not get better facilities, with other cities then bidding through ever escalating promises of generous subsidies. With community ownership of a team, the threat to leave is a moot point and the "arena arms race" will slow or even shut down, thus reducing the cost of subsidies.

The third option for cities is to get out of the professional team business. If cities must satisfy their urge to subsidize the affluent, then instead of revitalizing cities with shiny arenas for their professional teams, monies could be redirected toward revitalizing cities by subsidizing industries to the community that create good-paying jobs. Further, the cities could commit to the provision of better services, especially education in the inner city. The cities under these circumstances would be safer, with more hopeful and secure citizens from the top to the bottom of the socioeconomic strata.

The unequal cost of spectatorship

In 1990, Ronald Reagan received the Theodore Roosevelt Award, the highest honor bestowed on an individual by the National Collegiate Athletic Association. In his acceptance speech, Reagan said,

> When men and women compete on the athletics field, socioeconomic status disappears. Black or white, Christian or Jew, rich or poor . . . all that matters is that you're out there on the field giving your all. It's the same way in the stands, where corporate presidents sit next to janitors . . . and they high-five each other when their team scores . . . which makes me wonder if it [status] should matter at all. (cited in "Athletics a Great Equalizer," 1990, p. 1)

This observation, of course, is incredibly naive. Examining the last part, on the blurring of social class in the stands, two observations are noteworthy. First, the cost of attending sports contests is too costly for the poor, who, we need to remind ourselves, help to pay for the arenas in which the contests occur through sales taxes (used to fund the building of Coors Field in Denver and the Ballpark in Arlington, Texas) and "sin taxes" on tobacco and alcohol (which will pay for 48% of the cost of Jacobs Field in Cleveland). The 1994 average cost of tickets for National Football League (NFL) ranged from $39.75 for the 49ers to $25 for the Jets. In 1994 a day at an NFL game for a family of four averaged $184.19 (four tickets, two small beers, four small sodas, four hot dogs, parking, two game programs, and two twill caps) (Associated Press, 1994; Schefter, 1994). Baseball is cheaper, but at a ticket price at the lower end of the range at $10 or so, a family of four would spend about $75 for an evening's entertainment. At big-time college football and basketball programs, seats may be available only after a sizable contribution to the Athletic Department. These costs will likely keep the poorest away from the sports arenas except as workers (vendors, janitors). Even if the poor could afford seats for regular events, they are priced out completely from premier events. Because these games are sold out (with corporate sponsors holding huge blocks of seats), scalpers sell the precious few remaining seats at premium prices (1994 Super Bowl tickets with a face value of $175 sold for as much as $1,200; the 1994 Stanley Cup finals tickets with a face value of $125 brought as much as $5,000 at Madison Square Garden) (Castro, 1994; Madden, 1994). Sizing up this unfair situation, John Underwood (1993) has argued that the high cost of going to sports events had denied the underclass and even the lower-middle class from attending them.

For those attending sports events, seating is segregated by cost. Contrary to President Reagan's characterization, the rich and the middle classes do not sit side by side. The very rich are in luxury suites that cost from $50,000 to $200,000 a season. At basketball games, the affluent may sit in $500 courtside seats. The less well-to-do are dispersed by cost of seating, with the cheapest seats far from the action. The poor, of course, are not in the seats at all.

Three points are significant to this discussion. First, the high cost of seating in publicly subsidized arenas keeps some citizens, the poorest, from attending. This, despite their taxes that subsidized the building of these arenas and even the construction of the luxury suites that are exclusively for the very affluent. Second, the building of new arenas or the refurbishing of older ones, which usually means the construction of more luxury suites, and even costlier tickets, which, of course, shuts out the poor even more (Lopez, 1994). Finally, the affluent are often able to write off the purchase of tickets or luxury suites as a business expense, thus reducing their actual cost. The less well-to-do wage earners are not able to use the tax code to reimburse them in part for their tickets to sports events. The effect in this case is that the latter subsidize the former.

Policy recommendations

Ironically, even though communities under the current arrangements subsidize the owners of professional teams, they receive little in return (token rents, or perhaps a portion of the parking revenues). City governments should insist as part of the bargain that admission, parking, and concession prices be kept at a minimum so they would be more affordable to a larger portion of the community. This goal could also be accomplished by setting aside a generous portion of low-cost tickets. Also, cities should insist that fewer season tickets be sold so that a larger number of community citizens would have the opportunity to attend games. Finally, I recommend that the tax code be amended to eliminate the write-offs that affluent individuals and businesses receive for their purchase of sports tickets.

The exploitation of big-time college gladiators

The athletes in big-time college sports programs, by which I mean men's football and basketball programs at the National Collegiate Athletic Association (NCAA) Division I level, are dissimilar from the rest of their fellow students. They differ, of course, in size, strength, speed, and coordination; but, more to the point of this article, they differ by social-class origins. Three empirical observations underscore this crucial difference. A study by Allen Sack and Robert Thiel (1979) compared football players with nonathletes who had graduated from Notre Dame between 1946 and 1965 and found that the football players had come from poorer backgrounds. Second, the research by Peter Adler and Patty Adler (1985) of basketball players at a major school from 1980 to 1984 found that the athletes were isolated culturally by their racial and socioeconomic differences from the rest of the students. Third, African Americans comprise 60% of athletic scholarship holders in Division I basketball and 43% of them in Division I football (Lederman, 1992). Many of these Black athletes come from rural and urban pockets of poverty.

Herein lies the contradiction: The male athletes in big-time sports programs are disproportionately poor *and they are kept poor by NCAA rules*, yet they generate huge sums of money for the NCAA, various corporations, their schools, and their coaches. Full-scholarship athletes receive room, board, books, and tuition. To maintain the guise of amateur sport, the athletes are not allowed to work during the school year. They are not permitted to promote themselves through advertising or writing articles or books. Finally, they are not permitted to have financial consultants or agents prior to turning professional. The athletes must, according to the NCAA, be amateurs who are untainted by money. But this is a charade, as George Sage (1990) has argued:

> In reality, the scholarship is nothing but a work contract. What colleges are really doing is hiring entertainers. The deceit of claiming that educational purposes preclude salaried compensation for athletic performances is testimony to the extensive attempts of the collegiate establishment to avoid its financial responsibilities. Athletic scholarships are actually a form of economic exploitation, the establishment of a wage below the poverty level for student-athlete-entertainers who directly produce millions of dollars for athletic departments. . . . Paying as little as possible to operate a business is called keeping overhead low; it's what every business owner strives to do. The NCAA and major universities have mastered this principle. No other American business operates so pretentiously, making huge sums of money but insisting the enterprise be viewed as an educational service. (pp. 179–180)

These "amateur" athletes in big-time programs generate considerable wealth for others. A few examples make this point:

- Item: About $2.5 billion a year in college merchandise (e.g., caps, sweats, beer mugs) is sold under license, with an estimated $100 million going to the schools in royalties. In 1993 the University of Michigan's athletic department took in nearly $5.8 million from these royalties (17% of its athletic budget) (Rubin, 1994).
- Item: Big-time programs such as Michigan and Ohio State have annual athletic budgets in excess of $20 million, with almost all of the money generated from the men's football and basketball programs.
- Item: Each school in the 1994 Rose Bowl received $6.5 million, and each school in the Orange Bowl received $4.2 million. The total amount

paid to schools teams competing in postseason bowls exceeded $68 million.

- Item: The Columbia Broadcasting System (CBS) agreed to pay the NCAA $1 billion over 7 years ($143 million annually) for the television rights to the NCAA men's basketball tournament. In turn, General Motors agreed to pay CBS $400 million to be the exclusive advertiser of automobiles during those telecasts.
- Item: One school, Louisiana State University, through its athletics generates more than $65 million in sales for local merchants, another $25.5 million in household earnings, and supports 1,616 jobs in the Baton Rouge area ("Louisiana State Athletics," 1991).
- Item: Former Nevada-Las Vegas basketball coach Rollie Massimino's contract provided him with a compensation package of nearly $1 million a year ("Paper Says," 1994).
- Item: It was reported widely in 1993 that Mike Krzyzewski, basketball coach at Duke, received a $1 million bonus plus $375,000 per year for 15 years from Nike for having his players wear its shoes.

The wealth generated by college athletes, except for room, board, tuition, and books, is kept from them. Obviously, they are being exploited. The athletes are, as George Sage (1990) has suggested, amateurs in a big business environment. The average professional basketball player in 1994 made $1.4 million; the average professional football player made more than $700,000. College athletes, on the other hand, receive scholarships worth, depending on the institution, between $8,000 and $20,000. Top players are especially exploited. A study of Patrick Ewing's value to Georgetown University during his 4 years has been estimated at more than $12 million (Leslie, 1986). Economist Robert Brown has estimated that each player drafted in the National Basketball Association (NBA) produced about $1 million in *annual* revenues to his university, and each draftee into professional football netted his university more than $500,000 a year while he was in school (Blum, 1994).

The common argument is that student-athletes receive a college education, which is invaluable. This, however, is not true for two thirds of Black male athletes and 4 out of 10 White male athletes in big-time programs. NCAA data, using 6 years from entering school to graduate, show that only 33% of Black male basketball players had graduated (compared with 62% of White male players), and 34% of Black football players had graduated, compared with 58% of White players (Stacey, 1993).

In sum, many young men in big-time programs toil for minimum wages, whereas others prosper greatly from their labors. Many are physically injured in their jobs as athletes. Many do not even receive a college education. Most, of course, do not make it to the professional level. We must conclude, regrettably, that athletes in big-time programs who are disproportionately from disadvantaged backgrounds are exploited by their institutions.

Policy recommendations

I have two suggestions. First, athletes should receive fair compensation for the revenues they generate. Clearly, these scholarship recipients are not amateurs but, just as clearly, they are not well-paid professionals either. In addition to what they now receive, athletes should receive a monthly wage determined by a relatively small percentage of the monies generated from their sport, medical and dental insurance, eligibility for Worker's Compensation (the NCAA has fought this because, if players were eligible, they would be classified as workers rather than students), money for travel home twice a year, and money for their parents to visit the campus and attend games twice a year. Those athletes from economically disadvantaged backgrounds should also receive a supplementary stipend for incidentals, clothing, and entertainment.

Second, schools must provide a supportive climate to assist their athletes achieve a meaningful college experience and graduation. To the degree that athletes were truly student-athletes and universities were truly committed to the intellectual growth of their athletes, then big-time sport would be less exploitive.

Unequal financing of public school sports programs

Public school financing in the United States depends, for the most part, on the wealth of property within school districts. Schools receive some federal money, more state money, and, typically, about half of their budget from local property taxes. The result is a wide disparity in per-pupil expenditures among the states and within each state. The use of property taxes is discriminatory because rich school districts can spend more money than poor ones on each student, yet *at a lower taxing rate*. This last point is important— poor districts have higher mill levies than wealthy districts, yet they raise less money *because they are poor*. Thus those with property in poor districts make a greater sacrifice for the education of their children than do those with property in wealthier districts. The result is that suburban students are more advantaged than are students from the inner city, districts with business enterprises are favored over agricultural districts, and districts with natural resources are better able to provide for their children than are those districts with few resources (see Kozol, 1991). In Texas, for example, in 1992 the spending for each pupil ranged from $3,190 in the poorest school district to $11,801 in the richest school district (Cellis, 1992).

These disparities by school district have ramifications for sport. Wealthy districts provide more sports opportunities, more coaches, and better facilities and equipment than do the poorer districts. In the metropolitan Chicago area, for example, suburban schools in 1992 had sports budgets (not counting coaches' salaries) in excess of $200,000, whereas the city schools

340

each had sports budgets of only $750. Whereas the wealthy suburban schools had as many as 23 sports and state-of-the-art weight-training facilities, the have-nots, the schools in Chicago, had to do without adequate gymnasiums and weight rooms. They use public transportation to get to games. Their equipment is shabby. They have fewer and less well-paid coaches than do the suburban schools. Money must be raised through donations and car washes and from using the profits from candy and soda pop machines (Bell, 1992).

A common strategy for districts with inadequate budgets is to impose a fee to participate in sports. This "pay for play" cost is a flat fee (the average fee per sport across the United States in 1994 was $85), which, of course, is regressive. The financially strapped schools may also require athletes to provide some or all of their own equipment to participate. These regressive policies tend to restrict the opportunities for the poor to play.

Policy recommendations

The Supreme Court, regrettably, has ruled that school financing is a state issue, not a federal one. Therefore, it is up to state legislatures and state courts to work toward equity. These efforts are under way in many states but they typically meet resistance from the wealthier districts, which not so incidentally have more political power than the poorer districts. It seems obvious that a nation founded on the principle of "equality of opportunity" must provide this through more or less equal funding for schools.

Meanwhile, although schools remain unequal in funding, efforts must be used to reduce the burden on the poor. In metropolitan areas, suburban schools should be combined with urban schools into metropolitan school districts to equalize monies. Taxation to fund schools must be progressive. Also, if a program is deemed to have important educational outcomes—for example, interscholastic sports—then it should be provided to all children without cost to them in the form of fees or the provision of their own equipment.

To conclude, let me end, as I began, by paraphrasing Robert Hutchins. Hutchins (1976) argued that for freedom and justice to occur, all citizens must have equal access to educational opportunities, the legal system, health care, and housing.

Hutchins did not include sport in his discussion. He should have, because sport, just as the other institutions of society, reflects the inequalities and injustices found in society.

References

Adler, P., & Adler, P.A. (1985, October). From idealism to pragmatic detachment: The academic performance of college athletes. *Sociology of Education, 58,* 241–250.

Appelbome, P. (1994, October 9). An olympic renewal? Atlanta's big question. *New York Times*, p. 14.

Associated Press. (1994, August 9). NFL fans dig deep. *Fort Collins Coloradoan*, p. D1.

Athletics a great equalizer, Reagan tells NCAA. (1990, January 10), *NCAA News*, pp. 1–2.

Bartimole, R. (1994, June). If you build it, we will stay. *The Progressive, 58*, 28–31.

Bell, T. (1992, October 11). Chicago high schools have- nots of sports. *Chicago Sun-Times*, pp. 42A–43A.

Blum, D.E. (1994, April 13). Top players produce up to $1-million in revenue for their universities. *The Chronicle of Higher Education*, pp. A33–A34.

Castro, J. (1994, June 20). Rock "n" roll's holy war. *Time*, pp. 48–49.

Cellis, W.III. (1992, February 12). A Texas-size battle to rich and poor alike. *New York Times*, p. B8.

Eitzen, D.S., & Baca Zinn, M. (1994). *Social problems* (6th ed.) Boston: Allyn & Bacon.

Hutchins, R.M. (1976, January/February). Is democracy possible? *Center Magazine*, pp. 2–6.

Kidd, B. (1990). The men's cultural centre: Sports and the dynamic of women's oppression/men's repression. In M. A. Messner & D. F. Sabo (Eds.), *Sport, men, and the gender order* (pp. 31–43). Champaign, IL: Human Kinetics.

Kozol, J. (1991). *Savage inequalities: Children in America's schools*. New York: Crown.

Lederman, D. (1992, June 17). Blacks make up large proportion of scholarship athletes, yet their overall enrollment lags at Division I colleges. *The Chronicle of Higher Education*, pp. Al, A30–A34.

Leslie, G. (1986, January). Pick-and-bankroll. *Regardie's*, p. 17.

Lopez, C. (1994, August 25). New arenas often mean costlier tickets. *Denver Post*, p. 3B.

Louisiana State athletics shown to be an economic catalyst (1991, June 5), *NCAA News*, p. 5.

Madden, M. (1994, January 31). Scalpers able to name their price. *Boston Globe*, p. 45.

Nelson, M.B. (1994). *The stronger men get, the more men love football: Sexism and the American culture of sports*. New York: Harcourt Brace Jovanovich.

Paper says Massimino has secret deal. (1994, August 18), *USA Today*, p. 8C.

Rubin, D. (1994, September 11). You've seen the game. Now buy the underwear. *New York Times*, p. F5.

Sack, A.L., & Thiel, R. (1979, January). College football and social mobility: A case study of Notre Dame football players. *Sociology of Education, 52*, 60–66.

Sage, G.H. (1990). *Power and ideology in American sport: A critical perspective*. Champaign, IL: Human Kinetics.

Schefter, A. (1994, January 30), Broncos seats get pricier. *Rocky Mountain News*, pp. B1, B6.

Stacey, J. (1993, May 20). A look at graduation rates. *USA Today*, p. 10C.

Timmer, D.A., Eitzen, D.S., & Talley, K.D. (1994). Paths to homelessness: Extreme poverty and the urban housing crisis. Boulder, CO: Westview.

Underwood, J. (1993, October 31). From baseball and apple pie, to greed and sky boxes. *New York Times*, p. 22.

Part 16

SPORT AND THE BODY

57

THE BODY IN CULTURE
AND SPORT

John W. Loy, David L. Andrews and Robert E. Rinehart

Source: *Sport Science Review* 2 (1993): 69–91.

Drawing upon a review of related literature, our primary purpose in this paper is to outline and highlight the socially significant aspects of the body, with particular reference to active sport participation. First, we begin with an overview of social studies of the body during the past decade. Second, we focus on the social import of a variety of body techniques developed and displayed in sport situations. Third, we center attention on the self-control and the social control of the body in sport via institutionalized ideological and material constraints. Fourth, we address how sporting fields are contested terrains for the sociocultural construction, embodiment, and experienced meaning of class, gender, and race. Fifth, we review research concerning body politics and sport in modernity and postmodernity in the context of consumer culture.

The explicit purpose of our review is to highlight the socially significant aspects of the body with reference to sport involvement. The underlying premise is that the human body comprises the chief corporeal component of sporting practices. As Hargreaves (1987) well notes,

> Although the degree of physical input varies from sport to sport, the primary focus of attention in sport overall, is *the body and its attributes . . . it is the body* that constitutes the most striking symbol, as well as constituting the material core of sporting activity
>
> (p. 141, italics added)

Granted the premise that the body is the corporeal core of sport, an implicit objective of our review is to emphasize the prerequisites for a fully embodied sociology of sport.

Toward an embodied sociology of sport

In this first section of our review we note the non-body bias of sociology in general and sport sociology in particular; we suggest several reasons for the disembodied perspectives of general sociology and sport sociology; we list the major influences stimulating a marked interest in the scholarly study of the body during the past decade; we cite recent attempts to incorporate an embodied self into sociological theory; and we give a framework for the following sections of our review.

Absent bodies

In an essay titled "Bringing Society Into the Body," Freund (1988) starkly states,

> The subject matter of the social sciences is supposedly living, breathing human creatures of flesh and blood. Yet both psychology and anthropology,[1] as well as sociology in particular have a curiously "disembodied" view of human beings.
>
> (p. 839)

It is not entirely clear as to why the social sciences in general, and sociology in particular, have had a non-body bias, but a number of reasons have been offered. Freund (1988), for example, suggests that "Social science, in . . . dualistic thinking so characteristic of Western thought, assigns mind priority over body, and severs it from its embodied from" (p. 839).

Turner (1984), with specific reference to sociology, makes three telling observations about disembodied social theory. First, he records that "Any reference to the corporeal nature of human existence raises in the mind of the sociologist the specter of social Darwinism, biological reductionism or sociobiology" (p. 1). Second, he points out that "There exists a theoretical prudery with respect to human corporeality which constitutes an analytical gap at the core of sociological inquiry" (p. 30). Third, with respect to different levels of sociological analysis, he notes that "micro-sociology excludes the body because the self as social actor is socially constructed in action, macro-sociology excludes the body because its theoretical focus is on the 'social system' " (p. 33).

Most important for present considerations is the fact that the non-body bias of general sociology is also characteristic of sport sociology. As Theberge (1991) points out in a paper titled "Reflections on the Body in the Sociology of Sport,"

> In a quest to establish the social significance of sport . . . this field has had little to say about the body. It is ironic that in studying sport,

346

where the body is essential to the experience, we have largely missed its meaning and importance.[2]

(p. 124)

Perhaps sport sociologists have overlooked the body per se because they have been negatively influenced in two ways. On the one hand, they have been exposed to the non-body bias of general sociology just discussed. On the other hand, they have also been exposed to the disembodied discourses of physical education associated with its "scientization" (Whitson & Macintosh, 1990), performance enhancement ethos (Harris, 1992; Sage, 1992), and hegemonic image of the body-as-machine (Lawson, 1988; McKay, Gore, & Kirk, 1990).

However, notwithstanding the legacy of disembodied sociological discourses about society, sport, and culture, bodies are currently very much in fashion within many areas of the humanities and social sciences. Within the past dozen years bodies have come out of the closets of academia, and there is currently a boom in social studies of the body, as evidenced by the proliferation of publications on the topic of the body.

Bringing bodies back in

Frank (1990), in an article titled "Bringing Bodies Back In: A Decade Review," suggests that the relatively recent scholarly interest in the body stems largely from three forms of influence, namely feminism, the work of Michel Foucault, and "the contradictory impulses of modernity" (p. 132). In a more recent and more analytical review, Frank (1991) contends that "Current interest in the body as a topic of investigation seems to have proximate sources, which can be roughly labelled as modernism, postmodernism, and feminism" (p. 39).

In addition, we mention other forms of influence that we believe have excited interest in the sociological study of the body: (a) the re-reading of essays by Erving Goffman; (b) the re-discovery of the early writings of Norbert Elias; (c) the increased attention given to the contemporary work of Pierre Bourdieu; (d) recent alternative conceptualizations of paradigms in medical sociology and heightened interest in the sociology of emotions; (e) increased concern with aging and physically challenged populations; (f) the bodily problematics of consumer culture; and (g) the bodily implications of social controversies surrounding the problems of AIDS, women's reproductive rights, and men's sexual violence toward women.

These various forms of influence have resulted in renewed interest in the significance of the body for social practices in everyday life, and in re-evaluation of the importance of incorporating the body into sociological theory. Although one cannot readily point to a fully embodied sociological theory, several systematic sociological typologies of the body have been

347

produced which we believe contain the basic elements for developing a fully embodied social theory of human action.

Examples of recent typologies of the body include Turner (1984), O'Neill (1985), Feher, Naddaff, and Tazi (1989a, 1989b, 1989c), Frank (1990, 1991), and Maguire (1991). Within these materials, the most systematic sociological analysis of the body is given by Bryan Turner in *The Body and Society*. In brief, he argues,

> a sociology of the body is a study of the problem of social order and it can be organized around four issues. These are the reproduction and regulation of populations in time and space, and the restraint and representation of the body as a vehicle of the self.
>
> (1984, p. 41)

The import of Turner's functional framework for the sociology of sport is discussed by Theberge (1991) with special reference to sport involvement for women.

Frank (1991) argues that "Turner begins with the body as a functional problem for a society" (p. 47); while he proposes "instead to begin with how the body is a problem *for itself*, which is an action problem from a phenomenological orientation rather than a functional one" (p. 47). For Frank " 'the body' is constituted in the intersection of an equilateral triangle the points of which are *institutions, discourses and corporeality*" (p. 49).

Frank constructs four ideal-typical forms of body use in action, which he treats in terms of related sets of dimensions, mediums of activity, and action problems (addressed as questions) as follows: (a) The *body disciplined* represents the control dimension, within the medium of regimentation, wherein "The body must ask itself how predictable its performance will be" (p. 51). (b) The *mirroring body* represents the desire dimension, within the medium of consumption, wherein "the question is whether the body is lacking or producing" (p. 51). (c) The *dominating body* represents the relation-to-others dimension, within the medium of force, wherein the question is "Does the body relate to itself as monadic and closed in upon itself, or as dyadic, existing in relation of mutual constitution with others?" (p. 52). (d) The *communicative body* represents the self-relatedness dimension, within the medium of recognition, wherein the question is "Does the body consciousness associate with its own being, particularly its surface, or dissociate itself from that corporeality?" (p. 52).

Although Frank's conceptions of embodied action can be critically challenged (Maguire, 1991), we heuristically employ his topology of body use in action in order to organize our review of research related to the body in sport situations. Thus the four substantive sections of our review which follow address the communicative body, the disciplined body, the dominating body, and the mirroring body, respectively.

348

Communicative bodies and sport subcultures

Keeping with Frank's essential elements of the communicative body, we center attention in this section on the body's relation to others in terms of the medium of activity that Frank loosely labels recognition. Our review of related literature, however, is a very selective one. Specifically, within the context of sport subcultures, we focus on the body techniques and tactics related to career contingencies, and on the body styles and strategies associated with identity construction and character confirmation.

Body techniques and tactics

Marcel Mauss' essay titled "Techniques of the Body" (1973 [1935]), based on a lecture given at a meeting of the French Society of Psychology in 1934, represents the classical treatise on the subject. His several classifications of body techniques are now perhaps only of historical interest, but his concept of (body) habitus is a modern one. For Mauss, all body techniques, including athletic activities like climbing, running, and swimming, involve "physio-psycho-sociological assemblages of series of actions" (p. 85) which are more or less habitual. Presaging contemporary commentary on body habitus by sociologists such as Elias, Bourdieu, and Wacquant, Mauss observes,

> These "habits" do not just vary with individuals and their imitations, they vary especially between societies, educations, proprieties and fashions, prestiges. In them we should see the technique and work of collective and individual practical reason.
>
> (1973, p. 73)

The bio-psycho-sociological complex of body techniques is especially characteristic of the career contingencies associated with job related skills and traits in occupational sport subcultures.

By way of illustration, we cite studies of somewhat deviant occupational sport subcultures wherein the communicative body is often a deceitful one, and wherein athletes must often paradoxically disguise their true skills and athletic abilities. A classic case is Polsky's (1964, 1967) study of the poolroom hustler. He states that "the hustler's cardinal rule is: *don't show your real speed*" (1967, p. 52), and adds,

> The corollaries of the hustler's chief rule are: (a) The hustler must restrain himself from making many of the extremely difficult shots. Such restraint is not easy, because the thrill of making a fancy shot that brings applause from the audience is hard to resist. But the hustler must resist, or else it would make less believable his misses on

349

more ordinary shots. (b) He must play so that the games he wins are won by only a small margin. (c) He must let his opponent win an occasional game.

(1967, pp. 52–53)

Polsky (1967) further describes bodily job related skills and traits of the hustler such as having "heart" (courage) and stamina, and possessing a repertoire of bodily short-con techniques such as "pretending to be sloppy-drunk" (pp. 54–56).

Body communication strategies are also characteristic of the professional jockey. Scott (1968, pp. 42–43) points out that a jockey must simultaneously attempt to please fans, horsemen, and officials when these three separate audiences frequently make conflicting demands regarding performance expectations. He notes, however,

> What ever the orders, the jockey must at least *appear* to be riding energetically and cleanly. To bring off these appearances the jockey has developed certain communication strategies—*dramatic accentuation* and *concealment* or a combination of both.
>
> (p. 43)

An example of dramatic accentuation that may involve concealment is the jockey who pumps her or his arms furiously while riding a front running horse. Such pumping indicates an energetic effort to spectators, but it indicates to other riders that the jockey's horse will soon slow up, when in fact the jockey may actually whip the horse and speed ahead. In any event, as Scott suggests, "Even when the other jockeys suspect that pumping may be a deception, they can never be sure. Hence, at the very least, the strategy undercuts certainty" (1967, p. 44). Concealment strategies are particularly important in handicap races wherein the jockey, like the hustler, must disguise "true speed" and not win by too much (Scott, 1968, p. 44).

Professional wrestling provides additional examples of body communication strategies in a sport context. As Birrell and Turowetz (1979) indicate,

> Staging of the physical skills is an important aspect of the wrestler's world. The audience must be led to believe, however willingly, that the series of holds, moves, falls are not rehearsed. This contingency requires added levels of learning physical skill. Not only must the wrestler possess a degree of "real" physical skill, he must possess enough physical skill to provide the audience with a believable parody of legitimate wrestling.
>
> (p. 229)

In sum, the communicative strategies of the hustler, jockey, and professional wrestler highlight how body techniques are important for impression

350

management in contexts of total sport involvement. We expand upon the notion of bodily impression management in the following consideration of identity construction and character confirmation in sport subcultures.

Body styles and strategies

Drawing upon their respective ethnographies of mountain climbers (Donnelly, 1980) and rugby players (Young, 1983), Donnelly and Young (1988) offer a coherent conceptualization of the construction and confirmation of identity in sport subcultures with a special emphasis on career stages. In their discussion of the construction of identity, they highlight several bodily features of impression management. For example, they describe the bodily aspects of rookie misconceptions and gaffes; and they address the problematics of dress and demeanor in terms of subcultural identity and peer status. Related accounts of the bodily dimensions of identity construction within sport subcultures can be found in Rosenberg and Turowetz's (1975) comparison of wrestlers and physicians, Birrell and Turowetz's comparative analysis of collegiate gymnasts and professional wrestlers, and Klein's (1986) study of bodybuilders.

Donnelly and Young in their discussion of identity confirmation focus on the ways in which climbers and rugby players verify and validate their claims of physical prowess. However, except for a quote from Gross and Stone's (1964) examination of embarrassment, having obvious body implications, their account of identity construction is largely disembodied. We suggest that a focus on character confirmation rather than identity confirmation per se puts a greater body spin on matters.

The concepts of moral career, character, and character contest are implicit, if not explicit, in several ethnographies of sport subcultures. Harre, Clarke, and De Carlo (1985) note that "A moral career consists of the stages of acquisition or loss of honor and the respect due from other people as one passes through various systems of hazard characteristic of different social worlds" (p. 147). These systems of hazard constitute what Goffman (1967) refers to as contexts of action, that is, "activities that are consequential, problematic, and undertaken for what is felt to be their own sake" (p. 185). Character can only be developed and displayed in action situations involving character contests, or special kinds of moral games, in which contestants' moral attributes such as composure, courage, gameness, and integrity are displayed, tested, and subjected to social evaluation (Goffman, 1967, pp. 239–258).

Sport situations provide clear and concrete contexts for observing character and establishing moral careers through a variety of character contests. Ethnographies of sport subcultures suggest that the most highly valued character traits are those of coolness, heart, and honor. Coolness refers to poise under pressure (Goffman, 1967; Lyman & Scott, 1968). With reference to sport, Scott (1968) states that "Above all, the jockey with strong character possesses the perceived virtue of coolness" (p. 26); and Birrell and Turowetz (1979) note that "Cool competence is the mark of the superior gymnast and is displayed through face work and through body work" (p. 225).

Heart refers to courage and fighting spirit. Weinberg and Arond (1952) describe the "fighting heart" of the professional boxer; and Polsky (1967) notes that "Without exception, hustlers contend that 'heart' (courage or toughness) is as essential to hustling as playing ability is" (p. 71). Interestingly, heart is also attributed to courageous race horses (Scott, 1968, p. 18).

With respect to honor, Scott (1968) contends that "The jockey is one of the few survivals of the traditional concept of 'the man of honor' " (p. 25); and both Faulkner (1974) and Colburn (1985) describe the character testing nature of professional ice hockey and demonstrate that players engage in ritualized violence for the display of honorable, respectable occupational behavior. Their analyses also reflect the nature of disciplined bodies in sport situations with respect to both personal practices and public forms of social control.

Disciplined bodies and sporting practices

The sporting body is a key site for studying the dynamic relationship between power, knowledge, and corporeal existence. According to Hargreaves, the body is disciplined because

> Power is incorporated or invested in the body through meticulous, insistent work on people's bodies—on children in families and schools; on soldiers, prisoners and hospital patients; in the gym, or the dinner table, and in the bathroom (Foucault, 1976).
>
> (Hargreaves, 1987, p. 140).

Hence, the discursive practices surrounding sport, discipline and control the body by defining its socially preferred shape and the institutional regimes that act upon it.

Shaping the body

The body has inherent anatomical and biological constraints that are difficult, if not impossible, to modify. Nevertheless, the body can be significantly altered in terms of its shape, size, and volume; even the underlying biophysical structure of the body can be remodeled using artificial replacements for various body parts and organs. Although there is a substantive literature dealing with bodily disciplines in general, only a handful of studies in sport sociology have focused on bodywork related to personal fitness and athletic training for sport competition. However, recent ethnographic accounts of boxing and bodybuilding well illustrate the training and dietary regimes used for shaping the body.

Wacquant's (1992a; in press) studies of the bodily craft of boxing in a ghetto gym offer rich examples of a variety of regimes of body discipline. Interestingly, Wacquant (1992a) reports that boxers often compare the management of their bodies to military training, especially with respect to discipline and self-control (p. 236). He records that "The training of the boxer is an intensive exacting discipline . . . that aims at transmitting, in a practical manner, by way of *direct embodiment*, a practical mastery of the fundamental corporeal, visual, and mental schemata of boxing" (1992a, p. 237). With respect to body shaping per se, Wacquant's (in press) ethnographic research reveals numerous examples of boxers' efforts to trim down or bulk-up. Moreover, he notes, "Boxers also build a specific muscular armor through drills that enable them to reinforce and expand those parts of their body that they need most for protection (shoulders, abdominals, biceps), endurance, and punching power."

In a similar fashion, bodybuilders' overt aim is to reshape the body, to configure it to an aesthetic that transcends that of others. Aycock (1992) in his study of casual bodybuilders observes that "The lifter works upon the convexities and concavities of the flesh to discover a more powerful self . . . that is, the self even in casual training reveals a substantial being more competent, more attractive, more demanding of deference than in ordinary positionings of self and other" (p. 354). Klein (1992) in his study of elite competitive bodybuilders observes that "Contemporary elite bodybuilding has pushed the human form to its limits in terms of muscle density, symmetry, and striation" (p. 328).

In addition to following standardized training regimes in their respective sports, both boxers and bodybuilders conform to dietary regimes in efforts to shape their bodies. Dietary regimes are designed, of course, for purposes of both increasing and decreasing body weight. An extreme example of increasing body weight is the dietary regimes of sumo wrestlers, who daily consume massive amounts of food and drink in order to develop their gargantuan size (Adams & Newton, 1989, p. 58). Less dramatically, Wacquant (in press) records that Michael Spinks gained 30 pounds in 7 months by consuming three 5,500-calorie meals a day. More likely, however, boxers abide by a strict diet in order to reach their optimal fight weight (Wacquant, 1992a, p. 238).

Similarly, Bolin (1992, p. 384) notes that "The diet is regarded as an integral part of the bodybuilding lifestyle," and reports,

> When bodybuilders were asked to rank the diet in terms of its relative importance for competition, it was not uncommon for them to assign 90 to 98% of the precontest preparation, 3 to 4 months before the competition, to a strict eating program.
>
> (1992, p. 381)

Bolin further notes that "Foods prohibited during the precontest phase are those desired in the ritual binge" (p. 391) following competition.

Although perhaps not always medically correct or scientifically sound, most training and dietary regimes are perceived as proper and legitimate. But there are other procedures employed in sport to shape the body that are deviant at best and illegal at worst, as for example the use of human growth hormones and steroids.

Finally, we note that one may shape one's body—or rather, have it shaped— through surgical procedures. Such physical shaping may prolong the careers of high-level athletes. Surgery may also provide a radically new corporeality, as exemplified by Renee Richards (Birrell & Cole, 1990).

Sanctioning the body

During the course of his sociohistoric research, Michel Foucault explored various institutional settings including the asylum, the clinic, and the prison; and he studied the regimes designed to discipline and control the insane, ill, or criminal bodies that populated these institutions (Foucault, 1973, 1975, 1977). Given Foucault's intellectual interests, it is easy to see the logic behind Whitson's assertion that "the work of Foucault . . . on the discourses of discipline . . . that surround the body in modern societies, has much to offer students of sport" (1989, p. 62). And yet as Theberge (1991) points out, there have been few studies of sport, in an institutional context, that have adopted a Foucaultian perspective.

The work in this area that most explicitly utilizes Foucault's understanding of institutional regimes of bodily discipline and control has been carried out by John Hargreaves (1986, 1987) on the discourses of sport and physical education. He identifies physical education as a discipline in the Foucaultian sense of the term, in that it incorporates "strategies of control which involve the training and coercion of bodies into complying with and hence integrating into a particular hierarchical power structure" (Smart, 1985, p. 85).

Based on an in-depth genealogical analysis of the practices and ideologies surrounding the discourse of physical education in Great Britain, Hargreaves shows that "PE theory, its objectives and recommended practices, constitute a programme of control through sustained work on the body" (1986, p. 163). He points out that "The aims and objectives of physical education, as annunciated in official publications and by leading members of the profession in text and journals, not only encode, but in many cases are explicitly committed to, views concerning the nature of the social order, which find ready agreement among dominant groups" (1986, p. 164). Hargreaves shows how these official objectives, in conjunction with the actual disciplinary regimes of physical education, schools the body to accept and reproduce very definite class, gender, and ethnic divisions, identities, and experiences (1986, pp. 173–181).

Harvey and Sparks (1991) similarly drawn upon Foucault's ideas about disciplines in their analysis of how "Bodily practices such as physical education and sport are linked to political forces and indeed to the building of the modern state" (p. 40). They specifically show how the disciplines of the body centered around the discourse of gymnastics in 19th-century France acted as an emergent form "of domination and integration to the social order" (p. 35). Harvey and Sparks conclude that the sociohistoric understanding of sport and physical education, as prominent bodily practices, can only be fully realized if they are related to an understanding of the contemporary political positioning of the body.

It is often overlooked that Foucault's work on the body was preceded by Norbert Elias' (1978, 1982) understanding of the civilizing process. His analysis of this process focuses on the relationship between the microlevel (i.e., the development of constraints and controls upon bodily emotions and practices) and the macrolevel (i.e., the development of the state formation) of social discourse (Featherstone, 1987). Elias (1978, 1982) shows how the evolution of western societies from feudalism, through the emergence of the bourgeoisie, to the establishment of the modern nation-state, was concomitant with the civilizing of the body. In short, the increasing complexity, and hence influence, of the state formation came to define the acceptable standards of social conduct in terms of personal behaviors and emotions.

With the assistance of Eric Dunning, Elias came to view sport as a "topic of great sociological significance" (Mennell, 1992, p. 140). Undoubtedly a great impetus for Elias' adoption of sport as an area of inquiry was its relevance as a vehicle for vindicating his theory of the civilizing process. Elias enthusiastically depicted how the genesis of modern sports was pivotally linked to the encroaching influence of the modern nation-state, which suppressed the violence and brutality of earlier game forms and leisure pursuits. The civilizing and sportization of leisure was achieved through the development and promotion of more controlled modern sporting practices, wherein the degree of aggression and violence was significantly reduced (e.g., Brookes, 1978; Dunning, 1971; Murphy, & Sheard, 1979; Elias & Dunning, 1986).

Recently, sociologists influenced by Elias' configurational sociology have examined what might be termed the "decivilizing process" in the case of soccer hooliganism behavior (Dunning, 1990; Dunning, Murphy, & Williams, 1988; Murphy, Dunning, & Williams, 1988; Williams, Dunning, & Murphy, 1984).

Dominating bodies and contested terrains

Frank (1991) contends that "dominating bodies are, at least in the literature, exclusive male bodies" (p. 69). Contrarily, Maguire (1991) argues that "the idea that dominating bodies are exclusively male bodies is more contentious

355

than Frank asserts" (p. 8). Whether one sides with Frank or Maguire, it is evident that bodies are contested terrains for gender identities and relations. Above all, it is feminist analyses of sport that have most clearly demonstrated the centrality of gender in any sociological analysis of the dominating body in sport (e.g., Bennett, Whitaker, Smith, & Sablove, 1987; Birrell, 1984, 1988; Hall, 1984, 1990; Jarratt, 1990).

The body, gender, and sport

Theberge (1991) identifies three major areas of research related to the combined consideration of the body, gender, and sport, namely (a) the body, disciplinary practices, and domination; (b) gender, sport, and power; and (c) the structural bases of disciplinary power. We refer to these lines of investigation to organize our review of literature below.

With respect to disciplinary practices and domination, Theberge (1991) points out that "There is . . . a growing and increasingly sophisticated analysis of disciplinary practices and subjugation in contemporary sport and physical activity" (p. 128). General analyses of the ideology of male domination in sport can be found in Naison (1980), Walker (1988), and Willis (1982). Sociohistorical studies showing how women have been excluded from sport participation as a result of male control over female bodies are given in Atkinson (1978), Lenskyj (1986), and Vertinsky (1990; in press). We also mention Metheny's (1965) classic analysis of socially appropriate and inappropriate body techniques for women engaged in sport competition. Contemporary examinations of disciplinary practices reflecting male domination of women in sport include Birrell and Theberge (1989), Daniels (1992), Khoury-Murphy and Murphy (1992), and MacKinnon (1987).

Recent research in the sociology of sport reveals how gender identities are constructed and confirmed in the context of sport. The antecedents and consequents of the cultural production and reproduction of gender in sport situations is clearly shown in the work of Dewar (1987), Eder and Parker (1987), Jennifer Hargreaves (1986), Johnsen (1982), Leaman and Carrington (1985), and Messner and Sabo (1990). The means of constructing male identities and the mechanisms of maintaining masculine hegemony through sporting practices are examined in Bryson (1987), Crosset (1990), Connell (1990), Dunning (1986), Gillett and White (1992), Messner (1985, 1987, 1990), Sabo and Panepinto (1990), Sheard and Dunning (1973), and Whitson (1990). Striking illustrations of male sexuality in sport are given in the studies of bullfighting by Marvin (1988, pp. 143–165) and Mitchell (1991). However, the most substantive analysis of the embodiment of masculinity within the world of sport is presented in Messner (1992).

Carrigan, Connell, and Lee (1985) observe that "The most important feature of . . . masculinity, alongside its connection with dominance, is that it is heterosexual" (p. 393). Hence there are only a few embodied sociological accounts of lesbians and gays in sport (e.g., Pronger, 1990a, 1990b; Schulze, 1990). Studies of the embodiment of race and gender in sport are also rare; exceptions include Birrell (1990), Majors (1990), and Wacquant (1992a, in press).

Finally, with respect to disciplinary practices and domination, we follow Theberge's (1991) lead and note that "consideration of gender and power has also explored the possibilities of transformation so that sport becomes a measure of women's empowerment rather than their subjugation" (p. 129). Representative research regarding the embodied form of female empowerment and bodily resistance by women is found in Bloch (1987), Bryson (1990), Donnelly (1988), Duquin (1982), Gilroy (1989), Guthrie and Castelnuovo (1992), Markula (1992), and Theberge (1987).

We highlighted some of the structural bases of disciplinary power in our earlier discussion of sanctioning the body, especially with reference to schooling the body. But, as Theberge (1991) notes, "The structural base of the subordination of women has also been explored extensively in studies of media accounts of sport" (p. 130). Significant analyses of the sport media include Duncan and Hasbrook (1988); Duncan, Messner, Williams, and Jensen (1990); Duncan, Messner, and Williams (1991); Duncan and Sayaovung (1990); Holmlund (1989); Messner (1988); Klein (1988); and McNeill (1988).

The body, sport, and social class

Relevant to the notions of dominating bodies and contested ideological terrains, Bourdieu (1978) notes that "sport, like any other practice, is an object of struggles between the factions of the dominant class and also between the social classes" (p. 826). More specifically, he states that "the field of sporting practices is the site of struggles in which what is at stake, *inter alia*, is the monopolistic capacity to impose the legitimate definition of sporting practice and of the legitimate function of sporting activity—amateurism vs. professionalism, participant sport vs. spectator sport, distinctive (elite) sport vs. popular (mass) sport" (p. 826). Bourdieu further indicates the embodied nature of these struggles in pointing out that the field of sporting practices "is itself part of the larger field of struggles over the definitions of the *legitimate body* and the *legitimate use of the body*" (p. 826).

In a paper titled "Program for a Sociology of Sport" (1988), Bourdieu presents a specific framework for studying the kinds of struggles just mentioned. Critiques and explications of his core concepts and key themes relative to the combined consideration of the body, class, and sport are given in Gruneau (1991, in press); Kew (1986); MacAloon (1988); and Shilling (1991). Recent sociological studies of the body in sport based on Bourdieu's theoretical perspective include Harvey and Sparks (1991); Laberge and Sankoff (1988); Sack (1988); and Wacquant (1992a, in press).

Wacquant's (1992a) study of boxing in a ghetto gym links social class with race and fulfills a dual purpose. First, by drawing upon his 3 years of participant observation, he provides a fascinating ethnographic account of an occupational subculture of black boxers. Second, "by reflecting on the nature of a *practice of which the body is at once the seat, the instrument, and the target*" (p. 224), he provides added insight about what Bourdieu (1990) has conceptualized as the "logic of practice." In additions, extending Bourdieu's concepts of class habitus and body habitus, Wacquant proposes the particular concept of pugilistic habitus, which he describes in terms of "the specific set of bodily and mental schemata that define the competent boxer" (p. 224).

Utilizing key concepts underlying Bourdieu's (1984) influential study of social class and aesthetic taste, Sack (1988) shows the ties between social class and youth in his analysis of the relationship between sport involvement and lifestyle in German youth cultures. With particular reference to Bourdieu's concepts of class habitus and taste, Sack suggests, "(1) how elements of taste do penetrate sportive situations, (2) how and why sportive situations are not apt to integrate people of different tastes, [and] (3) that sport even in childhood and adolescence is a social system that helps to differentiate society vertically" (p. 214).

Employing relative sophisticated statistical procedures, Laberge and Sankoff (1988) provide the first quantitative study in sport sociology based on Bourdieu's theoretical perspective. With particular reference to Bourdieu's related concepts of class habitus and body habitus, they connect social class and gender in their analysis of the lifestyles and patterns of participation in physical activities for a sample of married (or formerly married) female Francophones, classified according to social class, and being neither athletes nor students. In conclusion, they state that "the structure of the relations between various physical practices, different types of attention to the body, and various leisure activities provides information about the social meaning of participation in physical activities, that is, about the social logics that govern these activities and the balance of power between the different classes and class segments with respect to the definition of legitimate physical activity" (p. 285).

The mirroring body and consumer culture

According to Frank (1991), the "medium of the mirroring body is consumption; based on consumption the body becomes as predictable as the objects made available for it" (p. 61). However, in his analytical account of the relationship between the mirroring body and consumption, Frank does not delineate the differing modes of commodity production and consumption that distinguish the industrial from the postindustrial periods. More specifically, despite his appropriation of both Pierre Bourdieu's critique of the distinctive modern body and Jean Baudrillard's depiction of the narcissistic postmodern body, Frank fails to contextualize the mirroring body in terms of modernity and postmodernity. Thus we focus our review on literature that reveals relations between the body and sport within the modern era of mass consumption and the postmodern era of hyperconsumption.

The body, modernity, and mass consumption

The onset of modernity refers to the changing nature of lived social reality associated with the systematic rationalization of administrative and economic institutions that accompanied the maturation of industrial capitalism. Modernity denotes the era of mechanized mass production in which a flourishing harvest of manufactured commodities became the dominant definer of existence within industrialized society.

The individual subject was crucially implicated in the process of industrialization, because the rational advancement of a modern society required that mass consumption become the necessary other of mass production. In order to create a mass of consumers, "more and more aspects of life were brought under the influence of the expanding market with its propaganda for commodities" (Featherstone, 1982, p. 19). In conjunction with the emergence of consumer culture was the progressive commercialization and commodification of sport and sporting bodies (e.g., Alt, 1983; Beamish, 1981; Brohm, 1978; John Hargreaves, 1986; Hoch, 1972; McKay & Miller, 1991; Rigauer, 1981; Sewart, 1987). Further, "what links up consumer culture with sports culture so economically is their common concern with, and capacity to, accommodate the body as a means of expression" (John Hargreaves, 1986, p. 134).

Body expression can, of course, range from the ostentatious forms of display characterized by Veblen (1899/1934) in his classic account of conspicuous consumption, to the subtle moves of synchronized swimmers, to bodily forms of resistance and political protest (Donnelly, 1988; Martin, 1990). However, the popular commercial media has articulated the body as the embodiment of individual accomplishment and personal success, as defined in terms of beauty, fitness, health, pleasure, sexuality, vitality, and youthfulness. As Featherstone (1982) contends,

> the closer the actual body approximates to the idealized images of youth, health, fitness, and beauty, the higher its exchange value. Consumer culture permits the unashamed display of the human body.
>
> (pp. 21–22)

Manipulated by a hedonistic ideology of consumerism, the discourses of sport, leisure, health, and exercise during the past decade were clearly directed at the mirroring body. Moreover, they typically focused on personal problems rather than public issues. Ingham (1985) and Howell (1990, 1991) well illustrate the individualized nature of these discourses in their analyses of the ideological construction of lifestyle by the New Right. Their analyses clearly show that discourses of the New Right couch problems of health and well-being in terms of personal, moral responsibility and thus avert attention from structural constraints and social inequalities related to well-being.

With reference to the fiscal crisis of the welfare state, Ingham (1985) summarizes his position as follows:

> In terms of lifestyle, voluntaristic policies of autonomous bodily drill as privatized, preventive medicine or as means to self-fulfillment in a consumerist body culture may be strategic for the new right and hegemonic for both the right-thinking and progressive segments of the middle class, given their relatively privileged access to resources. But such policies cannot mitigate the claims of those who lack the resources and opportunities to perform up to the standards of respectability or consumerism. For these people, the bootstraps cannot be raised up; they are already rooted in the social prophecies of poverty.
>
> (pp. 50–51)

Howell (1990, 1991) extends Ingham's critique of the "pull yourself up by the bootstraps" alternative to state intervention in health care in his examination of the quality-of-life debate in Reagan's America. For example, in discussing the politics of the fitness movement, he writes,

> Defining and measuring the quality of life now encompasses a self-preservationist conception of the body. Individuals are encouraged to adopt instrumental strategies to biologically better themselves so as to avoid deterioration and thus better the quality of their lives. Such strategies are politically encouraged and applauded by state bureaucracies who seek to reduce health costs by educating the public against bodily neglect, combining such encouragement with the notion that the body is a vehicle of pleasure and self-expression.
>
> (1991, p. 267)

The idea of the body as a vehicle of pleasure and an instrument of desire is further emphasized in postmodern thought.

The body, postmodernity, and hyperconsumption

Simply put, postmodernity is the age of instantaneous visual communication associated with the culture of late-capitalist society. The conditions of postmodernity refer to a historical juncture in which the output of hi-tech mass communication has replaced that of industrial production as the pivotal element in defining the experience of human existence. "Through the development of technology, mass media interpret, produce and distribute images in news ways and, in doing so, revolutionize the manner in which people apprehend and know reality" (Rail, 1991b, p. 731). This new "reality logic" (Luke, 1991, p. 349) results from the unremitting circulation of televisual images, which emanate from the expanding information and communication networks. The subjective experience of the postmodern world is thus dominated and defined by the mediated simulations of reality transmitted by the media.

The postmodern obsession with the production and consumption of images has heralded the emergence of a culture of signification in which the commodity-sign (Featherstone, 1991) has usurped the economic commodity as the dynamic force and structuring principle of everyday existence. What matters to contemporary social understanding is not the economic value of commodities but the contextual meaning and significance with which they are imbued. "No longer based on an economy seeking to fulfill the needs of modernization, [postmodern] societies correspond to a surplus economy which is driven to perpetually create new desires" (Rail, 1991b, p. 731). The postmodern body faithfully mirrors the commodity-signs it desires. Consequently, as Faurschou (1987) has indicated, the profoundity of commodity-signs which constitute the regime of hyperconsumption become responsible for creating "bodies for aerobics, bodies for sportscars, bodies for vacations, bodies for Pepsi, for Coke, and of course bodies for fashion" (p. 72).

Faurschou's (1987) work implicates the media in the creation of the sporting postmodern body and directs us to the most prominent theorist of postmodernism, Jean Baudrillard. Unfortunately, the challenging disposition of his writing has precluded many from drawing upon his theoretical perspective in the study of sport. However, Rojek (1990) has described the relevance of Baudrillard's ideas for leisure studies; Andrews (in press) has done the same for sport studies; and Glassner (1989, in press) and Rail (1991a, 1991b) have borrowed from Baudrillard in their respective analyses of fitness and mediated sport.

Within his analyses of fitness and the postmodern subject, Glassner (1989, in press) identifies how contemporary fitness practices have defused the body/self polarity that characterized the human experience during the modern era. Through the quintessential postmodern world of the exercise video, "The person experiences his or her own body within the context of a media environment of repeating images" (Glassner, 1989, p. 183). Hence, while exercising within a world of simulated images, the distinction between the human body and the self identity implodes as the postmodern subject becomes a mirroring screen of televisual circuitry.

Rail (1991a) complements Glassner (1989) in her synopsis of the modernist polarities dissolved by postmodern sport. Speaking epistemologically, she contends that "Through sport, the self becomes conscious of the body, the self is embodied, exteriorized. Not only bodily practices, but the body itself become a sign of the self" (p. 747). Rail (1991b) also appropriates a Baudrillardian perspective in her critique of postmodern mediated sport. This is most evident in her examination of the thesis that "Technology used to mediate sport is anti-mediatory in that it does not allow communication . . . [because] . . . the viewer is always positioned as a passive observer or listener and has no freedom but to consume or reject the sports spectacle" (p. 732). The anti-mediatory model implies an inert body caught in what Rail terms "the dead sporting spectacle."

Conclusion

In his insightful analysis of contemporary popular culture, Grossberg (1992) confesses that

> The simple fact of the matter is that no one can collect all of the material that is necessary or appropriate. And as the size and density of the field continuously expand, the contradictions multiply more rapidly than our writing.
>
> (p. 29)

His sentiment is most applicable to the ever expansive and dynamic discourse on the sporting body. Thus our review is largely a synopsis of significant sport related studies that implicate the body in the process of sociocultural production. We trust, however, that we have fulfilled our latent objectives to both inform and stimulate readers of our review.

We attempted to be informative by providing summaries of exemplary studies of contrasting theoretical perspectives pertaining to the explication of the sporting body's experience of differing social settings, regimes of power, and historical conjunctures. And we have tried to excite interest in research that interpretively connects sporting practices to corporeal existence in our discussions of four types of body usage. In conclusion, echoing the thoughts of Wacquant (1992b, p. xiv), we envision our review as both an invitation to the sporting body and as a body of work that readers may selectively utilize in their own specific studies of embodied sporting practices.[3]

Notes

1 Contrarily, it can be argued that anthropology has an embodied tradition. For example, Turner (1991) cites four examples of the body's prominence in anthropology.

2 Perhaps the initial call for an embodied sociology of sport came from Heinemann (1980), in his article titled "Sport and the Sociology of the Body."

3 Since writing the final draft of our review, several important works about the body in culture and sport have come to our attention, including Hoberman (1992), Kirk and Spiller (in press), Shilling (1992), and Shilling (in press).

References

Adams, A., & Newton, C. (1989). *Sumo*. New York: Gallery Books.

Alt, J. (1983). Sport and cultural reification: From ritual to mass consumption. *Theory, Culture and Society*, **1**(3), 93–107.

Andrews, D.L. (in press). All-consumed bodies: Baudrillard, hyperreality, and the cybernetic construction of the postmodern body. In C.L. Cole, J.W. Loy, & M.A. Messner, (Eds.), *Exercising power: The making and remaking of the body*. Albany, NY: SUNY Press.

Atkinson, P. (1978). Fitness, feminism and schooling. In S. Delamont & C. Duffin (Eds.), *The nineteenth century woman: Her physical and cultural world* (pp. 92–133). London: Croom Helm.

Aycock, A. (1992). The confession of the flesh: Disciplinary gaze in casual bodybuilding. *Play & Culture*, **5**, 338–357.

Baudrillard, J. (1988). *The ecstacy of communication*. New York: Semiotext(e).

Beamish, R. (1981). Sport, value and the fetishism of commodities: Central issues in the alienation of sport labour. In A.G. Ingham & E.F. Broom (Eds.), *Career patterns and career contingencies in sport: Proceedings of the First Regional Symposium International Committee for the Sociology of Sport* (pp. 81–102). Vancouver: University of British Columbia.

Bennett, R.S., Whitaker, K.G., Smith, N.J.W., & Sablove, A. (1987). Changing the rules of the game: Reflections toward a feminist analysis of sport. *Women's Studies International Forum*, **10**, 369–379.

Birrell, S. (1984). Studying gender in sport: A feminist perspective. In N. Theberge & P. Donnelly (Eds.), *Sport and the sociological imagination* (pp. 125–135). Fort Worth: Texas Christian University Press.

Birrell, S. (1988). Discourses on the gender/sport relationship: From women in sport to gender relations. *Exercise and Sport Sciences Reviews*, **16**, 159–200.

Birrell, S. (1990). Women of color, critical autobiography, and sport. In M.A. Messner & D.F. Sabo (Eds.), *Sport, men and the gender order* (pp. 185–200). Champaign, IL: Human Kinetics.

Birrell, S., & Cole, C.L. (1990). Double fault: Renee Richards and the construction and naturalization of difference. *Sociology of Sport Journal*, **7**, 1–21.

Birrell, S., & Theberge, N. (1989, June). *The fitness boom and the fragmentation of women's bodies*. Paper presented at meetings of the National Women's Studies Association, Towson, MD.

Birrell, S., & Turowetz, A. (1979). Character work-up and display. *Urban Life*, **8**, 219–246.

Bloch, C. (1987). Everyday life, sensuality, and body culture. *Women's Studies International Forum*, **10**, 433–442.

Bolin, A. (1992). Flex appeal, food, and fat: Competitive bodybuilding, gender, and diet. *Play & Culture*, **5**, 378–400.

Bourdieu, P. (1978). Sport and social class. *Social Science Information*, **17**, 819–840.

Bourdieu, P. (1984). *Distinction: A social critique of the judgement of taste*. Cambridge, MA: Harvard University Press.

Bourdieu, P. (1988). Program for a sociology of sport. *Sociology of Sport Journal*, **5**, 153–161.

Bourdieu, P. (1990). *The logic of practice*. Stanford: Stanford University Press.

Brohm, J-M. (1978). *Sport: A prison of measured time*. London: Ink Links.

Brookes, C. (1987). *English cricket*. London: Weidenfeld & Nicholson.

Bryson, L. (1987). Sport and the maintenance of masculine hegemony. *Women's Studies International Forum*, **10**, 349–360.

Bryson, L. (1990). Challenges to male hegemony in sport. In M.A. Messner & D.F. Sabo (Eds.), *Sport, men, and the gender order* (pp. 173–183). Champaign, IL: Human Kinetics.

Carrigan, T., Connell, B., & Lee, J. (1985). Toward a new sociology of masculinity. *Theory and Society*, **14**, 551–604.

Colburn, K. (1985). Honor, ritual and violence in ice hockey. *Canadian Journal of Sociology*, **10**, 153–170.

Connell, R.W. (1990). An iron man: The body and some contradictions of hegemonic masculinity. In M.A. Messner & D.F. Sabo (Eds.), *Sport, men, and the gender order* (pp. 83–96). Champaign, IL: Human Kinetics.

Crosset, T. (1990). Masculinity, sexuality, and the development of early modern sport. In M.A. Messner & D.F. Sabo (Eds.), *Sport, men, and the gender order* (pp. 45–54). Champaign, IL: Human Kinetics.

Daniels, P.B. (1992). Gender (body) verification (building), *Play & Culture*, **5**, 370–377.

Dewar, A. (1987). The social construction of gender in physical education. *Women's Studies International Forum*, **10**, 453–465.

Donnelly, P. (1980). *The subculture and public image of climbers*. Unpublished doctoral dissertation, University of Massachusetts.

Donnelly, P. (1988). Sport as a site for "popular" resistance. In R.S. Gruneau (Ed.), *Popular cultures and political practices* (pp. 69–82). Toronto: Garamond Press.

Donnelly, P., & Young, K. (1988). The construction and confirmation of identity in sport subcultures. *Sociology of Sport Journal*, **5**, 223–240.

Duncan, M.C., & Hasbrook, C.A. (1988). Denial of power in televised women's sports. *Sociology of Sport Journal*, **5**, 1–21.

Duncan, M.C., Messner, M.A., Williams, L., & the Amateur Athletic Foundation of Los Angeles. (1991). *Coverage of women's sports in four daily newspapers*. Los Angeles: AAF. (2141 West Adams Blvd., Los Angeles, CA 90018)

Duncan, M.C., Messner, M.A., Williams, L., Jensen, K., & the Amateur Athletic Foundation of Los Angeles. (1990). *Gender stereotyping in televised sports*. Los Angeles: AAF. (2141 West Adams Blvd., Los Angeles, CA 90018)

Duncan, M.C., & Sayaovong, A. (1990). Photographic images and gender in *Sports Illustrated for Kids*. *Play & Culture*, **3**, 91–116.

Dunning, E.G. (1971). *The sociology of sport: A selection of readings*. London: Frank Cass.

Dunning, E.G. (1986). Sport as a male preserve: Notes on the social sources of masculine identity and its transformations. *Theory, Culture and Society*, **3**, 79–90.

Dunning, E.G. (1990). Sociological reflections on sport, violence and civilization. *International Review for the Sociology of Sport*, **25**, 65–81.

Dunning, E.G., Murphy, P., & Williams, J. (1988). *The roots of football hooliganism: An historical and sociological study*. London: Routledge & Kegan Paul.

Dunning, E.G., & Sheard, K.S. (1979). *Barbarians, gentlemen and players*. Oxford: Martin Robertson.

Duquin, M.E. (1982). The importance of sport in building women's potential. *Journal of Physical Education, Recreation and Dance*, **53**(3), 18–20, 36.

Eder, D., & Parker, S. (1987). The cultural production and reproduction of gender: The effect of extracurricular activities on peer-group culture. *Sociology of Education*, **60**, 200–213.

Elias, N. (1978). *The civilizing process. Volume I: The history of manners*. Oxford: Basil Blackwell.

Elias, N. (1982). *The civilizing process. Volume II: State formation and civilization*. Oxford: Basil Blackwell.

Elias, N., & Dunning, E.G. (1986). *Quest for excitement: Sport and leisure in the civilizing process*. Oxford: Basil Blackwell.

Faulkner, R.R. (1974). Making violence by doing work. *Sociology of Work and Occupations*, **1**, 288–312.

Faurschou, G. (1987). Fashion and the cultural logic of postmodernity. *Canadian Journal of Political and Social Theory*, **11**(1–2), 68–82.

Featherstone, M. (1982). The body in consumer culture. *Theory, Culture and Society*, **1**(2), 18–33.

Featherstone, M. (1987). Norbert Elias and figurational sociology: Some prefatory remarks. *Theory, Culture and Society*, **4**, 197–211.

Featherstone, M. (1991). *Postmodernism and consumer culture*. London: Sage.

Feher, M., Naddaff, R., & Tazi, N. (1989a). *Fragments for a history of the human body, Part one*. New York: Zone.

Feher, M., Naddaff, R., & Tazi, N. (1989b). *Fragments for a history of the human body, Part two*. New York: Zone.

Feher, M., Naddaff, R., & Tazi, N. (1989c). *Fragments for a history of the human body, Part three*, New York: Zone.

Foucault, M. (1973). *Madness and civilization: A history of insanity in the age of reason*. New York: Vintage Books.

Foucault, M. (1975). *The birth of the clinic: An archaeology of medical perception*. New York: Vintage Books.

Foucault, M. (1976). *Nietzsche*. Paris: Cahiers de Royaumont.

Foucault, M. (1977). *Discipline and punish: The birth of the prison*. New York: Pantheon.

Frank, A.W. (1990). Bringing the bodies back in: A decade review. *Theory, Culture and Society*, **7**, 131–162.

Frank, A.W. (1991). For the sociology of the body: An analytical review. In M. Featherstone, M. Hepworth, & B.S. Turner (Eds.), *The body: Social process and cultural theory* (pp. 36–102). London: Sage.

Freund, P.E.S. (1988). Bringing society into the body. *Theory and Society*, **17**, 839–864.

Gillett, J., & White, P.G. (1992). Male bodybuilding and the reassertion of hegemonic masculinity: A critical feminist perspective. *Play & Culture*, **5**, 358–369.

Gilroy, S. (1989). The emBody-ment of power: Gender and physical activity. *Leisure Studies*, **8**, 163–171.

Glassner, B. (1989). Fitness and the postmodern self. *Journal of Health and Social Behavior*, **30**, 180–191.

Glassner, B. (in press). Fitness as postmodern action. In C.L. Cole, J.W. Loy, & M.A. Messner (Eds.), *Exercising power: The making and remaking of the body*. Albany, NY: SUNY Press.

Goffman, E. (1967). *Interaction ritual*. Garden City, NY: Anchor Books.

Gross, E., & Stone, G.P. (1964). Embarrassment and the analysis of role requirements. *American Journal of Sociology*, **70**, 1–15.

Grossberg, L. (1992). *We gotta get out of this place*. New York: Routledge.

Gruneau, R.S. (1991). Sport and "esprit de corps": Notes on power, culture and the politics of the body. In F. Landry, M. Landry, & M. Yerles (Eds.), *Sport . . . The third millennium* (pp. 169–186). Sainte-Foy, Quebec: Les Presses de L'Universite Laval.

Gruneau, R.S. (in press). The critique of sport in modernity: Theorizing power, culture and the politics of the body. In E.G. Dunning, J. Maguire, & R. Pearton (Eds.), *The sports process*. London: Human Kinetics.

Guthrie, S.R., & Castelnuovo, S. (1992). Elite women bodybuilders: Models of resistance or compliance? *Play & Culture*, **5**, 401–408.

Hall, M.A. (1984). Towards a feminist analysis of gender inequality in sport. In N. Theberge & P. Donnelly (Eds.), *Sport and the sociological imagination* (pp. 82–103). Fort Worth: Texas Christian University Press.

Hall, M.A. (1990). How should we theorize gender in the context of sport? In M.A. Messner & D.F. Sabo (Eds.), *Sport, men, and the gender order* (pp. 223–240). Champaign, IL: Human Kinetics.

Hargreaves, J[ennifer]. (1986). Where's the virtue? Where's the grace? A discussion of the social production of gender through sport. *Theory, Culture and Society*, **3**, 109–122.

Hargreaves, J[ohn]. (1986). *Sport, power and culture*. Cambridge, England: Polity Press.

Hargreaves, J[ohn]. (1987). The body, sport and power relations. In J. Horne, D. Jary, & A. Tomlinson (Eds.), *Sport, leisure and social relations* (pp. 139–159). London: Routledge & Kegan Paul.

Harre, R., Clarke, D., & De Carlo, N. (1985). *Motives and mechanisms*. London: Methuen.

Harris, J.C. (1992). Modifying the performance enhancement ethos: Disciplinary and professional implications. *American Academy of Physical Education Papers*, **25**, 96–103.

Harvey, J., & Sparks, R. (1991). The politics of the body in the context of modernity. *Quest*, **43**, 164–189.

Heinemann, K. (1980). Sport and the sociology of the body. *International Review of Sport Sociology*, **15**(3–4), 41–56.

Hoberman, J.M. (1992). *Mortal engines: The science of performance and the dehumanization of sport*. New York: Free Press.

Hoch, P. (1972). *Rip off the big game*. Garden City, NJ: Doubleday.

Holmlund, C.A. (1989). Visible difference and flex appeal: The body, sex, sexuality, and race in the *Pumping Iron* films. *Cinema Journal*, **28**(4), 38–51.

Howell, J. (1990). *Meanings go mobile: Fitness, health and the quality of life debate in contemporary America*. Unpublished doctoral dissertation, University of Illinois at Urbana–Champaign.

Howell, J. (1991). "A revolution in motion": Advertising and the politics of nostalgia. *Sociology of Sport Journal*, **8**, 258–271.

Ingham, A.G. (1985). From public issue to personal trouble: Well-being and the fiscal trouble of the state. *Sociology of Sport Journal*, **2**, 43–55.

Jarratt, E.H. (1990). Feminist issues in sport. *Women's Studies International Forum*, **13**, 491–499.

Johnsen, K.P. (1982). The development and maintenance of gender differentiation through sports. In R.M. Pankin (Ed.), *Social approaches to sport* (pp. 90–103). East Brunswick, NJ: Associated University Press.

Kew, F.C. (1986). Sporting practices as an endless play of self-relativising tastes: Insights from Pierre Bourdieu. In J.A. Mangan & R.B. Small (Eds.), *Sport, culture, society: International, historical and sociological perspectives* (pp. 306–313). London: E & FN Spon.

Khoury-Murphy, M., & Murphy, M.D. (1992). Southern (bar)belles: The cultural problematics of implementing a weight training program among older southern women. *Play & Culture*, **5**, 409–419.

Kirk, D., & Spiller, B. (in press). Schooling the docile body: Physical education, schooling and the myth of oppression. *Australian Journal of Education*.

Klein, A.M. (1986). Pumping irony: Crisis and contradiction in bodybuilding. *Sociology of Sport Journal*, **3**, 112–133.

Klein, A.M. (1988). The discourse of women in sports reports. *International Review for the Sociology of Sport*, **23**, 139–152.

Klein, A.M. (1992). Man makes himself: Alienation and self-objectification in bodybuilding. *Play & Culture*, **5**, 326–337.

Laberge, S., & Sankoff, D. (1988). Physical activities, body *habitus*, and lifestyles. In J. Harvey & H. Cantelon (Eds.), *Not just a game: Essays in Canadian sport sociology* (pp. 267–323). Ottawa: University of Ottawa Press.

Lawson, H. (1988). Occupational socialization, cultural studies, and the physical education curriculum. *Journal of Teaching in Physical Education*, **7**, 265–288.

Leaman, O., & Carrington, B. (1985). Athleticism and the reproduction of gender and ethnic marginality. *Leisure Studies*, **4**, 205–217.

Lenskyj, H. (1986). *Out of bounds: Women, sport and sexuality*. Toronto: Women's Press.

Luke, T. (1991). Power and politics in hyperreality: The critical project of Jean Baudrillard. *Social Science Journal*, **28**, 347–367.

Lyman, S.M., & Scott, M.B. (1968). Coolness in everyday life. In M. Truzzi (Ed.), *Sociology and everyday life* (pp. 92–101). Englewood Cliffs, NJ: Prentice Hall.

MacAloon, J.J. (1988). A prefatory note to Pierre Bourdieu's "Program for a Sociology of Sport." *Sociology of Sport Journal*, **5**, 150–152.

MacKinnon, C. (1987). Women, self-possession and sport. In C. MacKinnon, *Feminism unmodified: Discourses on life and law* (pp. 117–124). Cambridge, MA: Harvard University Press.

Maguire, J. (1991, November). *Looking for a synthesis: Bodies, cultures and societies: An evaluation and Critique*. Paper presented at the annual meetings of the North American Society for the Sociology of Sport, Milwaukee.

Majors, R. (1990). Cool pose: Black masculinity and sports. In M.A. Messner & D.F. Sabo (Eds.), *Sport, men and the gender order* (pp. 109–114). Champaign, IL: Human Kinetics.

Markula, P. (1992). *Total-body-tone-up: Paradox and women's realities in aerobics.* Unpublished doctoral dissertation, University of Illinois at Urbana-Champaign.

Martin, R. (1990). *Performance as political act.* New York: Bergin & Garvey.

Marvin, G. (1988). *Bullfight.* Oxford: Basil Blackwell.

Mauss, M. (1973). Techniques of the body. *Economy and Society,* **2**(1), 70–88.

McKay, J., Gore, J.M., & Kirk, D. (1990). Beyond the limits of technocratic physical education. *Quest,* **42**, 52–76.

McKay, J., & Miller, T. (1991). From old boys to men and women of the corporation: The Americanization and commodification of Australian sport. *Sociology of Sport Journal,* **8**, 86–94.

McNeill, M. (1988). Active women, media representations, and ideology. In J. Harvey & H. Cantelon (Eds.), *Not just a game: Essays in Canadian sport sociology* (pp. 195–211). Ottawa: University of Ottawa Press.

Mennell, S. (1992). *Norbert Elias: An introduction.* Oxford: Basil Blackwell.

Messner, M.A. (1985). The changing meaning of male identity in the lifecourse of the athlete. *Arena Review,* **9**(2), 31–60.

Messner, M.A. (1987). The meaning of success: The athletic experience and the development of male identity. In H. Brod (Ed.), *The making of masculinities: The new men studies* (pp. 193–209). Boston: Allen & Unwin.

Messner, M.A. (1988). Sports and male domination: The female athlete as contested ideological terrain. *Sociology of Sport Journal,* **5**, 197–211.

Messner, M.A. (1990). Masculinities and athletic careers: Bonding and status differences. In M.A. Messner & D.F. Sabo (Eds.), *Sport, men, and the gender order* (pp. 97–108). Champaign, IL: Human Kinetics.

Messner, M.A. (1992). *Power at play,* Boston: Beacon Press.

Messner, M.A., & Sabo, D.F. (Eds.) (1990). *Sport, men and the gender order.* Champaign, IL: Human Kinetics.

Metheny, E. (1965). Symbolic forms of movement: The feminine image in sports. In E. Metheny, *Connotations of movement in sport and dance* (pp. 43–56). Dubuque, IA: Wm. C. Brown.

Mitchell, T. (1991). *Blood sport,* Philadelphia: University of Pennsylvania Press.

Murphy, P., Dunning, E.G., & Williams, J. (1988). Soccer crowd disorder and the press: Processes of amplification and de-amplification in historical perspective. *Theory, Culture and Society,* **5**, 645–673.

Naison, M. (1980). Sports, women, and the ideology of domination. In D. Sabo & R. Runtola (Eds.), *Jock: Sports and male identity* (pp. 30–36). Englewood Cliffs, NJ: Prentice Hall.

O'Neill, J. (1985). *Five bodies: The human shape of modern society.* Ithaca, NY: Cornell University Press.

Polsky, N. (1964). The hustler. *Social Problems,* **12**(1), 3–15.

Polsky, N. (1967). *Husters, beats, and others.* Chicago: Aldine.

Pronger, B. (1990a). *The arena of masculinity.* New York: St. Martin's Press.

Pronger, B. (1990b). Gay jocks: A phenomenology of gay men in athletics. In M.A. Messner & D.F. Sabo (Eds.), *Sport, men, and the gender order* (pp. 141–152). Champaign, IL: Human Kinetics.

Rail, G. (1991a). The dissolution of polarities as a megatrend in postmodern sport. In F. Landry, M. Landry, & M. Yerles (Eds.), *Sport . . . The third millennium* (pp. 745–751). Sainte-Foy, Quebec: Les Presses de L'Universite Laval.

Rail, G. (1991b). Technologie post-moderne et culture: Un regard sur le sport media-tise [Postmodernity and mediated sport: The medium is the model]. In F. Landry, M. Landry, & M. Yerles (Eds.), *Sport . . . The third millennium* (pp. 731–739). SainteFoy, Quebec: Les Presses de L'Universite Laval.

Rigauer, B. (1981). *Sport and work*. New York: Columbia University Press.

Rojek, C. (1990). Baudrillard and leisure. *Leisure Studies*, **9**, 1–20.

Rosenberg, M.M., & Turowetz, A. (1975). The wrestler and the physician: Identity workup and organizational arrangements. In D.W. Ball & J.W. Loy (Eds.), *Sport and social order* (pp. 559–579). Reading, MA: Addison-Wesley.

Sabo, D.F., & Panepinto, J. (1990). Football ritual and the social reproduction of masculinity. In M.A. Messner & D.F. Sabo (Eds.), *Sport, men, and the gender order* (pp. 115–126). Champaign, IL: Human Kinetics.

Sack, H.G. (1988). The relationship between sport and involvement and life-style in youth cultures. *International Review for the Sociology of Sport*, **23**, 213–230.

Sage, G.H. (1992). Beyond enhancing performance in sport: Toward empowerment and transformation. *American Academy of Physical Education Papers*, **25**, 85–95.

Schulze, L. (1990). On the muscle. In J. Gaines & C. Herzog (Eds.), *Fabrications, costume and the female body* (pp. 59–78). New York: Routledge.

Scott, M.B. (1968). *The racing game*. Chicago: Aldine.

Sewart, J.J. (1987). The commodification of sport, *International Review for the Sociology of Sport*, **22**, 171–192.

Sheard, K.G., & Dunning, E.G. (1973). The rugby football club as a type of "male preserve": Some sociological notes. *International Review for the Sociology of Sport*, **8**(3/4), 5–24.

Shilling, C. (1991). Educating the body: Physical capital and the production of social inequalities. *Sociology*, **25**, 653–672.

Shilling, C. (1992). Schooling and the production of physical capital. *Discourse*, **13**(1), 1–19.

Shilling, C. (in press). The body, class and social inequalities. In J. Evans (Ed.), *Equality and physical education*. London: Falmer Press.

Smart, B. (1985). *Michel Foucault*, London: Tavistock.

Theberge, N. (1987). Sport and women's empowerment. *Women's Studies International Forum*, **10**, 387–393.

Theberge, N. (1991). Reflections of the body in the sociology of sport. *Quest*, **43**, 123–134.

Turner, B.S. (1984). *The body and society*. Oxford: Basil Blackwell.

Turner, B.S. (1991). Recent developments in the theory of the body. In M. Feather-stone, M. Hepworth, & B.S. Turner (Eds.), *The body: Social process and cultural theory* (pp. 1–35). London: Sage.

Veblen, T. (1934). *The theory of the leisure class*. New York: The Modern Library. (Original work published 1899).

Vertinsky, P. (1990). *The eternally wounded woman: Women, doctors and exercise in the late nineteenth century*. Manchester: Manchester University Press.

Vertinsky, P. (in press). Form, function and physical activity: The medicalization of women's bodies. In C.L. Cole, J.W. Loy, & M.A. Messner (Eds.), *Exercising power: The making and re-making of the body*. Albany, NY: SUNY Press.

Wacquant, L.J.D. (1992a). The social logic of boxing in black Chicago: Toward a sociology of pugilism. *Sociology of Sport Journal*, **9**, 221–254.

Wacquant, L.J.D. (1992b). Preface. In P. Bourdieu & L.J.D. Wacquant, *An invitation to reflexive sociology* (pp. ix–xiv). Oxford: Polity Press.

Wacquant, L. (in press). A sacred weapon: Bodily capital and bodily labor among professional boxers. In C.L. Cole, J.W. Loy, & M.A. Messner (Eds.), *Exercising power: The making and re-making of the body*. Albany, NY: SUNY Press.

Walker, J.C. (1988). The way men act: Dominant and subordinate male cultures in an inner-city school. *British Journal of the Sociology of Education*, **9**(1), 3–17.

Weinberg, S.K., & Arond, H. (1952). The occupational culture of the boxer. *American Journal of Sociology*, **62**, 460–469.

Whitson, D.J. (1989). Discourse of critique in sport sociology. *Sociology of Sport Journal*, **6**, 60–65.

Whitson, D.J. (1990). Sport in the social construction of masculinity. In M.A. Messner & D.F. Sabo (Eds.), *Sport, men, and the gender order* (pp. 19–30). Champiagn, IL: Human Kinetics.

Whitson, D.J., & Macintosh, D. (1990). The scientization of physical education: Discourse of performance. *Quest*, **42**, 40–51.

Williams, J., Dunning, E.G., & Murphy, P. (1984). *Hooligans abroad: The behaviour and control of English fans in continental Europe*. London: Routledge & Kegan Paul.

Willis, P. (1982). Women in sport in ideology. In J[ennifer] Hargreaves (Ed.), *Sport, culture and ideology* (pp. 117–135). London: Routledge & Kegan Paul.

Young, K. (1983). *The subculture of rugby players: A form of resistance and incorporation*. Unpublished master's thesis, McMaster University.

58

PUMPING IRONY

Crisis and contradiction in bodybuilding

Alan M. Klein

Source: *Sociology of Sport Journal* 3(2) (1986): 112–133.

While the projection of ideal images is very important in American culture, it is in the subculture and sport of bodybuilding that it gets carried to the extreme. A 4-year study of bodybuilding's mecca—Southern California—revealed a fundamental set of discrepancies between what the subculture projects as ideal and what actually goes on. These discrepancies are examined to determine which ones result from changes that have taken place in body-building and which are structural to it. It is shown that as the sport/subculture altered its image to achieve cultural respectability, it inadvertently created new problems. The shifts are examined within the context of studies of deviance and point to the need for long-term ethnography in sport sociology.

Sociologists and anthropologists have avoided disciplinary conflict in part because they have drawn territorial boundaries that complement each others' interests, a feat that has as much to do with avoidance as it does engagement. Subject matter and methodology were divided so as to avoid turf issues. According to this simplified scheme, anthropologists study exotic cultures (preferably non-White and non-European) while sociologists seek out Western societies. Anthropologists do qualitative analysis, while sociologists focus on quantitative. Enough is shared between them to constitute an intellectual demilitarized zone filled with anthropologists studying Western urban contexts and rural sociologists working in areas like Brazil and the Philippines.

The study of sport reflects both the separation and complementarity between sociology and anthropology. Sport sociology has been even more separate from anthropology than have other sociological fields, making the potential contributions from ethnography more promising. The following ethnographic study will speak to the fruitful relationships between the disciplines of sport sociology, urban anthropology, and studies of subculture. In particular, the relationship between cultural ideals and behavioral actuality will be examined. While both disciplines share an interest in this relationship, they have framed it somewhat differently (e.g., Durkheim, 1953; Becker, 1963; Diamond, 1972; Linton, 1945; Freilich, 1977). Using some of the more recent contributions from the field of subcultural studies, this paper focuses on the use of historical analysis and power relationship to look at discrepancies between ideal and real (Hebdige, 1983).

In sport analysis there is an immediate difference in the way the two fields define the appropriate subject of study. Sociologists study sport, while anthropologists deal with play. Play is certainly a broader category of behavior than sport, covering as it does, for instance, a child sitting alone making mudpies, as well as organized competition. By and large, however, anthropological studies of play view sport as less common in kin-based, nonstate societies, hence more properly the realm of other social scientists.

The association that each discipline forms also reflects these divisions. The North American Society for the Sociology of Sport (NASSS) studies Western sport or occasionally sport in Eastern industrial society (e.g., Cantelon & Gruneau, 1982; Eitzen, 1983). Exceptions are uncommon, such as Lever's study of soccer in Brazil (Lever, 1983). On the other hand, The Anthropological Association for the Study of Play (TAASP) tends to look at games and play in a Third World context (e.g., Stevens, 1977; Schwartzman, 1980; Blanchard & Cheska, 1983). The commitment to ethnography and fieldwork is noted in the work on sport carried out by anthropologists, while their sociologist colleagues lean heavily toward quantitative methods. It is the possibility of a *sport ethnography* within the sociological domain of contemporary industrial sport that represents a fruitful merger of anthropological orientation and sociological setting. This study attempts such a fusion.

Sport sociology and the ethnography of sport

Sport sociologists occupy a position of low status within the hierarchy of sociological specializations. Studying almost any institution, be it law, family, corporations, even deviance itself, seems more legitimate than the study of sport. Among sport sociologists there is an unstated consensus about the negative views their colleagues outside the specialty have of them.[1] In partial response to this, sport sociologists have compensated with a hyperempirical methodology. Quantitative sport studies predominate, as evidenced by the citations of work in leading texts (Coakley, 1982; Eitzen & Sage, 1978; Leonard, 1980). Journals such as the *Journal of Sport and Social Issues* and *Sociology of Sport Journal* also point to a gap at least as large as the one that separates the disciplines of sociology and anthropology.

Anthropologists have increasingly carried out ethnographies and fieldwork on games (Blanchard & Cheska, 1985). With few exceptions, however, these studies have been on nonindustrial peoples (e.g., Geertz, 1972) or marginal groups within industrial societies (e.g., Tindall, 1975). While these are worthwhile anthropological contributions that deepen our understanding of culture, they do little to inform our understanding of American or Western society as it is affected by and through sport. This reinforces the oft-held view of anthropology as having little to say about the dominant society. Anthropologists have developed their analysis of small-scale societies, however, seeing them as a set of institutions and cultural variables which act to integrate and alter that society through consensus and conflict. This is assessed through participant observation. More important, anthropologists stress the use of culture as a prism through which social life can be interpreted. While sociologists are aware of these techniques and perspectives, it is the anthropologists who have developed them more fully. As a result, they can be used to advantage where other perspectives have previously prevailed.

Sport ethnography is virtually nonexistent. Participant observation in the service of sport reporting is not in itself sufficient. On occasion, journalists with unusually keen insight and a sense of social analysis inadvertently cross over into the realm of ethnography (e.g., Lipsyte, 1975; Boswell, 1983). However, these efforts remain diletantish rather than being serious ethnography. The observations of Janet Lever in her thoughtful sociological work on Brazilian soccer (1983), or those of Brower (1975) or Devereux (1976) on Little Leaguers, are not the same as those of Colin Turnbull (1965) or Spradley (1970) or Lee (1979). Missing is the view of soccer or baseball as a self-contained, integrated whole, a cultural diarama. That totality and the insight and understanding that comes from the method and perspective of ethnography can be a critical element in the rise of sport sociology to a position of prominence.

Sport ethnography and subcultural studies

The gap between sport sociology and ethnography can be bridged by looking at the analysis of subcultures. Although primarily the contribution of sociologists, anthropologists have not been altogether absent (e.g., Liebow, 1969; Spradley & Mann, 1975; Daner, 1976; Keiser, 1979). The theoretical debates have centered on the function, origins, and systematic workings of subcultures but have mistakenly placed such work within the area of deviance. Periodic reassessments (e.g., Matza, 1969; Brake, 1980; Hebdige, 1983) have done little to change this view. Anthropologists are uncomfortable with the way in which sociologists have lumped disparate subcultures under the heading of deviance. Despite cautioning us about the larger society's method of stigmatizing and labeling deviants, sociologists' continued use of the label sanctions it (see Hebdige, 1983). In anthropology the tradition of cultural relativism is sufficiently strong to promote a view of subculture that avoids deviance connotations, in part by focusing on the study of cultural entities via ethnography. Through relativism, and by partially sacrificing the subculture's ties to the larger society, the ethnography can intensively examine a subculture, giving it an integrity that ethnographic tradition often bestows upon its subject. Admittedly, unless one is careful the relations between the part and the whole (i.e., the subculture and the larger society) can be sacrificed; this hurts analysis but is more than made up for by affording a view of the subculture freed of the deviance label.

Some sociologists distinguish between subcultures on the basis of delinquency, thereby dichotomizing between delinquent and occupational subculture (Downes, 1966) or delinquent and subterranean subcultures (Matza, 1964). Sport subculture would seemingly fall into the category of the more acceptable work and countercultural groups. Many assume that sport as a whole is synonymous with socialization of norms (e.g., Phillips & Schafer, 1971). Others see this as the province of specific sport subcultures (Loy, McPherson, & Kenyon, 1978). Clearly there is a need for the establishment of a sport ethnography in looking at the machinations and function of sport subculture.

The neat division between delinquent and subterranean subculture that Matza (1969) points to, and the view of sport subculture as fitting neatly into the mainstream, is somewhat rattled by the case of competitive bodybuilding in Southern California.

Bodybuilding as subculture

The respect by the larger society that has eluded bodybuilding for so long is finally within reach. This acceptance can be measured by the astounding growth in the past decade of competitive and noncompetitive bodybuilding. Trade publications estimate that as many as 85 million Americans engage in some form of weight training, and while only a tiny fraction will ever develop enough to compete, almost all of them are expecting to see bodily transformation. In that sense they are all bodybuilders, body shapers, or body designers. Over 100 countries now sanction and promote it as a sport, making bodybuilding the 7th largest sport federation in the world. Southern California, and Olympic Gym in particular, is the pulse of bodybuilding. It is the nexus between bodybuilding as sport and subculture, and as such it is the ideal place to study its cultural properties. As the self-styled core of bodybuilding, Olympic Gym has been home to almost every great bodybuilder of the past two decades.

Venice, California, is the perfect setting for a subculture as visually exotic as bodybuilding. Muscle Beach, Olympic, Gold's, and World's Gyms are all within a square mile of each other, making it easy for people to characterize the area as a haven for the practitioners of this sport. Venice, however, leads the entire complex a good deal of its own color. The ideologues of the sport —the Weider brothers who own the largest conglomerate of bodybuilding products in the world and who are headquartered nearby in Woodland Hills —view the free spirited and tolerant climate of Venice as somewhat excessive

374

and potentially embarrassing. They strive to gain respect by projecting a persona of wholesomeness. By dovetailing with the fitness movement, the behemoths who determine bodybuilding's cultural images through their magazines are concerned with gaining cultural respectability rather than trendy popular cultural status. To come closer to mainstream culture, three values are heavily projected to the public via the leading publications: health, heterosexuality, and rugged individualism. As mainstream values, these three differ from values sought by other subcultures. Bodybuilding does not perceive the larger society as malfunctioning and in need of alternatives. If anything, the bodybuilding subculture is conservative, or as Matza might claim, an occupational subculture (1969).

A tension exists within bodybuilding's subculture, one between the ideal image as expressed in the three values listed above, and bodybuilding institutions that foster different and often contradictory behavior. In anthropology these discrepancies have been called "ideal versus real" culture patterns. First the status of bodybuilding in sports must be discussed.

Bodybuilding: sport or spectacle?

Bodybuilding rests precipitously between sport and spectacle. If professional wrestling or roller derby have become synonymous with spectacle, it is not because of their inability to meet basic definitions of sport. Structurally, they meet the outlines presented by Coakley (1982), who cites physical exertion, competition, and organization as three key traits all sports must have. Bodybuilding has some unique problems in meeting these criteria.

All three of Coakley's traits can be found in bodybuilding. The International Federation of Body Building (IFBB) is the dominant organization in the sport. Contests are highly competitive, but the physical exertion and demonstration and of skills, which most people assume runs in tandem with organization and competition, is conspicuously absent. It takes place separately and is linked to the contest only as a visual reportage—a posing routine. This transforms the contest. into a nonphysical event that outsiders often see as being like a beauty contest. Insiders defend against this by claiming that the sport is both sport and art: weight training is the sport, and posing and competitions are the art. Regardless of how they divide their field, the physical component is not contemporaneous with the organized competition, raising a claim that it is not a sport at all but a spectacle. Belly dancing is not a sport, yet many of sits practitioners engage in weight training and enter competitions. Even within bodybuilding there has been a tendency of late to exaggerate the spectacle with the use of props and outrageous costuming and makeup (e.g., The Night of the Champions, a professional contest).

Definition of sport is mediated by other factors, however, most notably the media's willingness to accept an activity as such and the public's acceptance of that decision. Within the past decade just such a passive acquiescence seems to have occurred through the dramatic rise in popularity of "trash sports" (Sewart, 1983). Bodybuilding rode that crest, first through the attention received by the award-winning film *Pumping Iron*, and second with network telecasts of some of the better bodybuilding contests. This supported the view that virtually any sporting event would generate sufficient ratings, and contests along with prize money proliferated during the late 1970s. The advent of women's bodybuilding made the most dramatic impact, however, because it opened the sport/spectacle to a hitherto excluded group. And to the thousands of fans who willingly paid as much as $100 a seat to get into the Mr. Olympia contest, the temporal break meant nothing.

Closely related to bodybuilding is the internationally recognized sport of powerlifting. Here, one sees all three of Coakley's traits functioning at once. Both powerlifting and bodybuilding stemmed from the 19th-century strongman acts of Europe, with the former monopolizing the strength feature while bodybuilding focused on the physique. Between them exists an uneasy truce marked by the condescension of powerlifters toward their counterparts. The few powerlifters at Olympic (most prefer more utilitarian, austere gyms) were given a wide berth and respect granted only to the top people in the gym. Yet it is bodybuilding, not powerlifting, that has risen to cultural prominence, a rise that bears testimony to the media's ability to redefine cultural institutions and their definitions.

While the status of bodybuilding is not universally accepted, its position as a subculture is even more questioned. Many of the practices and beliefs held by bodybuilders have undergone a degree of change as a result of the newfound acceptance of the sport. Media attention exacerbates this, with the result being that discrepancies emerge between what is consciously being presented about the sport and what actually goes on. Three of the more glaring examples are (a) individualism as a self-definition versus socially determined self, (b) health versus illness, (c) heterosexual projection versus homosexuality.

Individualism versus socially determined self

Bodybuilders prefer to be thought of as rugged individuals. Their very presence in such an individualized sport speaks to that preference. Those who came to the sport with a previous sport background invariably note their disdain for team sports and what it implies:

> I began developing a strong sense of individuality quite early. I was always turned off by team sports. I just didn't like being part of a team and the back-slapping and groupie sweating and all that. I would rather spend time in my basement pumping iron.

376

I liked football and all, but there was too much sharing. I just didn't wanna depend on anyone. I wanted to do something totally by myself. Bodybuilding is it.

A recent study of bodybuilders (Sprague, n.d.) used the Cattell 16PF psychology test on a random sample of people and found that bodybuilders were significantly more self-sufficient and less group-dependent than the mean population.

Of the numerous interviews conducted between 1979 and 1984, the expressed lack of ties among bodybuilders was typical, with characteristic comments like, "I'm a loner" or "I'm not easy to make friends with."

Question: Do you hang around with anyone in the gym?
Answer: No, no. You don't hang around with those guys, You're not gonna get it [acknowledgement] from them. The gym isn't really a social situation for me.

I don't think these guys make friends. You know what the problem is? Bodybuilders are selfish, and I been around for 10 years. They have to be. All they do is think about themselves. That's why —— was so popular. Cuz in a sport where selfishness, size, and hustling count, he was the most selfish, the biggest hustler, and just the biggest.

Within the gym, however, there are distinct social[2] and psychological categories, the most significant being gender. Women are far more likely to be social, more likely to bond with others than men are. They are also more likely to lend mutual assistance (Klein, 1985b). However, because men make up the majority of the gym's population, and always have, the atmosphere still rings of indifference, and at times even surliness. The social solidarity of women is typified in the following:

Women are tighter. I've seen girls swap clothing, posing suits at contests. And they helped me with my hair and makeup when my hairdresser didn't show up on time.

Some of the girls really helped each other. Like P. She had gas. She said to C, "I gottas get rid of this gas." So C. Starts taking her through these stomach exercises that will help her move the gas around, and she massages her stomach for it. It was really neat the way she put her own considerations aside . . . People help each other and that's what I like about the competitions.

The daily routine of bodybuilders and the relations they fashion and act in are all couched in atomistic behavior. Special dietary restrictions makes eating fairly dull and a more or less isolated act. The entire day is built around training, and much of the mental preparation is of the self-motivating form: no team sessions or mutual psyching (with one notable exception) as found in other sports. At the gym no one dares to break into someone else's routine or approach equipment until relatively certain that it is unused. Conversation, especially as a contest nears, is often kept to a minimum while working out.

> While we're training, we don't wanna be bothered. It's much more social for non-serious bodybuilders. Those guys have time to bullshit in the gym.

> I'm very sociable really. But I know when to cut it off. When I'm training I don't want to be bothered, like right now.

> I can't talk now, man.

Thus while the gym may appear as if it is rocking in collective exertion, it is, with the exception of the training partnership, really a long sequence of individual efforts.

It is in competing, however, that one glimpses the extent of the individualism. All pretense at social bonding abandoned, each bodybuilder views others suspiciously. Competitors in bodybuilding (unlike most other sports) train together in the same place, and each day of contest preparation is dotted with confrontations and guarded acts lest one's physical condition be prematurely revealed. To assure this privacy the body is swaddled in sweat clothes, no information is given, and a hostile bravado supplants a tentative affability.

As the contest nears, conversation, which is already at a premium, virtually ceases. This is as much the result of the pernicious effects of dieting as it is the anxiety of competition. Men give and ask for nothing.[3] Backstage at the contest, sullen, scantily clad men stand alone in a crowd. The ruthlessness of actual competition is no more bruising than the isolated preparation that goes into it (Klein, n.d., chapter 4).

Economically, bodybuilders suffer as a result of their atomism. What each pro strives for are contest earnings as well as endorsements. Additionally, a world-class bodybuilder can parlay his or her winnings and titles into a lucrative mail order business. This is the economic ideal: individual competitive success followed by self-employment. The result is that every successful bodybuilder competes for a finite market against others, as well as the leading entrepreneurs. In the face of such fierce competition, more rational attempts to conduct business such as joining forces or not duplicating efforts would seem imminent. But the individualism that is so pervasive works to prevent this. Needless to say, the possibility of a bodybuilders' union, as was attempted in 1979, is doomed form the start.

Feudal organization and bodybuilding

Despite their individualism, bodybuilders do in fact form a community, rooted in their physical distinctiveness and what it symbolizes. Forced in upon themselves, bodybuilders have fashioned a subculture in Southern California's more tolerant climate. The gym, various contests, Muscle Beach, and media hype are additional factors making possible the expression of the subculture. In this context their individualism is actually fused into a social system that allows them their atomism while concealing social bonds. This social system has many traits in common with a feudal social system, yet exists within capitalism (Klein, 1981, 1985a).

To the outsider the gym appears as either a group-grope or a collection of individuals, yet there exists a clearly demarcated social hierarchy as well as different strata of political and economic entities. Beginning with the latter, and borrowing the feudal analogy, bodybuilding has a small class of powerful lords consisting of the largest entrepreneurs such as the Weider organization and to a lesser extent Olympic Gym. Beneath them and tied to individual lords through ties of dependence, one finds the various professional bodybuilders. These men and women vie with one another not only for prize money in contests but for closer political ties with the moguls. Amateurs competing for limited access to these same mentors, as well as the larger category of noncompetitive bodybuilders, are the serfs. They serve in the capacity of consumers for the products generated by the other strata.

The key to this feudal structure is the tie of personal dependence. Within each strata individuals compete for rank and economic opportunity, the result being the creation of vertical ties at the expense of horizontal ones. The primary relationship is one between a mentor and a subordinate, between a mogul and a bodybuilder. The paternalistic giants in turn vie with one another for the allegiance of the competitors. Group solidarity is virtually impossible in such a milieu, a condition that allows for an exaggerated view of individual autonomy.

One of the most sought after rewards for the aspiring bodybuilder is magazine space for one's ads.[4] Here is what several candid bodybuilders had to say about the control exercised over the access to ad space:

> Of course it [success in the magazines] all depends on who you are. Tom P. and R. get a gratis thing [free ad space]. I know that Joe Weider doesn't like me, but then he doesn't like others also. I remember he said that R. would never appear in *Muscle and Fitness* but he did an article on him anyway. And somebody said that they heard Weider say that I didn't exist as far as he was concerned. But then I know that Joe is considering me for *Flex* . . . oh he wants to sell me but he doesn't wanna work with me.

A. used to go to Joe [Weider]. He was one of the intermittent people. He wouldn't get a lot but he'd get something. He would never get a mail order ad, but he would get a couple hundred bucks when his face appeared in the magazine, whereas everybody else has to be perfect and kiss their ass to get in the mag. Then A. found out that if he asked Joe for help, "Joe, I need some help in my posing." Or "Joe, my diet. I can't get it quite right." You know, make him feel as if he's needed. Well it worked to get him in.

Responding to my question in 1979 regarding a failed attempt to put together a bodybuilders' union by some people at the gym, one top professional dismissed it, revealing the feudel-like political structure in the subculture:

I don't think bodybuilders need a union. The IFBB [the largest international federation in the sport, created and presided over by the Weiders] operates with the best interests of bodybuilders in mind. Whenever problems arise they're willing to listen and legislate or change the situation for the better. I think if things were so bad that there had to be a union, there would have been a union.

Social organization of olympic

Because of its influential position in the sport, a gym like Olympic has a unique social organization. Six distinct hierarchically organized groups exist. These are arranged in pyramid fashion, with the members constituting the largest group.

Owners
Professional bodybuilders
Amateur bodybuilders
Gym rats (noncompetitors)
Members at large
Onlookers and Pilgrims

The first three categories are self-explanatory and not particularly unusual except that at Olympic one tends to find whole clusters of professionals and amateurs, whereas at most gyms finding one is unusual. The category of gym rat is worth describing, however. All serious gyms have these men and women at their core. They come in religiously and train hard, but are distinguished from pros and amateurs because they do not compete. Hence, in gym hierarchies gym rats have less status. Members comprise that category of people who train less than the other categories. Of gym regulars, they have the least status, often not even looking like bodybuilders.

There's a pecking order with guys like Mike at the top. Maybe I'm put in there too. In terms of who gets to use a piece of equipment if three guys are waiting for it, and other things having to do with the gym.

Olympic, however, has another category of people who do not belong to the gym. Onlookers and pilgrims come there either to satisfy their curiosity or because they are bodybuilders who come to pay homage to the place. Since they are constant presences in the gym, they are given a place in the front of the gym. Commenting on the removal of one line of gym equipment that had brought in a flood of outsiders, one competitor summed up insider/ outsider relations:

I'm kinda glad the water machines are out of the gym. I felt like I was training in a showroom. Those machines brought in a lotta sales people . . . and there was always those weirdos in business suits watching us all the time.

Get outta here. Go up there [pointing to the balcony] where all the weirdos gawk. I mean, where people train, you gotta prove yourself to be accepted. There's a lotta non-people in the gym, people who shouldn't be here.

This pyramidal organization is not a conscious one. Little in the way of formal organizational properties can be found in bodybuilding other than the organizing bodies that govern competition. Within the gym the only formal relationship is the training partnership. Usually made up of two (but sometimes three) people, training partners are responsible for pushing each other to their limits to enhance physical goals. This bond is formal and recognized as distinct from all other relationships. It is also a brittle bond, often lasting only as long as the preparatory period before a contest. Yet, through these partnerships a sequence of tentative bonds emerges, linking people in the gym together. The rarified nature of these bonds was succinctly stated by one female competitor: "It's easy to find a boyfriend, but a training partner is hard to find."

Health versus illness

In the past few years fitness and health have been the bodybuilder's ticket to cultural respectability. Weider changed the name of his magazine to reflect his going from *Muscle Power* to *Muscle and Fitness*. Bodybuilders now view themselves as nutritional and kinesiological experts, and for a fee will counsel others on matters of diet and training. Up on all the latest research in pop kinesiology, each has his or her idiosyncratic road to vigor and health and hypes it in comic books, exercise books, mail order ads, or most recently as guru-trainers to the stars. Certainly, in terms of fashioning their bodies into whatever form they desire, bodybuilders are advanced. Not only do they know what combinations of goods to consume, but also how to bulk up (increase mass) or cut up (reduce subcutaneous fat) on demand. This is fused with a mind-boggling array of weight training routines.

Self-mastery is the goal. Experiencing each repetition and calorie in terms of an overall plan for physical transformation is the means. One man had so mastered himself in terms of diet, training, and routine that he had no need of an alarm clock. At precisely 7:30 each morning he awoke with the urge to evacuate his bowels; at 11:30 a.m. his breakfast and food supplements were just kicking in and he could commence a 3-hour workout. Another had not missed a daily or twice-daily workout in 5 years. Illness is anathema, an admission of having failed to do things properly. Nutritional Calvinism is the philosophical tenet: bodybuilding success is partially predetermined (i.e., genetic), but good protein, complex carbohydrates, training, and so forth can help one realize his or her predetermined potential.

In direct contradiction to their public boasting of fitness and strength, we find bodybuilders' use of steroids and other drugs to be widespread. Despite the profoundly negative effects of steroids on health (e.g., the carcinogenic effects and negative impact on the liver), steroid use is virtually universal among male competitors and increasingly frequent among women and noncompetitors:

> They all use drugs, even the Mr. Naturals. That year that S. won the Olympia [a professional contest], he told me that he used more drugs that year than he'd ever used in his whole life. They all use 'em, and when they say they don't, they're lying.

Drug peddling is so common among bodybuilders that conversations about drugs and drug deals are barely concealed. As well versed as these people are in matters of training and nutrition, they are equally unquestioning and naive on the subject of drugs. For instance, thyroid prescriptions from other countries are not even translated into English. In one instance this lead to an overdosing just before a contest:

> I had a reaction to thyroid medication . . . I heard so much about a European product, I did something I hadn't been guilty of in the past—using it without knowing about it . . . I had all the symptoms of hyperthyroidism: nervousness, irritability, weakness, dizziness. You kind a feel subjected which is stupid, but you change so much during the last weeks before a contest. I mean bodybuilding is obviously not a healthy endeavor.

Drug related conversations are, ironically, quite lively, with a considerable sharing of information and misinformation. This is in marked contrast to other kinds of conversations.

The schizophrenic relationship of bodybuilding to steroid use involves outright denial and manifests itself in accusing others of drug abuse:

> I think we [referring to himself and friend] have the potential to be the best. All these guys [pointing around the gym] take steroids and we don't. Our structure is perfect. We don't take a lot. We been on steroids three times now [in the past 12 months].

In magazines bodybuilders espouse a competitive life free of steroids. Advice columns reject drugs as dangerous and not all that effective. Yet, among themselves they continue to consume dangerous quantities:

Q. Did you use a lot of steroids over a long period?
A. When I quit using steroids I had trouble finding a spot on my ass that I could inject.
Q. Why?
A. Cuz, calcium deposits build up when you inject certain steroids. And I'd been on a long cycle [using the drug for a protracted period].

One well known pro read his own advice column aloud in the gym in mocking tones. As he read his quote on banning steroids, he and the others gathered around him rolled with laughter.

The top pros know best how to use as little of the "right" drugs and get the results needed. But lesser lights have little knowledge of drugs and experiment freely on themselves. First-timers on oral steroids were, from time to time, seen doubled over in the corner of the gym. Another man handed me a box of hormones he was taking. The label cautioned, "Not to be used on horses that will be used for food."

The reason for drug use is that they help resolve a physical dilemma. The bodybuilder has to be as big as possible, yet achieve maximum muscular striation (getting "cut up"). This combination is usually incompatible. To facilitate striation a bodybuilder must diet down (perhaps as little as 1,000 calories a day) near contest time, but in doing so jeopardizes strength and the ability to retain size. Steroids are allegedly capable of enhancing strength and granting size, and in so doing permit one to continue to be large and achieve striation through dieting.

The extreme dieting preceding a contest also exacts a toll on the body as well as on the psyche. In conjunction with the anxiety surrounding the competition, many are not only weak but irritable as well. This is a time when bodybuilders lash out. Steroids only increase aggressiveness, and confrontations are kept to a minimum by judiciously limiting all social interaction.

Immediately before the contest many even take diuretics to increase the striated look and overcome the bloating effect that many steroids create. As one pro said, "When we walk on stage we are closer to death than we are to life."

Courting dehydration and exhaustion, pumped with a variety of steroids and other drugs, many bodybuilders no longer represent the picture of health they so busily promote. Citing the prison he felt competition symbolized for him, one informant commented on his retirement that he was happy because, "I'll never have to take my shirt off again. From here on I train for me."

Following the contest there is an institutional gorging, accurately termed "pigging out." In groups and singly, bodybuilders go out to eat vast quantities of food. In a single evening some will gain 15 pounds. On one occasion an informant consumed 7 pies. Another downed 24 donuts. The way binging and dieting occur institutionalizes borderline bulemic and anorexic behavior. These we know are syndromes involving intrapsychic disorders, but in bodybuilding they become structured into an acceptable cultural product. Epidemiological research suggests, however, that rapid weight fluctuation is positively correlated with certain forms of cancer and cardiac irregularities.

As with so much of bodybuilding, the behavior is based on shortsightedness. Steroids foster short-term success at the risk of long-term illness. Underlying this preoccupation with the immediate is the demand for the new wealth coming to the sport. This collective grasping takes its sense of urgency from bodybuilding's past isolation and the fact it was held in disrepute. As late as the mid 1970s almost no practitioner could make a living from the sport. With the fitness movement in the United States came the opportunity for many who labored in obscurity to make money in the sport. Thus, the relative deprivation has had the effect of negating long-term, rational considerations. The apparent deleterious impact of drugs is explained away through a series of pseudoscientific facts that claim the contrary—that in moderation and in the right dosages one can use steroids without ill effects. Hence, the contradiction between health and illness is understood as an historico-economic problem, and one that will continue until the rewards are not so great.

Heterosexuality and hustling

Heterosexuality is enshrined in the pages of *Muscle and Fitness*. Each issue abounds with full-color ads of men and women together, enjoying each other in some wholesome way. Forty years ago Charles Atlas' ads ran in comic books and also reinforced heterosexuality. In both Weider's and Atlas' ads the message is that if one looks like a man some woman will drape herself over him.

> Ya know in every age the women, they always go for the guy with muscles, the bodybuilder. [The women] never go for the studious guy.
> (Weider interview, March 1980)

The Atlas ad scenario underscores the same perspective. It begins with a young man out to impress his girl. They run into the physically imposing beach bully who insults the skinny man and kicks sand in his face, all of which is perceived as being emasculated. The girl is miraculously impressed with the bully's display, or so we are led to believe. An ad in his comic book leaps out at our unlikely hero, promising him a secure and permanent grip on his masculinity: a big body. Weeks later he avenges himself upon the bully by outsizing him and meting out physical punishment. In the course of this ludicrous scenario the woman is impressed and content to become the prize.

Size, masculinity, and physical appeal are equated with bodybuilding, and through magazines and ads that work by invidious comparison, they are hyped to an insecure public. Weider's latter-day versions of Atlas ads have not changed. The sexism is still present in his images of fit women seemingly delighted in being dwarfed by their he-men. The men all hold large impressive weights, while the women hold smaller, chrome plated versions of the same. It exaggerates their weakness to be cast in these scenes, but sales of these magazines have risen dramatically in the past 6 years.

For all this heterosexual posturing, bodybuilding has long existed under a cloud of suspicion. Be it the inordinate attention paid to oneself, the preoccupation with prancing about on stage wearing as little as possible, or an awareness that for all that form there is little function behind bodybuilding, many outsiders see bodybuilders as somehow associated with homosexuality.

Americans are perhaps the most homophobic people in the world. Cross-cultural analysis on the subject indicates that most societies are not nearly as fearful of homosexuality (Karlen, 1971). In enculturating young men we seek to instill in them the notion that one's masculinity is determined in direct proportion to the repudiation of anything deemed homosexual. The latter is based in negative associations men have of women, and involves negating those traits. For many the ultimate man is the most macho-looking and sounding, the most aggressive-appearing and acting. "Real" men do not wince in the face of pain or trouble; they do not emote freely. Anything falling outside of this is considered weak and unfit, that is, womanly. The final link in this line of reasoning is that should one be biologically male, yet behave as a weakling or a woman, then he is an a priori candidate for homosexuality.

Building one's body becomes a necessary part of achieving the desired state of heterosexuality for many men. Hence, little boys are taught a modified version of the military male model: tough, disciplined, and stoic. Popular culture reinforces this as young boys are inundated with heroes such as Hulk Hogan, Rambo, or bodybuilder Arnold Schwarzenegger as Conan or the Terminator. Anthony Wallace (1970) has shown what the negative consequences of such one-dimensional expectations were for the 18th-century Iroquois Indian warriors. Buried under hypermasculine behavior, it was difficult for them to show need, dependency, or softness; and the greater the need the more it needed to be displaced. Caught in a similar quandry, many bodybuilders simultaneously search for requisite masculinity and a repudiation of homosexuality.

Ironically, the selling of sexual favors to gay men is widespread in Southern California bodybuilding. Estimates of the activity range from 40% to 75% depending on who is queried.[5] It is called "hustling" by people at the gym, but it only involves the male members of the community. Hustling is a range of transactions involving a bodybuilder and a gay male. Only on rare occasions is a woman the procurer of sexual favors. The act of hustling may entail selling one's time for "beefcake" photographs, or nude dancing at all-male events, but primarily it involves sexual acts. The latter might be passive or active, depending on one's conscience. Hustling is seen as distinct from being gay, a dichotomy made by both bodybuilders as well as myself. The two may merge, as when a gay bodybuilder engages in the act of hustling, but informants pointed out that very few of the bodybuilders they knew who hustled were also gay.

The process by which a bodybuilder moves from his conscious heterosexual upbringing to hustling is complex. Hustling is not found equally often among all strata in the gym. Pros, for instance, do not hustle that much, while amateurs do so relatively more frequently. The bulk of this behavior is found among males who compete but do not as yet earn any real income from bodybuilding. Elsewhere (Klein, n.d., chapter 8) I have interpreted male hustling as an "economic strategy," engaged in primarily by amateurs and noncompetitors. The reason for it is that amateurs have made the commitment to train full-time for competition but do not have enough economic security to do so. Proper training is an out-growth of leisure time and money —time to mentally prepare oneself, to engage in lengthy training sessions. Given the educational background and work histories of most male bodybuilders, it is unlikely they would have the sorts of jobs that would allow them to train effectively. In Southern California, men train for the most prestigious contests (e.g., the Mr. California, or Gold's Classic, or the pro Mr. Universe or Mr. Olympia shows). This increases the caliber of training needed. The economic dilemma is answered through the gay community (or segments of it) that exist on the periphery of the subculture. Hustling is easy to initiate because of the proximity of men willing to pay for it. Once a hustler achieves any degree of security and can generate his own money, hustling is usually left behind.

There is a second and growing category of hustler—the bodybuilder who trains full-time without intending to compete. This man hustles purely to pay for his bodybuilding lifestyle. He has no intention of working his way up the ranks, and the presence of greater numbers of these men has been noted by many of the older informants who have been at Olympic for years (Klein fieldnotes, October, 1985).

Jennifer James' (1973) analysis of female prostitution holds valuable insights for this interpretation of hustling. She points out that for many of the young runaways who venture into the world of prostitution, the path is lined with people offering shelter and friendship but who, after a time, demand a payment (most often sexual). For young girls faced with the sudden pressure to reciprocate sexually for favors they thought were offered freely, the response is often based on guilt, shame, and capitulation. The sex they experience with their one-time protector or friend is often seen as the fall that makes all subsequent sex a moot point, and so they can move on to prostitution.

For many of the young men who go to Southern California and expect to be instantly successful at bodybuilding, the initial indifference they encounter can be jolting. Few come prepared emotionally, or with enough money to pay the dues demanded by the sport and lifestyle. These men are often the targets of advances made by other men. At first it might be just a token of friendship as when someone offers a badly needed job, or steroids, but later it is for services rendered. The quandry is quickly realized and while some bodybuilders reject these advances, many do not. It should also be noted that many hustlers as well as homophobic bodybuilders tend to see advances even where they don't exist. Hustling represents quick money, freeing them to train and meet expenses. To assuage guilt and facilitate acceptance of their impending status change, the men flirting with hustling will list all the great bodybuilders who have engaged in this behavior.

> People don't realize that in any given lineup of 20 competitors 10 are hustling.

> We have always had gays in the gym. . . . I learned from —— who was hustling, that all the guys were doing it and that really opened my eyes. But now there is such a heavy gay concentration in the gym.

Hardly anyone is spared, allowing the novice to feel that hustling is a rite of passage rather than a deviant act.

Interviews taken also point to compartmentalization of experience, a psychological device that allows one to separate out kinds of behavior that might be contradictory or otherwise problematic. Hence, straight life is separated from the hustling life. As with any defensive strategy, however, it can at times break down. At that point the suppressed anxiety surrounding homophobia manifests itself in hostile encounters toward gays. The very people who hustle most often are the ones who talk endlessly about their women and sexual conquests around other bodybuilders, thereby denying anything that might implicate them. The following is typical of the line of reasoning given for *not* going out with women while hustling, that is, that they are too demanding.

On any given time I can go out with a woman, but it's not very satisfying like a regular relationship. Women demand time. I don't have that right now. I lived with that girl [points to a photo] for a year and a half, but it's not that good. Several know what I'm doing. Some can handle it, some can't. I can't lie so that's why I'm not living with anyone until I get older.

The Jekyll-and-Hyde life they fashion enables them to juggle opposing moralities, but often the contradictions surface as hatred (often violent) of gays. Sometimes it takes the form of self-loathing and guilt, which on more than a few occasions has led to repudiation of the lifestyle and replacing it with Born Again Christianity. At other times it has led to suicide attempts. Reiss (1973) in his study of street hustlers documents the hatred that the hustlers had for gays. This expression of homophobia performs the function of separating the "peer" (hustler) from the "queer" (Reiss, 1973:404–406). It is likewise found among bodybuilders I interviewed:

I'll tell you being involved with the whole thing [hustling] reaffirmed my whole thing [being straight]. I remember in Venice I was involved in that, you know, community and saw so much that I began to wonder about their sanity and mine.

Maybe 75% of the judges on any panel are gay. Well, they might understand this [the sane view of hustling] at the same time that they might hold it against you: the fact that you're working in that gay world, taking advantage of their people.

Here we see how hustling may fuel a hustler's homophobia as well as resentment on the part of gays. Viewing gays in a predatory way allows the hustler to continue the charade that lets him separate out his "straight self" identity from the hustling behavior he engages in. Gays who regularly seek sexual favors from bodybuilders often see the relation as predatory as well. Comments about getting the best of the deal are typical.

The positive role of gays in the world of bodybuilding, however, cannot be denied. As a group, bodybuilders tend to have (or have had) a poor sense of self. They generally require a strong dose of material and emotional support. It is in this context that various gay men have played a substantial role. When the society at large was indifferent or even hostile to bodybuilders, members of the gay community would lend support and admire them by acting in the capacity of fans and defenders. Gays essentially subsidized the sport in the difficult days of bodybuilding when the sport paid little.

The reasons for the attention paid by gays to bodybuilders stems from a psychological complex that merges heterosexual and homosexual issues. One is the notion that bodily form (and overall looks) is best understood and appreciated in a nonerotic way by members of the same sex. I refer here to the many studies pointing out that men dress for other men rather than for women, and the converse of that. This is based in part on self-love extended to encompass our gender, or appreciation of our gender as an extension of ourselves. I would call this *gender narcissism*, and it is universal, essential in the formation of bonds among members of the same sex. The excessive homophobia in our society, however, fosters a view of this otherwise healthy expression of gender narcissism as too close to homosexuality to allow expression. That gays have historically been supportive of bodybuilding therefore is seen in all cases to result from their erotic desires. The broader appreciation stemming from gender narcissism is fused with the erotic and suppressed. In doing so, however, we deny the capacity to appreciate any extension of our gender. Women, being less homophobic than men, are less likely to do this. It is, for instance, deemed suitable for women to state how attractive another woman may be, while one rarely hears something comparable from one man to/or about another.

The concern with presenting the sport in the best possible light has resulted in expunging any association with homosexuality and narcissism. The subculture of bodybuilding raises this possibility more than any other sport, but ultimately asks the question of sport itself.

Conclusion

In this study I have attempted to show how each publicly expressed value is created and then, because of the sport's need for acceptance, betrayed. New relations, within the subculture and between the subculture and society, stem from its increasing incorporation into contemporary capitalism. As a result a series of quasi-contradictions are brought to the fore. While the world of bodybuilding never envisioned itself as an alternative to status quo society, it nevertheless developed atypically and so fell within the domain of deviant subculture.

The sticking point that prevented greater cultural acceptance of the sport of bodybuilding has always been the vanity factor in addition to the sexual suspicions cast on its practitioners. Contrary to the Protestant Ethic, pre-occupation with the body was seen as a frivolous, self-indulgent exercise in vanity. Recruitment to the subculture, however, stems from real, felt unmet needs and personality deficiencies. In short, poor self-image lurks in the background of most bodybuilders.

> I got caught up in the sport just cuz I was thin, and I wanted to put some body weight on, you know, get big.

> I was picked on when I was a kid. There was no support from my parents. I was always wrong in my parents' eyes.

I was never dated, not even for the senior prom . . . People used to laugh at me when I'd wear a bikini. They'd call me chicken legs. Now I can walk through a crowd and people go. "Check her out, what a bod."

Poor body image also results from emotional and other handicaps. Dyslexia, stuttering, eye problems, along with short stature and weight problems, were all documented as factors contributing to low self-worth among people at Olympic Gym. Considering their low self-esteem, mainstream views of bodybuilders as narcissistic and vain misses the point (Klein, n.d., chapter 9). This study sees the narcissism institutionalized in bodybuilding as therapeutic, a view also shared with bodybuilders who see it as a mark of how far they've personally come.

Well, I would say that as a bodybuilder you have your mind so much into your body. You have to keep thinking positive. You may not be falling in love with your body, but you are positive that you're great in looking at yourself. I noticed that when I was more in love with my body and I'd look in the mirror; I dunno, it's something to do with muscle and pain. Your mind has to be so positive. In the gym you have to be in love with your workout. You have to think about your pump [muscle worked to the point of failure]. So in a way I would have to say that bodybuilders are in love with themselves.

These guys are drawn to bodybuilding for some reason, insecurities or whatever. That's why they flare their lats out like that.

Q. Do you think they're narcissistic?
A. Have you looked at the guys in this gym? Damn straight they're narcissistic. It's gotta be cuz of where these guys' heads are at, you know, insecurity.

It is at this point that deviant and occupational subcultures merge into a single category. The labeling of bodybuilders as deviant is then stood upon its head by the bodybuilders who turn the stigma into status-bearing criteria (c.f., Hebdige, 1983). Thus narcissism becomes essential, leading to perfection, and hypermasculinity becomes the Mr. Olympia form.

More recently, the society at large seems to be altering its views on bodybuilding. Matza and Sykes (1961) point out that values associated with the dramatic rise of leisure since World War II foster a change in views of deviance. Values centering on excitement, disdain for work, hedonism, masculinity, and toughness are socially more highly regarded, and these are traits central to the bodybuilding subculture. Bodybuilding, then, stands to gain cultural acceptance by virtue of being what was previously most reprehensible, that is, self-indulgent, narcissistic, excessive, and sexually exotic.

Ironically the sport of bodybuilding has, according to its premier publication, chosen just this time to stress traditionally held cultural values such as hard work, wholesomeness of family, filial piety, God and country. Ideologues in this sport have missed the point that it is the oft-held view of bodybuilding as lured, seamy, and excessive that is at the core of its new-found appeal. Instead, cover photos depict hulking men with their wives, girlfriends, or a model, but always lacking sexuality. Articles heralding the virtues of nutrition and drug-free lives abound, not to mention clinchés about hard work and Horatio Alger snippets by the truckload. It is likewise ironic that many suspicions once held by outsiders turn out to have more than an element of truth. However, now those suspicions are fashionable—vanity and hedonism is in, as attested to by the popularity of the looks and messages of rock stars such as Madonna, Prince, and David Lee Roth.

In the course of this obstacle-strewn path to success, bodybuilding seeks to pay homage to tradition while appearing postmodern. This often creates more questions. As with the adult who earlier suffered humiliation, much of later life is spend responding to that hurt. So it is with bodybuilding, which can never completely enjoy its newfound success. The wound is historic and institutionalized as a set of behaviors. The recent rise in popularity of that subculture has generated a crisis in confidence because so much of the subculture was premised on social stigma that removing the barriers threatens many of the institutions within the subculture.

The work done on subcultures (e.g., Becker, 1963; Cohen, 1955; Brake, 1980), it seems, has understood the need to look at origins of subculture but has missed the value of looking at subsequent developments, such as removal of the stigmatization that can create new problems. These problems foster conflicts within the subculture precisely, as I have tried to show, because of the change in rules and structures. Sport ethnography goes a long way toward helping social scientists discern these crises.

Notes

1 The feeling on the part of mainstream sociologists seems to be that if one teaches sport sociology, one suddenly has a joint appointment with the physical education department. Disparaging comments about those who study popular culture, media, and in this instance sports, are thinly veiled as jokes but show through as counter-productive elitism.

2 In 1983 the owners of Olympic Gym estimated their annual dues-paying members to be approximately 700, but as many as 2,000 come for shorter periods. The numbers of professional bodybuilders there range from 4 to 10 or more, amateurs from 10 to 30. Most gyms are fortunate to have a single pro or amateur in their ranks.

3 There is a term among Southern California bodybuilders for psyching out one's opponents: "the California treatment"; it is subtle, designed to destroy an

adversary's confidence. Men are experts at this sort of behavior. Women have until recently been less likely to use it.

4 Ads in Weider's magazines are for the individual's mail order business. The space sells for about $2,500 per page per month. To defray the cost, a bodybuilder will seek to endorse Weider products. In return he or she will pay a reduced fee for the ad.

5 No informant I asked felt that hustling was insignificant. Most feel that it has increased in the past several years.

References

Becker, Howard 1963 Outsiders: Studies in the Sociology of Deviance. New York: Glencoe Press.

Blanchard, Kendall and Alyce Cheska 1985 The Anthropology of Sport. South Hadley, MA: Bergin & Garvey.

Boswell, Thomas 1983 How Life Imitates the World Series. New York: Penguin Books.

Brake, Mike 1980 The Sociology of Youth Culture and Youth Subcultures. London: Routledge & Kegan Paul.

Brower, Jonathan 1975 Little League Baseballism: Adult Dominance in a Child's Game. Paper presented at Pacific Sociological Association meetings, Victoria, B.C.

Cantelon, H. and Richard Gruneau 1982 Sport, Culture, and the Modern State. Toronto: University Tornonto Press

Coakley, Jay 1982 Sport in Society. St. Louis: C.V. Mosby.

Cohen, Albert K. 1955 Delinquent Boys: The Culture of the Gang. New York: The Free Press.

Daner, Francine J. 1976 The American Children of Krsna: A Study of Hare Krsna Movement. New York: Holt, Rinehart & Winston.

Devereux, Edward C. 1976 Backward Versus Little Legaue Baseball: The Impoverishment of Children's Games. Pp. 179–192 in D. Landers (ed.), Social Problems in Athletics. Champaign, IL: University of Illinois Press.

Diamond, Stanley 1972 "Review, man and culture: a philosophical anthropology" (A.W. Levy, ed., Dell Publ., NY). American Anthropologist, 74(3):304–307.

Downes, D. 1966 The Delinquent Solution. London: Routledge & Kegan Paul.

Durkheim, Emile 1953 "Value judgements and judgements of reality." Pp. 37–55 in Society and Philosophy. New York: Free Press.

Eitzen, Stanley (ed.) 1983 Sport in Contemporary Society. New York: St. Martin's Press.

Eitzen, Stanley and George Sage 1978 Sport in American Society. Dubuque: IA: W.C. Brown.

Freilich, Morris 1977 "The meaning of sociocultural." Pp. 20–33 in D. Bernardi (ed.), Concepts and Dynamics of Culture. The Hague: Mouton.

Geertz, Clifford 1972 "Deep play: notes on the Balinese cockfight." Pp. 126–141 in The Interpretation of Culture. New York: Basic Books.

Hebdige, Dick 1983 Subculture: The Meaning of Style. London: Methuen.

James, Jennifer 1973 "The prostitute-pimp relationship." Medical Aspects of Human Sexuality, (Nov.), pp. 147–160.

Karlen, Arno 1971 Sexuality and Homosexuality. New York: Norton.

Keixer, Lincoln 1979 The Vice Lords: Warriors of the Streets (2nd Ed.). New York: Holt, Rinehart & Winston.

Klein, Alan M. 1981 "The master blaster: empire building and bodybuilding." Arena Review, 5(3):12–15.

1985a "Muscle manor: the use of sport metaphor and history in sport sociology." Journal of Sport and Social Issues, 9(1):4–19.

1985b "Pumping iron." Society, 22(6):68–75. n.d. No Pain, No Gain: The Subculture of Bodybuilding. In preparation.

Lee, Richard 1979 The Kung San: Men, Women, and Work in a Foraging Society, Cambridge: Cambridge University Press.

Leonard, W. 1980 A Sociological Perspective of Sport. Minneapolis: Burgess.

Lever, Janet 1983 Soccer Madness. Chicago: University of Chicago Press.

Liebow, Elliot 1969 Tally's Corner. Boston: Little, Brown & Co.

Linton, Ralph 1945 The Cultural Background of Personality. New York: Appleton-Century-Crofts.

Lipsyte, Robert 1975 Sportsworld: An American Dreamland. New York: New York Times Books.

Loy, J.W., B.D. McPherson and G.S. Kenyon (eds.) 1978 Sport and Social Systems. Reading, MA: Addison-Wesley.

Matza, David 1964 Delinquency and Drift. New York: Wiley & Sons.

1969 Becoming Deviant. Englewood Cliffs, NJ: Prenctice-Hall.

Matza, D. and G. Sykes 1961 "Techniques of neutralization." American Sociological Review, 27(4):667–670. Muscle and Fitness

1979–1984 Woodland Hills, CA: Weider Enterprises.

Phillips, J. and W. Shafer 1971 "Athletics, aspirations, and attainments." Sociology of Education, 42(1):102–113.

Reiss, A. 1973 "The social integration of peers and queers." In E. Rubington and M. Weinberg (eds.), Deviance: The Interactionist Perspective. New York: MacMillan.

Schwartzman, Helen B. (ed.) 1980 Play and Culture. West Point, NY: Leisure Press.

Sewart, John 1983 Trash Sports. Paper delivered at 4th Annual Meeting of North American Society for Sociology of Sport, St. Louis.

Spradley, James 1970 You Owe Yourself a Drunk. Boston: Little, Brown & Co.

Spradley, James and Patricia Mann 1975 The Cocktail Waitress. New York: Wiley & Sons.

Sprague, Homer n.d. Psychological profiles of bodybuilders. (unpublished manuscript)

Stevens, Phillips 1977 Studies in the Anthropology of Play. West Point: NY: Leisure Press.

Tindall, B. Allen 1975 "The cultural transmissive function of physical education." Council on Anthropology and Education Quarterly, 16(2):10–20.

Turnbull, Colin 1965 The Forest People. New York: Simon & Schuster.

Wallace, A.F.C. 1970 Death and Rebirth of the Seneca. New York: Alfred A. Knopf.

59

DISABILITY MANAGEMENT AMONG WOMEN WITH PHYSICAL IMPAIRMENTS

The contribution of physical activity

Sharon R. Guthrie and Shirley Castelnuovo

Source: *Sociology of Sport Journal* 18(1)(2001):5–20.

The purpose of this qualitative study was to describe the ways women with physical disabilities shape their identities and manage (i.e., cope or come to terms with) their disabilities while living in an able-bodyist culture. Particular emphasis was placed on how these women, all of whom were participating in sport or exercise, used physical activity in the management process. In-depth interviews were conducted with 34 women who had physical mobility disabilities. Findings indicated three different approaches to managing disability via physical activity: (a) management by minimizing the significance of the body, (b) management by normalization of the body, and (c) management by optimizing mind-body functioning. They also indicated that having a disability does not preclude positive physical and global self-perceptions. The implications of these findings for sport and society are discussed.

Three times a week during the early afternoon hours, when few people are around, we lift weights at a local health club. Rita, a woman with paraplegia, does the same. She knows that at this time of day there will be fewer people exercising, thus less traffic to negotiate in her motorized wheelchair and more chance that the few machines she is capable of accessing will be available.

Rita begins each exercise by carefully positioning her chair as close to the machine as possible and at a particular angle. Then, after slowly and methodically transferring her weight from the seat of the chair to that of the machine, she prepares herself for lifting. This arrangement of her body takes Rita at least as much time as the routines she executes. Moreover, her facial expressions suggest that the process, from beginning to end, is difficult and sometimes painful. Yet Rita persists, asking for no one's help, until her workout is completed. Watching and admiring the tenacity and focus of this woman, we have often wondered what motivates her to lift weights amid myriad physical and social obstacles, and how her bodily experience differs from those of persons without disabilities.

It is clear that when Rita works out, she pays attention to her body and the exercise environment in ways that persons without disabilities typically do not. For example, Rita does not take for granted her movement from machine to machine or her ability to get in and out of the machines as able-bodied weightlifters are prone to do. What takes relatively little attentional space for persons without disabilities, she has to seriously contemplate. Thus, Rita's body does not fade as easily from focal awareness.

This tendency of the "able" body to disappear from consciousness until some form of distress or dysfunction (e.g., pain, fatigue, hunger) is experienced encourages support for mind-body dualism, which has dominated much of Western thought for centuries (Leder, 1990). One of the central reasons dualistic thought has maintained its influential power, despite an ongoing critique, is because it is confirmed by everyday experience. That is, when our bodies function without problems, they are hardly noticeable, yet when we are sick or feel aches and pains, they become the focus of attention. It is at times such as these that we are most likely to experience the body as divorced from the mind and incapable of being fully determined or controlled by the will.

Our weightlifting experience and that of Rita reminds us, however, that the body is more than a complex physico-chemical object, subject to inclinations of the immaterial mind. Rather, it is the medium through which our perceptions and experiences of the world emerge. When we interact physically with the world, in this case with the weight-lifting equipment, we are engaging in the process of self-definition or what Merleau-Ponty (1962) referred to as "motility." That is, human identity and consciousness are embodied experiences, which can be enhanced by moving the body in skillful and intentional ways.

It does seem true that when we lift weights and thus improve our muscular strength and endurance, we experience improvements in the more global, less physical dimensions of self as well. We also gain greater clarity of mind-body unity and interdependence rather than separation and opposition. Rita most likely shares this experience. In fact, she may feel this sense of empowerment even more profoundly than we because she is engaged in a process that challenges stereotypes associated with physical disability, in addition to developing her own mind-body capabilities.

Unfortunately, however, Rita's empowerment emerges in a sociocultural context in which able-bodied norms are firmly entrenched. Most every aspect of this context, from the society at large to the structuring and placement of weight machines in this particular gym, reflect such norms. Being a person with a disability, Rita confronts the physical reality of her impairment, as well as social indicators that her body is "abnormal" and "lesser than" those of able-bodied persons. As a woman, she receives messages that her body should be a particular size and shape. Living in a society that fosters dualistic thinking and individual responsibility, she is told that because her mind can control her body, she is accountable for her own health and normalization. She may also be informed, in subtle and not so subtle ways, that she is incapable of developing abstract, rational thought because her disability makes transcending the physical realm difficult.

It therefore appears that Rita and other women with disabilities encounter at least four social forces, which we refer to as discourses of embodiment, that can influence their identity formation: (a) the discourse of disability (i.e., able-bodyism), (b) the discourse of feminine body-beauty, (c) the discourse of dualism, and (d) the discourse of personal responsibility.[1] Moreover, if they are women of color, lesbian, bisexual, or financially disadvantaged, they must contend with additional discourses. Given these physical and social constraints, how do women like Rita manage to develop a healthy sense of self?

Foucauldian analysis helps to explain how this is possible. According to Foucault (1990), although discourses, particularly those associated with sexual identity, have a profound impact on the way people constitute themselves, resistance to these discourses also occurs. Rita exemplifies such resistance. Indeed, one day she told us that her identity as a sexually attractive, professional woman was demolished the day she was forced to use a wheelchair and that, against her will, "disabled woman" became her master status, particularly in able-bodied circles. She confessed that such restrictive notions of who she is are deeply disturbing; however, she finds that the focus weight training requires helps her to cope with the discrimination she experiences, as well as to destabilize stereotypes associated with physical limitation. Rita's reactions to the discourse associated with disability (i.e., able-bodyism) confirm Foucault's relational understanding of power: where power exists, there will also be resistance.

Foucault (1985, 1988, 1989) posited two types of resistance, however: "reverse resistance," which involves continued support of a power-knowledge discourse, and "resistance as freedom," which requires developing a self that is not grounded in the limiting aspects of the discourse. For example, if Rita engages in weight training as a way to normalize or beautify herself—attempting to minimize her disability in the eyes of others—her actions reinforce the discourse associated with able-bodied norms. In contrast, if she uses weight training to develop herself physically and mentally in ways that transcend the discourse, she is engaging in resistance as freedom.

While the Foucauldian distinction between reverse resistance and resistance as freedom is useful in deciphering Rita's experiences, his notion of resistance as an intellectual enterprise is less so. For example, Rita's disability and weight training are not solely mental experiences, they are also physical processes. Therefore, her acts of resistance and self-transformation have a physical dimension as well. Moreover, Foucault claimed that resistance as freedom must remain an individual act because if the potentially liberating practice becomes part of a group dynamic, the possibility of a new, yet equally confining, discourse is created; thus, he did not allow for collective resistance.

Because Foucauldian logic does not fully elucidate Rita's physical activity experiences or those of the other women we studied, we found it necessary to meld Foucault's ideas with those of Merleau-Ponty, who provides another, yet complementary, theoretical framework to fill the explanatory gap. The strength of Merleau-Ponty's philosophy is his belief that human subjectivity is located in the body rather than the mind and that movement, what he called "motility," is the critical factor in the construction of human identity. Motility, he claimed, which involves moving one's body in space, always results in a new embodied reality. Therefore, it is through the process of movement, as opposed to sheer mental activity, that one's consciousness develops. Merleau-Ponty also argued, in contrast to Foucault, that resistance, and ultimately social transformation, can never be a solitary activity, but rather must involve the interaction of multiple individuals who are collectively engaged in resistant activities.

Grounding our work in this combined phenomenological Foucauldian perspective, we thus set out to answer the following questions: (a) how do women like Rita shape their identities and manage their physical disabilities while living in an able-bodyist culture and (b) what function does physical activity serve in the management process, if any?[2]

Method

Participants

Thirty-four physically active adult female volunteers, ranging in age from 20–72 (M = 29.2), participated in this study.[3] All of the participants had physical mobility disabilities, including spinal cord injury ($n = 12$), congenital limb deficiency ($n = 9$), amputation ($n = 5$), acquired brain injury ($n = 1$), post-polio syndrome ($n = 2$), multiple sclerosis ($n = 2$), amyotrophic lateral sclerosis ($n = 1$), spina bifida ($n = 1$), and dwarfism ($n = 1$). Twenty-two of the women had acquired disabilities while 12 had congenital disabilities. The disability ages (i.e., the amount of time one has had a disability or disabilities) ranged from 6 months to 42 years: 18 had disability ages of less than 5 years (defined in this study as a short disability age) while 16 had lived with their disabilities for 5 years or more (defined as a long disability age).

The racial/ethnic composition of this sample included 22 Caucasians, 4 African-Americans, 1 Asian American, 2 Hispanics, and 5 multiracial individuals (i.e., those identifying with more than one racial/ethnic category).

The majority ($n = 26$) had at least some college education ($n = 12$), or already possessed a bachelor's degree ($n = 12$), master's degree ($n = 1$), or doctoral degree ($n = 1$). Although the sample was comprised primarily of hetero-sexuals ($n = 25$), seven women identified themselves as lesbian and two as bisexual.

Ten of the participants were competing in various types of organized sports (i.e., basketball, tennis, marathon racing). The majority ($n = 24$) were not involved in sport but were exercising on a regular basis in non-competitive settings, that is, at least three times a week for at least 30 minutes. Of these regular exercisers, 10 had competed in sport in the past, most before they had acquired their disability ($n = 6$).

Procedures

The participants were recruited from various disability organizations (both sport and non-sport-related), the student populations at four universities, and by word of mouth. To be a participant in this study, a woman had to meet two criteria: (a) she had to have a physical mobility disability, and (b) she had to be participating in some form of regular physical activity (e.g., sport or exercise).

Instrumentation

An interview guide was developed specifically for the purposes of this study. The researchers drew upon their previous work with women with disabilities in constructing the interview questions and pilot-tested the guide with two women with physical disabilities—one with a physical mobility impairment and the other with congenital limb deficiency—to determine the appropriateness and clarity of the questions. As a result of these interviews, the questions were deemed appropriate and clear.

Interviews, all of which were conducted by the same person, consisted primarily of open-ended questions and were standardized to maximize con-sistency. Each question was read exactly as worded, only non-directive probes were used for clarification and elaboration (i.e., those that do not influence the content of the resulting answers), all responses were tape-recorded and transcribed without interviewer discretion, and the interviewer attempted to communicate a neutral, nonjudgmental perspective with regard to the respondents' answers. These procedures are accepted among qualitative researchers (Fowler & Mangione, 1990).

Each woman was interviewed privately in her home, by phone, or in the researcher's office for approximately 90 minutes. The interview began by ask-ing general questions about the nature of one's disability and physical activity history. It then became more focused by asking questions directly associated with the goal of the study (see Appendix A for sample interview questions).

All participants were made aware that they could refuse answering any question and terminate the interview at any time. At the end of the interview, they were allowed to add anything they believed to be important, and later, after the interviews were transcribed, participants also had the opportunity to review the transcripts and make corrections or additions.

Inductive content analysis

Each interview was transcribed verbatim in preparation for data analysis. After the transcripts were completed, each interview was read, question by question, and salient themes and illustrating quotes were recorded. The purpose of the inductive analysis was to synthesize specific perceptions reported by the participants into meaningful themes. To accomplish this, the data were first sorted into raw data themes associated with each of the research goals. Each of the raw data themes was then recorded on a separate sheet of paper. Quotations illustrating the theme were also written on the paper, in addition to a comment summarizing the quote. One reliability check was performed by having two other individuals trained in qualitative methods— one who was associated with the research investigation and another who was not—read all of quotes and summary comments to determine if the summaries accurately reflected the quotes. The reviewers found the summaries to be accurate reflections of the quotes.

After the list of raw data themes was compiled, an inductive analysis of the data was undertaken in order to generate lower order and higher order themes (i.e., merging similar raw data themes together into broader concepts). A second reliability check was performed by a fourth person, not associated with the investigation, who independently read the transcripts and subsequently categorized raw data themes into more general themes. These categories were compared to those established by the researchers and found to be 100% consistent at both the lower and higher order levels. The trustworthiness and credibility of qualitative analyses may be established through the use of such techniques (Lincoln & Guba, 1985; Patton, 1990).

Results

The primary purpose of this study was to determine how women with physical mobility disabilities manage their disabilities while living in an able-bodyist culture, and in particular, how physical activity was used in the process. A total of 47 lower order themes were extracted relative to this goal. Inductive analysis revealed that these lower order themes coalesced into three general dimensions; that is, three distinct approaches to managing disability were identified, each of which was characterized by a different way of perceiving and valuing physical activity (see Table 1).

Table 1 Disability management themes

Lower order themes	Higher order themes	General dimensions
Focus on: • Readings (i.e., fiction, autobiography, biography, poetry, religious/spiritual) • Artistic expression (i.e., painting, photography, sculpting, performing and composing music, writing) • Academic/job/professional aspirations	Mental strategies	All three groups ($N = 34$)
Focus on: • Involvement with religious/spiritual community • Religious/spiritual teachings • Trying to be a better, more moral person	Spiritual strategies	
Focus on: • Using the Internet to meet others • Social and professional support networks	Social strategies	
Physical activity (primarily exercise) used: • to control disease • to prevent further disability • to prevent disability-related complications • to avoid guilt, fear, worry, vacillation of negative emotions • to alleviate disability-related depression • to alleviate disability-related anger and frustration • to avoid self-pity	Physical activity for health and therapeutic purposes only	Minimalization of the body group ($n = 10$, 29.5%)

	Physical activity to fit able-body ideals of of beauty and mind-body function	Normalization/beautification of the body group (n = 14.41%)
Physical activity (primarily exercise) used: • to look and feel sexier • to look lose weight • to look athletic • to look and feel fit • to avoid looking abnormal (either functionally or aesthetically) • to look and feel more womanly • to gain muscle tone • to be more popular with males		
Physical activity (primarily sport) used: • to enhance self-efficacy • to enhance self-esteem • to enhance motor skill and control • to enhance perception of control (internal locus of control) • to enhance mind-body unity and awareness • to be stronger physically and mentally • to be a great athlete • to be less vulnerable to psychosexual abuse in relationships, at work, and in social settings	Physical activity: • to enhance mind-body functioning • to challenge one's own internalized ableism	Optimizing mind-body functioning group (n = 10, 29.5%) Non-collectives (n = 6)
	• to enhance mind-body functioning • to challenge one's own and others' internalized ableism, as well as disability oppression in society	Collectives (n = 4)

Management by minimizing bodily significance

The first group ($n = 10$, 29%), comparised primarily of women with acquired disabilities ($n = 7$) and an equal number of long and short disability ages, have managed their disabilities by minimizing, as much as possible, their focus on the body and the physical dimension of living. For most of these women, the body was viewed as an encumbrance, quite separate from the mind. Although they used physical activity to manage their disabilities to some extent (e.g., preventing further disability and disability-related complications), it was not a significant aspect of their lives, and for most of them, it had never been. Instead, mental, social, and spiritual activities were more often used to facilitate the development of a positive identity and to cope with disability (e.g., being a competent student, worker, or professional; meditating; taking a religious perspective on disability and life; using the Internet to communicate and develop support systems). Therefore, the discourse associated with dualism seemed to be very significant in shaping their attitudes and behaviors.

The most notable commonality among these women was that they viewed physical activity as unpleasant work and were active for physical health or therapeutic reasons only. Although two had been former athletes, the majority ($n = 8$) began their current exercise programs at the request of a doctor or physical therapist, mostly to avoid further physical disability. Moreover, none of these women reported physical activity to be helpful in coping with disability discrimination. The following comments made by one woman with an acquired spinal cord injury and another with multiple sclerosis (in response to the question, "what motivated you to become physically active?") illustrate the largely fear- and guilt-driven nature of this group's participation in physical activity:

> I began exercising, mostly swimming, only because I was told by my doctor that it would be good for my health. Being in a wheelchair all the time isn't good for my circulation, heart, and overall health. I know I'm supposed to exercise, so I do. And it's true—exercise does help me deal with some of the physical aspects of my condition. Exercising does very little, however, for my overall self-esteem, nor has it helped me to be more accepting of my disability. Only my religious beliefs and focusing on my work helping others as a teacher help me to do that. I think the emphasis this society places on physical fitness is a bit obsessive. I have always been more interested in activities that are less physical in nature.

> I started exercising regularly when I found out I have MS. The doctors told me it would be good for me. Even though I never cared much about exercising or other physical activites, it makes me feel

like I am doing something for myself . . . that I am taking care of myself physically. I know a positive attitude helps. When I exercise I feel less fearful of my future.

Another commonality among this group was that they preferred exercise over sport. For those who did not consider themselves athletic, exercise was their activity of choice because they felt less uncoordinated and vulnerable to injury when exercising than when playing sport ($n = 7$). In contrast, the athletes, both of whom had competed before acquiring their disabilities, preferred exercise because sport reminded them of how their lives and physical capabilities had been altered forever. As one woman with a recently acquired spinal cord injury remarked,

> I used to pride myself on my physical prowess, particularly in team sports. After my accident, all I did was feel sorry for myself. Someone recommended that I join a wheelchair basketball league. "Go back to sports," they said, "you can shine again, maybe be even more successful because there will be less competition!" No way was I going to play wheelchair basketball. I still haven't fully come to terms with my disability and playing sport makes it worse. All I do is think about how it used to be. I lift weights though because I want to keep my upper body as fit as possible so I will be less dependent on others.

Management by normalizing the body

Women in the second group ($n = 14$, 41%), who had predominantly acquired disabilities ($n = 11$) and short disability ages ($n = 11$), managed disability by trying to normalize themselves, particularly their bodies, as much as possible; they used physical activity for the same purpose (e.g., to improve their physical appearance and sexual attractability; to lose weight, gain muscle tone, or maximize their body's functional status so that their bodies and motor function did not appear abnormal or aesthetically displeasing). In other words, their physical activity, which was primarily in exercise ($n = 11$) rather than sport ($n = 3$), was an attempt to align or, more often, realign themselves as much as possible with feminine body-beauty and other able-bodied ideals.

Although this group used a variety of non-physical strategies to manage disability (e.g., focusing on professional aspirations, non-physical hobbies, social networks, and religious beliefs), they placed far more importance on physical appearance and the physical dimension of living than the first group, who minimized the body's importance. Such emphasis is reflected in the comments of three women with acquired disabilities (i.e., post-polio syndrome, acquired brain injury, and amputation) when asked their reasons for engaging in physical activity:

I have always been interested in keeping myself looking good and my body as sexually appealing as possible. Exercise helps me to feel better about my body and to feel more normal. This became particularly important after I got ill and realized that I am no longer able to have the life I took for granted. Feeling better about my body and my looks helps me feel OK about myself.

I hate looking weird, but I don't have much choice. I walk with a stagger because of my accident. Exercising and keeping myself fit helps me to feel more normal. I also feel like it will keep me from regressing even further physically. Who knows, maybe someday they [the doctors] will come up with something to make me normal again.

Before the accident, I was always known for my good body. Although I had to watch my weight, which I did with diet and exercise, I was considered very attractive. When I lost my leg and arm in the accident, I was really scared about whether anyone would find my attractive again. My boyfriend bagged out, almost immediately. I still have a lot of anger, and I hate the stares in the gym; I go there mostly to keep what body I've got left looking good so that I don't withdraw completely from the public life I used to have.

Thus, in comparison to the first group, these women had much more deeply internalized the discourse of feminine body-beauty. They also were much more influenced by the discourse of individual responsibility, which was reflected in their feeling pressure to "look like everyone else," at least as far as external appearance was concerned, and guilt when they felt they had failed (e.g., in their weight control). They were similar to the women in the first group in three ways, however: (a) they tended to view exercise as work and as a means to an end, in this case to normalize/beautify the body, (b) they were not participating in physical activity for political reasons (i.e., to challenge one's own or other's internalized ableism), and (c) they expressed little or no interest in being or becoming social change agents via any of their activities, physical or otherwise.

Management by optimizing mind-body functioning

The women in the third group ($n = 10$, 29%) had adopted what seemed to be a more balanced mind-body approach to living with disability than those in the first two groups. Rather than emphasizing the importance of either mental or physical strategies in managing disability, this group believed both to be important. They also seemed to be developing their identities, for the most part, according to their own criteria, as opposed to those considered acceptable by able-bodied society.

Although minimizing the negative influences of able-bodyism (i.e., the disability discourse) and the other discourses of embodiment was not an easy task for any of them, they had found ways of being in the world that challenged such constraints, thus allowing a more self-determined identity to emerge. As two participants (one with a spinal cord injury and another with congenital limb deficiency) remarked,

> When I became disabled I was freaked, literally and figuratively. It took about a year before I came around to realizing that although a precious part of me—the tall, forceful walker part—was gone, my true self was still very much present. I am trying to get in touch with that self in every way I can, and one of the ways I do that is by listening to my intuition and not so much to what society says I'm supposed to be like. Making yourself fit TAB [temporarily able-bodied individuals] standard is self-defeating for people like me. I tried that approach; it made me sick, mentally and physically. Now I'm listening to my own voice; as difficult as this can be at times, it has been my road to salvation.

> I was born without feet. By rights, I should feel sorry for myself or be angry at God, but I have never felt this to be healthy or productive. Most people who meet me seem surprised that I am confident and self-assured, that I expect to be loved for who I am and not necessarily how I look—even though I think I am attractive enough. When I was young, the doctors tried to get me to wear protheses so I would look more normal and probably because they felt bothered by my stumps. I refused because I felt they were cosmetic more than anything else and ultimately postponing the inevitable—me accepting my limitations.

This group used physical activity to optimize the functioning of their minds and bodies rather than to normalize or beautify themselves and tended to prefer competitive sport ($n = 7$) more than non-competitive exercise ($n = 3$) to achieve such goals. Also in contrast to the women in the other groups, they more often viewed physical activity as intrinsically rewarding, enjoyable, and a significant part of their lives and personal identities. As a result, most of those who were without disruptive health problems were trying to improve the quality or quantity of their motor performances (e.g., through increasing their training intensity or volume or taking advantage of advancements in prosthetic devices and sporting equipment for persons with disabilities) and to improve their physical fitness. For those with progressive medical conditions, physical exercise kept them in touch with their physical selves and satisfied their desire to do whatever movement was feasible. As a former elite athlete with advanced amyotrophic lateral sclerosis commented,

I exercise because my physical self is a central part of the whole. It is
the part of me that got the most fan-fare growing up. You can't just
turn that off, in your dreams or awake. Although I am no longer at
one with my body—I can't walk without help anymore and my body
does and does not do many things I can't control—I still take walks
around the house with my caregiver twice daily, and I still see myself
as an athlete in my dreams. I plan on exercising my body until I am
so weak it is impossible. It makes me feel like I am still engaged in
living.

Although all of the women in the "optimizing mind-body functioning"
group were constructing an identity at least partially rooted in their own
criteria, the majority ($n = 6$) did not take this a step further by joining others
in collective activities to contest ableism and disability oppression in society;
rather, they focused primarily on their own self-development. Moreover,
although they perceived, and even claimed to feel proud about, social change
occurring as a result of their individual actions (e.g., being a role model for
other disabled athletes or shattering negative stereotypes that women with
disabilities are weak and helpless), they admitted that they did not, for the
most part, consciously attempt to accomplish this goal.

In contrast, the remaining four, who were labeled "the collectives," were
committed not only to managing their disability and achieving personal
goals via physical and other forms of activity, but also to advancing social
justice for all persons with disabilities. Not surprisingly, they were all
involved in one or more civil rights movements (i.e., those associated with
disability, sex, race, and sexual orientation). Also not surprisingly, the discourse of feminine body-beauty had a lesser influence in their lives than the
women in the other groups. The collectives also raised questions about the
discourse of individual responsibility believing that individuals with disabilities often require social and institutional programs to facilitate their
independence.

Like the other members of their group, the collectives believed that liberating women with disabilities requires strategies designed to enhance both
physical and psychological aspects of the self. They believed, however, that
physical activity, particularly in organized sport, was more than just a tool to
develop oneself; it also served the political purpose of deconstructing their
own internalized ableism, as well as that of others with whom they come in
contact (e.g., able-bodied persons who believe disabled women cannot perform successfully in sport or exercise settings).

The collectives also tended to take a more metaphysical approach to life
than the other members of their group; that is, they believed there are
reasons, beyond mere coincidence, that explained their circumstances and life
experiences. Thus, the question, "why me?", often served as a stimulus for
personal growth and fulfillment of a felt-mission rather than as a constant

source of anger, frustration, and denial. For example, one woman with congenital limb deficiency felt that she had selected, while in a previous non-incarnate, non-temporal state of existence, to be disabled during this lifetime so that she could help others with disabilities accept themselves and teach able-bodied persons to be more humane:

> In the beginning when I became disabled, it was tough on me, just like it would be for anyone. I was fearful, angry, and feeling helpless. However, after a period of a few months, I said "that's it; get over it, get on with your life," and most importantly, I started moving and doing something, instead of moping around. Soon thereafter, I began to realize that I had a job to do—to help others with disability to realize or take back their power, to show the world that being disabled doesn't prevent you from being successful, or from experiencing joy and life satisfaction. This attitude came partially from my spiritual beliefs but also from being around others who see and believe the way I do.

Besides being a woman with a disability, all of the collectives were members of at least one additional marginalized group (e.g., lesbians, bisexuals, women of color or multiracial background). In this respect, they were different than the other members of their group, who were primarily Caucasian and heterosexual. As a whole, however, the "optimizing mind-body functioning" group was comprised of more women with congenital disabilities ($n = 6$ out of 10) and longer disability ages ($n = 8$ out of 10) than either of the other groups. This is particularly noteworthy in light of the fact that there were fewer women with congenital disabilities ($n = 12$), as opposed to acquired disabilities ($n = 22$) in this study.

Discussion

The findings of this study, which support our earlier work examining physical activity and disability management (Guthrie, 1999), indicate that this sample of women used a variety of strategies (i.e., mental, spiritual, social, and physical) in managing their disabilities and ultimately to enhance their overall identities. For most, participation in sport and/or exercise seemed valuable in this regard. There is no question that building a healthy sense of self is critical in confronting internalized ableism. If, however, oppressive notions and norms are to be seriously challenged at the societal level, individual resistance must eventually become collective and public in nature. That is, groups of women must commit themselves to work, collaboratively, to bring about social change. This requires extensive support and validation, which group activities often provide. Participation in sport may be more useful than individual exercise training in providing such affirmation.

This is not to deny the numerous health benefits women with physical disabilities can derive from regular exercise, nor the fact that physical and self-perceptions are often enhanced in exercise settings. Rita is a prime example, as are the many women in this study who found that exercise helped them manage both their disabilities and disability oppression. What makes sport different, however, is that it seems to provide a double benefit to its participants—personal and collective affirmation of the empowered self.

Contributing to this double sense of empowerment may be the fact that sporting participation allows more possibilities than individual exercise programs for public recognition of motor skill and efficiency because there is a greater likelihood of media coverage and spectators. When this occurs, the belief that women with disabilities are helpless and vulnerable and that physical activity, particularly sport, is an able-bodied domain can be more broadly challenged. This may help to explain why the collectives and the other women in their group, who were more often involved in sport than exercise, were using physical activity to extend their bodily capacities and were more likely than those in the other two groups to view their difference from able-bodied society as a source of pride.[4]

Did participation in sport play a critical role in fostering self-acceptance and esteem among the women who were optimizing mind-body functioning? It certainly could be argued that having congenital disabilities, and thus no "before and after" images with which to contend, and longer disability ages may have facilitated their ability to construct a healthy view of self apart from being physically active. The findings of this study provide compelling evidence, however, that sporting experience at least partially facilitated these positive self-perceptions; that is, all of the women who were using physical activity to maximize their mind-body powers believed sport, more than exercise alone, enhanced their sense of agency, as well as their pride in their bodies and themselves. Moreover, for the collectives whose physical activity was a form of political activism, sport was viewed as a site in which the discourses of embodiment and other restrictive notions of the body, ability, and physical performance could be effectively challenged.

It seems clear, then, that in order to produce the greatest good for the greatest number, more opportunities for women with disabilities in both sport and exercise must be made available, and those that do exist must be made more accessible and accommodating (Castelnuovo & Guthrie, 1998; DePauw, 1997; Guthrie, 1999, Henderson & Bedini, 1995, Sherill, 1997). Indeed, many of the participants in this study indicated that, despite disability legislation, persons with disabilities continue to have limited entrance to physical activity spaces. As long as such constraints continue, the ability of women with physical disabilities to transform themselves and able-bodyist notions of normality via physical activity is severely compromised. It is important to remember, however, that physical activity is not necessarily a remedy for problematic self- or societal perceptions of disability.

Indeed, there were women in this study who, while using physical activity to manage their disabilities on some level, found mental or spiritual activities to be far more helpful in this regard. There were also those who used their physical activity primarily to fit feminine body-beauty ideals. Although striving to normalize or beautify the body through physical activity (e.g., to appear sexier and thinner or more functionally normal) is certainly understandable considering the rigorous criteria to which all women are subjected, such actions ultimately reify able-bodied norms and images, and thus further the oppression of persons with disabilities. It is noteworthy, however, that the women with acquired disabilities and short disability ages were more likely than those with congenital disabilities and long disability ages to use physical activity for such purposes rather than for augmenting their mind-body capabilities. Such attitudes and behaviors can possibly be accounted for by the fact that those with recently acquired disabilities had a more vivid memory of their former able-bodied selves, as well as less time to come to terms with their disability; as a result, they were still trying to compensate for body image and self-esteem issues associated with their disabilities. The results of this study lend support for such an analysis.

They also suggest the complexity of identity formation among this sample of women, as well as the diverse ways disability is experienced in an able-bodyist culture. For example, although the four discourses of embodiment have been encountered by all of the participants, their responses (e.g., acceptance, resistance) to these discourses varied considerably. For the minimizing group, dualism was clearly evidenced in their devaluing of the body and physical activities; for the normalization group, feminine body-beauty ideals and individual responsibility for mainstreaming were particularly significant. Even the optimizing group was not immune to ideological forces. The women in the optimizing group did seem, however, to be more capable of resisting their negative potential.

Foucauldian discourse analysis was clearly helpful in identifying those discourses that most impact the lives of these women. Although the optimizing group was more actively involved in reconfiguring oppressive notions of disability on individual or societal levels, all of the women in this study challenge the postmodern notion that humans are merely products of the multiple discourses through which they are described and interpreted. That is, despite the restrictive notions and norms they regularly experience, these women have all found ways to successfully manage their disabilities, and thus enhance the quality of their lives.

Contesting the four discourses of embodiment, particularly that associated with disability, played an important role in this process, although oppositional strategies varied considerably. Foucault's distinction between reverse resistance and resistance as freedom was helpful here in differentiating the women who were reverse resistors, that is, those who were managing their disabilities via minimizing or beautifying the body, from those who were engaging in resistance as freedom (i.e., the optimizing group). Indeed, this latter group of women were striving to move beyond restrictive notions of embodiment by constructing identities grounded in their own criteria rather than those imposed by able-bodied norms. They also more often relied on a combination of mind-body strategies to manage their disabilities and more often used sport to achieve this goal. Such findings offer compelling evidence for Merleau-Ponty's conviction that we come to understand the world and ourselves through the lived-body and that our sense of identity is not simply the product of cognition.

The findings also support Merleau-Ponty's claim that group strategies facilitate the success of revolutionary acts. Although the "collectives" were most aware of the need for collaboration in combating oppressive structures and ideologies and the most involved in social activism, all of the women recognized that what is most disabling about their circumstances is not physical impairment per se, but a system of interlocking social forces that subjugates people with disabilities. They also realized that they cannot change the world, or their experience in the world, alone. Considering the magnitude of the social dictates with which women with disabilities must contend, this particular sample demonstrated a remarkable level of resiliency. Equally significant is the lesson they teach the rest of us: Living with disabilities does not preclude the development of a positive sense of self.

Acknowledgment

Adapted by permission, from Sharon Guthrie, 1999, "Managing imperfection in a perfectionistic culture: Physical activity and disability management among women with disabilities," *Quest*, **51**, 369–381.

Notes

1 The term discourse is used in the Foucauldian sense of power-knowledge structures and language that shape social institutions and individual attitudes and behaviors.
2 This study is both a replication and extension of an earlier study (Guthrie, 1999).
3 Part of this data set was analyzed in another article (Guthrie, 1999).
4 It should be noted that the women with recently acquired disabilities had to put a good deal of energy into seeking rehabilitation, accommodations, and support networks and addressing immediate financial concerns, thus taking part in activities like sport is likely to have been of secondary importance.

References

Castelnuovo, S., & Guthrie, S.R. (1998). *Feminism and the female body: Liberating the Amazon within*. Boulder, CO: Lynne Rienner.

DePauw, K.P. (1997). The invisibility of disability: Cultural context and "sporting bodies." *Quest*, **49**, 416–430.

Foucault, M. (1985). *The use of pleasure: The history of sexuality, Volume 2*. New York: Pantheon Books.

Foucault, M. (1988). *The care of the self: The history of sexuality, Volume 3*. New York: Vintage Books.

Foucault, M. (1989). *The return of morality: Foucault life*. New York: Semniotexte.

Foucault, M. (1990). *The history of sexuality, Volume I: An introduction*. New York: Vintage Books.

Fowler, F.J., & Mangione, T.W. (1990). *Standardized survey interviewing: Minimizing interviewer-related error*. Newbury Park, CA: Sage.

Guthrie, S.R. (1999). Managing imperfection in a perfectionistic culture: Physical activity and disability management among women with disabilities, *Quest*, **51**(4), 369–381.

Henderson, K.A., & Bedini, L.A. (1995). "I have a soul that dances like Tina Turner, but my body can't": Physical activity and women with mobility impairments. *Research Quarterly for Exercise and Sport*, **66**(2), 151–161.

Leder, D. (1990). *The absent body*. Chicago, IL: University of Chicago Press.

Lincoln, Y.S., & Guba, E.G. (1985). *Naturalistic inquiry*. Newbury Park, CA: Sage.

Merleau-Ponty, M. (1962). *Phenomenology of perception*. London: Routledge & Kegan Paul Ltd.

Patton, M.Q. (1990). *Qualitative evaluation and research methods*. Newbury Park, CA: Sage.

Sherill, C. (1997). Disability, identity, and involvement in sport and exercise. In K.R. Fox (Ed.), *The physical self: From motivation to well-being* (pp. 257–286). Champaign, IL: Human Kinetics.

Appendix

Sample Interview Questions

1. Please describe your disability and your physical activity experience.
2. What motivated you to begin playing sport or engaging in an exercise program?
3. What are the reasons why you remain involved in sport or exercise?
4. What benefits do you gain from sport or exercise?
5. Do you perceive a connection between your physical activity experiences and how you feel about your body and yourself? Between your physical activity experience and how you feel about your disability? If so, please tell me about this connection.
6. How do you believe you are doing in terms of managing (i.e., coping or coming to terms with) your disability?
7. What have you found helpful in managing your disability? Has sport or exercise been helpful in this regard? If so, how?
8. What do you find to be most difficult about being a woman with a physical disability? What benefits do you experience?

60

RETIREMENT FROM PROFESSIONAL SPORT

The process and problems of occupational
and psychological adjustment

Barry D. McPherson

Source: *Sociological Symposium* 30 (1980): 126–143.

The study of former athletes from a social scientific perspective can be approached from an analysis of both their career pattern while an athlete (cf., Kenyon, 1973) and their occupational and psychological adjustment to retirement. This paper examines the following social processes which account for the present social situation of former athletes: (1) socialization into the career; (2) career patterns and contingencies; (3) the decision-making process concerning retirement; and (4) adjustment to retirement (desocialization) and the transition (resocialization) to a "second career."

As a preface a few caveats should be noted. First, much of the information in this area is anecdotal and based on journalistic accounts, often about those who have not adjusted such as alcoholics, derelicts and those who meet an early death (e.g., through suicide). In fact, a search of the Sociology of Sport and Leisure Information Retrieval System at the University of Waterloo generated only 20 citations pertaining to retired athletes. Few of these were empirical studies. As a result, this paper blends the few empirical findings with a theoretical and conceptual analysis of the process and the problems from a sociological, social psychological and social gerontological perspective.

A second caveat is that empirical work of a survey nature is hampered by the problem of first trying to locate former athletes, and second, of obtaining their agreement and cooperation to complete a questionnaire or interview. With respect to the first problem, it is unusual for league or team officials to maintain contact with former athletes, and even when they are aware of their place of residence, they are reluctant to provide this information to social scientists. Moreover, they are especially reluctant to release information about former athletes who have not been successful in maintaining a middle-class image. For example, only after considerable groundwork did Roy (1974) obtain a list of current addresses for former National Hockey League play-ers. This list was produced (probably not randomly) by an official at league headquarters who, we suspect, was careful to include only certain players.

Even with the cooperation of league or team officials in obtaining addresses, it is a time consuming, expensive and difficult task to locate for-mer athletes (cf., Gustafson, 1973; Arviko, 1976; Kornheiser, 1976) since they are highly mobile (e.g., few settle permanently in the city in which they played). Nevertheless, there are some encouraging trends emerging in the sense that many athletes who have retired in recent years are more articulate and more responsive to questionnaires and interviews. In fact, many of them want to be consulted and remembered. To illustrate, one respondent in the Arviko (1976) study wrote on the questionnaire, "Thanks for remembering me"; while another, retired for over twenty years, sent along an autographed picture of himself as a player. Similarly, Lerch (1979:140) reported that 10 percent of his sample included with their responses some form of personal baseball memorablia such as, an autograph, a publicity photo or an old baseball card.

A third caveat to be noted is that there have been no theoretical or empir-ical studies or anecdotal accounts pertaining to retired female athletes (e.g., golf or tennis players), and few studies of former elite amateur (e.g., Olym-pic) athletes. For the most part then, the limited database refers to retired male professional athletes in the traditional spectator sports of baseball, football, boxing, hockey and soccer.

Socialization into a professional sport career

For those who attain a career in sport, the process of sport role socialization begins early in life (cf., Kenyon and McPherson, 1973; Loy, McPherson and Kenyon, 1978:215–241). For example, most elite athletes report that they competed in the traditional spectator sports (baseball, football or basketball) in early elementary school, and then in high school began to specialize in their present sport. As a result, early in life a sense of commitment to sport is established. This pattern of sport involvement is sanctioned by significant others (e.g., parents and coaches) who often encourage the child to strive for a career in sport. Furthermore, the future professional athlete is generally highly successful in sport as a child and thus receives additional attention and hence, prestige. This leads to a definition and ego-involvement of the self as an "athlete," which is later reinforced by being recruited by college coaches and professional scouts.

In short, it appears that early in life future professional athletes begin to base their self-esteem on athletic performance. This has potentially serious consequences in that most psychic and physical energy is directed toward sport, often to the neglect of education and participation in other social domains. As a result, in later life the individual may not have the prerequisite skills or the credentials to move into an occupation outside the sport milieu. That is, their life style for most of their first twenty to thirty years of life has been restricted almost exclusively to sport and interaction within that social world. In sum, because the career socialization process begins so early in life, one's definition of self is closely tied to involvement in sport. Moreover, there is a risk that a quality education may be devalued or ignored at some stage in the process, leading to unemployment or underemployment in the post-playing stage of the life cycle. To illustrate, John Updike, in his poem, "Ex-Basketball Player," comments on the status of Flick Webb who set a county high school scoring record:

> He never learned a trade; he just sells gas, checks oil and changes flats.

The career patterns and career contingencies of professional athletes

The career of the professional athlete is characterized by uncertainty; by upward, horizontal or downward mobility; by varying degrees of occupational prestige; by age-grading; and, by a unique life style comprised of unusual working hours, extensive travel and the necessity to develop a presentation of self which must vary in the "front" and "back" regions of professional sport (cf., Charnofsky, 1968). All of these factors may subsequently influence the occupational and psychological adjustment to retirement from this short-lived career.

The average career for professional athletes, if they survive the first two years, is between five and ten years depending on the sport (Blitz, 1973). While the career for some may last up to twenty years, many will not remain employed long enough (normally five years) to be eligible for pension benefits. The career, then, is characterized by uncertainty with athletes never knowing when they may be injured (thereby perhaps terminating the career) or traded or "cut" from the team. In fact, many athletes experience horizontal or downward mobility throughout their career when they are traded to another team in the league or sent down to a minor league affiliate. For example, Boulton (1975) traced the career of one journeyman hockey player who was a member of 16 major and minor league professional teams. Many athletes fail to see that these lateral or downward moves are indicative of marginal status or failure and that they should begin to develop alternative occupational goals.

Faced with the fact that they are unlikely to be promoted to the major leagues, many engage in structural or personal face-saving mechanisms to maintain a facade of success (cf., Faulkner, 1975). For example, Scott (1968) suggests that many aspiring but unsuccessful jockeys "cop out" by becoming exercise boys to save face. Further, many professional athletes terminate their sport career on a note of "downward skidding" since their career ends in the minor leagues (cf., Smith and Diamond, 1976). For some this trend may continue in their post-sport occupation as illustrated by Weinberg and Arond's (1969) statement that the general pattern for boxers is a rapid economic and status descent, often accompanied by severe emotional problems in adjusting to the world outside the boxing subculture.

During the playing career it is generally impossible to develop or pursue a second career outside sport, partly because of the length of the season and the extensive travel. Although the possibility of developing outside alternatives may exist for a few "stars" who have the capital and power to invest in their future, management normally discourages this practice. Hence, athletes seldom gain an opportunity to develop skills necessary for another occupation. Furthermore, it is often difficult to initiate a second occupation in the "off" season or while not training. To illustrate, Hare (1971:7) notes that boxers are inadequately prepared for another career since:

> Professional boxing fails to equip its graduates for other work. In fact, it tends to prejudice them against it. Managers and trainers are opposed to having their fighters learn other trades during their careers.

Similarly, in a recent study of former professional baseball players, one of the respondents complained:

> Baseball and professional athletics can often be a "pseudo-world" which allows people to think it is real. Forced or voluntary retirement is a "real world" and *will* happen. Management is *not* concerned with this and makes no effort to help players prepare for it . . . Preparing for retirement is *far* more important than the game itself and the Players Association should put on seminars, etc. with outside speakers several times a year to help in this preparation
> (Lerch, 1979:139).

Even where athletes do establish a successful side-bet during the playing career, they are often so far removed from the day-to-day operations that they serve as distant figureheads who are sometimes exploited.

Within professional sport, another contingency which influences the adjustment process is the varying degree of prestige and recognition which is attached to specific sport roles, especially in the major leagues. For example, the quarterback normally has greater status than the offensive tackle (cf., Abrahamson, 1979; Loy, 1979). Thus, similar to other occupations, the role of professional athlete provides varying degrees of status and self-definition for the individual. However, within the sport, this status changes more rapidly because the individual performs in public and is therefore constantly evaluated. As a result he or she either receives adulation or is ignored by the media and the public. In short, the status and ego of athletes are very much dependent on public interpretation and feedback concerning their performance. Moreover, the athlete's self-definition becomes dependent on this public recognition. But, the status and prestige normally last but a few years and are quickly lost after retirement. To illustrate, A. E. Houseman has a poignant description of this process in his poem. "To An Athlete Dying Young":

Now you will not swell the rout
of lads that wore their honours out
Runners whom reknown outran
And the name died before the man.

Thus, just as the senior citizen at age 65 faces a possible crisis brought about by the loss of social identity, so too the athlete experiences this loss of self-respect and the need to be socially significant. In the case of the athlete, the problem is more critical because he or she has been accustomed to living in the public eye and because retirement before 35 years of age is not normally socially sanctioned. Moreover, the adjustment process is likely to be more problematic because of the failure or inability to plan for retirement[1] and because the retired athlete is usually faced with supporting a young family.

A final career contingency is the presence of age-grading in professional sport. That is, the evaluation of an individual is influenced by informal norms which suggest that athletes are expected to be at a specific level of performance by a specific chronological age. If not, they receive little serious consideration as an employee. For example, Faulkner (1975) indicates that unless a player has played a significant number of games in the National Hockey League before 25 years of age, he is likely to be assigned permanently to the minor leagues or released outright.

The retirement decision: voluntary or involuntary

The process of retiring from professional sport occurs early in life (usually before 35 years of age) and the decision may be voluntary or involuntary. However, for those in a team sport the process is usually involuntary and is initiated by management. That is, unlike most high status professional occupations, the professional team athlete has little autonomy in the decision-making process. For those who retire voluntarily, many delay the retirement as long as possible, partly because they fear the loss of identity and partly because no one wants to be labelled a "quitter." A select few, however, know when to retire as illustrated by Jerry Kramer's (1973: 358–359) analysis of his own decision:

> Giving up football . . . is giving up the hero's role. I worry about that. I wonder how much I'll miss being recognized, being congratulated, being idolized . . . But then I thought of all the guys who've tried to hang on, who've tried to regain their peaks after their skills had left them. Joe Louis is probably the classic example. As great as he was, he really hurt his image by competing too long. . . . I realized that the odds had to be against me ever being All-Pro again. . . . I made up my mind, finally, definitely, absolutely, that I would quit.

Similarly, the loss of physical skills may lead to a rational decision as Carl Erskine explained to Roger Kahn (1971:260):

> I could look back and say I should have pitched a few more years. My arm doesn't hurt now . . . But in 1959 I walked into the office of Buzzy Bavasi and told him I'd had enough. I was thirty-two years old and my arm was 110 . . . Some of the time I could barely reach the plate.

Most recently Eric Nesterenko, in describing his love/hate relationship with hockey, comments ambivalently on the physical and mental need to retire, yet the loss at getting out:

> I couldn't wait to get out of it on the one hand, I just walked away from it as fast as I could. There was the pain thing . . . But the game – the game doesn't prepare you for anything else. And although I knew that mentally, you could say I never absorbed it emotionally. All it leaves you with, when you reduce it, is this memory of an incredible emotional high, an extraordinary alertness. Either you try to re-create that focus or you give it up . . . At my age (46) I'm casting about for something to do . . . This is something my wife just can't understand: what my skiing now is all about. It's wanting to live at a certain physical level you've grown used to (Teitel, 1980:24)

On the other hand, some athletes, especially in boxing, continue beyond the point at which they should have retired:

> . . . One estimate is that 60 percent of the boxers become mildly punch-drunk and 5 percent become severely punch-drunk. The severely punch-drunk fighters can be detected by an ambling gait, thickened or retarded speech, mental stereotyping, and a general decline in efficiency . . . Many boxers persist in fighting when they

have passed their prime and even when they have been injured. For example, one boxer, blind in one eye and barred from fighting in one state, was grateful to his manager for getting him matches in other states (Weinberg and Arond, 1969: 451–452).

In individual sports like golf, tennis, skating and skiing, the decision may be made voluntarily if the athlete is faced with declining success accompanied by continuing personal expenses. Here the decision may be objectively made for economic reasons. On the other hand, as in boxing, the need to earn additional income may serve as the stimulus to delay retirement in order to have one more "pay day."

Decision-making concerning retirement is partially related to the process whereby athletes initially enter the world of professional sport. To illustrate, in professional baseball there are basically two entry paths (Haerle, 1975). First, there is the noncollege player who appears to be more involved in the occupation and who signs a professional contract much earlier. This player is likely to spend a long period of time in professional baseball (17 or more years), to postpone planning for the retirement years, to resist retirement and to spend years at the end of the career in the low minor leagues prior to "getting out." Not surprisingly, this type of individual has limited options available once the playing career is ended. In short, withdrawal is traumatic because they have lived within the subculture for their entire adult life. Many, in fact, never leave as they search for and occupy insecure lesser status roles as scouts, coaches, or trainers. That is, faced with an identity crisis which often leads to maladjustment in the nonsport culture of mainstream society, they retreat to safety within the sport subculture.

The other career profile is represented by the college-educated player who enters professional baseball at a later age and who usually terminates the career at an earlier age. For these individuals, baseball serves as a mobility device wherein they transfer their visibility in sport into viable post-retirement positions in the "real" world. Thus, they may accept a career-oriented job offer outside baseball and voluntarily retire early. Moreover, these individuals are usually less committed during the playing career to the subcultural life surrounding professional sport. It is quite likely that similar career profiles for entry and exit are present in other professional sports, although they have yet to be studied.

Unfortunately, most athletes do not recognize, or are unwilling to accept the fact that their skills are declining (Weinberg and Arond, 1969; Kramer, 1969). For example, Mihovilovic (1968) found that soccer players in Yugoslavia were very resistant to relinquishing their playing positions to younger athletes. This behavioral pattern supports Sussman's (1972) general finding that the individual who retires involuntarily is less well-prepared for retirement compared to the individual who makes the decision himself.

Another factor influencing the retirement decision is the present and

418

future financial situation of the athlete and the size of the anticipated pension. In the future, former athletes should be more willing to consider voluntary retirement in light of higher salaries during the playing career and more adequate pension plans. As a result, there may also be less trauma due to economic problems associated with a forced retirement. Hence, more athletes may elect to retire voluntarily at the peak of their career, provided they can earn a satisfactory maintenance income in a meaningful second occupation.

It is this latter concern which may be most problematic for retired athletes; namely, how to find and move into a meaningful job with an adequate income. Basically, the retired athlete has two choices – to remain in sport in some lesser status position or to seek a career outside sport. To date, many have attempted to remain within their sport, despite relatively few positions being available. Moreover, in addition to personality considerations, there appear to be certain ascriptive and structural criteria which influence what kind of athlete is retained after the playing career. For example, there are few black managers or coaches in professional sport, and those who occupied central positions as a player (e.g., the infield in baseball and the backfield in football) seem to have greater access to coaching or management positions (Loy and McElvogue, 1970; Roy, 1974; Loy, Curtis and Sage, 1978).

Although data are unavailable to provide a complete picture of the second or subsequent occupations of former athletes, it appears that many go through more than one occupation as they search for a meaningful career that will match their skills and satisfy their interests and needs. Moreover, although a range of occupations have been selected, many former athletes are found in low status white collar or blue collar positions, although this pattern appears to vary between and within sports. For example, whereas the former Brooklyn Dodgers interviewed by Kahn (1971) were settled into comfortable middle-class careers (e.g., general manager, farm owner, insurance broker, vice-president of marketing, baseball manager), 37 of the 48 former boxers in Hare's (1971) study were employed as unskilled or semi-skilled laborers, and 60 percent of these were dissatisfied with their job. Haerle (1975) reported that 65 percent of the former baseball players in his sample occupied white collar occupations, while 11 percent held blue collar jobs. Only 29 percent were still employed in baseball.

In summary, barring serious injury the decision to retire is normally delayed as long as possible and is influenced by the level of educational attainment, the present and future financial position, the awareness and acceptance of declining athletic skills, the perceived career opportunities after the athletic career, and the amount of anticipatory socialization for the post-playing stage of the life cycle.

Occupational and psychological adjustment to retirement

The process of adjustment to a life style outside sport appears to be traumatic for some individuals. To illustrate, personality disorders appear as reflected in attempted or successful suicides, alcohol or drug addiction and a general orientation to the past rather than to the present or future. In addition, a number of former athletes have been arrested on a variety of criminal charges. These disorders may result from anxiety about the future or from a sudden loss of status and social identity. Whatever the explanation, these cases receive the most publicity, and hence generalizations are often drawn by the public. However, in fact, little empirical evidence is available to describe or explain the adjustment process encountered by former athletes. Nevertheless, this section attempts to account for some of the processes which operate.

Moving into a second career

The necessity to adjust to retirement and to begin another occupation between 25 and 35 years of age is atypical. The former athlete does not simply change jobs, but rather must be resocialized into a new occupational field. Haug and Sussman (1970) suggest that the factors associated with the choice and entrance into a second career are comprised of "push" and "pull" factors. A prime push factor is the inability to continue in a field of work. This inability may be structurally determined by subjective or objective age or performance criteria, as in the case of airline pilots and professional athletes. It may also result from physical problems such as those caused by injuries. A second push comes from the recognition that the first career is over or at a dead end. This could apply to an individual in the military who has reached the end of his career possibilities (Ullman, 1971), or to the athlete who has won an Olympic gold medal. A third push results from technological changes; however, this factor rarely, if ever, applies in sport. A fourth push simply results from an individual's desire to "get out of a rut," to innovate or to change his or her life style. This could apply to the athlete who tires of the training regimen, the travel, and the competition. Finally, a push toward a second career may arise from dissatisfaction with the status, the pay, or the insecurity of the first career.

The "pulls" of better status, higher pay, greater mobility and increased security are often mediated by the unique characteristics of the second career (Haug and Sussman, 1979). It is clear that many persons entering a second career will generally be older than those embarking on their first. Thus, careers such as medicine or law, with long periods of training, are usually ruled out. It is important to consider also the extent to which occupational skills can be transferred. In an examination of second careers for military retirees, Ullman (1971) noted that the transferability of military skills to civilian occupations was of central importance in increasing employability and adjustment. Within professional sport most retiring athletes do not have transferable skills which can be utilized in occupations outside the sport domain. Thus, they may have difficulty beginning a second occupation at age 30 to 40, unless they remain within the sport milieu where their athletic skills or knowledge can be transferred and utilized.

Reaction to failure in sport

The adjustment after the playing career can be satisfying, especially if the process is voluntary and well-planned, or can be traumatic, leading to psychological or life style adjustment problems. In many cases the reaction depends upon age, the options or alternative life styles available, the amount of anticipatory socialization for an alternative career, and the availability of support from significant others for desocialization from the athletic role. One way to view the desocialization or withdrawal process is to consider it as a form of failure.

An analysis of failure in sport (Ball, 1976) suggests that the process includes the reaction of members of the former group toward the failed individual, as well as the individual's reaction to his or her own failure. The reaction of the group involves either degradation, wherein the player is ignored as if he or she is not present (i.e., they are a nonperson), or cooling out, wherein sympathy and rationalizations are extended, expected and accepted. From the perspective of the individuals, they experience embarrassment since their expectations are left unfulfilled, and they must face significant others to whom they have expressed career plans (cf., Harris and Eitzen, 1978). The individual also utilizes new frames of reference by joining cliques on the new team (if he is sent to a lower level of competition) which are often comprised of other organizational failures.

Ball (1976) suggests that the reaction processes vary according to the structure of the sport. In baseball, which is a two-tiered caste system (comprised of major and minor leagues), players who fail at the major league level are usually "sent down" to a minor league affiliate. However, they are still visible to the public and their former peers. Thus, they have second class status and are constantly reminded of their marginality within the organizational set. Because the individual remains somewhere in the "system," degradation and embarrassment may operate more frequently. To illustrate the feeling experienced by such an individual, Ball (1976:731) cites from Bouton (1971:106):

> As I started throwing stuff into my bag. I could feel the wall, invisible but real, forming around me. I was suddenly an outsider, a different person, someone to be shunned, a leper.

This process operates in sports such as hockey and baseball, and in tennis and golf where there are satellite tours.

On the other hand, there are sports, such as football and basketball, where there is no formal minor league structure so that the player who fails is released outright, or remains on a "taxi squad." In this situation they are removed from public visibility and do not experience the public embarrassment of being seen in a marginal role. Moreover, many of the failures in these two sports are rookies who have a college education and therefore they have greater alternatives outside sport. Ball (1976) suggests that a "cooling-out" mechanism operates for failures in this type of sport structure because there are viable non-sport alternatives. Furthermore, because there is no lower subsystem, there is a higher expected rate of failure and therefore failure is less traumatic than in those sports where an option to perform at a lower level is available.

Another mechanism for handling failures was described by Goldner (1968) as "zigzag" mobility wherein a demotion is masked as a horizontal move. Here individuals are often given the implied hope that there may be a promotion in the future. A version of this strategy within sport occurs when a fading star is encouraged to become a playing coach with a minor league team or an assistant coach with the current team.

Adjustment to retirement from a sport career

The process of adjusting to retirement by former athletes has been described and analyzed in both qualitative and quantitative reports. The qualitative evidence can be found in poetry, fiction, non-fiction, interviews and journalistic articles about former Olympic athletes (Johnson, 1972; Kaplan, 1977), professional athletes (Jordan, 1975; Kahn, 1971; Kramer, 1969:3–10; Teitel, 1980) and Little League baseball players (Ralbovsky, 1974). Whether the process is voluntary or involuntary, these qualitative analyses reveal that athletes are handicapped by a failure to plan for their retirement, by not having an education or training suitable for a second occupation, and by a desire to remain within the game in some capacity in order to satisfy an ego which has been fed by adulation from the masses (cf., Kramer, 1969:3–10). In short, the athlete experiences an identity crisis[2] (cf., Hallden, 1965; Page, 1969:200; Cratty, 1974:154; Gilbert, 1974; Hill and Lowe, 1974).

One of the first empirical attempts to analyze this phenomenon was a study of 44 former soccer players in Yugoslavia by Mihovilovic (1968). He found that 95 percent of the athletes in his sample reported that the process of retirement was imposed on them, thereby suggesting that there is a conscious attempt to extend the playing career as long as possible. Retirement for those who had no profession to move into was a traumatic experience characterized by personal conflict, frustration, increased smoking and drinking and loss of friends on the team. One of the reasons for these side effects is that retirement has a negative connotation since it represents a devaluation in status, a reduction in income and necessitates the need to acquire other roles in a new social world.

In an extensive analysis Haerle (1975) examined the adjustment to retirement among former professional baseball players on both a social psychological and an occupational dimension. He found that 75 percent of the 312 respondents in his study did not begin to consider the post-career life until they were in their early or mid-thirties; approximately 50 percent reported that they were oriented more toward the past than to the future at the time of retirement; the forced decision led to feelings of regret, sadness and shock at the reality of the aging process; and, only 25 percent were future-oriented in the sense of accepting the inevitable fact of retirement. For example, compare the responses of a past-oriented with a future-oriented retiree from professional baseball: "It scared hell out of me. I wanted to stay in baseball in some capacity for the rest of my life," versus, 'I knew I was out of baseball so didn't worry too much. I had my mind made up that I could do anything I selected by hard work" (Haerle, 1975: 499–500).

The transition from one career to another seems to be more problematic for those who begin a "skidding" process late in the career by continuing to play until they are involuntarily removed. That is, those who end their career after a period of downward mobility may find that they continue sliding in their post-playing life (cf., Smith and Diamond, 1976). Haerle (1975) found that those who remained inside baseball as coaches, managers or scouts had a less stable career pattern in the post-playing years than those who moved into an occupation outside baseball immediately upon the conclusion of their playing career. Similar patterns have emerged among former professional hockey players (Roy, 1974). Moreover, there are other differences between those who remain in baseball and those who move into other careers. For example, Haerle (1975: 503) reported that those who retired as a player at a later age, often ending their career in a lower minor league, were more likely to remain in baseball in some capacity (e.g., scout, coach). Thus, for those employed outside baseball, the playing career may have been a stepping-stone to a more secure white collar occupation. In fact, in Haerle's (1975: 503–507) causal model, baseball fame acquired during the playing career was the most important predictor of immediate occupational attainment, with the respondents' educational attainment being second in importance. Thus, the athlete who is able to convert his or her athletic achievements into academic or social-mobility opportunities avoids "conversion failure" (cf., Bend and Petrie, 1977:40) and appears to adjust to the post-playing stage of the life cycle. However, over the long run, ability to perform at a high level and high educational attainment were found to be equally important by Haerle (1975). This suggests that fame may lead to occupational sponsorship for the first post-playing position, but that education is equally important, if not more important, in determining long-term success in a second career.

In an attempt to account for the present job and life satisfaction of former baseball players (N=153), Arviko (1976) found that the better adjusted were those who occupied a large number of social roles during the playing career, who were highly religious, who had attained a high level of education, who retired voluntarily, and who had a high level of present income. The following comments (Arviko, 1976; Appendix D) express the views of two former players concerning their adjustment to retirement:

A: The most difficult adjustment when I retired was to live more within our means and to adjust to a society that quickly forgets. I also have difficulty in understanding why there aren't more jobs in baseball for people who have given up 15 or more years of their lives to the profession. It is a very difficult adjustment back to private life and very hard to accept that you are "washed up."

B: As to my retirement from baseball, I myself do not know the situation I was in at the time. It wasn't until a year later that I found out. You see, I was an alcoholic and ex-drug addict (pills). I am now with A. A. Cunning, baffling and powerful is what they call alcohol. I prepared myself from the age of seven to become a professional ballplayer and within one year it was ALL GONE.

Similarly, Mihovilovic (1968:81) reports that:

An older sportsman who has dropped out of the team usually hides, escapes, looks for compensation in alcohol, blames others, weaves dreams, and creates various combinations for returning to the team, deceives himself as regards his possibilities, grows indifferent to events around him, etc.

Finally, in the most recent survey of former athletes, Lerch (1979) developed and tested a model to explain variation in life satisfaction among former major league baseball players. His results, almost identical to those reported by Arviko (1976), indicated that the following factors, in order of importance, accounted for 15 percent of the variance in post-playing life satisfaction: good health, a high level of present income, a high degree of education, a positive pre-retirement attitude and having a present job related to sport. He also found that 15 percent of the respondents were at the lower end of a scale measuring life satisfaction.

Conclusion

In general, studies suggest that most former athletes adjust successfully to retirement, although the second occupation and career may not be as psychologically and economically rewarding. However, in almost every sport there are some who never adjust to the termination of their career and who as a result become labeled as "psychologically crippled jocks." These individuals live in the past, fail to hold a job and often skid downward on the social scale. For them, lack of education, excessive ego-involvement in the role, mismanagement of earnings, and little emotional support from former peers or employers contribute to this downward mobility and poor adjustment.

Fortunately, professional athletes in the future may make a more satisfying transition since they are increasingly being made aware that their playing career will terminate, and that they should initiate skill training for another occupation after the playing years. Moreover, an increasing number are recognizing the importance of completing their education and investing their earnings in order to build equity for later life. Similarly, almost all professional sports now have a players' association which generates pension and disability programs to protect the retiree in later life. A future function of the players' associations may involve pre-retirement counselling similar to that occurring in the labor force for those in their late 50's and 60's. It is quite likely, then, that in the future former athletes will be less likely to experience economic problems. However, they may still experience psychological stress as they adjust their life style to a social world wherein they are not a central actor with high prestige. It is in this sociological and psychological domain that research is greatly needed.

In order to initiate this research concerning the adjustment of those who retire from a short-lived career, social scientists need to draw upon theories and findings from the field of gerontology.[3] To illustrate, the following three theoretical perspectives might have some utility in guiding future research concerning how and why adjustment does or does not occur: disengagement theory (Cumming and Henry, 1961), activity theory (Friedman and Havighurst, 1954) and continuity theory (Atchley, 1977).

Notes

1 Studies have indicated that few individuals approaching 65 years of age make plans for their post-retirement years (cf., McPherson and Guppy, 1978). Therefore, there is even a greater likelihood that little, if any, anticipatory socialization would be initiated by athletes for a second occupation.

2 While many authors have suggested that the identity crisis accompanying withdrawal from sport can be traumatic at any stage in the career (i.e., little league, high school, college, or international sport), Snyder and Baber (1979), in a study of the life-satisfaction of former college athletes and non-athletes, did not find that disengagement from inter-collegiate sport had any deleterious effects on adjustment at later stages in the life-cycle. However, anecdotal accounts often refer to the loss of status and feelings of inferiority experienced by the child who is "cut" from a little league team. Future research should focus on both the short and long-term effects on children who are involuntarily removed from competitive sport programs.

SPORT AND THE BODY

3 There is a large body of literature on retirement from a sociological, social psychological, psychological and economic perspective. Some general and specific sources worth consulting include: Carp, 1972; Atchley, 1976, 1977, 1979; Schulz, 1976; and Hendricks and Hendricks, 1977:231–260, 1979: 294–346.

References

Abrahamson, M. "A Functional Theory of Organizational Stratification," *Social Forces*, 58 (September, 1979), 128–145.

Arviko, I. "Factors Influencing the Job and Life Satisfaction of Retired Baseball Players," M.Sc. Thesis, Department of Kinesiology, University of Waterloo, Waterloo, Ontario, 1976.

Atchley, R. *The Sociology of Retirement*. Cambridge, Massachusetts: Schenkman, 1976.

Atchley, R. "Issues in Retirement Research," *The Gerontologist*, 19 (1/1979), 44–54.

Atchley, R. *The Social Forces in Later Life*. Belmont, California: Wadsworth Publishing Co., 1977.

Ball, D. W. "Failure in Sport," *American Sociological Review*, 41 (August, 1976), 726–739.

Bend, E. and B. Petrie. "Sport Participation, Scholastic Success, and Social Mobility," pp. 1–44 in R. Hutton (ed.). *Exercise and Sport Sciences Reviews*. Volume 5. Santa Barbara, California: Journal Publishing Affiliates, 1977.

Blitz, H. "The Drive to Win: Careers in Professional Sports," *Occupational Outlook Quarterly*, 17 (1973), 2–16.

Boulton, R. "Hello Goodbye," *The Canadian*, (January 11, 1975), 10–13.

Bouton, J. *Ball Four*. New York: Dell Publishing Co., 1971.

Carp, F. *Retirement*. New York: Behavioral Publications, 1972.

Charnofsky, H. "The Major League Baseball Player: Self-Conception Versus Popular Image," *International Review of Sport Sociology*, 3(1968), 39–55.

Cratty, B. J. *Psycho-Motor Behavior in Education and Sport*. Springfield, Illinios: Charles C. Thomas, 1974.

Cumming, E. and W. Henry. *Growing Old: The Process of Development*. New York: Basic Books Publishing Co., 1961.

Faulkner, R. "Coming of Age in Organizations: A Comparitive Study of Career Contingencies of Musicians and Hockey Players," pp. 525–558 in D. W. Ball and J. W. Loy (eds.). *Sport and Social Order*. Reading, Massachusetts: Addison-Wesley Publishing Co., 1975.

Friedman, E. and R. Havighurst. *The Meaning of Work and Retirement*. Chicago: University of Chicago Press, 1954.

Gilbert, B. "What Counsellors Need to Know About College and Pro Sports," *Phi Delta Kappan*, 61 (October, 1974), 121–124.

Goldner, F. "Demotion in Industrial Management," pp. 267–279 in B. Glaser (ed.). *Organized Careers: A Source Book for Theory*. Chicago: Aldine, 1968.

Gustafson, W. F. "Locating the Old-Time Players," *Baseball Research Journal*, 2(1973), 40–45.

Haerle, R. "Career Patterns and Career Contingencies of Professional Baseball Players: An Occupational Analysis," pp. 461–519 in D. W. Ball and J. W. Loy (eds.). *Sport and Social Order*. Reading, Massachusetts: Addison-Wesley Publishing Co., 1975.

426

Hallden, O. "The Adjustment of Athletes After Retiring from Sports," pp. 730–733 in F. Antonelli (ed.), *Psicologia Dello Sport. Proceedings of the First International Congress of Sports Psychology*. Rome, 1965.

Hare, N. "A Study of the Black Fighter," *The Black Scholar*, (November, 1971), 2–9.

Harris, D. S. and D. S. Eitzen. "The Consequences of Failure in Sport," *Urban Life*, 7 (July, 1978), 177–188.

Haug, M. and M. Sussman. "The Second Career-Variant of a Sociological Concept," in H. Sheppard (ed.). *Toward an Industrial Gerontology*. Cambridge, Massachusetts: Schenkman Publishing Co., 1970.

Hendricks, J. and C. Hendricks. *Aging in Mass Society*. Cambridge, Massachusetts: Winthrop Publishers, 1977.

Hendricks, J. and C. Hendricks (eds.). *Dimensions of Aging*. Cambridge, Massachusetts: Winthrop Publishers, 1979.

Hill, P. and B. Lowe. "The Inevitable Metathesis of the Retiring Athlete," *International Review of Sport Sociology*, 9(3–4/1974), 5–29.

Johnson, W. "After the Golden Moment," *Sports Illustrated*, 37(July, 1972), 28, 30–34, 39–41.

Jordan, P. *A False Spring*. New York: Bantam Books, 1975.

Kahn, R. *The Boys of Summer*. New York: Harper and Row, 1971.

Kaplan, J. "What Do You Do When You Grow Up?", *Sports Illustrated*, 47(July 4, 1977), 30–32, 37–38.

Kenyon, G. S. "Sport and Career: Patterns of Role Progression," pp. 359–364 in O. Grupe *et al.* (eds.). *Sport in the Modern World: Chances and Problems*. New York: Springer-Verlag, 1973.

Kenyon, G. S. and B. D. McPherson. "Becoming Involved in Physical Activity and Sport: A Process of Socialization," pp. 303–332 in G. L. Rarick (ed.). *Physical Activity: Human Growth and Development*. New York: Academic Press, 1973.

Kornheiser, T. "The Super Bowl Jets: What They Remember and Where They Went," *The New York Times*, (Sunday December 5, 1976).

Kramer, J. *Farewell to Football*. New York: World Books, 1969.

Kramer, J. "Getting Out: The Football Player," pp. 355–360 in J. Talamini and C. Page (eds.). *Sport and Society: An Anthology*. Boston: Little, Brown, 1973.

Lerch, S. H. "Adjustment to Early Retirement: The Case of Professional Baseball Players," Ph.D. Thesis, Purdue University, August, 1979.

Loy, J. W. "Implications of the Davis-Moore Theory of Social Stratification for the Study of Social Differentiation Within Sport Organizations," pp. 106–126 in M. Krotee (ed.). *The Dimensions of Sport Sociology*. West Point, New York: Leisure Press, 1979.

Loy, J. W., J. E. Curtis and J. N. Sage. "Relative Centrality of Playing Position and Leadership Recruitment in Team Sports," pp. 257–284 in R. Hutton (ed.). *Exercise and Sport Sciences Reviews*. Volume 6. Santa Barbara, California: Journal Publishing Affiliates, 1978.

Loy, J. W. and J. McElvogue. "Racial Segregation in American Sport," *International Review of Sport Sociology*, 5(1970), 5–24.

Loy, J. W., B. D. McPherson and G. S. Kenyon. *Sport and Social Systems*. Reading, Massachusetts: Addison-Wesley Publishing Co., 1978.

McPherson, B. D. and N. Guppy. "Pre-Retirement Life-Style and the Degree of Planning for Retirement," *Journal of Gerontology*, 34(2/1979), 254–263.

Mihovilovic, M. "The Status of Former Sportsmen," *International Review of Sport Sociology*, 3(1968), 73–93.

Page, C. "Symposium Summary With Reflections Upon the Sociology of Sport as a Research Field," pp. 189–209 in G. S. Kenyon (ed.). *Aspects of Contemporary Sport Sociology*. Chicago: The Athletic Institute, 1969.

Ralbovsky, M. *Destiny's Darlings*. New York: Hawthorn Books, Inc., 1974.

Roy, G. "The Relationship Between Centrality and Mobility: The Case of the National Hockey League," M.Sc. Thesis, Department of Kinesiology, University of Waterloo, 1974.

Schulz, J. H. *The Economics of Aging*. Belmont, California: Wadsworth Publishing Co., Inc. 1976.

Scott, M. *The Racing Game*. Chicago: Aldine Press, 1968.

Smith, M. and F. Diamond. "Career Mobility in Professional Hockey," pp. 275–293 in R. Gruneau and J. Albinson (eds.). *Canadian Sport: Sociological* Perspectives. Don Mills, Ontario: Addison-Wesley Publishing Co., 1976.

Synder, E. and L. Baber. "A Profile of Former Collegiate Athletes and Non-athletes: Leisure Activities, Attitudes Toward Work and Aspects of Satisfaction With Life," *Journal of Sport Behavior*, 2 (November, 1979), 211–219.

Sussman, M. "An Analytic Model for the Sociological Study of Retirement," in F. Carp (ed.). *Retirement*. New York: Behavioral Publications, Inc., 1972.

Teitel, J. "The New Magic Youth of Nesterenko," *Quest*, 9 (February/March, 1980), 20–30.

Weinberg, S. and H. Arond. "The Occupational Culture of the Boxer," pp. 439–452 in J. W. Loy and G. S. Kenyon (eds.). *Sport, Culture and Society*. New York: The Macmillan Co., 1969.

Ullman, C. "Second Careers for Military Retirees," *Vocational Guidance Quarterly*, 20 (December, 1971).

U.W.E.L. LEARNING RESOURCES